Using **MIS**

Dear Student,

Honestly, this is a fun class. It's fun to take because you'll learn about things that dominate news headlines every day. You'll learn about things like artificial intelligence, self-driving cars, 3D printing, social media, Big Data, virtual reality, the cloud, and cybersecurity. No, it's not a programming class. It's not intended to be a class where you learn a bunch of boring technical terms and computer code. Not at all.

This class is about using technology to create value. For example, the smartphone sitting next to you is a piece of technology that is probably very valuable to you. It's an amazing piece of hardware that contains software, databases, and artificial intelligent agents. You use it to browse the Web, collaborate with friends, take pictures, post to social media, and make online purchases. More than 85 percent of college students have a smartphone, and 46 percent say they can't live without it. That's value, and they're willing to pay for it.

And that's what information systems are all about. Innovators like Steve Jobs, Bill Gates, Larry Ellison, Mark Zuckerberg, Larry Page, Sergey Brin, and Jeff Bezos have used technology to create value for their customers. As a result, they have made billions of dollars, revolutionized commerce, and created some of the largest companies in the world. And you can do the same thing in your personal life.

You can use technology to get a great job, increase your earning potential, and become indispensable to your future employer. You may not be a superstar entrepreneur like Steve Jobs, but you can exceed beyond your expectations by applying the knowledge you learn in this class. Companies are becoming increasingly dependent on technology. They need people who understand how to use *new* technology to solve *new* types of problems. And that's you.

Think about it. Over time, technology creates new jobs that didn't exist before. Mobile application developers, social media analysts, information security specialists, business intelligence analysts, and data architects didn't exist 20—even 10—years ago. Similarly, the best jobs 20 years from now probably don't currently exist.

The trick to turning information systems to your advantage is being able to predict technological innovations and then get ahead of them. During your career, you will find many opportunities for the innovative application of information systems in business and government—but only if you know how to look for them.

Once found, those opportunities become your opportunities when you—as a skilled, creative, nonroutine problem solver—apply emerging technology to facilitate your organization's strategy. This is true whether your job is in marketing, operations, sales, accounting, finance, entrepreneurship, or another discipline.

Congratulations on deciding to study business. Use this course to help you obtain and then thrive in an interesting and rewarding career. Learn more than just the MIS terminology—understand the ways information systems are transforming business and the many, many ways you can participate in that transformation.

In this endeavor, we wish you, a future business professional, the very best success!

David Kroenke & Randy Boyle

The Guides

Each chapter includes three unique **guides** that focus on current issues in information systems. In each chapter, one of the guides focuses on an ethical issue in business, and the second focuses on security. The third guide focuses on careers in the field of information systems. The content of each guide is designed to stimulate thought, discussion, and active participation in order to help *you* develop your problem-solving skills and become a better business professional.

Chapter 1

Ethics: Ethics and Professional Responsibility   23
Security: Passwords and Password Etiquette   26
Career Guide: Five-Component Careers   28

Chapter 2

Ethics: The Lure of Love Bots   42
Security: Hacking Smart Things   54
Career Guide: Director of Architecture   57

Chapter 3

Ethics: MIS-Diagnosis   76
Security: Equihax   102
Career Guide: Manager, Data and Analytics   104

Chapter 4

Ethics: Free Apps for Data   143
Security: Poisoned App-les   150
Career Guide: Senior Software Engineer   152

Chapter 5

Ethics: Mining at Work   168
Security: Big Data . . . Losses   190
Career Guide: Director of Data Engineering   192

Chapter 6

Ethics: Reverse Engineering Privacy   216
Security: IRS Systems Overtaxed   238
Career Guide: Senior Network Manager   241

Chapter 7

Ethics: Big Brother Wearables   274
Security: Security in the Sharing Economy   284
Career Guide: Software Product Manager   286

Chapter 8

Ethics: Paid Deletion   310
Security: It's Not Me . . . It's You   322
Career Guide: Software/Platform Engineer   324

Chapter 9

Ethics: Synthetic Friends   354
Security: Social Engineering Bitcoin   366
Career Guide: Social Media/Online Reputation Manager   368

Chapter 10

Ethics: Web Recording Everything   394
Security: Largest! Data! Breach! Ever!   408
Career Guide: Manager, Cybersecurity and Privacy   410

Chapter 11

Ethics: Training Your Replacement   429
Security: Watching the Watchers   438
Career Guide: Data Governance Officer   440

Chapter 12

Ethics: Engineered Slowdown   462
Security: IoT and Mirai   484
Career Guide: Developing Your Personal Brand   486

LEARNING AIDS FOR STUDENTS

We have structured this book so you can maximize the benefit from the time you spend reading it. As shown in the following table, each chapter includes various learning aids to help you succeed in this course.

Resource	Description	Benefit	Example
Guides	Each chapter includes three guides that focus on current issues in information systems. One addresses ethics, one addresses security, and the third addresses information systems careers.	Stimulate thought and discussion. Address ethics and security once per chapter. Learn about real-world IS jobs.	Chapter 5, Ethics Guide: Mining at Work Chapter 8, Security Guide: It's Not Me . . . It's You Chapter 9, Career Guide: Social Media/Online Reputation Manager
Chapter Introduction Business Example	Each chapter begins with a description of a business situation that motivates the need for the chapter's contents. We focus on two different businesses over the course of the text: eHermes, an automated mobile storefront retailer; and ARES, an augmented reality exercise startup opportunity.	Understand the relevance of the chapter's content by applying it to a business situation.	Chapter 9, opening vignette: Social Media Information Systems and ARES
Query-Based Chapter Format	Each chapter starts with a list of questions, and each major heading is a question. The Active Review contains tasks for you to perform in order to demonstrate your ability to answer the questions.	Use the questions to manage your time, guide your study, and review for exams.	Chapter 1, Q1-4: How Can You Use the Five-Component Model? Chapter 6, Q6-4: How Does the Internet Work?
So What?	Each chapter of this text includes an exercise called "So What?" This feature challenges the students to apply the knowledge they've gained from the chapter to themselves, often in a personal way. The goal is to drive home the relevancy of the chapter's contents to their future professional lives. It presents a current issue in IS that is relevant to the chapter content and asks you to consider why that issue matters to you as a future business professional.	Understand how the material in the chapter applies to everyday situations.	Chapter 2, So What? Amazon Eats Whole Foods

Resource	Description	Benefit	Example
2029?	Each chapter concludes with a discussion of how the concepts, technology, and systems described in that chapter might change by 2029.	Learn to anticipate changes in technology and recognize how those changes may affect the future business environment.	Chapter 8, 2029? discusses the future of ERP applications
Active Review	This review provides a set of activities for you to perform in order to demonstrate your ability to answer the primary questions addressed by the chapter.	After reading the chapter, use the Active Review to check your comprehension. Use for class and exam preparation.	Chapter 9, Active Review
Using Your Knowledge	These exercises ask you to take your new knowledge one step further by applying it to a practice problem.	Test your critical-thinking skills.	Chapter 4, Using Your Knowledge
Collaboration Exercises	These exercises and cases ask you to collaborate with a group of fellow students, using collaboration tools introduced in Chapter 1.	Practice working with colleagues toward a stated goal.	Collaboration Exercise 2 discusses how to tailor a high-end resort's information system to fit its competitive strategy
Case Studies	Each chapter includes a case study at the end.	Apply newly acquired knowledge to real-world situations.	Case Study 6, Salesforce.com
Application Exercises	These exercises ask you to solve situations using spreadsheet (Excel), database (Access), or Web applications.	Develop your computer skills.	AE10-2 builds on your knowledge from Chapter 10 by asking you to score the Web sites you visit using WOT
International Dimension	This module at the end of the text discusses international aspects of MIS. It includes the importance of international IS, the localization of system components, the roles of functional and cross-functional systems, international applications, supply chain management, and challenges of international systems development.	Understand the international implications and applications of the chapters' content.	International Dimension QID-3, How Do Inter-enterprise IS Facilitate Global Supply Chain Management?

ELEVENTH EDITION

Using **MIS**

David M. Kroenke

Randall J. Boyle

 Pearson

Vice President of Courseware Portfolio Management: Andrew Gilfillan
Executive Portfolio Manager: Samantha Lewis
Team Lead, Content Production: Laura Burgess
Content Producer: Faraz Sharique Ali
Development Editor: Rachael Mann, Laura Town
Portfolio Management Assistant: Bridget Daly
Director of Product Marketing: Brad Parkins
Director of Field Marketing: Jonathan Cottrell
Product Marketing Manager: Heather Taylor
Field Marketing Manager: Bob Nisbet
Product Marketing Assistant: Liz Bennett
Field Marketing Assistant: Derrica Moser
Senior Operations Specialist: Diane Peirano

Senior Art Director: Mary Seiner
Interior and Cover Design: Pearson CSC
Cover Photo: Colin Anderson Productions Pty Ltd/DigitalVision/ Getty Images
Senior Product Model Manager: Eric Hakanson
Manager, Digital Studio: Heather Darby
Course Producer, MyLab MIS: Jaimie Noy
Digital Studio Producer: Tanika Henderson
Full-Service Project Management: Pearson CSC, Susan Hannahs and Padma Rekha Madhukannan
Composition: Pearson CSC
Operations Specialist: LSC Communications, Maura Zalidvar-Garcia
Text Printer: LSC Communications
Cover Printer: LSC Communications

Library of Congress Cataloging-in-Publication Data
Names: Kroenke, David M., | Boyle, Randall, author.
Title: Using MIS / David M. Kroenke, Randall J. Boyle.
Other titles: Using management information systems
Description: Eleventh edition. | New York : Pearson Education, [2020] | Includes index.
Identifiers: LCCN 2018043431 | ISBN 9780135191767 | ISBN 0135191769
Subjects: LCSH: Management information systems.
Classification: LCC HD30.213 .K76 2020 | DDC 658.4/038011--dc23
    LC record available at https://lccn.loc.gov/2018043431

10 9 8 7 6 5 4 3 2 1

ISBN 10:   0-13-519176-9
ISBN 13: 978-0-13-519176-7

BRIEF CONTENTS

Part 1: Why MIS? 1

1   The Importance of MIS   3

2   Strategy and Information Systems   37

3   Business Intelligence Systems   65

Part 2: Information Technology 113

4   Hardware, Software, and Mobile Systems   115

5   Database Processing   161

6   The Cloud   201

Part 3: Using IS for Competitive Advantage 249

7   Collaboration Information Systems   251

8   Processes, Organizations, and Information Systems   293

9   Social Media Information Systems   335

Part 4: Information Systems Management 377

10   Information Systems Security   379

11   Information Systems Management   419

12   Information Systems Development   447

The International Dimension   494

Application Exercises   515

Glossary   534

Index   551

Describes how this course teaches four key skills for business professionals. Defines *MIS, information systems,* and *information.*

Describes reasons why organizations create and use information systems: to gain competitive advantage, to solve problems, and to support decisions.

Describes business intelligence, data warehouses, data mining, Big Data, artificial intelligence (AI), and knowledge management systems.

Describes the manager's essentials of hardware and software technology. Discusses open source, Web applications, mobile systems, and BYOD policies.

Explores database fundamentals, applications, modeling, and design. Discusses the entity-relationship model. Explains the role of Access and enterprise DBMS products. Defines *Big Data* and describes nonrelational and NoSQL databases.

Explains why organizations are moving to the cloud and how they can use the cloud effectively. Describes basic network technology that underlies the cloud and how the Internet works. Explains Web servers, SOA, and Web services standards. Discusses how organizations, including eHermes, can use the cloud securely.

Describes characteristics, criteria for success, and the primary purposes of collaboration. Discusses components of collaboration IS and describes collaboration for communication and content sharing. Illustrates use of Google Drive, SharePoint, and other collaboration tools.

Discusses workgroup, enterprise, and inter-enterprise IS. Describes problems of information silos and cross-organizational solutions. Presents CRM, ERP, and EAI. Discusses ERP vendors and implementation challenges.

Describes components of social media IS (SMIS) and explains how SMIS can contribute to organizational strategy. Discusses the theory of social capital and how revenue can be generated using social media. Explains the ways organizations can use ESN and manage the risks of SMIS.

Describes organizational response to information security: security threats, policy, and safeguards.

Describes the role, structure, and function of the IS department; the role of the CIO and CTO; outsourcing; and related topics.

Discusses the need for BPM and the BPM process. Introduces BPMN. Differentiates between processes and information systems. Presents SDLC stages. Describes agile technologies and scrum and discusses their advantages over the SDLC.

CONTENTS

Part 1: Why MIS?

1: The Importance of MIS 3

Q1-1 Why Is Introduction to MIS the Most Important Class in the Business School? 5

The Digital Revolution 5
Evolving Capabilities 6
Moore's Law 6
Metcalfe's Law 7
Other Forces Pushing Digital Change 8
This Is the Most Important Class in the School of Business 8

Q1-2 How Will MIS Affect Me? 9

How Can I Attain Job Security? 9
How Can Intro to MIS Help You Learn Nonroutine Skills? 10
What Is the Bottom Line? 13

Q1-3 What Is MIS? 14

Components of an Information System 14
Management and Use of Information Systems 15
Achieving Strategies 16

Q1-4 How Can You Use the Five-Component Model? 16

The Most Important Component—You 17
All Components Must Work 17
High-Tech Versus Low-Tech Information Systems 17
• *So What?* A Is for Alphabet 18
Understanding the Scope of New Information Systems 19
Components Ordered by Difficulty and Disruption 19

Q1-5 What Is Information? 19

Definitions Vary 19
Where Is Information? 20

Q1-6 What Are Necessary Data Characteristics? 21

Accurate 21
Timely 21
Relevant 22
Just Barely Sufficient 22
Worth Its Cost 22

Q1-7   2029?   22

- *Ethics Guide:* Ethics and Professional Responsibility   *23*
- *Security Guide:* Passwords and Password Etiquette   *26*
- *Career Guide:* Five-Component Careers   *28*

Case Study 1: Pluralsight   33

2:   Strategy and Information Systems   37

Q2-1   How Does Organizational Strategy Determine Information Systems Structure?   39

Q2-2   What Five Forces Determine Industry Structure?   40

Q2-3   How Does Analysis of Industry Structure Determine Competitive Strategy?   41

- *Ethics Guide:* The Lure of Love Bots   *42*

Q2-4   How Does Competitive Strategy Determine Value Chain Structure?   44

Primary Activities in the Value Chain   *44*
Support Activities in the Value Chain   *45*
Value Chain Linkages   *45*

Q2-5   How Do Business Processes Generate Value?   46

Q2-6   How Does Competitive Strategy Determine Business Processes and the Structure of Information Systems?   48

Q2-7   How Do Information Systems Provide Competitive Advantages?   49

- *So What?* Amazon Eats Whole Foods   *50*
Competitive Advantage via Products   *51*
Competitive Advantage via Business Processes   *52*
How Does an Actual Company Use IS to Create Competitive Advantages?   *52*
How Does This System Create a Competitive Advantage?   *53*

Q2-8   2029?   53

- *Security Guide:* Hacking Smart Things   *54*
- *Career Guide:* Director of Architecture   *57*

Case Study 2: The Amazon of Innovation   60

3: Business Intelligence Systems   65

Q3-1   How Do Organizations Use Business Intelligence (BI) Systems?   68

How Do Organizations Use BI?   68

What Are the Three Primary Activities in the BI Process?   69

Using Business Intelligence to Find Candidate Parts   70

Q3-2   How Do Organizations Use Data Warehouses and Data Marts to Acquire Data?   73

Problems with Operational Data   74

Data Warehouses Versus Data Marts   75

• **Ethics Guide:** *MIS-Diagnosis*   76

Q3-3   What Are Three Techniques for Processing BI Data?   78

Reporting Analysis   78

Data Mining Analysis   80

Big Data   83

• **So What?** *Geofencing for Businesses?*   84

Q3-4   What Are the Alternatives for Publishing BI?   86

Characteristics of BI Publishing Alternatives   86

What Are the Two Functions of a BI Server?   87

What Is the Role of Knowledge Management Systems?   88

Resistance to Knowledge Sharing   88

What Are Content Management Systems?   89

What Are the Challenges of Content Management?   89

Q3-5   Why Is Artificial Intelligence (AI) Important?   89

Advances in AI   90

Q3-6   How Will Artificial Intelligence and Automation Affect Organizations?   91

Benefits of Automated Labor   92

How Will AI Affect Me?   94

Unwanted Dirty Jobs   94

Retraining and Retooling   94

Surviving a Shifting Workplace   95

Q3-7   What Is the Goal of AI?   95

Integrated Enabler of Other Technology   97

Q3-8   How Does AI Work?   97

Machine Learning   98

IBM's Watson   100

Q3-9   2029?   101

• **Security Guide:** *Equihax*   102

• **Career Guide:** *Manager, Data and Analytics*   104

Case Study 3: Hadoop the Cookie Cutter   108

Part 2: Information Technology

4:   Hardware, Software, and Mobile Systems   115

Q4-1 What Do Business Professionals Need to Know About Computer Hardware?   117
Hardware Components   118
Types of Hardware   118
Computer Data   119

Q4-2 How Can New Hardware Affect Competitive Strategies?   121
Internet of Things   121
Digital Reality Devices   123
Self-Driving Cars   125
3D Printing   127
Cryptocurrencies   127

Q4-3 What Do Business Professionals Need to Know About Software?   128
What Are the Major Operating Systems?   129
Virtualization   131
Own Versus License   133
What Types of Applications Exist, and How Do Organizations Obtain Them?   133
What Is Firmware?   134

Q4-4 Is Open Source Software a Viable Alternative?   135
Why Do Programmers Volunteer Their Services?   135
• *So What?* New from CES 2018   136
How Does Open Source Work?   137
So, Is Open Source Viable?   138

Q4-5 What Are the Differences Between Native and Web Applications?   138
Developing Native Applications   138
Developing Web Applications   139
Which Is Better?   140

Q4-6 Why Are Mobile Systems Increasingly Important?   140
Hardware   141
Software   142
Data   142
• *Ethics Guide:* Free Apps for Data   143
Procedures   145
People   146

Q4-7 What Are the Challenges of Personal Mobile Devices at Work?   146
Advantages and Disadvantages of Employee Use of Mobile Systems at Work   146
Survey of Organizational BYOD Policy   147

Q4-8   2029?   149

- **Security Guide:** *Poisoned App-les*   150
- **Career Guide:** *Senior Software Engineer*   152

Case Study 4: The Apple of Your i   156

5:   Database Processing   161

Q5-1   What Is the Purpose of a Database?   163

Q5-2   What Is a Database?   165

Relationships Among Rows   166
Metadata   167
- **Ethics Guide:** *Mining at Work*   168

Q5-3   What Is a Database Management System (DBMS)?   170

Creating the Database and Its Structures   170
Processing the Database   171
Administering the Database   171
- **So What?** *Slick Analytics*   172

Q5-4   How Do Database Applications Make Databases More Useful?   174

Traditional Forms, Queries, Reports, and Applications   174
Browser Forms, Reports, Queries, and Applications   176
Multi-User Processing   177

Q5-5   How Are Data Models Used for Database Development?   178

What Is the Entity-Relationship Data Model?   179

Q5-6   How Is a Data Model Transformed into a Database Design?   182

Normalization   182
Representing Relationships   184
Users' Role in the Development of Databases   187

Q5-7   How Can eHermes Benefit from a Database System?   187

Q5-8   2029?   189

- **Security Guide:** *Big Data . . . Losses*   190
- **Career Guide:** *Director of Data Engineering*   192

Case Study 5: Searching for Pianos . . .   195

6:   The Cloud   201

Q6-1   Why Are Organizations Moving to the Cloud?   203

Cloud Computing   204
Why Do Organizations Prefer the Cloud?   205
When Does the Cloud Not Make Sense?   207

Q6-2 How Do Organizations Use the Cloud? 207

Resource Elasticity 207
Pooling Resources 208
Over the Internet 209
Cloud Services from Cloud Vendors 209
Content Delivery Networks 212
Using Web Services Internally 213

Q6-3 What Network Technology Supports the Cloud? 214

What Are the Components of a LAN? 215
• *Ethics Guide: Reverse Engineering Privacy* 216
Connecting Your LAN to the Internet 218

Q6-4 How Does the Internet Work? 220

The Internet and the U.S. Postal System 220
Step 1: Assemble Package (Packets) 221
Step 2: Put Name on Package (Domain Names) 221
Step 3: Look Up Address (IP Address) 221
Step 4: Put Address on Package (IP Address on Packet) 222
Step 5: Put Registered Mail Sticker on Package (TCP) 222
Step 6: Ship Package (Packets Transported by Carriers) 223

Q6-5 How Do Web Servers Support the Cloud? 224

Three-Tier Architecture 225
Watch the Three Tiers in Action! 225
Service-Oriented Architecture (SOA) 226
A SOA Analogy 226
SOA for Three-Tier Architecture 228
Internet Protocols 229
TCP/IP Protocol Architecture 229

Q6-6 How Can eHermes Use the Cloud? 231

SaaS Services at eHermes 231
PaaS Services at eHermes Security 232
IaaS Services at eHermes 232

Q6-7 How Can Organizations Use Cloud Services Securely? 232

Virtual Private Networks (VPNs) 233
Using a Private Cloud 233
Using a Virtual Private Cloud 235
• *So What? Quantum Learning* 236

Q6-8 2029? 237

• *Security Guide: IRS Systems Overtaxed* 238
• *Career Guide: Senior Network Manager* 241

Case Study 6: Salesforce.com 245

Part 3: Using IS for Competitive Advantage

7:   Collaboration Information Systems   251

Q7-1   What Are the Two Key Characteristics of Collaboration?   253

Importance of Constructive Criticism   254
Guidelines for Giving and Receiving Constructive Criticism   255
Warning!   255

Q7-2   What Are Three Criteria for Successful Collaboration?   256

Successful Outcome   257
Growth in Team Capability   257
Meaningful and Satisfying Experience   257

Q7-3   What Are the Four Primary Purposes of Collaboration?   257

Becoming Informed   258
Making Decisions   258
Solving Problems   260
Managing Projects   260

Q7-4   What Are the Requirements for a Collaboration Information System?   262

The Five Components of an IS for Collaboration   262
Primary Functions: Communication and Content Sharing   263

Q7-5   How Can You Use Collaboration Tools to Improve Team Communication?   263

Q7-6   How Can You Use Collaboration Tools to Manage Shared Content?   267

Shared Content with No Control   269
Shared Content with Version Management on Google Drive   269
Shared Content with Version Control   272
• **Ethics Guide:** *Big Brother Wearables*   274

Q7-7   How Can You Use Collaboration Tools to Manage Tasks?   276

Sharing a Task List on Google Drive   276
Sharing a Task List Using Microsoft SharePoint   276
• **So What?** *Future of the Gig Economy*   277

Q7-8   Which Collaboration IS Is Right for Your Team?   279

Three Sets of Collaboration Tools   280
Choosing the Set for Your Team   281
Don't Forget Procedures and People!   282

Q7-9 2029? 283

- **Security Guide:** *Security in the Sharing Economy* 284
- **Career Guide:** *Software Product Manager* 286

Case Study 7: Airbnb 289

8: Processes, Organizations, and Information Systems 293

Q8-1 What Are the Basic Types of Processes? 295

How Do Structured Processes Differ from Dynamic Processes? 296
How Do Processes Vary by Organizational Scope? 297

Q8-2 How Can Information Systems Improve Process Quality? 299

How Can Processes Be Improved? 300
How Can Information Systems Improve Process Quality? 300

Q8-3 How Do Information Systems Eliminate the Problems of Information Silos? 301

What Are the Problems of Information Silos? 302
How Do Organizations Solve the Problems of Information Silos? 303
An Enterprise System for Patient Discharge 304

Q8-4 How Do CRM, ERP, and EAI Support Enterprise Processes? 304

The Need for Business Process Engineering 305
Emergence of Enterprise Application Solutions 305
Customer Relationship Management (CRM) 306
Enterprise Resource Planning (ERP) 307
- **So What?** *Digital Dining* 308
- **Ethics Guide:** *Paid Deletion* 310
Enterprise Application Integration (EAI) 312

Q8-5 What Are the Elements of an ERP System? 314

Hardware 314
ERP Application Programs 314
ERP Databases 315
Business Process Procedures 315
Training and Consulting 315
Industry-Specific Solutions 317
Which Companies Are the Major ERP Vendors? 317

Q8-6 What Are the Challenges of Implementing and Upgrading Enterprise Information Systems? 318

Collaborative Management 318
Requirements Gaps 318
Transition Problems 319
Employee Resistance 319
New Technology 319

Q8-7 How Do Inter-Enterprise IS Solve the Problems of Enterprise Silos? 320

Q8-8   2029?   321
- **Security Guide:** *It's Not Me . . . It's You*   322
- **Career Guide:** *Software/Platform Engineer*   324

Case Study 8: A Tale of Two Interorganizational IS   330

9:   Social Media Information Systems   335

Q9-1   What Is a Social Media Information System (SMIS)?   337

Three SMIS Roles   337
SMIS Components   340

Q9-2   How Do SMIS Advance Organizational Strategy?   342

Social Media and the Sales and Marketing Activity   342
Social Media and Customer Service   343
Social Media and Inbound and Outbound Logistics   344
Social Media and Manufacturing and Operations   344
Social Media and Human Resources   345

Q9-3   How Do SMIS Increase Social Capital?   345

What Is the Value of Social Capital?   346
How Do Social Networks Add Value to Businesses?   346
Using Social Networking to Increase the Number of Relationships   347
- **So What?** *Enhanced Golf Fan*   348
Using Social Networks to Increase the Strength of Relationships   349
Using Social Networks to Connect to Those with More Resources   350

Q9-4   How Do (Some) Companies Earn Revenue from Social Media?   351

You Are the Product   351
Revenue Models for Social Media   351
Does Mobility Reduce Online Ad Revenue?   352
- **Ethics Guide:** *Synthetic Friends*   354

Q9-5   How Do Organizations Develop an Effective SMIS?   355

Step 1: Define Your Goals   356
Step 2: Identify Success Metrics   356
Step 3: Identify the Target Audience   357
Step 4: Define Your Value   357
Step 5: Make Personal Connections   358
Step 6: Gather and Analyze Data   358

Q9-6   What Is an Enterprise Social Network (ESN)?   359

Enterprise 2.0   359
Changing Communication   360
Deploying Successful Enterprise Social Networks   360

Q9-7   How Can Organizations Address SMIS Security Concerns?   361

Managing the Risk of Employee Communication   361
Managing the Risk of Inappropriate Content   362

Q9-8   2029?   364

- *Security Guide:* Social Engineering Bitcoin   366
- *Career Guide:* Social Media/Online Reputation Manager   368

Case Study 9: LinkedIn   372

Part 4: Information Systems Management

10:   Information Systems Security   379

Q10-1   What Is the Goal of Information Systems Security?   382

The IS Security Threat/Loss Scenario   382
What Are the Sources of Threats?   383
What Types of Security Loss Exist?   384
Goal of Information Systems Security   386

Q10-2   How Big Is the Computer Security Problem?   386

Q10-3   How Should You Respond to Security Threats?   388

Q10-4   How Should Organizations Respond to Security Threats?   390

- *So What?* New From Black Hat 2017   391

Q10-5   How Can Technical Safeguards Protect Against Security Threats?   392

Identification and Authentication   393
Single Sign-on for Multiple Systems   393
- *Ethics Guide:* Web Recording Everything   394
Encryption   395
Firewalls   397
Malware Protection   398
Design for Secure Applications   399

Q10-6   How Can Data Safeguards Protect Against Security Threats?   399

Legal Safeguards for Data   400

Q10-7   How Can Human Safeguards Protect Against Security Threats?   401

Human Safeguards for Employees   401
Human Safeguards for Nonemployee Personnel   403
Account Administration   403
Systems Procedures   405
Security Monitoring   405

Q10-8 How Should Organizations Respond to Security Incidents?   406

Q10-9 2029?   407

- *Security Guide:* Largest! Data! Breach! Ever!   *408*
- *Career Guide:* Manager, Cybersecurity and Privacy   *410*

Case Study 10: Hitting the Target   414

11:   Information Systems Management   419

Q11-1 What Are the Functions and Organization of the IS Department?   421

How Is the IS Department Organized?   422
Security Officers   423
What IS-Related Job Positions Exist?   423

Q11-2 How Do Organizations Plan the Use of IS?   425

Align Information Systems with Organizational Strategy   425
- *So What?* Poor Data Management at Facebook   *426*
Communicate IS Issues to the Executive Group   427
Develop Priorities and Enforce Them Within the IS Department   427
Sponsor the Steering Committee   428

Q11-3 What Are the Advantages and Disadvantages of Outsourcing?   428

Outsourcing Information Systems   428
- *Ethics Guide:* Training Your Replacement   *429*
International Outsourcing   432
What Are the Outsourcing Alternatives?   432
What Are the Risks of Outsourcing?   433

Q11-4 What Are Your User Rights and Responsibilities?   435

Your User Rights   435
Your User Responsibilities   436

Q11-5 2029?   437

- *Security Guide:* Watching the Watchers   *438*
- *Career Guide:* Data Governance Officer   *440*

Case Study 11: Automating Labor   443

12:   Information Systems Development   447

Q12-1 How Are Business Processes, IS, and Applications Developed?   449

How Do Business Processes, Information Systems, and Applications Differ and Relate?   450
Which Development Processes Are Used for Which?   451

Q12-2 How Do Organizations Use Business Process
Management (BPM)? 453

Why Do Processes Need Management? 453
What Are BPM Activities? 454

Q12-3 How Is Business Process Modeling Notation (BPMN)
Used to Model Processes? 456

Need for Standard for Business Processing Notation 456
Documenting the As-Is Business Order Process 456

Q12-4 What Are the Phases in the Systems Development Life
Cycle (SDLC)? 459

Define the System 461
• **Ethics Guide:** *Engineered Slowdown* 462
Determine Requirements 464
Design System Components 466
System Implementation 467
Maintain System 468

Q12-5 What Are the Keys for Successful SDLC Projects? 469

Create a Work Breakdown Structure 469
Estimate Time and Costs 470
Create a Project Plan 471
Adjust Plan via Trade-Offs 472
Manage Development Challenges 474

Q12-6 How Can Scrum Overcome the Problems of the SDLC? 475

• **So What?** *Banking on IoT* 476
What Are the Principles of Agile Development Methodologies? 477
What Is the Scrum Process? 479
How Do Requirements Drive the Scrum Process? 480

Q12-7 2029? 482

Fetch! 483
User-Driven Systems 483
Industry Will Push Change 483
• **Security Guide:** *IoT and Mirai* 484
• **Career Guide:** *Developing Your Personal Brand* 486

Case Study 12: When Will We Learn? 491

The International Dimension 494

Application Exercises 515

Glossary 534

Index 551

PREFACE

In Chapter 1, we claim that MIS is the most important class in the business curriculum. That's a bold statement, and every year we ask whether it remains true. Is there any discipline having a greater impact on contemporary business and government than IS? We continue to doubt there is. Every year brings important new technology to organizations, and many of these organizations respond by creating innovative applications that increase productivity and help them accomplish their strategies.

Over the past year, we've seen long-discussed innovations take big leaps forward. Self-driving vehicles made huge strides over the past year. Tesla Motors logged 1.3 billion miles on its nearly autonomous (level 3) self-driving vehicles (with a few minor traffic incidents). Waymo (Google) logged more than 5 million fully autonomous (level 5) miles, and Uber logged more than 2 million autonomous miles. Nearly all other automobile manufacturers are running full-tilt to turn their traditional cars into fully autonomous smart cars. A recent study by Intel estimates that self-driving vehicle services will be worth $7 trillion by 2050.[1] Consider what would happen if Amazon started using self-driving trucks. It could reduce shipping costs by 80 percent!

At the annual Consumer Electronics Show (CES), Toyota announced an autonomous concept vehicle named the e-Palette that the company believes will fulfill a role in an emerging mobility as a service (MaaS) market. Smart devices were also a hit at CES again this year. A smart treadmill allows users to participate in live exercise classes led by expert trainers streamed right to their homes. A robotic Wi-Fi-enabled smart dog can recognize individuals and interact with them and recharge itself. Businesses see the potential value in smart devices such as these. They also recognize the need to collect, store, and analyze the data these devices generate. As a result, jobs in analytics, business intelligence, and Big Data are all in high demand right now.

Digital reality (sometimes called virtual reality) has really taken off. Microsoft announced that its second-generation device would be released in 2019 after a successful launch of its first mixed-reality device. Google showed off Magic Leap and indicated that it would debut in 2019. Expectations are high for Magic Leap considering that investors have put a record-breaking $4.5 billion into this secretive startup. The reviews for these devices from early adopters are glowing. These devices will create entirely new types of companies and could change the way people live, work, shop, and entertain themselves.

In addition to changing the ways individuals live and gather data, recent innovations are changing the way companies work, too. For example, over the past year Amazon experienced tremendous success using Kiva robots in its fulfillment centers. It expanded use of these robots to 26 warehouses around the world. These 100,000 Kiva robots have reduced operating costs by 20 percent ($22 million per warehouse); they have also reduced click-to-ship times by 75 percent.[2] If Amazon rolls out these robots to all of its 110 warehouses, it could save billions. Technology—in this case, an automated workforce—is fundamentally changing the way organizations operate. It's enabling them to be more productive, innovative, and adaptable.

Of course, not all of this year's technology news has been good. Large-scale data breaches continue to be a major problem. In fact, Yahoo! reluctantly disclosed that it experienced multiple data breaches during the previous 4 years totaling more than 3 billion lost records. Collectively, these data breaches represent the largest amount of compromised data in history, and Yahoo! chose not to notify users about these data breaches for years. Other notable data breaches this year included the loss of user accounts at DU Caller Group in China (2 billion), River City Media, LLC (1.3 billion), and FriendFinder Networks, Inc. (412 million).[3]

And these are just a fraction of the total number of organizations affected this year. Organizations saw a jump in the number of attacks from highly organized international hacking groups. The Mirai worm knocked more than 1 million German households offline, slowed large portions of the United States, and has spawned numerous variants that continue to affect IoT devices today.

This edition of the text has been updated for these developments as well as normal revisions that address emergent technologies like artificial intelligence, machine learning, cloud-based services, and so on.

All of these changes highlight the fact that more sophisticated and demanding users push organizations into a rapidly changing future—one that requires continual adjustments in business planning. In order to participate in this business environment, our graduates need to know how to apply emerging technologies to better achieve their organizations' strategies. Knowledge of MIS is critical to this endeavor. And this pace continues to remind us of Carrie Fisher's statement "The problem with instantaneous gratification is that it's just not fast enough."

Why This Eleventh Edition?

To reiterate the preface of earlier editions, we believe it is exceedingly important to make frequent adaptations to this text because of the delays associated with long textbook revision cycles. Text materials we develop in April of one year are published in January of the next year and are first used by students in September—a minimum 17-month delay.

For some areas of study, a year and a half may not seem long because little changes in that amount of time. But in MIS, entire companies can be founded and then sold for billions of dollars in just a few years. YouTube, for example, was founded in February 2005 and then sold in November 2006 to Google for $1.65B (21 months). And that wasn't just a one-time fluke. Facebook Inc. started in 2004, led the social media revolution, and became a public company currently (as of mid-2018) valued at $583B. That's a whopping $41B in growth per year for 14 years! MIS changes fast—very fast. We hope this new edition is the most up-to-date MIS textbook available.

The changes in this eleventh edition are listed in Table 1. The chapter on business intelligence systems was pulled forward to Chapter 3 because of the increased importance of these systems to all businesses. Every large tech company has spent considerable resources acquiring artificial intelligence (AI) companies in the past 10 years, including Google ($3.9 billion), Amazon ($871 million), Apple ($786 million), Intel ($776 million), and Microsoft ($690 million).[4] And that's not counting additional internal investments. AI and machine learning are becoming core parts of these companies' competitive advantage. Some of the highest-paying jobs are in AI, business analytics, Big Data, and data mining.

TABLE 1: CHANGES IN THE ELEVENTH EDITION

Chapter	Change
1	New eHermes introduction
	New and updated charts for CPU and data storage growth
	New job sector comparison statistics
	Discussion of the MIS skills gap
	Updated BLS job statistics for Business and MIS occupations
	New collaboration exercise (creating a collaboration system)

Chapter	Change
2	New eHermes introduction
	New So What? Guide: Amazon Eats Whole Foods
	Added discussion of first and second mover advantages
	Updated Amazon case study
3	New eHermes introduction
	New So What? Guide: Geofencing for Businesses
	New Security Guide: Equihax

Chapter	Change
	Reorganized chapter content for Q3-1 through Q3-4
	Simplified BI example in Q3-1 to find candidate 3D printing parts
	New Q3-5 discussion of why AI is important
	New Q3-6 discussion of how AI will affect organizations
	New Q3-7 discussion of the goals of AI
	New Q3-8 example of how AI works using machine learning and IBM's Watson
	New Q3-9 2029 discussion
	Updated Active Review questions
	New Using Your Knowledge questions
4	New eHermes introduction
	New So What? Guide: New from CES 2018
	New Career Guide: Senior Software Engineer
	Added discussion about cryptocurrencies, Bitcoin, blockchain, and phablets
	Updated Mac OS X to macOS
	Updated industry statistics throughout the chapter
	Updated Case Study and Ethics Guide
5	New eHermes introduction
	New Ethics Guide: Mining at Work
	New Career Guide: Director of Data Engineering
	New Q5-7 discussing databases at eHermes
	Updated images and statistics throughout the chapter
6	New eHermes introduction
	New Security Guide: IRS Systems Overtaxed
	New Ethics Guide: Reverse Engineering Privacy
	Updated industry statistics throughout the chapter
	Updated discussion about ICANN, net neutrality, and telemedicine
	Updated Q6-6 discussion of eHermes using the cloud
	New Case Study: Salesforce.com
7	New So What? Guide: Future of the Gig Economy
	New Security Guide: Security in the Sharing Economy
	New collaboration exercise
	New Case Study: Airbnb
	New Q7-9 2029 discussion about the sharing economy and the gig economy

Chapter	Change
	Updated chapter statistics and images
8	New ARES Systems introduction
	New So What? Guide: Digital Dining
	New Career Guide: Software/Platform Engineer
	Expanded discussion about major ERP vendors
9	New Security Guide: Social Engineering Bitcoin
	New Career Guide: Social Media Marketing
	New Case Study: LinkedIn
	New discussion about geofencing
	Updated collaboration exercise
	Updated industry statistics and charts throughout the chapter
	New Q7-9 2029 discussion
10	New So What? Guide: New from Black Hat 2017
	New Security Guide: Largest! Data! Breach! Ever!
	New Ethics Guide: Web Recoding Everything
	New industry statistics and charts throughout the chapter
	New discussion about legal safeguards for data
11	New So What? Guide: Poor Data Management at Facebook
	New Career Guide: Data Governance Officer
	Updated industry statistics and charts throughout the chapter
	New Q11-5 2029 discussion
12	New Security Guide: IoT and Mirai
	New Ethics Guide: Engineered Slowdown
	New charts and statistics about agile and scrum use
International Dimension	New Career Guide: Senior Learning and Development Specialist
	Updated statistics about international Internet access (fixed and mobile)
	New discussion of the General Data Protection Regulation (GDPR) law
	Updated examples of bribery and asset seizure
Appl Ex	New exercise AE3-3 Microsoft AI applications Fetch! and How-old
	New exercise AE6-4 Networking commands ping and ipconfig
	New exercise AE10-3 Recuva file recovery
	Updated data files and images

Even consumers are being affected. Consumers are interacting with AIs like Alexa, Google, and Siri in their homes on a daily basis. Machine learning is being used to make personalized recommendations for online shoppers. It's also being used to create automated Gmail replies, optimize Uber arrival times, and identify which songs you'll want to listen to.

Substantial changes were made in Chapter 3 with the addition of three new sections about artificial intelligence (AI). These sections focus on the impacts of AI on organizations and workers.

They look at why AI has become so important within the past few years and the long-term goals for this technology. We've included a simple machine learning example focused on spam filtering and a high-level look at IBM's Watson.

The chapter on collaboration information systems (now Chapter 7) was moved back to Part 3 ("MIS in Organizations") because it focuses on systems in organizations, much like Chapters 8 and 9 do. We hope this new organization of chapters will make the presentation of the chapters flow more naturally.

Chapters 1 through 6 begin with a new discussion of eHermes, a startup that provides mobile shopping experiences using self-driving vehicles. Chapters 7 through 12 continue to be introduced by the discussion of ARES Systems, a cloud-based augmented-reality exercise startup. In addition to motivating the chapter material, both case scenarios provide numerous opportunities for students to practice one of Chapter 1's key skills: "Assess, evaluate, and apply emerging technology to business."

This edition also continues to focus on teaching ethics. Every Ethics Guide asks students to apply Immanuel Kant's categorical imperative, Bentham and Mill's utilitarianism, or both to the business situation described in the guide. We hope you find the ethical considerations rich and deep with these exercises. The categorical imperative is introduced in the Ethics Guide in Chapter 1 (pages 23–24), and utilitarianism is introduced in the Ethics Guide in Chapter 2 (pages 42–43).

As shown in Table 1, additional changes were made to every chapter, including seven new So What? features, four new Ethics Guides, six new Career Guides, six new Security Guides, and four new chapter cases. Additional figures, like the one showing how machine learning works in Chapter 3, were added to make the text more accessible. Numerous changes were made throughout the chapters in an attempt to keep them up-to-date. MIS moves fast, and to keep the text current, we checked every fact, data point, sentence, and industry reference for obsolescence and replaced them as necessary.

Importance of MIS

As stated, we continue to believe we are teaching the single most important course in the business school. The rationale for this bold statement is presented in Chapter 1, starting on page 1. In brief, the argument relies on two observations.

First, processing power, interconnectivity of devices, storage capacity, and bandwidth are all increasing so rapidly that it's fundamentally changing how we use digital devices. Businesses are increasingly finding—and, more importantly, increasingly *required* to find—innovative applications for information systems. The incorporation of Facebook and Twitter into marketing systems is an obvious example, but this example is only the tip of the iceberg. For at least the next 10 years, every business professional will, at the minimum, need to be able to assess the efficacy of proposed IS applications. To excel, business professionals will also need to define innovative IS applications.

Further, professionals who want to emerge from the middle ranks of management will, at some point, need to demonstrate the ability to manage projects that develop these innovative information systems. Such skills will not be optional. Businesses that fail to create systems that take advantage of changes in technology will fall prey to competition that can create such systems. So, too, will business professionals.

The second premise for the singular importance of the MIS class relies on the work of Robert Reich, former Secretary of Labor for the Bill Clinton administration. In *The Work of Nations*,[5] Reich identifies four essential skills for knowledge workers in the 21st century:

- Abstract thinking
- Systems thinking
- Collaboration
- Experimentation

For reasons set out in Chapter 1, we believe the MIS course is the single best course in the business curriculum for learning these four key skills.

Today's Role for Professors

What is our role as MIS professors? Students don't need us for definitions; they have the Web for that. They don't need us for detailed notes; they have the PowerPoints. Consequently, when we attempt to give long and detailed lectures, student attendance falls. And this situation is even more dramatic for online courses.

We need to construct useful and interesting experiences for students to apply MIS knowledge to their goals and objectives. In this mode, we are more like track coaches than the chemistry professor of the past. And our classrooms are more like practice fields than lecture halls.[6]

Of course, the degree to which each of us moves to this new mode depends on our goals, our students, and our individual teaching styles. Nothing in the structure or content of this edition assumes that a particular topic will be presented in a nontraditional manner. But every chapter contains materials suitable for use with a coaching approach, if desired.

In addition to the chapter feature titled "So What?" all chapters include a collaboration exercise that students can use for team projects inside and outside of class. As with earlier editions, each chapter contains guides that describe practical implications of the chapter contents that can be used for small in-class exercises. Additionally, every chapter concludes with a case study that can be the basis for student activities. Finally, this edition contains 42 application exercises (see page 515).

eHermes and ARES Cases

Each part and each chapter opens with a scenario intended to get students involved emotionally, if possible. We want students to mentally place themselves in the situation and to realize that this situation—or something like it—could happen to them. Each scenario sets up the chapter's content and provides an obvious example of why the chapter is relevant to them. These scenarios help support the goals of student motivation and learning transfer.

Furthermore, both of these introductory cases involve the application of new technology to existing businesses. Our goal is to provide opportunities for students to see and understand how businesses are affected by new technology and how they need to adapt while, we hope, providing numerous avenues for you to explore such adaptation with your students.

In developing these scenarios, we endeavor to create business situations rich enough to realistically carry the discussions of information systems while at the same time simple enough that students with little business knowledge and even less business experience can understand. We also attempt to create scenarios that will be interesting to teach. This edition introduces the new eHermes case and continues the ARES case from the tenth edition.

eHermes

The chapters in Parts 1 and 2 are introduced with dialogue from key players at eHermes, a privately owned company that provides mobile shopping experiences using self-driving vehicles. We wanted to develop the case around an interesting business model that students would want to learn more about. Self-driving vehicles get a lot of attention in the press, but students may not know a lot about how they're used in business. Self-driving vehicles are on the road now. They should see widespread adoption in the next several years. It's likely that students will own or use a self-driving vehicle in the near future.

eHermes is considering strengthening its competitive advantage by using some type of artificial intelligence (AI) or machine learning to increase the efficiency of the fleet. However, were the company to do so, it would require a considerable capital investment. It would also need to hire a team of AI experts, develop new business processes, and modify its internal information systems. All of this is good fodder for Chapter 2 and for underlining the importance of the ways that IS needs to support evolving business strategy.

Ultimately, eHermes determines that it does not want to invest in an AI. It would be too costly, and it wants to use its capital to grow other parts of its business. The company doesn't have enough reliable data to train the AI, and it'd need to invest more in additional infrastructure. eHermes decides to focus on its core strength of selling items through its mobile storefronts.

Students may object that, in studying eHermes, they devoted considerable time to an opportunity that ultimately didn't make business sense and was rejected. But this outcome is at least as informative as a successful outcome. The example uses knowledge of processes as well as application of business intelligence to avoid making a serious blunder and wasting substantial money. eHermes didn't have to hire a dozen AI experts, buy new infrastructure, and build a complex AI just to find out it would be a mistake. It could try to make a prototype, analyze the costs and benefits, and then avoid making the mistake in the first place. The very best way to solve a problem is not to have it!

ARES

The Augmented Reality Exercise System (ARES) is an embryonic, entrepreneurial opportunity that uses digital reality devices (Microsoft HoloLens), data-gathering exercise equipment, and the cloud to share integrated data among users, health clubs, and employers. ARES allows users to virtually bike with friends, famous cyclists, or even "pacers" mimicking their previous performance.

ARES is based on a real-world prototype developed for the owner of a health club who wanted to connect the workout data of his club members to their workout data at home and to their employers, insurance companies, and healthcare professionals. The prototype was written in C#, and the code runs against an Azure database in the cloud. It used the Windows Phone emulator that is part of Visual Studio.

As reflected in the ARES case, the developers realized it was unlikely to succeed because Dr. Flores was too busy as a cardiac surgeon to make his startup a success. Therefore, he sold it to a successful businessman who changed the staff and the strategy and repurposed the software to take advantage of new digital reality hardware. All of this is described at the start of Chapter 7.

Use of the Categorical Imperative and Utilitarianism in Ethics Guides

Since the introduction of the Ethics Guides into the first edition of this text, we believe there has been a shift in students' attitudes about ethics. Students seem, at least many of them, to be more cynical and callous about ethical issues. As a result, in the seventh edition, we began to use Kant's categorical imperative and Bentham and Mill's utilitarianism to ask students, whose ethical standards are often immature, to adopt the categorical imperative and utilitarian perspectives rather than their own perspectives and, in some cases, in addition to their own perspectives. By doing so, the students are asked to "try on" those criteria, and we hope in the process they think more deeply about ethical principles than they do when we allow them simply to apply their personal biases.

The Ethics Guide in Chapter 1 introduces the categorical imperative, and the guide in Chapter 2 introduces utilitarianism. If you choose to use these perspectives, you will need to assign both of those guides.

2029?

Every chapter concludes with a question labeled "2029?" This section presents our guesses about how the subject of that chapter is likely to change between now and 2029. Clearly, if we had a crystal ball that would give good answers to that question, we wouldn't be writing textbooks.

However, we make what we believe is a reasonable stab at an answer. You will probably have different ideas, and we hope students will have different ideas as well. The goal of these sections is to prompt students to think, wonder, assess, and project about future technology. These sections usually produce some of the most lively in-class discussions.

Why Might You Want Your Students to Use SharePoint?

The difficult part of teaching collaboration is knowing how to assess it. Collaboration assessment is not simply finding out which students did the bulk of the work. It also involves assessing feedback and iteration; that is, identifying who provided feedback, who benefited from the feedback, and how well the work product evolved over time.

Microsoft SharePoint is a tool that can help assess collaboration. It automatically maintains detailed records of all changes that have been made to a SharePoint site. It tracks document versions, along with the date, time, and version author. It also maintains records of user activity—who visited the site, how often, what site features they visited, what work they did, what contributions they made, and so forth. SharePoint makes it easy to determine which students were making sincere efforts to collaborate by giving and receiving critical feedback throughout the project assignment and which students were making a single contribution 5 minutes before midnight the day before the project was due.

Additionally, SharePoint has built-in facilities for team surveys, team wikis, and member blogs as well as document and list libraries. All of this capability is backed up by a rich and flexible security system. To be clear, we do not use SharePoint to run our classes; we use either Blackboard or Canvas for that purpose. However, we do require students to use SharePoint for their collaborative projects. A side benefit is that they can claim, rightfully, experience and knowledge of using SharePoint in their job interviews.

You might also want to use Office 365 because it includes Skype, hosted Exchange, 1TB online storage, and SharePoint Online as an add-on. Microsoft offers Office 365 to academic institutions as a whole or to students directly at reduced educational rates.

Why Are the Chapters Organized by Questions?

The chapters of *Using MIS* are organized by questions. According to Marilla Svinicki,[7] a leading researcher on student learning at the University of Texas, we should not give reading assignments such as "Read pages 50 through 70." The reason is that today's students need help organizing their time. With such a reading assignment, they will fiddle with pages 50 through 70 while texting their friends, surfing the Internet, and listening to their iPods. After 30 or 45 minutes, they will conclude they have fiddled enough and will believe they have completed the assignment.

Instead, Svinicki states we should give students a list of questions and tell them their job is to answer those questions, treating pages 50 through 70 as a resource for that purpose. When students can answer the questions, they have finished the assignment.

Using that philosophy, every chapter in this text begins with a list of questions. Each major heading in the chapter is one of those questions, and the Active Review at the end of each chapter provides students a set of actions to take in order to demonstrate that they are able to answer the questions. Since learning this approach from Professor Svinicki, we have used it in our classes and have found that it works exceedingly well.

How Does This Book Differ from *Experiencing MIS* and from *Processes, Systems, and Information*?

In addition to *Using MIS*, we've written an MIS text titled *Experiencing MIS*. These two texts provide different perspectives for teaching this class. The principal difference between *Using MIS* and *Experiencing MIS* is that the latter is modular in design and has a more "in your face" attitude about MIS. Modularity definitely has a role and place, but not every class needs or appreciates the flexibility and brevity a modular text offers. A shorter, more custom version of *Experiencing MIS* is also available as *MIS Essentials*.

There is also a fourth MIS text titled *Processes, Systems, and Information: An Introduction to MIS* coauthored with Earl McKinney of Bowling Green State University. It represents a third approach to this class and is structured around business processes. It has a strong ERP emphasis and includes two chapters on SAP as well as two chapter tutorials for using the SAP Alliance Global Bikes simulation. Earl has taught SAP for many years and has extensive experience in teaching others how to use the Global Bikes simulation.

In *Using MIS*, we have endeavored to take advantage of continuity and to build the discussion and knowledge gradually through the chapter sequence, in many places taking advantage of knowledge from prior chapters.

The goal in writing these books is to offer professors a choice of approach. We are committed to each of these books and plan to revise them for some time. We sincerely hope that one of them will fit your style and objectives for teaching this increasingly important class.

Instructor Resources

At the Instructor Resource Center, *www.pearsonhighered.com/irc*, instructors can easily register to gain access to a variety of instructor resources available with this text in downloadable format. If assistance is needed, a dedicated technical support team is ready to help with the media supplements that accompany this text. Visit *http://support.pearson.com/getsupport* for answers to frequently asked questions and toll-free user support phone numbers.

The following supplements are available with this text:

- Instructor's Resource Manual
- Image Library
- Test Bank
- TestGen® Computerized Test Bank
- PowerPoint Presentation

AACSB Learning Standards Tags

What Is the AACSB?

The Association to Advance Collegiate Schools of Business (AACSB) is a nonprofit corporation of educational institutions, corporations, and other organizations devoted to the promotion and improvement of higher education in business administration and accounting. A collegiate institution offering degrees in business administration or accounting may volunteer for AACSB accreditation review. The AACSB makes initial accreditation decisions and conducts periodic reviews to promote continuous quality improvement in management education. Pearson Education is a proud member of the AACSB and is pleased to provide advice to help you apply AACSB Learning Standards.

What Are AACSB Learning Standards?

One of the criteria for AACSB accreditation is the quality of the curricula. Although no specific courses are required, the AACSB expects a curriculum to include learning experiences in such areas as:

- Communication Abilities
- Ethical Understanding and Reasoning Abilities
- Analytic Skills
- Use of Information Technology
- Dynamics of the Global Economy
- Multicultural and Diversity Understanding
- Reflective Thinking Skills

These seven categories are AACSB Learning Standards. Questions that test skills relevant to these standards are tagged with the appropriate standard. For example, a question testing the moral questions associated with externalities would receive the Ethical Understanding tag.

How Can I Use These Tags?

Tagged questions help you measure whether students are grasping the course content that aligns with AACSB guidelines. In addition, the tagged questions may help to identify potential applications of these skills. This, in turn, may suggest enrichment activities or other educational experiences to help students achieve these goals.

Available in MyLab MIS

- MIS Video Exercises—videos illustrating MIS concepts, paired with brief quizzes
- MIS Decision Simulations—interactive exercises allowing students to play the role of a manager and make business decisions
- Auto-Graded writing exercises—taken from the end of chapter
- Assisted-Graded writing exercises—taken from the end of chapter, with a rubric provided
- Chapter Warm Ups, Chapter Quizzes—objective-based quizzing to test knowledge
- Discussion Questions—taken from the end of chapter
- Dynamic Study Modules—on the go adaptive quizzing, also available on a mobile phone
- Learning Catalytics—bring-your-own-device classroom response tools
- Enhanced eText—an accessible, mobile-friendly eText
- Excel & Access Grader Projects—live in the application auto-graded Grader projects provided inside MyLab MIS to support classes covering Office tools

Acknowledgments

First, we wish to thank Earl McKinney, professor of information systems at Bowling Green University and author of *Processes, Systems, and Information*, for many hours of insightful conversation about the role of processes in this MIS course as well as for his deep insights into the theory of information. We also thank David Auer of Western Washington University for help with data communications technology and Jeffrey Proudfoot of Bentley University for his insights on information security.

Many thanks as well to Jeff Gains of San Jose State University for helpful feedback about prior editions of this text; Jeff's comments have strongly influenced revisions for years. Also, a special thanks to Harry Reif at James Madison University for most insightful observations about ways to improve this text.

At Microsoft, we are grateful for the help of Randy Guthrie, who supports MIS professors in many ways, including facilitating use of Microsoft Imagine as well as giving many presentations to students. Also, we thank Rob Howard for conversations and consulting about SharePoint and SharePoint Designer and Steve Fox for helpful conversations about both SharePoint and Microsoft Azure. Regarding our SharePoint program, a very special thanks to David Auer of Western Washington University and Laura Atkins of James Madison University, who serve as the community proctors for our SharePoint MIS community site, which enables dozens of professors and hundreds of students to learn how to use SharePoint. Our SharePoint solution is hosted by NSPI in Atlanta, Georgia. Additionally, we thank Don Nilson, a certified scrum master, for essential ideas and guidance on the new material on agile development and scrum.

We'd also like to thank all of the industry professionals that wrote Career Guides for this edition including Gabe Chino, Lindsey Tsuya, Marshall Pettit, Kailey Smith, Rebecca Cengiz-Robbs, Christie Wruck, Ben Peters, Adam Young, Marianne Olsen, Susan Jones, and Christin Dunlop. We hope their real-world advice provides students with insight into the daily lives of MIS professionals.

Laura Town and Rachael Mann are the development editors on all of our MIS books, and we continue to be grateful for their support, knowledge, expertise, and great attitude through thick and thin! The textbook industry is undergoing dramatic changes at this time, and their knowledge, guidance, and wisdom on the textbook production process are most appreciated.

We would like to thank those who contributed to the development of our excellent Instructor Resources: Instructor's Manual, Roberta M. Roth; PowerPoints, Steve Loy; and Test Bank, Katie Trotta/ANSR Source. We would also like to express our thanks to the following authors for creating a superb set of resources for our MyLab: Roberta M. Roth, University of Northern Iowa; Robert J. Mills, Utah State University; and John Hupp, Columbus State University.

Pearson Education is a great publishing company, chock-full of dedicated, talented, and creative people. We thank Samantha Lewis and Faraz Ali for taking over production management of a complex set of texts and doing it so efficiently and willingly. We also thank Susan Hannahs and Padma Rekha Madhukannan for managing the production of the book.

No textbook makes its way into the hands of students without the active involvement of a dedicated and professional sales force. We thank the Pearson sales team for their tireless efforts. Thanks also goes to our former, and now happily retired, editor Bob Horan for his years of friendship, support, and wise counsel. Finally, like so many authors in college publishing, we owe tremendous thanks to our current editor, Samantha Lewis. Samantha continues to provide us with the skilled guidance necessary to make these texts a great success.

David Kroenke
Randy Boyle

Thanks to Our Reviewers

The following people deserve special recognition for their review work on this and previous editions of the book—for their careful reading, thoughtful and insightful comments, sensitive criticism, and willingness to follow up with email conversations, many of which were lengthy when necessary. Their collaboration on this project is truly appreciated.

Dennis Adams, *University of Houston, Main*
Heather Adams, *University of Colorado*
Hans-Joachim Adler, *University of Texas, Dallas*
Mark Alexander, *Indiana Wesleyan University*
Paul Ambrose, *University of Wisconsin, Whitewater*

Craig Anderson, *Augustana College*
Michelle Ashton, *University of Utah*
Laura Atkins, *James Madison University*
Cynthia Barnes, *Lamar University*
Reneta Barneva, *SUNY Fredonia*

Michael Bartolacci, *Penn State Lehigh Valley*

Ozden Bayazit, *Central Washington University*

Jack Becker, *University of North Texas*

Paula Bell, *Lock Haven University*

Kristi Berg, *Minot State University*

Doug Bickerstaff, *Eastern Washington University*

Hossein Bidgoli, *California State University, Bakersfield*

James Borden, *Villanova University*

Mari Buche, *Michigan Technological University*

Sheryl Bulloch, *Columbia Southern University*

Thomas Case, *Georgia Southern University*

Thomas Cavaiani, *Boise State University*

Vera Cervantez, *Collin County Community College*

Siew Chan, *University of Massachusetts, Boston*

Andrea Chandler, *independent consultant*

Joey Cho, *Utah State University*

Jimmy Clark, *Austin Community College*

Tricia Clark, *Penn State University, Capital Campus*

Carlos Colon, *Indiana University Bloomington*

Daniel Connolly, *University of Denver*

Jeff Corcoran, *Lasell College*

Jami Cotler, *Siena University*

Stephen Crandell, *Myers University*

Michael Cummins, *Georgia Institute of Technology*

Mel Damodaran, *University of Houston, Victoria*

Charles Davis, *University of St. Thomas*

Roy Dejoie, *Purdue University*

Charles DeSassure, *Tarrant County College*

Carol DesJardins, *St. Claire Community College*

Dawna Dewire, *Babson College*

Michael Doherty, *Marian College of Fond du Lac*

Mike Doherty, *University of Wyoming*

Richard Dowell, *The Citadel*

Chuck Downing, *University of Northern Illinois*

Dave Dulany, *Aurora University*

Charlene Dykman, *University of St. Thomas*

William Eddins, *York College*

Lauren Eder, *Rider University*

Kevin Elder, *Georgia Southern Statesboro*

Kevin Lee Elder, *Georgia Southern University*

Sean Eom, *Southeast Missouri State University*

Patrick Fan, *Virginia Polytechnic Institute and State University*

Badie Farah, *Eastern Michigan University*

M. Farkas, *Fairfield University*

Lawrence Feidelman, *Florida Atlantic University*

Daniel Fischmar, *Westminster College*

Robert W. Folden, *Texas A&M University*

Charles Bryan Foltz, *University of Tennessee at Martin*

Jonathan Frank, *Suffolk University*

Jonathan Frankel, *University of Massachusetts, Boston Harbor*

Linda Fried, *University of Colorado, Denver*

William H. Friedman, *University of Central Arkansas*

Sharyn Gallagher, *University of Massachusetts, Lowell*

Gary Garrison, *Belmont University*

Beena George, *University of St. Thomas*

Biswadip Ghosh, *Metropolitan State College of Denver*

Dawn Giannoni, *Nova Southeastern University*

Ernest Gines, *Tarrant County College*

Steven Gordon, *Babson College*

Donald Gray, *independent consultant*

George Griffin, *Regis University*

Randy Guthrie, *California Polytechnic State University, Pomona*

Tom Hankins, *Marshall University*

Bassam Hasan, *University of Toledo*

Richard Herschel, *St. Joseph's University*

Vicki Hightower, *Elon University*

Bogdan Hoanca, *University of Alaska Anchorage*

Richard Holowczak, *Baruch College*

Walter Horn, *Webster University*

Dennis Howard, *University of Alaska Anchorage*

James Hu, *Santa Clara University*

Adam Huarng, *California State University, Los Angeles*

John Hupp, *Columbus State University*

Brent Hussin, *University of Wisconsin*

Mark Hwang, *Central Michigan University*

James Isaak, *Southern New Hampshire University*

Wade Jackson, *University of Memphis*

Thaddeus Janicki, *Mount Olive College*

Chuck Johnston, *Midwestern State University*

Susan Jones, *Utah State University*

Iris Junglas, *University of Houston, Main*

George Kelley, *Erie Community College-City Campus*

Richard Kesner, *Northeastern University*

Jadon Klopson, *United States Coast Guard Academy*

Brian Kovar, *Kansas State University*

Andreas Knoefels, *Santa Clara University*

Chetan Kumar, *California State University, San Marcos*

Subodha Kumar, *University of Washington*

Stephen Kwan, *San Jose State University*

Jackie Lamoureux, *Central New Mexico Community College*

Yvonne Lederer-Antonucci, *Widener University*

Joo Eng Lee-Partridge, *Central Connecticut State University*

Diane Lending, *James Madison University*

David Lewis, *University of Massachusetts, Lowell*

Keith Lindsey, *Trinity University*

Stephen Loy, *Eastern Kentucky University*

Steven Lunce, *Midwestern State University*

Efrem Mallach, *University of Massachusetts*

Purnendu Mandal, *Marshall University*

Ronald Mashburn, *West Texas A&M University*

Richard Mathieu, *James Madison University*

Sathasivam Mathiyalakan, *University of Massachusetts, Boston*

Dan Matthews, *Trine University*

Ron McFarland, *Western New Mexico University*

Patricia McQuaid, *California Polytechnic State University,*
  San Luis Obispo
Stephanie Miserlis, *Hellenic College*
Wai Mok, *University of Alabama in Huntsville*
Janette Moody, *The Citadel*
Ata Nahouraii, *Indiana University of Pennsylvania*
Adriene Nawrocki, *John F. Kennedy University*
Anne Nelson, *Nova Southeastern University*
Irina Neuman, *McKendree College*
Donald Norris, *Southern New Hampshire University*
Margaret O'Hara, *East Carolina University*
Ravi Patnayakuni, *University of Alabama, Huntsville*
Ravi Paul, *East Carolina University*
Lowell Peck, *Central Connecticut State University*
Richard Peschke, *Minnesota State University, Mankato*
Doncho Petkov, *Eastern Connecticut State University*
Olga Petkova, *Central Connecticut State University*
Leonard Presby, *William Paterson University of New Jersey*
Terry Province, *North Central Texas College*
Uzma Raja, *University of Alabama*
Adriane Randolph, *Kennesaw State University*
Harry Reif, *James Madison University*
Karl Reimers, *Mount Olive College*
Wes Rhea, *Kennesaw State University*
Frances Roebuck, *Wilson Technical Community College*
Richard Roncone, *United States Coast Guard Academy*
Roberta Roth, *University of Northern Iowa*
Cynthia Ruppel, *Nova Southeastern University*
Bruce Russell, *Northeastern University*
Ramesh Sankaranarayanan, *University of Connecticut*
Eric Santanen, *Bucknell University*
Atul Saxena, *Mercer University*
Charles Saxon, *Eastern Michigan University*
David Scanlan, *California State University, Sacramento*
Herb Schuette, *Elon University*
Ken Sears, *University of Texas, Arlington*
Robert Seidman, *Southern New Hampshire University*

Tom Seymour, *Minot State University*
Sherri Shade, *Kennesaw State University*
Ganesan Shankar, *Boston University*
Emily Shepard, *Central Carolina Community College*
Lakisha Simmons, *Belmont University*
David Smith, *Cameron University*
Glenn Smith, *James Madison University*
Stephen Solosky, *Nassau Community College*
Howard Sparks, *University of Alaska Fairbanks*
George Strouse, *York College*
Gladys Swindler, *Fort Hays State University*
Arta Szathmary, *Bucks County Community College*
Robert Szymanski, *University of South Carolina*
Albert Tay, *Idaho State University*
Winston Tellis, *Fairfield University*
Asela Thomason, *California State University, Long Beach*
Lou Thompson, *University of Texas, Dallas*
Anthony Townsend, *Iowa State University*
Goran Trajkovski, *Western Governors University*
Kim Troboy, *Arkansas Technical University*
Jonathan Trower, *Baylor University*
Ronald Trugman, *Cañada College*
Nancy Tsai, *California State University, Sacramento*
Betty Tucker, *Weber State University*
William Tucker, *Austin Community College*
David VanOver, *Sam Houston State University*
Therese Viscelli, *Georgia State University*
William Wagner, *Villanova University*
Rick Weible, *Marshall University*
Melody White, *University of North Texas*
Robert Wilson, *California State University, San Bernardino*
Elaine Winston, *Hofstra University*
Joe Wood, *Webster University*
Michael Workman, *Florida Institute of Technology*
Kathie Wright, *Salisbury University*
James Yao, *Montclair State University*
Don Yates, *Louisiana State University*

ENDNOTES

1. Wayne Cunningham, "Intel Finds Seven Trillion Reasons to Build Self-Driving Cars," CNET, June 1, 2017, accessed June 23, 2018, *www.cnet.com/roadshow/news/intel-finds-seven-trillion-reasons-to-build-self-driving-cars.*
2. SCDigest Editorial Staff, "Supply Chain News: The Future of Distribution Automation, It Seems, Is Here Right Now," *SupplyChainDigest.com,* June 20, 2018, accessed June 23, 2018, *www.scdigest.com/ontarget/18-06-20-2.php?cid=14351.*
3. Risk Based Security, "Data Breach QuickView Report Year End 2017," January 2017, *RiskedBasedSecurity.com,* accessed June 16, 2018, *www.rpsins.com/media/2884/mc_000063 4a-yearendreport.pdf.*
4. Olivia Krauth, "The 10 Tech Companies That Have Invested the Most Money in AI," *Tech Republic,* January 12, 2018 accessed June 23, 2018, *www.techrepublic.com/article/the-10-tech-companies-that-have-invested-the-most-money-in-ai.*
5. Robert B. Reich, *The Work of Nations* (New York: Alfred A. Knopf, 1991), p. 229.
6. Some instructors take the next step and replace their lectures with their own recorded PowerPoints, in what is coming to be known as flipping the classroom. The So What? features, guides, collaboration exercises, and case studies in this text support that approach if you choose it. See the article titled "How the Flipped Classroom Is Radically Transforming Learning" on *www.thedailyriff.com* for more about this technique.
7. Marilla Svinicki, *Learning and Motivation in the Postsecondary Classroom* (New York: Anker Publishing), 2004.

ABOUT THE AUTHORS

David Kroenke has many years of teaching experience at Colorado State University, Seattle University, and the University of Washington. He has led dozens of seminars for college professors on the teaching of information systems and technology; in 1991, the International Association of Information Systems named him Computer Educator of the Year. In 2009, David was named Educator of the Year by the Association of Information Technology Professionals-Education Special Interest Group (AITP-EDSIG).

David worked for the U.S. Air Force and Boeing Computer Services. He was a principal in the startup of three companies, serving as the vice president of product marketing and development for the Microrim Corporation and as chief of database technologies for Wall Data, Inc. He is the father of the semantic object data model. David's consulting clients have included IBM, Microsoft, and Computer Sciences Corporations, as well as numerous smaller companies. Recently, David has focused on using information systems for teaching collaboration and teamwork.

His text *Database Processing* was first published in 1977 and is now in its 15th edition. He has authored and coauthored many other textbooks, including *Database Concepts*, 8th ed. (2017), *Experiencing MIS*, 8th ed. (2018), *SharePoint for Students* (2012), *Office 365 in Business* (2012), and *Processes, Systems, and Information: An Introduction to MIS*, 3rd ed. (2018).

Randall J. Boyle received his Ph.D. in Management Information Systems from Florida State University in 2003. He also has a master's degree in Public Administration and a B.S. in Finance. He has received university teaching awards at Longwood University, the University of Utah, and the University of Alabama in Huntsville. He has taught a wide variety of classes, including Introduction to MIS, Cyber Security, Networking & Servers, System Analysis and Design, Telecommunications, Advanced Cyber Security, Decision Support Systems, and Web Servers.

His research areas include deception detection in computer-mediated environments, secure information systems, the effects of IT on cognitive biases, the effects of IT on knowledge workers, and e-commerce. He has published in several academic journals and has authored several textbooks, including *Experiencing MIS*, 8th ed., *Corporate Computer and Network Security*, 4th ed., *Applied Information Security*, 2nd ed., and *Applied Networking Labs*, 2nd ed.

To C.J., Carter, and Charlotte
—David Kroenke

To Courtney, Noah, Fiona, Layla, and Henry
—Randy Boyle

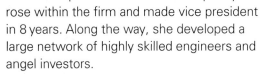

Why MIS?

eHermes is a 5-year-old, privately owned company that provides mobile shopping experiences using self-driving vehicles. Essentially, it's eBay on wheels that brings a mobile storefront right to your door. eHermes acts as a local classified broker that sells both used and new items. Its mobile storefronts pick up items customers want to sell and drop off items customers want to buy. Each of eHermes' mobile storefronts, which look like futuristic transparent shipping containers, can hold hundreds of different items.

eHermes mobile storefronts allow customers to physically inspect hundreds of similar items without having to meet sellers in person. Customers love this feature, and they often end up buying several items when the storefront stops in front of their house. eHermes charges a fee to put items up for sale for a set amount of time and receives a commission on each item purchased. The company also makes a moderate amount of ad revenue from its Web site and mobile app.

eHermes' CEO and cofounder is Jessica Ramma, a former VP at a midsized venture capital (VC) firm in California. Jessica got her MBA from the University of Chicago and immediately went to work analyzing high-tech startups for the VC firm. She quickly rose within the firm and made vice president in 8 years. Along the way, she developed a large network of highly skilled engineers and angel investors.

While investigating a startup, she met Victor Vazquez. At the time, Victor was managing a small artificial intelligence startup that was working on a groundbreaking vision system. Victor was charming, intelligent, and wealthy and had already run several successful startups. He had the uncanny ability to know which companies were going to be successful, and he could effectively work with the founders to grow their companies quickly.

Source: Chesky/Shutterstock

1

Source: Andrey Suslov/Shutterstock

Jessica asked Victor about the practical applications of his company's vision system, and he kept coming back to its potential use in self-driving vehicles. Victor explained that self-driving vehicles can see better than human drivers and can react much more quickly if something goes wrong. The conversation then shifted to a broader discussion of the impact of self-driving vehicles. Jessica was convinced of the inevitability of widespread self-driving vehicle adoption and wondered how this might affect existing business models. In fact, a friend of hers, Kamala Patel, had developed some of the first inter-vehicle protocols used to send information between vehicles. Kamala was passionate about automation and believed self-driving vehicles would affect nearly every industry. Jessica asked Victor if he would have lunch with her and Kamala the following week. She had an idea.

At the lunch, Jessica pitched Victor and Kamala on the eHermes idea, and the company was born a few months later. Fast forward 5 years. eHermes now has several dozen mobile storefronts with revenues of about $8 million per year. As the CEO, Jessica wants to grow the company more quickly by providing mobile storefronts to traditional companies like Walmart and local grocery stores as well as e-commerce retailers like Amazon. Victor is worried that the company is not ready. It's been a bumpy ride just to get the existing mobile storefronts working correctly.

Designing, building, and testing the storefronts have been expensive and, at times, frustrating. Creating the inventory tracking system was more complicated than initially thought. The routing, coordination, and optimization of the storefronts have been a nightmare, too. Inefficient routes increase fuel consumption, which has a big impact on the company's bottom line. And then there's the hugely expensive systems development project that's currently under way to automate the collection, storage, and analysis of storefront data. Currently, everything is recorded manually by sales associates who ride inside each storefront. Any new inventory is brought back to the warehouse, where it's photographed and entered into the online system.

Victor feels like they should wait to expand the business. The company doesn't have the money or the people to start a major expansion like the one Jessica is thinking about. But customers love buying from eHermes, and sales projections look promising. The company has gotten a lot of positive press lately, and investors are more than willing to throw money into the company.

Jessica also mentioned that they should explore the possibility of using some type of artificial intelligence (AI) or machine learning to increase the efficiency of the fleet. Coordinating all of the sales stops, inventory pickups, mobile storefront stocking, travel routes, charging and fueling times, and maintenance schedules is incredibly complex. The current system is working OK, but it's not optimal. And it's hurting eHermes financially. The company needs a fully integrated solution.

CHAPTER 1

The Importance of MIS

"Fired? You're firing me?"

"Well, *fired* is a harsh word, but . . . well, eHermes has no further need of your services."

"But, Victor, I don't get it. I really don't. I worked hard, and I did everything you told me to do."

"Amanda, that's just it. You did everything *I* told you to do."

"I put in so many hours. How could you fire me?"

"Your job was to find ways to reduce our costs using AI or machine learning."

"Right! And I did that."

"No, you didn't. You followed up on ideas *that I gave you.* But we don't need someone who can follow up on my plans. We need someone who can figure out what we need to do, create her own plans, and bring them back to me . . . and others."

"How could you expect me to do that? I've only been here 6 months!"

"It's called teamwork. Sure, you're just learning our business, but I made sure all of our senior staff would be available to you . . ."

"I didn't want to bother them."

MyLab MIS

Using Your Knowledge
Questions 1-1, 1-2, 1-3
Essay Questions 1-15, 1-16

"Well, you succeeded. I asked Kamala what she thought of the plans you're working on. 'Who's Amanda?' she asked."

"But doesn't she work down at the warehouse hub?"

"Right. She's in charge of operations . . . and it would seem to be worth talking to her."

"I'll go do that!"

"Amanda, do you see what just happened? I gave you an idea, and you said you'd do it. That's not what I need. I need you to find solutions on your own."

"I worked really hard. I put in a lot of hours. I've got all these reports written."

"Has anyone seen them?"

"I talked to you about some of them. But I was waiting until I was satisfied with them."

"Right. That's not how we do things here. We develop ideas and then kick them around with each other. Nobody has all the smarts. Our plans get better when we comment and rework them . . . I think I told you that."

"Maybe you did. But I'm just not comfortable with that."

"Well, it's a key skill here."

"I know I can do this job."

"Amanda, you've been here almost 6 months; you have a degree in business and information systems. Several weeks ago, I asked you for your first idea for a process that would identify which AIs or machine learning processes could be used to reduce costs and increase efficiency. Do you remember what you said?"

"But today, they're not enough."

Source: Haiyin Wang/Alamy Stock Photo

"Yes, I wasn't sure how to proceed. I didn't want to just throw something out that might not work."

"But how would you find out if it would work?"

"I don't want to waste money . . . "

"No, you don't. So, when you didn't get very far with that task, I backed up and asked you to send me a list of companies that are currently using AIs and machine learning. I wanted to know what *types* of problems they're solving, the magnitude of efficiency gains they're realizing, how long it took to implement these systems, and a basic description of how they might be used in our company. Not details, just an overview."

"Yes, I sent you those lists and descriptions."

"Amanda, they made no sense. Your lists included companies that use AI vision systems and natural language processing systems; and your description of how AI could be used at eHermes was focused on robotics."

"I know they can be used for planning and optimization too, I just didn't include it in the material I sent you. But I'll try again!"

Study QUESTIONS

Q1-1 Why is Introduction to MIS the most important class in the business school?

Q1-2 How will MIS affect me?

Q1-3 What is MIS?

Q1-4 How can you use the five-component model?

Q1-5 What is information?

Q1-6 What are necessary data characteristics?

Q1-7 2029?

"Well, I appreciate that attitude, but we're a small company, really still a startup in many ways. Everyone needs to pull more than their own weight here. Maybe if we were a bigger company, I'd be able to find for a spot for you, see if we could bring you along. But we can't afford to do that now."

"What about my references?"

"I'll be happy to tell anyone that you're reliable, that you work 40 to 45 hours a week, and that you're honest and have integrity."

"Those are important!"

"Yes, they are. But today, they're not enough."

Chapter PREVIEW

"But today, they're not enough."

Do you find that statement sobering? And if hard work isn't enough, what is? We'll begin this book by discussing the key skills that Amanda (and you) need and explaining why this course is the single best course in the business school for teaching you those key skills.

You may find that last statement surprising. If you are like most students, you have no clear idea of what your MIS class will be about. If someone were to ask you, "What do you study in that class?" you might respond that the class has something to do with computers and maybe computer programming. Beyond that, you might be hard-pressed to say more. You might add, "Well, it has something to do with computers in business," or maybe, "We are going to learn to solve business problems with computers using spreadsheets and other programs." So, how could this course be the most important one in the business school?

We begin with that question. After you understand how important this class will be to your career, we will discuss fundamental concepts. We'll wrap up with some practice on one of the key skills you need to learn.

Q1-1   Why Is Introduction to MIS the Most Important Class in the Business School?

Introduction to MIS is the most important class in the business school. This wasn't always the case. A couple decades ago, majoring in "computers" was considered a nerdy thing to do. But things have changed—a lot. Now the hottest jobs are found in tech companies. People brag about working for tech startups. Apple Inc. is the largest corporation in the world with a market cap of $919B. The largest IPO offering in history ($25B) came from the online e-commerce giant Alibaba (Alibaba Holdings Group) in 2014.

But why? Why has information technology changed from a minor corporate support function to a primary driver of corporate profitability? Why are tech jobs some of the highest paid? Why is working for a tech company considered über cool?

The answer has to do with the way technology is fundamentally changing business.

The Digital Revolution

You've probably heard that we live in the **Information Age**, or a period in history where the production, distribution, and control of information is the primary driver of the economy. The Information Age started in the 1970s with the **Digital Revolution**, or the conversion from mechanical and analog devices to digital devices. This shift to digital devices meant monumental changes for companies, individuals, and our society as a whole.

The problem was, people couldn't really understand how, or even why, this shift was going to affect them. Much like people today, they based their future projections on past events. They knew factories, bureaucracies, mass production, and operational efficiency. But this knowledge didn't prepare them for the changes that were coming.

The Digital Revolution didn't just mean that new "digital" equipment was replacing old mechanical, or analog, equipment. These new digital devices could now be connected to other digital devices and share data among themselves. They could also work faster as processor speed increased. This was groundbreaking. In 1972, computer scientist Gordon Bell recognized that these digital devices would change the world as they evolved and became widely used. He formulated **Bell's Law**, which states that "a new computer class forms roughly each decade establishing a new industry."[1] In other words, digital devices will evolve so quickly that they will enable new platforms, programming environments, industries, networks, and information systems every 10 years.

And it has happened just as Bell predicted. About every 10 years since 1970, entirely new classes of digital devices have emerged. They have created entirely new industries, companies, and platforms. In the 1980s, we saw the rise of the personal computer (PC) and small local networks. In the 1990s, we saw the rise of the Internet and widespread adoption of cellular phones. In the 2000s, we saw a push toward making all "things" network-enabled. Social networking and cloud-based services really took off, creating a flurry of new companies. In the 2010s, so far, we've seen huge advances in artificial intelligence, 3D printing, digital reality devices (e.g., Microsoft Hololens), self-driving vehicles, and cryptocurrencies.

The evolution of digital technology has fundamentally altered businesses and become a primary driver of corporate profitability. And it will probably continue to do so for at least the next few decades. The key to understanding how businesses will be affected by this digital evolution is understanding the forces pushing the evolution of these new digital devices.

Evolving Capabilities

To understand the fundamental forces pushing the evolution of digital devices, let's imagine your body is evolving at the same rate as digital devices. Suppose you can run 8 miles per hour today. That's about average. Now suppose, hypothetically, that your body is changing so quickly that you can run twice as fast every 18 months. In 18 months, you'd be able to run 16 mph. In another 18 months, you'd be at 32 mph. Then 64, 128, 256, and 512. Then, after 10 1/2 years of growth, you'd be running 1,024 mph—on foot! How would this change your life?

Well, you'd certainly give up your car. It would be much too slow. Air travel would also probably be a thing of the past. You could start a very profitable package delivery business and quickly corner the market. You could live outside of the city because your commute would be shorter. You'd also need new clothes and some really tough shoes! And this is the key point—not only would *you* change, but *what* you do and *how* you do it would also change. This is Bell's Law. This same thing is happening to digital devices.

This example may seem silly at first, but it helps you understand how exponential change is affecting digital devices. Processing power, interconnectivity of devices, storage capacity, and bandwidth are all increasing extremely rapidly—so rapidly that it's changing how these devices are used. Let's explore some of these forces by looking at the laws that describe them.

Moore's Law

In 1965, Gordon Moore, cofounder of Intel Corporation, stated that because of technology improvements in electronic chip design and manufacturing, "The number of transistors per square inch on an integrated chip doubles every 18 months." This became known as **Moore's Law**. His statement has been commonly misunderstood to be "The speed of a computer doubles every 18 months," which is incorrect but captures the sense of his principle.

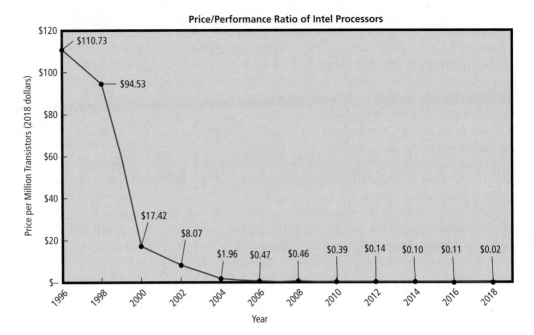

FIGURE 1-1
**Computer Price/
Performance Ratio
Decreases**

Source: © Based on data from
ark.intel.com#@Processors

Because of Moore's Law, the ratio of price to performance of computer processors has fallen dramatically. In 1996, when the Internet was really starting to take off, a standard CPU cost about $110 per million transistors. By 2018 that price had fallen to $0.02 per million transistors.[2] See Figure 1-1. Increasing processing power has had a greater impact on the global economy in the past 30 years than any other single factor. It has enabled new devices, applications, companies, and platforms. In fact, most tech companies would not exist today if processing power hadn't increased exponentially.

As a future business professional, however, you needn't care how fast of a computer your company can buy for $1,000. That's not the point. The point is, because of Moore's Law, the cost of data processing is approaching zero. Current applications like new drug development, artificial intelligence, and molecular modeling require massive amounts of processing power. Innovations in these areas are being held back because the cost of buying sufficient processing power is so high. But the good news is that the cost of processing is dropping—rapidly.

Metcalfe's Law

Another fundamental force that is changing digital devices is Metcalfe's Law, named after Robert Metcalfe, the inventor of Ethernet. **Metcalfe's Law** states that the value of a network is equal to the square of the number of users connected to it. In other words, as more digital devices are connected together, the value of that network will increase.[3] See Figure 1-2. Metcalfe's Law can be clearly seen in the dramatic rise of the Internet in the 1990s. As more users gained access to the Internet, it became more valuable. The dot-com boom ushered in tech giants like Google, Amazon, and eBay. None of these companies would have existed without large numbers of users connected to the Internet.

Metcalfe's Law isn't lost on tech companies, either. Google's Project Loon is a major effort to bring Internet access to everyone on the planet using a network of inflated balloons floating around the world. One of the primary metrics for social media companies is the number of monthly active users (MAU) using their social network. The more people they can get in their network, the more their company will be worth. And look at the network effects of using products like Microsoft Word. Why do you pay for Microsoft Word when you could use a free word processor like LibreOffice Writer? You pay for Microsoft Word because everyone else uses it.

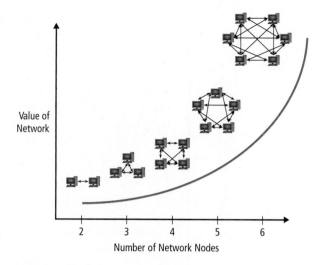

FIGURE 1-2
Increasing Value of Networks

Value of
Network

Number of Network Nodes

Other Forces Pushing Digital Change

And it's not just the number of users on the network that's changing the way we use digital devices—it's the *speed* of the network. **Nielsen's Law**, named after Jakob Nielsen, says that network connection speeds for high-end users will increase by 50 percent per year. As networks become faster, new companies, new products, and new platforms will emerge.

YouTube, for example, started in February 2005 when there wasn't a lot of video shared over the Internet. But average Internet speeds were increasing to the point where a typical Internet connection could handle a stream of YouTube videos. By November 2006, the company was bought by Google for $1.65B. If you're counting, that's less than 2 years to create a billion-dollar company. Network speed matters. The question is, why didn't Google, Microsoft, IBM, or Apple think of video sharing before the YouTube founders?

There are other forces changing digital devices beyond Nielsen's Law, Metcalfe's Law, and Moore's Law. See Figure 1-3. **Kryder's Law**, named after Mark Kryder, the former chief technology officer of Seagate Corp., says that the storage density on magnetic disks is increasing at an exponential rate. See Figure 1-4. Digital storage is so important that it's typically the first question you ask when you buy a new computer, smartphone, or tablet. There's also power consumption, image resolution, and interconnectivity between devices, all of which are changing, too. And this isn't a complete list.

This Is the Most Important Class in the School of Business

This takes us back to our original statement that Introduction to MIS is the most important class you will take in the school of business. Why? Because this class will show you how technology is fundamentally changing businesses. You'll learn why executives are constantly trying to find ways

Law	Meaning	Implications
Moore's Law	The number of transistors per square inch on an integrated chip doubles every 18 months.	Computers are getting exponentially faster. The cost of data processing is approaching zero.
Metcalfe's Law	The value of a network is equal to the square of the number of users connected to it.	More digital devices are connected together. The value of digital and social networks is increasing exponentially.
Nielsen's Law	Network connection speeds for high-end users will increase by 50 percent per year.	Network speed is increasing. Higher speeds enable new products, platforms, and companies.
Kryder's Law	The storage density on magnetic disks is increasing at an exponential rate.	Storage capacity is increasing exponentially. The cost of storing data is approaching zero.

FIGURE 1-3
Fundamental Forces
Changing Technology

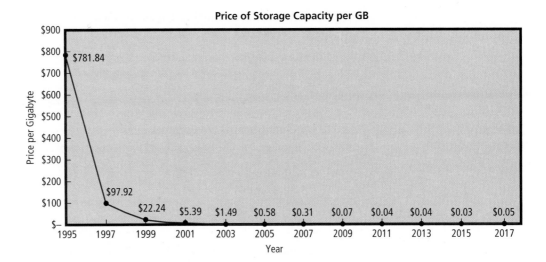

FIGURE 1-4
**Price of Storage Capacity
per GB**

to use new technology to create a sustainable competitive advantage. This leads us to the first reason Introduction to MIS is the most important course in the business school today:

> **Future business professionals need to be able to assess, evaluate, and apply emerging information technology to business.**

You need the knowledge of this course to attain that skill.

Q1-2 How Will MIS Affect Me?

Technological change is accelerating. So what? How is this going to affect you? You may think that the evolution of technology is just great. You can hardly wait for the next iGadget to come out.

But pause for a second and imagine you graduated from college in 2004 and went to work for one of the largest and most successful home entertainment companies in the United States—Blockbuster LLC. In 2004, Blockbuster had 60,000 employees and 9,000-plus stores with $5.9B in annual revenues. Everything looked peachy. Fast-forward 6 years to 2010 and Blockbuster was bankrupt! Why? Because streaming a video over the Internet is easier than driving to a store. High-speed Internet connections made it all possible.

The point is that after graduation you too may choose to go to work for a large, successful, well-branded company. And 6 years down the road, it could be bankrupt because technology changed and it didn't.

How Can I Attain Job Security?

Many years ago, I had a wise and experienced mentor. One day I asked him about job security, and he told me that the only job security that exists is "a marketable skill and the courage to use it." He continued, "There is no security in our company, there is no security in any government program, there is no security in your investments, and there is no security in Social Security." Alas, how right he turned out to be.

So, what is a marketable skill? It used to be that one could name particular skills, such as computer programming, tax accounting, or marketing. But today, because of Moore's Law, Metcalfe's Law, and Kryder's Law, the cost of data processing, storage, and communications is essentially zero. Any routine skill can and will be outsourced to the lowest bidder. And if you live in the United States, Canada, Australia, Europe, or another advanced economy, the lowest bidder is unlikely to be you.

Numerous organizations and experts have studied the question of what skills will be marketable during your career. Consider two of them. First, the RAND Corporation, a think tank located in Santa Monica, California, has published innovative and groundbreaking ideas for more than

70 years, including the initial design for the Internet. In 2004, RAND published a description of the skills that workers in the 21st century will need:

> Rapid technological change and increased international competition place the spotlight on the skills and preparation of the workforce, particularly the ability to adapt to changing technology and shifting demand. Shifts in the nature of organizations . . . favor strong nonroutine cognitive skills.[4]

Whether you're majoring in accounting, marketing, finance, or information systems, you need to develop strong nonroutine cognitive skills.

What are such skills? Robert Reich, former Secretary of Labor, enumerates four:[5]

- Abstract reasoning
- Systems thinking
- Collaboration
- Ability to experiment

Figure 1-5 shows an example of each. Reread the eHermes case that started this chapter, and you'll see that Amanda lost her job because of her inability to practice these key skills. Even though Reich's book was written in the early 1990s, the cognitive skills he mentions are still relevant today because humans, unlike technology, aren't changing that rapidly.[6]

How Can Intro to MIS Help You Learn Nonroutine Skills?

Introduction to MIS is the best course in the business school for learning Reich's four key skills because every topic requires you to apply and practice them. Here's how.

Abstract Reasoning

Abstract reasoning is the ability to make and manipulate models. You will work with one or more models in every course topic and book chapter. For example, later in this chapter you will learn about a *model* of the five components of an information system. This chapter will describe how to use this model to assess the scope of any new information system project; other chapters will build upon this model.

In this course, you will not just manipulate models that we have developed, you will also be asked to construct models of your own. In Chapter 5, for example, you'll learn how to create data models, and in Chapter 12 you'll learn to make process models.

Systems Thinking

Can you go to a grocery store, look at a can of green beans, and connect that can to U.S. immigration policy? Can you watch tractors dig up a forest of pulpwood trees and connect that woody trash

Skill	Example	Amanda's Problem at eHermes
Abstract Reasoning	Construct a model or representation.	Hesitancy and uncertainty when conceptualizing a method for using AI and machine learning.
Systems Thinking	Model system components and show how components' inputs and outputs relate to one another.	Inability to model eHermes' operational needs.
Collaboration	Develop ideas and plans with others. Provide and receive critical feedback.	Unwilling to work with others on works in progress.
Ability to Experiment	Create and test promising new alternatives, consistent with available resources.	Fear of failure prohibited discussion of new ideas.

FIGURE 1-5
Examples of Critical Skills for Nonroutine Cognition

to Moore's Law? Do you know why Cisco Systems is one of the major beneficiaries of YouTube? Answers to all of these questions require systems thinking. **Systems thinking** is the ability to model the components of the system to connect the inputs and outputs among those components into a sensible whole that reflects the structure and dynamics of the phenomenon observed.

As you are about to learn, this class is about information *systems*. We will discuss and illustrate systems; you will be asked to critique systems; you will be asked to compare alternative systems; you will be asked to apply different systems to different situations. All of those tasks will prepare you for systems thinking as a professional.

Collaboration

Collaboration is the activity of two or more people working together to achieve a common goal, result, or work product. Chapter 7 will teach you collaboration skills and illustrate several sample collaboration information systems. Every chapter of this book includes collaboration exercises that you may be assigned in class or as homework.

Here's a fact that surprises many students: Effective collaboration isn't about being nice. In fact, surveys indicate the single most important skill for effective collaboration is to give and receive critical feedback. Advance a proposal in business that challenges the cherished program of the VP of marketing, and you'll quickly learn that effective collaboration skills differ from party manners at the neighborhood barbeque. So, how do you advance your idea in the face of the VP's resistance? And without losing your job? In this course, you can learn both skills and information systems for such collaboration. Even better, you will have many opportunities to practice them.

Ability to Experiment

"I've never done this before."
"I don't know how to do it."
"But will it work?"
"Is it too weird for the market?"

Fear of failure: the fear that paralyzes so many good people and so many good ideas. In the days when business was stable, when new ideas were just different verses of the same song, professionals could allow themselves to be limited by fear of failure.

Let's look at an example of the application of social networking to the oil change business. Is there a legitimate application of social networking there? If so, has anyone ever done it? Is there anyone in the world who can tell you what to do? How to proceed? No. As Reich says, professionals in the 21st century need to be able to experiment.

Successful experimentation is not throwing buckets of money at every crazy idea that enters your head. Instead, **experimentation** is making a reasoned analysis of an opportunity, envisioning potential solutions, evaluating those possibilities, and developing the most promising ones, consistent with the resources you have.

In this course, you will be asked to use products with which you have no familiarity. Those products might be Microsoft Excel or Access, or they might be features and functions of Blackboard that you have not used. Or you may be asked to collaborate using OneDrive or SharePoint or Google Drive. Will your instructor explain and show every feature of those products that you'll need? You should hope not. You should hope your instructor will leave it up to you to experiment, to envision new possibilities on your own, and to experiment with those possibilities, consistent with the time you have available.

Jobs

Employment is another factor that makes the Introduction to MIS course vitally important to you. Accenture, a technology consulting and outsourcing company, conducted a survey of college graduates in 2017. It found that 84 percent of students expect their employer to provide them with

Occupations	2017 Median Wage	2016–26 Percent Job Growth
Management	$ 102,590	8.5
Computer and mathematical	$ 84,560	13.7
Legal	$ 80,080	9.1
Architecture and engineering	$ 79,180	7.5
Business and financial operations	$ 67,710	9.6
Healthcare practitioners and technical	$ 64,770	15.3
Life, physical, and social science	$ 64,510	9.6
Education, training, and library	$ 48,740	9.4
Arts, design, entertainment, sports, and media	$ 48,230	6.1
Construction and extraction	$ 44,730	11.0
Installation, maintenance, and repair	$ 44,520	6.6
Community and social service	$ 43,840	14.5
Protective service	$ 39,550	4.5
All	$ 37,690	7.4
Office and administrative support	$ 34,740	0.6
Production	$ 33,990	−4.3
Transportation and material moving	$ 31,600	6.2
Healthcare support	$ 28,710	23.6
Sales and related	$ 27,020	2.9
Building and grounds cleaning and maintenance	$ 25,620	9.3
Farming, fishing, and forestry	$ 24,390	−0.3
Personal care and service	$ 23,610	19.1
Food preparation and serving related	$ 21,910	9.3

FIGURE 1-6
Median Wage and Percent Job Growth by Sector
Source: Employment Projections program, U.S. Bureau of Labor Statistics.

additional formal training. Further, 54 percent of recent graduates were working in jobs that did not require their degree or were otherwise underemployed.[7] But this is not the case in job categories related to information systems.

The demand for information systems and business jobs is high and driving future wage growth. According to data from the U.S. Bureau of Labor Statistics, shown in Figure 1-6, the top five occupational categories with the highest median wages in 2017 were management, computer and mathematical, legal, architecture and engineering, and business and financial operations. Projected job growth in computer and mathematical jobs (13.7 percent) was nearly double the average for all occupations (7.4 percent). The mismatch between the high level of tech skills demanded by employers and the low level of tech skills held by employees is known as the **technology skills gap**.

Figure 1-7 shows a more detailed breakdown of salary growth from 2012 to 2016 for specific subcategories under business managers, computer and information technology, and other business occupations. It also shows job growth projections for the years 2016 to 2026.[8] Growth rates of all information systems–related jobs are above the 7 percent average for all occupations.

Information systems and computer technology provide job and wage benefits beyond just IS professionals. Acemoglu and Autor published an impressive empirical study of jobs and wages in the United States and parts of Europe from the 1960s to 2010. They found that early in this period, education and industry were the strongest determinants of employment and salary. However, since 1990, the most significant determinant of employment and salary is the nature of work

	2012 Median Pay	2014 Median Pay	2017 Median Pay	Job Growth (%) 2016–26	Job Growth (N) 2016–26
Business Managers					
Marketing Managers	$ 115,750	$ 123,450	$ 129,380	10%	23,800
Information Systems Managers	$ 120,950	$ 127,640	$ 139,220	12%	44,200
Financial Managers	$ 109,740	$ 115,320	$ 125,080	19%	108,600
Human Resources Managers	$ 99,720	$ 102,780	$ 110,120	9%	12,300
Sales Managers	$ 105,260	$ 110,660	$ 121,060	7%	28,900
Computer and Information Technology					
Computer Network Architects	$ 91,000	$ 98,430	$ 104,650	6%	10,500
Computer Systems Analysts	$ 79,680	$ 82,710	$ 88,270	9%	54,400
Database Administrators	$ 118,700	$ 80,280	$ 87,020	11%	13,700
Information Security Analysts	$ 87,170	$ 88,890	$ 95,510	28%	28,500
Network and Systems Administration	$ 72,560	$ 75,790	$ 81,100	6%	2,400
Software Developers	$ 93,350	$ 97,990	$ 103,560	24%	302,500
Web Developers	$ 62,500	$ 63,490	$ 67,990	15%	24,400
Business Occupations					
Accountants and Auditors	$ 63,550	$ 65,940	$ 69,350	10%	139,900
Financial Analysts	$ 76,950	$ 78,620	$ 84,300	11%	32,200
Management Analysts	$ 78,600	$ 80,880	$ 82,450	14%	115,200
Market Research Analysts	$ 60,300	$ 61,290	$ 63,230	23%	138,300
Logisticians	$ 72,780	$ 73,870	$ 74,590	7%	10,300
Human Resources Specialists	$ 55,640	$ 57,420	$ 60,350	7%	38,900

FIGURE 1-7
Bureau of Labor Statistics Occupational Outlook 2016–2026

Source: Based on Bureau of Labor Statistics, "Computer Systems Analysts," Occupational Outlook Handbook, accessed May 16, 2018, *www.bls.gov/ooh.*

performed. In short, as the price of computer technology plummets, the value of jobs that benefit from it increases dramatically.[9]

For example, plentiful, high-paying jobs are available to business professionals who know how to use information systems to improve business process quality, or those who know how to interpret data mining results for improved marketing, or those who know how to use emerging technology like 3D printing to create new products and address new markets. See the Career Guide on pages 28–29 for more thoughts on why you might consider an IS-related job.

What Is the Bottom Line?

The bottom line? This course is the most important course in the business school because:

1. **It will give you the background you need to assess, evaluate, and apply emerging information systems technology to business.**
2. **It can give you the ultimate in job security—marketable skills— by helping you learn abstraction, systems thinking, collaboration, and experimentation.**
3. **Many well-paid MIS-related jobs are in high demand.**

Q1-3 What Is MIS?

We've used the term *MIS* several times, and you may be wondering exactly what it is. **MIS** stands for **management information systems**, which we define as *the management and use of information systems that help organizations achieve their strategies*. MIS is often confused with the closely related terms *information technology* and *information systems*. An **information system (IS)** is an assembly of hardware, software, data, procedures, and people that produces information. In contrast, **information technology (IT)** refers to the products, methods, inventions, and standards used for the purpose of producing information.

How are MIS, IS, and IT different? You cannot buy an IS. But you can buy IT; you can buy or lease hardware, you can license programs and databases, and you can even obtain predesigned procedures. Ultimately, however, it is *your* people who will assemble the IT you purchase and execute those procedures to employ that new IT. Information technology drives the development of new information systems.

For any new system, you will always have training tasks (and costs), you will always have the need to overcome employees' resistance to change, and you will always need to manage the employees as they use the new system. Hence, you can buy IT, but you cannot buy IS. Once your new information system is up and running, it must be managed and used effectively in order to achieve the organization's overall strategy. This is MIS.

Consider a simple example. Suppose your organization decides to develop a Facebook page. Facebook provides the IT. It provides the hardware and programs, the database structures, and standard procedures. You, however, must create the IS. You have to provide the data to fill your portion of its database, and you must extend its standard procedures with your own procedures for keeping that data current. Those procedures need to provide, for example, a means to review your page's content regularly and a means to remove content that is judged inappropriate. Furthermore, you need to train employees on how to follow those procedures and manage those employees to ensure that they do. MIS is the management of your Facebook page to achieve your organization's overall strategy. Managing your own Facebook page is as simple an IS as exists. Larger, more comprehensive IS that involve many, even dozens, of departments and thousands of employees require considerable work.

The definition of MIS has three key elements: *management and use*, *information systems*, and *strategies*. Let's consider each, starting first with information systems and their components.

Components of an Information System

A **system** is a group of components that interact to achieve some purpose. As you might guess, an *information system (IS)* is a group of components that interacts to produce information. That sentence, although true, raises another question: What are these components that interact to produce information?

Figure 1-8 shows the **five-component framework**—a model of the components of an information system: **computer hardware**, **software**, **data**, **procedures**, and **people**. These five components are present in every information system, from the simplest to the most complex. For example, when you use a computer to write a class report, you are using hardware (the computer, storage disk, keyboard, and monitor), software (Word, WordPerfect, or some other word-processing program), data (the words, sentences, and paragraphs in your report), procedures (the methods you use to start the program, enter your report, print it, and save and back up your file), and people (you).

Consider a more complex example, say, an airline reservation system. It, too, consists of these five components, even though each one is far more complicated. The hardware consists of

FIGURE 1-8
Five Components of an Information System

Five-Component Framework

| Hardware | Software | Data | Procedures | People |

thousands of computers linked together by data communications hardware. Hundreds of different programs coordinate communications among the computers, and still other programs perform the reservations and related services. Additionally, the system must store millions upon millions of characters of data about flights, customers, reservations, and other facts. Hundreds of different procedures are followed by airline personnel, travel agents, and customers. Finally, the information system includes people, not only the users of the system but also those who operate and service the computers, those who maintain the data, and those who support the networks of computers.

The important point here is that the five components in Figure 1-8 are common to all information systems, from the smallest to the largest. As you think about any information system, including a new one like social networking, learn to look for these five components. Realize, too, that an information system is not just a computer and a program, but rather an assembly of computers, programs, data, procedures, and people.

As we will discuss later in this chapter, these five components also mean that many different skills are required besides those of hardware technicians or computer programmers when building or using an information system. See the Career Guide starting on pages 28–29 for more.

Before we move forward, note that we have defined an information system to include a computer. Some people would say that such a system is a **computer-based information system**. They would note that there are information systems that do not include computers, such as a calendar hanging on the wall outside of a conference room that is used to schedule the room's use. Such systems have been used by businesses for centuries. Although this point is true, in this book we focus on computer-based information systems. To simplify and shorten the book, we will use the term *information system* as a synonym for *computer-based information system*.

Management and Use of Information Systems

The next element in our definition of MIS is the *management and use* of information systems. Here we define management to mean develop, maintain, and adapt. Information systems do not pop up like mushrooms after a hard rain; they must be developed. They must also be maintained, and, because business is dynamic, they must be adapted to new requirements.

You may be saying, "Wait a minute, I'm a finance (or accounting or management) major, not an information systems major. I don't need to know how to manage information systems." If you are saying that, you are like a lamb headed for shearing. Throughout your career, in whatever field you choose, information systems will be built for your use and sometimes under your direction. To create an information system that meets your needs, you need to take an *active role* in that system's development. Even if you are not a programmer or a database designer or some other IS professional, you must take an active role in specifying the system's requirements and in managing the system's development project. You will also have an important role in testing the new system. Without active involvement on your part, it will only be good luck that causes the new system to meet your needs.

As a business professional, you are the person who understands business needs and requirements. If you want to apply social networking to your products, you are the one who knows how best to obtain customer responses. The technical people who build networks, the database designers who create the database, the IT people who configure the computers—none of these people know what is needed and whether the system you have is sufficient or whether it needs to be adapted to new requirements. You do!

In addition to management tasks, you will also have important roles to play in the *use* of information systems. Of course, you will need to learn how to employ the system to accomplish your job tasks. But you will also have important ancillary functions as well. For example, when using an information system, you will have responsibilities for protecting the security of the system and its data. You may also have tasks for backing up data. When the system fails (all do, at some point), you will have tasks to perform while the system is down as well as tasks to accomplish to help recover the system correctly and quickly.

Security is critically important when using information systems today. You'll learn much more about it in Chapter 10. But you need to know about strong passwords and their use now, before you get to that chapter. Read and follow the Security Guide on pages 26–27.

Achieving Strategies

The last part of the definition of MIS is that information systems exist to help organizations *achieve their strategies*. First, realize that this statement hides an important fact: Organizations themselves do not "do" anything. An organization is not alive, and it cannot act. It is the people within a business who sell, buy, design, produce, finance, market, account, and manage. So, information systems exist to help people who work in an organization to achieve the strategies of that business.

Information systems are not created for the sheer joy of exploring technology. They are not created so the company can be "modern" or so the company can show it has a social networking presence on the Web. They are not created because the information systems department thinks it needs to be created or because the company is "falling behind the technology curve."

This point may seem so obvious that you might wonder why we mention it. Every day, however, some business somewhere is developing an information system for the wrong reasons. Right now, somewhere in the world, a company is deciding to create a Facebook presence for the sole reason that "every other business has one." This company is not asking questions such as:

- "What is the purpose of our Facebook page?"
- "What is it going to do for us?"
- "What is our policy for employees' contributions?"
- "What should we do about critical customer reviews?"
- "Are the costs of maintaining the page sufficiently offset by the benefits?"

For more information on how an understanding of MIS can broaden your career options, see the Career Guide on pages 28–29.

But that company should ask those questions! Chapter 2 addresses the relationship between information systems and strategy in more depth. Chapter 9 addresses social media and strategy specifically.

Again, MIS is the development and use of information systems that help businesses achieve their strategies. You should already be realizing that there is much more to this class than buying a computer, working with a spreadsheet, or creating a Web page.

Q1-4   How Can You Use the Five-Component Model?

The five-component model in Figure 1-8 can help guide your learning and thinking about IS, both now and in the future. To understand this framework better, first note in Figure 1-9 that these five components are symmetric. The outermost components, hardware and people, are both actors; they can take actions. The software and procedure components are both sets of instructions: Software is instructions for hardware, and procedures are instructions for people. Finally, data is the bridge between the computer side on the left and the human side on the right.

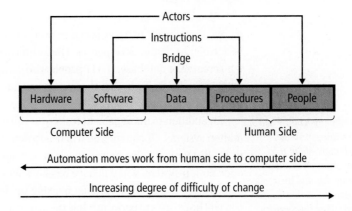

FIGURE 1-9

Characteristics of the Five Components

Now, when we automate a business task, we take work that people are doing by following procedures and move it so that computers will do that work, following instructions in software. Thus, the process of automation is a process of moving work from the right side of Figure 1-9 to the left.

The Most Important Component—You

You are part of every information system that you use. When you consider the five components of an information system, the last component, people, includes you. Your mind and your thinking are not merely a component of the information systems you use; they are the most important component.

As you will learn later in this chapter, computer hardware and programs manipulate data, but no matter how much data they manipulate, it is still just data. It is only humans that produce information. When you take a set of data, say, a list of customer responses to a marketing campaign, that list, no matter if it was produced using 10,000 servers and Hadoop, is still just data. It does not become information until you or some other human take it into your mind and are informed by it.

Even if you have the largest computer farm in the world and even if you are processing that data with the most sophisticated programs, if you do not know what to do with the data those programs produce, you are wasting your time and money. The quality of your thinking is what determines the quality of the information that is produced.

Substantial cognitive research has shown that although you cannot increase your basic IQ, you can dramatically increase the quality of your thinking. That is one reason we have emphasized the need for you to use and develop your abstract reasoning. The effectiveness of an IS depends on the abstract reasoning of the people who use it.

All Components Must Work

Information systems often encounter problems—despite our best efforts, they don't work right. And in these situations, blame is frequently placed on the wrong component. You will often hear people complain that the computer doesn't work, and certainly hardware or software is sometimes at fault. But with the five-component model, you can be more specific, and you have more suspects to consider. Sometimes the data is not in the right format or, worse, is incorrect. Sometimes, the procedures are not clear and the people using the system are not properly trained. By using the five-component model, you can better locate the cause of a problem and create effective solutions.

High-Tech Versus Low-Tech Information Systems

Information systems differ in the amount of work moved from the human side (people and procedures) to the computer side (hardware and programs). For example, consider two different versions of a customer support information system: A system that consists only of a file of email addresses and an email program is a very low-tech system. Only a small amount of work has been moved from the human side to the computer side. Considerable human work is required to determine when to send which emails to which customers.

In contrast, a customer support system that keeps track of the equipment that customers have and the maintenance schedules for that equipment and then automatically generates email reminders to customers is a higher-tech system. This simply means that more work has been moved from the human side to the computer side. The computer is providing more services on behalf of the humans.

Often, when considering different information systems alternatives, it will be helpful to consider the low-tech versus high-tech alternatives in light of the amount of work being moved from people to computers.

SO WHAT?   A IS FOR ALPHABET

We are living in an era referred to as the Information Age, a period in human history characterized by the shift from an economy based on industrial production to one based on information and computerization.[10] This shift has changed virtually every aspect of our lives, from the way we communicate with friends, coworkers, and loved ones to the way we purchase goods and carry out various financial transactions. What advancement made this shift possible? You guessed it—the Internet!

As with most technological innovations, the Internet started out as a project sponsored by both research and governmental entities. It took several decades to lay the groundwork for the Internet as we know it today, and the tipping point for widespread Internet use was the introduction of Netscape Navigator, the Web browser of choice in the mid-1990s. The adoption and use of Netscape was critical because it allowed fledgling Internet users to access information posted by other users around the world. At that time, the content available on the Internet was minimal and only tech-savvy users could create and manage content. Over time, the amount of information available became so great that new tools were needed to search the Internet. Enter Google.

Google Searches for a Better Future in Alphabet

Today, Google is the dominant Internet search engine and is one of the largest publicly traded companies in the world. What you may not realize is that Google's core search engine service (Google Search) is only one of many successful products in a larger portfolio. Google has turned Google Maps, YouTube, Chrome, and Android into successful standalone offerings. The success and diversity of Google's many projects led the company to announce that, as of August 10, 2015, it was a subsidiary of an overarching company named Alphabet Inc.[11]

Google founders Larry Page and Sergey Brin decided that it was time to reduce their involvement in the daily management of Google projects. To facilitate this change, each project was transitioned into a standalone company with its own CEO, and each standalone company is a subsidiary of Alphabet Inc. In this way, Page and Brin can manage the overall strategic objectives of the subsidiaries without having to immerse themselves in the daily operations of each company.

Why did they choose the name Alphabet? In a blog post about the new direction of the company, Page revealed that there are a number of meanings associated with this new name. First, an alphabet represents the collection of letters used to define a language, which Page classifies as one of humanity's

Source: Ian Dagnall Commercial Collection/Alamy Stock Photo

most profound creations. Second, alphabets serve as the basis for Google searches around the world. Finally, in the world of finance, alpha represents an investment return above the benchmark, which according to Page, is something the company is continuously striving to achieve.[12]

While Page's rationale about the restructuring makes sense, outsiders have identified this strategy as a direct response to Google's struggles to retain top talent in a highly competitive industry. Before restructuring, Google housed a wide variety of projects and research initiatives under one roof; this led to an increasingly bureaucratic climate and inherent limitations on the career trajectories of industry superstars.[13] Alphabet was born to create a new corporate environment in which top talent can thrive. In the Alphabet hierarchy, individual companies are much more nimble and better able to provide the autonomy and efficiency that smaller companies offer.

When future generations look back at the Information Age, it is likely Alphabet will be seen as playing a prominent role. With all of the projects the company is pursuing—everything from drones and robots to medical research and artificial intelligence—it is intriguing to think about the role Alphabet will play in shaping the next era of humanity.

Questions

1. The feature identifies the Internet as a catalyst for the Information Age. What other innovations have contributed to this era of unprecedented access to information via computers?

2. Think about your daily use of phones, tablets, and traditional desktop/laptop computers. How many searches do you perform each day? What types of things do you search for on the Internet? Do you use Google for these searches? If not, what search engine do you use? Why do you use that search engine?

3. Conduct an Internet search to find a project or product offered by Alphabet that you had not heard about before reading this feature. Are you surprised at the diversity of the company and its projects and research initiatives?

4. What technological innovation do you think will drive the next great era in humanity? What do you think the defining elements of that era will be?

The Ethics Guide in each chapter of this book considers the ethics of information systems use. These guides challenge you to think deeply about ethical standards, and they provide for some interesting discussions with classmates. The Ethics Guide on pages 23–24 considers the ethics of presenting data that deceives the viewer.

Understanding the Scope of New Information Systems

The five-component framework can also be used when assessing the scope of new systems. When in the future some vendor pitches the need for a new technology to you, use the five components to assess how big of an investment that new technology represents. What new hardware will you need? What programs will you need to license? What databases and other data must you create? What procedures will need to be developed for both use and administration of the information system? And, finally, what will be the impact of the new technology on people? Which jobs will change? Who will need training? How will the new technology affect morale? Will you need to hire new people? Will you need to reorganize?

Components Ordered by Difficulty and Disruption

Finally, as you consider the five components, keep in mind that Figure 1-9 shows them in order of ease of change and the amount of organizational disruption. It is a simple matter to order additional hardware. Obtaining or developing new programs is more difficult. Creating new databases or changing the structure of existing databases is still more difficult. Changing procedures, requiring people to work in new ways, is even more difficult. Finally, changing personnel responsibilities and reporting relationships and hiring and terminating employees are all very difficult and very disruptive to the organization.

Q1-5 What Is Information?

Based on our earlier discussions, we can now define an information system as an assembly of hardware, software, data, procedures, and people that interact to produce information. The only term left undefined in that definition is *information*, and we turn to it next.

Definitions Vary

Information is one of those fundamental terms that we use every day but that turns out to be surprisingly difficult to define. Defining information is like defining words such as *alive* and *truth*. We know what those words mean, we use them with each other without confusion, but nonetheless, they are difficult to define.

In this text, we will avoid the technical issues of defining information and will use common, intuitive definitions instead. Probably the most common definition is that **information** is knowledge derived from data, whereas *data* is defined as recorded facts or figures. Thus, the facts that employee James Smith earns $70.00 per hour and that Mary Jones earns $50.00 per hour are *data*. The statement that the average hourly wage of all the graphic designers is $60.00 per hour is *information*. Average wage is knowledge derived from the data of individual wages.

Another common definition is that *information is data presented in a meaningful context*. The fact that Jeff Parks earns $30.00 per hour is data.[14] The statement that Jeff Parks earns less than half the average hourly wage of the company's graphic designers, however, is information. It is data presented in a meaningful context.

Another definition of information that you will hear is that *information is processed data* or, sometimes, *information is data processed by summing, ordering, averaging, grouping, comparing, or other similar operations*. The fundamental idea of this definition is that we do something to data to produce information.

There is yet a fourth definition of information, which was set out by the great research psychologist Gregory Bateson. He defined information as *a difference that makes a difference*.

For the purposes of this text, any of these definitions of information will do. Choose the definition of information that makes sense to you. The important point is that you discriminate between data and information. You also may find that different definitions work better in different situations.

Where Is Information?

Suppose you create a graph of Amazon's stock price and net income over its history, like that shown in Figure 1-10. Does that graph contain information? Well, if it shows a difference that makes a difference or if it presents data in a meaningful context, then it fits two of the definitions of information, and it's tempting to say that the graph contains information.

However, show that graph to your family dog. Does your dog find information in that graph? Well, nothing about Amazon, anyway. The dog might learn what you had for lunch, but it won't obtain any information about Amazon 's stock price over time.

Reflect on this experiment and you will realize that the graph is not, itself, information. The graph is data that you and other humans *perceive*, and from that perception you *conceive* information. In short, if it's on a piece of paper or on a digital screen, it's data. If it's in the mind of a human, it's information.

Why, you're asking yourself, do I care? Well, for one, it further explains why you, as a human, are the most important part of any information system you use. The quality of your thinking, of your ability to conceive information from data, is determined by your cognitive skills. *The data is just the data; the information you conceive from it is the value that you add to the information system.*

Furthermore, people have different perceptions and points of view. Not surprisingly, then, they will conceive different information from the same data. You cannot say to someone, "Look, it's right there in front of you, in the data" because it's not right there in the data. Rather, it's in your head and in their heads, and your job is to explain what you have conceived so that others can understand it.

FIGURE 1-10
Amazon Stock Price and Net Income
Source: © Based on data from www .nasdaq.com/symbol/amzn/historical.

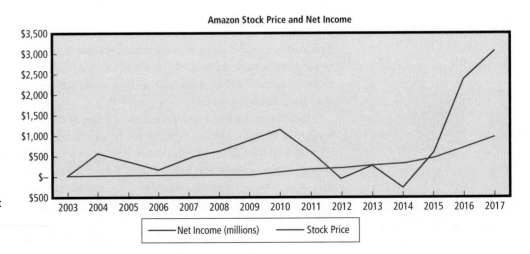

Finally, once you understand this, you'll understand that all kinds of common sentences make no sense. "I sent you that information" cannot be true. "I sent you the data, from which you conceived the information" is the most we can say. During your business career, this observation will save you untold frustration if you remember to apply it.

Q1-6 What Are Necessary Data Characteristics?

You have just learned that humans conceive information from data. As stated, the quality of the information that you can create depends, in part, on your thinking skills. It also depends, however, on the quality of the data you are given. Figure 1-11 summarizes critical data characteristics.

Accurate

First, good information is conceived from accurate, correct, and complete data that has been processed correctly as expected. Accuracy is crucial; business professionals must be able to rely on the results of their information systems. The IS function can develop a bad reputation in the organization if a system is known to produce inaccurate data. In such a case, the information system becomes a waste of time and money as users develop work-arounds to avoid the inaccurate data.

A corollary to this discussion is that you, a future user of information systems, ought not to rely on data just because it appears in the context of a Web page, a well-formatted report, or a fancy query. It is sometimes hard to be skeptical of data delivered with beautiful, active graphics. Do not be misled. When you begin to use a new information system, be skeptical. Cross-check the data you are receiving. After weeks or months of using a system, you may relax. Begin, however, with skepticism. Again, you cannot conceive accurate information from inaccurate data.

Timely

Good information requires that data be timely—available in time for its intended use. A monthly report that arrives 6 weeks late is most likely useless. The data arrives long after the decisions have been made that required the information. An information system that sends you a poor customer credit report after you have shipped the goods is unhelpful and frustrating. Notice that timeliness can be measured against a calendar (6 weeks late) or against events (before we ship).

When you participate in the development of an IS, timeliness will be part of the requirements you specify. You need to give appropriate and realistic timeliness needs. In some cases, developing systems that provide data in near real time is much more difficult and expensive than producing data a few hours later. If you can get by with data that is a few hours old, say so during the requirements specification phase.

Consider an example. Suppose you work in marketing and you need to be able to assess the effectiveness of new online ad programs. You want an information system that not only will deliver ads over the Web but that also will enable you to determine how frequently customers click on those ads. Determining click ratios in near real time will be very expensive; saving the data in a batch and

FIGURE 1-11
Data Characteristics Required for Good Information

- Accurate
- Timely
- Relevant
  - To context
  - To subject
- Just sufficient
- Worth its cost

processing it some hours later will be much easier and cheaper. If you can live with data that is a day or two old, the system will be easier and cheaper to implement.

Relevant

Data should be relevant both to the context and to the subject. Considering context, you, the CEO, need data that is summarized to an appropriate level for your job. A list of the hourly wage of every employee in the company is unlikely to be useful. More likely, you need average wage information by department or division. A list of all employee wages is irrelevant in your context.

Data should also be relevant to the subject at hand. If you want data about short-term interest rates for a possible line of credit, then a report that shows 15-year mortgage interest rates is irrelevant. Similarly, a report that buries the data you need in pages and pages of results is also irrelevant to your purposes.

Just Barely Sufficient

Data needs to be sufficient for the purpose for which it is generated, but just barely so. We are inundated with data; one of the critical decisions that each of us has to make each day is what data to ignore. The higher you rise into management, the more data you will be given, and because there is only so much time, the more data you will need to ignore. So, data should be sufficient, but just barely.

Worth Its Cost

Data is not free. There are costs for developing an information system, costs of operating and maintaining that system, and costs of your time and salary for reading and processing the data the system produces. For data to be worth its cost, an appropriate relationship must exist between the cost of data and its value.

Consider an example. What is the value of a daily report of the names of the occupants of a full graveyard? Zero, unless grave robbery is a problem for the cemetery. The report is not worth the time required to read it. It is easy to see the importance of economics for this silly example. It will be more difficult, however, when someone proposes new technology to you. You need to be ready to ask, "What's the value of the information I can conceive from this data?" "What is the cost?" "Is there an appropriate relationship between value and cost?" Information systems should be subject to the same financial analyses to which other assets are subjected.

 2029?

At the start of this chapter you read about how technology is changing exponentially. Processing power, connectivity of devices, network speed, and data storage are increasing so rapidly that they fundamentally change the way we use technology every 10 years (Bell's Law). Businesspeople need to be able to assess, evaluate, and apply emerging technology. They need to know how these changes affect businesses.

Let's take a guess at technology in the year 2029. Of course, we won't have perfect insight, and, in fact, these guesses will probably seem ludicrous to the person who finds this book for sale for a dollar at a Goodwill store in 2029. But let's exercise our minds in that direction.

Would you use your smartphone differently if it had a gigabyte network connection, an exabyte of data storage, and a battery that lasted a month on a single charge? What if it could connect to every device in your home, car, and office—and control them remotely? With this new device you could store every book, song, and movie ever created. You could capture, store, and stream 8K of UHD video with no delay at all.

On the other hand, maybe smartphones will fade away. Large tech companies are investing tremendous resources into mixed-reality devices like HoloLens, Meta, and Magic Leap that can

ETHICS GUIDE

ETHICS AND PROFESSIONAL RESPONSIBILITY

Suppose you're a young marketing professional who has just taken a new promotional campaign to market. The executive committee asks you to present a summary of the sales effect of the campaign, and you produce the graph shown in Figure 1. As shown, your campaign was just in the nick of time; sales were starting to fall the moment your campaign kicked in. After that, sales boomed.

But note the vertical axis has no quantitative labels. If you add quantities, as shown in Figure 2, the performance is less impressive. It appears that the substantial growth amounts to less than 20 units. Still the curve of the graph is impressive, and if no one does the arithmetic, your campaign will appear successful.

This impressive shape is only possible, however, because Figure 2 is not drawn to scale. If you draw it to scale, as shown in Figure 3, your campaign's success is, well, problematic, at least for you.

Which of these graphs do you present to the committee? Each chapter of this text includes an Ethics Guide that explores ethical and responsible behavior in a variety of MIS-related contexts. In this chapter, we'll examine the ethics of data and information.

Centuries of philosophical thought have addressed the question "What is right behavior?" and we can't begin to discuss all of it here. You will learn much of it, however, in your business ethics class. For our purposes, we'll use two of the major pillars in the philosophy of ethics. We introduce the first one here and the second in Chapter 2.

The German philosopher Immanuel Kant defined the *categorical imperative* as the principle that *one should behave only in a way that one would want the behavior to be a universal law.* Stealing is not such behavior because if everyone steals, nothing can be owned. Stealing cannot be a universal law. Similarly, lying cannot be consistent with the categorical imperative because if everyone lies, words are useless.

When you ask whether a behavior is consistent with this principle, a good litmus test is "Are you willing to publish your behavior to the world? Are you willing to put it on your Facebook page? Are you willing to say what you've done to all the players involved?" If not, your behavior is not ethical, at least not in the sense of Kant's categorical imperative.

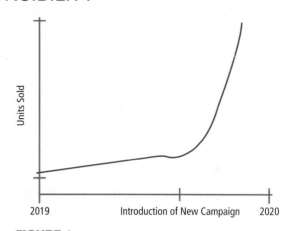

FIGURE 1

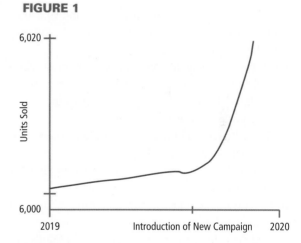

FIGURE 2

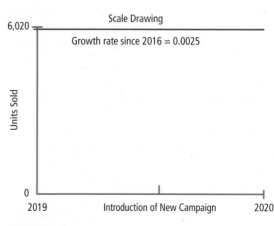

FIGURE 3

Kant defined *duty* as the necessity to act in accordance with the categorical imperative. *Perfect duty* is behavior that must always be met. Not lying is a perfect duty. *Imperfect duty* is action that is praiseworthy but not required according to the categorical imperative. Giving to charity is an example of an imperfect duty.

Kant used the example of cultivating one's own talent as an imperfect duty, and we can use that example as a way of defining professional responsibility. Business professionals have an imperfect duty to obtain the skills necessary to accomplish their jobs. We also have an imperfect duty to continue to develop our business skills and abilities throughout our careers.

We will apply these principles in the chapters that follow. For now, use them to assess your beliefs about Figures 1 through 3 by answering the following questions.

Source: Pressmaster/Fotolia

 # DISCUSSION QUESTIONS

1. Restate Kant's categorical imperative using your own words. Explain why cheating on exams is not consistent with the categorical imperative.
2. While there is some difference of opinion, most scholars believe that the Golden Rule ("Do unto others as you would have them do unto you.") is not equivalent to Kant's categorical imperative. Justify this belief.
3. Using the Bateson definition (discussed in Q1-5) that information is a difference that makes a difference:
   a. Explain how the features of the graph in Figure 1 influence the viewer to create information.
   b. Explain how the features of the graph in Figure 3 influence the viewer to create information.
   c. Which of these graphs is consistent with Kant's categorical imperative?
4. Suppose you created Figure 1 using Microsoft Excel. To do so, you keyed the data into Excel and clicked the Make Graph button (there is one, though it's not called that). Voilà, Excel created Figure 1 without any labels and drawn out of scale as shown. Without further consideration, you put the result into your presentation.
   a. Is your behavior consistent with Kant's categorical imperative? Why or why not?
   b. If Excel automatically produces graphs like Figure 1, is Microsoft's behavior consistent with Kant's categorical imperative? Why or why not?

5. Change roles. Assume now you are a member of the executive committee. A junior marketing professional presents Figure 1 to the committee, and you object to the lack of labels and the scale. In response, the junior marketing professional says, "Sorry, I didn't know. I just put the data into Excel and copied the resulting graph." What conclusions do you, as an executive, make about the junior marketing professional in response to this statement?
6. Is the junior marketing person's response in question 5 a violation of a perfect duty? Of an imperfect duty? Of any duty? Explain your response.
7. If you were the junior marketing professional, which graph would you present to the committee?
8. According to Kant, lying is not consistent with the categorical imperative. Suppose you are invited to a seasonal barbeque at the department chair's house. You are served a steak that is tough, overcooked, and so barely edible that you secretly feed it to the department chair's dog (who appears to enjoy it). The chairperson asks you, "How is your steak?" and you respond, "Excellent, thank you."
   a. Is your behavior consistent with Kant's categorical imperative?
   b. The steak seemed to be excellent to the dog. Does that fact change your answer to part a?
   c. What conclusions do you draw from this example?

create virtual objects within the real world (see Chapter 4). It's possible that changes in technology will make these devices commonplace. People didn't always carry a phone around with them. But now they're in nearly every pocket.

How would these new devices change your everyday life? Well, you wouldn't have to fight over the TV remote control any more. Everyone wearing a Microsoft HoloLens could sit on the couch and watch a *different* show at the same time. In fact, you might not have a two-dimensional TV hanging on the wall at all. 3D Holographic entertainment would take place in the *center* of the room, not on the walls.[15]

Your mixed-reality devices would also have gesture and voice control. That means you could turn your smart lightbulbs on or off by simply pointing to them. You could even see inside your smart refrigerator without leaving the couch! Nice. Also, thanks to increases in connectivity, all of your new smart devices could talk to each other. Imagine waking up in the morning and your smart home turning the lights on automatically. Your smart home then reads off your daily schedule (from your Internet-based calendar), starts your coffeepot, and tells your self-driving car to check for traffic delays.

Advances in technology will undoubtedly have a profound impact on your personal life. But what about the impact of these advances on business? How will they change the way you work? What new types of jobs will be created? What new companies will form to support these advances?

In 2013, then-CEO of Yahoo! Marissa Mayer required her employees to come to work and earned the disdain of many. She said important work gets done in informal meetings around the coffeepot. But what if you could virtually remote into work using a holographic interface and stay at home physically? You could still interact with your boss face-to-face and chat with coworkers at the coffee pot.[16] But you could live anywhere, skip the commute, and work for multiple companies at the same time.

These changes may improve the way you work, but they'll also change the *type* of work you do. People with the ability to effectively experiment will be able to adapt to changes in technology required by their employer. Companies that adapt more quickly will gain a competitive advantage, at least temporarily. For example, an innovative automaker may switch from using desktop computers and traditional CAD design software to using mixed-reality devices and 3D printing to shorten design time.

Systems thinking will also be important because of the need to predict changes caused by interconnected smart devices. For example, medical data (i.e., calories burned, heart rate, etc.) from your smart pacemaker and smartwatch could be integrated into other systems. It could be sent to your doctor, athletic trainer, and insurance company. Your doctor could know you're having a heart attack, call an ambulance, and forward your insurance information to the hospital before you even realize what's happening.

Advances in technology have a downside too. By 2029, privacy may be increasingly difficult to maintain. Your data will be collected by new kinds of apps, flowing through the cloud, and be packaged for sale by companies providing "free" services. Social relationships may suffer as well. We may become less connected to *people* as we become more connected to *systems*. Just look around at your family staring into their tiny phone screens at holiday parties. What will happen when they can watch a high-definition 3D holographic football game without anyone knowing?

We'll take a 2029 look at the end of each chapter. For now, just realize one certainty: Knowledge of information systems and their use in business will be more important, not less.

PASSWORDS AND PASSWORD ETIQUETTE

Many forms of computer security use passwords to control access to systems and data. Most likely, you have a university account that you access with a username and password. When you set up that account, you were probably advised to use a "**strong password**." That's good advice, but what is a strong password? Probably not "sesame," but what then?

Microsoft, a company that has many reasons to promote effective security, provides the following guidelines for creating a strong password. A strong password should:

- Have at least 12 characters; 14 is even better
- Not contain your username, real name, or company name
- Not contain a complete dictionary word in any language
- Be different from previous passwords you have used
- Contain both upper- and lowercase letters, numbers, and special characters (such as ~ ! @; # $ % ^ &; * () _+; =; { } | [] \: "; ' <; >;?,./)

Examples of good passwords are:

- Qw37^T1bb?at
- 3B47qq<3>5!7b

The problem with such passwords is that they are nearly impossible to remember. And the last thing you want to do is write your password on a piece of paper and keep it near the device where you use it. Never do that!

One technique for creating memorable, strong passwords is to base them on the first letter of the words in a phrase. The phrase could be the title of a song or the first line of a poem or one based on some fact about your life. For example, you might take the phrase "I was born in Rome, New York, before 2000." Using the first letters from that phrase and substituting the character < for the word *before*, you create the password IwbiR,NY<2000. That's an acceptable password, but it would be better if all of the numbers were not placed on the end. So, you might try the phrase, "I was born at 3:00 AM in Rome, New York." That phrase yields the password Iwba3:00AMiR,NY which is a strong password that is easily remembered.

Once you have a strong password you want to avoid *reusing* the same password at every site you visit. Not all sites provide the same level of protection for your data. In fact, sometimes they lose your password to hackers. Then hackers can use those passwords to access other sites that you regularly use. Password variety is your friend. Never use the same password for less important sites (e.g., social networking) that you'd use to access more important sites (e.g., online banking).

You also need to protect your password with proper behavior. Never write down your password, do not share it with others, and never ask others for their passwords. Occasionally, an attacker will pretend to be an administrator and ask users for their passwords. You'll never have to give your password to a real administrator. He or she doesn't need it and won't ask for it. He or she already has full access to all corporate computers and systems.

Source: Iqoncept/Fotolia

But what if you need someone else's password? Suppose, for example, you ask someone to help you with a problem on your computer. You sign on to an information system, and for some reason, you need to enter that other person's password. In this case, say to the other person, "We need your password," and then get out of your chair, offer your keyboard to the other person, and look away while she enters the password. Among professionals working in organizations that take security seriously, this little "do-si-do" move—one person getting out of the way so another person can enter her password—is common and accepted.

If someone asks for your password, do not give it out. Instead, get up, go over to that person's machine, and enter your own password yourself. Stay present while your password is in use, and ensure that your account is logged out at the end of the activity. No one should mind or be offended in any way when you do this. It is the mark of a professional.

DISCUSSION QUESTIONS

1. Here is a line from Shakespeare's *Macbeth:* "Tomorrow and tomorrow and tomorrow, creeps in its petty pace." Explain how to use these lines to create a password. How could you add numbers and special characters to the password in a way that you will be able to remember?

2. List two different phrases that you can use to create a strong password. Show the password created by each.

3. One of the problems of life in the cyberworld is that we all are required to have multiple passwords—one for work or school, one for bank accounts, another for eBay or other auction sites, and so forth. Of course, it is better to use different passwords for each. But in that case you have to remember three or four different passwords. Think of different phrases you can use to create a memorable, strong password for each of these different accounts. Relate the phrase to the purpose of the account. Show the passwords for each.

4. Explain proper behavior when you are using your computer and you need to enter, for some valid reason, another person's password.

5. Explain proper behavior when someone else is using her computer and that person needs to enter, for some valid reason, your password.

CAREER GUIDE

FIVE-COMPONENT CAREERS

Some years, even some decades, students can wait until their last semester to think seriously about jobs. They can pick a major, take the required classes, and prepare to graduate, all the while assuming that job recruiters will be on campus, loaded with good jobs, sometime during their senior year. *Alas, today is not one of those periods.*

In the current employment situation, you need to be proactive and aggressive in your job search. Think about it: You will be spending one-third of your waking life in your job. One of the best things you can do for yourself is to begin to think seriously about your career prospects now. You don't want to find yourself working as a barista after 4 years of business school, unless, of course, you're planning on starting the next Starbucks.

So, start here. Are you interested in a career in MIS? At this point, you don't know enough to know, but Figure 1-6 and Figure 1-7 should catch your attention. With job growth like that, in a category of jobs that is net of outsourcing, you should at least ponder whether there is a career for you in IS and related services.

But what does that mean? If you go to the U.S. Bureau of Labor Statistics, you can find that there are more than a million computer programmers in the United States today and more than 600,000 systems analysts. You probably have some notion of what a programmer does, but you don't yet know what a systems analyst is. Examine the five components in Figure 1-8, however, and you can glean some idea. Programmers work primarily with the software component, while systems analysts work with the entire system, with all five components. So, as a systems analyst, you work with

system users to determine what the organizational requirements are and then with technical people (and others) to help develop that system. You work as a cultural broker: translating the culture of technology into the culture of business, and the reverse.

Fortunately for you, many interesting jobs are not captured by the bureau's data. Why fortunate? Because you can use what you're learning in this course to identify and obtain jobs that other students may not think about or even know about. If so, you've gained a competitive advantage.

The chart on the next page provides a framework for thinking about careers in an unconventional way. As you can see, there are technical jobs in MIS but fascinating, challenging, high-paying, nontechnical ones as well. Consider, for example, professional sales. Suppose you have the job of

Source: Tyler Olson/Fotolia

selling enterprise-class software to the Mayo Clinic. You will sell to intelligent, highly motivated professionals with tens of millions of dollars to spend. Or suppose you work for the Mayo Clinic on the receiving end of that sales pitch. How will you spend your tens of millions? You will need knowledge of your business, and you will need to understand enough technology to ask intelligent questions and interpret the responses.

Give this some thought by answering the questions that follow, even if they aren't assigned for a grade!

	Hardware	Software	Data	Procedures	People
Sales & Marketing	Vendors (IBM, Cisco, etc.)	Vendors (Microsoft, Oracle, etc.)	Vendors (Acxiom, Google, etc.)	Vendors (SAP, Infor, Oracle)	Recruiters (Robert Half, Lucas Group)
Support	Vendors Internal MIS	Vendors Internal MIS	Database administration Security	Vendors and internal customer support	Customer support Training
Development	Computer engineering Internal MIS	Application programmer Quality test Engineer	Data modeler Database design	Business process management Process reengineering	Training Internal MIS recruiting
Management	Internal MIS	Internal MIS	Data administration	Project management	Technical management
Consulting	Project management, development, pre- and postsale support				

DISCUSSION QUESTIONS

1. What does the phrase *in a category of jobs that is net of outsourcing* mean? Reread the discussion of Figure 1-6 if you're not certain. Why is this important to you?

2. Examine the five-component careers chart and choose the row that seems most relevant to your interests and abilities. Describe a job in each component column of that row. If you are uncertain, Google the terms in the cells of that row.

3. For each job in your answer to question 2, describe what you think are the three most important skills and abilities for that job.

4. For each job in your answer to question 2, describe one innovative action that you can take this year to increase your employment prospects.

ACTIVE REVIEW

Use this Active Review to verify that you understand the ideas and concepts that answer the chapter's study questions.

Q1-1 Why is Introduction to MIS the most important class in the business school?

Define *Bell's Law* and explain why its consequences are important to business professionals today. Describe how *Moore's Law*, *Metcalfe's Law*, *Nielsen's Law*, and *Kryder's Law* are changing how digital devices are used. State how business professionals should relate to emerging information technology.

Q1-2 How will MIS affect me?

Give the text's definition of *job security* and use Reich's list to explain how this course will help you attain that security. Summarize IS-related job opportunities. According to the Bureau of Labor Statistics, how does the growth rate of IS-related jobs compare with the average growth rate of all jobs nationally?

Q1-3 What is MIS?

Explain why you can buy IT but you can never buy IS. What does that mean to you as a potential future business manager? Identify the three important phrases in the definition of *MIS*. Name the five components of an information system. Using the five-component model, explain the difference between IT and IS. Explain why end users need to be involved in the management of information systems. Explain why it is a misconception to say that organizations do something.

Q1-4 How can you use the five-component model?

Name and define each of the five components. Explain the symmetry in the five-component model. Show how automation moves work from one side of the five-component structure to the other. Name the most important component and state why it is the most important. Use the five-component model to describe the differences between high-tech and low-tech information systems. Explain how the components are ordered according to difficulty of change and disruption.

Q1-5 What is information?

State four different definitions of information. Identify the one that is your favorite and explain why. State the difference between data and information. Explain why information can never be written on a piece of paper or shown on a display device.

Q1-6 What are necessary data characteristics?

Create a mnemonic device for remembering the characteristics of good data. Explain how these data characteristics relate to information quality.

Q1-7 2029?

What trends do you expect to see in 2029? How might you use your smartphone differently in 2029? What everyday devices might be able to connect to the Internet in 2029? How might mixed-reality devices change your daily life? How could these devices change the way you work? Why would the ability to experiment and systems thinking be important in adapting to technological change? Summarize how answering these questions contributes to your skill as a nonroutine thinker.

Using Your Knowledge with eHermes

Reread the eHermes vignette at the start of this chapter. Using the knowledge you've gained from this chapter, especially that in Q1-2, identify five mistakes that Amanda made. For each, explain what you would do differently. Be specific.

Abstract reasoning   10
Bell's Law   6
Collaboration   11
Computer hardware   14
Computer-based information
    system   15
Data   14
Digital Revolution   5
Experimentation   11

Five-component framework   14
Information   19
Information Age   5
Information system (IS)   14
Information technology (IT)   14
Kryder's Law   8
Management information systems
    (MIS)   14
Metcalfe's Law   7

Moore's Law   6
Nielsen's Law   8
People   14
Procedures   14
Software   14
Strong password   26
System   14
Systems thinking   11
Technology skills gap   12

MyLab MIS

To complete the problems with MyLab MIS, go to EOC Discussion Questions in the MyLab.

USING YOUR KNOWLEDGE

1-1.
MyLab MIS
One of life's greatest gifts is to be employed doing work that you love. Reflect for a moment on a job that you would find so exciting that you could hardly wait to get to sleep on Sunday night so that you could wake up and go to work on Monday.

a. Describe that job. Name the industry, the type of company or organization for which you'd like to work, the products and services it produces, and your specific job duties.

b. Explain what it is about that job that you find so compelling.

c. In what ways will the skills of abstraction, systems thinking, collaboration, and experimentation facilitate your success in that job?

d. Given your answers to parts a through c, define three to five personal goals for this class. None of these goals should include anything about your GPA. Be as specific as possible. Assume that you are going to evaluate yourself on these goals at the end of the quarter or semester. The more specific you make these goals, the easier it will be to perform the evaluation.

1-2.
MyLab MIS
Consider costs of a system in light of the five components: costs to buy and maintain the hardware; costs to develop or acquire licenses to the software programs and costs to maintain them; costs to design databases and fill them with data; costs of developing procedures and keeping them current; and, finally, human costs both to develop and use the system.

a. Many experts believe that, over the lifetime of a system, the single most expensive component is people. Does this belief seem logical to you? Explain why you agree or disagree.

b. Consider a poorly developed system that does not meet its defined requirements. The needs of the business do not go away, but they do not conform themselves to the characteristics of the poorly built system. Therefore, something must give. Which component picks up the slack when the hardware and software programs do not work correctly? What does this say about the cost of a poorly designed system? Consider both direct money costs as well as intangible personnel costs.

c. What implications do you, as a future business manager, take from parts a and b? What does this say about the need for your involvement in requirements and other aspects of systems development? Who eventually will pay the costs of a poorly developed system? Against which budget will those costs accrue?

1-3.
MyLab MIS
Consider the four definitions of information presented in this chapter. The problem with the first definition, "knowledge derived from data," is that it merely substitutes one word we don't know the meaning of (*information*) for a second word we don't know the meaning of (*knowledge*). The problem with the second definition, "data presented in a meaningful context," is that it is too subjective. Whose context? What makes a context meaningful? The third definition, "data processed by summing, ordering, averaging, etc.," is too mechanical. It tells us what to do, but it doesn't tell us what information is. The fourth definition, "a difference that makes a difference," is vague and unhelpful.

Also, none of these definitions helps us to quantify the amount of information we receive. What is the information content of the statement that every human being has a navel? Zero—you already know that. In contrast, the statement that someone has just deposited $50,000 into your checking account is chock-full of information. So, good information has an element of surprise.

Considering all of these points, answer the following questions:

a. What is information made of?

b. If you have more information, do you weigh more? Why or why not?

c. When you give a copy of your transcript to a prospective employer, how is information produced? What part of that information production process do you control? What, if anything, can you do to improve the quality of information that the employer conceives?

d. Give your own best definition of information.

e. Explain how you think it is possible that we have an industry called the *information technology industry* but we have great difficulty defining the word *information*.

COLLABORATION EXERCISE 1

This chapter discussed why collaboration is a key skill to maintaining job security. In this exercise, you will build a collaboration IS and then use that IS to answer the questions below in a collaborative fashion. You might want to read the four questions below before you build your IS.

Until you answer question 1-4, you'll have to make do with email or face-to-face meeting. Once you've answered that question, use your communication method to answer question 1-5. Once you've answered question 1-5, use your communication method and your content-sharing method to answer question 1-6. Then use the full IS to answer questions 1-7 and 1-8.

1-4. Build a communication method:

a. Meet with your team and decide how you want to meet in the future.

b. From the discussion in step a, list the requirements for your communication system.

c. Select and implement a communication tool. It could be Skype, Google Hangouts, or Skype for Business.

d. Write procedures for the team to use when utilizing your new communication tool.

1-5. Build a content-sharing method:

a. Meet with your team and decide the types of content that you will be creating.

b. Decide as a team whether you want to process your content using desktop applications or cloud-based applications. Choose the applications you want to use.

c. Decide as a team the server you will use to share your content. You can use Google Drive, Microsoft OneDrive, Microsoft SharePoint, or some other server.

d. Implement your content-sharing server.

e. Write procedures for the team to use when sharing content.

1-6. Build a task management method:

a. Meet with your team and decide how you want to manage tasks. Determine the task data that you want to store on your task list.

b. Decide as a team the tool and server you will use for sharing your tasks. You can use Google Drive, Microsoft OneDrive, Microsoft SharePoint, or some other facility.

c. Implement the tool and server in step a.

d. Write procedures for the team to use when managing tasks.

1-7. Nonroutine skills:

a. Define *abstract reasoning* and explain why it is an important skill for business professionals. Give three other examples of abstractions commonly used in business.

b. Define *systems thinking* and explain why it is an important skill for business professionals. Give three other examples of the use of systems thinking with regard to consequences of Bell's Law, Moore's Law, or Metcalfe's Law.

c. Define *collaboration* and explain why it is an important skill for business professionals. Is the work product of your team better than any one of you could have done separately? If not, your collaboration is ineffective. If that is the case, explain why.

d. Define *experimentation* and explain why it is an important skill for business professionals. How does the fear of failure influence your willingness to engage in experimentation?

1-8. Job security:

a. State the text's definition of *job security*.

b. Evaluate the text's definition of job security. Is it effective? If you think not, offer a better definition of job security.

c. As a team, do you agree that improving your skills on the four dimensions in the Collaboration Exercise Questions will increase your job security?

d. Do you think technical skills (accounting proficiency, financial analysis proficiency, etc.) provide job security? Why or why not? Do you think you would have answered this question differently in 2000? Why or why not?

Pluralsight

The pace of technology innovation is increasing. For companies hiring tech professionals, there is no standardized way of knowing whether potential new employees have the tech skill sets that will be required of them. Even college degrees or professional certifications offer no guarantee of skill or aptitude. Techniques change, knowledge fades, and skills quickly become obsolete. Organizations struggle with knowing whom to hire and how to keep current employees up to date with the latest tech skills. The technology skills gap is widening at a rapid rate.

In 2004, Aaron Skonnard, Keith Brown, Fritz Onion, and Bill Williams founded a technology training company called Pluralsight that provided on-site technical and business management training in a classroom environment. Pluralsight's focus was on training people and organizations in the latest technology-related skills to help them keep pace with technology innovation.

Source: Pluralsight Headquarters

Filling the Gap

Pluralsight focuses on filling the skills gap between the high level of technology skills companies need and the relatively low level of technology skills that workers bring to the table. Pluralsight sees technology as an integral part of all modern companies and a force that is constantly pushing them forward. As such, companies become increasingly dependent on new technologies and need to retrain their employees in order to take advantage of these advances. Most employers and employees clearly see the need for constant technical skills training.

High-Speed Online Growth

Since Pluralsight's founding in 2004, the company has grown to more than 800 employees and 1,300 expert authors.[17] The company's mission is to provide a learning platform to everyone everywhere that enables them to gain the technology skills they need to create progress. In 2008, the company shifted focus from on-site classroom learning to online learning. The Pluralsight online learning library began with 10 courses based on Microsoft technologies.[18] Today more than 6,000 courses are available in more than 150 countries, covering a wide variety of software development and technology skills; these courses are delivered by carefully vetted instructors.[19]

In 2011, Pluralsight made some strategic changes in its pricing strategy and began offering monthly subscriptions for its learning platform. Since then, the company has enjoyed rapid growth, nearly doubling subscriptions in each subsequent year. Headquartered in Utah, Pluralsight was named the #9 Top Education Company on the Inc. 5000 list of fastest-growing companies. It was also named a 2017 Best Workplace by Great Place to Work and #20 on the Forbes Cloud 100 list.

Going Public

In April 2018, Pluralsight went public. Shares of Pluralsight closed at $20 on the first day of trading, up 33 percent from the company's list price of $15. At that share price, Pluralsight enjoyed a market capitalization of more than $2.5 billion, which far exceeded its last private valuation of about $1 billion.[20] Pluralsight reported annual 2017 revenues of $166 million, which was up 23 percent from the previous year. In interviews shortly after the IPO, founder Aaron Skonnard said one of Pluralsight's major areas of growth was training at large corporations.

Ultimately, Pluralsight succeeded because its founders developed an innovative application of information systems technology. Training isn't anything new. Neither is the Internet. Yet Pluralsight created a $2.5 billion company using common technology to provide online training. One of the keys to its success was finding a way to apply that technology to a business opportunity and then having the managerial skill to develop that idea into a thriving business.

QUESTIONS

1-9. Go to *http://pluralsight.com* and search for a course you might be interested in taking. What is attractive to you about online versus traditional training?

1-10. What advice would you give executives at Pluralsight if they wanted to grow their business? How could they increase revenues?

1-11. Why would corporate clients be interested in online technology training for their internal employees? How would they benefit from paying Pluralsight for training?

1-12. Why is there a technology skills gap? Why do employers have the need for highly skilled workers, and why do too few workers have these skills?

1-13. How might a traditional university benefit from a partnership with Pluralsight? Why might some universities see such a partnership as a threat to their existence while others might see it as a great opportunity?

1-14. Suppose you were considering buying stock in Pluralsight. What types of threats might Pluralsight face in the future? Could a large tech company mimic its business model and threaten its profitability? How could Pluralsight defend against this type of competition?

MyLab MIS

Go to the Assignments section of your MyLab to complete these writing exercises.

1-15. The text states that data should be worth its cost. Both cost and value can be broken into tangible and intangible factors. *Tangible* factors can be directly measured; *intangible* ones arise indirectly and are difficult to measure. For example, a tangible cost is the cost of a computer monitor; an intangible cost is the lost productivity of a poorly trained employee.

Give five important tangible and five important intangible costs of an information system. Give five important tangible and five important intangible measures of the value of an information system. If it helps to focus your thinking, use the example of the class scheduling system at your university or some other university information system. When determining whether an information system is worth its cost, how do you think the tangible and intangible factors should be considered?

1-16. The U.S. Department of Labor publishes descriptions of jobs, educational requirements, and the outlook for many jobs and professions. Go to its site at *www.bls.gov* and answer the following questions:

a. Search for the job title *systems analyst*. Describe what such people do. Is this a job that interests you? Why or why not? What education do you need? What is the median pay and job growth projection?

b. Click the Similar Occupations link at the bottom of the page. Find another job that you might want. Describe that job, median salary, and educational requirements.

c. The BLS data is comprehensive, but it is not up to date for fast-changing disciplines such as IS. For example, one very promising career today is social media marketing, a job that does not appear in the BLS data. Describe one way that you might learn about employment prospects for such emerging job categories.

d. Considering your answer to part c, describe an IS-related job that would be the best match for your skills and interests. Describe how you can learn if that job exists.

ENDNOTES

1. Gordon Bell. "Bell's Law for the Birth and Death of Computer Classes: A Theory of the Computer's Evolution," November 1, 2007, *http://research.microsoft.com/pubs/64155/tr-27-146.pdf*.
2. These figures were compiled from both Intel's specification archive (*http://ark.intel.com/*) and TechPowerUP's CPU Database (*www.techpowerup.com/cpudb/*).
3. Zipf's Law is a more accurate, though less easily understood, way of explaining how the value of a network increases as additional network nodes are added. See Briscoe, Odlyzko, and Tilly's 2006 article "Metcalfe's Law Is Wrong" for a better explanation: *http://spectrum.ieee.org/computing/networks/metcalfes-law-is-wrong*.

4. Lynn A. Kaoly and Constantijn W. A. Panis, *The 21st Century at Work* (Santa Monica, CA: RAND Corporation, 2004), p. xiv.

5. Robert B. Reich, *The Work of Nations* (New York: Alfred A. Knopf, 1991), p. 229.

6. In the 2011 book "Literacy Is NOT Enough: 21st Century Fluencies for the Digital Age," Lee Crockett, Ian Jukes, and Andrew Churches list problem solving, creativity, analytical thinking, collaboration, communication, and ethics, action, and accountability as key skills workers need for the 21st century.

7. Accenture, "Accenture 2017 College Graduate Employment Survey," last modified April 16, 2018, *www.accenture.com/ t20170901T080938Z__w__/us-en/_acnmedia/PDF-50/Accenture-Strategy-Workforce-Gen-Z-Rising-POV.pdf*.

8. Bureau of Labor Statistics, "Computer Systems Analysts," *Occupational Outlook Handbook*, accessed May 16, 2018, *www.bls.gov/ooh*.

9. Daron Acemoglu and David Autor, "Skills, Tasks, and Technologies: Implications for Employment and Earnings" (working paper, National Bureau of Economic Research, June 2010), *www.nber.org/papers/ w16082*.

10. Julian Birkinshaw, "Beyond the Information Age," *Wired*, June 2014, accessed May 21, 2018, *www.wired.com/insights/2014/06/ beyond-information-age/*.

11. Larry Page, "G Is for Google," *GoogleBlog*, August 10, 2015, accessed May 21, 2018, *https://googleblog.blogspot.com/2015/08/google-alphabet.html*.

12. Ibid.

13. Josh Constine, "Google Shreds Bureaucracy to Keep Talent Loyal to the Alphabet," *TechCrunch.com*, August 10, 2015, accessed May 21, 2018, *http://techcrunch.com/2015/08/10/google-of-thrones*.

14. Actually, the word *data* is plural; to be correct, we should use the singular form *datum* and say, "The fact that Jeff Parks earns $30.00 per hour is a datum." The word *datum*, however, sounds pedantic and fussy, and we will avoid it in this text.

15. James Risley, "Microsoft Shows Off HoloLens-Enabled 'Holographic Teleportation' and Predicts the Demise of 2D Technology," GeekWire, February 19, 2016, accessed May 21, 2018, *www.geekwire.com/2016/ microsoft-shows-off-hololens-enabled-teleportation-and-call-for-an-end-to-2d-tech*.

16. Edgar Alvarez, "Microsoft Shows How NFL Fans Could Use HoloLens in the Future," Engadget, February 2, 2016, accessed May 21, 2018, *www.engadget.com/2016/02/02/microsoft-hololens-nfl-concept-video*.

17. Pluralsight, "At a Glance," accessed June 4, 2018, *www.pluralsight. com/about*.

18. Tim Green, "How Pluralsight Grew an Online Learning Business That Made Its Tutors Millionaires," Hottopics, May 21, 2015, accessed May 26, 2018, *www.hottopics.ht/13976/how-pluralsight-grew-an-online-learning-business-that-made-its-tutors-millionaires*.

19. Sarah Buhr, "A Chat with Pluralsight Founder Aaron Skonnard on the Global Move to Sharpen Tech Skills Through Online Training," Techcrunch, April 20, 2017, accessed May 26, 2018, *https://techcrunch.com/2017/04/20/a-chat-with-pluralsight-founder-aaron-skonnard-on-the-global-move-to-sharpen-tech-skills-through-online-training*.

20. Alex Konrad, "Utah Ed Tech Leader Pluralsight Pops 33% in First-Day Trading, Keeping Window Open for Software IPOs," Forbes, May 17, 2018, accessed May 26, 2018, *www.forbes.com/sites/ alexkonrad/2018/05/17/utah-pluralsight-ipo*.

CHAPTER 2

Strategy and Information Systems

"**Hey Kamala,** let's get some lunch. I need to hear more about the new RFID inventory system we're going to start using," says a well-dressed Tess as she pops into a conference room in one of the main distribution warehouses. Tess is eHermes' vice president of sales.

Kamala is examining data visualizations from eHermes' fleet of self-driving vehicles and making changes to a diagram on a large whiteboard. Kamala is an expert in automation and robotics with a master's degree from MIT who grew up in India and London.

"Yeah, sure, I could use the break."

"What are you all working on?"

"Well. . .Jessica wants to see if we can feed all of our data into an AI to improve our operational efficiency. I know how computer vision systems and machine learning work with self-driving vehicles, but integrating all these different data feeds for planning and optimization is new to me."

MyLab MIS

Using Your Knowledge Questions 2-1, 2-2, 2-3

Essay Questions 2-13, 2-14, 2-15

CONFERENCE ROOM

"Sounds complex. I'm glad you're the engineer and I'm the salesperson."
Kamala motions to Tess to move out into the hall.

"Honestly, we'll get it figured out. But it will take a lot longer than anyone thinks. Eventually it will increase sales and decrease costs, but this project is the least of my worries." Kamala rolls her eyes and looks sincerely frustrated.

"What do you mean?"

"Who are we?"

"What do you mean?" Tess is a little taken aback.

"Well, as a company, who are we? We've made our reputation as a company that is essentially a mobile, door-to-door eBay. I get that. But . . . there's a lot of money we could make if we expanded into other areas."

"What do you mean? What other areas?"

"Well, Jessica mentioned the other day that we should consider partnering with local companies to sell *new* products, not just second-hand products. I totally agree. And we could do even more than that. What if we started delivering packages too?"

"You mean become a shipping company?"

"Yes. . .well, kind of. I realize we'd be helping potential competitors deliver their packages, but we'd also have a customer standing in front of our mobile storefronts ready to buy. I think we'll really miss out if we don't think more broadly."

"We can't be everything to everybody."

Source: Haiyin Wang/Alamy Stock Photo

"Have you talked with Jessica about this?"

"Yes, she agreed that these are all good ideas, but she wants to stay focused on expanding into carrying new products in our mobile storefronts. She even thinks we might be able to partner with local farmers and create mobile farmers' markets."

"And. . .what's the downside? It sounds like low-hanging fruit. We wouldn't have to change the way we do business very much, we'd get a lot of new products, and margins from corporate clients would probably be pretty good."

"Yeah, but what if we can't sign them? What if they realize we can essentially cut them out of the distribution chain? I mean, we'd be able to do to retailers what Netflix did to Blockbuster. Brick-and-mortar stores would

Study QUESTIONS

Q2-1   How does organizational strategy determine information systems structure?

Q2-2   What five forces determine industry structure?

Q2-3   How does analysis of industry structure determine competitive strategy?

Q2-4   How does competitive strategy determine value chain structure?

Q2-5   How do business processes generate value?

Q2-6   How does competitive strategy determine business processes and the structure of information systems?

Q2-7   How do information systems provide competitive advantages?

Q2-8   2029?

become a liability. Or, worse, what if we become dependent on them and they start to squeeze our margins?"

"I don't know. If the money's as good as Jessica thinks it is, it might be worth a shot."

"Yes, but we could be spending our time and money making eHermes into more than just a 'retail' company. There's so much money on the table if we become a shipping or even a transportation company." Kamala is clearly frustrated and shakes her head.

"Kamala, I completely agree. We could become the leader in automated shipping and delivery. There's no arguing that."

"Well?"

"Well, it comes down to focus. We can't be everything to everybody. Expanding our existing retail business is very different than becoming a shipping and transportation provider."

"But what about all the money we could be making right now? If we don't earn it, somebody else will. What if Amazon's drone delivery service takes off. . .literally?"

Tess starts to smile and says, "Hey, let's grab Victor on the way out to lunch. He's the one who really needs to hear this. You two can talk strategy while I get some pad thai!"

Chapter PREVIEW

Recall from Chapter 1 that MIS is the development and use of information systems that enables organizations to achieve their strategies. This chapter focuses on how information systems support competitive strategy and how IS can create competitive advantages. As you will learn in your organizational behavior classes, a body of knowledge exists to help organizations analyze their industry, select a competitive strategy, and develop business processes. In the first part of this chapter, we will survey that knowledge and show how to use it, via several steps, to structure information systems. Then, toward the end of the chapter, we will discuss how companies use information systems to gain a competitive advantage.

eHermes provides a good example. Its strategy has been to differentiate itself by providing mobile storefronts for users to buy and sell used items. It has systems and processes to do that. But, as Kamala states, what if eHermes can't secure new contracts with retail stores? If it can't get the new contracts, would it be best to try to move into the shipping business? Even if the company does get those new contracts, does it have the systems and process to handle them?

Q2-1 How Does Organizational Strategy Determine Information Systems Structure?

According to the definition of MIS, information systems exist to help organizations achieve their strategies. As you will learn in your business strategy class, an organization's goals and objectives are determined by its *competitive strategy*. Thus, ultimately, competitive strategy determines the structure, features, and functions of every information system.

Figure 2-1 summarizes this situation. In short, organizations examine the structure of their industry and determine a competitive strategy. That strategy determines value chains, which, in turn, determine business processes. The structure of business processes determines the design of supporting information systems.

Michael Porter, one of the key researchers and thinkers in competitive analysis, developed three different models that can help you understand the elements of Figure 2-1. We begin with his five forces model.

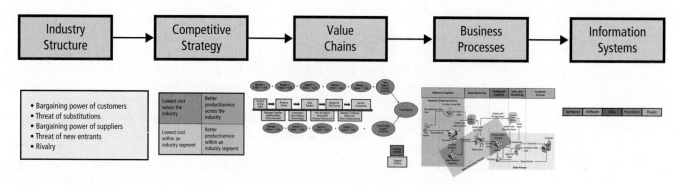

FIGURE 2-1

Organizational Strategy Determines Information Systems

Q2-2 What Five Forces Determine Industry Structure?

Organizational strategy begins with an assessment of the fundamental characteristics and structure of an industry. One model used to assess an industry structure is Porter's **five forces model**,[1] summarized in Figure 2-2. According to this model, five competitive forces determine industry profitability: bargaining power of customers, threat of substitutions, bargaining power of suppliers, threat of new entrants, and rivalry among existing firms. The intensity of each of the five forces determines the characteristics of the industry, how profitable it is, and how sustainable that profitability will be.

To understand this model, consider the strong and weak examples for each of the forces in Figure 2-3. A good check on your understanding is to see if you can think of different forces for each category in Figure 2-3. Also, take a particular industry—say, auto repair—and consider how these five forces determine the competitive landscape of that industry.

In the opening vignette of this chapter, Kamala is concerned that focusing only on selling products may place eHermes at a competitive disadvantage. She thinks the company could expand into shipping or transportation. She's also worried about being financially dependent on a few large corporate accounts. Figure 2-4 shows an analysis of the competitive landscape eHermes faces.

The large corporate accounts that eHermes serves could demand a greater share of the profits because they account for a large percentage of eHermes' revenue. The threat of substitutions, like a local eBay delivery service, is somewhat strong. But these substitutions may not be viable options for some of the corporate clients due to lack of technical skill or physical distance limitations. A new entrant, like Uber offering mobile retail services using its fleet of self-driving vehicles, could be a substantial threat. Or the new corporate clients could just build their own mobile marketplaces. But eHermes could respond to this by offering additional services like selling clothes, auto parts, or hot food. Or it could enter new markets like shipping, transportation, or entertainment.

The other forces are not as worrisome to eHermes. The bargaining power of the mobile storefront suppliers is weak because there are lots of companies willing to sell eHermes the underlying self-driving vehicle chassis. The competition among automakers for a share of the self-driving market is fierce. The threat from rivals isn't strong because eHermes has developed the custom mobile storefront platform and integrated the online retail system. It wouldn't be easy for rivals to replicate their system.

Like eHermes, organizations examine these five forces and determine how they intend to respond to them. That examination leads to competitive strategy.

FIGURE 2-2

Porter's Five Forces Model of Industry Structure

Source: Based on Michael E. Porter, *Competitive Advantage: Creating and Sustaining Superior Performance* (The Free Press, a Division of Simon & Schuster Adult Publishing Group). Copyright © 1985, 1998 by Michael E. Porter.

- Bargaining power of customers
- Threat of substitutions
- Bargaining power of suppliers
- Threat of new entrants
- Rivalry

Force	Example of Strong Force	Example of Weak Force
Bargaining power of customers	Toyota's purchase of auto paint (because Toyota is a huge customer that will purchase paint in large volume)	Your power over the procedures and policies of your university
Threat of substitutions	Frequent traveler's choice of auto rental	Patients using the only drug effective for their type of cancer
Bargaining power of suppliers	New car dealers (because they control what the "true price" of a vehicle is and the customer cannot reliably verify the accuracy of that price)	Grain farmers in a surplus year (an oversupply makes the product less valuable and less profitable)
Threat of new entrants	Corner latte stand (because it is an easy business to replicate)	Professional football team (because the number of teams is tightly controlled by the NFL)
Rivalry	Used car dealers (because there are many to choose from)	Google or Bing (expensive to develop and market a search engine)

FIGURE 2-3
Examples of Five Forces

Q2-3 How Does Analysis of Industry Structure Determine Competitive Strategy?

See the Ethics Guide on pages 42–43 to learn how new technologies may be used in questionable ways to achieve strategic goals.

An organization responds to the structure of its industry by choosing a **competitive strategy**. Porter followed his five forces model with the model of four competitive strategies, shown in Figure 2-5.[2] According to Porter, firms engage in one of these four strategies. An organization can focus on being the cost leader, or it can focus on differentiating its products or services from those of the competition. Further, the organization can employ the cost or differentiation strategy across an industry, or it can focus its strategy on a particular industry segment.

Consider the car rental industry, for example. According to the first column of Figure 2-5, a car rental company can strive to provide the lowest-cost car rentals across the industry, or it can seek to provide the lowest-cost car rentals to an industry segment—say, U.S. domestic business travelers.

As shown in the second column, a car rental company can seek to differentiate its products from the competition. It can do so in various ways—for example, by providing a wide range of

Force	eHermes Example	Force Strength	eHermes' Response
Bargaining power of customers	A large account wants a greater share of profits	Strong	Lower prices or diversify into other markets
Threat of substitutions	eBay offers local delivery service	Medium	Offer differentiating services, like shipping, transportation, or entertainment
Bargaining power of suppliers	We're increasing the cost of the self-driving vehicle chassis	Weak	We'll buy from a different manufacturer
Threat of new entrants	Ubers starts offering mobile retail services	Medium	Offer differentiating services and enter other markets
Rivalry	Amazon offers drone delivery	Weak	Offer additional services or create additional corporate partnerships

FIGURE 2-4
Five Forces at eHermes

THE LURE OF LOVE BOTS

Gary Lucas couldn't stop looking across the maze of cubicles into the conference room on the other side of the office. His boss, Richard Matthews, was having what looked like a spirited discussion with a group of five people Gary had never seen before. Even without being in the meeting or being close enough to read people's lips, Gary knew what the meeting was about.

The company he worked for, Why Wait, Date!, was struggling. Not only was competition fierce in the online matchmaking industry, but subscriptions at his company had been drying up due to a more challenging problem: The latest analysis of user statistics revealed that 15 percent of the total subscribers were female while 85 percent were male. How could the company retain subscribers if the competition between male users was so fierce? Many male subscribers were unable to find a match, even after months of trying. Unfortunately for Gary, the manager of customer retention, unhappy customers don't keep paying. Despite marketing efforts and discounted subscription offers aimed at female users, Gary had been unable to balance out the disproportionate customer base. He was worried that his job was on the line. His replacement might be sitting in that meeting with his boss right now.

Gary looked back over at the conference room just in time to see Richard open the door and wave him over. Gary hastily made his way to the conference room. As he took a seat at the end of the table, Richard smiled at him and said, "Gary, I think these consultants have a plan that can bring this company back to life!" Gary sighed with relief. It sounded like his job was safe for now—but what kind of miracle had the consultants promised to make Richard so optimistic about the future?

iMatch

Thomas, the lead consultant, began his pitch to save the company. Richard nodded and smiled as Thomas explained his idea. "The key to maintaining subscribers on this type of site," Thomas explained, "is keeping them interested. We need male users to have some sort of positive experience on the site before they reach their threshold of getting discouraged and cancel their subscription. Our consulting team has created a model based on all of your user data, and we are able to predict when a male user is on the verge of canceling his subscription with a high degree of accuracy."

Gary interrupted, "You have access to all of our user data?" He looked at Thomas with a distressed expression on his face, but Thomas motioned for him to calm down and keep listening to the pitch. Thomas continued, "Now that we can predict when a customer is about to leave, we can take action to keep him interested. We know when customers need a potential 'match' in order to keep paying for the service. All we have to do is send them some messages from a dummy account so they think someone is interested.

"Depending on how much you want to invest in our solution," Thomas continued, "we can even have these dummy accounts engage in complex interactions that take place over weeks or months. After several weeks or months, the dummy account will indicate that it has found someone else. There does not have to be any actual follow-through; the customer will just think that it didn't work out. The best part is that you won't have to pay employees to interact with customers—this can all be done with our AI platform. These long-term interactions will keep customers paying and inflate the hope that they will actually find someone using your site!"

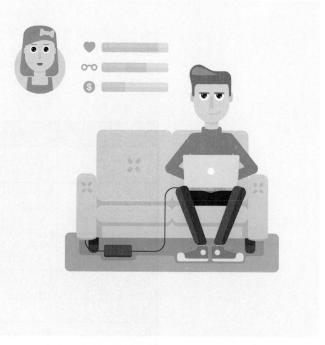

AI-Jedis

An hour after the meeting, Gary was sitting at his desk with his head spinning. He was still trying to come to terms with what had happened in the conference room. His boss had directed him to cut all marketing efforts by 80 percent and start looking to hire new people to take charge of creating the dummy accounts. Richard had also signed a 6-month contract with the consultants; they would begin implementation of their customer retention tool starting the next day.

Gary looked down at the business cards the consultants had given him after the meeting—they all worked for a company called AI-Jedis. Gary realized *AI* stood for "artificial intelligence." He couldn't believe they were going to essentially use robots to trick people into thinking they were about to find a match on the site. He suddenly felt chills down his spine. . .trick people? He was starting to wonder if this could be perceived as fraudulent or even illegal. What if someone found out about what they were doing? The company would be destroyed. Gary leaned back in his chair, stared at the ceiling, and let out a long sigh. Part of him wanted to go talk to Richard and tell him this was a bad idea; the other part of him decided that it might be time to start polishing his resume.

The Ethics Guide in Chapter 1 introduced Kant's categorical imperative as one way of assessing ethical conduct. This guide introduces a second way, one known as *utilitarianism*. According to utilitarianism, the morality of an act is determined by its outcome. Acts are judged to be moral if they result in the greatest good to the greatest number or if they maximize happiness and reduce suffering.

Using utilitarianism as a guide, killing can be moral if it results in the greatest good to the greatest number. Killing Adolf Hitler would have been moral if it stopped the Holocaust. Similarly, utilitarianism can assess lying or other forms of deception as moral if the act results in the greatest good to the greatest number. Lying to someone with a fatal illness that you're certain he or she will recover is moral if it increases that person's happiness and decreases his or her suffering.

DISCUSSION QUESTIONS

1. According to the definitions of the ethical principles defined in this book:
   a. Do you think that using automated bots on a dating site is ethical according to the categorical imperative (page 23-24)?
   b. Do you think that using automated bots on a dating site is ethical according to the utilitarian perspective?
2. While this scenario might seem like something out of a science fiction movie, the use of automated tools for decision making and customer interaction is widespread. Brainstorm examples of other companies or services that might be using automated tools right now.
3. If you were in this situation, would you leave the company?
4. Do you think Gary would benefit by trying to talk to Richard about the risk of using bots? How do you think people would respond if word got out that the company was using this type of technology to retain customers?

---

high-quality cars, by providing the best reservation system, by having the cleanest cars or the fastest check-in, or by some other means. The company can strive to provide product differentiation across the industry or within particular segments of the industry, such as U.S. domestic business travelers.

According to Porter, to be effective, the organization's goals, objectives, culture, and activities must be consistent with the organization's strategy. To those in the MIS field, this means that all information systems in the organization must reflect and facilitate the organization's competitive strategy.

	Cost	Differentiation
Industry-wide	Lowest cost across the industry	Better product/service across the industry
Focus	Lowest cost within an industry segment	Better product/service within an industry segment

FIGURE 2-5
Porter's Four Competitive Strategies

Q2-4   How Does Competitive Strategy DetermineValue Chain Structure?

Organizations analyze the structure of their industry, and, using that analysis, they formulate a competitive strategy. They then need to organize and structure the organization to implement that strategy. If, for example, the competitive strategy is to be *cost leader*, then business activities need to be developed to provide essential functions at the lowest possible cost.

A business that selects a *differentiation* strategy would not necessarily structure itself around least-cost activities. Instead, such a business might choose to develop more costly processes, but it would do so only if those processes provided benefits that outweighed their costs. Jessica at eHermes knows that creating mobile storefronts is expensive, and she judges the costs worthwhile. She may find that developing eHermes' own AI is worthwhile, too.

Porter defined **value** as the amount of money that a customer is willing to pay for a resource, product, or service. The difference between the value that an activity generates and the cost of the activity is called the **margin**. A business with a differentiation strategy will add cost to an activity only as long as the activity has a positive margin.

A **value chain** is a network of value-creating activities. That generic chain consists of five **primary activities** and four **support activities**.

Primary Activities in the Value Chain

To understand the essence of the value chain, consider a medium-sized drone manufacturer (see Figure 2-6). First, the manufacturer acquires raw materials using the inbound logistics activity. This activity concerns the receiving and handling of raw materials and other inputs. The accumulation of those materials adds value in the sense that even a pile of unassembled parts is worth something to some customer. A collection of the parts needed to build a drone is worth more than an empty space on a shelf. The value is not only the parts themselves, but also the time required to contact vendors for those parts, to maintain business relationships with those vendors, to order the parts, to receive the shipment, and so forth.

FIGURE 2-6
Drone Manufacturer's Value Chain

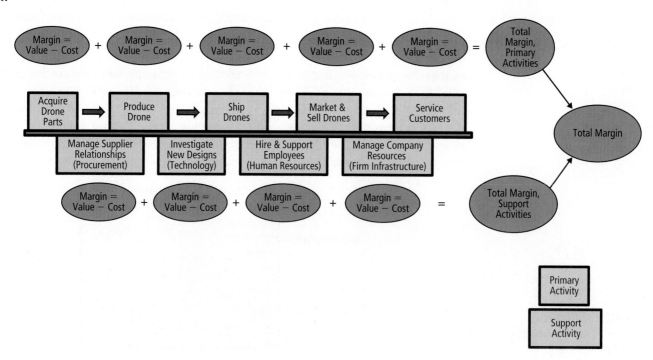

Primary Activity	Description
Inbound Logistics	Receiving, storing, and disseminating inputs to the products
Operations/Manufacturing	Transforming inputs into the final products
Outbound Logistics	Collecting, storing, and physically distributing the products to buyers
Sales and Marketing	Inducing buyers to purchase the products and providing a means for them to do so
Customer Service	Assisting customers' use of the products and thus maintaining and enhancing the products' value

FIGURE 2-7
Task Descriptions for Primary Activities of the Value Chain
Source: Based on Michael E. Porter, *Competitive Advantage: Creating and Sustaining Superior Performance* (The Free Press, a Division of Simon & Schuster Adult Publishing Group). Copyright © 1985, 1998 by Michael E. Porter.

In the operations activity, the drone maker transforms raw materials into a finished drone, a process that adds more value. Next, the company uses the outbound logistics activity to deliver the finished drone to a customer. Of course, there is no customer to send the drone to without the marketing and sales value activity. Finally, the service activity provides customer support to the drone users.

Each stage of this generic chain accumulates costs and adds value to the product. The net result is the total margin of the chain, which is the difference between the total value added and the total costs incurred. Figure 2-7 summarizes the primary activities of the value chain.

Support Activities in the Value Chain

The support activities in the generic value chain contribute indirectly to the production, sale, and service of the product. They include procurement, which consists of the processes of finding vendors, setting up contractual arrangements, and negotiating prices. (This differs from inbound logistics, which is concerned with ordering and receiving in accordance with agreements set up by procurement.)

Porter defined technology broadly. It includes research and development, but it also includes other activities within the firm for developing new techniques, methods, and procedures. He defined human resources as recruiting, compensation, evaluation, and training of full-time and part-time employees. Finally, firm infrastructure includes general management, finance, accounting, legal, and government affairs.

Supporting functions add value, albeit indirectly, and they also have costs. Hence, as shown in Figure 2-6, supporting activities contribute to a margin. In the case of supporting activities, it would be difficult to calculate the margin because the specific value added of, say, the manufacturer's lobbyists in Washington, D.C., is difficult to know. But there is a value added, there are costs, and there is a margin—even if it is only in concept.

Value Chain Linkages

Porter's model of business activities includes **linkages**, which are interactions across value activities. For example, manufacturing systems use linkages to reduce inventory costs. Such a system uses sales forecasts to plan production; it then uses the production plan to determine raw material needs and then uses the material needs to schedule purchases. The end result is just-in-time inventory, which reduces inventory sizes and costs.

By describing value chains and their linkages, Porter recognized a movement to create integrated, cross-departmental business systems. Over time, Porter's work led to the creation of a new discipline called business process design. The central idea is that organizations should not automate or improve existing functional systems. Rather, they should create new, more efficient business processes that integrate the activities of all departments involved in a value chain. You will see an example of a linkage in the next section.

Value chain analysis has a direct application to manufacturing businesses like the drone manufacturer. However, value chains also exist in service-oriented companies such as medical clinics. The difference is that most of the value in a service company is generated by the operations, marketing and sales, and service activities. Inbound and outbound logistics are not typically as important.

Q2-5 How Do Business Processes Generate Value?

A **business process** is a network of activities that generate value by transforming inputs into outputs. The **cost** of the business process is the cost of the inputs plus the cost of the activities. The margin of the business process is the value of the outputs minus the cost.

A business process is a network of activities. Each **activity** is a business function that receives inputs and produces outputs. An activity can be performed by a human, by a computer system, or by both. The inputs and outputs can be physical, like drone parts, or they can be data, such as a purchase order. A **repository** is a collection of something; a database is a repository of data, and a raw material repository is an inventory of raw materials. We will refine and extend these definitions in Chapter 8 and again in Chapter 12, but these basic terms will get us started.

Consider the three business processes for a drone manufacturer shown in Figure 2-8. The materials ordering process transforms cash[3] into a raw materials inventory. The manufacturing process transforms raw materials into finished goods. The sales process transforms finished goods into cash. Notice that the business processes span the value chain activities. The sales process involves sales and marketing as well as outbound logistics activities, as you would expect. Note, too, that while none of these three processes involve a customer-service activity, customer service plays a role in other business processes.

FIGURE 2-8
Three Examples of Business Processes

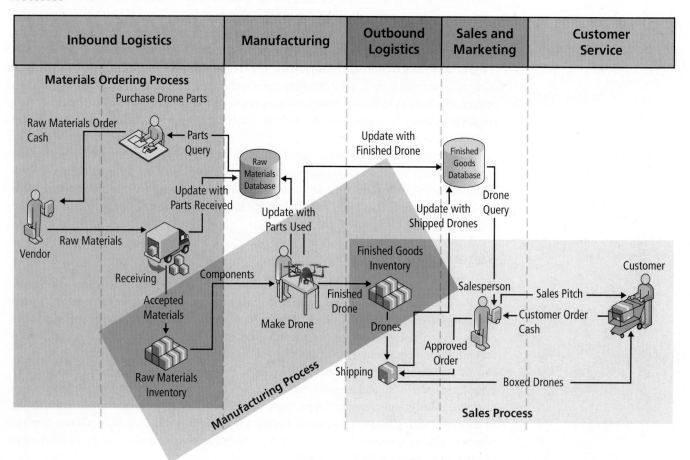

Also notice that activities get and put data resources from and to databases. For example, the purchase-drone parts activity queries the raw materials database to determine the materials to order. The receiving activity updates the raw materials database to indicate the arrival of materials. The make-drone activity updates the raw materials database to indicate the consumption of materials. Similar actions are taken in the sales process against the finished goods database.

Business processes vary in cost and effectiveness. In fact, the streamlining of business processes to increase margin (add value, reduce costs, or both) is key to competitive advantage. You will learn about process design when we discuss **business process management** in Chapter 12. To get a flavor of process design, however, consider Figure 2-9, which shows an alternate process for the drone manufacturer. Here the purchase-drone-parts activity not only queries the raw materials inventory database, it also queries the finished goods inventory database. Querying both databases allows the purchasing department to make decisions not just on raw materials quantities but also on customer demand. By using this data, purchasing can reduce the size of raw materials inventory, reducing production costs and thus adding margin to the value chain. This is an example of using a linkage across business processes to improve process margin.

As you will learn, however, changing business processes is not easy to do. Most process design requires people to work in new ways and to follow different procedures, and employees often resist such change. In Figure 2-9, the employees who perform the purchase-drone-parts activity need to learn to adjust their ordering processes to use customer purchase patterns. Another complication is that data stored in the finished goods database likely will need to be redesigned to keep track of customer demand data. As you will learn in Chapter 12, that redesign effort will require that some application programs be changed as well.

FIGURE 2-9
Improved Material Ordering Process

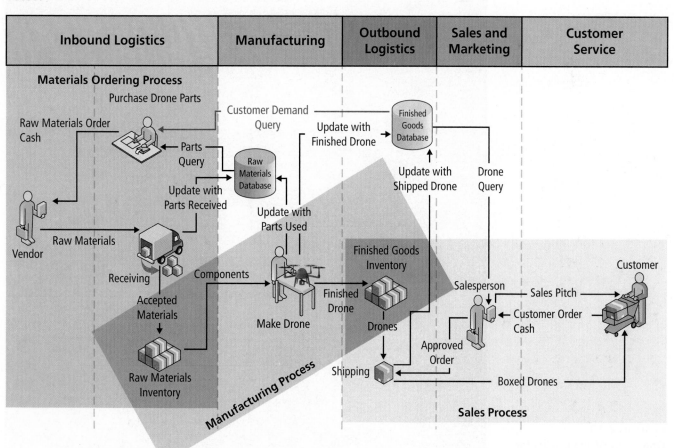

Q2-6 How Does Competitive Strategy Determine Business Processes and the Structure of Information Systems?

You can read about how IT architecture supports competitive strategy in the Career Guide on page 57.

Figure 2-10 shows a business process for renting bicycles. The value-generating activities are shown in the top of the table, and the implementation of those activities for two companies with different competitive strategies is shown in the rows below.

The first company has chosen a competitive strategy of low-cost rentals to students. Accordingly, this business implements business processes to minimize costs. The second company has chosen a differentiation strategy. It provides "best-of-breed" rentals to executives at a high-end conference resort. Notice that this business has designed its business processes to ensure superb service. To achieve a positive margin, it must ensure that the value added will exceed the costs of providing the service.

Now, consider the information systems required for these business processes. The student rental business uses a shoebox for its data facility. The only computer/software/data component in its business is the machine provided by its bank for processing credit card transactions.

The high-service business, however, makes extensive use of information systems, as shown in Figure 2-11. It has a sales tracking database that tracks past customer rental activity and an inventory database that is used to select and up-sell bicycle rentals as well as to control bicycle inventory with a minimum of fuss to its high-end customers.

	Value-Generating Activity	Greet Customer →	Determine Needs →	Rent Bike →	Return Bike & Pay
Low-cost rental to students	Message that implements competitive strategy	"You wanna bike?"	"Bikes are over there. Help yourself."	"Fill out this form, and bring it to me over here when you're done."	"Show me the bike." "OK, you owe $23.50. Pay up."
	Supporting business process	None.	Physical controls and procedures to prevent bike theft.	Printed forms and a shoebox to store them in.	Shoebox with rental form. Minimal credit card and cash receipt system.
High-service rental to business executives at conference resort	Message that implements competitive strategy	"Hello, Ms. Henry. Wonderful to see you again. Would you like to rent the WonderBike 4.5 that you rented last time?"	"You know, I think the WonderBike Supreme would be a better choice for you. It has . . ."	"Let me just scan the bike's number into our system, and then I'll adjust the seat for you."	"How was your ride?" "Here, let me help you. I'll just scan the bike's tag again and have your paperwork in just a second." "Would you like a beverage?" "Would you like me to put this on your hotel bill, or would you prefer to pay now?"
	Supporting business process	Customer tracking and past sales activity system.	Employee training and information system to match customer and bikes, biased to "up-sell" customer.	Automated inventory system to check bike out of inventory.	Automated inventory system to place bike back in inventory. Prepare payment documents. Integrate with resort's billing system.

FIGURE 2-10
Operations Value Chains for Bicycle Rental Companies

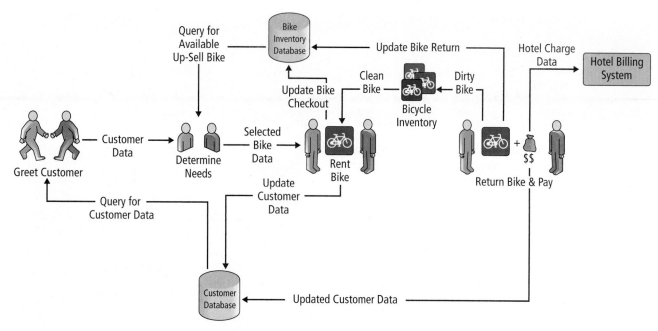

FIGURE 2-11
Business Process and Information Systems for High-Service Bike Rental

Q2-7 How Do Information Systems Provide Competitive Advantages?

In your business strategy class, you will study the Porter models in greater detail than we have discussed here. When you do so, you will learn numerous ways that organizations respond to the five competitive forces. For our purposes, we can distill those ways into the list of principles shown in Figure 2-12. Keep in mind that we are applying these principles in the context of the organization's competitive strategy.

Some of these competitive techniques are created via products and services, and some are created via the development of business processes. Consider each.

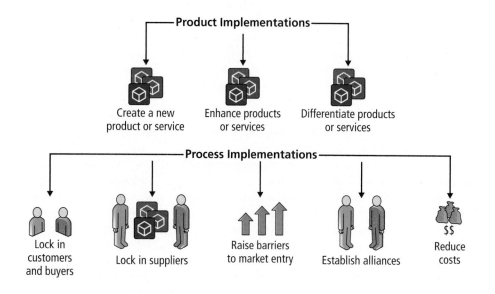

FIGURE 2-12
Principles of Competitive Advantage

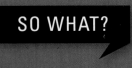

AMAZON EATS WHOLE FOODS

When was the last time that you bought something? How was this transaction processed? Did you shop around for a number of alternatives before making the purchase? Could you have found a better price if you had taken the time to conduct some research? In today's economy, you are presented with countless resources to help you make a purchase. Using Internet retailers, you can quickly and easily perform research about competing products, find the best price, choose between payment options, and process your transactions rapidly. However, it was not always this easy or convenient for consumers to shop around and buy goods.

Imagine living on a farm somewhere in rural America just over a century ago. How would you procure food and supplies for your farm and your family? The reality is that most Americans outside of cities relied on small general stores that offered narrow selections of goods. And with little or no competition nearby, prices were often inflated.

Years ago, a young entrepreneur obtained some watches at a good price and began a mail-order watch business. This seemingly insignificant business deal evolved into a roaring mail-order company with catalogues containing hundreds of pages of products. The business was named Sears, Roebuck and Company. Its business model provided consumers around the country—and especially in remote areas—with the variety and competitive pricing that they were seeking.

Amazon Prime Beef

In a way, Amazon feels like a newer, digital version of the Sears, Roebuck and Company catalogue. Even today, many people in the world live in areas where brick-and-mortar shopping options are limited. Amazon has created a digital marketplace offering a virtually limitless number of products and services, and in doing so, it has facilitated competitive pricing for anyone in the world with a computer and an Internet connection. And despite its already extensive product line, the company continues to expand into new markets.

For example, Amazon recently announced its purchase of the grocery retailer Whole Foods for more than $13 billion. Amazon has been dabbling in selling groceries for several years, but this move is perceived by many as strategic in nature and not just a simple expansion of a product line.

The purchase of Whole Foods is seen as a strategic move against Amazon's major competitor—Walmart. Walmart sells more groceries than any other company in the United States, and Amazon wants a piece of that pie. The acquisition of Whole Foods will help Amazon increase its grocery business. Walmart faces a similar dilemma. Amazon is an online e-commerce

Source: Wiskerke/Alamy Stock Photo

juggernaut that's hurting Walmart's brick-and-mortar business. Walmart wants to boost its online sales. To do so, it acquired retailers like Bonobos and Jet.com.[4]

It is interesting to note that Amazon's acquisition of Whole Foods will result in Amazon managing more than 450 brick-and-mortar stores, which is quite a departure from its primary business model of online retail.

Amazon Goes Big

Since Amazon announced its acquisition of Whole Foods, there has been speculation about the extent to which Amazon will change Whole Foods stores. Amazon is currently testing a variety of technologies in the new Amazon Go convenience store located in Seattle. The Amazon Go store appears to be just like most convenience stores in many ways. But there are a few obvious differences, such as no checkout lines or point-of-sale terminals. Shoppers just walk through a pair of gates, and their Amazon account is charged for all items in their cart.[5] The store is able to identify customers as they enter the store, and using hundreds of cameras, the system tracks customer movements, including taking an item off the shelf and placing it in a shopping bag. Even concerted attempts to shoplift by rapidly concealing items taken off the shelf were futile—the faux criminal received a receipt for the goods within minutes of leaving the store.[6]

The long-term strategy for Amazon's grocery business remains unclear. Is it possible that the Amazon Go model could be merged with Whole Foods to create a massive grocery network in which customers shop with ease (and without checkout lines)? Or, in an even more radical play, could Whole Foods stores simply become launching points for Amazon delivery drones (either quadcopters or self-driving vehicles) to ferry grocery orders to customers so they can shop from their living room sofa? No one knows for sure. But it is clear that the grocery industry is on the verge of serious changes. The shelf life of certain business models may be shorter than people think.

Questions

1. The feature begins with a description of the Sears, Roebuck and Company business model and then makes a comparison between that company and Amazon. Can you think of any other businesses that successfully sold goods to consumers located in more remote parts of the United States on a large scale? How and why did these companies succeed?

2. It has been stated that even the suggestion that Amazon will enter an industry causes fear in the existing companies operating in that market. Do you think other grocery chains are concerned about this move by Amazon?

3. The Amazon Go convenience store presents yet another example of using technology to increase efficiency. However, do you see any downsides of the Amazon Go model?

4. Based on Amazon's strategic decision to compete in the grocery market, can you identify any other industries that Amazon may choose to enter in the next 5 years?

Competitive Advantage via Products

The first three principles in Figure 2-12 concern products or services. Organizations gain a competitive advantage by creating *new* products or services, by *enhancing* existing products or services, and by *differentiating* their products and services from those of their competitors.

Information systems create competitive advantages either as part of a product or by providing support to a product. Consider, for example, a car rental agency like Hertz or Avis. An information system that produces information about the car's location and provides driving instructions to destinations is part of the car rental, and thus is part of the product itself (see Figure 2-13a). In contrast, an information system that schedules car maintenance is not part of the product but instead supports the product (see Figure 2-13b). Either way, information systems can help achieve the first three principles in Figure 2-12.

a. Information System as Part of a Car Rental Product

b. Information System That Supports a Car Rental Product

Daily Service Schedule – June 15, 2020

StationID   22

StationName   Lubrication

ServiceDate	ServiceTime	VehicleID	Make	Model	Mileage	ServiceDescription
06/15/2020	12:00 AM	155890	Ford	Explorer	2244	Std. Lube
06/15/2020	11:00 AM	12448	Toyota	Tacoma	7558	Std. Lube

StationID   26

StationName   Alignment

ServiceDate	ServiceTime	VehicleID	Make	Model	Mileage	ServiceDescription
06/15/2020	9:00 AM	12448	Toyota	Tacoma	7558	Front end alignment inspect

StationID   28

StationName   Transmission

ServiceDate	ServiceTime	VehicleID	Make	Model	Mileage	ServiceDescription
06/15/2020	11:00 AM	155890	Ford	Explorer	2244	Transmission oil change

FIGURE 2-13

Two Roles for Information Systems Regarding Products

The remaining five principles in Figure 2-12 concern competitive advantage created by the implementation of business processes.

First Mover Advantage

It's a common misconception that in order to create a competitive advantage a company has to be the pioneering creator of a new technology. This **first mover advantage**, or gaining market share by being the first to develop a new technology in a market segment, doesn't guarantee an advantage over rivals. On the contrary, it's often detrimental because pioneering companies have to spend considerable resources on research and development (R&D) and educating the public about the new product or service. In this way, the cutting edge of technological development can quickly turn into the bleeding edge.

Many of the leading companies you know today obtained a **second mover advantage**, gaining market share by following a pioneering company and imitating its product or service, thereby reducing costly R&D expenditures. Google, for example, wasn't the first search engine. Altavista, WebCrawler, Lycos, and Ask.com were available before Google registered its domain name in 1997. But Google (Alphabet) is currently the dominant search engine. In fact, some of the largest tech companies in the world (e.g., Apple and Facebook) are second movers behind their early competitors (e.g., Motorola and MySpace). The old adage "the second mouse gets the cheese" is often repeated by investors hoping to avoid costly R&D expenditures.

Competitive Advantage via Business Processes

Organizations can *lock in customers* by making it difficult or expensive for customers to switch to another product. This strategy is sometimes called establishing high **switching costs**. Organizations can *lock in suppliers* by making it difficult to switch to another organization or, stated positively, by making it easy to connect to and work with the organization. Finally, competitive advantage can be gained by *creating entry barriers* that make it difficult and expensive for new competition to enter the market.

One advantage a company can create is ensuring that it produces secure products. For more information, see the Security Guide on pages 54–55.

Another means to gain competitive advantage is to *establish alliances* with other organizations. Such alliances establish standards, promote product awareness and needs, develop market size, reduce purchasing costs, and provide other benefits. Finally, organizations can gain competitive advantage by *reducing costs*. Such reductions enable the organization to reduce prices and/or to increase profitability. Increased profitability means not just greater shareholder value but also more cash, which can fund further infrastructure development for even greater competitive advantage.

All of these principles of competitive advantage make sense, but the question you may be asking is "How do information systems help to create competitive advantage?" To answer that question, consider a sample information system.

How Does an Actual Company Use IS to Create Competitive Advantages?

ABC, Inc., a major transportation company that did not want its name published in this textbook, is a worldwide shipper with sales well in excess of $1B. From its inception, ABC invested heavily in information technology and led the shipping industry in the application of information systems for competitive advantage. Here we consider one example of an information system that illustrates how ABC successfully uses information technology to gain competitive advantage.

ABC maintains customer account data that include not only the customer's name, address, and billing information but also data about the people, organizations, and locations to which the customer ships. ABC provides customers with a Web interface that automatically populates drop-down lists with the names of companies that the customer has shipped to in the past.

When the user clicks the company name, the underlying ABC information system reads the customer's contact data from a database. The data consist of names, addresses, and phone numbers of recipients from past shipments. The user then selects a contact name, and the system inserts that contact's address and other data into the form using data from the database. Thus, the system saves customers from having to reenter data for recipients to whom they have shipped in the past. Providing the data in this way also reduces data-entry errors.

Using ABC's system, customers can also request that email messages be sent to the sender (the customer), the recipient, and others as well. The customer can opt for ABC to send an email when the shipment is created and when it has been delivered. The customer can choose who receives delivery notifications, but only the sender will receive shipment notification. The customer can add a personal message and generate a shipping label. Automatically generating a shipping label on the customer's premises reduces errors in the preparation of shipping labels and results in considerable cost savings to the company. By adding these capabilities to the shipment scheduling system, ABC has extended its product from a package-delivery service to a package- and information-delivery service.

How Does This System Create a Competitive Advantage?

Now consider the ABC shipping information system in light of the competitive advantage factors in Figure 2-12. This information system *enhances* an existing service because it eases the effort of creating a shipment to the customer while reducing errors. The information system also helps to *differentiate* the ABC package delivery service from competitors that do not have a similar system. Further, the generation of email messages when ABC picks up and delivers a package could be considered a *new* service.

Because this information system captures and stores data about recipients, it reduces the amount of customer work when scheduling a shipment. Customers will be *locked in* by this system: If a customer wants to change to a different shipper, he or she will need to rekey recipient data for that new shipper. The disadvantage of rekeying data may well outweigh any advantage of switching to another shipper.

This system achieves a competitive advantage in two other ways as well. First, it raises the barriers to market entry. If another company wants to develop a shipping service, it will not only have to be able to ship packages, but it will also need to have a similar information system. In addition, the system reduces costs. It reduces errors in shipping documents, and it saves ABC paper, ink, and printing costs.

Of course, to determine if this system delivers a *net savings* in costs, the cost of developing and operating the information system will need to be offset against the gains in reduced errors and paper, ink, and printing costs. It may be that the system costs more than the savings. Even still, it may be a sound investment if the value of intangible benefits, such as locking in customers and raising entry barriers, exceeds the net cost.

Before continuing, review Figure 2-12. Make sure you understand each of the principles of competitive advantage and how information systems can help achieve them. In fact, the list in Figure 2-12 probably is important enough to memorize because you can also use it for non-IS applications. You can consider any business project or initiative in light of competitive advantage.

Q2-8 2029?

In the next 10 years, business models, strategies, and competitive advantages are unlikely to change. Their relationships to business processes and IS are also unlikely to change. They may evolve and new models may rise to the surface, but those new models will likely be extensions of existing models within existing paradigms.

What is likely to change, however, is pace. The speed of business is continuing to accelerate because of faster Internet speeds, new networked devices, and improved hardware. The Web and other social sites (e.g., Twitter, Facebook, etc.) enable the rapid spread of new ideas and innovations. They also require businesses to constantly be on alert for changes that may affect their strategy in the near future.

SECURITY GUIDE

HACKING SMART THINGS

You may have noticed a recent trend in TV commercials for cars. Many car manufacturers are focusing on technology-centric special features. One of the most popular add-ons right now is adding the capability to turn your car into an Internet hot spot. Sure, allowing your friends to check their social media updates using your car's Wi-Fi sounds pretty cool. But there may be some unintended risks associated with incorporating this capability into your car—or any device, for that matter. What if one of your passengers used that Wi-Fi connection to access your car's brakes?

Internet of Things (IoT)

You may have already heard of the *Internet of Things* (IoT), or the idea that objects are becoming connected to the Internet so they can interact with other devices, applications, or services. Countless companies are working to capitalize on the possibilities of new "smart" products designed to automatically communicate with other devices and exchange data with little or no intervention by the user. The trend of developing new Internet-enabled devices is so widespread that some estimates place the number of IoT devices at roughly 21 billion by 2021.[7]

But what can all of these new smart devices be used for? Take home automation, for example. The home automation market is growing rapidly with new Internet-enabled devices like thermostats, smoke detectors, light bulbs, surveillance cameras, and door locks gaining in popularity.[8] These devices allow a homeowner to remotely monitor the temperature of the home, turn lights on or off, or remotely keep an eye on the family dog by tapping into a webcam feed. While all of these capabilities seem like a great idea and add convenience to daily life, the trend of outfitting every object with Internet access may prove to be a hazardous, even dangerous, proposition.

Internet of Threats

You might already be aware of some of the types of security threats on the Internet. If you tune in to the evening news on any given night, you will see stories about data stolen from

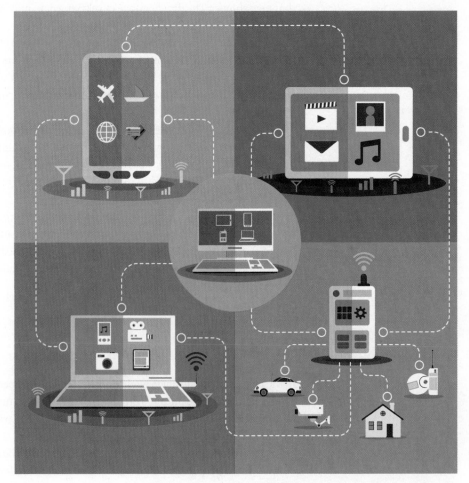

Source: Macrovector/Fotolia

large corporations, government insiders leaking sensitive information, or cyberattacks launched from around the globe.

What does this have to do with you? Well, you have sensitive information, too. How would you feel if your bank statements, medical records, and email history for the past 5 years were stolen and posted online? You probably are taking steps to avoid these threats like running antivirus software, enabling automatic updates, using your operating system's default firewall, avoiding suspicious emails, and staying away from shady Web sites.

But what about securing your data stored on these new Internet-enabled smart devices? Think about the security implications of having to protect 10, 20, or 30 different Internet-enabled devices in your home. Will you have to buy antivirus software for your refrigerator or configure a firewall on your thermostat? Could a hacker hijack the webcam in your living room or, worse, actually hijack your car?

Taking Back-Seat Driver to a Whole New Level

Yes, a hacker could potentially compromise your car if it is connected to the Internet. If a hacker takes control of your vehicle, he or she could then remotely control various functions of the vehicle (e.g., the brakes), keep tabs on your GPS coordinates, activate the Bluetooth microphone and listen to anything taking place inside of the car, or access data about the vehicle's operations and performance.[9] The thought of someone eavesdropping on your conversations in the car is bad enough. But what would happen if the hacker activates the brakes, or disables them, while you are driving? What happens when driverless cars become widely adopted and hackers could have complete control over the vehicle?

As more and more devices are accessible over some form of network, users will have to weigh the pros and the cons of using them. But securing these new smart devices will take additional work. The same thing that makes these devices great will also make them vulnerable to attack. Yes, of course, a smart thermostat will save you money. But what happens when it gets a virus? Will you be the one running a temperature?

 DISCUSSION QUESTIONS

1. How many devices in your home are connected to the Internet? How much time do you spend daily, weekly, or monthly trying to ensure that these devices have the latest updates and are secure? What are the implications of maintaining dozens of smart devices?

2. The guide discusses the potential threat of a hacker accessing a vehicle and downloading data about the car's performance and operations. Aside from a malicious hacker acting alone, are there any businesses or government agencies that could benefit from accessing these data? How?

3. Has this guide changed your perception of the Internet of Things? Do the benefits of smart devices outweigh the risk of data loss or your personal privacy? Why or why not?

4. The Internet of Things is not solely focused on home automation or private consumer products. Businesses are using the Internet of Things to manage supply chains and streamline various business processes. What benefits or risks are associated with businesses adopting new Internet-enabled devices?

To look forward, it is sometimes helpful to look back. Consider the innovations shown in Figure 2-14. These are innovative new products developed by five of the largest technology companies in the world. Many of them weren't around 10 years ago (i.e., in 2007). Google (1998) and Facebook (2004) were up and running, and the first iPhone had just been released. Smartphone competitors and the first AIs wouldn't come into being for about 5 years. Smartwatches wouldn't appear for about 7 years. Augmented reality (AR) and virtual reality devices (VR) are just now being released to consumers. Drones are currently used by hobbyists and some small companies, but large-scale commercial use is still in the experimental stage. Self-driving cars are in the late development to early adoption phases and are getting a lot of attention from manufacturers and consumers.

Company	Market Cap. In Billions	Search	Smartphone	AI	Smartwatch	AR/VR	Drones	Self-driving Car
Apple	$898		iPhone (2007)	Siri (2011)	Apple Watch (2015)	? (dev.)		? (dev.)
Alphabet	$711	Google (1998)	Nexus (2013)	Assistant (2016)	Wear (os) (2014)	Magic Leap (2018)	Wing (dev.)	Waymo
Microsoft	$723	Bing (2009)	Lumia (2011)	Cortana (2014)	Band (2014)	Hololens (2016)		
Facebook	$504	Facebook (2004)		FAIR (dev.)		Oculus Rift (2016)	Ascenta (dev.)	
Samsung	$295		Galaxy S (2010)	S Voice (2012)	Gear S2 (2013)	Gear VR (2015)		

FIGURE 2-14
Innovations by Technology Companies

This isn't a complete list, either—3D printing, cloud computing, software, hardware, e-commerce, and social media were left out of this chart. You'll learn more about innovations in hardware and software in Chapter 4. Companies such as IBM, Oracle, and Amazon could be included in this comparison as potential competitors as well. The point of this chart is to show the pace of technological development over time. Consider how quickly corporate strategies must adapt to this development. Strategically speaking, should each company have a product in each category like Alphabet does? Or would it be smarter to focus on fewer products?

By 2029, it's very likely that AR/VR will be commonplace. New 3D applications, games, and user interfaces will be developed. Consequently, companies may need to redesign their business processes. Drones and self-driving cars will see widespread use and have a major effect on competitive strategies. For many products, transportation is a major cost. Entire value chains will be disrupted as transportation and delivery costs plummet.

Robotics will likely be the next big area of technological expansion. Even now, companies are introducing robotics into areas outside of manufacturing. The strategic implications of a robotic workforce cannot be understated. Robots don't require health care, time off, vacations, breaks, sick days, or workman's compensation. They don't join unions, get mad, sue their employer, harass coworkers, or drink on the job. They also work 24 hours a day without a paycheck! Combine that with a great AI like IBM's Watson, and you've got an entirely different workforce. By 2029 we may understand "labor" in an entirely different way.

So, we can reasonably assume that the pace of change and the pace at which new technology is integrated will be fast and increasing, possibly accelerating, in the next 10 years. We can lament this fact or we can ignore it, but doing either is like standing on the shore of the Mississippi River and telling it to flow elsewhere.

Instead, we, and especially *you*, need to view this increased pace as rapidly creating opportunities in which you can excel. You know it's coming. You know that, if not self-driving vehicles, then some other new technology-based product that is being constructed in someone's garage today will change the competitive landscape for the company for which you will work. Knowing that, how can you take advantage of it?

Maybe you want to be an innovator and use technology to create new products like self-driving cars, drones, or 3D printers. If so, do it. But, maybe, like eHermes, you want to use the innovative products that others are making and create new strategies or build new businesses that take advantage of the opportunities that new products create. You can be certain that, 10 years from now, you will have even more opportunity to do so.

CAREER GUIDE

Name: Gabe Chino
Company: Financial Services
Job Title: Director of Architecture
Education: Weber State University, University of Utah

Source: Gabriel Chino, Director of architecture, Financial Services

1 How did you get this type of job?

I took an internship as a Software Engineer at a small company while completing my undergraduate work in computer science. I stayed with the company for 3 years as a web developer. During that time, I learned SQL, application development, and front-end development. I eventually left the company to broaden my experience in IT. After working at a few more companies, I programmed in numerous languages, managed servers, managed networks, and even did some desktop support. I then went on to do my graduate work in IS. These experiences prepared me to be a director at a large financial services company where I manage IT teams and have broad influence on IT decisions for the organization.

2 What attracted you to this field?

I have always been interested in how technology can enhance our lives. After getting some exposure to programming in college, I was hooked. I realize there is no end to innovation and creativity in this field, so I am never bored.

3 What does a typical workday look like for you (duties, decisions, problems)?

I provide solutions. Depending on the day, these could be technology solutions, including code, data, and infrastructure. They can be team solutions, including relationships, communication, or efficiency. They can also be organizational and business solutions. When you are on the technology side of the organization, you get a reputation for being the person who can figure anything out.

4 What do you like most about your job?

I like to come up with creative solutions to business problems. I pretty much get to define how I get work done. I am expected to be a thought leader in the organization, and I feel like there is a high level of respect between my peers and me.

5 What skills would someone need to do well at your job?

The skills needed to be an IT architect are (1) a solid technical background with exposure to many platforms and systems and (2) very strong communication skills. In IT, there are many ways to solve a problem. The architect's job is to find the right solution for the company's needs. I always have to be prepared to have my ideas challenged.

6 Are education or certifications important in your field? Why?

An education is a must for this field. I have met amazing IT architects from a variety of majors. The most common majors in this field are information systems and computer science. Certifications can really set you apart as an architect as well. Networking, programming, and security certifications are most common. I recently completed my TOGAF certification, which is an architect certification.

7 What advice would you give to someone who is considering working in your field?

My advice would be to always watch where the tech field is going. If this field is really for you, stay current with the latest IT trends.

8 What do you think will be hot tech jobs in 10 years?

IT security professionals will be in very high demand as businesses continue to put more and more online. Data scientists will continue to grow in importance as businesses try to target the right customers in the right way.

ACTIVE REVIEW

Use this Active Review to verify that you understand the ideas and concepts that answer the chapter's study questions.

Q2-1 How does organizational strategy determine information systems structure?

Diagram and explain the relationship of industry structure, competitive strategy, value chains, business processes, and information systems. Working from industry structure to IS, explain how the knowledge you've gained in these first two chapters pertains to that diagram.

Q2-2 What five forces determine industry structure?

Name and briefly describe the five forces. Give your own examples of both strong and weak forces of each type, similar to those in Figure 2-3.

Q2-3 How does analysis of industry structure determine competitive strategy?

Describe four different strategies as defined by Porter. Give an example of four different companies that have implemented each of the strategies.

Q2-4 How does competitive strategy determine value chain structure?

Define the terms *value*, *margin*, and *value chain*. Explain why organizations that choose a differentiation strategy can use value to determine a limit on the amount of extra cost to pay for differentiation. Name the primary and support activities in the value chain and explain the purpose of each. Explain the concept of linkages.

Q2-5 How do business processes generate value?

Define *business process*, *cost*, and *margin* as they pertain to business processes. Explain the purpose of an activity and describe types of repository. Explain the importance of business process redesign and describe the difference between the business processes in Figure 2-8 and those in Figure 2-9.

Q2-6 How does competitive strategy determine business processes and the structure of information systems?

In your own words, explain how competitive strategy determines the structure of business processes. Use the examples of a clothing store that caters to struggling students and a clothing store that caters to professional businesspeople in a high-end neighborhood. List the activities in the business process for the two companies and create a chart like that in Figure 2-9. Explain how the information systems' requirements differ between the two stores.

Q2-7 How do information systems provide competitive advantages?

List and briefly describe eight principles of competitive advantage. Consider your college bookstore. List one application of each of the eight principles. Strive to include examples that involve information systems.

Q2-8 2029?

Describe how technological innovations have developed in the past 10 years. What new innovations currently under development will likely be adopted in the next 10 years? Explain how business strategies might change due to these new innovations. Describe the strategic implications of self-driving cars or robotics on traditional companies.

Using Your Knowledge with eHermes

Explain in your own words how eHermes competitive strategy might be threatened by relying on a large corporate account. Describe eHermes' planned response and summarize the problems that Kamala perceives with that response. Recommend a course of action for eHermes. Use Kamala's idea of diversifying the types of services the company provides to illustrate your answer.

KEY TERMS AND CONCEPTS

Activity   46
Business process   46
Business process management   47
Competitive strategy   41
Cost   46
First mover advantage   52

Five forces model   40
Linkages   45
Margin   44
Primary activities   44
Repository   46
Second mover advantage   52

Support activities   44
Switching costs   52
Value   44
Value chain   44

MyLab MIS

To complete the problems with MyLab MIS, go to EOC Discussion Questions in the MyLab.

USING YOUR KNOWLEDGE

2-1.
MyLab MIS
Apply the value chain model to a mail-order company such as L.L.Bean (*www.llbean.com*). What is its competitive strategy? Describe the tasks L.L.Bean must accomplish for each of the primary value chain activities. How does L.L.Bean's competitive strategy and the nature of its business influence the general characteristics of its information systems?

2-2.
MyLab MIS
Suppose you decide to start a business that recruits students for summer jobs. You will match available students with available jobs. You need to learn what positions are available and what students are available for filling those positions. In starting your business, you know you will be competing with local newspapers, Craigslist (*www.craigslist.org*), and your college. You will probably have other local competitors as well.

a. Analyze the structure of this industry according to Porter's five forces model.

b. Given your analysis in part a, recommend a competitive strategy.

c. Describe the primary value chain activities as they apply to this business.

d. Describe a business process for recruiting students.

e. Describe information systems that could be used to support the business process in part d.

f. Explain how the process you describe in part d and the system you describe in part e reflect your competitive strategy.

2-3.
MyLab MIS
Consider the two different bike rental companies in Q2-6. Think about the bikes they rent. Clearly, the student bikes will be just about anything that can be ridden out of the shop. The bikes for the business executives, however, must be new, shiny, clean, and in tip-top shape.

a. Compare and contrast the operations value chains of these two businesses as they pertain to the management of bicycles.

b. Describe a business process for maintaining bicycles for both businesses.

c. Describe a business process for acquiring bicycles for both businesses.

d. Describe a business process for disposing of bicycles for both businesses.

e. What roles do you see for information systems in your answers to the earlier questions? The information systems can be those you develop within your company or they can be those developed by others, such as Craigslist.

COLLABORATION EXERCISE 2

Using the collaboration IS you built in Chapter 1 (page 32), collaborate with a group of students to answer the following questions.

Singing Valley Resort is a top-end 50-unit resort located high in the Colorado mountains. Rooms rent for $400 to $4,500 per night, depending on the season and the type of accommodations.

Singing Valley's clientele are well-to-do; many are famous entertainers, sports figures, and business executives. They are accustomed to, and demand, superior service.

Singing Valley resides in a gorgeous mountain valley and is situated a few hundred yards from a serene mountain lake. It prides itself on superior accommodations; tip-top service; delicious, healthful, organic meals; and exceptional wines. Because it has been so successful, Singing Valley is 90 percent occupied except during the "shoulder seasons" (November, after the leaves change and before the snow arrives, and late April, when winter sports are finished but the snow is still on the ground).

Singing Valley's owners want to increase revenue, but because the resort is nearly always full and because its rates are already at the top of the scale, it cannot do so via occupancy revenue. Thus, over the past several years it has focused on up-selling to its clientele activities such as fly-fishing, river rafting, cross-country skiing, snowshoeing, art lessons, yoga and other exercise classes, spa services, and the like.

To increase the sales of these optional activities, Singing Valley prepared in-room marketing materials to advertise their availability. Additionally, it trained all registration personnel on techniques of casually and appropriately suggesting such activities to guests on arrival.

The response to these promotions was only mediocre, so Singing Valley's management stepped up its promotions. The first step was to send emails to its clientele advising them of the activities available during their stay. An automated system produced emails personalized with names and personal data.

Unfortunately, the automated email system backfired. Immediately upon its execution, Singing Valley management received numerous complaints. One long-term customer objected that she had been coming to Singing Valley for 7 years and asked if they had yet noticed that she was confined to a wheelchair. If they had noticed, she said, why did they send her a personalized invitation for a hiking trip? The agent of another famous client complained that the personalized email was sent to her client and her husband, when anyone who had turned on a TV in the past 6 months knew the two of them were involved in an exceedingly acrimonious divorce. Yet another customer complained that, indeed, he and his wife had vacationed at Singing Valley 3 years ago, but he had not been there since. To his knowledge, his wife had not

been there, either, so he was puzzled as to why the email referred to their visit last winter. He wanted to know if, indeed, his wife had recently been to the resort, without him. Of course, Singing Valley had no way of knowing about customers it had insulted who never complained.

During the time the automated email system was operational, sales of extra activities were up 15 percent. However, the strong customer complaints conflicted with its competitive strategy so, in spite of the extra revenue, Singing Valley stopped the automated email system, sacked the vendor who had developed it, and demoted the Singing Valley employee who had brokered the system. Singing Valley was left with the problem of how to increase its revenue.

Your team's task is to develop two innovative ideas for solving Singing Valley's problem. At the minimum, include the following in your response:

a. An analysis of the five forces of the Singing Valley market. Make and justify any necessary assumptions about their market.

b. A statement of Singing Valley's competitive strategy.

c. A statement of the problem. If the members of your group have different perceptions of the problem, all the better. Use a collaborative process to obtain the best possible problem description to which all can agree.

d. Document in a general way (like the top row of Figure 2-10) the process of up-selling an activity.

e. Develop two innovative ideas for solving the Singing Valley problem. For each idea, provide:
   - A brief description of the idea.
   - A process diagram (like Figure 2-11) of the idea. Figure 2-11 was produced using Microsoft Visio; if you have access to that product, you'll save time and have a better result.
   - A description of the information system needed to implement the idea.

f. Compare the advantages and disadvantages of your alternatives in part e and recommend one of them for implementation.

CASE STUDY 2

The Amazon of Innovation

On Cyber Monday, November 27, 2017, Amazon customers ordered more than 1,400 electronics per second from a mobile device.[10] And shopping on Amazon's app increased 70 percent over the previous year. On its busiest day, Amazon packed and shipped more than 1 million packages. Amazon's last same-day delivery order for the holiday season was ordered on Christmas Eve and delivered in 58 minutes, arriving at 11:58 PM just in time for Christmas. (Some of Amazon's major innovations are listed in Figure 2-15.)

You may think of Amazon as simply an online retailer, and that is indeed where the company achieved most of its success. To do this, Amazon had to build enormous supporting infrastructure—just imagine the information systems and fulfillment facilities needed to ship electronics ordered at a rate of 1,400 per second. That infrastructure, however, is needed only during the busy holiday season. Most of the year, Amazon is left with excess infrastructure capacity. Starting in 2000, Amazon began to lease some of that capacity to other companies. In the process, it played a key role in the creation of what are termed *cloud services*, which you will learn about in Chapter 6. For now, just think of cloud

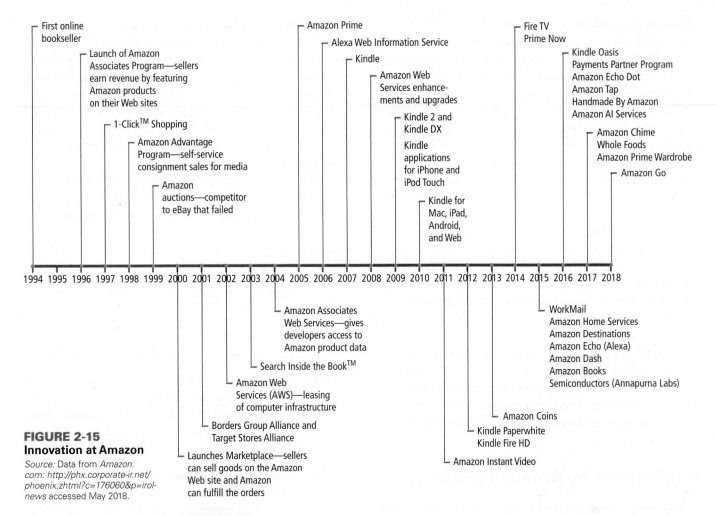

FIGURE 2-15
Innovation at Amazon
Source: Data from *Amazon. com: http://phx.corporate-ir.net/ phoenix.zhtml?c=176060&p=irol-news* accessed May 2018.

services as computer resources somewhere out in the Internet that are leased on flexible terms.

Today, Amazon's business lines can be grouped into three major categories:

- Online retailing
- Order fulfillment
- Cloud services

Consider each.

Amazon created the business model for online retailing. It began as an online bookstore, but every year since 1998 it has added new product categories. The company is involved in all aspects of online retailing. It sells its own inventory. It incentivizes you, via the Associates program, to sell its inventory as well. Or it will help you sell your inventory within its product pages or via one of its consignment venues. Online auctions are the major aspect of online sales in which Amazon does not participate. It tried auctions in 1999, but it could never make inroads against eBay.[11]

Today, it's hard to remember how much of what we take for granted was pioneered by Amazon. "Customers who bought this, also bought that;" online customer reviews; customer ranking of customer reviews; books lists; Look Inside the Book; automatic

free shipping for certain orders or frequent customers; and Kindle books and devices were all novel concepts when Amazon introduced them.

Amazon's retailing business operates on very thin margins. Products are usually sold at a discount from the stated retail price, and 2-day shipping is free for Amazon Prime members (who pay an annual fee of $119). How does it do it? For one, Amazon drives its employees incredibly hard. Former employees claim the hours are long, the pressure is severe, and the workload is heavy. But what else? It comes down to Moore's Law and the innovative use of nearly free data processing, storage, and communication.

In addition to online retailing, Amazon also sells order fulfillment services. You can ship your inventory to an Amazon warehouse and access Amazon's information systems just as if they were yours. Using technology known as Web services (discussed in Chapter 6), your order processing information systems can directly integrate, over the Web, with Amazon's inventory, fulfillment, and shipping applications. Your customers need not know that Amazon played any role at all. You can also sell that same inventory using Amazon's retail sales applications.

Amazon Web Services (AWS) allow organizations to lease time on computer equipment in very flexible ways. Amazon's Elastic Cloud 2 (EC2) enables organizations to expand and contract the computer resources they need within minutes. Amazon has a variety of payment plans, and it is possible to buy computer time for less than a penny an hour. Key to this capability is the ability for the leasing organization's computer programs to interface with Amazon's to automatically scale up and scale down the resources leased. For example, if a news site publishes a story that causes a rapid ramp-up of traffic, that news site can, programmatically, request, configure, and use more computing resources for an hour, a day, a month, whatever.

With its Kindle devices, Amazon has become both a vendor of tablets and, even more importantly in the long term, a vendor of online music and video. Amazon Echo (Alexa-enabled ordering system) and Amazon Dash (a one-button reordering device) have become two of Amazon's top-selling products.

In late 2016, Jeff Bezos announced the first package delivery by drone via Amazon Prime Air in the UK.[12] But regulations have slowed it's adoption in the United States. While drone delivery is something that will happen in the future, consider a service that Amazon is offering right now.

In mid-2017 Amazon made news by acquiring grocery giant Whole Foods. By 2018 Amazon had opened its own automated grocery store named Amazon Go, which didn't use cashiers or checkout terminals. Amazon's expansion into the traditional grocery store space drove speculation about how far Amazon's reach would extend.

Fulfillment by Amazon (FBA)

Fulfillment by Amazon (FBA) is an Amazon service by which other sellers can ship goods to Amazon warehouses for stocking, order packaging, and shipment. FBA customers pay a fee for the service as well as for inventory space. Amazon uses its own inventory management and order fulfillment business processes and information systems to fulfill the FBA customers' orders.

FBA customers can sell their goods on Amazon, sell them via their own sales channels, or both. If the FBA customer sells on Amazon, Amazon will provide customer service for order processing (handling returns, fixing erroneously packed orders, answering customer order queries, and the like).

The costs for Fulfillment by Amazon depend on the type and size of the goods to be processed. The FBA fees for standard-size products as of May 2018 are shown in the table.

Standard Size	FBA Costs[13]
Small (1 lb. or less)	$2.41
Large (1 lb. or less)	$3.19
Large (1 to 2 lb.)	$4.71
Large (over 2 lb.)	$4.71 + $0.38/lb. above first 2 lb.
Storage (cubic foot per month)	$0.69

If goods are sold via Amazon, Amazon uses its own information systems to drive the order fulfillment process. However, if the goods are sold via an FBA customer's sales channel, then the FBA customer must connect its own information systems with those at Amazon. Amazon provides a standardized interface by which this is done called Amazon Marketplace Web Service (MWS). Using Web-standard technology (see Chapter 6), FBA customers' order and payment data are directly linked to Amazon's information systems.

FBA enables companies to outsource order fulfillment to Amazon, thus avoiding the cost of developing their own processes, facilities, and information systems for this purpose.

QUESTIONS

2-4. Based on the facts presented in this case, what do you think is Amazon's competitive strategy? Justify your answer.

2-5. Jeff Bezos, CEO of Amazon, has stated that the best customer support is none. What does that mean?

2-6. Suppose you work for Amazon or a company that takes innovation as seriously as Amazon does. What do you suppose is the likely reaction to an employee who says to his or her boss, "But, I don't know how to do that!"?

2-7. Using your own words and your own experience, what skills and abilities do you think you need to have to thrive at an organization like Amazon?

2-8. What should UPS and FedEx be doing in response to Amazon's interest in drone delivery via Amazon Prime Air?

2-9. Summarize the advantages and disadvantages for brick-and-mortar retailers to sell items via Amazon. Would you recommend that they do so?

2-10. If a brick-and-mortar retailer were to use FBA, what business processes would it not need to develop? What costs would it save?

2-11. If a brick-and-mortar retailer were to use FBA, what information systems would it not need to develop? What costs would it save?

2-12. If a brick-and-mortar retailer were to use FBA, how would it integrate its information systems with Amazon's? (To add depth to your answer, Google the term *Amazon MWS.*)

MyLab MIS

Go to the Assignments section of your MyLab to complete these writing exercises.

2-13. Samantha Green owns and operates Twigs Tree Trimming Service. Samantha graduated from the forestry program of a nearby university and worked for a large landscape design firm, performing tree trimming and removal. After several years of experience, she bought her own truck, stump grinder, and other equipment and opened her own business in St. Louis, Missouri. Although many of her jobs are one-time operations to remove a tree or stump, others are recurring, such as trimming a tree or groups of trees every year or every other year. When business is slow, she calls former clients to remind them of her services and of the need to trim their trees on a regular basis. Samantha has never heard of Michael Porter or any of his theories. She operates her business "by the seat of her pants."

    a. Explain how an analysis of the five competitive forces could help Samantha.

    b. Do you think Samantha has a competitive strategy? What competitive strategy would seem to make sense for her?

    c. How would knowledge of her competitive strategy help her sales and marketing efforts?

    d. Describe, in general terms, the kind of information system that she needs to support sales and marketing efforts.

2-14. YourFire, Inc., is a small business owned by Curt and Julie Robards. Based in Brisbane, Australia, YourFire manufactures and sells a lightweight camping stove called the YourFire. Curt, who previously worked as an aerospace engineer, invented and patented a burning nozzle that enables the stove to stay lit in very high winds—up to 90 miles per hour. Julie, an industrial designer by training, developed an elegant folding design that is small, lightweight, easy to set up, and very stable. Curt and Julie manufacture the stove in their garage, and they sell it directly to their customers over the Internet and via phone.

    a. Explain how an analysis of the five competitive forces could help YourFire.

    b. What does the YourFire competitive strategy seem to be?

    c. Briefly summarize how the primary value chain activities pertain to YourFire. How should the company design these value chains to conform to its competitive strategy?

    d. Describe business processes that YourFire needs in order to implement its marketing and sales and its service value chain activities.

    e. Describe, in general terms, information systems to support your answer to part d.

2-15. A friend of yours from college, who you haven't talked to in 3 years, sends you an email asking you to meet him for lunch. He says he's got a great idea for a business and wants to run it by you. At first you're hesitant because your friend, while obviously intelligent, doesn't always think things though. You agree to meet for lunch and talk about the idea. At lunch, he explains that he's been developing new flexible screens for his employer that are incredibly tough, waterproof, and use very little energy. His idea is to use these new flexible screens to create wearable computing clothing that can connect directly to smartphones and push ads, promotions, and video. His only problem is that he knows nothing about business. He's not sure where to start.

    a. Explain how you could use the five forces model to help your friend understand the potential success of his wearable flex screens.

    b. How might understanding the unique forces affecting this industry determine the competitive advantage for your friend's new company?

ENDNOTES

1. Michael Porter, *Competitive Strategy: Techniques for Analyzing Industries and Competitors* (New York: Free Press, 1980).
2. Based on Michael Porter, *Competitive Strategy* (New York: Free Press, 1985).
3. For simplicity, the flow of cash is abbreviated in Figure 2-8. Business processes for authorizing, controlling, making payments, and receiving revenue are, of course, vital.
4. Nick Wingfield, "Amazon to Buy Whole Foods for $13.4 Billion," *The New York Times*, April 7, 2018, *www.nytimes.com/2017/06/16/business/dealbook/amazon-whole-foods.html*.
5. Nick Wingfield, "Inside Amazon Go, a Store of the Future," *The New York Times*, April 7, 2018, *www.nytimes.com/2018/01/21/technology/inside-amazon-go-a-store-of-the-future.html*.
6. Ibid.
7. Julia Boorstin, "An Internet of Things That Will Number Ten Billions," *CNBC.com*, Feburary 1, 2016, accessed April 24, 2016, *www.cnbc.com/2016/02/01/an-internet-of-things-that-will-number-ten-billions.html*.
8. *https://nest.com/works-with-nest/*
9. Michael Miller, "'Car Hacking' Just Got Real: In Experiment, Hackers Disable SUV on Busy Highway," *Washington Post*, July 22, 2015, accessed April 24, 2016, *www.washingtonpost.com/news/morning-mix/wp/2015/07/22/car-hacking-just-got-real-hackers-disable-suv-on-busy-highway*.
10. Amazon.com Inc., "Amazon Celebrates Biggest Holiday; More Than Four Million People Trialed Prime in One Week Alone This Season," Press release, December, 26, 2017, accessed May 22, 2018, *http://phx.corporate-ir.net/phoenix.zhtml?c=176060&p=irol-newsArticle&ID=2324045*.
11. For a fascinating glimpse of this story from someone inside the company, see "Early Amazon: Auctions" at *http://glinden.blogspot.com/2006/04/early-amazon-auctions.html*, accessed April 28, 2016.
12. Frederic Lardinois, "Amazon Starts Prime Air Drone Delivery Trial in the UK—but Only with Two Beta Users," TechCrunch, December 14, 2016, accessed May 22, 2018, *https://techcrunch.com/2016/12/14/amazons-prime-air-delivery-uk/*.
13. "Fulfillment by Amazon (FBA) Fees and Rate Structure," *Amazon.com*, accessed June 6, 2018, *https://services.amazon.com/fulfillment-by-amazon/pricing.htm*.

CHAPTER 3

Business Intelligence Systems

"Any progress with the new corporate accounts? Are they interested in eHermes?" Seth Wilson, director of IT services at eHermes, asks as he sets down his lunch.

"Pretty good." Tess, the VP of sales, responds nodding slightly as she unwraps her sandwich. "I decided to focus on grocery stores. They're worried about competition from online grocery sales through Walmart and Amazon, so it wasn't hard to get them to try something new."

"And?"

"A large regional grocery chain is interested in giving it a try. The company leaders liked the idea that customers could walk out their doors and pick out their own produce right from a mobile eHermes storefront. They said some of

MyLab MIS

Using Your Knowledge
Questions 3-1, 3-2, 3-3

Essay Questions 3-20, 3-21, 3-22

their customers are hesitant to buy groceries online because they worry about the quality of the produce picked out by grocery store employees. eHermes might solve that problem and increase their online sales."

Seth looks surprised. "Hmm . . . interesting. I didn't think about that. What about the partnership with eHermes? Are they worried that we might cut them out and work directly with their distributors?"

"No. Actually, they see it as a way to strategically compete with the online sales of Walmart and Amazon. They view themselves as the butcher, baker, pharmacist, and acquirer of fresh produce. They see us as a new type of delivery service and an online sales channel. They don't think we'll threaten their core business."

"They're probably right. Well, for most of their products, anyway."

"Yes, it's really a win-win for everyone," Tess says nodding her head. "They get increased online sales and automated delivery without having to develop any of the underlying technology. We get to expand our product lines and reach our customers more often. Everyone does what they do best, and we're able to compete with the biggest online retailers."

"Hmm . . . and what about their customer data? How much are they willing to share with us?"

"Unfortunately, not much," Tess says, grimacing.

"Why not? Don't they understand the benefits of sharing data with us?"

"No, they understand the benefits. They know we'd be able to accurately target their customers with the products they buy most often and offer

"Data analysis where you don't know the second question to ask until you see the answer to the first one."

Source: Haiyin Wang/Alamy Stock Photo

them right when they need them. It would be super convenient and likely increase sales dramatically."

"Well, what's their hang-up?" Seth says, shaking his head.

"It's their existing privacy policy. It says they can't share customers' personally identifiable information with affiliates like us. And they don't want to revise the policy. This is a new partnership, and they don't know us or trust us yet."

"Bummer. What are you going to do?"

"I've got an idea," Tess says, smiling. "But I'll need your help."

"OK, I'll bite. What do you need?"

Study QUESTIONS

Q3-1   How do organizations use business intelligence (BI) systems?

Q3-2   How do organizations use data warehouses and data marts to acquire data?

Q3-3   What are three techniques for processing BI data?

Q3-4   What are the alternatives for publishing BI?

Q3-5   Why is artificial intelligence (AI) important?

Q3-6   How will Artificial Intelligence and automation affect organizations?

Q3-7   What is the goal of AI?

Q3-8   How does AI work?

Q3-9   2029?

Tess grabs a marker and starts drawing on a whiteboard. "The grocery store chain is willing to share 'anonymized' customer data with us that doesn't have customer names or addresses. By itself, it's not very valuable. We need individualized customer data. But I might be able to identify individual customers if I can combine the grocery store's data with our data and some publicly available voter data. By triangulating these different data sources, I should be able to identify each customer. Then we would know their individual buying habits."

"Wow! So, what do you need from me?"

"I think I can identify most customer records with just zip code, gender, and date of birth. But honestly, I'm not quite sure what I want."

"That's typical for BI."

"What's BI?"

"Business intelligence. Data analysis where you don't know the second question to ask until you see the answer to the first one."

"Yeah. That's it exactly! That's where I am."

"OK, let me gather some data from our existing system and put it in a spreadsheet for you. Then you can combine it with your other data sets and see how far you get."

"That should work," Tess says, sitting back in her chair.

"Yes, well, if it does work and you want to set up a data mart, then you'll need to come up with some money for my budget." Seth turns to make a few notes on the whiteboard.

Tess laughs. "If I can turn your data into dollars, that won't be a problem."

Seth smiles as he picks up his sandwich. "That's always the tricky part."

Chapter PREVIEW

Information systems generate enormous amounts of data. This data might be used for operational purposes, such as tracking orders, inventories, payables, and so forth. It also has a potential windfall: It contains patterns, relationships, and clusters and can be used to classify, forecast, and predict.

This chapter considers business intelligence (BI) systems: information systems that can produce patterns, relationships, and other information from organizational data (structured and unstructured) as well as from external, purchased data. Analysts can use BI systems to create value for the organization, or they can direct an artificial intelligence (AI) system to achieve a specific goal.

As a future business professional, using business intelligence is a critical skill. According to a recent survey by PricewaterhouseCoopers, 50 percent of U.S. CEOs see *very high value* of digital technology in data analytics (business intelligence). Eighty percent reported that data mining and analytics were strategically important to their organizations.[1] In 2016, Gartner found that one of the top priorities for CEOs is managing the digital transformation of their businesses (e.g., Internet of Things, self-driving cars, etc.). More than half of CEOs believe that their industries will undergo such tremendous digital transformations in the next 5 years that they will be nearly unrecognizable. As you will learn, business intelligence is a key technology supporting such digital transformation.[2]

This chapter begins by summarizing the ways organizations use business intelligence. It then describes the three primary activities in the BI process and illustrates those activities using a parts selection problem. The discussion then moves to the role of data warehouses and data marts. This is followed by a discussion of reporting analysis, data mining, and Big Data and alternatives for publishing BI. After that, you'll learn about the importance of AI and how it will affect organizations. The chapter then looks at the goals of AI and walks through a simple example. We will wrap up the chapter with a 2029 observation that many people find frightening.

Q3-1 How Do Organizations Use Business Intelligence (BI) Systems?

Business intelligence (BI) systems are information systems that process operational, social, and other data to identify patterns, relationships, and trends for use by business professionals and other knowledge workers. These patterns, relationships, trends, and predictions are referred to as **business intelligence**. As information systems, BI systems have the five standard components: hardware, software, data, procedures, and people. The software component of a BI system is called a **BI application**.

In the context of their day-to-day operations, organizations generate enormous amounts of data. AT&T, for example, processes 1.9 trillion call records in its database, and Google stores a database with more than 33 trillion entries.[3] Business intelligence is buried in that data, and the function of a BI system is to extract it and make it available to those who need it.

The boundaries of BI systems are blurry. In this text, we will take the broad view shown in Figure 3-1. Source data for a BI system can be the organization's own operational data, social media data, data that the organization purchases from data vendors, or employee knowledge. The BI application processes the data with reporting applications, data mining applications, and Big Data applications to produce business intelligence for knowledge workers.

How Do Organizations Use BI?

See what a typical workday would look like for someone who manages data and analytics in the Career Guide on page 104.

Starting with the first row of Figure 3-2, business intelligence can be used just for informing. For example, retail grocery store managers can use a BI system to see which products are selling quickly. At the time of the analysis, they may not have any particular purpose in mind but are just browsing

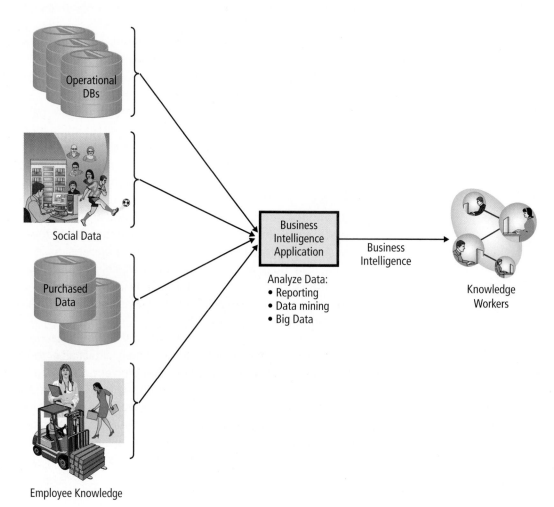

FIGURE 3-1

Components of a Business Intelligence System

Task	Grocery Store Example
Informing	Which products are selling quickly? Which products are most profitable?
Deciding	Which customers shop at each location? Create custom marketing plans per store.
Problem Solving	How can we increase sales? How can we reduce food waste?
Project Management	Build in-store cafés. Expand to other locations.

FIGURE 3-2
Types of Business Intelligence Systems

the BI results for some future, unspecified purpose. They may have no particular purpose in mind; they just want to know "how we're doing."

Moving down a row in Figure 3-2, some managers use BI systems for decision making. Managers could use a BI system or its user data to determine the location of the closest retail store to each user. They could then create customized marketing plans for each store, targeting the products those specific customers buy most often. So, for example, a grocery store chain may market expensive lobster tails at one location (the more affluent part of town) and less expensive hamburgers in another part of town. Profits might go up, and waste would probably go down.

(By the way, some authors define BI systems as supporting decision making only, in which case they use the older term **decision support systems** as a synonym for decision-making BI systems. We take the broader view here to include all four of the tasks in Figure 3-2 and will avoid the term *decision support systems*.)

Problem solving is the next category of business intelligence use. Again, a problem is a perceived difference between what is and what ought to be. Business intelligence can be used for both sides of that definition: determining *what is* as well as *what should be*. If revenue is below expectations, a grocery store manager can use BI to learn what factors to change to increase sales and reduce food waste. They could buy the right types of food in the correct quantities.

Finally, business intelligence can be used during project management. A grocery store manager can use BI to support a project to build an in-store café. If the café is successful, it can use BI to determine which locations would be good future expansion targets.

As you study Figure 3-2, recall the hierarchical nature of these tasks. Deciding requires informing; problem solving requires deciding (and informing); and project management requires problem solving (and deciding [and informing]).

What Are the Three Primary Activities in the BI Process?

Figure 3-3 shows the three primary activities in the BI process: acquire data, perform analysis, and publish results. These activities directly correspond to the BI elements in Figure 3-1. **Data acquisition** is the process of obtaining, cleaning, organizing, relating, and cataloging source

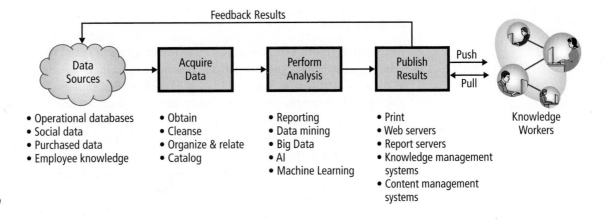

FIGURE 3-3
Three Primary Activities in the BI Process

data. We will illustrate a simple data acquisition example later in this question and discuss data acquisition in greater detail in Q3-2.

BI analysis is the process of creating business intelligence. The three fundamental categories of BI analysis are reporting, data mining, and Big Data. We will describe each of the categories of BI analysis and illustrate a simple example of a reporting system later in this question and in greater detail in Q3-3 and Q3-4. We will also look at automated analysis using AI and machine learning later in Q3-5 and Q3-8.

Publish results is the process of delivering business intelligence to the knowledge workers who need it. **Push publishing** delivers business intelligence to users without any request from the users; the BI results are delivered according to a schedule or as a result of an event or particular data condition. **Pull publishing** requires the user to request BI results. Publishing media include print as well as online content delivered via Web servers, specialized Web servers known as *report servers*, automated applications, knowledge management systems, and content management systems. We will discuss these publishing options further in Q3-4. For now, consider a simple example of the use of business intelligence.

Using Business Intelligence to Find Candidate Parts

3D printing offers the possibility for customers to print parts they need rather than order them from a retailer or distributor. One large distributor of bicycle parts wanted to stay on top of this potential change in demand and decided to investigate the possibility of selling 3D printing files for the parts rather than the parts themselves. Accordingly, it created a team to examine past sales data to determine which part designs it might sell. To do so, the company needed to identify qualifying parts and compute how much revenue potential those parts represent.

To address this problem, the team obtained an extract of sales data from its IS department and stored it in Microsoft Access. It then created five criteria for parts that might quality for this new program. Specifically, it looked for parts that were:

1. Provided by certain vendors (starting with just a few vendors that had already agreed to make part design files available for sale)
2. Purchased by larger customers (individuals and small companies would be unlikely to have 3D printers or the expertise needed to use them)
3. Frequently ordered (popular products)
4. Ordered in small quantities (3D printing is not suited for mass production)
5. Simple in design (easier to 3D print)

The team knew that the fifth criterion would be difficult to evaluate because the company doesn't store data on part complexity per se. After some discussion, the team decided to use part weight and price as surrogates for simplicity, operating under the assumption that "If it doesn't weigh very much or cost very much, it probably isn't complex." At least, the team decided to start that way and find out. Accordingly, the team asked the IS department to include part weight in the extract.

Acquire Data

As shown in Figure 3-3, acquiring data is the first step in the BI process. In response to the team's request for data, the IS department extracted operational data to produce the table shown in Figure 3-4. This table is a combination of data from the Sales table (CustomerName, Contact, Title, Bill Year, Number Orders, Units, Revenue, Source, PartNumber) and the Part table (PartNumber, Shipping Weight, Vendor) for select vendors willing to release 3D part design files.

As team members examined this data, they concluded they had what they needed and actually wouldn't need all of the data columns in the table. Notice there are some missing and questionable values. Numerous rows have missing values of Contact and Title, and some rows have a value of zero for Units. The missing contact data and title data weren't a problem. But the values of zero

CustomerName	Contact	Title	Bill Year	Number Orders	Units	Revenue	Source	PartNumber	Shipping Weight	Vendor
Gordos Dirt Bikes	Sergio Gutiérrez	Sales Represe	2020	43	107	$26,234.12	Internet	100-108	3.32	Riley Manufacturing
Island Biking			2021	59	135	$25,890.62	Phone	500-2035	9.66	ExtremeGear
Big Bikes			2019	29	77	$25,696.00	AWS	700-1680	6.06	HyperTech Manufacturing
Lazy B Bikes			2018	19	30	$25,576.50	Internet	700-2280	2.70	HyperTech Manufacturing
Lone Pine Crafters	Carlos Hernández	Sales Represe	2021	1	0	$25,171.56	Internet	500-2030	4.71	ExtremeGear
Seven Lakes Riding	Peter Franken	Marketing Ma	2018	15	50	$25,075.00	Internet	500-2020	10.07	ExtremeGear
Big Bikes			2021	10	40	$24,888.00	Internet	500-2025	10.49	ExtremeGear
B' Bikes	Georg Pipps	Sales Manage	2021	14	23	$24,328.02	Internet	700-1680	6.06	HyperTech Manufacturing
Eastern Connection	Isabel de Castro	Sales Represe	2021	48	173	$24,296.17	AWS	100-105	10.73	Riley Manufacturing
Big Bikes	Carine Schmitt	Marketing Ma	2018	22	71	$23,877.48	AWS	500-2035	9.66	ExtremeGear
Island Biking	Manuel Pereira	Owner	2020	26	45	$23,588.86	Internet	500-2045	3.22	ExtremeGear
Mississippi Delta Riding	Rene Phillips	Sales Represe	2021	9	33	$23,550.25	Internet	700-2180	4.45	HyperTech Manufacturing
Uncle's Upgrades			2021	9	21	$22,212.54	Internet	700-1680	6.06	HyperTech Manufacturing
Big Bikes			2019	73	80	$22,063.92	Phone	700-1680	6.06	HyperTech Manufacturing
Island Biking			2021	18	59	$22,025.88	Internet	100-108	3.32	Riley Manufacturing
Uncle's Upgrades			2020	16	38	$21,802.50	Internet	500-2035	9.66	ExtremeGear
Hard Rock Machines			2021	42	57	$21,279.24	Internet	100-108	3.32	Riley Manufacturing
Kona Riders			2021	11	20	$21,154.80	Internet	700-1880	2.28	HyperTech Manufacturing
Moab Mauraders			2021	6	20	$21,154.80	Internet	700-2180	4.45	HyperTech Manufacturing
Lone Pine Crafters			2021	35	58	$21,016.59	Internet	100-106	6.23	Riley Manufacturing
Big Bikes	Carine Schmitt	Marketing Ma	2019	9	36	$20,655.00	Internet	500-2035	9.66	ExtremeGear
East/West Enterprises			2020	14	60	$20,349.00	Internet	100-104	5.80	Riley Manufacturing
Jeeps 'n More	Yvonne Moncada	Sales Agent	2021	47	50	$20,230.00	AWS	500-2030	4.71	ExtremeGear
East/West Enterprises			2018	14	60	$20,178.15	AWS	500-2035	9.66	ExtremeGear
Lone Pine Crafters			2021	20	54	$20,159.28	Internet	100-106	6.23	Riley Manufacturing
Lone Pine Crafters	Carlos Hernández	Sales Represe	2021	1	0	$20,137.27	Internet	500-2030	4.71	ExtremeGear
Lazy B Bikes			2021	21	29	$19,946.78	AWS	700-1580	7.50	HyperTech Manufacturing
Eastern Connection	Isabel de Castro	Sales Represe	2021	42	173	$19,907.06	Phone	100-105	10.73	Riley Manufacturing
Lazy B Bikes			2021	8	30	$19,724.25	AWS	700-1580	7.50	HyperTech Manufacturing
Sedona Mountain Trails			2019	12	22	$19,677.29	Internet	700-2080	8.63	HyperTech Manufacturing
Mississippi Delta Riding	Maria Larsson	Owner	2019	17	20	$19,507.50	Internet	700-1880	2.28	HyperTech Manufacturing
Seven Lakes Riding	Peter Franken	Marketing Ma	2020	39	53	$19,400.40	AWS	500-2020	10.07	ExtremeGear
Lazy B Bikes			2020	6	20	$19,218.50	Internet	700-1580	7.50	HyperTech Manufacturing
Kona Riders			2021	25	50	$19,209.69	AWS	700-2180	4.45	HyperTech Manufacturing
Gordos Dirt Bikes	Sergio Gutiérrez	Sales Represe	2019	89	164	$18,772.79	Phone	100-108	3.32	Riley Manufacturing
Moab Mauraders			2021	20	50	$18,518.10	Internet	100-108	3.32	Riley Manufacturing
Mountain Traders			2021	5	18	$18,480.11	Internet	700-1580	7.50	HyperTech Manufacturing
Mountain Traders			2019	16	20	$18,062.50	Internet	700-1480	5.12	HyperTech Manufacturing
Kona Riders	Janete Limeira	Assistant Sale	2018	10	36	$18,054.00	Internet	500-2025	10.49	ExtremeGear
Hard Rock Machines			2021	6	17	$17,981.58	Internet	700-1980	0.48	HyperTech Manufacturing

FIGURE 3-4

Sample Extracted Data

Source: Windows 10, Microsoft Corporation.

units might be problematic. At some point, the team might need to investigate what these values mean and possibly correct the data or remove those rows from the analysis. In the immediate term, however, the team decided to proceed even with these incorrect values. Such problematic data is common in data extracts.

Analyze Data

The data in Figure 3-4 has been filtered for the team's first criterion to consider parts only from particular vendors. For their next criterion, team members needed to decide how to identify large customers. To do so, they created a query that sums the revenue, units, and average price for each customer. Looking at the query results in Figure 3-5, team members decided to consider only customers having more than $200,000 in total revenue; they created a query having just those customers and named that query *Big Customers.*

Next, team members discussed what they meant by frequent purchase and decided to include items ordered an average of once a week or roughly 50 times per year. They set that criterion for Number Orders in the query to select only parts that were ordered in small quantities. They first created a column that computes average order size (Units/[Number Orders]) and then set a criterion on that expression that the average must be less than 2.5. Their last two criteria were that the part be relatively inexpensive and that it be lightweight. They decided to select parts with a unit price (computed as Revenue/Units) less than 100 and a shipping weight less than 5 pounds.

The results of this query are shown in Figure 3-6. Of all the parts that the company sells, these 12 fit the criteria that the team created. The next question was how much revenue potential these parts represent. Accordingly, the team created a query that connected the selected parts with their past sales data. The results are shown in Figure 3-7.

Customer Summary			
CustomerName	SumOfRevenue	SumOfUnits	Average Price
Great Lakes Machines	$1,760.47	142	12.3976535211268
Seven Lakes Riding	$288,570.71	5848	49.3451963919289
Around the Horn	$16,669.48	273	61.0603611721612
Dewey Riding	$36,467.90	424	86.0092018867925
Moab Mauraders	$143,409.27	1344	106.7033234375
Gordos Dirt Bikes	$113,526.88	653	173.854335068913
Mountain Traders	$687,710.99	3332	206.395855432173
Hungry Rider Off-road	$108,602.32	492	220.736416056911
Eastern Connection	$275,092.28	1241	221.669848186946
Mississippi Delta Riding	$469,932.11	1898	247.593315542676
Island Biking	$612,072.64	2341	261.457770098249
Big Bikes	$1,385,867.98	4876	284.222310233798
Hard Rock Machines	$74,853.22	241	310.594267219917
Lone Pine Crafters	$732,990.33	1816	403.629038215859
Sedona Mountain Trails	$481,073.82	1104	435.755269474638
Flat Iron Riders	$85,469.20	183	467.044808743169
Bottom-Dollar Bikes	$72,460.85	154	470.52502012987
Uncle's Upgrades	$947,477.61	1999	473.975794047023
Ernst Handel Mechanics	$740,951.15	1427	519.236962438683
Kona Riders	$511,108.05	982	520.476624439919
Lazy B Bikes	$860,950.72	1594	540.119648619824
Jeeps 'n More	$404,540.62	678	596.667583185841
French Riding Masters	$1,037,386.76	1657	626.063224984912
B' Bikes	$113,427.06	159	713.377735849057
East/West Enterprises	$2,023,402.09	2457	823.525474074074
Bon App Riding	$65,848.90	60	1097.48160833333

FIGURE 3-5
Customer Summary
Source: Windows 10, Microsoft Corporation.

Qualifying Parts				
Number Orders	Average Order Size	Unit Price	Shipping Weight	PartNumber
275	1	9.14173854545455	4.14	300-1016
258	1.87596899224806	7.41284524793388	4.14	300-1016
110	1.18181818181818	6.46796923076923	4.11	200-205
176	1.66477272727273	12.5887211604096	4.14	300-1016
139	1.0431654676259	6.28248965517241	1.98	200-217
56	1.83928571428571	6.71141553398058	1.98	200-217
99	1.02020202020202	7.7775	3.20	200-203
76	2.17105263157895	12.0252206060606	2.66	300-1013
56	1.07142857142857	5.0575	4.57	200-211
73	1.15068493150685	5.0575	4.57	200-211
107	2.02803738317757	6.01096405529954	2.77	300-1007
111	2.07207207207207	6.01096434782609	2.77	300-1007

FIGURE 3-6
Qualifying Parts Query Results
Source: Windows 10, Microsoft Corporation.

Revenue Potential		
Total Orders	Total Revenue	PartNumber
3987	$84,672.73	300-1016
2158	$30,912.19	200-211
1074	$23,773.53	200-217
548	$7,271.31	300-1007
375	$5,051.62	200-203
111	$3,160.86	300-1013
139	$1,204.50	200-205

FIGURE 3-7
Sales History for Selected Parts
Source: Windows 10, Microsoft Corporation.

Publish Results

Publish results is the last activity in the BI process shown in Figure 3-3. In some cases, this means placing BI results on servers for publication to knowledge workers over the Internet or other networks. In other cases, it means making the results available via a Web service for use by other applications. In still other cases, it means creating PDFs or PowerPoint presentations for communicating to colleagues or management.

In this case, the team reported these results to management in a team meeting. Judging just by the results in Figure 3-7, there seems to be little revenue potential in selling designs for these parts. The company would earn minimal revenue from the parts themselves; the designs would have to be priced considerably lower, and that would mean almost no revenue.

In spite of the low revenue potential, the company might still decide to offer 3D designs to customers. It might decide to give the designs away as a gesture of goodwill to its customers; this analysis indicates it will be sacrificing little revenue to do so. Or it might do it as a PR move intended to show that it's on top of the latest manufacturing technology. Or it might decide to postpone consideration of 3D printing because it doesn't see that many customers ordering the qualifying parts.

Of course, there is the possibility that the team members chose the wrong criteria. If they have time, it might be worthwhile to change their criteria and repeat the analysis. Such a course is a slippery slope, however. They might find themselves changing criteria until they obtain a result they want, which yields a very biased study.

This possibility points again to the importance of the human component of an IS. The hardware, software, data, and query-generation procedures are of little value if the decisions that the team made when setting and possibly revising criteria are poor. Business intelligence is only as intelligent as the people creating it!

With this example in mind, we will now consider each of the activities in Figure 3-3 in greater detail.

Q3-2   How Do Organizations Use Data Warehouses and Data Marts to Acquire Data?

Although it is possible to create basic reports and perform simple analyses from operational data, this course is not usually recommended. For reasons of security and control, IS professionals do not want data analysts processing operational data. If an analyst makes an error, that error could cause a serious disruption in the company's operations. Also, operational data is structured for fast and reliable transaction processing. It is seldom structured in a way that readily supports BI analysis. Finally, BI analyses can require considerable processing; placing BI applications on operational servers can dramatically reduce system performance.

For these reasons, most organizations extract operational data for BI processing. For small organizations, the extraction may be as simple as an Access database. Larger organizations, however,

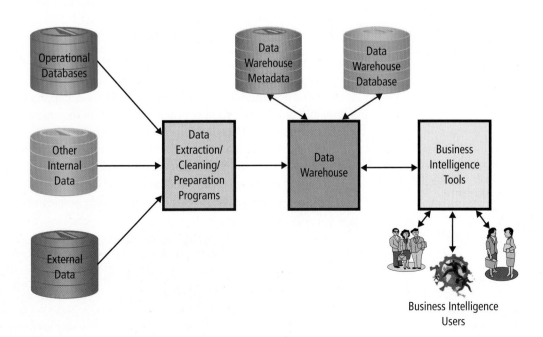

FIGURE 3-8
Components of a Data Warehouse

• Name, address, phone	• Magazine subscriptions
• Age	• Hobbies
• Gender	• Catalog orders
• Ethnicity	• Marital status, life stage
• Religion	• Height, weight, hair and eye color
• Income	• Spouse name, birth date
• Education	• Children's names and birth dates
• Voter registration	
• Home ownership	
• Vehicles	

FIGURE 3-9
Examples of Consumer Data That Can Be Purchased

typically create and staff a group of people who manage and run a **data warehouse**, which is a facility for managing an organization's BI data. The functions of a data warehouse are to:

- Obtain data
- Cleanse data
- Organize and relate data
- Catalog data

Figure 3-8 shows the components of a data warehouse. Programs read operational and other data and extract, clean, and prepare that data for BI processing. The prepared data is stored in a data warehouse database. Data warehouses include data that is purchased from outside sources. The purchase of data about organizations is not unusual or particularly concerning from a privacy standpoint. However, some companies choose to buy personal consumer data (e.g., marital status) from data vendors such as Acxiom Corporation. Figure 3-9 lists some of the consumer data that can be readily purchased. An amazing (and, from a privacy standpoint, frightening) amount of data is available.

Metadata concerning the data—its source, its format, its assumptions and constraints, and other facts about the data—is kept in a data warehouse metadata database. The data warehouse extracts and provides data to BI applications.

The term *business intelligence users* is different from *knowledge workers* in Figure 3-1. BI users are generally specialists in data analysis, whereas knowledge workers are often non-specialist users of BI results. A loan approval officer at a bank is a knowledge worker but not a BI user.

Problems with Operational Data

Most operational and purchased data has problems that inhibit its usefulness for business intelligence. Figure 3-10 lists the major problem categories. First, although data that is critical for successful operations must be complete and accurate, marginally necessary data need not be. For example, some systems gather demographic data in the ordering process. But, because such data is not needed to fill, ship, and bill orders, its quality suffers.

Security concerns about access to data are problematic. See the Security Guide on pages 102–103 for more information.

Problematic data is termed dirty data. Examples are a value of B for customer gender and of 213 for customer age. Other examples are a value of 999-999-9999 for a U.S. phone number, a part color of *gren*, and an email address of *WhyMe@GuessWhoIAM.org*. The value of zero for units in Figure 3-4 is dirty data. All of these values can be problematic for BI purposes.

• Dirty data	• Wrong granularity – Too fine – Not fine enough
• Missing values	• Too much data – Too many attributes – Too many data points
• Inconsistent data	
• Data not integrated	

FIGURE 3-10
Possible Problems with Source Data

Purchased data often contains missing elements. The contact data in Figure 3-4 is a typical example; orders can be shipped without contact data, so its quality is spotty and has many missing values. Most data vendors state the percentage of missing values for each attribute in the data they sell. An organization buys such data because for some uses, some data is better than no data at all. This is especially true for data items whose values are difficult to obtain, such as Number of Adults in Household, Household Income, Dwelling Type, and Education of Primary Income Earner. However, care is required here because for some BI applications a few missing or erroneous data points can seriously bias the analysis.

Data can also have the wrong **granularity**, a term that refers to the level of detail represented by the data. Granularity can be too fine or too coarse. For example, a file of regional sales totals cannot be used to investigate the sales in a particular store in a region, and total sales for a store cannot be used to determine the sales of particular items within the store. Instead, we need to obtain data that is fine enough for the lowest-level report we want to produce. In general, it is better to have too fine a granularity than too coarse. If the granularity is too fine, the data can be made coarser by summing and combining. If the granularity is too coarse, however, there is no way to separate the data into constituent parts.

The final problem listed in Figure 3-10 is to have too much data. As shown in the figure, we can have either too many attributes or too many data points. We can also have too many columns or too many rows.

Consider the first problem: too many attributes. Suppose we want to know the factors that influence how customers respond to a promotion. If we combine internal customer data with purchased customer data, we will have more than a hundred different attributes to consider. How do we select among them? In some cases, analysts can ignore the columns they don't need. But in more sophisticated data mining analyses, too many attributes can be problematic. Because of a phenomenon called the *curse of dimensionality*, the more attributes there are, the easier it is to build a model that fits the sample data but that is worthless as a predictor.

The second way to have an excess of data is to have too many data points—too many rows of data. Suppose we want to analyze clickstream data on CNN.com, or the clicking behavior of visitors to that Web site. How many clicks does that site receive per month? Millions upon millions! In order to meaningfully analyze such data, we need to reduce the amount of data. One good solution to this problem is statistical sampling. Organizations should not be reluctant to sample data in such situations.

Data Warehouses Versus Data Marts

To understand the difference between data warehouses and data marts, think of a data warehouse as a distributor in a supply chain. The data warehouse takes data from the data manufacturers (operational systems and other sources), cleans and processes the data, and locates the data on the shelves, so to speak, of the data warehouse. The data analysts who work with a data warehouse are experts at data management, data cleaning, data transformation, data relationships, and the like. However, they are not usually experts in a given business function.

A **data mart** is a data collection, smaller than the data warehouse, that addresses the needs of a particular department or functional area of the business. If the data warehouse is the distributor in a supply chain, then a data mart is like a retail store in a supply chain. Users in the data mart obtain data that pertain to a particular business function from the data warehouse. Such users do not have the data management expertise that data warehouse employees have, but they are knowledgeable analysts for a given business function.

Figure 3-11 illustrates these relationships. In this example, the data warehouse takes data from the data producers and distributes the data to three data marts. One data mart is used to analyze clickstream data for the purpose of designing Web pages. A second analyzes store sales data and determines which products tend to be purchased together. This information is used to train salespeople on the best way to up-sell to customers. The third data mart is used to analyze

MIS-DIAGNOSIS

Fred Bolton stared at his computer screen until his eyes glazed over. He had been working 15-hour days for the past week trying to solve a serious problem that could have a devastating impact on the future of his employer. Fred had worked at A+Meds for almost a decade, and he was proud to be affiliated with a world-leading pharmaceutical company. He had started out at the bottom of the IT department but had moved up quickly. He was a fast learner with a never-give-up attitude. But today he was on the verge of giving up.

Fred was astounded at how much the pharmaceutical industry had changed over the previous 10 years. When he first started at A+Meds, the company could drive up sales using direct marketing techniques. Doctors met with company representatives who convinced them that A+Meds were the best on the market. Now, technology had started to permeate every aspect of the healthcare industry. Doctors were relying more and more on artificial intelligence (AI)-driven expert systems to select the most appropriate medications and treatments. These systems made recommendations based on drug profiles submitted to the system by pharmaceutical companies. The companies could update the drug profiles if any aspect of the drug changed, but this didn't happen very often if the changes were minor.

Recently, the sales of a new drug had been underperforming. A+Meds had invested tens of millions of dollars in developing it. Company executives and new product developers were convinced that the product was superior to competing drugs. The problem, they believed, was that the expert systems used by doctors were not recommending the product. Sales were suffering, profitability was down, and employee compensation was in jeopardy.

Fred had been tasked with doing a rigorous investigation of the AI recommendation system. He was supposed to identify the problem and see if there was something the company could do to improve the system's "perception" of the product. During his testing, Fred found that minor modifications to the drug's profile made a big difference. But some of the numbers he used to modify the profile were not accurate. Even if they were, the changes he made would warrant a regulatory review, which could take an extensive amount of time. The financial damage to the company would be done long before the review was complete. Fred was not looking forward to reporting his findings.

Information Manipulation

Fred kept looking at the clock on his computer monitor. It was time for his meeting, but he was trying to find an excuse to linger at his desk. He came up empty handed and headed over to the boardroom. He took a seat at the end of a long conference table and joined Patricia Tanner, a high-level A+Meds sales executive. "So, Fred, what did you find out?" Patricia asked. "Good news, I hope!" Fred explained that, in spite of his extensive analysis of the recommendation system, he was unable to identify a solution that would cause the system to

Source: Sergey/Fotolia

select their product over competing products—unless they tweaked the profile.

"But our drug is superior and safer!" she exclaimed. "I was a sales executive at our competitor when they were putting a similar drug through trials, and I know for a fact that our drug is the better choice."

"That may be," Fred replied cautiously, "but our profile is based on our current approval guidelines. The drug's current profile is causing us to lose out to competing drugs."

They both sat for a minute before Patricia slowly replied, "What if we submit a new profile that the system perceives as more favorable, even though some of the data is a bit of a stretch?"

Fred couldn't believe she'd just asked that question. He wasn't sure how to respond without putting his job in jeopardy. "Wouldn't the addition of inaccurate information to the system be considered a violation? Wouldn't we be liable if something happened to a patient who took our drug based on *altered* information?" Fred asked. Patricia replied that drug companies did stuff like this all of the time. Investigations were extremely rare and only occurred if there were numerous patient-related incidents of a serious nature.

Patricia looked over at him with a funny look on her face and said, "Do you think it is right to have people using what we *know* to be an inferior drug simply based on how this system interprets drug profiles? What if people get sick or if something more serious happens to them because they should have taken our drug but didn't because of the system? Wouldn't you feel bad about that?" Fred hadn't thought about it like that. Maybe Patricia was right. Fred did believe their drug was the better choice. But he wasn't a doctor. Adhering to federal regulations seemed like the right choice, but not at the risk of keeping people from the medication they *should* be getting. He let out a sigh and leaned back in his chair. He wasn't sure what to say.

 DISCUSSION QUESTIONS

1. According to the definitions of the ethical principles defined previously in this book:
   a. Do you think that manipulating the recommendation of an AI system even though the new recommendation may be for the better drug is ethical according to the categorical imperative (page 23-24)?
   b. Do you think that manipulating the recommendation of an AI system even though the new recommendation may be for the better drug is ethical according to the utilitarian perspective (page 42-43)?
2. How would you respond if you were placed in Fred's shoes? Do you think it is appropriate to submit inaccurate information because the drug may be better and safer than the competition?
3. How should Fred handle the fact that Patricia made the suggestion to manipulate the drug's profile? Is her willingness to use this type of tactic cause for concern in its own right?
4. How do you feel about the growing use of AI and other technological solutions in helping people make decisions? Would you want a doctor treating you based on recommendations from an automated system? Consider other arenas as well. For example, would you trust the recommendation of an automated financial investment system over the advice of a human financial advisor?

customer order data for the purpose of reducing labor for item picking from the warehouse. A company like Amazon, for example, goes to great lengths to organize its warehouses to reduce picking expenses.

As you can imagine, it is expensive to create, staff, and operate data warehouses and data marts. Only large organizations with deep pockets can afford to operate a system like that shown in Figure 3-8. Smaller organizations operate subsets of this system, but they must find ways to solve the basic problems that data warehouses solve, even if those ways are informal.

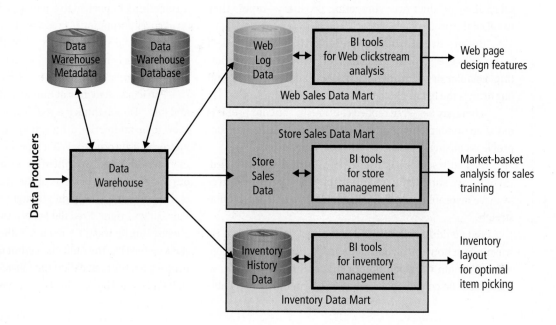

FIGURE 3-11
Data Mart Examples

Q3-3 What Are Three Techniques for Processing BI Data?

Figure 3-12 summarizes the goals and characteristics of three fundamental types of BI analysis. In general, reporting analyses are used to create information about past performance, whereas data mining is used primarily for classifying and predicting. There are exceptions, but these statements are reasonable rules of thumb. The goal of Big Data analysis is to find patterns and relationships in the enormous amounts of data generated from sources like social media sites or Web server logs. As indicated, Big Data techniques can include reporting and data mining as well. Consider the characteristics of each type.

Reporting Analysis

Reporting analysis is the process of sorting, grouping, summing, filtering, and formatting structured data. **Structured data** is data in the form of rows and columns. Most of the time structured data means tables in a relational database, but it can refer to spreadsheet data as well. A **reporting application** is a BI application that inputs data from one or more sources and applies reporting processes to that data to produce business intelligence.

The team that analyzed parts in Q3-1 used Access to apply all five of these operations. Examine, for example, Figure 3-7. The results are *sorted* by Total Revenue and *filtered* for particular parts, sales

BI Analysis Type	Goal	Characteristics
Reporting	Create information about past performance.	Process structured data by sorting, grouping, summing, filtering, and formatting.
Data mining	Classify and predict.	Use sophisticated statistical techniques to find patterns and relationships.
Big Data	Find patterns and relationships in Big Data.	Volume, velocity, and variety force use of MapReduce techniques. Some applications use reporting and data mining as well.

FIGURE 3-12
Three Types of BI Analysis

are *grouped by* PartNumber, Total Orders and Total Revenue are *calculated*, and the calculations for Total Revenue are *formatted* correctly as dollar currency.

Another type of report, **exception reports** are produced when something out of predefined bounds occurs. For example, a hospital might want an exception report showing which doctors are prescribing more than twice the amount of pain medications than the average doctor. This could help the hospital reduce the potential for patient addiction to pain medications.

The simple operations mentioned previously can be used to produce complex and highly useful reports. Consider RFM analysis and online analytical processing as two prime examples.

RFM Analysis

RFM analysis, a technique readily implemented with basic reporting operations, is used to analyze and rank customers according to their purchasing patterns.[4] RFM considers how *recently* (R) a customer has ordered, how *frequently* (F) a customer ordered, and how much *money* (M) the customer has spent.

To produce an RFM score, the RFM reporting tool first sorts customer purchase records by the date of their most recent (R) purchase. In a common form of this analysis, the tool then divides the customers into five groups and gives customers in each group a score of 5 to 1. The 20 percent of the customers having the most recent orders are given an R score of 5, the 20 percent of the customers having the next most recent orders are given an R score of 4, and so forth, down to the last 20 percent, who are given an R score of 1.

The tool then re-sorts the customers on the basis of how *frequently* (F) they order and assigns values in the same way. Finally, the tool sorts the customers again according to the amount of *money* (M) spent on their orders assigns similar rankings.

Figure 3-13 shows sample RFM results for Big 7 Sports (R=5, F=5, and M=3). Big 7 sports has ordered recently and orders frequently. But its M score of 3 indicates that it does not order the most expensive goods. From these scores, the sales team can conclude that Big 7 Sports is a good, regular customer and that it should attempt to up-sell more expensive goods to Big 7 Sports. No one on the sales team should even think about the third customer, Miami Municipal. This company has not ordered for some time; it did not order frequently; and, when it did order, it bought the least expensive items and not many of them. Let Miami Municipal go to the competition; the loss will be minimal.

Online Analytical Processing (OLAP)

Online analytical processing (OLAP), a second type of reporting application, is more generic than RFM. OLAP provides the ability to sum, count, average, and perform other simple arithmetic operations on groups of data. The defining characteristic of OLAP reports is that they are dynamic. The viewer of the report can change the report's format—hence the term *online*.

An OLAP report has measures and dimensions. A **measure** is the data item of interest. It is the item that is to be summed or averaged or otherwise processed in the OLAP report. Total sales, average sales, and average cost are examples of measures. A **dimension** is a characteristic of a measure. Purchase date, customer type, customer location, and sales region are all examples of dimensions.

Customer	RFM Score		
Big 7 Sports	5	5	3
St. Louis Soccer Club	1	5	5
Miami Municipal	1	2	1
Central Colorado State	3	3	3

FIGURE 3-13
Example RFM Scores

Store Sales Net	Store Type					
Product Family	Deluxe Supermarket	Gourmet Supermarket	Midsize Grocery	Small Grocery	Supermarket	Grand Total
Drink	$8,119.05	$2,392.83	$1,409.50	$685.89	$16,751.71	$29,358.98
Food	$70,276.11	$20,026.18	$10,392.19	$6,109.72	$138,960.67	$245,764.87
Nonconsumable	$18,884.24	$5,064.79	$2,813.73	$1,534.90	$36,189.40	$64,487.05
Grand Total	$97,279.40	$27,483.80	$14,615.42	$8,330.51	$191,901.77	$339,610.90

Figure 3-14 shows a typical OLAP report. Here, the measure is *Store Sales Net*, and the dimensions are *Product Family* and *Store Type*. This report shows how net store sales vary by product family and store type. Stores of type *Supermarket* sold a net of $36,189 worth of nonconsumable goods, for example.

A presentation like that in Figure 3-14 is often called an **OLAP cube** or sometimes simply a *cube*. The reason for this term is that some software products show these displays using three axes, like a cube in geometry. The origin of the term is unimportant here, however. Just know that an *OLAP cube* and an *OLAP report* are the same thing.

As stated earlier, the distinguishing characteristic of an OLAP report is that the user can alter the format of the report. Figure 3-15 shows such an alteration. Here, the user added another dimension, *Store Country* and *Store State*, to the horizontal display. Product-family sales are now broken out by store location. Observe that the sample data only includes stores in the United States and only in the western states of California, Oregon, and Washington.

With an OLAP report, it is possible to **drill down** into the data. This term means to further divide the data into more detail. In Figure 3-16, for example, the user has drilled down into the stores located in California; the OLAP report now shows sales data for the four cities in California that have stores.

Notice another difference between Figures 3-15 and 3-16. The user has not only drilled down, but she has also changed the order of the dimensions. Figure 3-15 shows *Product Family* and then store location within *Product Family*. Figure 3-16 shows store location and then *Product Family* within store location.

Both displays are valid and useful, depending on the user's perspective. A product manager might like to see product families first and then store location data. A sales manager might like to see store locations first and then product data. OLAP reports provide both perspectives, and the user can switch between them while viewing the report.

Data Mining Analysis

Data mining is the application of statistical techniques to find patterns and relationships among data for classification and prediction. As shown in Figure 3-17, data mining resulted from a convergence of disciplines, including artificial intelligence and machine learning.

Sum of store_sales			Column Labels					
Row Labels	Store Country	Store State	Deluxe Superma	Gourmet Supermar	Midsize Groce	Small Grocery	Supermarket	Grand Total
Drink	USA	CA		$3,940.54		$373.72	$9,888.98	$14,203.24
		OR	$7,394.25				$4,743.04	$12,137.29
		WA	$6,092.91		$2,348.79	$768.89	$13,285.09	$22,495.68
	USA Total		$13,487.16	$3,940.54	$2,348.79	$1,142.61	$27,917.11	$48,836.21
Drink Total			$8,119.05	$2,392.83	$1,409.50	$685.89	$16,751.71	$29,358.98
Food	USA	CA		$33,424.17		$3,275.80	$78,493.20	$1,15,193.17
		OR	$62,945.01				$39,619.66	$1,02,564.67
		WA	$54,143.86		$17,314.24	$6,899.50	$1,12,920.15	$1,91,277.75
	USA Total		$1,17,088.87	$33,424.17	$17,314.24	$10,175.30	$2,31,033.01	$4,09,035.59
Food Total			$70,276.11	$20,026.18	$10,392.19	$6,109.72	$138,960.67	$245,764.87
Nonconsumable	USA	CA		$8,385.53		$791.66	$20,594.24	$29,771.43
		OR	$16,879.02				$10,696.09	$27,575.11
		WA	$14,607.19		$4,666.20	$1,776.81	$28,969.59	$50,019.79
	USA Total		$31,486.21	$8,385.53	$4,666.20	$2,568.47	$60,259.92	$1,07,366.33
Nonconsumable Total			$18,884.24	$5,064.79	$2,813.73	$1,534.90	$36,189.40	$64,487.05
Grand Total			$1,62,062.24	$45,750.24	$24,329.23	$13,886.38	$3,19,210.04	$5,65,238.13

	A	B	C	D	E	F	G
1	Sum of store_sales	Column Labels					
2	Row Labels	Deluxe Supermarket	Gourmet Supermarket	Midsize Grocery	Small Grocery	Supermarket	Grand Total
3	USA	$162,062.24	$45,750.24	$24,329.23	$13,886.38	$319,210.04	$565,238.13
4	CA		$45,750.24		$4,441.18	$108,976.42	$159,167.84
5	Beverly Hills		$45,750.24				$45,750.24
6	Drink		$3,940.54				$3,940.54
7	Food		$33,424.17				$33,424.17
8	Nonconsumable		$8,385.53				$8,385.53
9	Los Angeles					$54,545.28	$54,545.28
10	Drink					$4,823.88	$4,823.88
11	Food					$39,187.46	$39,187.46
12	Nonconsumable					$10,533.94	$10,533.94
13	San Diego					$54,431.14	$54,431.14
14	Drink					$5,065.10	$5,065.10
15	Food					$39,305.74	$39,305.74
16	Nonconsumable					$10,060.30	$10,060.30
17	San Francisco				$4,441.18		$4,441.18
18	Drink				$373.72		$373.72
19	Food				$3,275.80		$3,275.80
20	Nonconsumable				$791.66		$791.66
21	OR	$87,218.28				$55,058.79	$142,277.07
22	Portland					$55,058.79	$55,058.79
23	Salem	$87,218.28					$87,218.28
24	WA	$74,843.96		$24,329.23	$9,445.20	$155,174.83	$263,793.22
25	Bellingham				$4,739.23		$4,739.23
26	Bremerton					$52,896.30	$52,896.30
27	Seattle					$52,644.07	$52,644.07
28	Spokane					$49,634.46	$49,634.46
29	Tacoma	$74,843.96					$74,843.96
30	Walla Walla				$4,705.97		$4,705.97
31	Yakima			$24,329.23			$24,329.23
32	Grand Total	$162,062.24	$45,750.24	$24,329.23	$13,886.38	$319,210.04	$565,238.13

FIGURE 3-16

Example of Drilling Down into Expanded Grocery Sales OLAP Report

Source: Windows 10, Microsoft Corporation.

Most data mining techniques are sophisticated, and many are difficult to use well. Such techniques are valuable to organizations, however, and some business professionals, especially those in finance and marketing, have become expert in their use. Today, in fact, there are many interesting and rewarding careers for business professionals who are knowledgeable about data mining techniques.

Data mining techniques fall into two broad categories: unsupervised and supervised. We explain both types in the following sections.

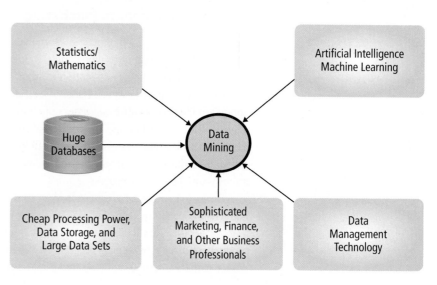

FIGURE 3-17

Source Disciplines of Data Mining

Unsupervised Data Mining

With **unsupervised data mining**, analysts do not create a model or hypothesis before running the analysis. Instead, they apply a data mining application to the data and observe the results. With this method, analysts create hypotheses *after the analysis*, in order to explain the patterns found.

One common unsupervised technique is **cluster analysis**. With it, statistical techniques identify groups of entities that have similar characteristics. A common use for cluster analysis is to find groups of similar customers from customer order and demographic data.

Artificial intelligence (AI) applications are being used to help users process large amounts of data and make decisions. What happens when these decisions include recommendations for competing products? The Ethics Guide on pages 76–77 considers these questions.

For example, suppose a cluster analysis finds two very different customer groups: One group has an average age of 33, owns four Android phones and three iPads, has an expensive home entertainment system, drives a Lexus SUV, and tends to buy expensive children's play equipment. The second group has an average age of 64, owns Arizona vacation property, plays golf, and buys expensive wines. Suppose the analysis also finds that both groups buy designer children's clothing.

These findings are obtained solely by data analysis. There is no prior model about the patterns and relationships that exist. It is up to the analyst to form hypotheses, after the fact, to explain why two such different groups are both buying designer children's clothes.

Supervised Data Mining

With **supervised data mining**, data miners develop a model *prior to the analysis* and apply statistical techniques to data to estimate parameters of the model. For example, suppose marketing experts in a communications company believe that cell phone usage on weekends is determined by the age of the customer and the number of months the customer has had the cell phone account. A data mining analyst would then run an analysis that estimates the effect of customer and account age.

One such analysis, which measures the effect of a set of variables on another variable, is called a **regression analysis**. A sample result for the cell phone example is:

$$\text{CellphoneWeekendMinutes} = 12 + (17.5 \times \text{CustomerAge}) + (23.7 \times \text{NumberMonthsOfAccount})$$

Using this equation, analysts can predict the number of minutes of weekend cell phone use by summing 12, plus 17.5 times the customer's age, plus 23.7 times the number of months of the account.

As you will learn in your statistics classes, considerable skill is required to interpret the quality of such a model. The regression tool will create an equation, such as the one shown. Whether that equation is a good predictor of future cell phone usage depends on statistical factors, such as *t* values, confidence intervals, and related statistical techniques.

Identifying Changes in Purchasing Patterns

Most students are aware that business intelligence is used to predict purchasing patterns. Amazon made the phrase "Customers who bought . . . also bought" famous; when we buy something today, we expect the e-commerce application to suggest what else we might want.

More interesting, however, is identifying changes in purchasing patterns. Retailers know that important life events cause customers to change what they buy and, for a short interval, to form new loyalties to new brands. Thus, when people start their first professional job, get married, have a baby, or retire, retailers want to know. Before BI, stores would watch the local newspapers for graduation, marriage, and baby announcements and send ads in response. That was a slow, labor-intensive, and expensive process.

Target wanted to get ahead of the newspapers and in 2002 began a project to use purchasing patterns to determine that someone was pregnant. By applying business intelligence techniques to its sales data, Target was able to identify a purchasing pattern of lotions, vitamins, and other products that reliably predicts pregnancy. When Target observed that purchasing pattern, it sent ads for diapers and other baby-related products to those customers.

Its program worked—too well for one teenager who had told no one she was pregnant. When she began receiving ads for baby items, her father complained to the manager of the local Target store, who apologized. It was the father's turn to apologize when he learned that his daughter was, indeed, pregnant.

Big Data

Big Data (also spelled *BigData*) is a term used to describe data collections that are characterized by huge *volume*, rapid *velocity*, and great *variety*. Considering volume, Big Data refers to data sets that are at least a petabyte in size, and usually larger. A data set containing all Google searches in the United States on a given day is Big Data in size. Additionally, Big Data has high velocity, meaning that it is generated rapidly. (If you know physics, you know that *speed* would be a more accurate term, but *speed* doesn't start with a *v*, and the *vvv* description has become a common way to describe Big Data.) The Google search data for a given day is generated in, well, just a day. In the past, months or years would have been required to generate so much data.

Finally, Big Data is varied. Big Data may have structured data, but it also may have free-form text, dozens of different formats of Web server and database log files, streams of data about user responses to page content, and possibly graphics, audio, and video files.

MapReduce

Because Big Data is huge, fast, and varied, it cannot be processed using traditional techniques. **MapReduce** is a technique for harnessing the power of thousands of computers working in parallel. The basic idea is that the Big Data collection is broken into pieces, and hundreds or thousands of independent processors search these pieces for something of interest. That process is referred to as the *Map* phase. In Figure 3-18, for example, a data set having the logs of Google searches is broken into pieces, and each independent processor is instructed to search for and count search keywords. Figure 3-18, of course, shows just a small portion of the data; here you can see a portion of the keywords that begin with *H*.

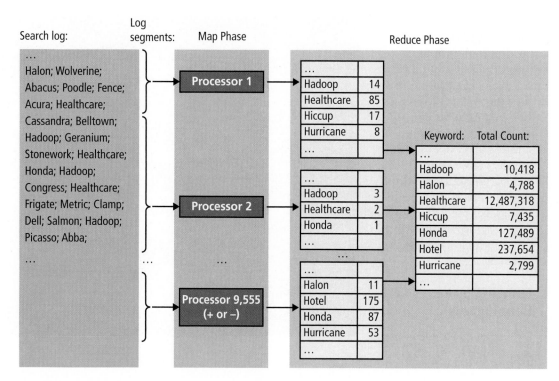

FIGURE 3-18
MapReduce
Processing Summary

SO WHAT? GEOFENCING FOR BUSINESSES?

Have you ever thought about all of the different types of data that are being transmitted through you and around you on a continuous basis? A few decades ago, these data transmissions were limited to only a few sources, like radio and television stations operating in your area. However, the number of transmission devices in and around your community continues to grow (e.g., cell phone towers). On a smaller scale, you have likely purchased numerous transmission devices and set them up around your home. For example, Wi-Fi base stations, smart speakers, wireless security cameras, and streaming entertainment devices all broadcast data streams. Other, smaller devices that transmit these signals include smartphones, tablets, and smartwatches (especially the newer ones with cell phone capabilities).

There is an entire invisible world of data transmissions that is bombarding us around the clock, and many businesses are pursuing novel ways to add new dimensions to, and create new profit streams from, this invisible world. One technology that companies are exploring in this area is geofencing. **Geofencing** is a location service that allows applications to know when a user has crossed a virtual fence (specific location) and then trigger an automated action.

For example, suppose a user enters a coffee shop and her phone automatically connects to the free Wi-Fi. An app on her phone recognizes the coffee shop wireless network and pushes an in-store ad to her phone for a free donut. Her phone might also be able to use her cellular network to determine her location, and she could see that there's a sale on shoes at the outdoor mall down the street.

To set up a geofence, boundaries must first be established and then parameters must be established to track a person's location. Triggers can then be used to automate a response whenever a person crosses that boundary. Geofencing has the potential to make a tremendous impact on a massive number of people because geofencing is technically supported by more than 90 percent of smartphones in the United States.[5]

Growing by Leaps and Boundaries

Consider the example of a shopping mall that has developed a

smartphone application to help improve shoppers' experience. Not only does this application provide general alerts about coupons and sales at stores in the mall, but the app also employs geofencing to track information about the location of shoppers in the mall. As a customer wanders around a large department store, beacons are used to identify the areas in the department store that are visited for longer periods of time. The app is programmed to know the types of goods sold in each part of the store and can make recommendations about other stores that sell those same types of products after the consumer leaves the department store. For example, a shopper lingers in the shoe department for 15 minutes, and upon leaving the department store, they receive an alert about other shoe stores in the mall that may be of interest to them. There are promising indicators that this type of approach works. A recent study found that more than half of shoppers would visit a certain retailer after getting this type of alert.[6]

On a larger scale, geofencing is also starting to be used for employee recruitment. As the economy has continued improving over the past several years, jobless rates have decreased, and it has become difficult for employers to fill positions with qualified personnel, especially in the medical industry. One hospital is fighting this employment battle through the use of geofencing. It is using geofencing to send recruiting ads to qualified nurses who live in or frequent certain geofenced zones.[7] While both of these examples demonstrate the value that can be created by

Source: Sergey/Fotolia

geofencing, some wonder if this strategy is becoming invasive and too much of a privacy concern.

Crossing the Line?

Any technology that seemingly tracks the location of people and links their movements with personally identifiable information can present a legitimate privacy concern. In fact, the state of Massachusetts enacted a law to protect against the use of location-based advertising.[8] Not to mention, receiving a geofence alert can present the same kind of inconvenience that a pop-up ad on a Web site brings—it is a message that the recipient might not have wanted to receive in the first place. In spite of these factors, the possible applications of geofencing appear limitless, and considering that a recent study found that 80 percent of people surveyed want to receive location-based alerts from businesses,[9] there are clearly a lot of people who embrace the value that this technology can provide.

Questions

1. The Internet of Things (IoT) and consumer products for smart homes have become extremely popular. How could geofencing be integrated with these products to create an even more efficient home ecosystem?

2. Develop a use case proposal that you could pitch to a company about how it could improve its marketing and increase its sales by using geofencing.

3. How would you feel about receiving alert messages from a store or potential employer that is using geofencing? Would you consider it an annoyance and/or a privacy concern?

4. How could a university leverage the benefits of geofencing on campus to improve student life and safety?

As the processors finish, their results are combined in what is referred to as the *Reduce* phase. The result is a list of all the terms searched for on a given day and the count of each. The process is considerably more complex than described here, but this is the gist of the idea.

By the way, you can visit Google Trends to see an application of MapReduce. There you can obtain a trend line of the number of searches for a particular term or terms. Figure 3-19 compares the search trends for the terms *Web 2.0* and *Hadoop*. Go to *www.google.com/trends* and enter the terms *Big Data* and *data analytics* to see why learning about them is a good use of your time.

Hadoop

Hadoop is an open source program supported by the Apache Foundation[10] that implements MapReduce on potentially thousands of computers. Hadoop could drive the process of finding and counting the Google search terms, but Google uses its own proprietary version of MapReduce to do so instead. Some companies implement Hadoop on server farms they manage themselves, and others, as you'll read more about in Chapter 6, run Hadoop in the cloud. Amazon supports Hadoop as part of its EC3 cloud offering. Microsoft offers Hadoop on its Azure platform as a service named HDInsight. Hadoop includes a query language titled **Pig**.

FIGURE 3-19

Google Trends on the Terms *Web 2.0* and *Hadoop*

Source: ©2018 Google LLC, used with permission. Google and the Google logo are registered trademarks of Google LLC.

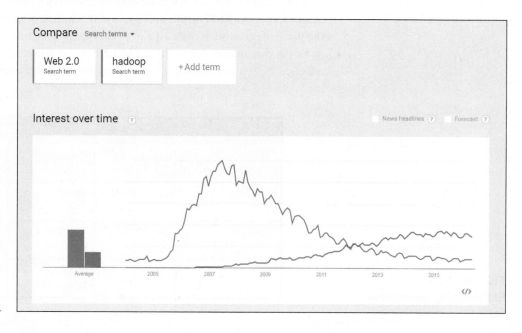

At present, deep technical skills are needed to run and use Hadoop. Judging by the development of other technologies over the years, it is likely that higher-level, easier-to-use query products will be implemented on top of Hadoop. For now, understand that experts are required to use it; you may be involved, however, in planning a Big Data study or in interpreting results.

Big Data analysis can involve both reporting and data mining techniques. The chief difference is, however, that Big Data has volume, velocity, and variation characteristics that far exceed those of traditional reporting and data mining.

Q3-4   What Are the Alternatives for Publishing BI?

The previous discussions have illustrated the power and utility of reporting, data mining, and Big Data BI applications. But, for BI to be actionable, it must be published to the right user at the right time. In this question, we will discuss primary publishing alternatives including BI servers, knowledge management systems, and content management systems.

Characteristics of BI Publishing Alternatives

Figure 3-20 lists four server alternatives for BI publishing. **Static reports** are BI documents that are fixed at the time of creation and do not change. A printed sales analysis is an example of a static report. In the BI context, most static reports are published as PDF documents.

Dynamic reports are BI documents that are updated at the time they are requested. A sales report that is current at the time the user accessed it on a Web server is a dynamic report. In almost all cases, publishing a dynamic report requires the BI application to access a database or other data source at the time the report is delivered to the user.

Pull options for each of the servers in Figure 3-20 are the same. The user goes to the site, clicks a link (or opens an email), and obtains the report. Because these options are the same for all four server types, they are not shown in Figure 3-20 .

Push options vary by server type. For email or collaboration tools, push is manual; someone— say, a manager, an expert, or an administrator—creates an email with the report as an attachment (or URL to the collaboration tool) and sends it to the users known to be interested in that report. For Web servers and SharePoint—which you will learn about in Chapter 7—users can create alerts and RSS feeds to have the server push content to them when the content is created or changed, with the expiration of a given amount of time, or at particular intervals. SharePoint workflows can also push content.

A BI server extends alert/RSS functionality to support user **subscriptions**, which are user requests for particular BI results on a particular schedule or in response to particular events. For example, a user can subscribe to a daily sales report, requesting that it be delivered each morning. Or the user might request that RFM analyses be delivered whenever a new result is posted on the server, or a sales manager might subscribe to receive a sales report whenever sales in his

Server	Report Type	Push Options	Skill Level Needed
Email or collaboration tool	Static	Manual	Low
Web server	Static/Dynamic	Alert/RSS	Low for static High for dynamic
SharePoint	Static/Dynamic	Alert/RSS Workflow	Low for static High for dynamic
BI server	Dynamic	Alert/RSS Subscription	High

FIGURE 3-20
BI Publishing Alternatives

region exceed \$1M during the week. We explain the two major functions of a BI server in the next section.

The skills needed to create a publishing application are either low or high. For static content, little skill is needed. The BI author creates the content, and the publisher (usually the same person) attaches it to an email or puts it on the Web or a SharePoint site, and that's it. Publishing dynamic BI is more difficult; it requires the publisher to set up database access when documents are consumed. In the case of a Web server, the publisher will need to develop or have a programmer write code for this purpose. In the case of SharePoint and BI servers, program code is not necessarily needed, but dynamic data connections need to be created, and this task is not for the technically faint of heart. You'll need knowledge beyond the scope of this class to develop dynamic BI solutions. You should be able to do this, however, if you take a few more IS courses or major in IS.

What Are the Two Functions of a BI Server?

A **BI server** is a Web server application that is purpose-built for the publishing of business intelligence. The Microsoft SQL Server Report manager (part of Microsoft SQL Server Reporting Services) is the most popular such product today, but there are other products as well.

BI servers provide two major functions: management and delivery. The management function maintains metadata about the authorized allocation of BI results to users. The BI server tracks what results are available, what users are authorized to view those results, and the schedule upon which the results are provided to the authorized users. It adjusts allocations as available results change and users come and go.

As shown in Figure 3-21, all management data needed by any of the BI servers is stored in metadata. The amount and complexity of such data depends, of course, on the functionality of the BI server.

BI servers use metadata to determine what results to send to which users and, possibly, on which schedule. Today, the expectation is that BI results can be delivered to "any" device. In practice, *any* is interpreted to mean computers, smartphones, tablets, applications such as Microsoft Office, and standardized Web applications.

FIGURE 3-21
Elements of a BI System

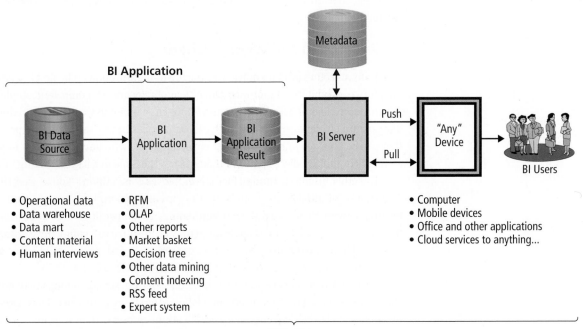

BI System

What Is the Role of Knowledge Management Systems?

Nothing is more frustrating for a manager to contemplate than the situation in which one employee struggles with a problem that another employee knows how to solve easily. Or to learn of a customer who returns a large order because the customer could not perform a basic operation with the product that many employees (and other customers) can readily perform. Even worse, someone in the customer's organization may know how to use the product, but the people who bought it didn't know that.

Knowledge management (KM) is the process of creating value from intellectual capital and sharing that knowledge with employees, managers, suppliers, customers, and others who need that capital. The goal of knowledge management is to prevent the kinds of problems just described.

Knowledge management was done before social media. Before we turn to specific technologies, however, consider the overall goals and benefits of KM. KM benefits organizations in two fundamental ways:

- It improves process quality.
- It increases team strength.

Process quality is measured by effectiveness and efficiency, and knowledge management can improve both. KM enables employees to share knowledge with each other and with customers and other partners. By doing so, it enables the employees in the organization to better achieve the organization's strategy. At the same time, sharing knowledge enables employees to solve problems more quickly and to otherwise accomplish work with less time and other resources, hence improving process efficiency.[11]

Additionally, successful teams not only accomplish their assigned tasks, but they also grow in capability, both as a team and as individuals. By sharing knowledge, team members learn from one another, avoid making repetitive mistakes, and grow as business professionals.

For example, consider the help desk at any organization, say, one that provides support for electronic components like iPhones. When a user has a problem with an iPhone, he or she might contact Apple support for help. The customer service department has, collectively, seen just about any problem that can ever occur with an iPhone. The organization as a whole knows how to solve the user's problem. However, that is no guarantee that a particular support representative knows how to solve that problem. The goal of KM is to enable employees to be able to use knowledge possessed collectively by people in the organization. By doing so, both process quality and team capability improve.

Resistance to Knowledge Sharing

Two human factors inhibit knowledge sharing in organizations. The first is that employees can be reluctant to exhibit their ignorance. Out of fear of appearing incompetent, employees may not submit entries to blogs or discussion groups. Such reluctance can sometimes be reduced by the attitude and posture of managers. One strategy for employees in this situation is to provide private media that can be accessed only by a smaller group of people who have an interest in a specific problem. Members of that smaller group can then discuss the issue in a less-inhibiting forum.

The other inhibiting human factor is employee competition. "Look," says the top salesperson. "I earn a substantial bonus from being the top salesperson. Why would I want to share my sales techniques with others? I'd just be strengthening my competition." This understandable perspective may not be changeable. A KM application may be ill-suited to a competitive group. Or the company may be able to restructure rewards and incentives to foster sharing of ideas among employees (e.g., giving a bonus to the group that develops the best idea).

If these two factors are limiting knowledge sharing, strong management endorsement can be effective, especially if that endorsement is followed by strong positive feedback. Overcoming employee resistance can be difficult, but remember, "Nothing wrong with praise or cash . . . especially cash."

What Are Content Management Systems?

One form of knowledge management concerns knowledge that is encoded in documents. **Content management systems (CMS)** are information systems that support the management and delivery of documents including reports, Web pages, and other expressions of employee knowledge.

Typical users of content management systems are companies that sell complicated products and want to share their knowledge of those products with employees and customers. Someone at Toyota, for example, knows how to change the timing belt on the four-cylinder 2020 Toyota Camry. Toyota wants to share that knowledge with car owners, mechanics, and Toyota employees.

What Are the Challenges of Content Management?

Content management systems face serious challenges. First, most content databases are huge; some have thousands of individual documents, pages, and graphics. Second, CMS content is dynamic. Imagine the frequency of Web page changes at Apple or Google or Amazon that must occur each day!

Another complication for content management systems is that documents do not exist in isolation from each other. Documents refer to one another, and when one changes, others must change as well. To manage these connections, content management systems must maintain linkages among documents so that content dependencies are known and used to maintain document consistency.

A fourth complication is that document contents are perishable. Documents become obsolete and need to be altered, removed, or replaced. For example, Microsoft's new release of Microsoft Office 2019 likely affects thousands of internal documents, external facing pages, blogs, etc. All of that has to be changed in a matter of hours.

Finally, content is provided in many languages. 3M has tens of thousands of products, some of which are harmful when used improperly. 3M must publish product safety data for all such products in several dozen languages. Every document, in whatever language it was authored, must be translated into all languages before it can be published on 3M's site. And when one document changes, all of the translated versions must change as well.

Q3-5 Why Is Artificial Intelligence (AI) Important?

Artificial intelligence (AI) is the ability of a machine to simulate human abilities such as vision, communication, recognition, learning, and decision making in order to achieve a goal. Organizations hope to use AI to increase the **automation**, or the process of making systems operate without human intervention, of mundane tasks typically done by humans. For example, a professor at Georgia Tech trained IBM's AI, named Watson, to be a teaching assistant in his class. The AI was responsible for answering a portion of nearly 10,000 student questions. None of the students realized "Jill Watson" was a machine until the end of the semester when the professor identified their cybernetic classmate.[12]

Tim Cook, CEO of Apple, recently talked about the company's efforts to make a self-driving car code-named Project Titan. Cook said Apple is focusing on creating the "mother of all AI projects" to make the brain of an autonomous system. This AI could then be used in many different autonomous Apple systems beyond self-driving cars. These could include robots, commercial drones, agricultural systems, military platforms, surgical systems, and other smart devices.

A recent report by Bank of America Merrill Lynch suggests that the AI and automated robotic market could be valued at $153 billion by 2020.[13] The resulting efficiency gains and cost reductions over the subsequent 10 years could be as large as $14 to $33 trillion. That's an enormous economic impact in a short period of time. To put that number in perspective, the entire annual gross domestic product (GDP) for the U.S. is about $18 trillion.

Advances in AI

The potential benefits of AI are mind boggling. Studies throw out many statistics; for example, there's a 50 percent chance AI will outperform humans in all tasks in 45 years, or there's an 83 percent chance AI will take over all jobs paying less than $20 an hour within a few years.[14] But are these studies right?

Historically, studies such as these have not been right. But they might be right in the near future. In the 1950s, 1980s, and late 1990s AI research went through several waves of innovation. During each wave, there was a lot of discussion about how AI would revolutionize the world. Some people got excited about it, and some got nervous about it. In the end, it led to a bunch of great science-fiction movies. AI research was slow and incremental during each of these periods. Unfortunately, AI started to develop a bad reputation. In fact, the term *AI* was so loaded with historical false-starts that when IBM started developing its Watson, it used the term *cognitive computing* rather than *AI*.

But, significant innovations in the past couple of decades have advanced AI to the point that it's now starting to be successful. Figure 3-22 shows the six main forces that have helped advance AI in recent years.

First, *computing power* has been increasing exponentially for several decades (Moore's Law), while earlier waves of AI lacked the necessary computing power. The computers during those time periods were just not fast enough to process the data necessary to make AI work. Just like an airplane during takeoff, AI must reach critical speed before it can get off the ground. IBM's Watson, for example, operates at about 80 teraflops per second.

Second, the *availability* of large data sets has advanced to the point that AI is viable technology. AI applications require a surprisingly large amount of data in order to learn, represent knowledge, and process natural language. Watson, for example, can read 800 million pages per second. AI applications need both large amounts of rich data and the accompanying processing power to sift through it.

Third, *cloud* computing has advanced AI development because it has made scalable resources available at very low costs. AI development could now be done by more people at a much lower cost. The cloud allows developers to access existing AI applications through online interfaces. IBM offers developers access to a variety of online AI applications including Conversation, Discovery, Document Conversion, Language Translator, Tone Analyzer, Speech to Text, and Visual Recognition.

Fourth, the rapid increase in *network connected smart devices* is producing vast amounts of data for AI applications. These devices are more than just desktops, laptops, and smartphones; they also include a variety of network-enabled optical, motion, temperature, audio, and magnetic sensors. There are thousands of IoT devices that can provide the data AI applications use to learn.

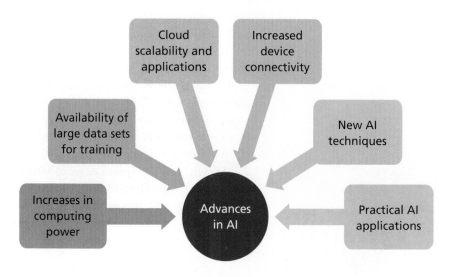

FIGURE 3-22
Forces Driving AI Innovation

Company	Practical Artificial Intelligence Applications
Amazon	Alexa, Echo, Amazon Rekognition, Amazon Polly, Amazon Lex, Amazon Machine Learning, Amazon EMR, Spark & Sparkml, AWS Deep Learning AMI
Facebook	DeepText, DeepFace, News Feed, targeted advertising, filtering offensive content, search rankings, application design
Google	Google Assistant, Google Translate, Home, Google Brain, TensorFlow, Cloud ML, DeepMind Lab, Convnet.js, OpenFrameworks, Wekinator
Microsoft	Cortana, Computer Vision, Face, Content Moderator, Translator Speech, Translator Text, Language Understanding Intelligent Service, Recommendations, QnA Maker, Bing Image Search Integrated into Microsoft Suite
Apple	Integrated into all Apple products and services (Siri, iPhone, HomePod, iWatch, etc.)

FIGURE 3-23
Examples of Practical AI Applications

AI applications are also used by these connected devices. For example, CogniToys Dino is a small green plastic dinosaur toy powered by IBM's Watson. It answers questions, tells jokes, plays interactive games, and automatically adapts to the age of the child playing with it. It also sends data to a "parental panel" that gives parents detailed feedback about the child's interactions with Dino.

Fifth, *fundamental breakthroughs* in AI techniques have made AI useful for a variety of tasks. For example, in 2006, AI researcher Geoffrey Hinton developed a method for simulating multiple layers of artificial neural networks rather than just a single layer.[15] A **neural network** is a computing system modelled after the human brain that is used to predict values and make classifications. This multilayered neural network technique was applied to learning tasks and is now commonly known as **deep learning**. Deep learning has greatly increased the accuracy and practical usefulness of AI.

Finally, recent advances in AI have been driven by the demand for applications that *solve practical problems*. Figure 3-23 shows a few examples of practical AI applications produced by a handful of the largest tech companies. These are not academic theories or artificial simulations; these are applications focused on solving real-world problems for organizations. There are many more applications than those shown in Figure 3-23. In fact, Google has more than 1,000 working AI projects, and Apple and Microsoft are integrating AI into all of their hardware and software.

These six forces have driven innovations in AI to the point that AI is now becoming widely used, and it's becoming a core part of many tech companies' strategic advantage. AI has already been widely adopted by all of the major tech companies, and users are interacting with it (sometimes unknowingly) on a daily basis. It's also being used to create innovative new products by smaller companies. Traditional organizations are starting to see the value of AI, too.

Q3-6 How Will Artificial Intelligence and Automation Affect Organizations?

Artificial intelligence sounds like a great innovation—it will reduce costs, increase productivity, create new services, find unique solutions to age-old problems, and enable an army of smart devices with new capabilities. But, as a business leader, you need to understand the broader implications of using AI and automated machines. You need to understand how this new wave of AI is going to affect you and your organization.

For example, suppose you own a chain of fast-food restaurants. You're considering buying a fully automated hamburger-making machine powered by an AI. It can make 400 custom hamburgers an hour. It does it safely, cleanly, and without any human intervention. It's so efficient that it can replace three full-time cooks, potentially saving you $90,000 per year. It doesn't take breaks, call in sick, steal food, or sue you for lost wages. This robotic fast-food worker may sound far-fetched, but these types of machines already exist: Both Momentum Machines and Miso Robotics make robots with these capabilities.[16]

Will this new AI-powered hamburger-making machine really save you money? If so, how much? And how will your human employees react to their new cybernetic coworker?

Benefits of Automated Labor

First, let's consider the reduction in labor costs that come from using automated labor. According to the U.S. Bureau of Labor Statistics, the average employee in the United States makes $24.10 per hour.[17] But that's not the true cost. As shown in Figure 3-24, benefits add an additional 46 percent ($11.19) per hour to the true cost. So, a $24-per-hour employee actually costs *at least* $35 per hour. If you buy an automated system, you won't have to pay for any of the additional benefits required with human labor. You won't have to pay for overtime, leave, insurance, or retirement contributions.

In the case of your AI-powered hamburger machine, suppose you're replacing three cooks who each make $15.00 per hour plus $6.90 in benefits. That's a cost of $21.90 per cook per hour, for a total cost of $65.70 per hour. An AI-powered hamburger machine pays itself off pretty quickly at that rate. Suppose the machine costs $100,000 and runs 12 hours per day. You would recoup your investment in 4.2 months.

There are other productivity gains to consider beyond wages and benefits. Figure 3-25 lists a few examples of productivity gains you could realize from using an automated hamburger machine instead of a human laborer. Each of these productivity gains could be quantified, but the actual gains would vary substantially depending on the specific circumstances. For example, if your restaurants were open 24 hours per day, you would realize sizable productivity gains from an automated hamburger machine. But if the restaurants were only open 8 hours per day, the gains might be less.

A good example of an organization benefiting from an automated system is online banking. Banks that offer consumers online banking have seen both increases in productivity and decreases

FIGURE 3-24
Employee Costs per Hour (U.S.)

Source: Based on Data from Bureau of Labor Statistics

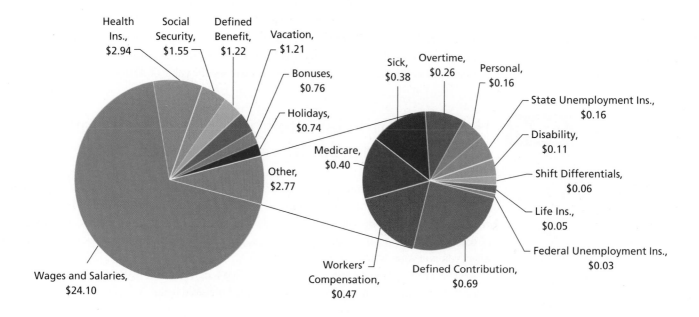

Employee Costs per Hour (U.S.)

Health Ins., $2.94
Social Security, $1.55
Defined Benefit, $1.22
Vacation, $1.21
Bonuses, $0.76
Holidays, $0.74
Sick, $0.38
Overtime, $0.26
Personal, $0.16
State Unemployment Ins., $0.16
Disability, $0.11
Shift Differentials, $0.06
Life Ins., $0.05
Federal Unemployment Ins., $0.03
Medicare, $0.40
Other, $2.77
Workers' Compensation, $0.47
Defined Contribution, $0.69
Wages and Salaries, $24.10

Productivity Gains from Automation
Can work 24 hours, 365 days
Immediately trained, no "onboarding"
No breaks during work hours
No impaired workers
No time-wasting activities
No accidents or injuries
No arguments with other employees or managers
No scheduling issues
All holiday shifts covered
More accurate, precise, and consistent

FIGURE 3-25
Productivity Gains from Automation

in costs. For example, the average cost per transaction to talk with a teller at the bank is about $4. But per-transactions costs drop to $0.17 for online transactions and $0.08 for mobile transactions.[18] Consumers can access their accounts online at any time without traveling to the bank to talk with a human teller. Online banking has allowed banks to reduce their labor costs and boost profitability.

Beyond productivity gains and reductions in labor costs, other factors may impact your decision to adopt the automated hamburger machine. Some of these factors aren't pleasant to think about because people don't want them to happen. Let's look at one of the costlier factors—employee fraud.

Managers don't want employees to steal from the company. It's no fun to think your workers are stealing from the company. But employee fraud happens, and it is extremely costly. The Association of Certified Fraud Examiners (ACFE) 2016 Report to the Nations estimates the median loss for employee fraud is $150,000 per incident.[19]

Figure 3-26 shows the type of employee fraud by frequency and median loss per incident. Not all types of fraud are the same. Some types of fraud, like financial statement fraud, don't occur that often but have large median losses. The ACFE estimates that a typical organization loses 5 percent of its annual revenue to employee fraud. To get an idea of the size of these losses, consider that the U.S. gross domestic product (GDP) was $18 trillion in 2015. That would mean the estimated amount of employee fraud losses would be $900 billion per year in the United States.

If you bought an automated machine, you would reduce the amount of employee fraud within your organization dramatically. An automated machine won't steal from you. It doesn't want to or

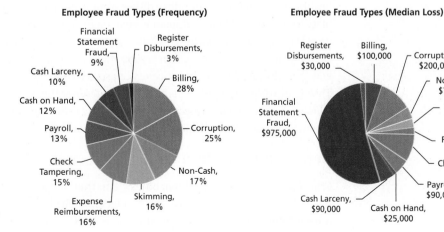

FIGURE 3-26
Employee Fraud Frequency and Median Loss

Source: Based on Report to the Nations on Occupational fraud and abuse

need to. It doesn't feel financial pressures or look for opportunities to steal. It just performs its task. It may also indirectly add 5 percent to your bottom line by reducing employee fraud.

Finally, there are a few additional benefits of automated labor that you must consider. Automated machines don't need severance packages, don't have union overhead, can't go on strike, don't steal intellectual property, won't file discrimination lawsuits, and can't harass coworkers. With human labor, all of these add costs to your organization's bottom line. They consume your time and energy as a manger, and they affect your organization's ability to remain competitive.

How Will AI Affect Me?

Whenever people start talking about the impacts of AI and automation, there are typically two distinct reactions. The first reaction is from the group of people who see AI as an incredible opportunity. They get excited about the gains in productivity, profitability, and competitive advantages. They want to be on the cutting edge and be the first to implement it in their industry.

The second reaction is from the group of people who see AI as a serious threat. They're worried about their jobs. They are concerned about what happens if they get replaced by a machine or an AI bot. They worry that their years of education and training will become worthless or that they may have to change careers. These are valid concerns, and this group of people is right to be concerned. Major seismic shifts in global workforces are imminent.

Jobs requiring routine physical and mental tasks are prime candidates for automation. Experts on AI and automation estimate that by 2025, nearly 100 million workers could be taken out of the current U.S. labor force (146 million workers).[20] They will be replaced by robots with IQs higher than 90 percent of the U.S. population. In developing countries, the labor replacement rates could be as high as 70 or 80 percent.[21] As a manager, you need to understand the economic implications of these historic changes. They're important for your organization, and they might be important to you personally.

Unwanted Dirty Jobs

While workers may not want their *incomes* to go away, they may not mind seeing certain *jobs* go away (assuming they can transition to a different job that still pays a good salary). Some jobs are dirty, stinky, boring, and even dangerous. AI and automation could do jobs that humans don't really want to do. Take waste disposal, for example. Twenty years ago, there were three workers on a garbage truck. One would drive, and two would fill the truck. Today, one person drives the truck and operates the side loader arm. In another twenty years, the truck will be self-driving, and garbage collection will be fully autonomous.

On a personal level, AI and autonomous machines could do other things you may not want to do. Home repairs, house cleaning, car washing, auto repairs, gardening, and cooking could all be done autonomously. Thanks to your new "gardener," you could have fresh homegrown food every day. You wouldn't have to buy as much food from the grocery store. Your personal AI could cook healthy meals and wash your dirty dishes. Your personal costs would go down, and your productivity would go up. AI and autonomous machines could also take care of the elderly and disabled, provide companionship, train "energetic" puppies, and teach children without becoming frustrated.

Similarly, there are jobs within organizations that humans may not want to do. Manufacturing and agricultural jobs have historically been seen as monotonous, backbreaking, and low-paying. They've also been decreasing in the United States over the past 40 years. Automated systems may allow workers to shift from assembling and making existing products to designing and creating new products. The key will be helping workers make that shift.

Retraining and Retooling

Critics of AI and automated machines claim that adoption of these systems will lead to mass unemployment. Similar predictions of a technological apocalypse have been made before, but it hasn't happened. For example, in the late 1990's, online shopping started to become more commonplace. Businesses weren't sure if brick-and-mortar businesses were going to be taken over by their online competition. Were they going to have to fire their traditional employees and transition to an online presence? A period of excessive speculation in tech companies called the dot-com boom began. Investors poured money into tech startups in hopes of making billions. Most of them failed by 2001.

The spectacular boom and bust of these tech companies got a lot of attention in the media. But the underlying shift in the global workforce was an equally important, yet subtle, change. New *types* of jobs were available to workers. Jobs in networking, database development, Web development, and programming paid well and were in high demand. Workers retrained for the new digital era. They sought out skills demanded by organizations that shifted their strategic priorities. A similar retooling of the existing workforce will be necessary when AI and automated machines take a more prominent role in our economy. There will be new *types* of jobs for humans to do. Lots of them.

Surviving a Shifting Workplace

How are human workers going to survive the workplace shift caused by AI? First, human workers need to develop skills that machines can't do. Back in Chapter 1 we touched on a few non-routine cognitive skills that help keep you competitive in a changing job market. These included *abstract reasoning*, *systems thinking*, *collaboration*, and *experimentation*. This is a good start. Humans excel in these areas. But there are a few other things that machines still can't do. *Creativity, adaptability*, and *new undefined problem solving* are human skills that give you a competitive advantage over your synthetic counterparts.

Second, lots of human workers will be needed to take care of these new machines. Even the best AIs need *training*. IBM's Watson needs experts to train it so it knows if it's getting the right answers. Human domain experts will always be needed. As a result, you'll change jobs much more quickly than workers did in the past. Human workers will need to adapt quickly to their synthetic coworkers.

AI-enabled machines will also need humans for the foreseeable future because they lack something humans have—instincts. Machines don't have the basic internal unlearned driving forces that humans have. These forces ensured the survival of the human species. Without instincts, machines won't last long at all. Machines don't need or desire anything. Instincts drive humans to stay alive, procreate, improve their position, and seek the protection of others. Without these instincts, machines don't care if they die, and they won't replicate and won't improve. Machines *need* humans to survive. They also need humans to help them to improve. Humans and machines need each other. That's why we'll be working together for a long time to come.

Q3-7 What Is the Goal of AI?

The goal of AI research is to create *artificial general intelligence*, or **strong AI** that can complete *all* of the same tasks a human can. This includes the ability to process natural language; to sense, learn, interact with the physical world; to represent knowledge; to reason; and to plan. Most AI researchers believe this will happen sometime around 2040.[22] Currently, as shown in Figure 3-27, we have **weak AI** which is focused on completing a *single* specific task. There is speculation that someday we may be able to create an AI that moves beyond strong AI to create a **superintelligence** capable of intelligence more advanced than human intelligence. Some researchers see superintelligence as a potential threat to humans. Others disagree and argue that this level of AI is hundreds of years away.[23]

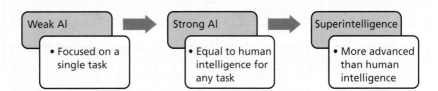

FIGURE 3-27
Evolution of AI Abilities

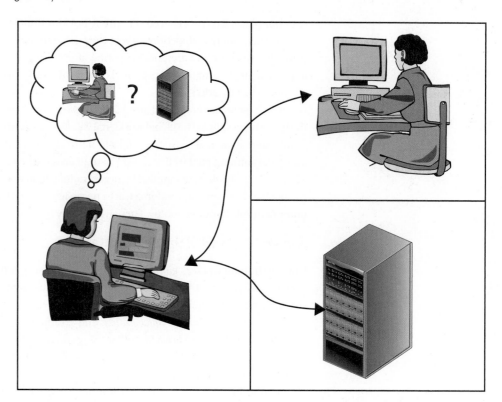

FIGURE 3-28
Turing Test

There is considerable disagreement about what it means to actually create an artificial intelligence. An early computer scientist named Alan Turing said a machine could be considered intelligent if a human could have a conversation with it and not be able to tell if it was a machine or a human. This standard, shown in Figure 3-28, became known as the **Turing test**. There are other standards for judging AI, but they're beyond the scope of this book. Again, the overall goal of AI is to create a machine that can complete the same tasks as a human.

But AI is much more than just the ability of a chat bot to simulate a human conversation. It's the ability of a machine to simulate *all* human abilities. Consider the scope of the major research areas within AI as well as a few select sub-areas, as shown in Figure 3-29. These major areas focus

FIGURE 3-29
Major AI Research Areas

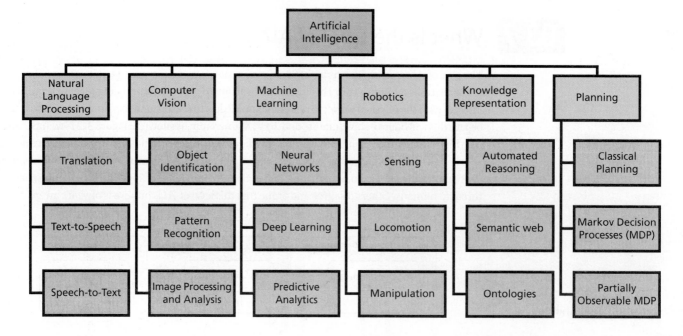

on different aspects of human abilities. In fact, AI as a research area is much broader than can be shown here. *AI* is a general term that means different things to different people depending on their area of interest. However, the implementation of AI into real-world technology usually involves combining multiple different areas together.

Integrated Enabler of Other Technology

Organizations see AI as an enabler of new technologies. Their goal is to use AI to enhance their existing products and services. For example, consider the amount of AI required for a fully autonomous self-driving car. A self-driving car will have multiple *computer vision* systems including GPS, gyroscopes, accelerometers, LIDAR, RADAR, 360-degree cameras, and possibly even night-vision capability. It will also have a *robotics* component that governs locomotion, sensing, and navigation. Future self-driving cars will automatically learn from your past transportation needs and environmental preferences (*machine learning*), preplan your routes, and monitor for delays (*planning*). You'll probably even be able to give your car instructions by talking with it normally (*natural language processing*).

   Technology companies like Apple want to put AI into more than just self-driving cars. Their goal is to put it into *all* of their devices and services. They want all of their devices to be more than just "smart" (i.e., connected to the Internet); they want them to be intelligent (i.e., powered by an AI back-end system). They want all IoT devices to be AI driven. Think about the new products and services that could be created if AI was applied to areas like manufacturing, finance, medicine, cybersecurity, transportation, education, entertainment, and agriculture. Major technology companies are investing heavily in AI to make this happen.

Saying No to AI

Widespread adoption of AI is going to cause a lot of changes in organizations. As organizations change, so will the types of jobs they need filled. Workers are going to have to continually develop new skills for new types of jobs. They might find themselves doing work that has little to do with their formal education. People don't like change in general. Change introduces risk, uncertainty, and loss of control. It will be tempting to say "no" to AI and automation. Governments may feel pressure to place restrictions on implementations of AI and automation to protect workers.

   But what will happen if you don't automate, and your competitors do? You may lose a competitive advantage if your competitor can produce a higher-quality product at one-third the price. Imagine banning online banking because it might cost tellers their jobs or banning Netflix because it might reduce the demand for labor at local brick-and-mortar video stores. That may sound silly to most people, but innovations have caused substantial shifts in the workforce. They always have. There's a long list of jobs that once existed that don't anymore. But there's also a list of new jobs that were created because of technological innovations. Adopting AI and automation at an *appropriate* pace may be the only way to keep organizations viable.

   Looking at the adoption of AI more broadly, it may solve some of the financial woes of certain world economies. Costs for health care and manufacturing could be reduced by $8 trillion over 10 years.[24] Employment costs could be reduced by $9 trillion. World economies could also see productivity gains of at least 30 percent. Governments may not *want* to see their citizens forced into new types of jobs, but they may *need* the economic gains AI and automation represent. Saying "yes" to AI may be a painful but necessary decision.

Q3-8   How Does AI Work?

AI has become somewhat of a buzzword in the tech and business worlds. People talk about the amazing things AI can do, but they don't really understand how it works. As a business professional, you need to have a basic understanding of how AI works. You don't have to become an expert, but you do need to understand the ways it might be applied to solve organizational problems. This will enable you to actually create value within your organization rather than just being awed by the productivity gains AI has created in other organizations.

The following example looks at the way AI can be used to solve a real-world problem—spam filtering. There are many other areas of AI that can produce applications with similarly compelling results, but this will give you an idea of what's possible.

Machine Learning

A subset of AI is **machine learning**, or the extraction of knowledge from data based on algorithms created from training data. Essentially, machine learning is focused on predicting outcomes based on *previously known* training data. For example, machine learning can be used to teach a system to recognize and classify dog breeds. A machine learns to recognize each breed of dog by analyzing millions of dog images. In fact, Microsoft has made an app named Fetch! that does just that. You can even submit your own photo and see what dog breed you most closely resemble (*www.what-dog.net*).

Machine learning can also help you make decisions. Suppose you meet a new dog at the park. You have to decide if you should pet the dog. It might bite you, but it might not. Through your experiences, you've established a set of criteria that helps you determine if you should or should not pet a dog. You probably take into account growling, bared teeth, barking, body posture, or foaming at the mouth. One of these factors alone may not be enough to prevent you from petting the dog, but combined with other factors it might be enough. Machines learn the same way you do—through experience.

Using Machine Learning to Automatically Detect Spam

Now let's apply machine learning to a real-world problem that can help an organization. We'll use machine learning to automatically classify email as either spam or legitimate email as described by Paul Graham.[25] In order to do so, we'll need to choose an **algorithm**, or a set of procedures used to solve a mathematical problem, that best fits our situation. We'll use an algorithm called a **Naïve Bayes Classifier** that predicts the probability of a certain outcome based on prior occurrences of related events. In other words, we're going to try to predict whether a new email is spam or not based on attributes of *previous* spam messages.

To do this, we first collect a large number of previous emails. Then we classify each email as either "spam" or "legitimate," as shown in Figure 3-30a. Next, we search all of the emails for the word *promotion* and see how many matches we get. As shown in Figure 3-30b we found 5 legitimate emails and 40 spam emails containing the word *promotion*. Some of the legitimate emails may have used the word *promotion* in the context of an advancement in your job. On the other hand, the spam emails likely used the word *promotion* in terms of a special sale.

In this case, 88 percent of previous emails containing the word *promotion* were spam. So, in the future, if a new email comes in containing the word *promotion*, we will say there is an 88 percent chance that it is spam. That doesn't mean the word *promotion* can be used to perfectly identify all spam, but it's a strong indicator. Combining it with other key words could really boost spam detection accuracy.

Machine learning automates this process and looks for spelling mistakes, words like *madam*, and other key terms common to spam emails. The result is a list of terms and associated probabilities that can be used to automatically assess all new incoming emails. Machine learning allows automated systems to *learn* from users as they tag emails as spam and then filters future emails based on the content of those spam messages. Again, it's not perfect, but it's amazingly accurate.

Machine learning can be used in a wide variety of tasks including college admissions decisions, credit approvals, fraud detection, search result optimization, and dating site matching. It can use other algorithms (like decision trees, linear regression, and logistic regression) depending on the type of data being analyzed. It can also use neural networks to predict values and make classifications such as "good prospect" or "poor prospect" based on a complicated set of possibly nonlinear

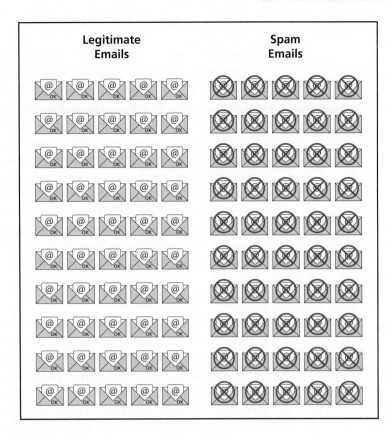

FIGURE 3-30A
Classifying Emails as Spam or Legitimate

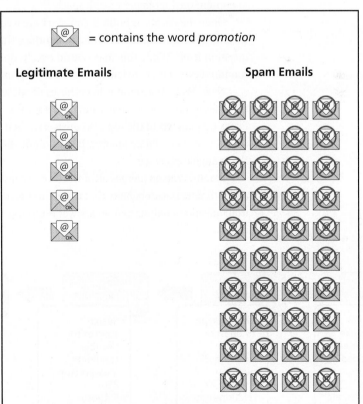

FIGURE 3-30B
Emails Containing the Word *Promotion*

equations. Or it can use deep learning techniques that allow the system to classify data by itself. Explaining these techniques is beyond the scope of this text. If you want to learn more, search *http://kdnuggets.com* for the term *neural network*.

IBM's Watson

Now that you've seen a simple example of how AI works, let's take a closer look at a more complex AI. IBM's artificial intelligence named Watson is a question answering system that draws on several areas of AI. First, it uses **natural language processing (NLP)**, or the ability of a computer system to understand spoken human language, to answer questions. It was designed to play against world champions on the quiz show *Jeopardy!*, and in 2011 it won.

But so what? Why spend millions of dollars to build a great AI that can win a trivia game? Isn't that trivial by definition? No. The trivia game was meant to be an exhibition of Watson's ability to answer difficult questions asked by humans in a natural way. The implications of Watson's win are profound. Watson can provide evidence-based answers for questions in fields like health care, transportation, education, social media, customer service, and security.[26] For example, H&R Block is using Watson to help do taxes, and LegalMation is using Watson to help automate litigation. The list of potential applications for Watson is long. To better understand Watson's capabilities, you need to understand the basics of how Watson works.

How Does Watson Work?

Figure 3-31 shows a shortened version of how Watson works. The actual DeepQA architecture is much more complex, and it is beyond the scope of this book.[27] As a business manager it's important to understand how Watson works so you can identify potential applications for this type of AI.

First, Watson acquires content from sources like dictionaries, encyclopedias, literature, reports, and databases. It extracts valuable pieces of data from these structured and semi-structured data sources. It then takes these extracted pieces of data and adds them to a **corpus of knowledge**, or a large set of related data and texts. During the *Jeopardy!* challenge, Watson used 200 million pages of content on 4 terabytes of disk space.[28]

Once the corpus is built, it can start answering questions. Each question that comes in goes through question analysis. Watson identifies the type of question being asked and analyzes the question itself. While this may sound overly simplistic, it's good to remember that it takes most humans several years to learn to speak their primary language.

Next, Watson generates hypotheses about what might be the right answer to the question. It searches its data for possible candidate answers. It takes the top 250 candidate answers and then filters them down to the top 100 answers. Then it goes back to its data and looks for evidence to support each candidate answer. It uses many different techniques to score each answer based on the available evidence.

Finally, Watson merges all of the scored candidate answers, identifies the best possible answer, and estimates the probability that the answer is correct. And here's the best part—it does everything from question analysis to final answer estimation in 3 seconds! That's powerful.

FIGURE 3-31
IBM's Question-and-Answer Process

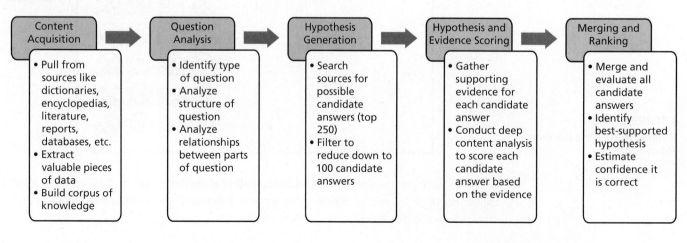

The Future for Watson

IBM's Watson is an amazing system. Watson can read hundreds of millions of pages per second, can interact with people all over the world at the same time, and speaks nine languages. But Watson still needs to be trained for different tasks. That might take more than we think. It took Watson 5 years to become the best at answering trivia questions. But Watson did it. And remember that Watson will live longer than any human and can get processor upgrades on demand that are twice as fast every 18 months (Moore's Law). Twenty years from now, Watson may be doing many things we thought were reserved for human workers.

Q3-9 2029?

BI systems are widely used today. Simple systems using RFM and OLAP are easy to use and truly do add value. More complex systems like AI machine learning are starting to be used by large companies with success. But they must be correctly designed and implemented and applied to problems appropriately.

Companies are already pretty savvy when it comes to using BI to effectively target customers with products they will likely buy. They use BI to know what you want to buy, when you'll buy it, and how you'll buy it. They can detect fraudulent credit card purchases, automatically lock your credit card, and resolve the unauthorized charges quickly. But there's much more that BI can do beyond retail.

By 2029, data storage, processing power, and network speeds will have increased exponentially. Most of the devices around you will be collecting and transmitting data. Companies will know more about you than just your purchasing habits. They will know your location throughout the day. They'll know your sleeping patterns, exercise routines, stress levels, and food preferences. They will even know what you talk about in your home. All of these types of data can be used for beneficial outcomes. But they could also be used for malicious outcomes. Privacy will become an increasing concern as BI develops over time.

There's also the real possibility that many jobs will be automated by 2029. What happens when an AI becomes sophisticated enough to replace BI analysts? What happens when the AI has the ability to find its own data sets, perform its own analysis, make decisions, and then decide which analysis to perform next? AI will likely automate many of the routine analytical tasks we now know we want to perform. But it also has the potential to find *new* patterns, correlations, and insights. In the future, AIs may do as much teaching as they do learning. They may even move beyond us.

Ray Kurzweil developed a concept he calls **the Singularity**, which is the point at which an AI becomes sophisticated enough that it can adapt and create its own software and, hence, adapt its behavior without human assistance. Apply this idea to unsupervised data mining.[29] What happens when machines can direct their own data mining activities? There will be an accelerating positive feedback loop among AIs. A single AI will have more processing power than all possible human cognitive power combined. We may even have the technology to merge human intelligence with AIs and gain knowledge that we could never have comprehended before. Kurzweil predicts this could happen by 2045.

By 2029 we'll start to see that future. We'll start to see machines as more than just *things* we create to augment ourselves (e.g., right now, we create cars because we can't run fast enough or far enough). We'll probably start seeing machines as assistants, coworkers, advisors, even friends. They may become the creators of things. They probably will be our caretakers. Hopefully, they will not be our overlords.

SECURITY GUIDE

EQUIHAX

We have all felt the sinking sensation that comes from sticking a hand into a pocket or bag to grab something only to find that it is not there. That feeling is soon followed by a rush of adrenaline and frenzied mental gymnastics as we try to remember the last time we saw or used that item. Often, we resort to checking other pockets or bags, retracing our steps, and even reaching out to friends or family who might have found the missing item. Sometimes these tactics prove successful; other times, they're not, and the item is never reclaimed.

In many cases, the lost item is a wallet. As a result, we bemoan any cash that was lost and face the frustration of contacting financial institutions to cancel debit and credit cards. While unpleasant, the overall magnitude of one person losing a wallet is relatively small. However, imagine the angst and frustration of something like this happening to more than 140 million people at the exact same time.

The Breach

It is not uncommon for headline stories on the nightly news to include cybersecurity breaches involving large corporations. However, a staggering headline in the summer of 2017 was the unveiling of a massive breach at Equifax, one of the three primary consumer credit reporting agencies. (The other two are Experian and Trans-Union.) The breach included the theft of highly sensitive personally identifiable information (PII), including the names, addresses, birth dates, and Social Security numbers associated with 143 million people.[30] Follow-up reports indicated that data for several million additional people were also compromised.

Equifax ultimately became the target of considerable criticism because the breach was carried out by exploiting Apache Struts, a publicly available piece of software for creating Web sites that had been identified by Cisco as having a vulnerability earlier in the year.[31] While Equifax had addressed the vulnerability to a large degree, some of its systems remained susceptible, and this susceptibility was sufficient for its infrastructure to be compromised.[32]

The nature of the Equifax breach was especially devastating because it gave criminals everything needed to commit massive fraud in a single data trove, compared with many previous breaches that included only email addresses and passwords or names and credit card numbers. Equifax and security experts recommended that affected individuals—who included just under half of the U.S. population—freeze their credit with all three credit reporting agencies. (This means changing the status of credit such that new accounts cannot be opened without direct authorization from an individual to "unfreeze" their credit.)

In spite of these recommendations, countless individuals have had their identities stolen and become victims of fraud. For example, one victim became aware that something was wrong when they received information in the mail about a credit card account that they had never actually opened.[33] Upon looking into this rogue account, they found that 15

Source: Izel Photography - A/Alamy Stock Photo

different fraudulent accounts had also been opened using their information. Similar stories have been shared by other victims, and the fraudulent activity has affected everything from bank accounts and car loans to home mortgages and drivers' licenses.[34]

Insult to Injury

The backlash against Equifax for this incident has been severe. Security experts contend that much more rigorous security controls should have been in place due to the extremely sensitive nature of the PII that Equifax possesses. There have also been questions as to whether Equifax and other companies that store PII should use a centralized data storage approach because this type of architecture becomes a huge target for hackers. Consumers are frustrated for many reasons, including the risk of fraud and the fact that they have no power over their own PII (i.e., the credit agencies collect data about everyone and there is no choice to "opt out" of having these companies store data about you).

Equifax made matters worse with a number of blunders in the way it handled the breach. For example, shortly after reporting the breach, the company created a support site for people to check whether their data had been compromised, but the site it created was external to its corporate domain (i.e., not related to its main Web site). This enabled cybercriminals to exploit unwary individuals by creating a variety of false Web sites with similar URLs. To make this point, a Web developer created a *fake* site that was subsequently referenced by a few Equifax employees. Incredibly, they erroneously tweeted out a link to the fraudulent site—multiple times![35] One estimate reported that almost 200 fake sites had been created by phishers within a day of the support site being created.[36]

DISCUSSION QUESTIONS

1. Have you or someone you know been the victim of any kind of theft (either personal possessions or identify theft)? How did you or this other person respond? What course of action was taken to remedy the situation? How long did it take for this incident to be resolved?

2. What do you think should happen to Equifax as a result of this breach? Should consumers have the option/right to have their data deleted by a company at any time upon request? Should the government step in and become the clearinghouse for consumer credit reporting in an effort to provide more robust security?

3. The article mentions Equifax's use of a centralized structure for storing data, which results in a very appealing target for hackers. Can you think of other companies/contexts in which a centralized structure is used? Do you think this should be avoided in light of the Equifax breach?

4. Equifax employees made the mistake of tweeting out a URL for a site that was not actually associated with the company's response efforts. How can you verify that a site is legitimate?

CAREER GUIDE

Name: Lindsey Tsuya
Company: American Express Company
Job Title: Manager, Data and Analytics
Education: University of Utah

Source: Lindsey Tsuya, American Express Company, Manager, Data and Analytics

1 **How did you get this type of job?**

I was referred by a friend who was already working at American Express. Luckily, I have been referred for every position I have held since graduation. In addition, upon graduation I entered into a technology rotation program that enabled me to explore different areas of technology. This allowed me to determine the type of technology that best suited me. The program enabled me to understand what I was passionate about in technology. I strongly recommend that anyone who has a similar opportunity take it.

2 **What attracted you to this field?**

As a college student, I worked in the service industry. When I was selecting my degree, I knew I wanted two things. First, I wanted a degree that made money. Second, I wanted a job that did not involve direct provision of service to the public. By choosing information systems, I knew I would be doing more of a behind-the-scenes job.

3 **What does a typical workday look like for you (duties, decisions, problems)?**

I am responsible for the majority of the reporting needs for my department. We have multiple weekly reports that must be sent out. We have monthly and quarterly reports as well. I also handle the majority of ad hoc requests from the department. We are a global team located in Singapore, London, Sydney, New York, and Salt Lake City. These reports may be ad hoc data analyses or data mining that looks for certain things in the data.

4 **What do you like most about your job?**

I love my job because I am passionate about what I do. I love data. I love analyzing data and determining what story the data is telling me. Because I am in a financial services company, I have to look at many drivers to determine the story. What I like most about my job is that it is always different. No two ad hoc requests are the same. Every day is different, and I like that.

5 **What skills would someone need to do well at your job?**

Good analytical skills and the ability to analyze large amounts of data are essential. Critical thinking skills and the ability to think outside the box are also important. Soft skills that differentiate people are passion and a can-do attitude. Those two things coupled together will take anyone far in life.

6 **Are education or certifications important in your field? Why?**

I would say in any field, education and certifications assist with career development and credibility.

7 **What advice would you give to someone who is considering working in your field?**

No matter what field you choose, make sure it is something you are passionate about because if you are not passionate about it, work will feel like . . . work. If you are passionate about what you do, then work feels like play. You will spend so many hours of your life working, and you should not waste them doing something you don't love.

ACTIVE REVIEW

Use this Active Review to verify that you understand the ideas and concepts that answer the chapter's study questions.

Q3-1   How do organizations use business intelligence (BI) systems?

Define *business intelligence* and *BI system*. Explain the components in Figure 3-1. Give an example, other than one in this text, of one way that an organization could use business intelligence for each of the four tasks in Figure 3-2. Name and describe the three primary activities in the BI process. Using Figure 3-3 as a guide, describe the major tasks for each activity. Summarize how the team at the parts distribution company used these activities to produce BI results. Explain the process shown in Figures 3-4 through 3-7.

Q3-2   How do organizations use data warehouses and data marts to acquire data?

Describe the need and functions of data warehouses and data marts. Name and describe the role of data warehouse components. List and explain the problems that can exist in data used for data mining and sophisticated reporting. Use the example of a supply chain to describe the differences between a data warehouse and data mart.

Q3-3   What are three techniques for processing BI data?

Name the three types of BI analysis and describe how the goal of each differs. Name and describe five basic reporting operations in reporting analysis. Define *RFM analysis* and explain the actions that should be taken with customers who have the following scores: [5, 5, 5,], [1, 5, 5,], [5, 5, 3], and [5, 2, 5]. Explain OLAP and describe its unique characteristics. Explain the roles for measure and dimension in an OLAP cube. Define *data mining* and explain how its use typically differs from reporting applications. Describe the differences between *unsupervised* and *supervised* data mining. Name and explain the three v's of Big Data. Describe the general goal of MapReduce and explain, at a conceptual level, how it works. Explain the purpose of Hadoop and describe its origins. Describe the ways organizations can deploy Hadoop. Define *Pig*.

Q3-4   What are the alternatives for publishing BI?

Name four alternative types of server used for publishing business intelligence. Explain the difference between static and dynamic reports; explain the term *subscription*. Describe why

dynamic reports are difficult to create. Define *knowledge management*. Explain five key benefits of KM. Briefly describe one type of KM system. Summarize possible employee resistance to hyper-social knowledge sharing and name two management techniques for reducing it. Define *content management system (CMS)*. Name two CMS application alternatives and explain the use of each. Describe five challenges organizations face for managing content.

Q3-5   Why is artificial intelligence (AI) important?

Define *artificial intelligence* and *automation*. Describe how organizations hope to use AI to increase automation. List each of the forces shown in Figure 3-22 that have driven recent advances in AI. Explain why each of these forces has been important to the current success of AI. Define *deep learning*. Describe how users may already be using AI applications like those shown in Figure 3-23.

Q3-6   How will Artificial Intelligence and automation affect organizations?

Explain how AI and automation could be used to reduce the costs and increase productivity for a fast-food restaurant. List some of the cost savings beyond wages and salaries shown in Figure 3-24 that organizations might see from adopting automated labor. Summarize some of the potential impacts of automated labor on organizational productivity as shown in Figure 3-25. Describe how the adoption of automated labor may reduce employee fraud and its potential impact on profitability. Describe two possible reactions people might have when their organizations implement widespread automation. List some jobs that humans may not want to do but that would be good for an automated worker. Describe how AI and automation will create new types of jobs to replace those that will be lost and why workers will have to adapt to these changes. List skills that can help you adapt to a shifting workplace caused by AI and automation.

Q3-7   What is the goal of AI?

Define *strong AI*, *weak AI*, and *superintelligence*. Describe the *Turing test*. Explain why the major AI research areas shown in Figure 3-29 seek to simulate all human abilities. Describe how each of these major AI research areas might be used in a self-driving car. Describe the potential effects of saying "no" to AI.

Q3-8   How does AI work?

Define *machine learning*, *algorithm*, and *Naïve Bayes Classifier*. Describe how machine learning uses training data to predict future outcomes. Summarize how machine learning can be used to detect spam as shown in Figure 3-30. Define *natural language processing*. Describe how IBM's AI named Watson could be used by organizations to help answer user questions. Summarize how the question and answer process used by IBM's Watson works as shown in Figure 3-31.

Q3-9   2029?

Summarize how retailers can use BI to target customers. Explain why companies in the future will know more about you than just your purchasing habits. What are some positives and negatives to analyzing this kind of data? Describe how AI might automate certain types of BI analyst jobs. Summarize the way AI could

spiral out of human control. In your opinion, is this a problem? Why or why not? Describe how Kurzweil's singularity might affect humanity.

Using Your Knowledge with eHermes

From this chapter, you know the three phases of BI analysis, and you have learned common techniques for acquiring, processing, and publishing business intelligence. This knowledge will enable you to imagine innovative uses for the data that your employer generates and also to know some of the constraints of such use. At eHermes, the knowledge of this chapter will help you understand possible ways to use customer sales data to increase revenue, or possibly an AI to help optimize eHermes' operational efficiency.

KEY TERMS AND CONCEPTS

Algorithm   98
Artificial intelligence (AI)   89
Automation   89
BI analysis   70
BI application   68
Big Data   83
BI server   87
Business intelligence (BI)   68
Business intelligence (BI) systems   68
Cluster analysis   82
Content management systems
    (CMS)   89
Cookie   108
Corpus of knowledge   100
Data acquisition   69
Data mart   75
Data mining   80
Data warehouse   74
Decision support systems   69

Deep learning   91
Dimension   79
Drill down   80
Dynamic reports   86
Exception reports   79
Geofencing   84
Granularity   75
Hadoop   85
Knowledge management (KM)   88
Machine learning   98
MapReduce   83
Measure   79
Naïve Bayes Classifier   98
Natural language processing
    (NLP)   100
Neural network   91
OLAP cube   80
Online analytical processing
    (OLAP)   79

Pig   85
Publish results   70
Pull publishing   70
Push publishing   70
Regression analysis   82
Reporting analysis   78
Reporting application   78
RFM analysis   79
Static reports   86
Strong AI   95
Structured data   78
Subscriptions   86
Superintelligence   95
Supervised data mining   82
The Singularity   101
Third-party cookie   108
Turing test   96
Unsupervised data mining   82
Weak AI   95

MyLab MIS

To complete the problems with MyLab MIS, go to EOC Discussion Questions in the MyLab.

USING YOUR KNOWLEDGE

3-1. Suppose a hospital adopts a BI system paid for by a large pharmaceutical company. The system provides automated drug recommendations to doctors for each patient. According to the categorical imperative, is this ethical? Is it ethical according to utilitarianism? Do you believe it is ethical?

3-2. Explain in your own words how the sales analysis team in Q3-1 implemented each of the five criteria it developed. Use the data and tables shown in Q3-1 in your answer.

3-3. In Q3-1, the sales analysis team created a query that connected the selected parts with their past sales data (Sales History for Selected Parts). Explain why the query results do not show promise for the selling of these part designs. In light of these results, should the team look at changing its criteria? If so, how? If not, why not?

3-4. Given the results from the Sales History for Selected Parts query, list three actions that the company can take. Recommend one of these actions and justify your recommendation.

3-5. Describe a use for RFM analysis for Costco. Explain what you would do for customers who have the following scores: [5, 5, 5], [3, 5, 5], [5, 2, 5], [3, 3, 5], [5, 5, 3]. Is this analysis useful to Costco? Explain your answer.

3-6. Define the characteristics of Big Data. Identify and describe three student-related applications at your university that meet Big Data characteristics. Describe patterns and relationships that might be found within that data.

3-7. CogniToys uses IBM's Watson to power its Dino toy. Dino answers questions children (or grown-ups) ask it but in a customized way. It remembers the age of the person asking the questions and gives more complex answers to older children. It also plays games, tells jokes, and keeps track of the child's progress in a variety of subjects. Parents can access online reports to see how well their child is progressing. Describe how IBM's Watson could change formal education. How might Watson be used to help educate children in developing countries?

3-8. Thought leaders like Bill Gates, Elon Musk, and the late Stephen Hawking have expressed concerns about the potential harm that could come from AI. For example, Stephen Hawking warned that AI could evolve beyond the control of humans and cause the end of mankind. Describe some of the potential harmful effects that could come from advanced AI (superintelligence). If AI-powered robots could do 95 percent of current human jobs, what will humans do?

COLLABORATION EXERCISE 3

Using the collaboration IS you built in Chapter 1 (page 32), collaborate with a group of students to answer the following questions.

Read Case Study 3 (pages 108–109) if you have not already done so. Undeniably, third-party cookies offer advantages to online sellers. They also increase the likelihood that consumers will receive online ads that are close to their interests; thus, third-party cookies can provide a consumer service as well. But at what cost to personal privacy? And what should be done about them? Working with your team, answer the following questions:

3-9. Summarize the ways that third-party cookies are created and processed. Even though cookies are not supposed to contain personally identifying data, explain how such data can readily be obtained. (See question 3-19.)

3-10. Numerous browser features, add-ins, and other tools exist for blocking third-party cookies. Search the Web for *block third-party cookies for xxx* and fill in the *xxx* with the name and version of your browser. Read the instructions and summarize the procedures that you need to take to view the cookies issued from a given site.

3-11. In large measure, ads pay for the free use of Web content and even Web sites themselves. If, because of a fear of privacy, many people block third-party cookies, substantial ad revenue will be lost. Discuss with your group how such a movement would affect the valuation of Facebook and other ad-revenue-dependent companies. Discuss how it would affect the delivery of free online content such as that supplied by *Forbes* or other providers.

3-12. Many companies have a conflict of interest with regard to third-party cookies. On the one hand, such cookies help generate revenue and pay for Internet content. On the other hand, trespassing on users' privacy could turn out to be a PR disaster. As you learned in your answer to question 3-10, browsers include options to block third-party cookies. However, in most cases, those options are turned off in the default browser installation. Discuss why that might be so. If sites were required to obtain your permission before installing third-party cookies, how would you determine whether to grant it? List criteria that your team thinks would actually be used (as opposed to what the team thinks *should* be used). Assess the effectiveness of such a policy.

3-13. The processing of third-party cookies is hidden; we don't know what is being done behind the scenes with the data about our own behavior. Because there is so much of it and so many parties involved, the possibilities are difficult to comprehend, even if the descriptions were available. And if your privacy is compromised by the interaction of seven different companies working independently, which company is to be held accountable? Summarize consequences of these facts to consumers.

3-14. Summarize the benefits of third-party cookies to consumers.

3-15. Given all you have learned about third-party cookies, what does your team think should be done about them? Possible answers are: (a) nothing, (b) require Web sites to ask users before installing third-party cookies, (c) require browsers to block third-party cookies, (d) require browsers to block third-party cookies by default but enable them at the users' option, and (e) something else. Discuss these alternatives among your team, and recommend one. Justify your recommendation.

CASE STUDY 3

Hadoop the Cookie Cutter

A **cookie** is data that a Web site stores on your computer to record something about its interaction with you. The cookie might contain data such as the date you last visited, whether you are currently signed in, or something else about your interaction with that site. Cookies can also contain a key value to one or more tables in a database that the server company maintains about your past interactions. In that case, when you access a site, the server uses the value of the cookie to look up your history. Such data could include your past purchases, portions of incomplete transactions, or the data and appearance you want for your Web page. Most of the time cookies ease your interaction with Web sites.

Cookie data includes the URL of the Web site of the cookie's owner. Thus, for example, when you go to Amazon, it asks your browser to place a cookie on your computer that includes its name, *www.amazon.com*. Your browser will do so unless you have turned cookies off.

A **third-party cookie** is a cookie created by a site other than the one you visited. Such cookies are generated in several ways, but the most common occurs when a Web page includes content from multiple sources. For example, Amazon designs its pages so that one or more sections contain ads provided by the ad-servicing company, DoubleClick. When the browser constructs your Amazon page, it contacts DoubleClick to obtain the content for such sections (in this case, ads). When it responds with the content, DoubleClick instructs your browser to store a Double-Click cookie. That cookie is a third-party cookie. In general, third-party cookies do not contain the name or any value that identifies a particular user. Instead, they include the IP address to which the content was delivered.

On its own servers, when it creates the cookie, DoubleClick records that data in a log, and if you click on the ad, it will add the fact of that click to the log. This logging is repeated every time DoubleClick shows an ad. Cookies have an expiration date, but that date is set by the cookie creator, and they can last many years. So, over time, DoubleClick and any other third-party cookie owner will have a history of what they've shown, what ads have been clicked, and the intervals between interactions.

But the opportunity is even greater. DoubleClick has agreements not only with Amazon but also with many others, such as Facebook. If Facebook includes any DoubleClick content on its site, DoubleClick will place another cookie on your computer. This cookie is different from the one that it placed via Amazon, but both cookies have your IP address and other data sufficient to associate the second cookie as originating from the same source as the first. So, DoubleClick now has a record of your ad response data on two sites. Over time, the cookie log will contain data to show not only how you respond to ads but also your pattern of visiting various Web sites on all those sites in which it places ads.

You might be surprised to learn how many third-party cookies you have. The browser Firefox has an optional feature called *Lightbeam* that tracks and graphs all the cookies on your computer. Figure 3-32 shows the cookies that were placed on my computer as I visited various Web sites. As you can see, in Figure 3-32a, when I started my computer and browser, there were no cookies. The cookies on my computer after I visited *www.msn.com* are shown in Figure 3-32b. At this point, there are already eight third-party cookies tracking. After I visited five sites, I had 27 third-party cookies, and after I visited seven sites I had 69, as shown in Figures 3-32c and d.

Who are these companies that are gathering my browser behavior data? If you hold your mouse over one of the cookies, Lightbeam will highlight it in the data column on the right. As you can see in Figure 3-30d , after visiting seven sites, Double-Click was connected to a total of 16 other sites, only seven of which are sites I visited. So, DoubleClick is connecting to sites I don't even know about and on my computer. Examine the connection column on the right. I visited MSN, Amazon, MyNorth-west, and WSJ, but who are Bluekai and Rubiconproject? I never

a. Display on Startup

b. After MSN.com and gmail

c. Five Sites Visited Yield 27 Third Parties

d. Sites Connected to DoubleClick

FIGURE 3-32
Third-Party Cookie Growth
Source: © Mozilla Corporation.

heard of them until I saw this display. They, apparently, have heard of me, however!

Third-party cookies generate incredible volumes of log data. For example, suppose a company, such as DoubleClick, shows 100 ads to a given computer in a day. If it is showing ads to 10 million computers (possible), that is a total of 1 billion log entries per day, or 365 billion a year. Truly this is Big Data.

Storage is essentially free, but how can they possibly process all that data? How do they parse the log to find entries just for your computer? How do they integrate data from different cookies on the same IP address? How do they analyze those entries to determine which ads you clicked on? How do they then characterize differences in ads to determine which characteristics matter most to you? The answer, as you learned in Q3-6, is to use parallel processing. Using a MapReduce algorithm, they distribute the work to thousands of processors that work in parallel. They aggregate the results of these independent processors and then, possibly, move to a second phase of analysis where they do it again. Hadoop, the open source program that you learned about in Q3-6, is a favorite for this process.

(See the collaboration exercise on page 107 for a continuation of the discussion: third-party cookies—problem? Or opportunity?)

QUESTIONS

3-16. Using your own words, explain how third-party cookies are created.

3-17. Suppose you are an ad-serving company, and you maintain a log of cookie data for ads you serve to Web pages for a particular vendor (say, Amazon).

    a. How can you use this data to determine which are the best ads?

    b. How can you use this data to determine which are the best ad formats?

    c. How could you use records of past ads and ad clicks to determine which ads to send to a given IP address?

    d. How could you use this data to determine how well the technique you used in your answer to question c was working?

    e. How could you use this data to determine that a given IP address is used by more than one person?

    f. How does having this data give you a competitive advantage vis-à-vis other ad-serving companies?

3-18. Suppose you are an ad-serving company, and you have a log of cookie data for ads served to Web pages of all your customers (Amazon, Facebook, etc.).

   a. Describe, in general terms, how you can process the cookie data to associate log entries for a particular IP address.

   b. Explain how your answers to question 3-10 change, given that you have this additional data.

   c. Describe how you can use this log data to determine users who consistently seek the lowest price.

   d. Describe how you can use this log data to determine users who consistently seek the latest fashion.

   e. Explain why users like those in parts c and d above are only possible with MapReduce or a similar technique.

3-19. As stated, third-party cookies usually do not contain, in themselves, data that identifies you as a particular person. However, Amazon, Facebook, and other first-party cookie vendors know who you are because you signed in. Only one of them needs to reveal your identity to the ad server and your identity can then be correlated with your IP address. At that point, the ad server and potentially all of its clients know who you are. Are you concerned about the invasion of your privacy that third-party cookies enable? Explain your answer.

MyLab MIS

Go to the Assignments section of your MyLab to complete these writing exercises.

3-20. Reflect on the differences among reporting systems, data mining systems, and Big Data systems. What are their similarities and differences? How do their costs differ? What benefits does each offer? How would an organization choose among them?

3-21. Install Firefox, if you do not already have it, and then install the Lightbeam add-on. Visit the sites you normally visit first thing in your day.

   a. How many third-party sites are you connected to?

   b. Find DoubleClick in the Lightbeam display. List the companies that DoubleClick is connected to that you did not visit.

   c. Choose one of the companies in your answer to question 3-21b. Google it and describe what it does.

3-22. Suppose you work for an online sporting goods retailer. You've been hired as a business analyst with the task of increasing sales. Describe how you could use RFM to increase the sales of sporting goods. If used effectively, how could RFM affect customer satisfaction?

ENDNOTES

1. PricewaterhouseCoopers. *2015 U.S. CEO Survey*, accessed May 24, 2018, *www.pwc.com/us/en/ceo-survey/index.html*.

2. Clint Boulton, "Why CEOs Must Go Big in Digital (or Go Home)," *CIO.com*, May 2, 2016, accessed May 24, 2018, *www.cio.com/article/3064592/cio-role/why-ceos-must-go-big-in-digital-or-go-home.html*.

3. Nipun Gupta, "Top 10 Databases in the World," May 4, 2014, accessed May 24, 2018, *http://csnipuntech.blogspot.com/2014/05/top-10-largest-databases-in-world.html*.

4. Arthur Middleton Hughes, "Quick Profits with RFM Analysis," *Database Marketing Institute*, May 31, 2016, *www.dbmarketing.com/articles/Art149.htm*.

5. Salesforce, "The Power of Geofencing and How to Add It to Your Marketing," *Salesforce*, April 18, 2018, *www.salesforce.com/products/marketing-cloud/best-practices/geofencing-marketing/*.

6. Yuki Noguchi, "Recruiters Use 'Geofencing' to Target Potential Hires Where They Live and Work," *All Tech Considered*, July 7, 2017, *www.npr.org/sections/alltechconsidered/2017/07/07/535981386/recruiters-use-geofencing-to-target-potential-hires-where-they-live-and-work*.

7. Ibid.

8. Salesforce, "The Power of Geofencing and How to Add It to Your Marketing," *Salesforce*, April 18, 2018, *www.salesforce.com/products/marketing-cloud/best-practices/geofencing-marketing/*.

9. Yuki Noguchi, "Recruiters Use 'Geofencing' to Target Potential Hires Where They Live and Work," *All Tech Considered*, July 7, 2017, *www.npr.org/sections/alltechconsidered/2017/07/07/535981386/recruiters-use-geofencing-to-target-potential-hires-where-they-live-and-work*.

10. A nonprofit corporation that supports open source software projects, originally those for the Apache Web server but today for a large number of additional major software projects.

11. Meridith Levinson, "Knowledge Management Definition and Solutions," *CIO Magazine*, accessed May 29, 2016, *www.cio.com/article/2439279/enterprise-software/knowledge-management-definitionand-solutions.html*.

12. Paul Miller, "Professor Pranksman Fools His Students with a TA Powered by IBM's Watson," *The Verge*, May 6, 2016, accessed May 26, 2018, *www.theverge.com/2016/5/6/11612520/ta-powered-by-ibm-watson*.

13. Beijia Ma, Sarbjit Nahal, and Felix Tran, "Robot Revolution—Global Robot & AI Primer," Bank of America Merrill Lynch, December 16, 2015, accessed May 26, 2018, *www.bofaml.com/content/dam/boamlimages/documents/PDFs/robotics_and_ai_condensed_primer.pdf.*

14. Cheyenne Macdonald, "Artificial Intelligence Will Outperform Humans in All Tasks in Just 45 Years and Could Take Over EVERY Job in the Next Century, Experts Claim," *Dailymail.com,* May 31, 2017, accessed May 26, 2018, *www.dailymail.co.uk/sciencetech/article-4560824/AI-outperform-humans-tasks-just-45-years.html.*

15. Robert D. Hof, "Deep Learning," *TechnologyReview.com,* April 23, 2013, accessed May 26, 2018, *www.technologyreview.com/s/513696/deep-learning/.*

16. Stefanie Fogel, "Burger-Flipping Robot Has Its First Day on the Job in California," *Engadget.com,* March 8, 2017, accessed May 26, 2018, *www.engadget.com/2017/03/08/burger-flipping-robot-flippy/.*

17. *www.bls.gov/news.release/ecec.toc.htm.*

18. David Migoya, "More Consumers Banking by Mobile App," *DenverPost.com,* April 11, 2013, accessed May 26, 2018, *www.denverpost.com/2013/04/11/more-consumers-banking-by-mobile-app.*

19. Association of Certified Fraud Examiners, "Report to the Nations on Occupational Fraud and Abuse," *ACFE.com,* March 30, 2016, accessed May 26, 2018, *www.acfe.com/rttn2016.aspx.*

20. William H. Davidow and Michael S. Malone, "What Happens to Society When Robots Replace Workers?" *Harvard Business Review,* December 10, 2014, accessed May 26, 2018, *https://hbr.org/2014/12/what-happens-to-society-when-robots-replace-workers.*

21. Carl Benedikt Frey and Ebrahim Rahbari, "Technology at Work v2.0," Citi GPS, January 2016, accessed May 26, 2018, *www.oxfordmartin.ox.ac.uk/downloads/reports/Citi_GPS_Technology_Work_2.pdf.*

22. Chris Kreinczes, "Artificial Intelligence Innovation Report 2016," Deloitte and Springwise Intelligence Ltd., 2016, accessed May 26, 2018, *www2.deloitte.com/content/dam/Deloitte/at/Documents/human-capital/artificial-intelligence-innovation-report.pdf.*

23. Rodney Brooks, "Artificial Intelligence Is a Tool, Not a Threat," *RethinkRobotics.com,* November 10, 2014, accessed May 26, 2018, *www.rethinkrobotics.com/blog/artificial-intelligence-tool-threat.*

24. Beijia Ma, Sarbjit Nahal, and Felix Tran, "Robot Revolution—Global Robot & AI Primer," Bank of America Merrill Lynch, December 16, 2015, accessed May 26, 2018, *www.bofaml.com/content/dam/boamlimages/documents/PDFs/robotics_and_ai_condensed_primer.pdf.*

25. Paul Graham, "A Plan for Spam," *PaulGraham.com,* August 2002, accessed May 26, 2018, *www.paulgraham.com/spam.html.*

26. Christina Mercer, "17 Innovative Businesses Using IBM Watson," *ComputerWorldUK.com,* June 29, 2017, accessed May 26, 2018, *www.computerworlduk.com/galleries/it-vendors/16-innovative-ways-companies-are-using-ibm-watson-3585847/.*

27. David Ferrucci, Eric Brown, Jennifer Chu-Carroll, James Fan, David Gondek, Aditya A. Kal-yanpur, Adam Lally, J. William Murdock, Eric Nyberg, John Prager, Nico Schlaefer, and Chris Welty, "Building Watson: An Overview of the DeepQA Project," *AI Magazine,* Fall 2010, accessed May 26, 2018, *www.aaai.org/Magazine/Watson/watson.php.*

28. Ian Paul, "IBM Watson Wins Jeopardy, Humans Rally Back," *PCWorld.com,* February 17, 2011, accessed May 26, 2018, *www.pcworld.com/article/219900/IBM_Watson_Wins_Jeopardy_Humans_Rally_Back.html.*

29. Ben Algaze, "The Singularity Is Near," *ExtremeTech,* March 15, 2018, accessed May 29, 2018, *www.extremetech.com/extreme/265673-ai-sxsw-2018-hives-ethics-morals-singularity.*

30. AnnaMaria Andriotis, Michael Rapoport, and Robert McMillan, "'We've Been Breached': Inside the Equifax Hack," *The Wall Street Journal,* March 26, 2018, *www.wsj.com/articles/weve-been-breached-inside-the-equifax-hack-1505693318.*

31. Ibid.

32. Ibid.

33. Anna Werner, "Months After Massive Equifax Data Breach, Victims Struggling to Recover," *CBS News,* March 26, 2018, *www.cbsnews.com/news/equifax-data-breach-victims-struggling-to-recover/.*

34. Ibid.

35. Brett Molina, "Equifax Support Team Sent Victims of Breach to Fake Site," *USA Today,* March 26, 2018, *www.usatoday.com/story/tech/talkingtech/2017/09/21/equifax-support-team-sent-victims-breach-phishing-site/688188001/.*

36. Ibid.

Information Technology

The next three chapters address the technology that underlies information systems. You may think that such technology is unimportant to you as a business professional. However, as you will see, today's managers and business professionals work with information technology all the time as consumers, if not in a more involved way.

Chapter 4 discusses hardware, software, and open source alternatives and defines basic terms and fundamental computing concepts. It briefly touches on new developments in the Internet of Things, augmented reality, self-driving cars, 3D printing, and cryptocurrencies. It also looks at the importance of Web applications and mobile systems.

Chapter 5 addresses the data component of information systems by describing database processing. You will learn essential database terminology and will be introduced to techniques for processing databases. We will also introduce data modeling because you may be required to evaluate data models for databases that others develop for you.

Source: Chesky/Shutterstock

Chapter 6 continues the discussion of computing devices begun in Chapter 4 and describes data communications, Internet technologies, and cloud-based services. It looks at how organizations can use the cloud effectively and addresses potential security problems that may come from using the cloud.

The purpose of these three chapters is to teach technology sufficient for you to be an effective IT consumer, like Jessica, Victor, Kamala, Tess, and Seth at eHermes. You will learn basic terms, fundamental concepts, and useful frameworks so that you will have the knowledge to ask good questions and make appropriate requests of the information systems professionals who will serve you.

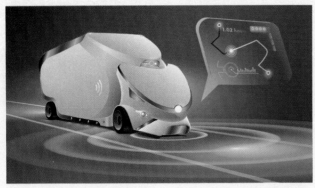

Source: Andrey Suslov/Shutterstock

It's difficult to stay up to date on the latest technology changes because things are changing so quickly. Every year, a slew of new innovations come out. Some of them may represent real threats to your organization's strategy. Others may represent potential new opportunities for growth. It's important to be able to understand the strategic implications these new technologies represent. You need to be able to ask the right questions.

The concepts and frameworks presented in these chapters will be far more useful to you than learning the latest technology trends. Trends come and go. The technology you're using now will be outdated in 10 years. Understanding how to assess the business implications behind any new innovation will be a benefit to you through your entire career.

CHAPTER 4

Hardware, Software, and Mobile Systems

"How is the AI project going, Kam?" asks Jessica with a smile on her face, hoping for good news. Kamala Patel, eHermes' automation subject matter expert (SME), has asked Jessica Ramma, CEO; Victor Vazquez, COO; and Tess Visser, VP of Sales, to come down to the large warehouse to see how the AI project is coming along. Jessica asked Kamala to see if she could feed the company's data into an AI and improve operational efficiency. If the project is successful, it could save the company a lot of money.

"It's going OK. Well, actually, it's going much more slowly than we thought," Kamala says, shaking her head slightly and pointing to a map of the city on a large monitor showing multicolored routes, destinations, and mobile storefronts. "Putting it all together is turning out to be a lot more work than we initially thought. My expertise is self-driving vehicles, not AI. I think I've gotten in over my head. We really need an AI expert to make this work."

MyLab MIS

Using Your Knowledge
Questions 4-1, 4-2, 4-3
Essay Questions 4-17, 4-18

"When we talked about this a couple of months ago, you said it could work. What's changed?" Jessica asks with a disappointed tone in her voice.

"Nothing has changed. It will still work. It will save us a lot of money, too. It could cut our costs by at least 20 percent and double our operational efficiency. But, to get to that point, it will take a lot more time and money than we initially thought," Kamala says, nodding with a hint of encouragement.

Tess spins around and points to one of the screens. "You see, right now we load up each mobile storefront with similar types of items that we think a person might buy. Say a customer wants to buy baby clothes. Well, they might be interested in buying other baby-related items. So, we send a storefront full of baby items to that location, and the customer usually ends up buying more than just baby clothes."

"And then we get the ice-cream-truck effect when people hear our eHermes chimes being played in the neighborhood," Kamala adds. "Multiple neighbors come out and buy items from that same truck. They also bring out their own items for sale. The time spent at each stop varies. There's a lot of time spent selling items and logging new items that customers want to sell. It's difficult to predict how long a storefront will stay at a given location."

Jessica looks slightly confused. "But we've seen this for the past couple of years. As people became more aware of eHermes, the duration of stops has increased. Why would this affect the AI project?"

"For a couple of reasons. First, we don't have enough data to train the AI. It takes a lot of data to train an AI to come up with optimal solutions. The variability in the way our business operates doesn't help. We're growing quickly, and the data from a few years ago isn't good training data. Second, I've been leaning on a friend of mine from graduate school to help me figure this all out. It's extraordinarily complex, and I'm not an AI expert. We're trying to optimize more than just a supply chain. We're really a company that combines shipping, online retailing, and physical retailing. We have to optimize routes, stops, probable sales, customer buying habits, inventory management—"

"We don't have enough data to train the AI."

Source: Haiyin Wang/Alamy Stock Photo

Study QUESTIONS

Q4-1 What do business professionals need to know about computer hardware?

Q4-2 How can new hardware affect competitive strategies?

Q4-3 What do business professionals need to know about software?

Q4-4 Is open source software a viable alternative?

Q4-5 What are the differences between native and Web applications?

Q4-6 Why are mobile systems increasingly important?

Q4-7 What are the challenges of personal mobile devices at work?

Q4-8 2029?

Victor interrupts Kamala with a look of concern on his face. "What would it take to make this work? How much would it cost?"

"At this point, probably more than we've got. We'd have to hire at least two AI experts and a team of mid-level people. That won't be cheap. We'd also need to spend more on infrastructure for the additional processing power, data storage, and back-end systems. Our cash burn rate will increase substantially."

Jessica looks visibly disappointed. "What if we hired a few more people for you to manage? Would that be enough?"

Kamala smiles. "No, not even close. I was swamped before we even started this project. I've been neglecting software upgrades to our self-driving vehicles, and more importantly, I need to finish the new systems development project to automate the data collection from the storefronts. We'll make a lot more money if we can log new inventory into our system as soon as we receive it from sellers and then sell it immediately."

Jessica looks disappointed. "Well, maybe you're right. I really wish there was some way to make it work. We can't grow quickly enough without an optimization system that doesn't even exist yet. It's really frustrating being on the cutting edge."

"You mean the bleeding edge. . .right?" Victor asks with a smirk.

Chapter PREVIEW

What would you do if you were Jessica? Or Victor? Would you go ahead and build your own AI? It would save you money down the road. It might even give you a competitive advantage over potential entrants into your market. You might be able to hire a team of AI people without breaking the bank. Is Kamala being too conservative? If you're wondering why, as a future business professional, you need to know about hardware and software, think about those questions. Those questions and others of greater complexity—most likely ones involving technology that will be invented between now and the time you start working—will come your way.

You don't need to be an expert. You don't need to be a hardware engineer or a computer programmer. You do need to know enough, however, to be an effective consumer. You need the knowledge and skills to ask important, relevant questions and understand the answers.

We begin with basic hardware concepts and how innovations in hardware could affect businesses. Next, we will discuss software concepts, open source software development, and the differences between native and Web applications. Following that, we'll discuss the importance of mobile systems and the challenges created when employees bring their computers to work. Finally, we'll wrap up by forecasting trends in hardware and software in 2029.

Q4-1 What Do Business Professionals Need to Know About Computer Hardware?

Most people think of computer hardware as a laptop, a desktop, a server, or maybe even a tablet. As time passes, the way we think of computer hardware is changing. Take phones as an example. Twenty-five years ago, they were strictly used for voice communication. No one would have considered a phone a piece of computer hardware.

Fast-forward to today. Smartphones have substantial processing power, the ability to connect to networks, internal memory, and virtual keyboards and can interconnect with other devices. Now a "phone" is essentially a powerful piece of computing hardware. Computing hardware is also being integrated into other devices such as watches, glasses, TVs, cars, and even toothbrushes.

Computer hardware consists of electronic components and related gadgetry that input, process, output, and store data according to instructions encoded in computer programs or software. All hardware today has more or less the same components, at least to the level that is important to us. We'll begin with those components, and then we'll quickly survey basic types of computers.

Hardware Components

Every computer has a **central processing unit (CPU)**, which is sometimes called "the brain" of the computer. Although the design of the CPU has nothing in common with the anatomy of animal brains, this description is helpful because the CPU does have the "smarts" of the machine. The CPU selects instructions, processes them, performs arithmetic and logical comparisons, and stores results of operations in memory. Some computers have two or more CPUs. A computer with two CPUs is called a **dual-processor** computer. **Quad-processor** computers have four CPUs. Some high-end computers have 16 or more CPUs.

CPUs vary in speed, function, and cost. Hardware vendors such as Intel, Advanced Micro Devices, and National Semiconductor continually improve CPU speed and capabilities while reducing CPU costs (as discussed under Moore's Law in Chapter 1). Whether you or your department needs the latest, greatest CPU depends on the nature of your work.

The CPU works in conjunction with **main memory**. The CPU reads data and instructions from memory and then stores the results of computations in main memory. Main memory is sometimes called **RAM**, for random access memory.

All computers include **storage hardware**, which is used to save data and programs. Magnetic disks (also called hard disks) are the most common storage device. **Solid-state storage (SSD)** (or an SSD drive) is much faster than traditional magnetic storage because it stores information using nonvolatile electronic circuits. SSD drives are gaining in popularity but are several times more expensive than magnetic hard disks. USB flash drives are small, portable solid-state storage devices that can be used to back up data and transfer it from one computer to another. Optical disks such as CDs and DVDs are also popular portable storage media.

Types of Hardware

Figure 4-1 lists the basic types of hardware. **Personal computers** (PCs) are classic computing devices that are used by individuals. In the past, PCs were the primary computer used in business. Today, they are gradually being supplanted by tablets and other mobile devices. The Mac Pro is an example of a modern PC. Apple brought **tablets** to prominence with the iPad. In 2012, Microsoft announced Surface and Google announced the Nexus series, all tablets. Moving down the list of hardware, a mobile device called a **phablet** combines the functionality of a smartphone with the larger screen of a tablet. Devices like Samsung's Galaxy Note or Apple's iPhone 8 Plus would fall into this crossover category. **Smartphones** are cell phones with processing capability; the Samsung Galaxy S9 and iPhone 8 are good examples. Today, because it's hard to find a cell phone that isn't "smart," people often just call them phones.

Hardware Type	Example(s)
Personal computer (PC) *Including desktops and laptops*	Apple Mac Pro
Tablet *Including e-book readers*	iPad, Microsoft Surface, Google Nexus, Kindle Fire
Phablet	Samsung Galaxy Note, iPhone 8 Plus
Smartphone	Samsung Galaxy, iPhone
Server	Dell PowerEdge Server
Server farm	Racks of servers (Figure 4-2)

FIGURE 4-1
Basic Types of Hardware

FIGURE 4-2
Server Farm
Source: Andrew Twort/Alamy Stock Photo

A **server** is a computer that is designed to support processing requests from many remote computers and users. A server is essentially a PC on steroids. A server differs from a PC principally because of what it does. The relationship between PCs and servers is similar to the relationship between clients and servers at a typical restaurant. Servers take requests from clients and then bring them things. In restaurants this is food and silverware. In computing environments servers can send Web pages, email, files, or data to PCs. PCs, tablets, and smartphones that access servers are called **clients**. As of 2018, a good example of a server is the Dell PowerEdge server.

Finally, a **server farm** is a collection of, typically, thousands of servers. (See Figure 4-2.) Server farms are often placed in large truck trailers that hold 5,000 servers or more. Typically a trailer has two large cables coming out of it; one is for power, and the other is for data communications. The operator of the farm backs a trailer into a pre-prepared slab (in a warehouse or sometimes out in the open air), plugs in the power and communications cables, and, voilà, thousands of servers are up and running!

Increasingly, server infrastructure is delivered as a service via the Internet that is often referred to as *the cloud*. We will discuss cloud computing in Chapter 6, after you have some knowledge of data communications.

The capacities of computer hardware are specified according to data units, which we discuss next.

Computer Data

Computers represent data using **binary digits**, called **bits**. A bit is either a zero or a one. Bits are used for computer data because they are easy to represent physically, as illustrated in Figure 4-3. A switch can be either closed or open. A computer can be designed so that an open switch represents zero and a closed switch represents one. Or the orientation of a magnetic field can represent a bit: magnetism in one direction represents a zero; magnetism in the opposite direction represents a one. Or, for optical media, small pits are burned onto the surface of the disk so that they will reflect light. In a given spot, a reflection means a one; no reflection means a zero.

Computer Data Sizes

All forms of computer data are represented by bits. The data can be numbers, characters, currency amounts, photos, recordings, or whatever. All are simply a string of bits. For reasons that interest many but are irrelevant for future managers, bits are grouped into 8-bit chunks called **bytes**. For

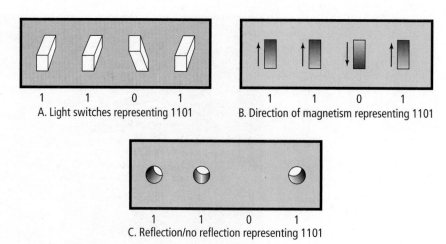

FIGURE 4-3
Bits Are Easy to Represent Physically

A. Light switches representing 1101

B. Direction of magnetism representing 1101

C. Reflection/no reflection representing 1101

character data, such as the letters in a person's name, one character will fit into one byte. Thus, when you read a specification that a computing device has 100 million bytes of memory, you know that the device can hold up to 100 million characters.

Bytes are used to measure sizes of noncharacter data as well. Someone might say, for example, that a given picture is 100,000 bytes in size. This statement means the length of the bit string that represents the picture is 100,000 bytes or 800,000 bits (because there are 8 bits per byte).

The specifications for the size of main memory, disk, and other computer devices are expressed in bytes. Figure 4-4 shows the set of abbreviations that are used to represent data storage capacity. A **kilobyte**, abbreviated **KB**, is a collection of 1,024 bytes. A **megabyte**, or **MB**, is 1,024 kilobytes. A **gigabyte**, or **GB**, is 1,024 megabytes; a **terabyte**, or **TB**, is 1,024 gigabytes; a **petabyte**, or **PB**, is 1,024 terabytes; an **exabyte**, or **EB**, is 1,024 petabytes; and a **zettabyte**, or **ZB**, is 1,024 exabytes. Sometimes you will see these definitions simplified as 1KB equals 1,000 bytes and 1MB equals 1,000KB, and so on. Such simplifications are incorrect, but they do ease the math.

To put these sizes in perspective consider that Walmart processes about 40 PB worth of customer data per day.[1] Facebook processes about 600 TB each day, in a 300PB data warehouse.[2] The super-secret NSA data center in Utah is estimated to hold about 12 EB of data.[3] And Cisco estimates that annual global Internet traffic volume will exceed 3.3 ZB by the end of 2021.[4]

Specifying Hardware with Computer Data Sizes

Computer disk capacities are specified according to the amount of data they can contain. Thus, a 5TB disk can contain up to 5TB of data and programs. There is some overhead, so it is not quite 5TB, but it's close enough.

Term	Definition	Abbreviation
Byte	Number of bits to represent one character	
Kilobyte	1,024 bytes	KB
Megabyte	1,024 KB = 1,048,576 bytes	MB
Gigabyte	1,024 MB = 1,073,741,824 bytes	GB
Terabyte	1,024 GB = 1,099,511,627,776 bytes	TB
Petabyte	1,024 TB = 1,125,899,906,842,624 bytes	PB
Exabyte	1,024 PB = 1,152,921,504,606,846,976 bytes	EB
Zettabyte	1,024 EB = 1,180,591,620,717,411,303,424 bytes	ZB

FIGURE 4-4
Important Storage-Capacity Terminology

You can purchase computers with CPUs of different speeds. CPU speed is expressed in cycles called *hertz*. In 2018, a slow personal computer had a speed of 3.0 Gigahertz with multiple processors. A fast personal computer had a speed of 3.5+ Gigahertz, with multiple processors. An employee who does only simple tasks such as word processing does not need a fast CPU; a multi-core 3.0 Gigahertz CPU will be fine. However, an employee who processes large, complicated spreadsheets or who manipulates large database files or edits large picture, sound, or video files needs a fast computer like a multi-processor workstation with 3.5 Gigahertz or more. Employees whose work requires them to use many large applications at the same time need 32 GB or more of RAM. Others can do with less.

One last comment: The cache and main memory are **volatile**, meaning their contents are lost when power is off. Magnetic and optical disks are **nonvolatile**, meaning their contents survive when power is off. If you suddenly lose power, the contents of unsaved memory—say, documents that have been altered—will be lost. Therefore, get into the habit of frequently (every few minutes or so) saving documents or files that you are changing. Save your documents before your roommate trips over the power cord.

Q4-2 How Can New Hardware Affect Competitive Strategies?

Organizations are interested in new hardware because they represent potential opportunities, or threats, to their ability to generate revenue. It's important to keep an eye on new tech hardware for the same reason you watch the weather forecast. You care about how the future will affect you.

Next, we will look at five new hardware developments that have the potential to disrupt existing organizations.

Internet of Things

The first disruptive force that has the power to change business is the **Internet of Things (IoT)**. This is the idea that objects are becoming connected to the Internet so they can interact with other devices, applications, or services. Everyday objects are being embedded with hardware capable of sensing, processing, and transmitting data. Objects can then connect to a network and share data with any other application, service, or device.

Take your mobile phone, for example; it's probably a smartphone. But it wasn't always "smart." It started out as a simple device that just handled voice calls. Over time it became a **smart device** by adding more processing power, more memory, Internet access, Wi-Fi connectivity, and the ability to interconnect with other devices and applications (Figure 4-5). People began to use their mobile phones much differently than before. It also changed the way businesses operate. In 2017, Amazon reported that more than 70 percent of its customers shopped using a mobile device.[5]

What happens when other devices become smart? How would your life change if you had access to a smart car, smart home appliances, or an entire smart building? Within a few short decades it's possible that you could interact with nearly every object around you from your smartphone. In fact, your devices will be able to talk to other devices, anticipate your actions, make changes, and configure themselves.

This shift away from "dumb" devices to interconnected smart devices is not lost on businesses. Consumers like smart devices and are willing to pay more for them. Businesses want to improve the existing devices they manufacture into a smart devices and then sell them for twice as much. If they don't, someone else will.

The iPhone, for example, was introduced by Apple Inc., a computing hardware and software company. The mobile phone market was already mature. Industry leaders could have created a

FIGURE 4-5
Smartphone Development
Source: Grgroup/Fotolia

smartphone, but they didn't. Apple's success with portable audio players (iPod) and mobile phones (iPhone) was a shot across the bow of other hardware manufacturers. A wave of smart devices is coming.

Impact of the Internet of Things

The impact of IoT will be felt by many different high-tech industries. Smart devices need microprocessors, memory, wireless network connections, a power source, and new software. These devices will also need new protocols, more bandwidth, and tighter security, and they will consume more energy.

A good example of this push toward smart devices is General Electric's (GE) Industrial Internet.[6] GE's Industrial Internet is a broad program focused on creating smart devices, analyzing the data from these devices, and then making changes that increase efficiencies, reduce waste, and improve decision making. GE sees the greatest potential for smart devices in hospitals, power grids, railroads, and manufacturing plants.

GE estimates that an average airline using smart devices in its jet aircraft could save an average of 2 percent in fuel consumption. The resulting fuel and carbon dioxide savings would be the equivalent of removing 10,000 cars from the road.[7]

Microsoft has also made tremendous gains using smart devices. Microsoft has created a network of 125 smart buildings spread over 500 acres in Redmond, Washington (Figure 4-6).[8] Its operations center processes 500 million data transactions every day from 30,000 devices, including heaters, air conditioners, lights, fans, and doors.

Microsoft engineers were able to reduce energy costs by 6 percent to 10 percent a year by identifying problems like wasteful lighting, competing heating and cooling systems, and rogue fans. For Microsoft, that's millions of dollars. What if every corporate building were a smart building? When you consider that 40 percent of the world's energy is consumed in corporate buildings, you can start to get an idea of the immense financial cost savings. Indirectly, this would also have a huge environmental and economic impact worldwide.

FIGURE 4-6
Microsoft's Redmond, WA, Campus
Source: Ian Dagnall/Alamy Stock Photo

Digital Reality Devices

The second disruptive force that has the power to change business is digital reality devices. Digital reality devices are an emerging technology with tremendous potential to revolutionize our daily lives. Much like the emergence of the Internet in the mid-1990s, these devices will create entirely new types of companies and change the way people live, work, shop, and entertain themselves. It's estimated that the digital reality market will be $160 billion by 2021.[9]

There are different levels of digital reality on a continuum from completely *real* environments to completely **virtual** environments, or simulated nonphysical environments. Before you start to think about how digital reality devices will affect business, you need to understand how the levels of digital reality differ. First, **reality** is the state of things as they actually exist. If you're reading the paper version of this textbook with your eyes, contact lenses, or glasses, you're seeing the real world without any digital alteration. You are (hopefully) experiencing reality.

Next comes augmented reality. **Augmented reality (AR)** is the altering of reality by overlaying digital information on real-world objects. Examples of AR devices include Google Glass ($1,250), Epson's Moverio Smart Glasses ($700), and Daqri Smart Helmet (est. $5,000 to $15,000). Essentially, these devices work like heads-up displays, giving users information about the real world they're experiencing. For example, an AR device could provide users directions in the form of virtual arrows being displayed on the roadway. Users could also read virtual emails displayed in the air or see virtual health data projected in front of them as they exercise.

The next step on the digital reality continuum, as shown in Figure 4-7, is mixed reality. **Mixed reality (MR)** is the combination of the real physical world with interactive virtual images or objects.

	Reality	Augmented Reality	Mixed Reality	Virtual Reality
Example	Glasses	Google Glass	Microsoft HoloLens	Facebook's Oculus Rift
Virtual Information	No	Yes	Yes	Yes
Virtual Objects	No	No	Yes	Yes
Virtual World	No	No	No	Yes

FIGURE 4-7
Levels of Digital Reality

Microsoft (HoloLens, $3,000) and Meta (Meta 2, $1,495) released their MR devices in early 2016. Both companies are marketing these devices to developers interested in creating digital reality applications. MR devices are generally perceived as having greater potential than AR devices due to their ability to interact with virtual objects in real time.

For example, using AR you could view a 2D virtual weather forecast projected on your wall. But with MR you would see a real-time 3D virtual model of your city created on your coffee table (Figure 4-8). It would show a virtual tornado moving toward the city, and you could interact with the 3D weather application to see its projected path. And this is just one example. Imagine watching sporting events live in high-definition 3D in the middle of your room.

There's one problem when discussing AR and MR devices. Currently, the term *augmented reality* isn't applied consistently. It's common to hear AR used to describe both AR and MR devices.[10] But this is normal for emerging technologies. Terms are created, refined, and stored in common speech as the technology develops. So don't be surprised to hear AR used to describe both types of digital reality.

The last step on the digital reality continuum is **virtual reality (VR)**, or a completely computer-generated virtual world with interactive digital objects. Here you'll find devices like Facebook's Oculus Rift ($465), Sony's PlayStation VR ($349), and Samsung Gear VR ($129). These are completely immersive experiences that try to create a strong **sense of presence**, or the illusion that a virtual experience is real. In other words, if a device were able to create a strong sense of presence, you'd lean back and hold on tight if you were on a virtual roller coaster about to go off the track.

Impact of Digital Reality Devices

Digital reality devices are developing in much the same way cellular phones developed over the past 20 years. In fact, it's entirely possible that the AR market could disrupt the smartphone market. Imagine taking calls, browsing the Web, messaging friends, and watching a movie without ever taking your smartphone out of your pocket.

The application of digital reality devices extends beyond personal use as well. Organizations are currently building digital reality applications for education, training, collaboration, new product design, "holoportation," gaming, sports, advertising, tourism, and shopping. For example, Lowe's new Holoroom allows customers to design and visualize their ideal room before they commit to major changes. Case Western Reserve University has partnered with Microsoft to develop 3D mixed-reality applications to teach anatomy in an interactive environment.[11]

The full impact of digital reality devices won't be understood for years—we just don't know how they'll be used. Even experts in the field are just starting to understand the implications of how digital reality devices will change organizations. The shift from 2D flat screens to a 3D virtual world

FIGURE 4-8
Digital Reality Applications
Source: Peshkov/Fotolia

is like changing vocations from being a painter to being a sculptor. It requires new skills, processes, tools, and ways of thinking. Digital reality devices are truly one of the most transformative innovations in hardware to come along in the past 20 years.

Self-Driving Cars

The third disruptive force that could change the way businesses operate is self-driving cars. A **self-driving car** (also known as a driverless car) uses a variety of sensors to navigate like a traditional car but without human intervention. It will be full of advanced hardware and integrated software and is the epitome of a mobile system. In fact, it will be so mobile that it will be able to move without anyone being in the car (Figure 4-9). Yes, self-driving cars are in your very near future.

A recent report by KPMG indicates that self-driving cars could reach nearly full adoption by 2050.[12] Most auto manufacturers (GM, Toyota, BMW, Ford, etc.) say they will have self-driving cars by 2021.[13] Uber, Waymo (Google), and Tesla have been testing self-driving cars for a few years now with more than 1 billion miles driven. Toyota announced its ePalette self-driving mobile store at the 2018 CES show. And Apple announced it is partnering with Volkswagen to make its first self-driving shuttles for its employees.[14] It looks like the race to develop self-driving cars is heating up. The competition will be fierce.

Self-driving cars will make things easier, cheaper, and safer. They'll also disrupt well-established industries.

Self-Driving Cars Make Things Easier

Imagine how a self-driving car will change the lives of a typical family. A self-driving car could allow Dad to review sales reports while "driving" to work. He's much less stressed out—and more

FIGURE 4-9
Future Cars Will Drive Themselves
Source: Dan Race/Fotolia

productive—during his commute than he was with his old car. The self-driving car could then drop off the kids at school—without Dad in the car—and return home to take Mom to work.

After work the family goes shopping and is dropped off curbside at the store. No need to park anymore. It's safer, too. While shopping, Dad gets a message from his college-aged daughter that she needs the car sent to pick her up from the airport. Dad's glad he won't have to drive all the way out there. Self-driving cars can also plan routes, fill themselves up with gas, take themselves to get repaired, and reroute themselves if there's an accident or traffic. There's no more stress or aggressive driving either.

Self-Driving Cars Make Things Cheaper

You've seen how a self-driving car can make your life easier. But what about cost? Will it be more expensive or less expensive than the car you have now? Self-driving cars will probably be much less expensive over time than your current car. Early adopters will pay a premium when self-driving cars first hit the market, but that's true of most new products. Cost savings will show up in several ways. In the preceding scenario, you may have noticed that the family had only one car. Self-driving cars will be used more effectively than cars are used now. Most cars sit dormant for 22 hours a day. Sharing a self-driving car could eliminate the need to have multiple cars. That's a big cost savings.

You'll see more cost savings because a self-driving car will drive more efficiently (less braking, revving the engine, and street racing!). You will avoid costly traffic tickets, parking tickets, accidents, and DUI citations. Your car insurance will drop dramatically. It may be so low that you won't even need it anymore. In a report about the effect of self-driving cars on the insurance industry, KPMG estimated that accident frequency will drop by 90 percent by the year 2050. Subsequently, the personal automobile industry will shrink to 22 percent of its current size.[15] The analysis is probably right. Self-driving cars will probably take a big chunk out of the $150B paid each year in car insurance premiums.

Self-Driving Cars Will Make Things Safer

Yes, you read that right—safer. Currently, 90 percent of motor vehicle crashes are caused by human error.[16] Motor vehicle crashes are the leading cause of death for people ages 3 to 33. Spending time driving may be the most dangerous thing you do all day. Your self-driving car will be able to see better than you, react more quickly than you, and have better information about your driving environment. It will be able to communicate with other cars around it, dynamically analyze traffic patterns, avoid construction sites, and contact emergency services if needed.

Self-driving cars will mean safer driving, fewer accidents, fewer drunk drivers, fewer road-rage incidents, and fewer auto–pedestrian accidents. Cars will be able to go faster with fewer accidents. In the future, manual driving may be a risky and expensive hobby.

Self-Driving Cars Will Disrupt Businesses

Self-driving cars have the potential to disrupt well-established industries. Self-driving cars may mean fewer cars on the road. Fewer cars on the road may mean fewer cars sold (transportation), fewer auto loans written (finance), fewer automobile insurance policies underwritten (insurance), fewer auto parts sold due to fewer accidents (manufacturing), and fewer parking lots (real estate). If they didn't have to drive, consumers might take more trips by car than by plane or train (transportation).

The production of self-driving cars will mean more jobs for engineers, programmers, and systems designers. There will be more computer hardware, sensors, and cameras in the vehicle. Corporations may not completely see the far-reaching effects of self-driving cars on existing industries. They may even fundamentally change our society. What if driving a "manual" car becomes too costly? Teenagers in the future may never learn how to drive a car. Ask yourself: Do you know how to ride a horse? Your ancestors did.

3D Printing

The fourth disruptive force that has the power to change businesses is 3D printing. 3D printing will not only change the competitive landscape, but it may change the nature of businesses themselves.

Consider how Nike has used 3D printing to improve the way it designs and creates shoes. It recently used a 3D printer to create the world's first 3D-printed cleat plate for a shoe called the Nike Vapor Laser Talon.[17] Nike chose to use a 3D printer to produce the cleat because it could create the optimal geometric shapes for optimal traction. Using a 3D printer, it could design and produce a lighter and stronger cleat much more quickly than before. In fact, Nike did just that when it produced a pair of custom-designed sprinting shoes (the Nike Zoom Superfly Flyknit) for gold-medal Olympian Allyson Felix to be worn at the 2016 Olympic games in Rio.[18]

3D printers have the potential to affect a broad array of industries beyond sporting equipment. You can get an idea of the scope of change when you realize that 3D printers can print in more than just plastics (Figure 4-10). They can print in metal, wood, ceramics, foods, and biological material too.

Take the ability to 3D-print in a variety of materials and look for opportunities across the aerospace, defense, automotive, entertainment, and healthcare industries. What happens when it becomes feasible to 3D-print extra-large objects like cars,[19] planes, boats, houses, and drones?

Cryptocurrencies

The fifth disruptive force that has the power to change businesses is cryptocurrencies. **Cryptocurrencies** are digital-only currencies that use cryptographic protections to manage and record secure transactions. **Bitcoin**, introduced in 2009, is currently the most well-known cryptocurrency among the thousands available today. Cryptocurrencies are an important disruptive force because of their potential to transform world economies.

Benefits of Cryptocurrencies

There are lots of reasons to love cryptocurrencies. Compared to traditional payment methods, cryptocurrency transactions are faster and easier and have few to no fees. Governments can't easily monitor, tax, or seize cryptocurrencies. Consumers holding cryptocurrencies are protected from inflation, too.

FIGURE 4-10
3D Printer
Source: Seraficus/iStock/Getty Images

For example, there are only 21 million possible bitcoins. Each bitcoin can be broken down into smaller fractions of a bitcoin, with the smallest unit, a **satoshi**, being 1/100,000,000 of one bitcoin. But there won't be any more bitcoins created beyond the original 21 million. The same is not true of traditional **fiat currencies**, or government-approved legal tender. Historically, when governments run up huge debts, they just print more money to pay for those debts. This causes inflation, which increases prices and decreases the purchasing power of your money. Consumers around the world like cryptocurrencies because they protect their users from inflation.

Risks of Cryptocurrencies

There are risks to cryptocurrencies, too. The value of a cryptocurrency can drop to zero if enough big holders of the currency sell their coins. Bitcoin, for example, derives its value because enough people *perceive* it as valuable. There is nothing like gold backing its value, and it is not government-approved legal tender. It's all perception. That can lead to extreme price volatility. Bitcoin also suffers from the fact that relatively few businesses accept it as payment, and it initially got a bad reputation for being used by organized crime.

The Future of Cryptocurrencies

Cryptocurrencies are slowly gaining acceptance. Banks and even some governments are launching their own cryptocurrencies. Business are using **blockchain**, or the decentralized public ledgering system used to record cryptocurrency transactions, to manage transactions in traditional sectors like shipping, real estate, voting, and stock trading. Even if they don't replace traditional fiat currencies, the underlying technology behind cryptocurrencies is making all types of transactions more secure and easier to manage.

Q4-3 What Do Business Professionals Need to Know About Software?

Innocuous-looking applications can be custom-made for malicious purposes. Read the Security Guide on pages 150–151 to learn more.

As a future manager or business professional, you need to know the essential terminology and software concepts that will enable you to be an intelligent software consumer. To begin, consider the basic categories of software shown in Figure 4-11.

Every computer has an **operating system (OS)**, which is a program that controls that computer's resources. Some of the functions of an operating system are to read and write data, allocate main memory, perform memory swapping, start and stop programs, respond to error conditions, and facilitate backup and recovery. In addition, the operating system creates and manages the user interface, including the display, keyboard, mouse, and other devices.

Although the operating system makes the computer usable, it does little application-specific work. If you want to check the weather or access a database, you need application programs such as an iPad weather application or Oracle's customer relationship management (CRM) software.

Both client and server computers need an operating system, though they need not be the same. Further, both clients and servers can process application programs. The application's design determines whether the client, the server, or both process it.

	Operating System	Application Programs
Client	Programs that control the client computer's resources	Applications that are processed on client computers
Server	Programs that control the server computer's resources	Applications that are processed on server computers

FIGURE 4-11
Categories of Computer Software

You need to understand two important software constraints. First, a particular version of an operating system is written for a particular type of hardware. For example, Microsoft Windows works only on processors from Intel and companies that make processors that conform to the Intel instruction set (the commands that a CPU can process). With other operating systems, such as Linux, many versions exist for many different instruction sets.

Second, two types of application programs exist. **Native applications** are programs that are written to use a particular operating system. Microsoft Access, for example, will run only on the Windows operating system. Some applications come in multiple versions. For example, there are Windows and Macintosh versions of Microsoft Word. But unless you are informed otherwise, assume that a native application runs on just one operating system. Native applications are sometimes called **thick-client applications**.

A **Web application** (also known as a **thin-client application**) is designed to run within a computer browser such as Firefox, Chrome, Opera, or Edge (formerly Internet Explorer). Web applications run within the browser and can run on any type of computer. Ideally, a Web application can also run within any browser, though this is not always true as you will learn.

Consider next the operating system and application program categories of software.

What Are the Major Operating Systems?

The major operating systems are listed in Figure 4-12. Consider each.

FIGURE 4-12
Major Operating Systems

Category	Operating System	Used for	Remarks
Nonmobile Clients	Windows	Personal computer clients	Most widely used operating system in business. Current version is Windows 10. Includes a touch interface.
	macOS	Macintosh clients	First used by graphic artists and others in arts community; now used more widely. First desktop OS to provide a touch interface. Current version is the macOS High Sierra.
	Unix	Workstation clients	Popular on powerful client computers used in engineering, computer-assisted design, architecture. Difficult for the nontechnical user. Almost never used by business clients.
	Linux	Just about anything	Open source variant of Unix. Adapted to almost every type of computing device. On a PC, used with Libre Office application software. Rarely used by business clients.
Mobile Clients	Symbian	Nokia, Samsung, and other phones	Popular worldwide, but less so in North America.
	BlackBerry OS	Research in Motion BlackBerries	Device and OS developed for use by business. Very popular in beginning, but losing market share to iOS and Android.
	iOS	iPhone, iPod Touch, iPad	Rapidly increasing installed base with success of the iPhone and iPad. Based on macOS.
	Android	Samsung, Google, HTC, and Sony smartphones; tablets	Linux-based phone/tablet operating system from Google. Rapidly increasing market share.
	Windows 10 (mobile)	Nokia and Microsoft Surface	Windows 10 tailored specifically for mobile devices. Full Windows 10 on Surface Pro.
Servers	Windows Server	Servers	Businesses with a strong commitment to Microsoft.
	Unix	Servers	Fading from use. Replaced by Linux.
	Linux	Servers	Very popular. Aggressively pushed by IBM.

Nonmobile Client Operating Systems

Nonmobile client operating systems are used on personal computers. The most popular is **Microsoft Windows**. Some version of Windows resides on more than 88 percent of the world's desktops, and, if we consider just business users, the figure is more than 95 percent. The most recent version of Windows is Windows 10. Net Applications estimates that overall market share of Windows as of 2018 is Windows 7 at 44 percent, Windows 10 at 31 percent, Windows XP at 6 percent, Windows 8.1 at 6 percent, and Windows 8 at 1 percent.[20] It's interesting to note that Windows 7 remains the most popular version of Windows despite the fact that Microsoft ended mainstream support for it in January 2015.

Windows 8 was a major rewrite of prior versions. Windows 8 was distinguished by what Microsoft calls **modern-style applications**.[21] These applications, now carried over into Windows 10, are touch-screen oriented and provide context-sensitive, pop-up menus. They can also be used with a mouse and keyboard. Microsoft claims that modern-style applications work just as well on portable, mobile devices, such as tablet computers, as they do on desktop computers. One key feature of modern-style applications is the minimization of menu bars, status lines, and other visual overhead. Figure 4-13 shows an example of a modern-style version of searching for images in Windows Explorer.

Apple Computer, Inc., developed its own operating system for the Macintosh, **macOS**. The current version is macOS High Sierra. Apple touts it as the world's most advanced desktop operating system. Windows 10 now gives it a run for the money in terms of that title.

Until recently, macOS was used primarily by graphic artists and workers in the arts community. But for many reasons, macOS has made headway into the traditional Windows market. According to Net Applications, as of 2018, desktop operating system market share was divided between versions of Windows (88.8 percent), macOS (Mac OS X) (8.6 percent), and Linux (2.3 percent).[22]

macOS was designed originally to run the line of CPU processors from Motorola, but today a Macintosh with an Intel processor is able to run both Windows and the macOS.

Unix is an operating system that was developed at Bell Labs in the 1970s. It has been the workhorse of the scientific and engineering communities since then. Unix is seldom used in business.

Linux is a version of Unix that was developed by the open source community. This community is a loosely coupled group of programmers who mostly volunteer their time to contribute code to

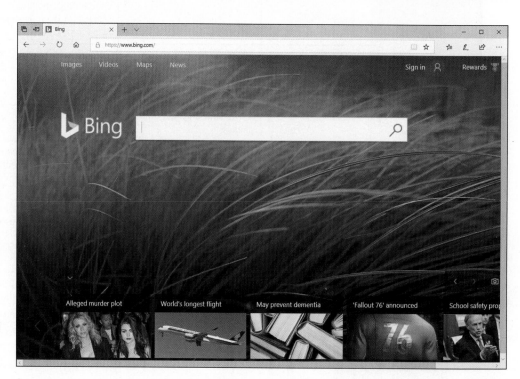

FIGURE 4-13
Example of the Modern-Style Interface

Source: Microsoft Edge, Windows 10, Microsoft Corporation.

develop and maintain Linux. The open source community owns Linux, and there is no fee to use it. Linux can run on client computers, but usually only when budget is of paramount concern. By far, Linux is most popular as a server OS. According to *DistroWatch.com*, the top five most popular versions of Linux as of 2018 were Linux Mint, Manjaro, Debian GNU/Linux, Ubuntu, and Solus.[23]

Mobile Client Operating Systems

Figure 4-12 also lists the five principal mobile operating systems. **Symbian** is popular on phones in Europe and the Far East, but less so in North America. **BlackBerry OS** was one of the most successful early mobile operating systems and was used primarily by business users on BlackBerry devices. It has lost market share to iOS, Android, and Windows 10.

iOS is the operating system used on the iPhone, iPod Touch, and iPad. When first released, it broke new ground with its ease of use and compelling display, features that are now being copied by the BlackBerry OS and Android. With the popularity of the iPhone and iPad, Apple has been increasing its market share of iOS, and, according to Net Applications, it is used on 28 percent of mobile devices.[24] The current version of iOS is iOS 11.

Android is a mobile operating system licensed by Google. Android devices have a very loyal following, especially among technical users. Net Applications estimates Android's market share to be nearly 69 percent.

Most industry observers would agree that Apple has led the way, both with the macOS and the iOS, in creating easy-to-use interfaces. Certainly, many innovative ideas have first appeared in a Macintosh or iSomething and then later were added, in one form or another, to Android and Windows.

Users who want Windows 10 on mobile devices will get either **Windows 10 (mobile)** on smartphones or a full version of Windows 10 on Surface Pro devices. Windows garners less than 1 percent of the mobile OS market share.

The smartphone market has always been huge, but recently, e-book readers and tablets have substantially increased the market for mobile client operating systems. As of 2018, 77 percent of Americans owned a smartphone, and 53 percent owned a tablet in addition to their smartphone.[25]

Server Operating Systems

The last three rows of Figure 4-12 show the three most popular server operating systems. **Windows Server** is a version of Windows that has been specially designed and configured for server use. It has much more stringent and restrictive security features than other versions of Windows and is popular on servers in organizations that have made a strong commitment to Microsoft.

Unix can also be used on servers, but it is gradually being replaced by Linux.

Linux is frequently used on servers by organizations that want, for whatever reason, to avoid a server commitment to Microsoft. IBM is the primary proponent of Linux and in the past has used it as a means to better compete against Microsoft. Although IBM does not own Linux, IBM has developed many business systems solutions that use Linux. By using Linux, neither IBM nor its customers have to pay a license fee to Microsoft.

Virtualization

Virtualization is the process by which one physical computer hosts many different virtual (not literal) computers within it. One operating system, called the **host operating system**, runs one or more operating systems as applications. Those hosted operating systems are called **virtual machines (vm)**. Each virtual machine has disk space and other resources allocated to it. The host operating system controls the activities of the virtual machines it hosts to prevent them from interfering with one another. With virtualization, each vm is able to operate exactly the same as it would if it were operating in a stand-alone, nonvirtual environment.

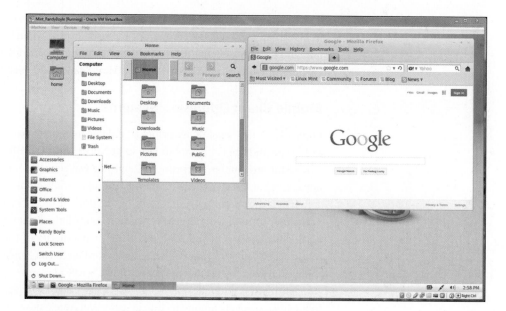

FIGURE 4-14

Linux Mint Virtual Machine Running in Microsoft Windows

Source: Windows 10, Microsoft Corporation.

Three types of virtualization exist:

- PC virtualization
- Server virtualization
- Desktop virtualization

With **PC virtualization**, a personal computer, such as a desktop or laptop, hosts several different operating systems. Say a user needs to have both Linux and Windows running on a computer for a training or development project. In that circumstance, the user can load software like Oracle VirtualBox or VMWare Workstation on the host operating system in order to create Linux and Windows virtual machines. The user can run both systems on the same hardware at the same time if the host operating system has sufficient resources (i.e., memory and CPU power) as shown in Figure 4-14.

With **server virtualization**, a server computer hosts one or more other server computers. In Figure 4-15, a Windows Server computer is hosting multiple virtual machines. Users can log on to any of those virtual machines, and they will appear as normal desktop computers. Figure 4-16 shows how one of those virtual machines would appear to a user of that virtual desktop. Notice

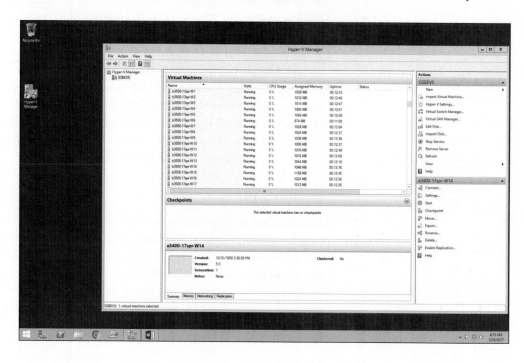

FIGURE 4-15

Windows Server Computer Hosting Virtual Machines

Source: Windows 10, Microsoft Corporation.

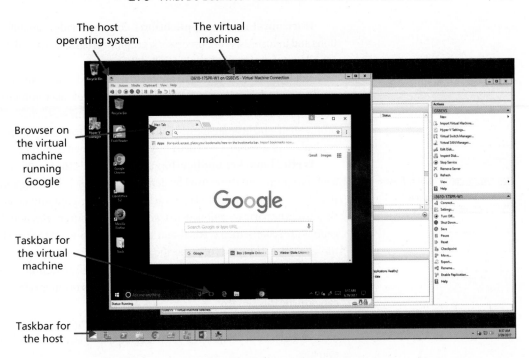

FIGURE 4-16
Virtual Machine Example
Source: Windows 10, Microsoft Corporation.

that the user of that virtual machine is running a Web browser as if it is a local desktop. Server virtualization plays a key role for cloud vendors, as you'll learn in Chapter 6.

PC virtualization is interesting as well as quite useful, as you will learn in Chapter 6. Desktop virtualization, on the other hand, has the potential to be revolutionary. With **desktop virtualization**, a server hosts many versions of desktop operating systems. Each of those desktops has a complete user environment and appears to the user to be just another PC. However, the desktop can be accessed from any computer to which the user has access. Thus, you could be at an airport and go to a terminal computer and access your virtualized desktop. To you, it appears as if that airport computer is your own personal computer. Using a virtual desktop also means that you wouldn't have to worry about losing a corporate laptop or confidential internal data. Meanwhile, many other users could have accessed the computer in the airport, and each thought he or she had his or her personal computer.

Desktop virtualization is in its infancy, but it might have major impact during the early years of your career.

Own Versus License

When you buy a computer program, you are not actually buying that program. Instead, you are buying a **license** to use that program. For example, when you buy a macOS license, Apple is selling you the right to use macOS. Apple continues to own the macOS program. Large organizations do not buy a license for each computer user. Instead, they negotiate a **site license**, which is a flat fee that authorizes the company to install the product (operating system or application) on all of that company's computers or on all of the computers at a specific site.

In the case of Linux, no company can sell you a license to use it. It is owned by the open source community, which states that Linux has no license fee (with certain reasonable restrictions). Large companies such as IBM and smaller companies such as RedHat can make money by *supporting* Linux, but no company makes money selling Linux licenses.

What Types of Applications Exist, and How Do Organizations Obtain Them?

Some applications are designed to be free but gather data about the people who use them. Read the Ethics Guide on pages 143–145 about how this is done.

Application software performs a service or function. Some application programs are general purpose, such as Microsoft Excel or Word. Other application programs provide specific functions. QuickBooks, for example, is an application program that provides general ledger and other accounting functions. We begin by describing categories of application programs and then describe sources for them.

Horizontal-market application software provides capabilities common across all organizations and industries. Word processors, graphics programs, spreadsheets, and presentation programs are all horizontal-market application software.

Examples of such software are Microsoft Word, Excel, and PowerPoint. Examples from other vendors are Adobe's Acrobat, Photoshop, and PageMaker and Jasc Corporation's Paint Shop Pro. These applications are used in a wide variety of businesses across all industries. They are purchased off the shelf, and little customization of features is necessary (or possible). They are the automobile equivalent of a sedan. Everybody buys them and then uses them for different purposes.

Vertical-market application software serves the needs of a specific industry. Examples of such programs are those used by dental offices to schedule appointments and bill patients, those used by auto mechanics to keep track of customer data and customers' automobile repairs, and those used by parts warehouses to track inventory, purchases, and sales. If horizontal-market applications are sedans, then vertical-market applications would be construction vehicles, like an excavator. They meet the needs of a specific industry.

Read more about how software is developed and managed in the Career Guide on page 152.

Vertical applications usually can be altered or customized. Typically, the company that sold the application software will provide such services or offer referrals to qualified consultants who can provide this service.

One-of-a-kind application software is developed for a specific, unique need. The U.S. Department of Defense develops such software, for example, because it has needs that no other organization has.

You can think of one-of-a-kind application software as the automotive equivalent of a military tank. Tanks are developed for a very specific and unique need. Tanks cost more to manufacture than sedans, and cost overruns are common. They take longer to make and require unique hardware components. However, tanks are highly customizable and fit the requirements of a heavy-duty battle vehicle very well.

If you're headed into battle, you wouldn't want to be driving a four-door sedan. Sometimes paying for a custom vehicle, while expensive, is warranted. It all depends on what you're doing. Militaries, for example, purchase sedans, construction vehicles, and tanks. Each vehicle fills its own need. You can buy computer software in exactly the same ways: **off-the-shelf software**, **off-the-shelf with alterations software**, or **custom-developed software**.

Organizations develop custom application software themselves or hire a development vendor. Like buying a tank, such development is done in situations where the needs of the organization are so unique that no horizontal or vertical applications are available. By developing custom software, the organization can tailor its application to fit its requirements.

Custom development is difficult and risky. Staffing and managing teams of software developers is challenging. Managing software projects can be daunting. Many organizations have embarked on application development projects only to find that the projects take twice as long—or longer—to finish than planned. Cost overruns of 200 percent and 300 percent are not uncommon. We will discuss such risks further in Chapter 12.

In addition, every application program needs to be adapted to changing needs and changing technologies. The adaptation costs of horizontal and vertical software are amortized over all the users of that software, perhaps thousands or millions of customers. For custom-developed software, however, the using organization must pay all of the adaptation costs itself. Over time, this cost burden is heavy.

Because of the risk and expense, custom development is the last-choice alternative, used only when there is no other option. Figure 4-17 summarizes software sources and types.

What Is Firmware?

Firmware is computer software that is installed into devices such as printers, print servers, and various types of communication devices. The software is coded just like other software, but it is installed into special, read-only memory of the printer or other device. In this way, the program

Software Source

	Off-the-shelf	Off-the-shelf and then customized	Custom-developed
Horizontal applications			
Vertical applications			
One-of-a-kind applications			

Software Type

FIGURE 4-17
Software Sources and Types

becomes part of the device's memory; it is as if the program's logic is designed into the device's circuitry. Therefore, users do not need to load firmware into the device's memory. Firmware can be changed or upgraded, but this is normally a task for IS professionals.

Q4-4 Is Open Source Software a Viable Alternative?

To answer this question, you first need to know something about the open source movement and process. Most computer historians would agree that Richard Matthew Stallman is the father of the movement. In 1983, he developed a set of tools called **GNU** (a self-referential acronym meaning *GNU Not Unix*) for creating a free Unix-like operating system. Stallman made many other contributions to open source, including the **GNU general public license (GPL) agreement,** one of the standard license agreements for open source software. Stallman was unable to attract enough developers to finish the free Unix system but continued making other contributions to the open source movement.

In 1991 Linus Torvalds, working in Helsinki, began work on another version of Unix, using some of Stallman's tools. That version eventually became Linux, the high-quality and very popular operating system discussed previously.

The Internet proved to be a great asset for open source, and many open source projects became successful, including:

- LibreOffice (default office suite in Linux distributions)
- Firefox (a browser)
- MySQL (a DBMS, see Chapter 5)
- Apache (a Web server, see Chapter 6)
- Ubuntu (a Windows-like desktop operating system)
- Android (a mobile device operating system)
- Cassandra (a NoSQL DBMS, see Chapter 5)
- Hadoop (a Big Data processing system, see Chapter 3)

Why Do Programmers Volunteer Their Services?

To a person who has never enjoyed writing computer programs, it is difficult to understand why anyone would donate his or her time and skills to contribute to open source projects. Programming is, however, an intense combination of art and logic, and designing and writing a complicated computer program can be exceedingly pleasurable (and addictive). Many programmers joyfully write computer programs—day after day. If you have an artistic and logical mind, you ought to try it.

The first reason that people contribute to open source is that it is great fun! Additionally, some people contribute to open source because it gives them the freedom to choose the projects they work on. They may have a programming day job that is not terribly interesting—say, writing a program to manage a computer printer. Their job pays the bills, but it's not fulfilling.

SO WHAT? NEW FROM CES 2018

What's new in hardware? It's the Consumer Electronics Show (CES) held in Las Vegas every January: 4,000 exhibitors and 180,000 hardware-gawking attendees whipped to a frenzy by loud music, screaming video, and hyperventilating media. It's a show that only Las Vegas can do!

What's hot this year? How about:

- **Toyota e-Palette**: At CES 2018, Toyota announced an autonomous concept vehicle named the e-Palette that the company believes will fill a role in an emerging mobility as a service (MaaS) market. The vehicle's bizarre design looks like a rectangular cube on wheels with transparent panels that can be customized to display digital signage based on whatever the vehicle is tasked with doing at the time. The e-Palette vehicle can be configured for a variety of uses, including ridesharing, package delivery, mobile stores, temporary lodging, food trucks, or temporary entertainment at large events.

  The implications of Toyota's e-Palette are even more profound if you consider that the vehicle is completely autonomous. Mobile clothing stores can bring products right to your front door to try on. You can order dinner from hundreds of different food trucks that will bring it wherever you are. Traditional and highly inefficient city buses will be replaced with smaller transport modules that can pick you up anywhere at any time for a fraction of the cost. Because drivers aren't needed, the entire shipping sector will be revolutionized by dramatically lower costs.

  Toyota's e-Palette may cause a fundamental transformation in commerce similar to the change that occurred with the emergence of the Internet. The Internet allowed certain companies to transform from traditional brick-and-mortar businesses to online businesses. Similarly, e-Palette may cause a transformation from brick-and-mortar and online businesses to *mobile* businesses.

- **Peloton Tread**: The Peloton Tread is a treadmill with a 32-inch HD touchscreen that allows users to participate in at least 10 live exercise classes per day. Users get live instruction by expert trainers streamed right to their homes. Users can see their real-time ranking on a live leaderboard as they're running and get detailed workout metrics.

  Users don't have to go to the gym anymore. They can get guided workouts that fit their schedule and have access to more than 1,000 prerecorded workouts. Users don't have to worry about the weather, uneven terrain, or dodging cars. It's a safe, convenient workout. The Peloton Tread will retail for about $4,000. These same features also come on Peloton's stationary bike ($2,000).

Source: Haiyin Wang/Alamy Stock Photo

- **Sony Aibo**: One of the most talked about innovations at CES 2018 was Sony's robotic dog named Aibo. The newest version of Aibo is Wi-Fi enabled and integrated with an AI. It has sensors all over its plastic body that recognize when people pet it. It has a camera built into its nose that can be used to recognize individual family members. Another camera on its back is pointed upward and used for navigation. In fact, Aibo learns the layout of the rooms and can even walk back to its charging station when it's low on power. Aibo will retail for about $1,800 and will require a $27-per-month subscription. Unfortunately, it's currently only for sale in Japan.

Questions

1. What impact do you think Toyota's e-Palette will have on traditional brick-and-mortar businesses?

2. How could Toyota's e-Palette affect e-commerce?

3. Why would consumers prefer Peloton Tread over a traditional treadmill or running outside?

4. Peloton has transformed traditional treadmills and stationary bikes into IoT devices. Which other workout devices would benefit from being smart IoT devices?

5. What are the benefits of a robot dog over a biological dog? What might be some of the drawbacks of a robot dog?

In the 1950s, Hollywood studio musicians suffered as they recorded the same style of music over and over for a long string of uninteresting movies. To keep their sanity, those musicians would gather on Sundays to play jazz, and a number of high-quality jazz clubs resulted. That's what open source is to programmers: a place where they can exercise their creativity while working on projects they find interesting and fulfilling.

Another reason for contributing to open source is to exhibit one's skill, both for pride and to find a job or consulting employment. A final reason is to start a business selling services to support an open source product.

How Does Open Source Work?

The term **open source** means that the source code of the program is available to the public. **Source code** is computer code as written by humans and understandable by humans. Figure 4-18 shows a portion of the computer code written for the ARES project (see Chapter 7 opener).

Source code is compiled into **machine code** that is processed by a computer. Machine code is, in general, not understandable by humans and cannot be modified. When a user accesses a Web site, the machine code version of the program runs on the user's computer. We do not show machine code in a figure because it would look like this:

1101001010010111111001110111100100011100000111111011101111100111...

In a **closed source** project, say, Microsoft Office, the source code is highly protected and only available to trusted employees and carefully vetted contractors. The source code is protected like gold in a vault. Only those trusted programmers can make changes to a closed source project.

With open source, anyone can obtain the source code from the open source project's Web site. Programmers alter or add to this code depending on their interests and goals. In most cases,

FIGURE 4-18
Source Code Sample

```
/// <summary>
/// Allows the page to draw itself.
/// </summary>
private void OnDraw(object sender, GameTimerEventArgs e)
{
    SharedGraphicsDeviceManager.Current.GraphicsDevice.Clear(Color.CornflowerBlue);

    SharedGraphicsDeviceManager.Current.GraphicsDevice.Clear(Color.Black);

    // Render the Silverlight controls using the UIElementRenderer.
    elementRenderer.Render();

    // Draw the sprite
    spriteBatch.Begin();

    // Draw the rectangle in its new position
    for (int i = 0; i < 3; i++)
    {
        spriteBatch.Draw(texture[i], bikeSpritePosition[i], Color.White);
    }

    // Using the texture from the UIElementRenderer,

    // draw the Silverlight controls to the screen.
    spriteBatch.Draw(elementRenderer.Texture, Vector2.Zero, Color.White);

    spriteBatch.End();
}
```

programmers can incorporate code they find into their own projects. They may be able to resell those projects depending on the type of license agreement the project uses.

Open source succeeds because of collaboration. A programmer examines the source code and identifies a need or project that seems interesting. He or she then creates a new feature, redesigns or reprograms an existing feature, or fixes a known problem. That code is then sent to others in the open source project who evaluate the quality and merits of the work and add it to the product, if appropriate.

Typically, there are many cycles of iteration and feedback. Because of this iteration, a well-managed project with strong peer reviews can result in very high quality code, like that in Linux.

So, Is Open Source Viable?

The answer depends on to whom and for what. Open source has certainly become legitimate. According to *The Economist*, "It is now generally accepted that the future will involve a blend of both proprietary and open-source software."[26] During your career, open source will likely take a greater and greater role in software. However, whether open source works for a particular situation depends on the requirements and constraints of that situation. You will learn more about matching requirements and programs in Chapter 12.

In some cases, companies choose open source software because it is "free." It turns out that this advantage may be less important than you'd think because in many cases support and operational costs swamp the initial licensing fee.

Q4-5 What Are the Differences Between Native and Web Applications?

Applications can be categorized as native applications that run on just one operating system or Web applications that run in browsers. In the latter case, the browser provides a more or less consistent environment for the application; the peculiarities of operating systems and hardware are handled by the browser's code and hidden from the Web application.

Figure 4-19 contrasts native and Web applications on their important characteristics. Consider the Native Applications column first.

Developing Native Applications

Native applications are developed using serious, heavy-duty, professional programming languages. macOS and iOS applications are constructed using Objective-C or the **Swift** programming language. Linux (Android) applications are constructed using Java, and Windows applications are constructed using C#, VB.NET, C++, and others. All of these languages are **object-oriented**, which means they can be used to create difficult, complex applications and, if used properly, will result in high-performance code that is easy to alter when requirements change. The particular characteristics of object-oriented languages are beyond the scope of this text.

Object-oriented languages can be used only by professional programmers who have devoted years to learning object-oriented design and coding skills. Typically, such developers were computer science majors in college.

The benefit of such languages is that they give programmers close control over the assets of the computing device and enable the creation of sophisticated and complex user interfaces. If the programs are well written, they perform fast and use memory efficiently. The limits on native applications are usually budgetary, not technological. As a businessperson, you can get just about any application you can afford.

The downside of native applications is that they are, well, native. They only run on the operating system for which they are programmed. An iOS application must be completely recoded in order

	Native Applications	Web Applications
Development Languages	Objective-C Java C#, C++, VB.NET, Swift (object-oriented languages)	html5 css3 JavaScript (scripting language)
Developed by	Professional programmers only	Professional programmers and technically oriented Web developers and business professionals
Skill level required	High	Low to high
Difficulty	High	Easy to hard, depending on application requirements
Developer's Degree	Computer science	Computer science Information systems Graphics design
User Experience	Can be superb, depending on programming quality	Simple to sophisticated, depending on program quality
Possible applications	Whatever you can pay for…	Some limits prohibit very sophisticated applications
Dependency	iOS, Android, Windows	Browser differences, only
Cost	High. Difficult work by highly paid employees, multiple versions required.	Low to high … easier work by lesser-paid employees, only multiple browser files necessary. Sophisticated applications may require high skill and pay.
Application distribution	Via application stores (e.g., Apple Store)	Via Web sites
Example	Vanguard iPad application (free in Apple's iTunes store)	Seafood Web site: *www.wildrhodyseafood.com* Picozu editor: *www.picozu.com/editor*

FIGURE 4-19
Characteristics of Native and Web Applications

to run on Android and recoded again to run on Windows.[27] Thus, to reach all users, an organization will need to support and maintain three separate versions of the same application. It will also have to staff and manage three different development teams, with three different skill sets.

As a general rule, the cost of native applications is high. Many organizations reduce that cost by outsourcing development to India and other countries (see the introduction to Chapter 11), but native applications are still expensive relative to Web applications. The standard way to distribute native applications is via a company store, such as iTunes, owned by Apple. An excellent example of a native application is Vanguard's iPad application. It is easy to use, has complex functionality, and is highly secure, as you would expect. Companies such as Vanguard must and can afford to pay for exceedingly high-quality applications.

Developing Web Applications

The third column in Figure 4-19 summarizes Web application characteristics. Such applications run inside a browser such as Firefox, Chrome, Opera, or Edge. The browser handles the idiosyncrasies of the operating system and underlying hardware. In theory, an organization should be able to develop a single application and have it run flawlessly on all browsers on all devices. Unfortunately, there are some differences in the way that browsers implement the Web code. This means that some applications won't run correctly in some browsers.

As shown in the first row of Figure 4-19, Web development languages are html5, css3, and Javascript. html5 is the latest version of html, which you will learn about in Chapter 6. The advantages of this version are support for graphics, animation, 2D animations, and other sophisticated user experiences. css3 is used with html5 to specify the appearance of content coded in html.

JavaScript is a scripting programming language that is much easier to learn than native-client languages. It is used to provide the underlying logic of the application.

Web applications can be written by professional programmers, and, indeed, most are. However, it is possible for technically oriented Web developers and business professionals to develop them as well. The entry-level technical skill required is low, and simple applications are relatively easy to develop. But sophisticated user experiences are difficult. Web application developers may have degrees in computer science, information systems, or graphics design.

The user experience provided by a Web application varies considerably. Some are simply fancy Web-based brochures (*www.wildrhodyseafood.com*); others are quite sophisticated, such as Spiro-Canvas (*www.gethugames.in/*) or, even more impressive, *www.biodigital.com*.

Web applications are limited by the capabilities of the browser. While browsers are becoming increasingly sophisticated, they cannot offer the full capabilities of the underlying operating system and hardware. Thus, Web applications are unable to support very specialized and complex applications, though this becomes less true each year.

As stated, the major advantage of Web over native applications is that they will run on any operating system and device. There are some browser differences, but these differences are very minor when compared with the differences among iOS, Android, and Windows. In general, unlike native applications, you can assume that a Web application has one code base and one development team.

Because Web applications can be developed by less skilled, lesser-paid employees and because only one code base and one development team are necessary, they are considerably cheaper to develop than native applications. However, this statement assumes applications of equivalent complexity. A simple native application can be cheaper to develop than a complex Web application.

Users obtain Web applications via the Internet. For example, when you go to *www.picozu.com/editor*, the required html5, css3, and JavaScript files are downloaded automatically over the Web. Updates to the application are automatic and seamless. You need not install (or reinstall) anything. This difference is an advantage to the user; it makes it more difficult, however, to earn money from your application. Amazon, for example, will sell your native application and pay you a royalty. However, unless you require users to buy your Web application (which is possible but rare), you'll have to give it away.

Which Is Better?

You know the answer to that question. If it were clear-cut, we'd only be discussing one alternative. It's not. The choice depends on your strategy, your particular goals, the requirements for your application, your budget, your schedule, your tolerance for managing technical projects, your need for application revenue, and other factors. In general, Web applications are cheaper to develop and maintain, but they may lack the wow factor. You and your organization have to decide for yourselves!

Q4-6 Why Are Mobile Systems Increasingly Important?

Mobile systems are information systems that support users in motion. Mobile systems users access the system from *any place*—at home, at work, in the car, on the bus, or at the beach—using any smart device, such as a smartphone, tablet, or PC. The possibilities are endless.

Mobile systems users move not only geographically but also from device to device. The user who starts reading a book on an iPad on a bus, continues reading that book on a PC at work, and finishes it on a Kindle Fire at home is mobile both geographically and across devices.

As shown in Figure 4-20, the major elements in a mobile system are *users in motion, mobile devices, wireless connectivity*, and a *cloud-based resource*. A **mobile device** is a small, lightweight, power-conserving, computing device that is capable of wireless connectivity. Almost all mobile

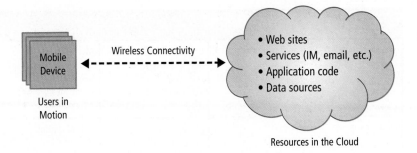

FIGURE 4-20
Elements of a Mobile Information System

devices have a display and some means for data entry. Mobile devices include smartphones, tablets, smartwatches, and small, light laptops. Desktop computers, Xboxes, and large, heavy, power-hungry laptops are not mobile devices.

You will learn about wireless connectivity and the cloud in Chapter 6. For now, just assume that the cloud is a group of servers on the other end of a connection with a mobile device. When downloading a book for a Kindle, for example, the cloud is one or more servers on the other end that store that book and download a copy of it to your device.

The major reason for the importance of mobile systems is the size of their market. According to Cisco, at the end of 2016 there were 8 billion mobile devices generating 7.2 exabytes of traffic per month.[28] By 2021, this will jump to 11.6 billion mobile devices generating more than 49 exabytes per month. That's 1.5 devices for every person on the planet. Smartphones will account for nearly 86 percent of global mobile traffic.[29]

It took seven years after the launch of the first iPhone (2007–2014) for smartphones to achieve mainstream use by 70 percent of the U.S. market.[30] That's faster than any other technology except television in the early 1950s, which tied the smartphone adoption rate. The February 2018 Pew Research Center Mobile Fact Sheet shows that 95 percent of people in the United States owned a mobile phone and 77 percent owned a smartphone.[31] The size of the mobile e-commerce, or **m-commerce**, market is expected to exceed $420B by 2021.[32]

Additionally, mobile use is favored by the young. According to Pew Research Center's measures of mobile device use, the younger the age group, the greater the percentage of people with mobile devices. Further, younger people have more devices per capita than older groups.[33] These young cohorts will further increase mobile systems use in the years to come.

Because of this vast and growing market, mobile systems are having a major impact on business and society today—impact that is forcing industry change while creating new career opportunities for mobile-IS-savvy professionals, as well as large numbers of new, interesting mobile-IS-related jobs.

Figure 4-21 summarizes the mobile-system impact for each of the five components of an information system. We will discuss each of the components in this figure, starting with hardware.

Hardware

Clearly, increasing demand for mobile systems means the sales of many more mobile devices, often at the expense of PC sales. Hewlett-Packard, a large PC manufacturer, learned this fact when it didn't respond quickly enough to the onslaught of mobile devices and was forced to eliminate 27,000 jobs in 2012. In the future, there will be high demand for innovative mobile devices as well as cheap copycats.

If you're reading this book, you're unlikely to be a hardware engineer, and if you're not living in Asia, you're also unlikely to be involved in hardware manufacturing. However, any market having 3.9 billion prospects is ripe with opportunities in marketing, sales, logistics, customer support, and related activities.

	Hardware	Software	Data	Procedures	People
Impact of mobile systems growth	Many, many more mobile devices will be sold.	Compact interfaces; new technology for active users; application scaling.	More data, but more information? Less device real estate means fewer ads possible.	Always on, always at work. Employee lifestyle becomes hybrid of personal and professional.	Ability to thrive in a dynamic environment more important.
Industry changes	PCs less important; high demand (and requirement) for innovative devices as well as cheap copycats.	html5, css3, and JavaScript increase capability of thin-clients.	Loss of control. Ad model in danger?	Personal mobile devices at work.	More part-time employees and independent contractors.
Career opportunities	Jobs for mobile device sales, marketing, support.	New technology levels the playing field for html5. Business expertise needed for mobile requirements. New companies!	Reporting and data mining even more important. Design of effective mobile reports.	Innovative use of just-in-time data. Need for adjusting business processes gives another premium to non-routine problem solvers.	Independent contractors (and some employees) work where and when they want. What is this new social organism?

FIGURE 4-21
Five Components of Mobile Change and Opportunity

Software

The reduced size of mobile devices requires the invention of new, innovative interfaces. The mobile user is an active user and expects an active screen experience. The premium will be for moving graphics, changing Web pages, and animation. Applications will need to scale from the very smallest to the very largest, while providing a user experience appropriate to the device's size.

Rapid technology change in mobile software continually levels the playing field. Today, for example, expert programmers in Objective-C better not relax. html5 and css3 are gaining popularity, and they will reduce the need for Objective-C expertise. Further, as you learned in Q4-5, while languages like Objective-C are difficult and time-consuming to learn, html5, css3, and JavaScript are less so. With the reduced barrier to entry, hordes of less experienced and less educated new entrants will appear as competitors. You might be one of them.

Additionally, continually evolving software means new and exciting entrepreneurial opportunities. Are you sorry that you missed the early days working at Facebook? Right now, somewhere, there is another Mark Zuckerberg starting. . . well, what? Because of the continually changing software environment, new opportunities abound and will continue to do so for decades.

Data

Many more mobile systems mean an incredible amount of new data, data that professionals can use to create much more information. But, as you learned in Chapter 1, more data doesn't necessarily mean more information. In fact, many business professionals believe they're drowning in data while starving for information. What can be done with all of this mobile-systems data to enable humans to conceive information of greater value to them? Data mining and better reporting are good options that were discussed in Chapter 3.

On the other hand, not all the news is good, at least not for many organizations. For one, smaller screens means less room for advertising, a factor that limited the success of the Facebook public offering in May 2012. Also, mobile systems increase the risk of organizations losing control over their data. In the past, employees used only computer equipment provided by the employer and connected only via employer-managed networks. In that situation, it is possible for the organization

ETHICS GUIDE

FREE APPS FOR DATA

You're sitting in your Introduction to MIS class, and the professor starts talking about how profitable software development can be. He points out that billionaires like Bill Gates (Microsoft), Larry Ellison (Oracle), Larry Page (Google), and Mark Zuckerberg (Facebook) all made their fortunes by developing useful software. But a vocal classmate jumps in and points out that he's never paid any of those people a penny. He uses Google Search, Gmail, and Facebook all for free. Yes, he uses Microsoft Office, but it's the free online version through OneDrive. Even the apps on his smartphone are free.

Then comes the perennial question, which also happens to be a major point of frustration for the tech industry: How do you make money from free apps? The professor says something about capturing market share, potential income, and future innovation. You're not buying it. You're interested in *real* income, not *potential* income.

Nick the Data Broker

The person sitting next to you, Nick, starts smiling broadly and nods his head. He's in your group for your big class project. He leans over and whispers, "If you're not paying for it, *you* are the product. Data is where you make money, not software. Give them the software, take the data, and make the money. It's simple."

You're a little confused at first. But then you think back to last Wednesday when you first met Nick. He said he was coming back to school to get a degree in MIS because he needed the technical knowledge for his new job with his brother's company. He explained that his brother was a data broker (sometimes called an information broker). He buys data about individuals from companies and then sells it to other companies for a profit. It sounded like they were doing really well. Before you could even ask if it was legal or ethical, Nick quipped, "Yes, of course it's legal. Everyone does it." He had obviously gotten this question before.

But was Nick right? He isn't a billionaire like Bill Gates. Nick was only concerned with buying and selling data. He wasn't interested in application development. But he did make a good point, and it got you thinking. What if you started a business that made applications that were designed to collect individual data? You could make dozens of useful apps, collect individual data, and then sell it to Nick.

But what data would Nick pay for? How much of it could you get? He wouldn't care about gaming data. But he would pay for data about user behavior like which Web sites they visit, where they're located, who their friends are, and what they purchase.

Flashlight Apps

At lunch, you do a few searches about how mobile applications can access data on smartphones. It turns out that users just have to grant the application permission(s), and it can access *any* data on the phone. Could that be right? *Any* data? This could be a gold mine. You get excited at the prospect of harvesting thousands of terabytes of data and selling them to Nick. You could retire in a month.

But then a sinking feeling comes over you. What if you're not the first person to think of this idea? What if someone else is already giving away apps and harvesting users' data. You decide to check the permissions for one of the most useful free applications you have on your phone—your flashlight app. You search for "flashlight app permissions" and you see dozens of news articles referencing a threat report by SnoopWall.[34]

The SnoopWall report looked at the permissions required by the top 10 flashlight apps for Android smartphones. The results were shocking. All of these apps did more than just turn a light on and off. They required permission to access data about your location, network connectivity, and USB storage. They also required permissions to install shortcuts, receive data to/from the Internet, modify your system settings, and disable your screen lock.

The app you use was third on the list. Not good. You decide to check to see whether the report was accurate. Were these apps harvesting all this data? You look at the first six flashlight apps that show up in Google Play. The results are shown in the following table. The bottom three rows show the changes in the number of permissions from 2013, 2014, 2016, and 2018.

Seeing all of the permissions required by these simple flashlight apps is distressing. Why would your flashlight need your GPS coordinates? Who was getting this data? What were they using it for? It looks like someone had already thought of your data-harvesting idea. It may be too late to make any money off the free-app-for-individual-data scheme. All of a sudden, these free apps don't look as attractive to you—as a consumer.

143

Permissions	Super-Bright LED Flashlight	Brightest Flashlight Free	Brightest LED Flashlight	Flashlight	High-Powered Flashlight	Tiny Flashlight + LED
Take pictures and videos	X	X	X	X	X	X
Receive data from Internet	X	X**	X		X	X**
Control flashlight	X	X	X	X*	X	X
Change system display settings	X**		X**		X**	
Modify system settings	X**		X**		X**	
Prevent device from sleeping	X	X	X	X*	X	X
View network connections	X	X	X	X	X	X
Full network access	X	X	X	X	X	X
Run at startup			X**			X
Control vibration				X**		X
Retrieve running apps						
Modify or delete the contents of your storage		X				
Read the contents of your storage		X		X**		
View Wi-Fi connections		X				
Read phone status and identity		X	X*			
Read Home settings and shortcuts		X				
Write Home settings and shortcuts						
Disable your screen lock						
Install shortcuts		X				
Uninstall shortcuts		X				
Approximate location		X		X**		
Precise location		X		X**		
Disable or modify status bar		X**				
Draw over other apps			X		X**	
Other					3	
Count 2013	20	15	13	9	15	6
Count 2014	8	15	13	9	15	7
Count 2016	6	14	8	5	6	7
Count 2018	8	16	10	7	12	8
* Dropped for 2018 ** Added for 2018						

DISCUSSION QUESTIONS

1. Consider the decision to create a free application designed to harvest individual data.
   a. Is this decision ethical according to the categorical imperative (page 23-24)?
   b. Is this decision ethical according to the utilitarian perspective (page 42-43)?
   c. How would users react if they knew their data was being harvested in exchange for a free app?
2. Suppose Google becomes aware that apps in the Google Play store are harvesting user data unrelated to the function of the application.
   a. Does it have a *legal* obligation to find out which apps are harvesting data inappropriately?
   b. Does it have an *ethical* obligation to find out which apps are harvesting data inappropriately?

   c. Does Google provide free apps in exchange for individual data? Why?
3. How hard should Google work at curating apps in Google Play to ensure that appropriate permissions are set?
4. In 2014, Symantec found that 17 percent of all Android apps were malware in disguise.[35] But a report by Google found that less than 1 percent of all Android devices had a potentially harmful application installed.[36]
   a. Is it ethical for Google to remove applications it considers inappropriate? Consider both the categorical imperative and utilitarian perspectives.
   b. Is it ethical for Google to limit permissions for certain applications? Consider both the categorical imperative and utilitarian perspectives.

to control who does what with which data and where. No longer. Employees come to work with their own mobile devices. Data leakage is inevitable.

With more people switching to mobile devices and with less room for ads, online advertising revenue may be sharply reduced, possibly endangering the revenue model that supports most of the Web's free content. If this happens, dramatic change is just around the corner!

Procedures

Mobile systems are always on. They have no business hours. And people who use mobile systems are equally always on. In the mobile world, we're always open for business. It is impossible to be out of the office. One consequence of always-on is the blending of our personal and professional lives. Such blending means, in part, that business will intrude on your personal life, and your personal life will intrude on your business. This intrusion can be distracting and stressful; on the other hand, it can lead to richer, more complex relationships.

Employees will expect to use their mobile devices at work, but should they? In truth, who can keep them from it? If the organization blocks them from connecting to the work-related networks, they can connect over the wireless networks that they pay for themselves. In this case, the organization is entirely out of the loop. Could employees send confidential corporate information through their personal mobile devices? We will discuss these issues in more detail in Q4-7.

Mobile systems offer the potential of **just-in-time data**, which is data delivered to the user at the precise time it is needed. A pharmaceutical salesperson uses just-in-time data when she accesses a mobile system to obtain the latest literature on a new drug while waiting for the doctor to whom she will pitch it. She needn't remember the drug's characteristics any longer than it takes her to walk down the hallway and make the sale.

Furthermore, some organizations will passively wait for change to happen, while others will proactively reengineer their processes to incorporate mobile systems for higher process quality. Either way, the need for business process change creates opportunity for creative, nonroutine business problem solvers.

People

Mobile systems change the value of our thinking. For example, just-in-time data removes the premium on the ability to memorize vast quantities of product data, but creates a premium for the ability to access, query, and present that data. Mobile systems increase the speed of business, giving an advantage to those who can nimbly respond to changing conditions and succeed with the unexpected.

With the ability to be connected and always on, organizations may find they can be just as effective with part-time employees and independent contractors. The increasing regulatory complexity and cost of full-time employees will create an incentive for organizations to do just that.

As that occurs, professionals who can thrive in a dynamic environment with little need for direct supervision will find that they can work both where and when they want, at least a good part of the time. Once you're always on and remote, it doesn't matter if you're always on in New Jersey or at a ski area in Vermont. New lifestyle choices become possible for such workers.

These mobile workers can work where they want and for whom they want. There won't be a boss looking over their shoulder. They can work multiple jobs with different companies at the same time! Companies may have to change the way they pay workers. Instead of paying employees by the hour, they would need to focus more on paying for productivity. This shift toward focusing on performance will empower great employees and make it harder for slackers to hide out in an organization. Companies will benefit from mobile workers too. They won't need as much expensive commercial office space. What an incredible time to be starting a business career!

Q4-7 What Are the Challenges of Personal Mobile Devices at Work?

So far, we've focused on mobile applications that organizations create for their customers and others to use. In this question we will address the use of mobile systems *within* organizations.

In truth, organizations today have a love/hate relationship with their employees' use of their own mobile devices at work. They love the cost-saving possibility of having employees buy their own hardware, but they hate the increased vulnerability and loss of control. The result, at least today, is a wide array of organizational attitudes.

Consider a recent report by Tech Pro Research that estimates 74 percent of companies have adopted BYOD or are planning to do so.[37] If you aren't already bringing your own device to work, you'll soon have to. Yet only 43 percent of all organizations have created an official mobile-use policy.[38]

Advantages and Disadvantages of Employee Use of Mobile Systems at Work

Figure 4-22 summarizes the advantages and disadvantages of employee use of mobile systems at work. Advantages include the cost savings just mentioned as well as greater employee satisfaction of using devices that they chose according to their own preferences rather than organization-supplied PCs. Because employees are already using these devices for their own purposes, they need less training and can be more productive. All of this means reduced support costs.

On the other hand, employee use of mobile devices has significant disadvantages. First, there is the real danger of lost or damaged data. When data is brought into employee-owned computing devices, the organization loses control over where it goes or what happens to it. IBM, for example, disallowed the use of Apple's voice searching application, Siri, on employees' mobile devices for just that reason.[39] Also, if an employee loses his or her device, the data goes with it, and when employees leave the organization, the data on their personal devices needs to be deleted somehow.

Advantages	Disadvantages
Cost savings	Data loss or damage
Greater employee satisfaction	Loss of control
Reduced need for training	Compatibility problems
Higher productivity	Risk of infection
Reduced support costs	Greater support costs

FIGURE 4-22
Advantages and Disadvantages of Employee Use of Mobile Systems at Work

Organizations also lose control over the updating of software and the applications that users employ. This control loss leads to compatibility problems; users can process data, for example edit documents, with software that is incompatible with the organization's standard software. The result to the organization is a mess of inconsistent documents.

Possibly the greatest disadvantage of employee use of their own devices is the risk of infection. The organization cannot know where the users have been with their devices or what they've done when they've been there. The possibility of severe viruses infecting the organization's networks is real. Finally, all of these disadvantages can also lead, ironically, to greater support costs.

Given all that, organizations cannot avoid the issue. Whatever the costs and risks, employees are bringing their own devices to work. Ignoring the issue will simply make matters worse.

Survey of Organizational BYOD Policy

A **bring your own device (BYOD) policy** is a statement concerning employees' permissions and responsibilities when they use their own device for organizational business. Figure 4-23 arranges BYOD policies according to functionality and control. Starting in the lower left-hand corner, the most primitive policy is to ignore mobile use. That posture, which provides neither functionality to the employee nor control to the organization, has no advantages and, as just stated, cannot last.

The next step up in functionality is for the organization to offer its wireless network to mobile devices, as if it were a coffee shop. The advantage to the organization of this policy is that the organization can sniff employees' mobile traffic, thus learning how employees are using their devices (and time) during work.

Control

		Low ←				→ High
High	Full VPN Access to Organizational Systems			You're responsible for damage	We'll check it out, reload software and data, and manage it remotely	If you connect it, we own it
Functionality	Organizational Services on Public Internet		We'll offer limited systems you can access from any device			
	Access to Internet	We'll be a coffee shop				
Low	None	They don't exist				

FIGURE 4-23
Six Common BYOD Policies

The next policy provides more functionality and somewhat more control. Here the organization creates secure application services using https (explained in Chapter 10) that require employee sign-on and can be accessed from any device, mobile or not. Such applications can be used when employees are at work or elsewhere. These services provide controlled access to some organizations' assets.

A fourth policy is more of a strategic maneuver than a policy. The organization tells employees that they can sign on to the organization's network with their mobile devices, but the employee is financially responsible for any damage he or she does. The hope is that few employees know what their exposure is and hence decide not to do so.

A more enlightened policy is to manage the users' devices as if they were owned by the organization. With this policy, employees turn over their mobile devices to the IS department, which cleanses and reloads software and installs programs that enable the IS department to manage the device remotely. Numerous vendors license products called **mobile device management (MDM) software** that assist this process. These products install and update software, back up and restore mobile devices, wipe employer software and data from devices in the event the device is lost or the employee leaves the company, report usage, and provide other mobile device management data.

This policy benefits the organization, but some employees resist turning over the management of their own hardware to the organization. This resistance can be softened if the organization pays at least a portion of the hardware expense.

The most controlling policy is for the organization to declare that it owns any mobile device that employees connect to its network. To be enforceable, this policy must be part of the employee's contract. It is taken by organizations that manage very secure operations and environments. In some military/intelligence organizations, the policy is that any smart device that ever enters the workplace may never leave it. The advantages of these six policies are summarized in Figure 4-24.

BYOD policies are rapidly evolving, and many organizations have not yet determined what is best for them. If your employer has a committee to develop such policies, join it if you can. Doing so will provide a great way to gain exposure to the leading technology thinkers at your organization.

BYOD Policy	Description	Advantage to Organization
They don't exist	Organization looks the other way when employees bring mobile devices to work.	None
We'll be a coffee shop	You'll be able to sign in to our wireless network using your mobile device.	Packet sniffing of employee mobile device use at work.
We'll offer limited systems you can access from any device	Organization creates https applications with sign-in and offers access to noncritical business systems.	Employees gain public access from any device, not just mobile devices, without having to use VPN accounts.
You're responsible for damage	Threatening posture to discourage employee use of mobile devices at work.	Appear to be permissive without actually being so.
We'll check it out, reload software, and then manage remotely	Employees can use their mobile devices just as if they were computers provided by the corporate IS department.	Employee buys the hardware (perhaps with an employer's contribution).
If you connect it, we own it	Employees are not to use mobile devices at work. If they do, they lose them. Part of employment agreement.	Ultimate in control for highly secure work situations (intelligence, military).

FIGURE 4-24
Advantages of Example BYOD Policies

Q4-8 2029?

There's a really old movie called *You've Got Mail* (1998) starring Tom Hanks and Meg Ryan. In it, the characters get really excited when they get "mail." The term *email* was so new at the time that it hadn't even caught on yet. You can see people in the movie reading newspapers and paper books. Oh, how times have changed.

Fast-forward to today. Email now comes in seconds after it's sent. You check your email during commercial breaks while you're watching TV, while you're driving in traffic, and while you're sitting on the toilet. Instead of checking your email with bated breath, you're dreading seeing more work pile up in your inbox. Or worse—bills, spam, and viruses.

New hardware and software have changed everyday life. People are always on, always connected, always communicating, always working and playing. This trend will continue. The Internet of Things will allow us to be continually connected to more and more devices. You'll be able to control your home, and everything in it, from your smartphone. Your home will be so smart that it will analyze you. It will see what, how, and when you do things and then anticipate your needs.

Imagine your TV turning on every morning at just the right time so you can watch the markets open (see Figure 4-25). You smell fresh-baked bread, your shower turns on by itself, and your car

FIGURE 4-25
Smart Home
Source: Si-Gal/iStock Vectors/Getty Images

SECURITY GUIDE

POISONED APP-LES

Have you ever stopped to look up at the stars on a clear night and seen a faint white light tracking slowly across the sky? If so, you've seen a satellite orbiting the earth at speeds exceeding thousands of miles per hour. What may surprise you is that early spacecraft launched by NASA had less computing power than your smartphone. That's right—the small handheld device you use for checking social media and email and for playing games is more powerful than the first spacecraft. But why do you need all of that computing power? Phone calls and text messages don't seem to require massive processing power. Welcome to the era of the "app"!

Apps are the drivers of faster and more powerful smartphones. Apple and other smartphone manufacturers release new versions of their phones on an annual basis. Keeping up with the flashiest and most powerful apps drives the demand for faster processing chips and more memory. Advancements in both of these areas often happen without increasing the form factor of the phone or reducing battery life.

Smartphone users have a seemingly insatiable appetite for apps. In 2017, the Apple App Store contained more than 2.2 million apps, reported 197 billion app downloads, and listed 12 million registered app developers.[40] These apps allow you to do everything from making stock trades on the go to checking the latest weather conditions anywhere in the world. While most apps cost only a few dollars, many of them are free. You may be wondering, "How is this possible?" and "Are there any hidden costs?" You may be surprised to learn that free apps may not be such a great deal after all.

XcodeGhost Haunts iOS

The App Store is generally a well-regulated marketplace. Apps are screened for security vulnerabilities and vulgar content in order to create a safe experience for users. However, with more than 2 million applications available to consumers, it is inevitable that some malicious apps clear the screening process.

Apple recently reported that dozens of apps available on the App Store contained a malware application named XcodeGhost. Apps containing this malware reportedly accessed user credentials, hijacked URLs, were able to read and write data on devices, and compromised other iOS apps. WeChat, an app used extensively in China, was affected by XcodeGhost and contributed heavily to the tally of more than 500 million iOS users who could have been exposed to this dangerous malware.[41]

The malware was embedded in apps available on the App Store because developers chose to install a compromised version of the Xcode developers kit despite warnings that the software had been altered. Developers were downloading the compromised software because it had been posted on a server offering faster-than-standard download speeds.

Once this vulnerability had been identified, Apple notified users that the dangerous apps had been removed from the

Source: © CarmenMurillo/iStock/Getty Images Plus

App Store and that they were collaborating with developers to ensure that this type of incident does not happen again. However, even with these apps identified and removed, this security breach begs the question "What other vulnerabilities are lurking in the App Store, and have you already downloaded any of these potential threats?"

Installation App-rehension

Have you ever been using your phone and seen an alert message indicating that one of the apps on your phone was accessing your location information in the background? If so, were you worried? Did you allow the app to continue monitoring your location, or did you shut it off? A key point to consider is that an app does not have to be considered malware to be dangerous or invasive. In fact, many of the apps on your phone are likely accessing data that are unrelated to the app's specific purpose. For example, a survey of apps with built-in networking tools revealed that 13 out of 15 of these apps uploaded all user contacts on the phone to remote servers managed by the app developers.[42] Contact information can then be sold to advertisers and other third parties for a profit.

This type of indirect information gathering is why many of the apps downloaded from the App Store are free. End users end up paying for them with their privacy. But why do users tolerate an invasion of their privacy? Users often fail to review the usage agreement for each app.[43] Even more striking is that developers can change the terms of privacy agreements after a user has agreed to a prior version of the terms.

Despite the tremendous convenience, productivity, and entertainment afforded by our phones and apps, there are hidden costs. These hidden costs may include the risk of downloading dangerous software or inadvertently allowing apps access to private data. A little app-rehension may help users prevent a serious privacy invasion or data theft.

DISCUSSION QUESTIONS

1. Think about your use of various phone and computer apps and your interactions on social media. Have you ever experienced a breach of your privacy or personal data? What was the impact of this breach? Were you able to resolve it, or were you forced to live with the consequences?

2. Try to identify three different strategies that any smartphone user could follow in an attempt to minimize the risk of installing and using dangerous/risky apps.

3. Reflect on the trade-off between free apps and the potential privacy risks that these apps may introduce. Has this article changed your perception of free apps? If so, how?

4. Conduct an Internet search to identify if there have been any recent security vulnerabilities introduced through an app store (e.g., the App Store, Google Play, or Windows Phone Store). If so, conduct a brief investigation to see which apps are involved, how many people have been affected, and whether the vulnerability has been resolved.

knows exactly when to self-start so it's warm when you get in. Your self-driving car will let you work on your way to work. You'll see these anticipatory systems at your job too.

How will advances in hardware and software affect the types of jobs you'll go to? Ten years from now, the best-paying jobs will be ones that don't currently exist. The following are hot jobs today: IoT architect, marketing technologist, Big Data architect, and DevOps manager. These job titles didn't exist 10 years ago. Ten years from now, there will be an entirely new set of jobs that you haven't heard of before.

How do you prepare for future jobs? What types of jobs will pay well? Regardless of your current college major, your future job will probably require a high level of tech skill. The best way to prepare for these types of jobs is to cultivate creativity, novel problem solving, and good judgment and have a sincere desire to learn new things.

CAREER GUIDE

Name: Marshall Pettit
Company: Preparis, Inc.
Job Title: Senior Software Engineer
Education: University of Utah

Source: Marshall Pettit, Preparis, Inc.
Sr. Software Engineer

1 How did you get this type of job?

Networking. Never underestimate the value of professional lunches and close friends. Although my education and earlier experience differed substantially from my current job, a brilliant friend encouraged me to pursue my dreams as a software developer and gave me a strong referral to a company that had recently offered him a job. We started together, and he became an important mentor for me.

2 What attracted you to this field?

Web software development has always fascinated me since taking an elective during my undergraduate business management studies. Building complex yet elegant business systems using commands in a text editor is as fulfilling as building a home from raw materials and seeing it take shape.

3 What does a typical workday look like for you (duties, decisions, problems)?

Each workday requires self-motivation and a strong commitment to our team. I meet briefly each morning with my team to review our progress and make sure it is in line with the goals and objectives we select at the beginning of each iteration, spanning 2 or 3 weeks. I also make myself available throughout the day to review their code and individual work, as they do for me.

4 What do you like most about your job?

My home is my office, and my schedule is flexible. This allows me opportunities to coach my children's sports teams, help with their homework, and support their daily needs.

5 What skills would someone need to do well at your job?

Learning quickly! Programming languages, platforms, and paradigms consistently change. Staying abreast of these changes is important for making positive contributions on a continuing basis.

6 Are education or certifications important in your field? Why?

Formal education is important in every field. Although my education differs from my current responsibilities, it provides me greater depth when interacting with business leaders as we develop solutions for the customers we serve. Certificates are not as important in my field. Instead, consistent informal study and practice at coding challenge websites pay greater dividends.

7 What advice would you give to someone who is considering working in your field?

Just do it. Take a leap of faith and run with the challenges ahead. Courageously tackling your dream job in spite of the imaginary barriers around it will be both fun and rewarding.

8 What do you think will be hot tech jobs in 10 years?

Artificial intelligence will provide the most intriguing opportunities in the coming years. Opportunities in machine learning, data science, and business intelligence will grow substantially.

ACTIVE REVIEW

Use this Active Review to verify that you understand the ideas and concepts that answer the chapter's study questions.

Q4-1   What do business professionals need to know about computer hardware?

List types of hardware and give an example of each. Define *bit* and *byte*. Explain why bits are used to represent computer data. Define the units of bytes used to size memory.

Q4-2   How can new hardware affect competitive strategies?

Define *IoT* and describe a smart device. Explain why smart devices are desirable. Give two examples of how businesses could benefit from smart devices. Describe the difference between AR, MR, and VR. Explain why sense of presence is important in virtual environments. Describe how self-driving cars could be safer and cheaper and make life easier. Explain how 3D printing works and how it could affect new product design, manufacturing, distribution, and consumer purchasing. Describe some of the benefits and risks of using a cryptocurrency like Bitcoin.

Q4-3   What do business professionals need to know about software?

Review Figure 4-12 and explain the meaning of each cell in this table. Describe three kinds of virtualization and explain the use of each. Explain the difference between software ownership and software licenses. Explain the differences among horizontal-market, vertical-market, and one-of-a-kind applications. Describe the three ways that organizations can acquire software.

Q4-4   Is open source software a viable alternative?

Define *GNU* and *GPL*. Name three successful open source projects. Describe four reasons programmers contribute to open source projects. Define *open source, closed source, source code,* and *machine code.* In your own words, explain why open source is a legitimate alternative but might or might not be appropriate for a given application.

Q4-5   What are the differences between native and Web applications?

In your own words, summarize the differences between native applications and Web applications. In high-level terms, explain the difference between object-oriented languages and scripting languages. Explain each cell of Figure 4-19. State which is better: native or Web applications. Justify your answer.

Q4-6   Why are mobile systems increasingly important?

Define *mobile systems.* Name and describe the four elements of a mobile system. Describe the size of the mobile market and explain why there are 3.9 billion mobile prospects. Explain why the mobile market will become stronger in the future. Explain why a problem for one organization is an opportunity for another. Using the five-component model, describe particular opportunities for each component. Define *just-in-time data* and explain how it changes the value of human thinking.

Q4-7   What are the challenges of personal mobile devices at work?

Summarize the advantages and disadvantages of employees' using mobile systems at work. Define *BYOD* and *BYOD policy.* Name six possible policies and compare them in terms of functionality and organizational control. Summarize the advantage of each to employers.

Q4-8   2029?

Explain how email usage has changed over the past 20 years. Describe how an anticipatory system might work. Explain how advances in hardware and software might change the types of jobs you take in the future.

Using Your Knowledge with eHermes

Suppose you are part of this eHermes team. Briefly summarize how the knowledge in this chapter would help you contribute. Explain why eHermes decided not to develop its own AI. Summarize the challenges it would face if it did decide to develop its own AI.

KEY TERMS AND CONCEPTS

Android   131
Application software   133
Augmented reality (AR)   123
Binary digits   119
Bitcoin   127
Bits   119
BlackBerry OS   131
Blockchain   128
Bring your own device (BYOD)
    policy   147
Bytes   119
Central processing unit (CPU)   118
Client   119
Closed source   137
Computer hardware   118
Cryptocurrencies   127
Custom-developed software   134
Desktop virtualization   133
Dual processor   118
Exabyte (EB)   120
Fiat currencies   128
Firmware   134
Gigabyte (GB)   120
GNU   135
GNU general public license (GPL)
    agreement   135
HoloLens   155
Horizontal-market application   134
Host operating system   131
Internet of Things (IoT)   121
iOS   131

Just-in-time data   145
Kilobyte (KB)   120
License   133
Linux   130
Machine code   137
macOS   130
Main memory   118
M-commerce   141
Megabyte (MB)   120
Microsoft Windows   130
Mixed reality (MR)   123
Mobile device   140
Mobile device management (MDM)
    software   148
Mobile systems   140
Modern-style application   130
Native application   129
Nonvolatile   121
Object-oriented   138
Off-the-shelf software   134
Off-the-shelf with alterations
    software   134
One-of-a-kind application   134
Open source   137
Operating system (OS)   128
PC virtualization   132
Personal computers   118
Petabyte (PB)   120
Phablet   118
Quad processor 118
RAM   118

Reality   123
Satoshi   128
Self-driving car   125
Sense of presence   124
Server   131
Server farm   119
Server virtualization   132
Site license   133
Smart device   121
Smartphone   118
Solid-state storage (SSD)   118
Source code   137
Storage hardware   118
Swift   138
Symbian   131
Tablets   118
Terabyte (TB)   120
Thick-client application   129
Thin-client application   129
Unix   130
Vertical-market application   134
Virtual   123
Virtualization   131
Virtual machines (vm)   131
Virtual reality (VR)   124
Volatile   121
Web application   129
Windows 10 (mobile)   131
Windows Server   131
Zettabyte (ZB)   120

MyLab MIS

To complete the problems with MyLab MIS, go to EOC Discussion Questions in the MyLab.

USING YOUR KNOWLEDGE

4-1. Microsoft offers free licenses of certain software products to students at colleges and universities that participate in its Microsoft Imagine program (formerly known as the Microsoft DreamSpark program). If your college or university participates in this program, you have the opportunity to obtain hundreds of dollars of software for free. Here is a partial list of the software you can obtain:

MyLab MIS

- Microsoft Access 2016
- Microsoft OneNote 2016
- Microsoft Windows Server 2016

- Microsoft Project 2016
- Microsoft Visual Studio 2017
- Microsoft SQL Server 2017
- Microsoft Visio 2016

a. Search *www.microsoft.com*, *www.google.com*, or *www.bing.com* and determine the function of each of these software products.

b. Which of these software products are operating systems, and which are application programs?

c. Which of these programs are DBMS products (the subject of the next chapter)?

d. Which of these programs should you download and install tonight?

e. Either (1) download and install the programs in your answer to part d or (2) explain why you would choose not to do so.

f. Does Microsoft Imagine provide an unfair advantage to Microsoft? Why or why not?

4-2. Visit the Open Source Initiative's Web site at *www.open-source.org*. Summarize the mission of this foundation. Find the definition of open source on this site, and summarize that definition in your own words. Explain this foundation's role with regard to open source licenses. Summarize the process for having a license approved by the foundation. Describe the advantage of having the foundation's approval.
MyLab MIS

4-3. Suppose that you are Kamala at eHermes. List five criteria you would use in helping eHermes decide whether it should make its own AI. Justify your criteria.
MyLab MIS

4-4. Describe how the class enrollment application at your university could benefit from a mobile application that uses the cloud.

4-5. Judging from your personal experience, describe the BYOD policy that appears to be in place at your university. Explain the advantages and disadvantages of the policy to you as a student and to the organization as a whole. How do you think that BYOD policy will change in the next five years? Explain your answer.

4-6. Read Q4-2 if you have not already done so. Critically evaluate the opinions of the author. Do you agree that advances in the IoT and self-driving cars will make life easier? Better? If so, say why. If not, explain what you think will happen when more smart devices and self-driving cars are adopted. Explain how you could prepare for a future high-tech job market.

COLLABORATION EXERCISE 4

Using the collaboration IS you built in Chapter 1 (page 32), collaborate with a group of students to answer the following questions.

In March 2016, Microsoft released the development edition of its new mixed-reality head-mounted device named Microsoft **HoloLens**. HoloLens differs from digital reality devices like Meta 2 or Oculus Rift because it is a stand-alone, untethered computing device. In other words, it doesn't have to be plugged into a computer. It's a complete Windows 10 computer.[44]

HoloLens has a custom-built holographic CPU, an Intel 32-bit processor, 2 GB of RAM, and 64 GB of storage. It can be used for 2 to 3 hours without being recharged, and it comes with Bluetooth/Wi-Fi connectivity. It also comes with a 2-megapixel HD video camera, four microphones, motion sensors, light sensors, environmental cameras, and a depth-sensing camera.

As a result, HoloLens can do some pretty amazing things. It accepts voice commands and gesture commands (e.g., air tapping), it maps spaces in a room, and, most importantly, it creates holograms (virtual objects) in thin air. You can watch videos of how HoloLens works on its YouTube channel.

In a recent demonstration, Microsoft showed how HoloLens could be used collaboratively by having two people in different locations fix a plumbing problem together. A person with a broken pipe was wearing HoloLens, and a person who knew how to fix the pipe was in a separate location. The person wearing the HoloLens could see 3D holographic arrows appear on the pipes indicating what needed to be done to fix the problem. The arrows were being hand-drawn on a tablet showing a live video feed from the HoloLens.

In another example, designers and engineers at Autodesk use HoloLens to collaboratively create new products.[45] Mechanical engineers, industrial designers, and marketing managers can all see the product as it's being designed. They don't have to iterate through numerous physical prototypes. They can make immediate changes to a virtual prototype before it's even built.

Volvo is using HoloLens in a similar way. The company has been able to reduce design times and potentially improve its manufacturing processes with the device. HoloLens also helps with sales. Using the device, customers can change the color of the car they're looking at with one click. Salespeople can also show customers interactive demonstrations of a car's built-in safety features (like automatic breaking sensors) in 3D holographic environments.

The potential uses for HoloLens are staggering. Gamers won't be stuck on the couch playing video games anymore; they will be able to play multiplayer holographic games anywhere with anyone—for 2 hours. HoloLens will also change the way people communicate. Microsoft engineers recently gave a demonstration of "holoportation" in which a real-time interactive 3D hologram of a person was holoported into another room. Users wearing HoloLens could interact with the person as if they were in the same room.

Many other applications in education, entertainment, tourism, design, engineering, and movies are being developed. And, because HoloLens is one of the first mixed-reality devices to become commercially available, it's likely that the best applications for this technology are still unknown. We simply don't know what people will use it for. What is clear, however, is that big names like Google, Microsoft, and Apple are making large investments into mixed-reality devices like HoloLens. They see the potential and are voting with their wallets.

Recall the RAND study cited in Chapter 1 that stated there will be increased worldwide demand for workers who can apply new technology and products to solve business problems in innovative ways. Microsoft HoloLens is an excellent example of a new technology that will be applied innovatively.

4-7. Consider uses for HoloLens at your university. How might HoloLens be used in architecture, chemistry, law, medicine, business, geography, political science, art, music, or any other discipline in which your team has interest? Describe one potential application for HoloLens for five different disciplines.

4-8. List specific features and benefits for each of the five applications you selected in question 4-7.

4-9. Describe, in general terms, the work that needs to be accomplished to create the applications you identified in question 4-7.

4-10. Some people buy gaming consoles like Sony PlayStation and Microsoft Xbox because of exclusive games. Not all video games are available on all consoles. How important might applications be in the success of digital reality devices like HoloLens, Meta 2, and Oculus Rift?

4-11. You will sometimes hear the expression "Emerging technology is constantly leveling the playing field." In other words, technology eliminates competitive advantages of existing companies and enables opportunities for new companies. How does this statement pertain to HoloLens, iPad, Windows 10, Apple, and Google?

CASE STUDY 4

The Apple of Your i

A quick glance at Apple's stock history in Figure 4-26 will tell you that Apple is an incredibly successful and dramatic company, having peaks around the turn of the century, in 2007–2008, 2012, 2015, and again in 2018. It currently has the highest market value of any public company worldwide. Apple has been so successful that the NASDAQ stock exchange concluded Apple's price was skewing the price of the NASDAQ 100 Index and reduced Apple's weight in that index from 20 percent to 12

percent. As of this writing, Apple stock is trading at $190 after hitting a recent low of $56 in 2013.

But since Steve Jobs's death (October 5, 2011), there haven't been any groundbreaking products like the iPod, iPhone, and iPad. iWatch was released in 2015, but many initial reviews were tepid at best.[46] There were already several smartwatches on the market that had similar functionality, and it had performance issues. Most importantly, it wasn't clear if the iWatch provided enough value over the iPhone that was already in users' pockets. In short, it wasn't an immediate hit. So, what does the future look

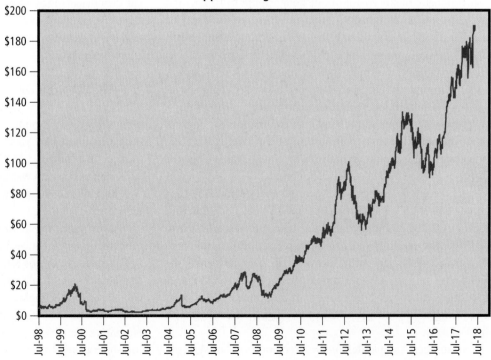

FIGURE 4-26
Growth in Apple Stock Price
Source: Financial data from *finance.yahoo.com*

like for Apple and its shareholders? Uncertain, especially if you consider its past history without Jobs.

Early Success and Downfall

At the dawn of the personal computer age, in the early 1980s, Apple pioneered well-engineered home computers and innovative interfaces with its Apple II PC for the home and its Macintosh computer for students and knowledge workers. At one point, Apple owned more than 20 percent of the PC market, competing against many other PC vendors, most of which are no longer relevant (or in business).

However, Apple lost its way. In 1985, Steve Jobs, Apple's chief innovator, lost a fight with the Apple board and was forced out. He founded another PC company, NeXT, which developed and sold a groundbreaking PC product that was too innovative to sell well in that era. Meanwhile, Apple employed a succession of CEOs, starting with John Sculley, who was hired away from Pepsi-Cola where he'd enjoyed considerable success. Sculley's knowledge and experience did not transfer well to the PC business, however, and the company went downhill so fast that CNBC named him the 14th worst American CEO of all time.[47] Two other CEOs followed in Sculley's footsteps.

During this period, Apple made numerous mistakes, among them not rewarding innovative engineering, creating too many products for too many market segments, and losing the respect of the retail computer stores. Apple's PC market share plummeted.

Steve Jobs, Second Verse

In 1996, Apple bought Jobs's NeXT computing and gained technology that became the foundation of macOS High Sierra, today's Macintosh operating system. The true asset it acquired, however, was Steve Jobs. Even he, however, couldn't create an overnight miracle. It is exceedingly difficult to regain lost market share and even more difficult to regain the respect of the retail channel that had come to view Apple's products with disdain. Even by 2011, Apple's PC market share was in the range of 10 percent to 12 percent, down from a high of 20 percent in the 1980s.

In response to these problems, Apple broke away from the PC and created new markets with its iPod, iPhone, and iPad. It also countered retailer problems by opening its own stores. In the process, it pioneered the sale of music and applications over the Internet.

iPod, iPhone, and iPad devices are a marvel of creativity and engineering. They exude not only ease of use, but also now/wow/fun coolness. By selling hot music for the iPod, Apple established a connection with a dynamic segment of the market that was willing to spend lots of money on bright, shiny objects. The ability to turn the iPhone on its side to rotate images probably sold more iPhones than anything else. With the iPad, portable devices became readable, and the market responded by awarding Apple

a 54 percent share of the mobile market.[48] And Apple's success continues with the iPhone 8, which, as of this writing, is selling well.

All of this success propelled Apple's stores not only beyond vanilla retailers like Murphy USA but also beyond the lofty heights of Tiffany & Co. In 2017, Apple stores were grossing more than $5,546 per square foot, compared with $2,951 for Tiffany and $3,721 for Murphy USA. Apple currently operates more than 500 such retail outlets and welcomes more than 1 million customers per day.[49]

Apple encourages customer visits and loyalty with its open and inviting sales floor, its Genius Bar help desk, and its incredibly well-trained and disciplined sales force. Salespeople, who are not commissioned, are taught to be consultants who help customers solve problems. Even some vocabulary is standardized. When an employee cannot solve a customer's problem, the word *unfortunately* is to be avoided; employees are taught to use the phrase *as it turns out* instead.[50] Try that on your next exam!

Apple has sold more than 25 billion songs through its iTunes online store, 130 million books through its iBookstore, and a mere 75 billion applications downloaded through its App Store. Apple is now the number-one PC software channel.[51]

To encourage the development of iPhone and iPad apps, Apple shares its revenue with application developers. That would be more than $70B paid to developers over the years![52] Developers responded by creating 1,000,000 iOS applications, and an army of developers are at work building thousands more while you read this.

By the way, if you want to build an iOS application, what's the first thing you need to do? Buy a Macintosh. Apple closed its development to any other development method. Adobe Flash? No way. Apple claims that Flash has too many bugs, and perhaps so. Thus, Flash developers are excluded. Microsoft Silverlight? Nope. Microsoft developers are out in the cold too. The non-Apple development community was furious, and Apple's response was, in essence, "Fine, we'll pay our $70B to someone else."

The bottom line? Until Jobs's death, every sales success fed every other sales success. Hot music fed the iPod. The iPod fed iTunes and created a growing customer base that was ripe for the iPhone. Sales of the iPhone fed the stores, whose success fed the developer community, which fed more applications, which fed the iPhone and set the stage for the iPad, which fed the App Store, which led to more loyal customers and, of course, to more developers.

Apple Without Steve Jobs

Apple's future is uncertain. It floundered when Jobs was fired in the 1990s, and it could flounder again. Sure, it'll be around for a long time, but the days of its incredible innovative leadership could be, alas, over. Smart investors must consider the innovations coming from Apple in a post-Steve-Jobs world. Will Apple's new CEO, Tim Cook, take the same bold risks that Steve Jobs did? In the years since Tim took over, we've seen improvements to existing products like the iPhone, iPad, iMac, and iPod, but few new innovations beyond Apple Watch and Apple Pay.

Will Apple come out with an iCar and iGoggles (mixed reality device) like many are hoping? Or will innovation at Apple be limited to incremental improvements to existing products? That's the trillion dollar question.

QUESTIONS

4-12. Which of Porter's four competitive strategies does Apple engage in? Explain.

4-13. What do you think are the three most important factors in Apple's past success? Justify your answer.

4-14. Steve Jobs passed away in October 2011. Until his death, he had been the heart and soul of Apple's innovation. Today, 123,000 Apple employees continue onward in his absence with Tim Cook as the new CEO.

A huge question for many investors is whether the company can be successful without Steve Jobs. What do you think? Has Tim Cook been innovative enough since taking over Apple? Will he be a bold innovator like Steve Jobs? Would you be willing to invest in Apple with Tim Cook at the helm? Why or why not?

4-15. Microsoft took an early lead in the development of tablet devices (like the iPad), and it had the world's leading operating system and applications for more than 20 years. Provide five reasons why Microsoft has not been able to achieve the same success that Apple has. Most industry analysts would agree that the skills and abilities of Microsoft's 124,000 employees are as good, on average, as Apple's.

4-16. Considering your answers to the previous four questions if you had a spare $5,000 in your portfolio and wanted to buy an equity stock with it, would you buy AAPL (Apple)? Why or why not?

MyLab MIS

Go to the Assignments section of your MyLab to complete these writing exercises.

4-17. Suppose your first job after graduating from college is working at a large insurance company. Your boss asks you to analyze the impact self-driving cars will have on revenues from car insurance policies. List four ways self-driving cars could impact the insurance industry. Justify your answers.

4-18. Visit *www.distrowatch.com*. Click on one of the top five listed Linux distributions (like Mint, Manjaro, Debian, Ubuntu, or Solus). Click on the Screenshots link for that distribution. List some similarities between this operating system and your current operating system. Summarize the advantages and disadvantages of switching from your current operating system to a Linux distribution.

ENDNOTES

1. Bernard Marr, "Really Big Data at Walmart: Real-Time Insights from Their 40+ Petabyte Data Cloud," *Forbes*, January 23, 2017, accessed May 30, 2018, *www.forbes.com/sites/bernardmarr/2017/01/23/really-big-data-at-walmart-real-time-insights-from-their-40-petabyte-data-cloud*.
2. Pamela Vagata and Kevin Wilfong, "Scaling the Facebook Data Warehouse to 300 PB," *Facebook.com*, accessed May 30, 2018, *https://code.facebook.com/posts/229861827208629/scaling-the-facebook-data-warehouse-to-300-pb*.
3. Kashmir Hill, "Blueprints of NSA's Ridiculously Expensive Data Center in Utah Suggest It Holds Less Info Than Thought," *Forbes.com*, accessed May 30, 2018, *www.forbes.com/sites/kashmirhill/2013/07/24/blueprints-of-nsa-data-center-in-utah-suggest-its-storage-capacity-is-lessimpressive-than-thought*.
4. Cisco Systems, Inc., "VNI Forecast Highlights," *Cisco.com*, accessed May 30, 2018, *www.cisco.com/c/m/en_us/solutions/service-provider/vni-forecast-highlights.html*.
5. Amazon, "Amazon Celebrates Biggest Holiday; More Than Four Million People Trialed Prime in One Week Alone This Season," press release,

December 26, 2017, accessed May 30, 2018, *http://phx.corporate-ir.net/phoenix.zhtml?c=176060&p=irol-newsArticle&ID=2324045*.
6. General Electric, "Industrial Internet," accessed May 30, 2018, *www.ge.com/reports/tag/industrial-internet/*.
7. Ibid.
8. Jennifer Warnick, "88 Acres: How Microsoft Quietly Built the City of the Future," Microsoft Corp., accessed May 30, 2018, *www.microsoft.com/en-us/news/stories/88acres/88-acres-how-microsoft-quietly-builtthe-city-of-the-future-chapter-1.aspx*.
9. Allan V. Cook, Ryan Jones, Ash Raghavan, and Irfan Saif, "Digital Reality: The Focus Shifts from Technology to Opportunity," *Deloitte Insights*, December 5, 2017, accessed May 30, 2018, *www2.deloitte.com/insights/us/en/focus/tech-trends/2018/immersive-technologies-digital-reality.html*.
10. Eric Johnson, "Choose Your Reality: Virtual, Augmented or Mixed," *Re/code*, July 27, 2015, accessed May 30, 2018, *www.casact.org/community/affiliates/bace/0517/KPMG.pdf*.
11. See Microsoft's site for the latest MR applications being developed for HoloLens: *www.microsoft.com/microsoft-hololens/en-us*.

12. KPMG, "The Chaotic Middle: The Autonomous Vehicle, Insurance and Potential New Market Entrants," May 12, 2017, accessed May 30, 2018, *www.kpmg.com/US/en/IssuesAndInsights/ArticlesPublications/Documents/automobile-insurancein-the-era-of-autonomous-vehicles-survey-results-june-2015.pdf.*

13. Saeed Elnai, "The Uber Accident, Waymo Technology and the Future of Self-Driving Cars," *Forbes,* May 24, 2018, accessed May 30, 2018, *www.forbes.com/sites/forbestechcouncil/2018/05/24/the-uber-accident-waymo-technology-and-the-future-of-self-driving-cars.*

14. Jack Nicas, "Apple, Spurned by Others, Signs Deal with Volkswagen for Driverless Cars," *The New York Times,* May 23, 2018, accessed May 30, 2018, *www.nytimes.com/2018/05/23/technology/apple-bmw-mercedes-volkswagen-driverless-cars.html.*

15. KPMG, "The Chaotic Middle: The Autonomous Vehicle, Insurance and Potential New Market Entrants," May 12, 2017, accessed May 30, 2018, *www.kpmg.com/US/en/IssuesAndInsights/ArticlesPublications/Documents/automobile-insurancein-the-era-of-autonomous-vehicles-survey-results-june-2015.pdf.*

16. Network of Employers for Traffic Safety, "10 Facts Employers Must Know," accessed May 30, 2018, *http://trafficsafety.org/safety/fleet-safety/10-facts-employers-must-know.*

17. Liz Stinson, "For Super Bowl, Nike Uses 3-D Printing to Create a Faster Football Cleat," *Wired,* January 10, 2014, accessed May 30, 2018, *www.wired.com/2014/01/nike-designed-fastest-cleat-history.*

18. Scott Grunewald, "Nike's 3D Printed Sprinting Shoe the Zoom Superfly Flyknit Will Be Worn at the 2016 Olympic Games in Rio," *3DPrint.com,* April 27, 2016, accessed May 30, 2018, *https://3dprint.com/131549/nike-zoom-superfly-flyknit.*

19. See EDAG's GENESIS prototype car at *www.EDAG.de.*

20. "Net Applications," accessed May 30, 2018, *www.netapplications.com.*

21. Previously called metro-style. Name change by Microsoft, reputedly because of a trademark lawsuit from Europe.

22. "Net Applications," accessed May 30, 2018, *www.netapplications.com.*

23. *DistroWatch.com,* accessed May 30, 2018, *www.distrowatch.com.*

24. "Net Applications," accessed May 30, 2018, *www.netapplications.com.*

25. Pew Research Center, "Device Ownership," February 1, 2018, accessed May 30, 2018, *www.pewinternet.org/fact-sheet/mobile.*

26. "Unlocking the Cloud," *The Economist,* May 28, 2009.

27. Not quite true. Much of the design and possibly some of the code can be reused between native applications. But, for your planning, assume that it all must be redone. Not enough will carry over to make it worth considering.

28. Cisco Systems Inc., "Cisco Visual Networking Index: Global Mobile Data Traffic Forecast Update, 2016–2021 White Paper," *Cisco.com,* March 28, 2017, accessed May 31, 2018, *www.cisco.com/c/en/us/solutions/collateral/service-provider/visual-networking-index-vni/mobile-white-paper-c11-520862.html.*

29. Ibid.

30. Horace Dediu, "Late Late Majority," *Asymco.com,* May 4, 2016, accessed May 30, 2018, *www.asymco.com/2014/07/08/late-late-majority.*

31. Pew Research Center, "Device Ownership," February 1, 2018, accessed May 30, 2018, *www.pewinternet.org/fact-sheet/mobile.*

32. Statista, "Mobile Retail E-commerce Sales in the United States from 2013 to 2021 (in Billion U.S. Dollars)," *Statista.com,* accessed May 30, 2018, *www.statista.com/statistics/249855/mobile-retail-commerce-revenue-in-the-united-states/.*

33. Pew Research Center, "Device Ownership," February 1, 2018, accessed May 30, 2018, *www.pewinternet.org/fact-sheet/mobile.*

34. SnoopWall, "SnoopWall Flashlight Apps Threat Assessment Report," October 1, 2014, *SnoopWall.com,* accessed May 30, 2018, *www.snoopwall.com/threat-reports-10-01-2014.*

35. Symantec Corporation, "Internet Security Report," *Symantec.com,* Volume 20, April 2015, accessed May 30, 2018, *www4.symantec.com/mktginfo/whitepaper/ISTR/21347932_GA-internet-security-threatreport-volume-20-2015-social_v2.pdf.*

36. Google, "Android Security 2014 Year in Review," *GoogleUserContent.com,* accessed May 30, 2018, *http://static.googleusercontent.com/media/source.android.com/en/us/devices/tech/security/reports/Google_Android_Security_2014_Report_Final.pdf.*

37. Teena Maddox, "Research: 74 Percent Using or Adopting BYOD," *ZDNet,* January 5, 2015, accessed May 30, 2018, *www.zdnet.com/article/research-74-percent-using-or-adopting-byod.*

38. "CDH," accessed May 30, 2018, *www.cdh.com.*

39. Robert McMillan, "IBM Worries iPhone's Siri Has Loose Lips," last modified May 24, 2012, *www.cnn.com/2012/05/23/tech/mobile/ibmsiri-ban/index.html?iphoneemail.*

40. Artyom Dogtiev, "App Download and Usage Statistics," BusinessofApps, May 25, 2018, *www.businessofapps.com/data/app-statistics/.*

41. Joe Rossignol, "What You Need to Know About iOS Malware XcodeGhost," *MacRumors,* March 4, 2016, *www.macrumors.com/2015/09/20/xcodeghost-chinese-malware-faq.*

42. Larry Magid, "App Privacy Issues Deeply Troubling," *The Huffington Post,* March 4, 2016, *www.huffingtonpost.com/larry-magid/iphone-appprivacy_b_1290529.html.*

43. Terrie Morgan-Besecker, "Cellphone Apps Can Invade Your Privacy," *Government Technology,* March 4, 2016, *www.govtech.com/applications/Cellphone-Apps-Can-Invade-Your-Privacy.html.*

44. Horia Ungureanu, "TAG Microsoft, HoloLens, Augmented Reality Microsoft HoloLens Full Processor, RAM and Storage Specs Revealed: All You Need to Know," *Tech Times,* May 4, 2016, accessed May 30, 2018, *www.techtimes.com/articles/155683/20160504/microsofthololens-full-processor-ram-and-storage-specs-revealed-all-you-need-toknow.htm.*

45. Ken Yeung, "Microsoft Partners with Autodesk to Bring 3D Product Design to HoloLens," *VentureBeat,* November 30, 2015, accessed May 30, 2018, *http://venturebeat.com/2015/11/30/microsoft-partners-with-autodesk-to-bring-3d-product-design-to-hololens.*

46. Will Shanklin, "Apple Watch Review: Elegant, Delightful . . . and Completely Optional," April 29, 2015, *Gizmag.com,* accessed May 30, 2018, *www.gizmag.com/apple-watch-review-iwatch-review/37244.*

47. "Portfolio's Worst American CEOs of All Time," *CNBC.com,* accessed May 30, 2018, *www.cnbc.com/id/30502091?slide=8.*

48. "Net Applications," accessed May 30, 2018, *www.netapplications.com.*

49. Marketing Charts, "Apple Remains the Retail Leader in Sales per Square Foot," *Marketingcharts.com,* August 7, 2017, accessed May 30, 2018, *www.marketingcharts.com/industries/retail-and-e-commerce-79421.*

50. Yukari Iwatani Kane and Ian Sherr, "Secrets from Apple's Genius Bar: Full Loyalty, No Negativity," *Wall Street Journal,* last modified June 15, 2011, *http://online.wsj.com/article/SB10001424052702304563104576364071955678908.html.*

51. Apple presentation at the Apple Worldwide Developers Conference, June 6, 2011.

52. Apple Inc., "Developer Earnings from the App Store Top $70 Billion," *Apple.com,* June 1, 2017, accessed May 30, 2018, *www.apple.com/newsroom/2017/06/developer-earnings-from-the-app-store-top-70-billion/.*

CHAPTER 5

Database Processing

"The tricky part is correctly identifying the inventory item," says Seth Wilson, eHermes' director of IT services. "We've tested hundreds of inventory items, and we're seeing about 85 percent accuracy in identifying items. The item needs to be positioned and lighted correctly, and then the system identifies items pretty well. But it doesn't do well with one-of-a-kind items or items that are really old."

"That sounds pretty good to me," says Victor Vazquez, eHermes' COO.

"Yes, it would really help us get items into inventory more quickly and accurately. Currently, customers have to manually upload images and a short description of each item. But sometimes the description isn't that great. That makes it hard for buyers to find the item they want. If we had more information about each item—say, color, age, brand name, or type—it would be much easier for customers to find the types of items they really want."

Seth reaches over and puts a small toy tractor in the portable photography light-box and clicks his mouse. The image appears on his monitor, and data starts filling in below it. Pointing at the screen, he says, "Once we correctly identify the item, we can also pull in customer reviews, product review videos, and links to the manufacturers' sites, and we can show comparative prices of previously sold items."

MyLab MIS

Using Your Knowledge
Questions 5-1, 5-2, 5-3
Essay Questions 5-20, 5-21

Victor smiles broadly. "Wow, this is great. Customers will love it. How long before we can push this out?"

Seth winces slightly. "We're still working out some of the details. We're using Google's image classifier API to identify the images. Depending on the features we want, it could cost us a few dollars per 1,000 images searched. But we'll need more data storage, a redesigned database, a new application front end, and possibly a new DBMS."

"Hmm . . . the image search doesn't sound too expensive. But the database redesign and the new application sound pricey," Victor says with a concerned tone.

"Not really. We can do the database redesign in house. We created it ourselves, so it won't cost much to redesign it. And I know a good local application developer, so that cost will be minimal. The increased storage costs will be minimal because we've got a fairly large NAS [Network Attached Storage] in our data center. It's just figuring out all the data flows, APIs, storage requirements, and security protections that are worrisome. We're sending and receiving data from multiple different data sources."

Victor nods understandingly. "I see. It sounds like the data sources might be an issue going forward."

"For sure. We'd be relying on Google for all of our image identification. If they increased their prices, we'd be at their mercy. We'd also be linking to videos on YouTube and product pages at manufacturers' sites, and we'd be pulling product reviews from other online Web sites. Internally we'd be tying in past sales data. That would increase our data processing needs. I just want to make sure it's all going to work together."

"That's understandable. But don't you think the rewards outweigh the risks?" Victor says, shaking his head.

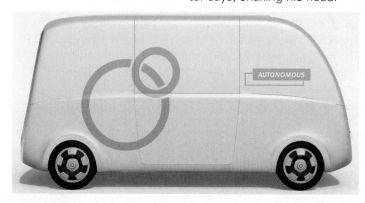

"We're seeing about 85 percent accuracy in identifying items."

Source: Haiyin Wang/Alamy Stock Photo

"Of course," Seth says, smiling. "It will be awesome. We can install these lightboxes in each mobile storefront with built-in digital cameras. Sellers will place their items in the lightboxes, and the boxes will automatically recognize the items. In seconds the system will fill in all related data fields, suggest an approximate sale price, and start marketing the item to potential buyers. Items would sell much more quickly because sellers would more accurately price their items based on the past sales of similar items. Sellers wouldn't have to write lengthy descriptions anymore."

"Sounds great. What's our next step?"

"We've got some database redesign and application development work to do. Then we'll install a lightbox in a mobile storefront and test the data transfers and new systems. We've got a lot of work ahead of us."

Study QUESTIONS

Q5-1	What is the purpose of a database?
Q5-2	What is a database?
Q5-3	What is a database management system (DBMS)?
Q5-4	How do database applications make databases more useful?
Q5-5	How are data models used for database development?
Q5-6	How is a data model transformed into a database design?
Q5-7	How can eHermes benefit from a database system?
Q5-8	2029?

Chapter PREVIEW

Although you may not realize it, you access dozens, if not hundreds, of databases every day. Every time you make a cell phone call, log on to the Internet, or buy something online using a credit card, applications behind the scenes are processing numerous databases. Use Snapchat, Facebook, Twitter, or LinkedIn, and again applications are processing databases on your behalf. Google something, and yet again dozens of databases are processed to obtain the search results.

As a user, you need know nothing about the underlying technology. From your perspective, "It just works," to quote the late Steve Jobs. However, as a business professional in the 21st century, it's a different story. You need the knowledge of this chapter for four principal reasons:

1. When you participate in the development of any new business initiative, you need to know if database technology can facilitate your project goals. If so, you need sufficient knowledge to assess whether building that database is akin to building a small shed or is closer to building a skyscraper. Victor, in the opening vignette of this chapter, needs to have some knowledge to assess how hard (and thus how expensive) building that new database will be.

2. Because databases are ubiquitous in commerce, billions upon billions of bytes of data are stored every day. You need to know how to turn that data into a format from which you can construct useful information. To that end, you might use one of many different graphical tools to query that data. Or, to become truly proficient, you might learn SQL, an international standard language for querying databases. Many business professionals have done just that.

3. Business is dynamic, and information systems must adapt. Often such adaptation means that the structure of the database needs to be changed. Sometimes it means that entirely new databases must be created. As you will learn in this chapter, only the users, such as yourself, know what and how details should be stored. You may be asked to evaluate a data model like those described in Q5-4 to facilitate database change and creation.

4. Finally, you might someday find yourself or your department in a material mess. Maybe you don't know who has which equipment, or where certain tools are located, or what's really in your supply closet. In that case, you might choose to build your own database. Unless you're an IS professional, that database will be small and relatively simple, but it can still be very useful to you and your colleagues. Case Study 5 on page 195 illustrates one such example.

This chapter addresses the why, what, and how of database processing. We begin by describing the purpose of a database and then explain the important components of database systems. Next, we discuss data modeling and show how IS professionals use data models to design database structure. We then discuss how a redesigned database system could be used to solve the item identification and inventory problem at eHermes. We'll wrap up with pondering where database technology might be in 2029.

Q5-1 What Is the Purpose of a Database?

The purpose of a database is to keep track of things. When most students learn that, they wonder why we need a special technology for such a simple task. Why not just use a list? If the list is long, put it into a spreadsheet.

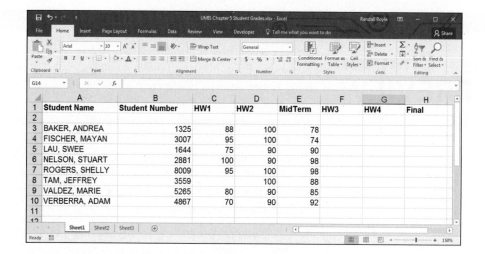

FIGURE 5-1

A List of Student Grades Presented in a Spreadsheet

Source: Excel 2016, Windows 10, Microsoft Corporation.

In fact, many professionals do keep track of things using spreadsheets. If the structure of the list is simple enough, there is no need to use database technology. The list of student grades in Figure 5-1, for example, works perfectly well in a spreadsheet.

Suppose, however, that the professor wants to track more than just grades. Say that the professor wants to record email messages as well. Or perhaps the professor wants to record both email messages and office visits. There is no place in Figure 5-1 to record that additional data. Of course, the professor could set up a separate spreadsheet for email messages and another one for office visits, but that awkward solution would be difficult to use because it does not provide all of the data in one place.

Instead, the professor wants a form like that in Figure 5-2. With it, the professor can record student grades, emails, and office visits all in one place. A form like the one in Figure 5-2 is difficult, if not impossible, to produce from a spreadsheet. Such a form is easily produced, however, from a database.

The key distinction between Figures 5-1 and 5-2 is that the data in Figure 5-1 is about a single theme or concept. It is about student grades only. The data in Figure 5-2 has multiple themes; it shows student grades, student emails, and student office visits. We can make a general rule from these examples: Lists of data involving a single theme can be stored in a spreadsheet; lists that involve data with multiple themes require a database. We will say more about this general rule as this chapter proceeds.

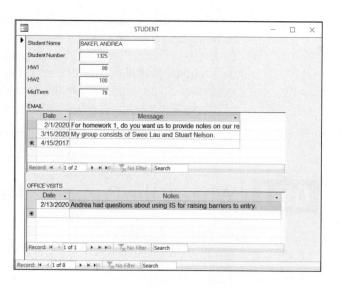

FIGURE 5-2

Student Data Shown in a Form from a Database

Source: Access 2016, Windows 10, Microsoft Corporation.

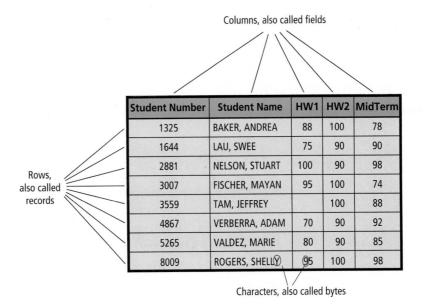

FIGURE 5-3
Student Table (also called a file)

Q5-2 What Is a Database?

A **database** is a self-describing collection of integrated records. To understand the terms in this definition, you first need to understand the terms illustrated in Figure 5-3. As you learned in Chapter 4, a **byte** is a character of data. In databases, bytes are grouped into **columns**, such as *Student Number* and *Student Name*. Columns are also called **fields**. Columns or fields, in turn, are grouped into **rows**, which are also called **records**. In Figure 5-3, the collection of data for all columns (*Student Number, Student Name, HW1, HW2,* and *MidTerm*) is called a *row* or a *record*. Finally, a group of similar rows or records is called a **table** or a **file**. From these definitions, you can see a hierarchy of data elements, as shown in Figure 5-4.

It is tempting to continue this grouping process by saying that a database is a group of tables or files. This statement, although true, does not go far enough. As shown in Figure 5-5, a database is a collection of tables *plus* relationships among the rows in those tables, *plus* special data, called

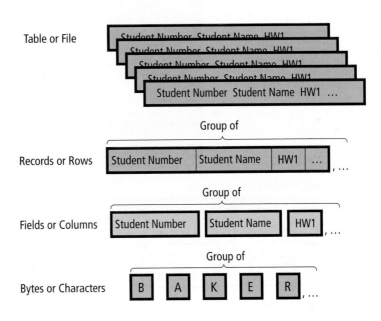

FIGURE 5-4
Hierarchy of Data Elements

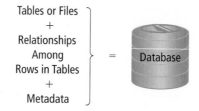

FIGURE 5-5
Components of a Database

metadata, that describes the structure of the database. By the way, the cylindrical symbol ▊ labeled "database" in Figure 5-5 represents a computer disk drive. It is used like this because databases are most frequently stored on disks.

Relationships Among Rows

Consider the terms on the left-hand side of Figure 5-5. You know what tables are. To understand what is meant by *relationships among rows in tables*, examine Figure 5-6. It shows sample data from the three tables *Email, Student,* and *Office_Visit*. Notice the column named *Student Number* in the *Email* table. That column indicates the row in *Student* to which a row of *Email* is connected. In the first row of *Email*, the *Student Number* value is 1325. This indicates that this particular email was received from the student whose *Student Number* is 1325. If you examine the *Student* table, you will see that the row for Andrea Baker has this value. Thus, the first row of the *Email* table is related to Andrea Baker.

FIGURE 5-6
Example of Relationships Among Rows

Email Table

EmailNum	Date	Message	Student Number
1	2/1/2020	For homework 1, do you want us to provide notes on our references?	1325
2	3/15/2020	My group consists of Swee Lau and Stuart Nelson.	1325
3	3/15/2020	Could you please assign me to a group?	1644

Student Table

Student Number	Student Name	HW1	HW2	MidTerm
1325	BAKER, ANDREA	88	100	78
1644	LAU, SWEE	75	90	90
2881	NELSON, STUART	100	90	98
3007	FISCHER, MAYAN	95	100	74
3559	TAM, JEFFREY		100	88
4867	VERBERRA, ADAM	70	90	92
5265	VALDEZ, MARIE	80	90	85
8009	ROGERS, SHELLY	95	100	98

Office_Visit Table

VisitID	Date	Notes	Student Number
2	2/13/2020	Andrea had questions about using IS for raising barriers to entry.	1325
3	2/17/2020	Jeffrey is considering an IS major. Wanted to talk about career opportunities.	3559
4	2/17/2020	Will miss class Friday due to job conflict.	4867

Now consider the last row of the *Office_Visit* table at the bottom of the figure. The value of *Student Number* in that row is 4867. This value indicates that the last row in *Office_Visit* belongs to Adam Verberra.

From these examples, you can see that values in one table relate rows of that table to rows in a second table. Several special terms are used to express these ideas. A **key** (also called a **primary key**) is a column or group of columns that identifies a unique row in a table. *Student Number* is the key of the *Student* table. Given a value of *Student Number*, you can determine one and only one row in *Student*. Only one student has the number 1325, for example.

Every table must have a key. The key of the *Email* table is *EmailNum*, and the key of the *Office_Visit* table is *VisitID*. Sometimes more than one column is needed to form a unique identifier. In a table called *City*, for example, the key would consist of the combination of columns (*City, State*) because a given city name can appear in more than one state.

Student Number is not the key of the *Email* or the *Office_Visit* tables. We know that about *Email* because there are two rows in *Email* that have the *Student Number* value 1325. The value 1325 does not identify a unique row; therefore, *Student Number* cannot be the key of *Email*.

Nor is *Student Number* a key of *Office_Visit*, although you cannot tell that from the data in Figure 5-6. If you think about it, however, there is nothing to prevent a student from visiting a professor more than once. If that were to happen, there would be two rows in *Office_Visit* with the same value of *Student Number*. It just happens that no student has visited twice in the limited data in Figure 5-6.

In both *Email* and *Office_Visit*, *Student Number* is a key, but it is a key of a different table, namely *Student*. Hence, the columns that fulfill a role like that of *Student Number* in the *Email* and *Office_Visit* tables are called **foreign keys**. This term is used because such columns are keys, but they are keys of a different (foreign) table than the one in which they reside.

Before we go on, databases that carry their data in the form of tables and that represent relationships using foreign keys are called **relational databases**. (The term *relational* is used because another, more formal name for a table like those we're discussing is **relation**.) You'll learn about another kind of database, or data store, in Q5-8 and in Case Study 5.

Metadata

Recall the definition of database: A database is a self-describing collection of integrated records. The records are integrated because, as you just learned, rows can be linked together by their key/foreign key relationship. Relationships among rows are represented in the database. But what does *self-describing* mean?

Databases and information systems can be complex enough that only a few internal employees know how to operate them. What happens when these employees use them for their own gain? See the Ethics Guide on pages 168–169 for an example case.

It means that a database contains, within itself, a description of its contents. Think of a library. A library is a self-describing collection of books and other materials. It is self-describing because the library contains a catalog that describes the library's contents. The same idea also pertains to a database. Databases are self-describing because they contain not only data, but also data about the data in the database.

Metadata is data that describes data. Figure 5-7 shows metadata for the *Email* table. The format of metadata depends on the software product that is processing the database. Figure 5-7 shows the metadata as it appears in Microsoft Access. Each row of the top part of this form describes a column of the *Email* table. The columns of these descriptions are *Field Name*, *Data Type*, and *Description*. *Field Name* contains the name of the column, *Data Type* shows the type of data the column may hold, and *Description* contains notes that explain the source or use of the column. As you can see, there is one row of metadata for each of the four columns of the *Email* table: *EmailNum*, *Date*, *Message*, and *Student Number*.

The bottom part of this form provides more metadata, which Access calls *Field Properties*, for each column. In Figure 5-7, the focus is on the *Date* column (note the light rectangle drawn around the *Date* row). Because the focus is on *Date* in the top pane, the details in the bottom pane pertain to the *Date* column. The Field Properties describe formats, a default value for Access to supply when a new row is created, and the constraint that a value is required for this column. It is not important

MINING AT WORK

Richard pulled into the employee lot and steered his shiny new sedan into a front-row spot. The office looked entirely different at night with the lot empty and only a handful of the offices illuminated. The new car was his first splurge since graduating from a graduate program a few years earlier. In spite of being in the field for a relatively short time, Richard had already moved up in the technology group and was one of two key system administrators at the company. He swiped his badge at the side entrance and heard the familiar click as the lock released. He worked his way up the dimly lit staircase to the server room on the tenth floor. As he moved toward the end of the hallway, Richard could smell the aroma of burgers and fries, his boss' staple meal on these overnight systems upgrade projects. He wasn't sure which was harder for him to tolerate—the greasy odor of the food or the presence of his boss, Steve.

Crypto-holic

Steve had been working for the company for several decades. The only thing rivaling his expertise was his propensity to complain. Steve's rants focused mainly on the incompetence of company executives and the salary increase he thought he deserved. When Richard grudgingly joined him for lunch a few times a week, Steve tended to go on and on about a variety of tech-related topics. However, lately Steve seemed interested in the surging popularity and value of cryptocurrencies. Hackers, college students, and tech startups were not only buying cryptocurrencies like bitcoin, but they were setting up computer "rigs" to mine them.

Richard didn't quite understand all of the technical nuances of Steve's tirades, but he surmised that cryptocurrency mining is based on computers compiling the most recent transactions for that type of cryptocurrency and performing complex mathematical calculations. When a "miner's" system successfully contributed to the update of this digital ledger, they received payment in that type of cryptocurrency. As the value of bitcoin increased, for example, more and more people were investing in top-of-the-line computer hardware to increase the odds that their mining system could successfully compete against other miners, helping them accrue as much cryptocurrency as possible.

Richard was especially interested to learn that the demand for these powerful mining rigs was dramatically increasing. High-end graphics processing cards were becoming hard to find, much to the chagrin of the gaming community.[1] Even more interesting was the pilgrimage of crypto-miners to Iceland due to the naturally cold climate that made it easier to keep their systems cool and the geothermal and hydroelectric resources that kept electricity prices low.[2] In fact, the power consumed by mining rigs in Iceland was exceeding that used by the country's residents!

Source: Alexander Blinov/Alamy Stock Photo

Son-of-a-Bitcoin

Richard exchanged pleasantries with Steve, received his instructions for the night, and retreated to his office adjacent to the server room. They would begin rolling out a number of system updates over the next several hours, but Steve insisted on finishing his dinner before starting. Richard opted to cut through the server room, even though it was not the most direct route to his office. As he entered the room, he noticed more activity and noise than usual. "Better check on this," he thought as he unlocked the door to his office. He pulled up a couple monitoring tools he used to manage the servers; everything seemed normal. He then ran a few scripts he had developed on his own, and within a few minutes he found himself staring at his monitor in shock. He slowly pushed back his keyboard and rolled his chair away from the terminal.

Steve had taken his fixation with cryptocurrency mining to a new level. He was not just talking about it, he was actually doing it—on the company's machines! Richard had discovered a rogue program that Steve had installed on all of the servers. It was programmed to run only after hours when employees were home and the processing capabilities of the servers were largely underutilized. This explained the frenzy of light and noise Richard had noticed in the server room—the servers were running the mining program. Steve had clearly underestimated Richard's technical abilities because he had done little to conceal his program.

Richard wasn't sure what to do about his discovery. It was not like Steve was overtly harming the company—the systems were just sitting around idling at night anyway, right? And even if running this program was putting wear and tear on the servers, they were replaced regularly and almost never failed before the replacement cycle began. The only thing it might cost the company was some extra power, but who would know or care about an uptick in the power bill, especially when the company was rapidly growing and regularly adding new staff and offices?

Beyond all of that, Steve was the last person Richard wanted to confront or make angry. He could seriously affect Richard's long-term employment at the company and his job prospects elsewhere. Steve was very well-connected in the tech world. On the other hand, if someone else figured out what was going on, would Richard be accused of complicity? He let out a groan and kept pondering what to do.

DISCUSSION QUESTIONS

1. According to the definitions of the ethical principles previously defined in this book:
   a. Do you think using company resources to mine cryptocurrency is ethical according to the categorical imperative (page 23-24)?
   b. Do you think using company resources to mine cryptocurrency is ethical according to the utilitarian perspective (page 42-43)?
2. Richard is probably the only other person in the company who could detect Steve's mining scheme. How important is it to have ethical employees in positions that can't be easily audited or checked? For these types of positions, is it better to hire a person who behaves ethically but has limited technical skills, or is it better to hire a highly skilled person with moral flexibility?
3. It's unlikely the company has a policy against using too much CPU power; this wasn't even an issue before crypto-mining became popular. Even if Richard turned Steve in, could Steve simply claim he wasn't violating corporate policy? How might Steve justify his mining activities and avoid being fired?
4. Suppose Steve goes to his boss and tells her about his idea. He reminds her that the main corporate office pays all the power bills, so they could just keep the profits within the IT group. Essentially, they could increase their departmental budget by "efficiently" using existing resources. Steve could covertly skim a small percentage off the top for himself and be protected from getting fired at the same time. He might even get a raise. How would you feel if you were the CEO of the company and found out about this sort of crypto-mining activity? How would you respond to the IT group?

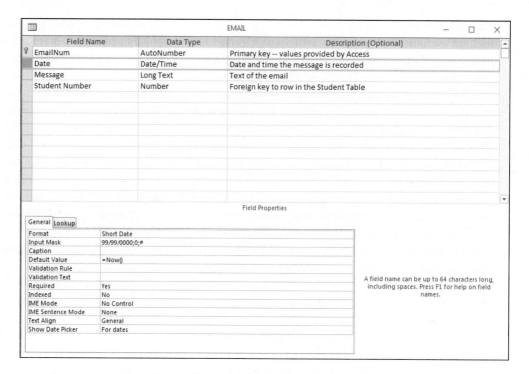

FIGURE 5-7
Sample Metadata (in Access)
Source: Access 2016, Windows 10, Microsoft Corporation.

for you to remember these details. Instead, just understand that metadata is data about data and that such metadata is always a part of a database.

The presence of metadata makes databases much more useful. Because of metadata, no one needs to guess, remember, or even record what is in the database. To find out what a database contains, we just look at the metadata inside the database.

Q5-3   What Is a Database Management System (DBMS)?

A **database management system (DBMS)** is a program used to create, process, and administer a database. As with operating systems, almost no organization develops its own DBMS. Instead, companies license DBMS products from vendors such as IBM, Microsoft, Oracle, and others. Popular DBMS products are **DB2** from IBM, **Access** and **SQL Server** from Microsoft, and **Oracle Database** from the Oracle Corporation. Another popular DBMS is **MySQL**, an open source DBMS product that is license-free for most applications.[3] Other DBMS products are available, but these five process the great bulk of databases today.

Note that a DBMS and a database are two different things. For some reason, the trade press and even some books confuse the two. A DBMS is a software program; a database is a collection of tables, relationships, and metadata. The two are very different concepts.

Creating the Database and Its Structures

Database developers use the DBMS to create tables, relationships, and other structures in the database. The form in Figure 5-7 can be used to define a new table or to modify an existing one. To create a new table, the developer just fills the new table's metadata into the form.

To modify an existing table—say, to add a new column—the developer opens the metadata form for that table and adds a new row of metadata. For example, in Figure 5-8 the developer has added a new column called *Response?*. This new column has the data type *Yes/No*, which means that the column can contain only one value—*Yes* or *No*. The professor will use this column to indicate whether he has responded to the student's email. A column can be removed by deleting its row in this table, though doing so will lose any existing data.

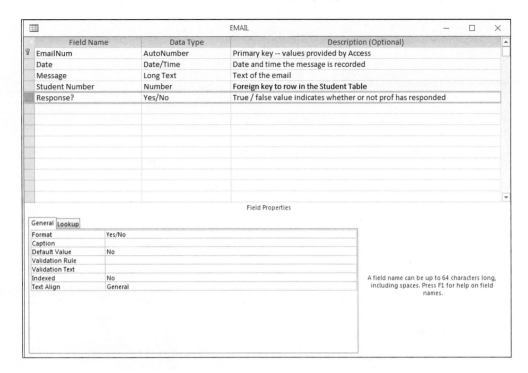

FIGURE 5-8
Adding a New Column to a Table (in Access)

Source: Access 2016, Windows 10, Microsoft Corporation.

Processing the Database

Organizations are collecting large amounts of data. Big data becomes a big target for hackers as described in the Security Guide on pages 190–191.

The second function of the DBMS is to process the database. Such processing can be quite complex, but, fundamentally, the DBMS provides applications for four processing operations: to read, insert, modify, or delete data. These operations are requested in application calls upon the DBMS. From a form, when the user enters new or changed data, a computer program behind the form calls the DBMS to make the necessary database changes. From a Web application, a program on the client or on the server calls the DBMS to make the change.

Structured Query Language (SQL) is an international standard language for processing a database. All five of the DBMS products mentioned earlier accept and process SQL (pronounced "see-quell") statements. As an example, the following SQL statement inserts a new row into the *Student* table:

```
INSERT INTO Student
([Student Number], [Student Name], HW1, HW2, MidTerm)
VALUES
(1000, 'Franklin, Benjamin', 90, 95, 100);
```

As stated, statements like this one are issued "behind the scenes" by programs that process forms and reports. Alternatively, they can be issued directly to the DBMS by an application program.

You do not need to understand or remember SQL language syntax. Instead, just realize that SQL is an international standard for processing a database. SQL can also be used to create databases and database structures. You will learn more about SQL if you take a database management class.

Administering the Database

A third DBMS function is to provide tools to assist in the administration of the database. **Database administration** involves a wide variety of activities. For example, the DBMS can be used to set up a security system involving user accounts, passwords, permissions, and limits for processing the database. To provide database security, a user must sign on using a valid user account before she can process the database.

Permissions can be limited in very specific ways. In the Student database example, it is possible to limit a particular user to reading only *Student Name* from the *Student* table. A different user could be given permission to read the entire *Student* table, but limited to update only the *HW1, HW2,* and *MidTerm* columns. Other users can be given still other permissions.

SO WHAT?
SLICK ANALYTICS

Spreadsheet software designed for small businesses is often misused. For example, if you use spreadsheet software to manage a dataset with several hundreds of thousands of rows of data, you will find that simple operations like sorting and saving updates to the data take several minutes. It is difficult to work effectively and efficiently when minutes are wasted on rudimentary operations. As companies continue to collect larger and larger datasets, there is demand for more robust and scalable data management solutions. These solutions must facilitate rather than hinder the rapid collection and analysis of important data.

Nowadays, a great deal of data collection, storage, and analysis has moved to the cloud. You may not realize it, but you are probably taking advantage of some sort of cloud-based storage solution right now. If you use applications like Dropbox, OneDrive, or Google Drive, you're using the cloud. You no longer need to transfer files from one device to the next using a flash drive or other physical storage medium. You can access your files on any device with Internet connectivity.

As a student, you've probably found cloud storage tremendously convenient (e.g., when sharing large files for a group project with peers). Businesses are harnessing the same power and convenience offered by the cloud, but on a much larger scale. Companies aren't just looking for the convenient file access, though; chief information officers (CIOs) are looking to merge the *storage* and *analysis* of data into one synergistic operation.

Drilling for Answers

Laredo Petroleum is an example of a company that has recognized the benefits offered by cloud analytics.[4] In a recent interview, the CIO described the cumbersome data analysis process the company had been using to improve its drilling operations. The company's old approach entailed the use of numerous spreadsheets and manual calculations that took a long time to perform. By the time actionable insights had been extracted from the data, the value of the information had already been diminished due to old age.

One important question Laredo Petroleum must answer is when it should clean chemical deposits in its wells. Cleaning these deposits boosts the efficiency of wells, but sending maintenance teams to clean the wells is costly. Laredo Petroleum transitioned from the antiquated spreadsheet-based approach of analyzing this problem to using a cloud-based analytics platform. This new approach made data management more scalable, data analysis more robust, and data accessibility better. Data could now be accessed on both traditional PCs and mobile devices at any time and in any location.[5]

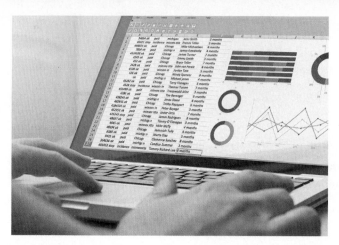

Source: Georgejmclittle/Fotolia

Cloud analytics provide a much nimbler information systems architecture. It can respond to changes in market conditions more easily (e.g., the dramatic drops in oil prices in 2008 and 2015 have affected how Laredo Petroleum does business). Laredo Petroleum isn't the only company that has identified cloud analytics as a viable solution for surviving and thriving in a world driven by Big Data. A recent study reported that global cloud analytics would grow by 46 percent through 2020.[6] The widespread interest in cloud analytics is likely driven by improvements in data storage and analysis functionality like enhanced scalability, parallelism across devices, resource pooling, and agile virtualization.[7]

Cloudburst?

It's easy to tout the benefits of cloud services, but you may be wondering if there are downsides. Think about your own use of cloud services. Are there any aspects of storing your files in the cloud that concern you? Some people are apprehensive about storing their photos and financial data (e.g., tax returns) in the cloud. Are their data being stored securely? Is it safe to allow your personal data out in the "wild" where it is out of your control?

There are other risks too. Could your data be permanently lost due to a system failure or a malicious insider at your cloud service provider?[8] Could a denial-of-service attack against your cloud service provider render your data inaccessible for an extended period of time?[9] As with any system, security often comes at the expense of convenience. As a business leader, you must consider if the *benefits* of cloud-based services outweigh the potential *risks*, which in some cases may turn into real losses.

Questions

1. Have you chosen to store any of your personal data in the cloud? If so, do you store all of your data or only certain types of data? If not, what factors have inhibited you from putting your data in the hands of a cloud provider? If you don't use cloud-based storage, how do you back up your data?

2. This article discussed the specific example of a petroleum company using cloud-based data analytics to improve decision making. What other industries can you identify that would benefit from the ability to capture large quantities of data in real time, analyze the data, and then use the results of those analyses to make better decisions?

3. This article mentions that some users may decide to manage their data "in house" rather than use cloud-based services and risk losing access to their data in the event of a denial-of-service (DoS) attack. Take a few minutes to research what a DoS attack is and how it could prevent users from accessing their data. Be prepared to explain this concept to another classmate or the class.

4. In a business setting, what types of organizations would place greater value on security rather than convenience? What types of organizations would prioritize convenience over security?

In addition to security, DBMS administrative functions include backing up database data, adding structures to improve the performance of database applications, removing data that are no longer wanted or needed, and similar tasks.

For important databases, most organizations dedicate one or more employees to the role of database administration. Figure 5-9 summarizes the major responsibilities for this function. You will learn more about this topic if you take a database management course.

Category	Database Administration Task	Description
Development	Create and staff DBA function	Size of DBA group depends on size and complexity of database. Groups range from one part-time person to small group.
	Form steering committee	Consists of representatives of all user groups. Forum for community-wide discussions and decisions.
	Specify requirements	Ensure that all appropriate user input is considered.
	Validate data model	Check data model for accuracy and completeness.
	Evaluate application design	Verify that all necessary forms, reports, queries, and applications are developed. Validate design and usability of application components.
Operation	Manage processing rights and responsibilities	Determine processing rights/restrictions on each table and column.
	Manage security	Add and delete users and user groups as necessary; ensure that security system works.
	Track problems and manage resolution	Develop system to record and manage resolution of problems.
	Monitor database performance	Provide expertise/solutions for performance improvements.
	Manage DBMS	Evaluate new features and functions.
Backup and Recovery	Monitor backup procedures	Verify that database backup procedures are followed.
	Conduct training	Ensure that users and operations personnel know and understand recovery procedures.
	Manage recovery	Manage recovery process.
Adaptation	Set up request tracking system	Develop system to record and prioritize requests for change.
	Manage configuration change	Manage impact of database structure changes on applications and users.

FIGURE 5-9
Summary of Database Administration (DBA) Tasks

How Do Database Applications Make Databases More Useful?

A set of database tables, by itself, is not very useful; the tables in Figure 5-6 contain the data the professor wants, but the format is awkward at best. The data in database tables can be made more useful, or more available for the conception of information, when it is placed into forms like that in Figure 5-2 or other formats.

A **database application** is a collection of forms, reports, queries, and application programs[10] that serves as an intermediary between users and database data. Database applications reformat database table data to make it more informative and more easily updated. Application programs also have features that provide security, maintain data consistency, and handle special cases.

The specific purposes of the four elements of a database application are:

Forms	View data; insert new, update existing, and delete existing data
Reports	Structured presentation of data using sorting, grouping, filtering, and other operations
Queries	Search based on data values provided by the user
Application programs	Provide security, data consistency, and special purpose processing, (e.g., handle out-of-stock situations)

Database applications came into prominence in the 1990s and were based on the technology available at that time. Many existing systems today are long-lived extensions to those applications; the ERP system SAP (discussed in Chapter 8) is a good example of this concept. You should expect to see these kinds of applications during the early years of your career.

Today, however, many database applications are based on newer technology that employs browsers, the Web, and related standards. These browser-based applications can do everything the older ones do, but they are more dynamic and better suited to today's world. To see why, consider each type.

Traditional Forms, Queries, Reports, and Applications

In most cases, a traditional database is shared among many users. In that case, the application shown in Figure 5-10 resides on the users' computers and the DBMS and database reside on a server computer. A network, in most cases *not* the Internet, is used to transmit traffic back and forth between the users' computers and the DBMS server computer.

FIGURE 5-10
Components of a Database Application System

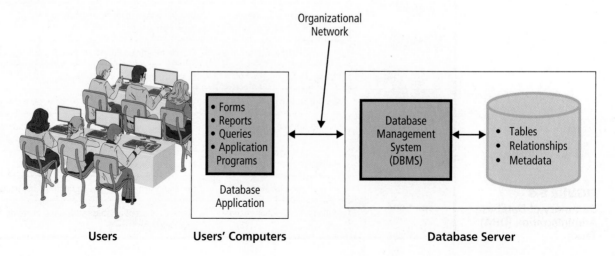

Student Homework Progress with Emails

Student Name	Student Number	HW1	HW2
BAKER, ANDREA	1325	88	100

Email Date	Message
3/15/2020	My group consists of Swee Lau and Stuart Nelson.
2/1/2020	For homework 1, do you want us to provide notes on our references?

Student Name	Student Number	HW1	HW2
LAU, SWEE	1644	75	90

Email Date	Message
3/15/2020	Could you please assign me to a group?

FIGURE 5-11
Example of a Student Report

Single-user databases like those in Microsoft Access are an exception. With such databases, the application, the DBMS, and the database all reside on the user's computer.

Traditional forms appeared in window-like displays like that in Figure 5-2. They serve their purpose; users can view, insert, modify, and delete data with them, but by today's standards, they look clunky.

Figure 5-11 shows a traditional report, which is a static display of data, placed into a format that is meaningful to the user. In this report, each of the emails for a particular student is shown after the student's name and grade data. Figure 5-12 shows a traditional query. The user specifies query criteria in a window-like box (Figure 5-12a), and the application responds with data that fit those criteria (Figure 5-12b).

Traditional database application programs are written in object-oriented languages such as C++ and VisualBasic (and even in earlier languages like COBOL). They are thick applications that need to be installed on users' computers. In some cases, all of the application logic is contained in a program on users' computers and the server does nothing except run the DBMS and serve up data. In other cases, some application code is placed on both the users' computers and the database server computer.

As stated, in the early years of your career, you will still see traditional applications, especially for enterprise-wide applications like ERP and CRM. Most likely, you will also be concerned, as a user if not in a more involved way, with the transition from such traditional applications into browser-based applications.

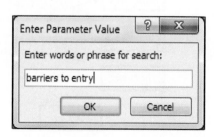

FIGURE 5-12A
Sample Query Form Used to Enter Phrase for Search
Source: Access 2016, Windows 10, Microsoft Corporation.

FIGURE 5-12B
Sample Query Results of Query Operation
Source: Access 2016, Windows 10, Microsoft Corporation.

Student Name	Date	Notes
BAKER, ANDREA	2/13/2020	Andrea had questions about using IS for raising barriers to entry.

Office Visits Keyword Query

Record: 1 of 1 — No Filter — Search

Browser Forms, Reports, Queries, and Applications

The databases in browser-based applications are nearly always shared among many users. As shown in Figure 5-13, the users' browsers connect over the Internet to a Web server computer, which in turn connects to a database server computer (often many computers are involved on the server side of the Internet).

Browser applications are thin-client applications that need not be preinstalled on the users' computers. In most cases, all of the code for generating and processing the application elements is shared between the users' computers and the servers. JavaScript is the standard language for user-side processing. Languages like C# and Java are used for server-side code, though JavaScript is starting to be used on the server with an open source product named Node.js.

Browser database application forms, reports, and queries are displayed and processed using html and, most recently, using html5, css3, and JavaScript as you learned in Chapter 4. Figure 5-14 shows a browser form that is used to create a new user account in Office 365. The form's content is dynamic; the user can click on the blue arrow next to *Additional Details* to see more data. Also, notice the steps on the left-hand side that outline the process that the administrator will follow when creating the new account. The current step is shown in color. Compare and contrast this form with that in Figure 5-2; it is cleaner, with much less chrome.

Figure 5-15 illustrates a browser report that shows the content of a SharePoint site. The content is dynamic; almost all of the items can be clicked to produce other reports or take other actions. The user can search the report in the box in the upper-right-hand corner to find specific items. Browser-based applications can support traditional queries, but more exciting are **graphical queries**, in which query criteria are created when the user clicks on a graphic.

Security requirements are more stringent for browser-based Internet applications than for traditional ones. Most traditional applications run within a corporate network protected from threats common on the Internet. Browser-based applications that are open to the public, over the Internet, are far more vulnerable. Thus, protecting security is a major function for browser-based Internet application programs. Like traditional database application programs, they need to provide for data

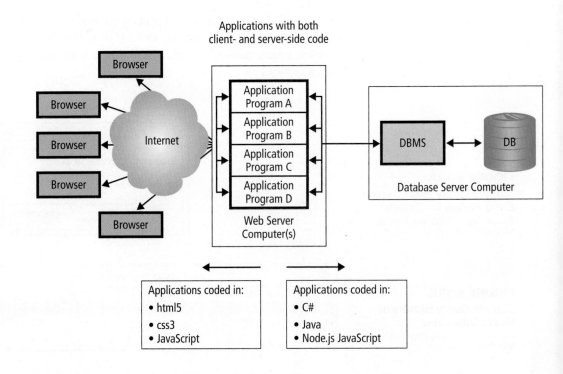

FIGURE 5-13
Four Application Programs on a Web Server Computer

Microsoft
Online Services

New user

1. **Details**
2. Settings
3. Licenses
4. Email
5. Results

Details
Name

* Required

First name: Drew
Last name: Mills
* Display name: Drew
* User name: Drew   @   Office365inBusiness.com

Additional details ▾

Next   Cancel

FIGURE 5-14
Account Creation Browser Form
Source: Windows 10, Microsoft Corporation.

consistency and to handle special conditions as well. As an example of the need for data consistency, consider the problems introduced by multi-user processing.

Multi-user Processing

Most traditional and browser-based applications involve multiple users processing the same database. While such **multi-user processing** is common, it does pose unique problems that you, as a future manager, should know about. To understand the nature of those problems, consider the following scenario, which could occur on either a traditional or browser-based application.

At a ticket vendor's Web site, two customers, Andrea and Jeffrey, are both attempting to buy tickets to a popular event. Andrea uses her browser to access the site and finds that two tickets are available. She places both of them in her shopping cart. She doesn't know it, but when she opened

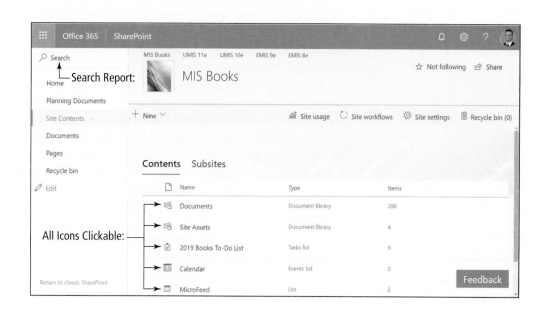

FIGURE 5-15
Browser Report
Source: Access 2016, Windows 10, Microsoft Corporation.

the order form, she invoked an application program on the vendor's servers that read a database to find that two tickets are available. Before she checks out, she takes a moment to verify with her friend that they still want to go.

Meanwhile, Jeffrey uses his browser and also finds that two tickets are available because his browser activates that same application that reads the database and finds (because Andrea has not yet checked out) that two are available. He places both in his cart and checks out.

Meanwhile, Andrea and her friend decide to go, so she checks out. Clearly, we have a problem. Both Andrea and Jeffrey have purchased the same two tickets. One of them is going to be disappointed.

This problem, known as the **lost-update problem**, exemplifies one of the special characteristics of multi-user database processing. To prevent this problem, some type of locking must be used to coordinate the activities of users who know nothing about one another. Locking brings its own set of problems, however, and those problems must be addressed as well. We will not delve further into this topic here, however.

Be aware of possible data conflicts when you manage business activities that involve multi-user processing. If you find inaccurate results that seem not to have a cause, you may be experiencing multi-user data conflicts. Contact your IS department for assistance.

Q5-5 How Are Data Models Used for Database Development?

In Chapter 12, we will describe the process for developing information systems in detail. However, business professionals have such a critical role in the development of database applications that we need to anticipate part of that discussion here by introducing two topics—data modeling and database design.

Because the design of the database depends entirely on how users view their business environment, user involvement is critical for database development. Think about the Student database. What data should it contain? Possibilities are: *Students, Classes, Grades, Emails, Office_Visits, Majors, Advisers, Student_Organizations*—the list could go on and on. Further, how much detail should be included in each? Should the database include campus addresses? Home addresses? Billing addresses?

In fact, there are unlimited possibilities, and the database developers do not and cannot know what to include. They do know, however, that a database must include all the data necessary for the users to perform their jobs. Ideally, it contains that amount of data and no more. So, during database development, the developers must rely on the users to tell them what to include in the database.

Database structures can be complex, in some cases very complex. So, before building the database the developers construct a logical representation of database data called a **data model**. It describes the data and relationships that will be stored in the database. It is akin to a blueprint. Just as building architects create a blueprint before they start building, so, too, database developers create a data model before they start designing the database.

To learn more about a career as a data engineer, see the Career Guide on page 192.

Figure 5-16 summarizes the database development process. Interviews with users lead to database requirements, which are summarized in a data model. Once the users have approved (validated) the data model, it is transformed into a database design. That design is then implemented into database structures. We will consider data modeling and database design briefly in the next two sections. Again, your goal should be to learn the process so that you can be an effective user representative for a development effort.

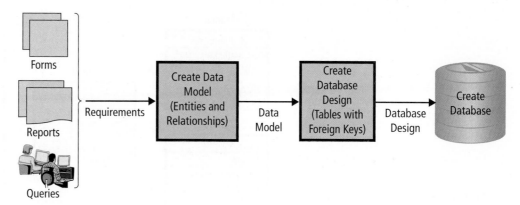

FIGURE 5-16
Database Development Process

What Is the Entity-Relationship Data Model?

The **entity-relationship (E-R) data model** is a tool for constructing data models. Developers use it to describe the content of a data model by defining the things (*entities*) that will be stored in the database and the *relationships* among those entities. A second, less popular tool for data modeling is the **Unified Modeling Language (UML)**. We will not describe that tool here. However, if you learn how to interpret E-R models, with a bit of study you will be able to understand UML models as well.

Entities

An **entity** is some thing that the users want to track. Examples of entities are *Order, Customer, Salesperson,* and *Item.* Some entities represent a physical object, such as *Item* or *Salesperson;* others represent a logical construct or transaction, such as *Order* or *Contract.* For reasons beyond this discussion, entity names are always singular. We use *Order,* not *Orders; Salesperson,* not *Salespersons.*

Entities have **attributes** that describe characteristics of the entity. Example attributes of *Order* are *OrderNumber, OrderDate, SubTotal, Tax, Total,* and so forth. Example attributes of *Salesperson* are *SalespersonName, Email, Phone,* and so forth.

Entities have an **identifier**, which is an attribute (or group of attributes) whose value is associated with one and only one entity instance. For example, *OrderNumber* is an identifier of *Order* because only one *Order* instance has a given value of *OrderNumber.* For the same reason, *CustomerNumber* is an identifier of *Customer.* If each member of the sales staff has a unique name, then *SalespersonName* is an identifier of *Salesperson.*

Before we continue, consider that last sentence. Is the salesperson's name unique among the sales staff? Both now and in the future? Who decides the answer to such a question? Only the users know whether this is true; the database developers cannot know. This example underlines why it is important for you to be able to interpret data models because only users like you will know for sure.

Figure 5-17 shows examples of entities for the Student database. Each entity is shown in a rectangle. The name of the entity is just above the rectangle, and the identifier is shown in a section at the top of the entity. Entity attributes are shown in the remainder of the rectangle. In Figure 5-18, the *Adviser* entity has an identifier called *AdviserName* and the attributes *Phone, CampusAddress,* and *EmailAddress.*

Observe that the entities *Email* and *Office_Visit* do not have an identifier. Unlike *Student* or *Adviser,* the users do not have an attribute that identifies a particular email. We *could* make one up. For example, we could say that the identifier of *Email* is *EmailNumber,* but if we do so we are not modeling how the users view their world. Instead, we are forcing something onto the

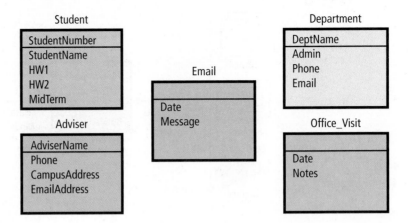

FIGURE 5-17
Student Data Model Entities

users. Be aware of this possibility when you review data models about your business. Do not allow the database developers to create something in the data model that is not part of your business world.

Relationships

Entities have **relationships** to each other. An *Order*, for example, has a relationship to a *Customer* entity and also to a *Salesperson* entity. In the Student database, a *Student* has a relationship to an *Adviser*, and an *Adviser* has a relationship to a *Department*.

Figure 5-19 shows sample *Department, Adviser,* and *Student* entities and their relationships. For simplicity, this figure shows just the identifier of the entities and not the other attributes. For this sample data, *Accounting* has three professors—Jones, Wu, and Lopez—and *Finance* has two professors—Smith and Greene.

The relationship between *Advisers* and *Students* is a bit more complicated because in this example, an adviser is allowed to advise many students and a student is allowed to have many advisers. Perhaps this happens because students can have multiple majors. In any case, note that Professor Jones advises students 100 and 400 and that student 100 is advised by both Professors Jones and Smith.

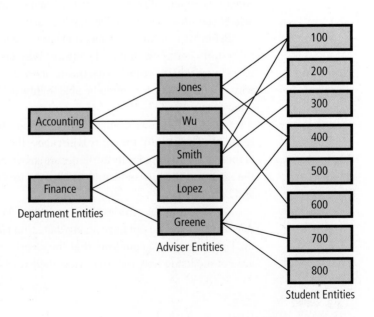

FIGURE 5-18

Example of Department, Adviser, and Student Entities and Relationships

FIGURE 5-19
Sample Relationships Version 1

Diagrams like the one in Figure 5-18 are too cumbersome for use in database design discussions. Instead, database designers use diagrams called **entity-relationship (E-R) diagrams**. Figure 5-19 shows an E-R diagram for the data in Figure 5-18. In this figure, all of the entities of one type are represented by a single rectangle. Thus, there are rectangles for the *Department*, *Adviser*, and *Student* entities. Attributes are shown as before in Figure 5-17.

Additionally, a line is used to represent a relationship between two entities. Notice the line between *Department* and *Adviser*, for example. The vertical bar on the left side of the relationship means that an adviser works in just one department. The forked lines on the right side of that line signify that a department may have more than one adviser. The angled lines, which are referred to as **crow's feet**, are shorthand for the multiple lines between *Department* and *Adviser* in Figure 5-18. Relationships like this one are called **1:N**, or **one-to-many relationships**, because one department can have many advisers, but an adviser has at most one department.

Now examine the line between *Adviser* and *Student*. Notice the crow's feet that appear at each end of the line. This notation signifies that an adviser can be related to many students and that a student can be related to many advisers, which is the situation in Figure 5-18. Relationships like this one are called **N:M**, or **many-to-many relationships**, because one adviser can have many students and one student can have many advisers.

Students sometimes find the notation N:M confusing. Interpret the N and M to mean that a variable number, greater than one, is allowed on each side of the relationship. Such a relationship is not written N:N because that notation would imply that there are the same number of entities on each side of the relationship, which is not necessarily true. N:M means that more than one entity is allowed on each side of the relationship and that the number of entities on each side can be different.

Figure 5-20 shows the same entities with different assumptions. Here, advisers may advise in more than one department, but a student may have only one adviser, representing a policy that students may not have multiple majors.

Which, if either, of these versions is correct? Only the users know. These alternatives illustrate the kinds of questions you will need to answer when a database designer asks you to check a data model for correctness.

Figures 5-19 and 5-20 are typical examples of an entity-relationship diagram. Unfortunately, there are several different styles of entity-relationship diagrams. This one is called, not surprisingly, a **crow's-foot diagram** version. You may learn other versions if you take a database management class.

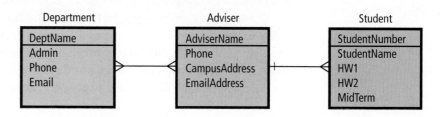

FIGURE 5-20
Sample Relationships Version 2

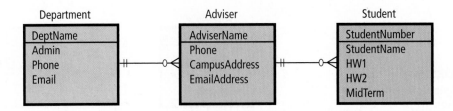

FIGURE 5-21
Sample Relationships Showing Both Maximum and Minimum Cardinalities

The crow's-foot notation shows the maximum number of entities that can be involved in a relationship. Accordingly, they are called the relationship's **maximum cardinality**. Common examples of maximum cardinality are 1:N, N:M, and 1:1 (not shown).

Another important question is "What is the minimum number of entities required in the relationship?" Must an adviser have a student to advise, and must a student have an adviser? Constraints on minimum requirements are called **minimum cardinalities**.

Figure 5-21 presents a third version of this E-R diagram that shows both maximum and minimum cardinalities. The second vertical bar on the lines means that at least one entity of that type is required. The small oval means that the entity is optional; the relationship *need not* have an entity of that type. Using this notation, if there are two vertical bars, both the minimum and maximum cardinality are one. If there is a vertical bar with a crow's foot, then the minimum cardinality is one and the maximum is many.

Thus, in Figure 5-21 a department is not required to have a relationship to any adviser, but an adviser is required to belong to a department. Similarly, an adviser is not required to have a relationship to a student, but a student is required to have a relationship to an adviser. Note, also, that the maximum cardinalities in Figure 5-21 have been changed so that both are 1:N.

Is the model in Figure 5-21 a good one? It depends on the policy of the university. Again, only the users know for sure.

Q5-6 How Is a Data Model Transformed into a Database Design?

Database design is the process of converting a data model into tables, relationships, and data constraints. The database design team transforms entities into tables and expresses relationships by defining foreign keys. Database design is a complicated subject; as with data modeling, it occupies weeks in a database management class. In this section, however, we will introduce two important database design concepts: normalization and the representation of two kinds of relationships. The first concept is a foundation of database design, and the second will help you understand important design considerations.

Normalization

Normalization is the process of converting a poorly structured table into two or more well-structured tables. A table is such a simple construct that you may wonder how one could possibly be poorly structured. In truth, there are many ways that tables can be malformed—so many, in fact, that researchers have published hundreds of papers on this topic alone.

Consider the *Employee* table in Figure 5-22a. It lists employee names, hire dates, email addresses, and the name and number of the department in which the employee works. This table seems innocent enough. But consider what happens when the Accounting department changes its name to Accounting and Finance. Because department names are duplicated in this table, every row that has a value of "Accounting" must be changed to "Accounting and Finance."

FIGURE 5-22

A Poorly Designed Employee Table

Employee

Name	HireDate	Email	DeptNo	DeptName
Jones	Feb 1, 2018	Jones@ourcompany.com	100	Accounting
Smith	Dec 3, 2020	Smith@ourcompany.com	200	Marketing
Chau	March 7, 2020	Chau@ourcompany.com	100	Accounting
Greene	July 17, 2019	Greene@ourcompany.com	100	Accounting

(a) Table Before Update

Employee

Name	HireDate	Email	DeptNo	DeptName
Jones	Feb 1, 2018	Jones@ourcompany.com	100	Accounting and Finance
Smith	Dec 3, 2020	Smith@ourcompany.com	200	Marketing
Chau	March 7, 2020	Chau@ourcompany.com	100	Accounting and Finance
Greene	July 17, 2019	Greene@ourcompany.com	100	Accounting

(b) Table with Incomplete Update

Data Integrity Problems

Suppose the Accounting name change is correctly made in two rows, but not in the third. The result is shown in Figure 5-22b. This table has what is called a **data integrity problem:** Some rows indicate that the name of Department 100 is "Accounting and Finance," and another row indicates that the name of Department 100 is "Accounting."

This problem is easy to spot in this small table. But consider a table like the *Customer* table in the Amazon database or the eBay database. Those databases have millions of rows. Once a table that large develops serious data integrity problems, months of labor will be required to remove them.

Data integrity problems are serious. A table that has data integrity problems will produce incorrect and inconsistent results. Users will lose confidence in the data, and the system will develop a poor reputation. Information systems with poor reputations become serious burdens to the organizations that use them.

Normalizing for Data Integrity

The data integrity problem can occur only if data are duplicated. Because of this, one easy way to eliminate the problem is to eliminate the duplicated data. We can do this by transforming the table design in Figure 5-22a into two tables, as shown in Figure 5-23. Here the name of the department is stored just once; therefore, no data inconsistencies can occur.

Of course, to produce an employee report that includes the department name, the two tables in Figure 5-23 will need to be joined back together. Because such joining of tables is common, DBMS products have been programmed to perform it efficiently, but it still requires work. From this example, you can see a trade-off in database design: Normalized tables eliminate data duplication, but they can be slower to process. Dealing with such trade-offs is an important consideration in database design.

The general goal of normalization is to construct tables such that every table has a *single* topic or theme. In good writing, every paragraph should have a single theme. This is true of databases

FIGURE 5-23
Two Normalized Tables

Employee

Name	HireDate	Email	DeptNo
Jones	Feb 1, 2018	Jones@ourcompany.com	100
Smith	Dec 3, 2020	Smith@ourcompany.com	200
Chau	March 7, 2020	Chau@ourcompany.com	100
Greene	July 17, 2019	Greene@ourcompany.com	100

Department

DeptNo	DeptName
100	Accounting
200	Marketing
300	Information Systems

as well; every table should have a single theme. The problem with the table design in Figure 5-22 is that it has two independent themes: employees and departments. The way to correct the problem is to split the table into two tables, each with its own theme. In this case, we create an *Employee* table and a *Department* table, as shown in Figure 5-23.

As mentioned, there are dozens of ways that tables can be poorly formed. Database practitioners classify tables into various **normal forms** according to the kinds of problems they have. Transforming a table into a normal form to remove duplicated data and other problems is called *normalizing* the table.[11] Thus, when you hear a database designer say, "Those tables are not normalized," she does not mean that the tables have irregular, not-normal data. Instead, she means that the tables have a format that could cause data integrity problems.

Summary of Normalization

As a future user of databases, you do not need to know the details of normalization. Instead, understand the general principle that every normalized (well-formed) table has one and only one theme. Further, tables that are not normalized are subject to data integrity problems.

Be aware, too, that normalization is just one criterion for evaluating database designs. Because normalized designs can be slower to process, database designers sometimes choose to accept non-normalized tables. The best design depends on the users' processing requirements.

Representing Relationships

Figure 5-24 shows the steps involved in transforming a data model into a relational database design. First, the database designer creates a table for each entity. The identifier of the entity becomes the key of the table. Each attribute of the entity becomes a column of the table. Next, the resulting tables are normalized so that each table has a single theme. Once that has been done, the next step is to represent the relationships among those tables.

- Represent each entity with a table
  - Entity identifier becomes table key
  - Entity attributes become table columns
- Normalize tables as necessary
- Represent relationships
  - Use foreign keys
  - Add additional tables for N:M relationships

FIGURE 5-24
Transforming a Data Model into a Database Design

For example, consider the E-R diagram in Figure 5-25a. The *Adviser* entity has a 1:N relationship to the *Student* entity. To create the database design, we construct a table for *Adviser* and a second table for *Student*, as shown in Figure 5-25b. The key of the *Adviser* table is *AdviserName*, and the key of the *Student* table is *StudentNumber*.

Further, the *EmailAddress* attribute of the *Adviser* entity becomes the *EmailAddress* column of the *Adviser* table, and the *StudentName* and *MidTerm* attributes of the *Student* entity become the *StudentName* and *MidTerm* columns of the *Student* table.

The next task is to represent the relationship. Because we are using the relational model, we know that we must add a foreign key to one of the two tables. The possibilities are: (1) place the foreign key *StudentNumber* in the *Adviser* table or (2) place the foreign key *AdviserName* in the *Student* table.

The correct choice is to place *AdviserName* in the *Student* table, as shown in Figure 5-25c. To determine a student's adviser, we just look into the *AdviserName* column of that student's row. To

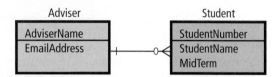

(a) 1:N Relationship Between Adviser and Student Entities

Adviser Table—Key Is AdviserName

AdviserName	EmailAddress
Jones	Jones@myuniv.edu
Choi	Choi@myuniv.edu
Jackson	Jackson@myuniv.edu

Student Table—Key Is StudentNumber

StudentNumber	StudentName	MidTerm
100	Lisa	90
200	Jennie	85
300	Jason	82
400	Terry	95

(b) Creating a Table for Each Entity

Adviser Table—Key Is AdviserName

AdviserName	EmailAddress
Jones	Jones@myuniv.edu
Choi	Choi@myuniv.edu
Jackson	Jackson@myuniv.edu

Foreign key column represents relationship

Student—Key Is StudentNumber

StudentNumber	StudentName	MidTerm	AdviserName
100	Lisa	90	Jackson
200	Jennie	85	Jackson
300	Jason	82	Choi
400	Terry	95	Jackson

(c) Using the *AdviserName* Foreign Key to Represent the 1:N Relationship

FIGURE 5-25
Representing a 1:N Relationship

determine the adviser's students, we search the *AdviserName* column in the *Student* table to determine which rows have that adviser's name. If a student changes advisers, we simply change the value in the *AdviserName* column. Changing *Jackson* to *Jones* in the first row, for example, will assign student 100 to Professor Jones.

For this data model, placing *StudentNumber* in *Adviser* would be incorrect. If we were to do that, we could assign only one student to an adviser. There is no place to assign a second adviser.

This strategy for placing foreign keys will not work for N:M relationships, however. Consider the data model in Figure 5-26a; here advisers and students have a many-to-many relationship. An adviser may have many students, and a student may have multiple advisers (for multiple majors).

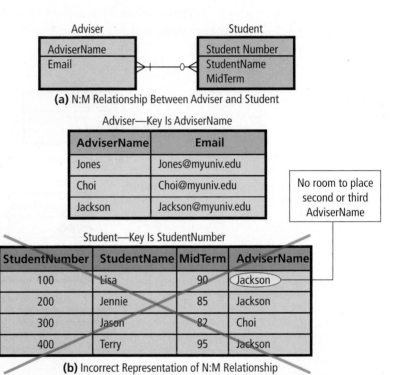

(a) N:M Relationship Between Adviser and Student

Adviser—Key Is AdviserName

AdviserName	Email
Jones	Jones@myuniv.edu
Choi	Choi@myuniv.edu
Jackson	Jackson@myuniv.edu

No room to place second or third AdviserName

Student—Key Is StudentNumber

StudentNumber	StudentName	MidTerm	AdviserName
100	Lisa	90	Jackson
200	Jennie	85	Jackson
300	Jason	82	Choi
400	Terry	95	Jackson

(b) Incorrect Representation of N:M Relationship

Adviser—Key Is AdviserName

AdviserName	Email
Jones	Jones@myuniv.edu
Choi	Choi@myuniv.edu
Jackson	Jackson@myuniv.edu

Student—Key Is StudentNumber

StudentNumber	StudentName	MidTerm
100	Lisa	90
200	Jennie	85
300	Jason	82
400	Terry	95

Adviser_Student_Intersection

AdviserName	StudentNumber
Jackson	100
Jackson	200
Choi	300
Jackson	400
Choi	100
Jones	100

Student 100 has three advisers

FIGURE 5-26

Representing an N:M Relationship

(c) Adviser_Student_Intersection Table Represents the N:M Relationship

To see why the foreign key strategy we used for 1:N relationships will not work for N:M relationships, examine Figure 5-26b. If student 100 has more than one adviser, there is no place to record second or subsequent advisers.

To represent an N:M relationship, we need to create a third table, as shown in Figure 5-26c. The third table has two columns, *AdviserName* and *StudentNumber*. Each row of the table means that the given adviser advises the student with the given number.

As you can imagine, there is a great deal more to database design than we have presented here. Still, this section should give you an idea of the tasks that need to be accomplished to create a database. You should also realize that the database design is a direct consequence of decisions made in the data model. If the data model is wrong, the database design will be wrong as well.

Users' Role in the Development of Databases

As stated, a database is a model of how the users view their business world. This means that the users are the final judges as to what data the database should contain and how the records in that database should be related to one another.

The easiest time to change the database structure is during the data modeling stage. Changing a relationship from one-to-many to many-to-many in a data model is simply a matter of changing the 1:N notation to N:M. However, once the database has been constructed and loaded with data and forms, reports, queries, and application programs have been created, changing a one-to-many relationship to many-to-many means weeks of work.

You can glean some idea of why this might be true by contrasting Figure 5-25c with Figure 5-26c. Suppose that instead of having just a few rows, each table has thousands of rows; in that case, transforming the database from one format to the other involves considerable work. Even worse, however, is that someone must change application components as well. For example, if students have at most one adviser, then a single text box can be used to enter *AdviserName*. If students can have multiple advisers, then a multiple-row table will need to be used to enter *AdviserName* and a program will need to be written to store the values of *AdviserName* into the *Adviser_Student_Intersection* table. There are dozens of other consequences, consequences that will translate into wasted labor and wasted expense.

Thus, *user review of the data model is crucial.* When a database is developed for your use, you must carefully review the data model. If you do not understand any aspect of it, you should ask for clarification until you do. *Entities must contain all of the data you and your employees need to do your jobs, and relationships must accurately reflect your view of the business.* If the data model is wrong, the database will be designed incorrectly, and the applications will be difficult to use, if not worthless. Do not proceed unless the data model is accurate.

As a corollary, when asked to review a data model, take that review seriously. Devote the time necessary to perform a thorough review. Any mistakes you miss will come back to haunt you, and by then the cost of correction may be very high with regard to both time and expense. This brief introduction to data modeling shows why databases can be more difficult to develop than spreadsheets.

Q5-7   How Can eHermes Benefit from a Database System?

eHermes wants to speed up the process of inventorying the new items it receives from sellers. Currently, sales associates have to wait for customers to enter lengthy product descriptions that are often incomplete or incorrect. If associates can take a picture of the new item and use Google's image classifier to automatically recognize it, eHermes will be able to automatically fill in its database. The information would likely be more detailed and accurate than what eHermes is currently getting, and items could be sold much more quickly.

This process would require a lot of data storage and multiple data flows. Images would be sent from mobile storefronts and stored either locally or on the cloud. Then the images would be sent to cloud services to be processed. Once an item is identified, eHermes would query additional sites for product information, reviews, and past sales data. The entire process needs to be fast and scalable as eHermes grows.

eHermes can choose one of two database architectures. For the first one, it can store the images on a file server and keep metadata about each image in a relational database that it can query. That metadata will include the address of the image on the file server. Alternatively, eHermes can utilize one of the new NoSQL DBMS products like **MongoDB**—an open source document-oriented DBMS—to store the images in the same database as the metadata. (See Q5-8.)

Seth Wilson, director of IT services, investigates these two alternatives and discusses his findings with Kamala Patel, an automation expert. They are both intrigued by the possible use of MongoDB, but they know that their interest is, in part, a desire to learn something new. They don't really know how well that product works, nor do they know how robust the MongoDB query facility will be.

On the other hand, they can readily modify their existing Microsoft SQL Server database to store the metadata. In the metadata, they can store the URL of the file server location that has the images (for example, *https://abc.ehermes.com/image1*). In this way, they can use the Microsoft SQL Server to store the data and then query it using the graphical query designer. Because Microsoft SQL Server can also process native SQL, they can use it for the most sophisticated query operations if needed.

Seth and Kamala discuss these alternatives and decide to use Microsoft SQL Server to store the metadata. They know this approach is less risky because it uses known technology. Also, both of them are skilled at using Microsoft SQL Server, and they can develop the database and application quickly with less risk. Seth and Kamala create a short presentation of this recommendation and present it to Jessica Ramma, eHermes' CEO, who approves it.

After the approval, Seth creates the E-R diagram shown in Figure 5-27 and discusses it with Kamala. She thinks that they might want to add an Employee entity rather than just the employee's name in the Analysis entity. They decide, however, that they don't yet have that many employees and that adding the extra entity might make the application too hard to use, at least at present. So, with that decision, they proceed to create the database and related applications. You'll have an opportunity to do the same with a team of your colleagues in Collaboration Exercise 5, page 195.

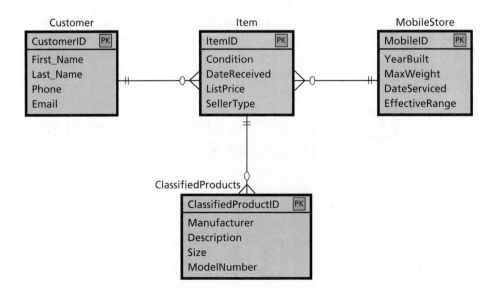

FIGURE 5-27
E-R Diagram for eHermes' Database

Q5-8   2029?

With ever-cheaper data storage and data communications, we can be sure that the volume of database data will continue to grow, probably exponentially, through 2029. All that data contains patterns that can be used to conceive information to help businesses and organizations achieve their strategies. That will make business intelligence, discussed in Chapter 3, even more important. Furthermore, as databases become bigger and bigger, they're more attractive as targets for theft or mischief, as we saw in recent attacks at Yahoo (3 billion accounts), Twitter (330 million accounts), Under Armour (150 million accounts), and Equifax (145 million accounts). Those risks will make database security even more important, as we discuss in Chapter 10.

Additionally, the DBMS landscape is changing. While for years relational DBMS products were the only game in town, the Internet changed that by posing new processing requirements. As compared to traditional database applications, some Internet applications process many, many more transactions against much simpler data. A tweet has a much simpler data structure than the configuration of a Kenworth truck, but there are so many more tweets than truck configurations!

Also, traditional relational DBMS products devote considerable code and processing power to support what are termed **ACID** (atomic, consistent, isolated, durable) transactions. In essence, this acronym means that either all of a transaction is processed or none of it is (atomic), that transactions are processed in the same manner (consistent) whether processed alone or in the presence of millions of other transactions (isolated), and that once a transaction is stored it never goes away—even in the presence of failure (durable).

ACID transactions are critical to traditional commercial applications. Even in the presence of machine failure, Vanguard must process both the sell and the buy sides of a transaction; it cannot process part of a transaction. Also, what it stores today must be stored tomorrow. But many new Internet applications don't need ACID. Who cares if, one time out of 1 million, only half of your tweet is stored? Or if it's stored today and disappears tomorrow?

These new requirements have led to three new categories of DBMS:

1. **NoSQL DBMS**. This acronym is misleading. It really should be non-relational DBMS. It refers to new DBMS products that support very high transaction rates processing relatively simple data structures, replicated on many servers in the cloud, without ACID transaction support. MongoDB, Cassandra, Bigtable, and Dynamo are NoSQL products.
2. **NewSQL DBMS**. These DBMS products process very high levels of transactions, like the NoSQL DBMS, but provide ACID support. They may or may not support the relational model. Such products are a hotbed of development with new vendors popping up nearly every day. Leading products are yet unknown.
3. **In-memory DBMS**. This category consists of DBMS products that process databases in main memory. This technique has become possible because today's computer memories can be enormous and can hold an entire database at one time, or at least very large chunks of it. Usually these products support or extend the relational model. SAP HANA is a computer with an in-memory DBMS that provides high volume ACID transaction support simultaneously with complex relational query processing. Tableau Software's reporting products are supported by a proprietary in-memory DBMS using an extension to SQL.

Does the emergence of these new products mean the death knell for relational databases? It seems unlikely because organizations have created thousands of traditional relational databases with millions of lines of application code that process SQL statements against relational data structures. No organization wants to endure the expense and effort of converting those databases and code to something else. There is also a strong social trend among older technologists to hang onto the relational model. However, these new products are loosening the stronghold that relational

BIG DATA . . . LOSSES

Do you enjoy trivia games? If so, you have probably flipped through the channels on a weeknight and stopped on the trivia game show *Jeopardy!* Successful contestants can quickly answer questions across a range of categories. Winners often repeat their success over several episodes. Long winning streaks are fairly uncommon, however, because they require mastery of an extensive set of topics. Viewers at home often resort to using their phones or computers to look up answers. If you have ever resorted to such tactics, you may have wondered how a computer would fare on *Jeopardy!*

Researchers at IBM had the same question in 2011. They had developed Watson, a supercomputer with advanced functionality that includes natural language processing and data mining. The data accessed by Watson when it competed on *Jeopardy!* included 500 gigabytes worth of dictionaries, encyclopedias, and other reference materials.[12] Since Watson's stunning defeat of two former *Jeopardy!* champions, IBM has been working to leverage Watson for a number of Big Data applications, including health care and marketing analytics.

Other companies witnessed the impressive performance of Watson on *Jeopardy!* and scrambled to develop their own Big Data analytics tools. However, some companies are still trying to figure out how Big Data applications can be used effectively. Furthermore, when focusing on perfecting powerful Big Data tools, some companies consider securing the data collected as an afterthought, if they consider it at all.

Security Loses, Again

Neglecting security for the sake of functionality and convenience is a common thread that runs through decades of technological advancement. For example, many car manufacturers now boast Internet connectivity in their advertisements but have done little to ensure the security and privacy of vehicles connected to the Internet. Technology-focused trade shows focus on the Internet of Things and feature home automation gadgets like Internet-connected lights, thermostats, door locks, and toasters. Unfortunately, the security features in these devices are often lacking or nonexistent.

The Big Data movement is another victim of the march toward technological advancement without thought of security ramifications. Many companies lack the ability to effectively use Big Data tools. As a result, their ability to secure these tools and the data that accompanies them is a grave concern.[13] Based on a recent scan of Big Data apps, a security audit conducted by a Swiss security company confirmed this suspicion. The company's analysis revealed that data on more than 39,000 NoSQL databases are exposed and 1.1 petabytes of this data were also available online.[14]

But what leads to poor security protocols for these Big Data applications?

Rich in Data, Poor in Security

It turns out that security shortcomings in Big Data practices are not isolated. In fact, it is likely that poor database management practices translate into larger and more specialized Big Data "transfers." A recent survey conducted by *InformationWeek* reveals some troubling findings concerning the security issues plaguing Big Data. The survey identified poor database security practices in roughly 20 percent of survey respondents. They found that (1) databases containing sensitive information are not secured, (2) data breaches have occurred or it cannot be confirmed breaches have not occurred, and (3) security evaluations are not regularly conducted on respondents' databases.[15] These factors are driven by the larger problem of Big Data tools prioritizing security below other objectives like functionality, flexible access, and convenience.

In light of these security deficiencies, a number of best practices have been recommended to improve the state of Big Data security. These include logging and auditing all activity to permit the identification of unauthorized access, implementing strict access management protocols, and using better encryption to safeguard sensitive data.[16] Ultimately, securing the data generated and used by data-driven applications is as important as the accuracy and reporting capabilities of the applications themselves!

DISCUSSION QUESTIONS

1. Think about how the trend of capturing and storing data has affected you. What types of data have been generated about you, and where are these data located? What data have you generated yourself? Can you do anything to manage access to or the security of these data?

2. Search the Web to identify a new data-driven application being used by IBM's Watson. Describe how this new application might provide a competitive advantage for the adopting organization.

3. The feature mentions the continuing technological tension between security and convenience. How has this tension affected your own interactions with computers? Do you err on the side of security or convenience when creating and managing your own security "policies"?

4. Have you or anyone you know purchased home-automation devices? Based on a lack of security found in many of these devices, are you willing to accept the risk that comes with these devices in exchange for the convenience they provide?

technology has enjoyed for decades, and it is likely that by 2029 many NoSQL, NewSQL, and in-memory databases will exist in commerce.

Furthermore, existing DBMS vendors like Oracle, Microsoft, and IBM will not sit still. With substantial cash and highly skilled developers, they will likely incorporate features of these new categories of DBMS into their existing or new products. Acquisitions of some of the NewSQL start-ups, in particular, are likely.

What does that mean to you as a business professional? First, such knowledge is useful; stay abreast of developments in this area. When you are given a problem, you might choose to utilize one of these new types of database. Unless you are an IT professional, however, you won't work with them directly. It will be to your advantage to know about them, however, and to suggest their use to the IS personnel who support your requirements.

Also, watch these developments from an investor's perspective. Not all such products will be open source; even if they are, there will be companies that integrate them into their product or service offerings, and those companies may well be good investment opportunities.

If you're interested in IS as a discipline or as a second major, pay attention to these products. You still need to learn the relational model and the processing of relational databases; they will be the bread-and-butter of the industry, even in 2029. But exciting new opportunities and career paths will also develop around these new DBMS products. Learn about them as well, and use that knowledge to separate yourself from the competition when it comes to job interviews.

CAREER GUIDE

Name: Kailey Smith
Company: Artemis Health
Job Title: Director of Data Engineering
Education: University of Utah

Source: Kailey Smith, Artemis Health,
Director of Data Engineering

1 How did you get this type of job?

I started at Artemis Health as a senior data quality engineer after being recruited by one of the co-founders on LinkedIn due to my experience with healthcare data. Because we're a startup, everyone is required to wear a lot of hats, and because of my eagerness to get things done and follow up with the people I was working with, they asked me to manage the team.

2 What attracted you to this field?

I've always enjoyed working with computers and figuring things out, but after taking my first information systems course at the University of Utah, I was sold. This is a field that will be growing and expanding with new and exciting opportunities. There are so many different areas to explore, and you can definitely be paid pretty well!

3 What does a typical workday look like for you (duties, decisions, problems)?

I manage the data team of ETL and SQL engineers, so we work very closely with our customers' data. I work with our COO to find different ways to improve our existing processes, making high-level decisions about how we can migrate to a different system or how we can better implement our next client, but I also jump in on client issues to determine where the bad data is coming from.

4 What do you like most about your job?

I like that there are a variety of things for me to do on a daily basis, and I love solving problems! My company is helping our clients find different ways they can save money on their employee benefits, and a lot of that has to do with the healthcare industry. We have been able to uncover some very interesting things that our customers haven't even thought of.

5 What skills would someone need to do well at your job?

Working with data really takes someone who is analytical and has an eye for detail. Patience is also important. You can spend a whole day going down the wrong path and start over the next day and find the answer within an hour. As far as technical skills, you need to understand data modeling, SQL, and data analysis.

6 Are education or certifications important in your field? Why?

Continually educating yourself on new technology is important for anyone going into the information systems world. If you can show that you're willing to learn on your own as well as on the job, employers will be far more willing to hire you. Microsoft certifications are only really useful if the company you are going to work for uses those applications.

7 What advice would you give to someone who is considering working in your field?

Keep an open mind. Try out new things. When I was in school, I was focused on the security side of things because it sounded more exciting, but I ended up working more on the data side. Figure out what really excites you, but the more you learn, the more opportunities will open up to you.

8 What do you think will be hot tech jobs in 10 years?

Big Data is definitely the "next big thing," but as technology becomes increasingly used in different ways, security is going to be more and more important. It's really so hard to predict because things are changing so rapidly!

ACTIVE REVIEW

Use this Active Review to verify that you understand the ideas and concepts that answer the chapter's study questions.

Q5-1   What is the purpose of a database?

State the purpose of a database. Explain the circumstances in which a database is preferred to a spreadsheet. Describe the key difference between Figures 5-1 and 5-2.

Q5-2   What is a database?

Define the term *database*. Explain the hierarchy of data and name three elements of a database. Define *metadata*. Using the example of *Student* and *Office_Visit* tables, show how relationships among rows are represented in a database. Define the terms *primary key*, *foreign key*, and *relational database*.

Q5-3   What is a database management system (DBMS)?

Explain the acronym *DBMS* and name its functions. List five popular DBMS products. Explain the difference between a DBMS and a database. Summarize the functions of a DBMS. Define *SQL*. Describe the major functions of database administration.

Q5-4   How do database applications make databases more useful?

Explain why database tables, by themselves, are not very useful to buiness users. Name the four elements of a database application and describe the purpose of each. Explain the difference between a database application and a database application program. Describe the nature of traditional database applications. Explain why browser-based applications are better than traditional ones. Name the primary technologies used to support browser-based applications.

Q5-5   How are data models used for database development?

Explain why user involvement is critical during database development. Describe the function of a data model. Sketch the database development process. Define *E-R model, entity, relationship, attribute,* and *identifier*. Give an example, other than one in this text, of an E-R diagram. Define *maximum cardinality* and *minimum cardinality*. Give an example of three maximum cardinalities and two minimum cardinalities. Explain the notation in Figures 5-20 and 5-21.

Q5-6   How is a data model transformed into a database design?

Name the three components of a database design. Define *normalization* and explain why it is important. Define *data integrity problem* and describe its consequences. Give an example of a table with data integrity problems and show how it can be normalized into two or more tables that do not have such problems. Describe two steps in transforming a data model into a database design. Using an example not in this chapter, show how 1:N and N:M relationships are represented in a relational database. Describe the users' role in the database development. Explain why it is easier and cheaper to change a data model than to change an existing database. Use the examples of Figures 5-25c and 5-26c in your answer.

Q5-7   How can eHermes benefit from a database system?

Summarize the two database architectures that eHermes could use for its image database. Describe the architecture it used and explain the rationale for that choice.

Q5-8   2029?

Explain how an increase in database data in the next decade will affect business intelligence and security. Summarize two major requirements that some Internet database applications created. Explain the characteristics of the ACID processing of a transaction. Briefly describe the characteristics of NoSQL, NewSQL, and in-memory DBMS products. Summarize how you should respond to these developments.

Using Your Knowledge with eHermes

You can readily understand why the knowledge of this chapter would be useful to you if you have a job like Seth or Kamala. But what if you are Jessica (the CEO) or Victor (the COO)? The knowledge in this chapter will prepare you to make better decisions like the one that Jessica made in Q5-7. It will also help Victor understand the level of budget required to fund this project. Even if you never create a single query during your career, you will make many decisions that involve the use, creation, and maintenance of databases.

KEY TERMS AND CONCEPTS

Access   170
ACID   189
Attributes   179
Byte   165
Columns   165
Crow's feet   181
Crow's-foot diagram   181
Data integrity
    problem   183
Data model   178
Database   165
Database administration   171
Database application   174
Database management system
    (DBMS)   170
DB2   170
Entity   179
Entity-relationship (E-R)
    data model   179

Entity-relationship (E-R)
    diagrams   181
Fields   165
File   165
Foreign keys   167
Graphical queries   176
Identifier   179
In-memory DBMS   189
Key   167
Lost-update
    problem   178
Many-to-many (N:M)
    relationships   181
Maximum cardinality   182
Metadata   167
Minimum cardinality   182
MongoDB   188
Multi-user processing   177
MySQL   170

NewSQL DBMS   189
Normal forms   184
Normalization   182
NoSQL DBMS   189
One-to-many (1:N)
    relationships   181
Oracle Database   170
Primary key   167
Records   165
Relation   167
Relational databases   167
Relationships   180
Rows   165
SQL server   170
Structured Query Language
    (SQL)   171
Table   165
Unified Modeling Language
    (UML)   179

MyLab MIS

To complete the problems with MyLab MIS, go to EOC Discussion Questions in the MyLab.

USING YOUR KNOWLEDGE

5-1. Draw an entity-relationship diagram that shows the relationships among a database, database applications, and users.
MyLab MIS

5-2. Consider the relationship between *Adviser* and *Student* in Figure 5-21. Explain what it means if the maximum cardinality of this relationship is:
MyLab MIS
   a. N:1
   b. 1:1
   c. 5:1
   d. 1:5

5-3. Identify two entities in the data entry form in Figure 5-28. What attributes are shown for each? What do you think are the identifiers?
MyLab MIS

5-4. Visit *www.acxiom.com*. Navigate the site to answer the following questions.
   a. According to the Web site, what is Acxiom's privacy policy? Are you reassured by its policy? Why or why not?

   b. Make a list of 10 different products that Acxiom provides.
   c. Describe Acxiom's top customers.
   d. Examine your answers in parts b and c and describe, in general terms, the kinds of data that Acxiom must be collecting to be able to provide those products to those customers.
   e. What is the function of InfoBase?
   f. What is the function of PersonicX?
   g. In what ways might companies like Acxiom need to limit their marketing so as to avoid a privacy outcry from the public?
   h. Should there be laws that govern companies like Acxiom? Why or why not?
   i. Should there be laws that govern the types of data services that governmental agencies can buy from companies like Acxiom? Why or why not?

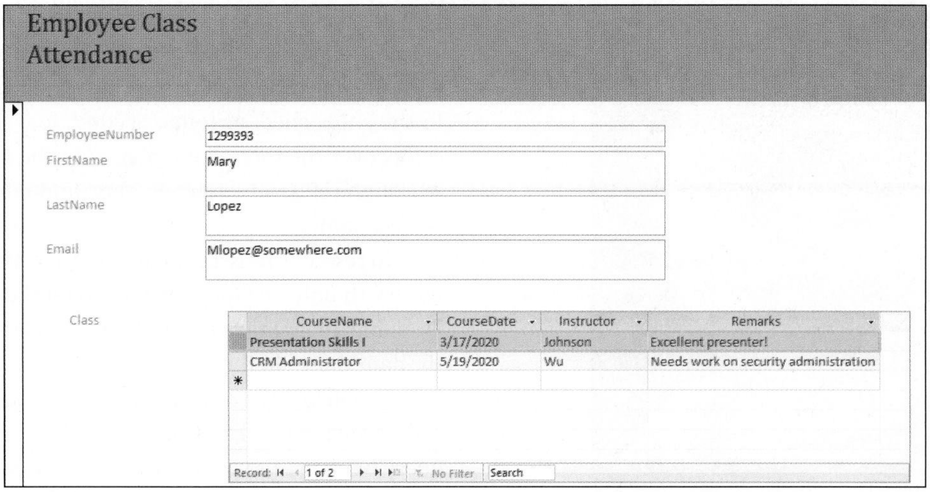

FIGURE 5-28
Sample Data Entry Form

COLLABORATION EXERCISE 5

Using the collaboration IS you built in Chapter 1 (page 32), collaborate with a group of students to answer the following questions.

The eHermes problem is an excellent example of the use of databases in business. It is also within reach for you to develop as a practice exercise. To do so, work with your team to answer the following questions:

5-5. Study Figure 5-27 to understand the entities and their relationships. Justify each of the cardinalities in this model.

5-6. Working with your team, develop a list of seven queries that together use all of the entities in Figure 5-27.

5-7. Modify the E-R model in Figure 5-27 to include a *Manufacturer* entity that is related to the *ClassifiedProducts* entity. Create the relationship, and specify and justify the relationship's cardinalities.

5-8. Discuss the advantages and disadvantages of the model you created in your answer to question 5-7 and the model in Figure 5-27.

5-9. Transform the data model in Figure 5-27 into a relational database design. *Hint:* Create a table for each entity and relate those tables as shown in question 5-6.

5-10. Create an Access database for your design in question 5-9.

5-11. Fill your database with sample data. Because you do not have files on a server, leave the URL column blank.

5-12. Using the Access query facility, process each of the seven queries that you created in your answer to question 5-6.

CASE STUDY 5

Searching for Pianos . . .

Dean Petrich is a certified piano tuner and technician who has been repairing and restoring pianos since 1973. He also has a career as Deano the Clown, a clown entertainer who performs at children's parties in the Seattle, WA, metro area. (See Figure 5-29, *http://deanotheclown.com.*) The schedule of his two businesses balance each other: He's busy as a clown in the late spring, summer, and fall, and during the rest of year, he repairs and restores pianos.

Over the past 20 years, the demand for pianos has dramatically declined. When Grandma dies or the kids move out or some other

life change occurs, families have no further use for their piano, and when they find there is no market for it, they call Dean, who picks up that piano for a modest fee. For a number of years, Dean restored those pianos and either resold or rented them. Since the turn of the century, however, the decreasing demand for pianos has affected him as well, and over time, he's accumulated far too many pianos. Even discarding the worst of them, he has, today, nearly 100.

As you can imagine, 100 pianos consume considerable storage. At first, Dean stored them in his workshop. When he ran out of room in his workshop, he built and stored them in a large

FIGURE 5-29
Deano the Clown
Source: Dean Petrich

best pianos—those he hopes to sell—but he offers many quality pianos for free. However, Dean has two problems. First, he doesn't know which pianos are best and where they are located in the shop, shed, or tents. Second, few people are willing to crawl over the tops of the pianos in the large shed and tents (through refuse of squirrels, rats, and mice) looking for their perfect piano.

To resolve this issue, Dean created a Microsoft Access database with only one table: Piano. To fill the database with data, Dean had to first take an inventory of all the pianos and record the data shown in the columns of Figure 5-32.

As you know, a one-table database could just as easily have been stored in Excel, but Dean used Access because he wants to query his data in a variety of ways. He wants to know, for example, all of the pianos located in a tent that have a sound quality of 4 or higher. And he wants to know which pianos have a sound quality of 1 or less so he can dispose of them. Further, customers have particular needs. One might, for example, want a Baldwin spinet (a type of piano); without a database he has no idea whether he has one or where. Or, when he needs a replacement key top, he might want to know the location of all the pianos in the workshop that have ivory keys and a sound quality of 2 or less, and so on.

Because of the dynamic nature of his needs, Dean uses the Access query facility. Figure 5-33 shows an example query that returns all of the pianos of a sound quality higher than 4 that are located in a tent and Figure 5-34 shows the result of that query. Dean also suspects that the quality deteriorates faster in the tents than in the shed or the shop. To determine if this is the case, he created the report shown in Figure 5-35.

metal shed (Figure 5-30). When the shed overflowed with pianos, he moved them to plastic tents in a meadow on his property (Figure 5-31). Unfortunately, the plastic tents are prone to rips and tears, and because Dean lives in the Pacific Northwest, many pianos have been ruined by rain, even when he covers them with plastic tarps inside the plastic tents.

Two years ago, sinking in his steadily increasing piano inventory, Dean began to offer pianos for free. Not the very

FIGURE 5-30
Pianos in Storage
Source: David Kroenke

FIGURE 5-31
Pianos in Tent
Source: David Kroenke

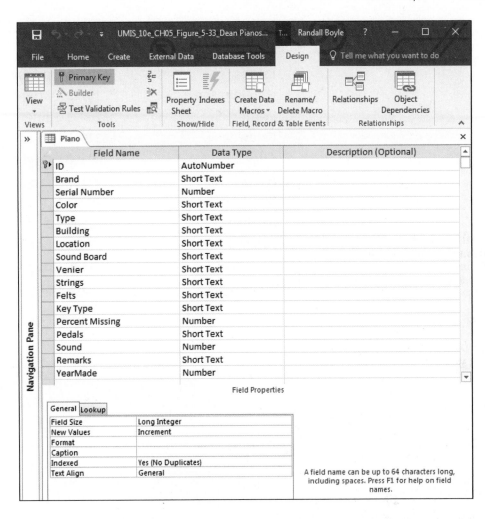

FIGURE 5-32
Columns in the Piano Table
Source: Microsoft Access, Microsoft Corporation.

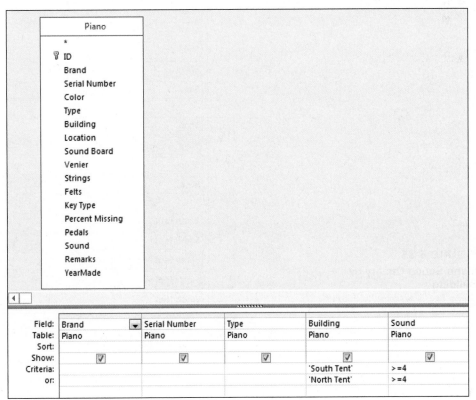

FIGURE 5-33
Example Query
Source: Microsoft Access, Microsoft Corporation.

Brand	Serial Number	Type	Building	Sound
Baldwin	70452	Spinet	South Tent	4
Esteu	20158	Upright	North Tent	4
H.G. Johnson	10749	Upright	North Tent	4
Winter ???	326493	Spinet	North Tent	4
Baldwin	637957	Spinet	North Tent	4
Briggs	80360	Upright	North Tent	4
Hobart Cable	77182	Upright	North Tent	4
Mehlin	28733	Upright	North Tent	4
Aeolian	182562	Spinet	North Tent	4
Farrand	27631	Upright	South Tent	4
Kurtzman	21398	Upright	South Tent	5
Mathushek	12963	Upright	South Tent	4

FIGURE 5-34
Results from Query in Figure 5-33
Source: Microsoft Access, Microsoft Corporation.

Piano Sound Quality by Building

Building	Sound Quality	Number Pianos
North Tent	1	1
North Tent	3	3
North Tent	4	8
Shed	0	10
Shed	1	1
Shed	2	7
Shed	3	13
Shed	4	12
Shop	0	2
Shop	1	2
Shop	3	5
Shop	4	2
South Tent	0	6
South Tent	2	3
South Tent	3	2
South Tent	4	3
South Tent	5	1

FIGURE 5-35
Piano Sound Quality by Building
Source: Microsoft Access, Microsoft Corporation.

QUESTIONS

5-13. Explain why a one-table database could be stored just as readily in Excel as in Access.

5-14. Justify the decision to use Access to store the piano database.

5-15. Examine the columns in Figure 5-32. Name three characteristics of pianos that are not represented in this table.

    a. If you were a consultant advising Dean, what criteria should you and he use in deciding whether to include that additional data?

    b. Is this database a model of an inventory of pianos, or is it a model of Dean's model of an inventory of pianos? Explain the difference.

5-16. Suppose, in addition to the data about pianos, Dean wants to store data about the manufacturer such as its address (or last known address), its years of operation, and general comments about that manufacturer.

    a. Design a Manufacturer table.

    b. Alter the design of the Piano table (Figure 5-32) to represent the relationship between Piano and Manufacturer. State and justify any assumptions.

5-17. Using the data in Figure 5-35, draw conclusions about the effect of location on piano sound quality. Justify your statements using this data.

5-18. Explain the statement "A database is an abstraction of some aspect of a business." Using this example, explain the ways that processing an abstraction is more effective than examining pianos. Explain the ways that processing an abstraction is more efficient that examining pianos. Generalize your observation to databases for business in general.

5-19. This database will soon become useless if it is not kept up to date. List procedures that Dean needs to create and follow to keep his database current.

MyLab MIS

Go to the Assignments section of your MyLab to complete these writing exercises.

5-20. Go to *http://aws.amazon.com* and search for AWS database offerings. Explain the differences among Amazon's RDS, DynamoDB, ElastiCache, and Redshift services. Which of these would you recommend for storing eHermes' data? (By the way, whenever you query the Internet for any AWS product, be sure to include the keyword "AWS" in your search. Otherwise, your search will result in Amazon's lists of books about the item you're searching for.)

5-21. Suppose you are the accounts manager at a wholesale auto parts distributor. You use spreadsheets to keep track of just about everything. So do your employees. You have hundreds of different spreadsheets to update, back up, and share. Some of them are getting extremely large and unwieldy. You're worried about losing track of them or, worse, having a malicious employee permanently destroy them. A new hire fresh out of college says building a database would solve most of your problems. How would you determine if a database would really solve your problems? If you chose to develop a centralized database, how would you choose the employees to create the database? What criteria would you use to select those employees? How would you justify allocating people and money to developing this database?

ENDNOTES

1. Sarah Needleman, "The Computer Part People Are Hoarding: 'I Felt Like I Was Buying Drugs,'" *The Wall Street Journal*, March 27, 2018, www.wsj.com/articles/the-computer-part-people-are-hoarding-i-felt-like-i-was-buying-drugs-1518195876.

2. William Alden, "The Bitcoin Mines of Iceland," *The New York Times*, March 27, 2018, *https://dealbook.nytimes.com/2013/12/23/morning-agenda-the-bitcoin-mines-of-iceland/*.

3. MySQL was supported by the MySQL Company. In 2008, that company was acquired by Sun Microsystems, which was, in turn, acquired by Oracle later that year. However, because MySQL is open source, Oracle does not own the source code.

4. Clint Boulton, "Oil Company Hopes to Strike Efficiency with Cloud Analytics," *CIO.com*, November 10, 2015, accessed June 2, 2018, *www.cio.com/article/3003498/cloud-computing/oil-company-hopes-to-strike-efficiency-with-cloud-analytics.html*.

5. Ibid.

6. James Kobielus, "The All-Consuming Future of Cloud Analytics," *InfoWorld.com*, March 20, 2015, accessed June 2, 2018, *www.infoworld.com/article/2899662/big-data/the-all-consuming-future-ofcloud-analytics.html*.

7. Ibid.

8. Ibid.

9. Fahmida Y. Rashid, "The Dirty Dozen: 12 Cloud Security Threats," InfoWorld.com, March 11, 2016, accessed June 2, 2018, *www.infoworld.com/article/3041078/security/the-dirty-dozen-12-cloudsecurity-threats.html*.

10. Watch out for confusion between a *database application* and a *database application program*. A database application includes forms, reports, queries, and database application programs.

11. See David Kroenke and David Auer, *Database Concepts*, 8th ed., pp. 81–86 (Upper Saddle River, NJ: Pearson Education, 2017) for more information.

12. Elizabeth Dwoskin, "IBM to Sell Watson as a Big-Data Tool," *Digits: Tech Tools & Analysis from the WSJ*, March 6, 2016, *http://blogs.wsj.com/digits/2014/09/16/ibms-watson-computer-now-has-analytics*.

13. John Jordan, "The Risks of Big Data for Companies," *The Wall Street Journal*, March 6, 2016, www.wsj.com/articles/SB10001424052702304526204579102941708296708.

14. John Leyden, "Misconfigured Big Data Apps Are Leaking Data Like Sieves," *The Register*, March 6, 2016, *www.theregister.co.uk/2015/08/13/big_data_apps_expose_data*.

15. Lorna Garey, "Big Data Brings Big Security Problems," *InformationWeek*, March 6, 2016, *www.informationweek.com/big-data/big-data-analytics/big-data-brings-big-security-problems/d/d-id/1252747*.

16. Ibid.

CHAPTER 6

The Cloud

"So, you think the cloud is the answer to our problems?" Jessica Ramma, CEO of eHermes, is meeting with Seth Wilson, director of IT services, and Victor Vazquez, COO, to discuss eHermes' data storage costs.

"Yes, that's right. We could substantially reduce our costs if we outsourced our data storage to the cloud," Seth says confidently.

"The *what?*" Victor says, annoyed.

"The cloud. We move all of our data to the cloud."

Jessica is curious. "OK, Seth, I'll bite. What's the cloud?"

"We lease storage capacity from a third party and access it over the Internet."

Victor is confused. "You mean we'd lease hard drives rather than buy them?"

MyLab MIS

Using Your Knowledge
Questions 6-1, 6-2, 6-3

Essay Questions 6-21, 6-22

"Well, not exactly. We wouldn't be installing any more hard drives in our data center. The cloud would allow us to lease online storage on very, very flexible, pay-as-you-go terms. As our business grows, we can acquire more storage and scale it to meet our needs."

"You mean each day? We can change the terms of our lease on a daily basis?" Victor is skeptical. "OK, so how much does it cost? This can't be cheap."

"How about $10 per terabyte?"

Jessica's puzzled at that. "What do you mean $10 per terabyte?"

"I mean we can get 1 terabyte of online storage for about $10 per month." Seth grins as he says this.

"*What?*" Victor is dumbfounded.

"Yeah, that's it. We can get as much storage as we want, and our systems automatically upload all incoming data from our mobile storefronts. The net difference would be that our average monthly storage costs would be at least 50 percent less than they are now. And that's not counting the power savings, the time saved doing backups, or the fact that we wouldn't have to configure any additional new hardware." Seth isn't quite sure, but he thinks the actual storage costs could be less.

"Seth, you've got to be kidding. We can save tens of thousands of dollars in storage costs. This is *huge*. The money we spend on storage has increased 350 percent in the past year. The company is growing so quickly, we'll need these cost savings. Plus you have the new automated inventory identification development project you're working on. The data storage costs on that project will be considerable." As Victor says this, in the back of his mind he's thinking, "If it's true."

"Well, it's good; I don't know about huge. We'd have additional development costs to set up our systems, and that will take some time. I also worry about being locked into a single vendor, and I have some security concerns."

"Seth, give me a plan. I want a plan," Jessica says, thinking what these savings could mean to the next two quarters . . . and beyond.

"I'll give you something next week."

"I want it by Friday, Seth."

"How about $10 per terabyte?"

Source: Haiyin Wang/Alamy Stock Photo

Study QUESTIONS

Q6-1   Why are organizations moving to the cloud?

Q6-2   How do organizations use the cloud?

Q6-3   What network technology supports the cloud?

Q6-4   How does the Internet work?

Q6-5   How do Web servers support the cloud?

Q6-6   How can eHermes use the cloud?

Q6-7   How can organizations use cloud services securely?

Q6-8   2029?

Chapter PREVIEW

If you go into business for yourself, there's an excellent chance you'll have a problem just like eHermes'. What is the best way to support your information systems? Should you use the cloud? Most likely, the answer will be yes. So, then, which of your applications should use it and how? You need the knowledge of this chapter to partici-pate in the conversations you'll have. Of course, you could just rely on outside experts, but that doesn't work in the 21st century. Many of your competitors will be able to ask and understand those questions—and use the money their knowledge saves them for other purposes.

Or what if you work for a large company that has embraced the Internet of Things (IoT)? Will you make products that send and receive data across the Internet? How will your products connect to the cloud? Will a cloud offering make sense for you and your customers? How will you know without some knowledge of the cloud?

We begin this chapter with an overview of where the cloud came from, why organizations are moving toward it, and how they use it. Then, in Q6-3 and Q6-4, we will discuss local area networks and the fundamentals of the Internet. We then look at how Web servers function, basic steps for setting up a cloud presence, and cloud security. We'll wrap up with the cloud in 2029.

Q6-1 Why Are Organizations Moving to the Cloud?

We define the **cloud** as the *elastic* leasing of *pooled* computer resources *over the Internet*. The term *cloud* is used because most early diagrams of three-tier and other Internet-based systems used a cloud symbol to represent the Internet, and organizations came to view their infrastructure as being "somewhere in the cloud." To understand its importance, you need to first know where the term *the cloud* came from.

From about the early 1960s to the late 1980s, organizations primarily used **mainframes**, or large-scale high-speed centralized computers, for their internal data processing needs (see Figure 6-1). A **mainframe architecture** supported connections between a central mainframe and numerous **thin clients** (sometimes called **computer terminals**) which were essentially a screen, a keyboard, and a network connection. All applications, data, and processing power were located on the mainframe. There was no cloud as we currently understand it because the Internet had not yet arrived.

By the early 1990s, Internet usage had started taking off. Users were connecting their personal computers (stand-alone clients) to the Internet and organizations were buying servers to host their Web sites and data (in-house hosting). As you read in Chapter 4, a **client-server architecture** allows clients (users) to send requests across the Internet to severs. Servers respond to requests by sending data back to clients. For example, a user sitting at home can click on a link that sends a Web request to a Web server. The Web server then sends a copy of the Web page back to the user. As shown in Figure 6-2, applications and data storage can reside on clients, servers, or both. Processing load can also be shared between clients and servers.

FIGURE 6-1
The Mainframe Era (1960s–1980s)

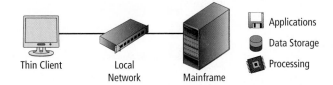

FIGURE 6-2
The Client-Server Era
(1990s–2000s)

The client-server architecture was more appealing to organizations than mainframes because servers were much less expensive. Mainframes cost millions of dollars, but servers only cost thousands of dollars. Servers were also more **scalable**—or easily able to respond to incremental growth in demand—than mainframes because their incremental cost was lower. The client-server architecture also allowed users to access systems from anywhere in the world as long as they had an Internet connection. What we now know as the cloud had arrived, but modern cloud computing was still a few years away. Mainframes didn't entirely go away with the advent of the client-server architecture. In fact, there are still some large organizations (e.g., large banks) that use mainframes to process daily transactions.

Cloud Computing

Until about 2008 or so, most organizations constructed and maintained their own computing infrastructure. Organizations purchased or leased hardware; installed it on their premises; and used it to support organizational email, Web sites, e-commerce sites, and in-house applications such as accounting and operations systems. After 2008, however, organizations began to move their computing infrastructure to the cloud.

Cloud computing architecture allows employees and customers to access organizational data and applications located in the cloud. As shown in Figure 6-3, applications, data, and processing power can be used remotely with a variety of devices including PCs, thin clients, mobile devices, and IoT devices. Organizations no longer need to purchase, configure, and maintain expensive computing infrastructure. Organizations are shifting to the cloud for some of the same reasons they shifted to a client-server architecture—reduced costs and improved scalability.

But there are additional benefits to using the cloud. At the beginning of this chapter we defined the cloud as the *elastic* leasing of *pooled* computer resources *over the Internet*. Consider each of the italicized terms in the definition to explore these benefits.

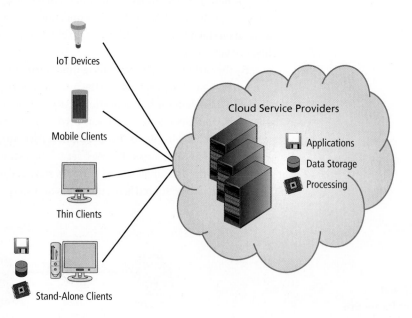

FIGURE 6-3
The Cloud Computing Era
(2008–Current)

Elastic

The term **elastic**, which was first used this way by Amazon.com, means that leased computing resources can be increased or decreased dynamically, programmatically, in a short span of time and that organizations pay for only the resources they use.

Elasticity is not the same thing as scalability, which is the ability to respond to slow incremental growth in demand. A system's ability to add 1,000 new clients per year for the next 10 years (an increase) is an example of scalability. A small local news channel's ability to handle Web page requests from everyone on the planet about a one-time news story (massive increase *and decrease*) is an example of elasticity.

Cloud-based hosting offers considerable elasticity that traditional client-server environments don't offer. An organization could purchase enough server capacity to respond to any increase in demand, but it would be extremely expensive. The same organization could lease the capacity from a cloud vendor on an as-needed basis for a fraction of the price.

Pooled

The second key in the definition of the cloud is *pooled*. Cloud resources are **pooled** because many different organizations use the same physical hardware; they share that hardware through virtualization. Virtualization technology enables the rapid creation of new virtual machines. The customer provides (or creates in the cloud) a disk image of the data and programs of the machine it wants to provision. Virtualization software takes it from there.

Virtualization increases the scalability of an organization's systems because it can quickly respond to incremental growth in demand. New virtual machines can be created in a few minutes. But ordering, shipping, installing, and configuring a physical server can take days. Virtualization also reduces costs. Hundreds of virtual machines (virtual servers) can reside on a single physical server. Thus, the cost of the physical server is spread across each of the individual virtual machines.

Over the Internet

Finally, with the cloud, the resources are accessed **over the Internet**. "Big deal," you're saying. "I use the Internet all the time." Well, think about that for a minute. Accessing resources over the Internet means they aren't stored locally. From an organization's point of view, it doesn't have to have any servers on its premises anymore. It doesn't have to pay for power to run its servers, buy backup generators in case the power goes out, lease the additional commercial space to store the servers, heat and cool the server room, or install specialized fire suppression systems in case a fire breaks out. It also doesn't have to pay for someone to physically care for its servers by replacing broken parts or upgrading components. Physically managing your own computing infrastructure is costly. For many companies it has become too costly.

Why Do Organizations Prefer the Cloud?

It is likely that in the future all or nearly all computing infrastructure will be leased from the cloud, but we're not there yet. Not all organizations have fully embraced cloud computing. There are still racks of servers filling up in-house data centers. But the list of companies that have embraced cloud computing is growing rapidly. Well-known organizations like Netflix, Verizon, Disney, GE, and Comcast have all shifted to the cloud.[1]

In fact, most people don't realize how quickly organizations have shifted to the cloud. Amazon launched Amazon Web Services (AWS) in 2006 largely as an experiment. Most industry analysts saw it as a cost center that probably wouldn't generate revenue for many years, if ever. As shown in Figure 6-4, by the first quarter of 2018 revenue from AWS was $5.44B,[2] and annual revenue was expected to be $26.1B.[3] That's tremendous growth in a short period of time. AWS

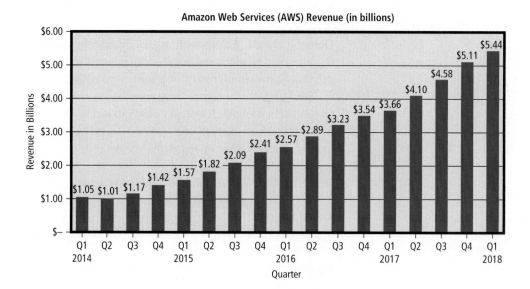

FIGURE 6-4
AWS Revenue Growth

also generated more than half of the operating income for Amazon as a whole and was growing twice as fast as its e-commerce counterpart. What is even more amazing is that Amazon boasts 33 percent market share of the cloud computing market with more than a million active customers![4] A million customers may not sound like a lot, but these aren't individual consumers buying items on Amazon.com; they are large companies like Adobe Systems ($124B market cap), Netflix Inc. ($157B market cap), and Pfizer Inc. ($213B market cap). One million of this type of customer is a lot.

Several factors have pushed organizations toward cloud-based hosting, including lower costs, ubiquitous access, improved scalability, and elasticity. But there are other reasons to shift to the cloud. Figure 6-5 compares and contrasts cloud-based and in-house (client-server) hosting. As you can see, the positives are heavily tilted toward cloud-based hosting. The cloud vendor Rackspace will lease you one medium server for less than a penny per hour. You can obtain and access that server today, actually within a few minutes. Tomorrow, if you need thousands of servers, you can readily scale up to obtain them. Furthermore, you know the cost structure; although you might have a surprise in terms of how many customers want to access your Web site, you won't have any surprises about how much it will cost.

Another positive is that as long as you're dealing with large, reputable organizations, you'll be receiving best-of-breed security and disaster recovery (discussed in Chapter 10). In addition, you need not worry that you're investing in technology that will soon be obsolete; the cloud vendor is taking that risk. All of this is possible because the cloud vendor is gaining economies of scale by selling to an entire industry, not just to you. Finally, cloud computing allows you to focus on your business, not spend time maintaining infrastructure. You can outsource functions that are not your core competency and focus on those that give you a competitive advantage (discussed in Chapter 2).

The negatives of cloud computing involve loss of control. You're dependent on a vendor; changes in the vendor's management, policy, and prices are beyond your control. Further, you don't know where your data—which may be a large part of your organization's value—is located. Nor do you know how many copies of your data there are or even if they're located in the same country as you are. Finally, you have no visibility into the security and disaster preparedness that is actually in place. Your competition could be stealing your data and you won't know it.

The positives and negatives of in-house hosting are shown in the second column of Figure 6-5. For the most part, they are the opposite of those for cloud-based hosting; note, however, the need for personnel and management. With in-house hosting, not only will you have to construct your own data center, you'll also need to acquire and train the personnel to run it and then manage those personnel and your facility.

Companies that harvest user data from network-enabled devices and then sell them can create privacy concerns. The Ethics Guide on pages 216–217 examines these concerns.

Cloud	In-house
Positive:	
Small capital requirements	Control of data location
Speedy development	In-depth visibility of security and disaster preparedness
Superior scalability to growing or fluctuating demand	
Known cost structure	
Possibly best-of-breed security/disaster preparedness	
No obsolescence	
Industry-wide economies of scale, hence cheaper	
Focus on core business, not infrastructure	
Negative:	
Dependency on vendor	Significant capital required
Loss of control over data location	Significant development effort
Little visibility into true security and disaster preparedness capabilities	Difficult (impossible?) to accommodate fluctuating demand
	Ongoing support costs
	Staff and train personnel
	Increased management requirements
	Annual maintenance costs
	Cost uncertainties
	Obsolescence

FIGURE 6-5
Comparison of Cloud and In-House Alternatives

The cloud can help keep critical systems online during periods of extreme demand. The Security Guide on pages 238–239 looks at how the cloud could have helped one such system.

When Does the Cloud Not Make Sense?

Cloud-based hosting makes sense for most organizations. The only organizations for which it may not make sense are those required by law or by industry standard practice to have physical control over their data. Such organizations might be forced to create and maintain their own hosting infrastructure. A financial institution, for example, might be legally required to maintain physical control over its data. Even in this circumstance, however, it is possible to gain many of the benefits of cloud computing using private clouds and virtual private clouds, possibilities we consider in Q6-7.

Q6-2 How Do Organizations Use the Cloud?

Now that you know *what* the cloud is, we will look at specific examples of *how* organizations use the cloud. We'll look at how a car manufacturer can benefit from the cloud's resource elasticity, pooling, and unique Internet connectivity.

Resource Elasticity

Suppose a car manufacturer creates an ad to run during the Academy Awards. It believes it has a fantastic ad that will result in millions of hits on its Web site. However, it doesn't know ahead of time if there will be a thousand, a million, 10 million, or even more site visits. Further, the ad may appeal more to one nationality than to another. Will 70 percent of those visits arise in the United States and the rest in Europe? Or will there be millions from Japan? Or Australia? Given this uncertainty, how does the car manufacturer prepare its computing infrastructure? The car manufacturer knows that if it cannot provide very short response time (say, a fraction of a second), it will lose the benefit of an incredibly expensive ad. On the other hand, if the ad is a flop, preprovisioning of thousands of servers will add to the accumulation of wasted money.

Figure 6-6 shows an example of this situation, based on a real case supported by Amazon's CloudFront. Suppose Figure 6-6 shows the processing on the car manufacturer's Web site during the Academy Awards. Throughout the day, the car manufacturer is delivering less than 10 Gbps of its content to users. However, as soon as its ad runs (2 PM in the Hawaii-Aleutian time zone where the data was collected), demand increases sevenfold and stays high for half an hour. After the announcement of Best Picture, when the ad runs again, demand again increases to 30 and 40 Gbps for an hour and then returns to its base level.

Without an increase in servers, response time will be 3 or 5 seconds or more, which is far too long to maintain the attention of an Academy Awards viewer. However, the car manufacturer has contracted with its cloud vendor to add servers, wherever needed worldwide, to keep response time to less than 0.5 seconds. Using cloud technology, the cloud vendor will programmatically increase its servers to keep response time below the 0.5-second threshold. As demand falls after the ad runs a second time, it will release the excess servers and reallocate them at the end of the awards.

In this way, the car manufacturer need not build or contract for infrastructure that supports maximum demand. Had it done so, the vast majority of its servers would have been idle for most of the evening. And, as you'll learn, the cloud vendor can provision servers worldwide using the cloud; if a good portion of the excess demand is in Singapore, for example, it can provision extra servers in Asia and reduce wait time due to global transmission delays.

Pooling Resources

The servers that the car manufacturer needed for these few hours were much less costly because it only needed them for a short time. The servers that it used for the Academy Awards can be real-located to CPA firms that need them later that same day, to textbook publishers who need them for online student activity on Monday, or to the hotel industry that needs them later the next week.

An easy way to understand the essence of this development is to consider electrical power. In the very earliest days of electric power generation, organizations operated their own generators to create power for their company's needs. Over time, as the power grid expanded, it became possible to centralize power generation so that organizations could purchase just the electricity they needed from an electric utility.

Both cloud vendors and electrical utilities benefit from *economies of scale*. According to this principle, the average cost of production decreases as the size of the operation increases. Major cloud

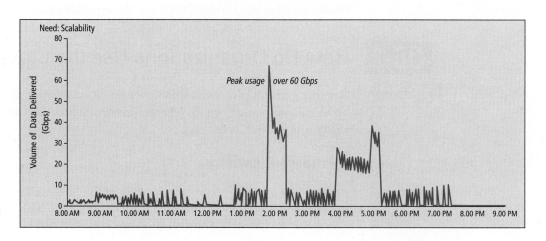

FIGURE 6-6
Example Video Banner Ad Customer

FIGURE 6-7
Apple Data Center in Maiden, NC
Source: ©2018 Google LLC, used with permission. Google and the Google logo are registered trademarks of Google LLC.

vendors operate enormous Web farms. Figure 6-7 shows the building that contains the computers in the Web farm that Apple constructed in 2011 to support its iCloud offering. This billion-dollar facility contains 505,000 square feet.[5] Amazon, IBM, Google, Microsoft, Oracle, and other large companies each operate several similar farms worldwide.

Over the Internet

The car manufacturer in the previous example has contracted with the cloud vendor for a maximum response time; the cloud vendor adds servers as needed to meet that requirement. As stated, the cloud vendor may be provisioning, nearly instantaneously, servers all over the world. How does it do that? And not for just one customer, like the car manufacturer, but for thousands?

In the old days, for such interorganizational processing to occur, developers from the car manufacturer had to meet with developers from the cloud vendor and design an interface. "Our programs will do this, providing this data, and we want your programs to do that, in response, sending us this other data back." Such meetings took days and were expensive and error-prone. Given the design, the developers then returned home to write code to meet the agreed-on interface design, which may not have been understood in the same way by all parties.

It was a long, slow, expensive, and prone-to-failure process. If organizations had to do that today, cloud provisioning would be unaffordable and infeasible.

Instead, the computer industry settled on a set of standard ways of requesting and receiving services over the Internet. You will learn about some of these standards in Q6-5. For now, just realize those standards enable computers that have never "met" before to organize a dizzying, worldwide dance to deliver and process content to users on PCs, iPads, Google phones, Xboxes, and even exercise equipment in a tenth of second or less. It is absolutely fascinating and gorgeous technology! Unfortunately, you will have the opportunity to learn only a few basic terms in Q6-3 and Q6-4.

Cloud Services from Cloud Vendors

Organizations can use the cloud in several different ways. The first and most popular way is obtaining cloud services from cloud service vendors. But not all organizations use cloud services to the same *extent*. You can use more of the cloud or less. It's up to you. As a business professional, you'll need to understand the differences in cloud service levels.

To help you understand these differences, we'll use a metaphor related to transportation and then relate it to cloud service offerings.

Transportation as a Service

Suppose you need to get to and from work each day. You have four options for satisfying your transportation needs. You can build a car, buy a car, rent a car, or take a taxi. Each has its own advantages and disadvantages. As shown in Figure 6-8, at one end of the spectrum, you manage your own transportation completely (building a car). At the other end of the spectrum, your transportation is managed by someone else (a taxi service).

For example, if you decide to buy a car rather than build one, you are essentially outsourcing some of your transportation to a car manufacturer. You don't have to buy the car parts, assemble the car, or test it to make sure it works properly. It might initially seem cheaper to build your own car. But realistically, you may not have the time, knowledge, skill, or patience to actually build a reliable car. It may end up cheaper to buy a car rather than build one.

Similarly, if you decide to rent a car, you're essentially outsourcing more of your transportation to someone else. By renting a car you don't have to pay for vehicle registration and taxes. You also don't have to make any repairs or clean the car. You're doing less work but potentially paying more. The same is true of the difference between renting a car and taking a taxi. If you take a taxi, you don't have to buy car insurance, drive the car, or buy gas. In fact, you don't even need a driver's license. Again, you're accomplishing the same thing—getting to and from work. You're just managing less of your transportation.

Types of Cloud Service Offerings

The "transportation as a service" metaphor helps explain how organizations use cloud services to move away from a traditional on-premises model in which they must provide all services internally. Depending on their choice of cloud services, organizations manage less of their infrastructure, platform, and software functions. In general, one type of service isn't necessarily better than another. What is best for an individual organization depends upon the way in which its managers want to use the cloud. Cloud-based service offerings can be organized into the three categories shown in Figure 6-9.

As shown in Figure 6-10, the most basic cloud offering is **infrastructure as a service (IaaS)**, which is the cloud hosting of a bare server computer, data storage, network, and virtualization. Rackspace Inc. provides hardware for customers to load whatever operating system they want, and

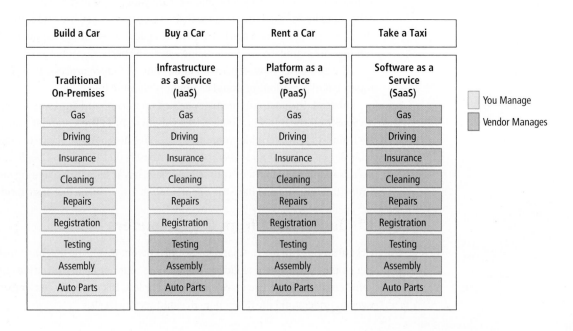

FIGURE 6-8
Transportation as a Service

Build a Car	Buy a Car	Rent a Car	Take a Taxi
Traditional On-Premises	**Infrastructure as a Service (IaaS)**	**Platform as a Service (PaaS)**	**Software as a Service (SaaS)**
Gas	Gas	Gas	Gas
Driving	Driving	Driving	Driving
Insurance	Insurance	Insurance	Insurance
Cleaning	Cleaning	Cleaning	Cleaning
Repairs	Repairs	Repairs	Repairs
Registration	Registration	Registration	Registration
Testing	Testing	Testing	Testing
Assembly	Assembly	Assembly	Assembly
Auto Parts	Auto Parts	Auto Parts	Auto Parts

You Manage
Vendor Manages

Cloud Service	Users	Examples
SaaS	Employees Customers	Salesforce.com iCloud Office 365
PaaS	Application developers Application testers	Google App Engine Microsoft Azure AWS Elastic Beanstalk
IaaS	Network architects Systems administrators	Amazon EC2 (Elastic Compute Cloud) Amazon S3 (Simple Storage Service)

FIGURE 6-9
Three Fundamental Cloud Types

Amazon licenses S3 (Simple Storage Service), which provides unlimited, reliable data storage in the cloud. The cost savings of IaaS over traditional on-premises hosting can be substantial.

The second category of cloud hosting is **platform as a service (PaaS)**, whereby vendors provide hosted computers with an operating system, runtime environment, and middleware like a Web server or a DBMS. Microsoft Windows Azure, for example, provides servers installed with Windows Server. Customers of Windows Azure then add their own applications on top of the hosted platform. Microsoft SQL Azure provides a host with Windows Server and SQL Server. Oracle On Demand provides a hosted server with Oracle Database. Again, for PaaS, organizations add their own applications to the host. Amazon EC2 provides servers with Windows Server or Linux installed.

An organization that provides **software as a service (SaaS)** provides not only hardware infrastructure and an operating system but application programs and databases as well. For example, Salesforce.com provides hardware and programs for customer and sales tracking as a service. Similarly, Google provides Google Drive and Microsoft provides OneDrive as a service. With Office 365, Exchange, Skype for Business, and SharePoint applications are provided as a service "in the cloud."

For each of these applications, you just sign up for them and learn how to use them. You don't have to worry about buying hardware, loading an operating system, setting up a database, or installing software. All of that is managed by the cloud service provider. Much like using a taxi—you just jump in and go.

As a business professional you'll need to know the advantages and disadvantages of on-premises hosing, IaaS, PaaS, and SaaS. Your choice of cloud service will be driven by your competitive environment, business strategy, and technical resources. Much like the "transportation as a service" metaphor mentioned earlier, not everyone should build, own, or even rent a car.

If you're a working professional living in a big city, maybe taking a taxi is your best transportation option (SaaS). If you're always on the road traveling for business, renting a car in each city might be the right choice (PaaS). If you own a large package delivery company, you might want

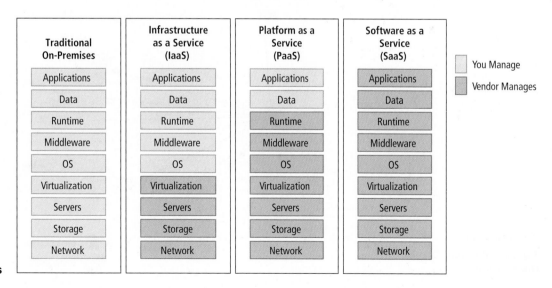

FIGURE 6-10
Cloud Service Offerings

to buy a fleet of trucks (IaaS). If you're a high-performance racecar driver, you may need to build your own specialized racing vehicle (on-premises). Making the right choice between cloud services is really more about finding the right fit with your organization's needs.

Content Delivery Networks

Another major use of the cloud is to deliver content from servers placed around the world. A **content delivery network (CDN)** is a system of hardware and software that stores user data in many different geographical locations and makes those data available on demand. A CDN provides a specialized type of PaaS but is usually considered in its own category, as it is here. To understand how a CDN delivers content, let's compare it to how traditional servers deliver content.

Figure 6-11 shows a server located in California delivering content to users around the United States. Suppose this hypothetical California-based media company streams HD movies to millions of homes around the country. The bandwidth usage from this company would be tremendous. To give you an idea of how much this might be, reports indicate that Netflix traffic consumes 35 percent of all Internet traffic in North America during peak evening hours.[6] This level of bandwidth consumption would be costly to deliver and would slow content delivery from other companies.

Figure 6-12 shows how this online media company could use a CDN to store copies of its movies. The CDN vendor replicates movies on servers, possibly worldwide, in order to speed up response time. When a user at home requests a movie, the request is transmitted to a routing server that determines which CDN server will deliver the movie to the user the fastest. Because traffic changes rapidly, such determinations are made in real time. A request for content at one moment in time could be served by a computer in, say, San Diego, and a few moments later, that same request from that same user might be served by a computer in Seattle.

In addition to movies, CDNs are often used to store and deliver content that seldom changes. For example, the company banner on an organization's Web page might be stored on many CDN servers. Various pieces of the Web page could be obtained from different servers on the CDN; all such decisions are made in real time to provide the fastest content delivery possible.

Figure 6-13 summarizes CDN benefits. The first two are self-explanatory. Reliability is increased because data are stored on many servers. If one server fails, any of a potentially large number of other servers can deliver the content. You will learn about denial-of-service (DoS) attacks in Chapter 10. For now, just understand that such security threats send so much data to a given server that the server's performance for legitimate traffic becomes unacceptable. By having multiple servers, CDNs help to protect against such attacks.

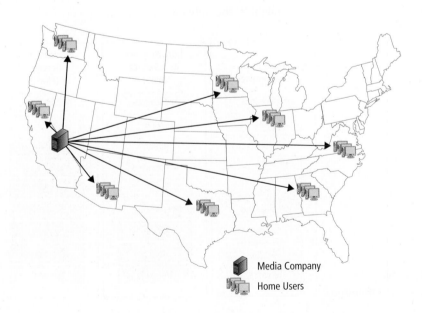

FIGURE 6-11
Traditional Server Content Distribution

Media Company

Home Users

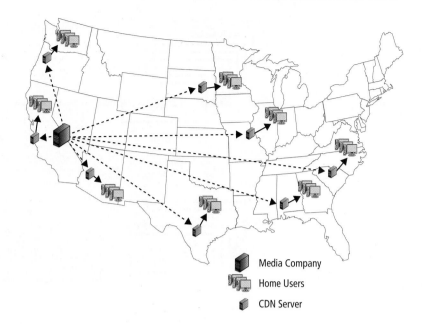

FIGURE 6-12
Distributed CDN Servers

In some cases, CDNs reduce access costs for mobile users (those who have a limited data account). By delivering the data faster, site connection charges can be reduced. Finally, many (but not all) CDN services are offered on a flexible, pay-as-you-go basis. Customers need not contract for fixed services and payments; they pay only for what they use, when they use it. Some of the leading CDN vendors include Amazon CloudFront, Akamai, CloudFlare CDN, and MaxCDN.

Using Web Services Internally

The final way that organizations can use cloud technology is to build internal information systems using Web services. Strictly speaking, this is not using the cloud because it does not provide elasticity or the advantages of pooled resources. It does advantageously use cloud standards, however, so we include it here.

Figure 6-14 shows a Web services inventory application at a hypothetical online bicycle part retailer named Best Bikes. In this example, Best Bikes is running its own servers on its own infrastructure. To do so, Best Bikes sets up a private internet within the company, an internet that is generally not reachable from outside the company. Best Bikes writes the applications for processing inventory using Web services standards, applications publish a WSDL, the Web services are accessed by other applications within the company using SOAP, and data are delivered using JSON. Application users access the inventory Web services using JavaScript that is sent down to the users' browsers. All of these will be discussed later in this chapter in Q6-5.

Users of the inventory Web services include Sales, Shipping, Customer Service, Accounting, and other departments. Internal applications can use the inventory Web services like building blocks. They can use the services that they need—and no more. Because the Web services are

```
Benefits of Content Delivery Networks

• Decreased, even guaranteed, loadtime
• Reduced load on origin server
• Increased reliability
• Protection from DoS attacks
• Reduced delivery costs for mobile users
• Pay-as-you-go
```

FIGURE 6-13
Benefits of Content Delivery Networks

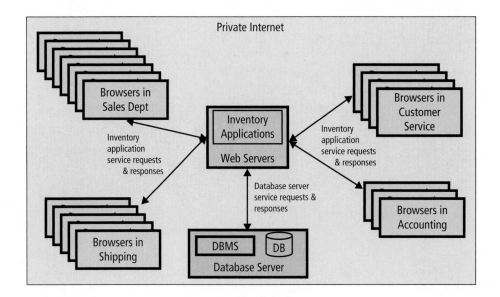

FIGURE 6-14
Web Services Principles Applied to Inventory Applications

encapsulated, the inventory system can be altered without affecting other applications. In this way, systems development is more flexible, and it will be faster and hence less costly.

As stated, however, this is not a cloud. In this example, Best Bikes has a fixed number of servers; no attempt is made to make them elastic. Also, the servers are dedicated to inventory. During idle periods, they are not dynamically reused for other purposes. Some organizations remove this limit by creating a private cloud, as discussed in Q6-7.

Q6-3 What Network Technology Supports the Cloud?

A computer **network** is a collection of computers that communicate with one another over transmission lines or wirelessly. As shown in Figure 6-15, the four basic types of networks are personal area networks, local area networks, wide area networks, and internets.

A **personal area network (PAN)** connects devices located around a *single person*. Most PAN devices connect wirelessly to other devices located within 10 meters. A **local area network (LAN)** connects computers that reside in a single geographic location on the premises of the company that operates the LAN. The number of connected computers can range from two to several hundred. The distinguishing characteristic of a LAN is *a single location*. A **wide area network (WAN)** connects computers at different geographic locations. The computers in two separated company sites must be connected using a WAN. To illustrate, a smartwatch or fitness tracker will create a PAN by connecting to a student's smartphone. The computers for a college of business located on a single campus can be connected via a LAN. The computers for a college of business located on multiple campuses must be connected via a WAN.

Type	Characteristic
Personal area network (PAN)	Devices connected around a single person
Local area network (LAN)	Computers connected at a single physical site
Wide area network (WAN)	Computers connected between two or more separated sites
The Internet and internets	Networks of networks

FIGURE 6-15
Basic Network Types

The single- versus multiple-site distinction between LANs and WANs is important. With a LAN, an organization can place communications lines wherever it wants because all lines reside on its premises. The same is not true for a WAN. A company with offices in Chicago and Atlanta cannot run a wire down the freeway to connect computers in the two cities. Instead, the company contracts with a communications vendor licensed by the government and that already has lines or has the authority to run new lines between the two cities.

An **internet** is a network of networks. Internets connect LANs, WANs, and other internets. The most famous internet is "**the Internet**" (with an uppercase letter *I*), the collection of networks you use when you send email or access a Web site. In addition to the Internet, private networks of networks, called *internets*, also exist. A private internet used exclusively within an organization is sometimes called an **intranet**.

The networks that make up an internet use a large variety of communication methods and conventions, and data must flow seamlessly across them. To provide seamless flow, an elaborate scheme called a *layered protocol* is used. The details of protocols are beyond the scope of this text. Just understand that a **protocol** is a set of rules and data structures for organizing communication. Computers need to use protocols so they can exchange data. People use similar protocols to communicate. People, for example, follow a conversational protocol that says when one person talks, the other person listens. They switch back and forth until they are done communicating. Without a protocol for conversations, people would continually talk over each other and nothing would be communicated.

There are many different protocols; some are used for PANs, some are used for LANs, some are used for WANs, some are used for internets and the Internet, and some are used for all of these. We will identify several common protocols in this chapter.

What Are the Components of a LAN?

See what a typical workday would look like for someone who manages networks in the Career Guide on page 241.

As stated, a LAN is a group of computers connected together on a single site. Usually the computers are located within a half-mile or so of each other. The key distinction, however, is that all of the computers are located on property controlled by the organization that operates the LAN. This means that the organization can run cables wherever needed to connect the computers.

Figure 6-16 shows a LAN typical of those in a **small office or home office (SOHO)**. Typically, such LANs have fewer than a dozen or so computers and printers. Many businesses, of course, operate LANs much larger than this one. The principles are the same for a larger LAN, but the additional complexity is beyond the scope of this text.

The computers and printers in Figure 6-16 communicate via a mixture of wired and wireless connections. Some devices use wired connections, and others use wireless connections. The devices and protocols used differ for wired and wireless connectivity.

The Institute for Electrical and Electronics Engineers (IEEE, pronounced "I triple E") sponsors committees that create and publish protocol and other standards. The committee that addresses LAN standards is called the *IEEE 802 Committee*. Thus, IEEE LAN protocols always start with the numbers 802.

The **IEEE 802.3 protocol** is used for wired LAN connections. This protocol standard, also called **Ethernet**, specifies hardware characteristics, such as which wire carries which signals. It also describes how messages are to be packaged and processed for wired transmission over the LAN.

Most personal computers today support what is called **10/100/1000 Ethernet**. These products conform to the 802.3 specification and allow for transmission at a rate of 10, 100, or 1,000 Mbps (megabits per second). Switches detect the speed a given device can handle and communicate with it at that speed. If you check computer listings at Dell, Lenovo, and other manufacturers, you will see PCs advertised as having 10/100/1000 Ethernet. Today, speeds of up to 1 Gbps are possible on wired LANs.

By the way, the abbreviations used for communications speeds differ from those used for computer memory. For communications equipment, *K* stands for 1,000, not 1,024 as it does for

ETHICS GUIDE

REVERSE ENGINEERING PRIVACY

Wendy entered the classroom and made her way up the stairs to the back row. She normally didn't like to sit in the back of the room, but she had been late on the first day of class, and the instructor had mandated assigned seating during that session. The semester felt like it was dragging on, and she couldn't wait to begin her marketing internship in the city that summer. She had worked for the same company the previous summer, and she was confident that she would be offered a full-time position once she graduated. Her thoughts of city life were interrupted when the instructor entered at the front and abruptly started class.

The class was required for business students, and it covered a variety of technology-related topics. The session began in the usual way—with an overview of current popular press articles. The instructor started the class by discussing an article that quickly grabbed the attention of the class. "Did you know that billboards are spying on you?" he said. "Well, let me rephrase that—they are not exactly *spying*, but they do know more about you than you think."

The Billboards Are Watching

"You may have noticed a number of digital billboards popping up around the city," the instructor continued. "They can be programmed to display a variety of ads throughout the day. If you've seen one, you may have thought it just cycles through a fixed set of advertisements over the course of the day, changing about every 10 seconds. However, the ad selection process is very dynamic, and the time of day that each advertisement is displayed is quite intentional. In fact, the billboard knows which types of demographic and socioeconomic segments are driving by the billboard throughout the day."[7] The class seemed skeptical about this statement—how could this be possible?

The instructor then explained how it worked. "Cell phone companies collect vast quantities of location data about their customers. This is because customers' phones are continuously communicating their location to cell towers in order to send and receive data. They also manage the process of identifying the nearby towers with the strongest signal. As a by-product of this process, phone companies know where you are at all times of the day as long as you are carrying your phone."

The instructor smiled matter-of-factly and continued, "They then take these massive data sets containing customer location data and sell them to third parties, in this case, companies advertising via billboards. These companies then analyze the location data and segment people into various groups—sports fans who have been to a stadium several times, people who like sailing and spend time at the yacht club every weekend, people who stop at a specific coffee shop every morning. Once these segments are identified, advertising companies determine when the highest number of people in each segment are driving by the digital billboards and display targeted ads accordingly."

Privacy Please

After describing the general process of how these billboards work, the instructor opened up the floor for students to comment. The students seemed to fall into one of two distinct

Source: Aurélio Scetta/Alamy Stock Vector

opinions. Some thought the technology was cool and that billboards displaying targeted advertisements based on their data was yet another example of the innovation and limitless reach of the information age. Others found the billboards to be another egregious example of companies operating with reckless abandon concerning the privacy and security of consumer data. After a number of students on each side shared their thoughts, the instructor offered some new insights to take the discussion a step further.

"Those of you who are concerned about the security of your data are justified in your position. There was a recent article that discussed the agreement you make when you allow apps on your phone to access your location data—you are essentially agreeing that they can take your data and sell it, and it may pass between any number of third parties before it is actually used for targeted advertising. This clearly poses a potential security risk if the data is compromised. This is especially worrisome because companies are not diligent about removing personally identifiable information (PII).[8] And to make matters worse, it was recently revealed that Android phones were collecting and storing location data even when location-based services were disabled."[9]

These revelations riled up the class even more and further polarized the two groups of students. Wendy wasn't exactly sure to which camp she belonged. As a marketing major, she recognized the tremendous potential in creating targeted advertising campaigns. However, as a private citizen, the thought of companies knowing everywhere she had been since she started using her cell phone and the ease with which these companies shared this data with other organizations without her permission felt wrong and unsettling. She started wondering about her future career in marketing. Could she work for a company that takes advantage of consumer data—her data—in this way?

DISCUSSION QUESTIONS

1. According to the definitions of the ethical principles defined previously in this book:
   a. Do you think tracking a customer's physical location throughout the day is ethical according to the categorical imperative (page 23-24)?
   b. Do you think tracking a customer's physical location throughout the day is ethical according to the utilitarian perspective (page 42-43)?

2. Why do you think Wendy is conflicted? Is it OK to track other people but not want your own movements tracked? Why?

3. Most people don't read the terms when they sign up for a new service. Do you think it's OK for a company to do whatever it wants with customer data if it specifically notes it in the terms of the contract? If the contract is extraordinarily lengthy, written in legalese, and displayed in a tiny font, is it reasonable to assume that a typical person will read and understand it? Is it the company's responsibility to make sure its customers understand it?

4. Suppose the cellular company shares network signal strength data from the customer's phone with a third-party marketing company. The marketing firm can then use the data to compute the customer's location throughout the day. How might sharing corporate "network" data be a potential customer privacy violation?

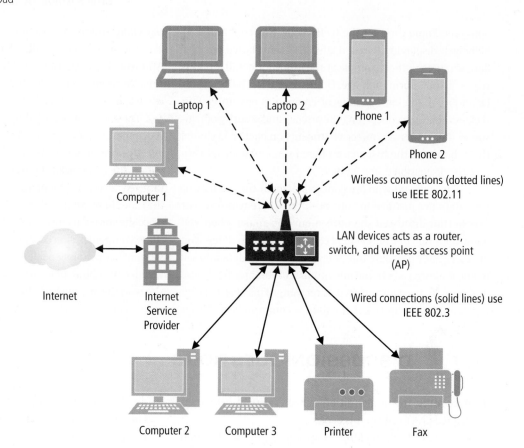

FIGURE 6-16
Typical Small Office/Home Office (SOHO) LAN

In figure: Laptop 1, Laptop 2, Phone 1, Phone 2, Computer 1, Internet, Internet Service Provider, Wireless connections (dotted lines) use IEEE 802.11, LAN devices acts as a router, switch, and wireless access point (AP), Wired connections (solid lines) use IEEE 802.3, Computer 2, Computer 3, Printer, Fax

memory. Similarly, *M* stands for 1,000,000, not 1,024 * 1,024; *G* stands for 1,000,000,000, not 1,024 * 1,024 * 1,024. Thus, 100 Mbps is 100,000,000 bits per second. Also, communications speeds are expressed in *bits,* whereas memory sizes are expressed in *bytes.* These are different units of measurement. One byte consists of eight bits. This means a 1 MB file would consist of 8,388,608 bits. If you sent a 1 MB file over a 1 Mbps connection, it would take more than 8 seconds to send because your connection speed is measured in bits per second, not bytes per second.

Wireless LAN connections use the **IEEE 802.11 protocol**. Several versions of 802.11 exist, and as of 2018, the most current one is IEEE 802.11ac. The differences among these versions are beyond the scope of this discussion. Just note that the current standard, 802.11ac, allows speeds of up to 1.3 Gbps, though few users have an Internet connection fast enough to take full advantage of that speed. The next version, 802.11ax, promises speeds around 10 Gbps.

Bluetooth is another common wireless protocol used to make PAN connections. It is designed for transmitting data over short distances, replacing cables. Devices, such as wireless mice, keyboards, printers, and headphones, use Bluetooth to connect to desktop computers. Other devices like smartwatches and fitness trackers can use Bluetooth to connect to smartphones and send data over the Internet. More and more devices like clothing, automobiles, and sports equipment are becoming Bluetooth enabled.

Connecting Your LAN to the Internet

Although you may not have realized it, when you connect your SOHO LAN, phone, iPad, or Kindle to the Internet, you are connecting to a WAN. You must do so because you are connecting to computers that are not physically located on your premises. You cannot start running wires down the street to plug in somewhere.

When you connect to the Internet, you are actually connecting to an **Internet service provider (ISP)**. An ISP has three important functions. First, it provides you with a legitimate

Internet address. Second, it serves as your gateway to the Internet. The ISP receives the communications from your computer and passes them on to the Internet, and it receives communications from the Internet and passes them on to you. Finally, ISPs pay for the Internet. They collect money from their customers and pay access fees and other charges on your behalf.

Figure 6-17 shows the three common alternatives for connecting to the Internet. Notice that we are discussing how your computer connects to the Internet via a WAN; we are not discussing the structure of the WAN itself. WAN architectures and their protocols are beyond the scope of this text. Search the Web for "leased lines" or "PSDN" if you want to learn more about WAN architectures.

SOHO LANs (such as that in Figure 6-16) and individual home and office computers are commonly connected to an ISP in one of three ways: a special telephone line called a DSL, a cable TV line, or a wireless-phone-like connection.

Digital Subscriber Line (DSL)

A **digital subscriber line (DSL)** operates on the same lines as voice telephones, but it operates so it does not interfere with voice telephone service. Because DSL signals do not interfere with telephone signals, DSL data transmission and telephone conversations can occur simultaneously. A device at the telephone company separates the phone signals from the computer signals and sends the latter signal to the ISP. Digital subscriber lines use their own protocols for data transmission.

Cable Line

A cable line is the second type of WAN connection. **Cable lines** provide high-speed data transmission using cable television lines. The cable company installs a fast, high-capacity optical fiber cable to a distribution center in each neighborhood it serves. At the distribution center, the optical fiber cable connects to regular cable-television cables that run to subscribers' homes or businesses. Cable signals do not interfere with TV signals.

Because as many as 500 user sites can share these facilities, performance varies depending on how many other users are sending and receiving data. At the maximum, users can download

FIGURE 6-17
Summary of LAN Networks

Type	Topology	Transmission Line	Transmission Speed	Equipment Used	Protocol Commonly Used	Remarks
Local area network	Local area network	UTP or optical fiber	Common: 10/100/1000 Mbps Possible: 1 Gbps	Switch NIC UTP or optical	IEEE 802.3 (Ethernet)	Switches connect devices, multiple switches on all but small LANs.
	Local area network with wireless	UTP or optical for nonwireless connections	Up to 1.3 Gbps	Wireless access point Wireless NIC	IEEE 802.11ac, (802.11ax not yet common)	Access point transforms wired LAN (802.3) to wireless LAN (802.11).
Connections to the Internet	DSL modem to ISP	DSL telephone	Personal: Upstream to 1 Mbps, downstream to 40 Mbps (max 10 likely in most areas)	DSL modem DSL-capable telephone line	DSL	Can have computer and phone use simultaneously. Always connected.
	Cable modem to ISP	Cable TV lines to optical cable	Upstream to 1 Mbps Downstream 20 Mbps to 100 Mbps	Cable modem Cable TV cable	Cable	Capacity is shared with other sites; performance varies depending on others' use.
	WAN wireless	Wireless connection to WAN	500 Kbps to 1.7 Mbps	Wireless WAN modem	One of several wireless standards	Sophisticated protocols enable several devices to use the same wireless frequency.

data up to 50 Mbps and can upload data at 512 Kbps. Typically, performance is much lower than this. In most cases, the download speed of cable lines and DSL lines is about the same. Cable lines use their own protocols.

WAN Wireless Connection

A third way you can connect your computer, mobile device, or other communicating device is via a **WAN wireless** connection. Amazon's Kindle, for example, uses a Sprint wireless network to provide wireless data connections. The iPhone uses a LAN-based wireless network if one is available and a WAN wireless network if not. The LAN-based network is preferred because performance is considerably higher. As of 2018, WAN wireless provides average performance of 1.0 Mbps with peaks of up to 3.0 Mbps, as opposed to the typical 50 Mbps for LAN wireless.

Q6-4 How Does the Internet Work?

This section will give you the basic understanding of how the Internet works and enable you to be an effective consumer of cloud services. The cloud resides in the Internet. So, in order to learn how the cloud works, you need a basic understanding of how the Internet works. With that background, you will learn how it is possible for a cloud vendor to provide dramatic elasticity to support the workload shown in Figure 6-6.

The Internet and the U.S. Postal System

The technology that underlies the Internet and the additional technology that enables the cloud to work are complicated. To explain how the Internet works, we'll use a simplified example, shown in Figure 6-18, comparing the movement of packages in the U.S. postal system to the movement of packets through the Internet. This is a highly simplified, but useful, example for explaining the basics of how the Internet works. We will stay at a high level and help you learn overarching concepts and basic definitions.

The Internet works much like the U.S. postal system in that both systems transport things from one location to another. The Internet transports email, while the U.S. postal system sends paper mail. Comparing the Internet to the U.S. postal system allows you to relate new Internet terms to a system with which you're already familiar (the U.S. postal system).

FIGURE 6-18
Comparison of the Postal System and the Internet

Steps to Send Package	Postal System	Internet Equivalent
1. Assemble package	Package	Packet
2. Put name on package	Person's name (e.g., BigBank Inc. or Jane Smith)	Domain name (e.g., www.BigBank.com)
3. Look up address	Phone book	DNS
4. Put address on package	Mailing address (e.g., 123 Park Ave, New York, NY, 10172)	IP address (e.g., 10.84.8.154)
5. Put registered mail sticker on package	Registered Mail	TCP
6. Ship package	Airlines (e.g., Delta Air Lines, Inc.) Airports (e.g., Seattle-Tacoma International Airport)	Carriers (e.g., Sprint Corp.) Routers

Step 1: Assemble Package (Packets)

Suppose you are sitting in your apartment in Seattle and you want to send a box of cookies to your friend, Jane Smith, working at BigBank Inc. in New York City. The Internet equivalent of this is sending a **packet**, or a formatted message that passes through networks, to BigBank's Web server requesting a copy of its main Web page. Packets wind their way through the Internet much the same way packages wind their way through the U.S. postal system. The cookies are created and boxed up by you, a person. The contents of the packet, on the other hand, are created by applications like Google Chrome, Firefox, Safari, Skype, or FileZilla.

Step 2: Put Name on Package (Domain Names)

The next step in sending a package through the U.S. postal system is to put a name on the package. On your package of cookies you might write "BigBank Inc." or "Jane Smith." On the packet you put a **domain name**, or a worldwide-unique name affiliated with a public IP address (discussed in Step 3). Examples of domain names include www.bigbank.com, www.microsoft.com, or www.university.edu.

It is not necessary for packets to contain a domain name. In fact, many don't. Just like with the U.S. postal system, the address is more important than the recipient name.

Step 3: Look Up Address (IP Address)

Before you can send your box of cookies to your friend you need to put a shipping address on the package (e.g., 123 Park Ave, New York, NY, 10172). Just like regular postal mail, every location on the Internet needs a unique address. For reasons beyond this discussion, an Internet address is called an **IP address**, which is a number that identifies a particular device. **Public IP addresses** identify a particular device on the public Internet. In order to get on the Internet, every device must have access to a public IP address.

IP Addresses

IP addresses have two formats. The most common form, called **IPv4**, has a four-decimal dotted notation such as 137.190.8.10. Unfortunately, there are only 4 billion IPv4 addresses that can be used by all 7 billion people on the earth. As a result, a second format of IP addresses called **IPv6** is being adopted—slowly. It has a longer format (e.g., 0:0:0:0:0:ffff:89be:80a), which accommodates 340 undecillion addresses. That's plenty of IP addresses—for now. In your browser, if you enter an IPv4 address like *http://137.190.8.10* or an IPv6 address like 0:0:0:0:0:ffff:89be:80a, your browser will connect with the device on the public Internet that has been assigned to this address.

DNS

Most people don't remember addresses. It's easier to remember a name like Jane Smith or Big-Bank Inc. and look up the mailing address in a phone book (or an Internet-based phone book). The Internet works the same way. Nobody wants to type IP addresses like *http://165.193.140.14* to find a particular site. It is easier to enter names like *www.pandora.com* or *www.woot.com* or *www.pearsonhighered.com*.

Because public IP addresses must be unique worldwide, their assignment is controlled by a centralized organization named **ICANN (Internet Corporation for Assigned Names and Numbers)**. ICANN administers a directory naming system, like a phone book, called **Domain Name System (DNS)** that assigns domain names to IP addresses. When an organization or individual wants to register a domain name, it goes to a company that applies to an ICANN-approved agency to do so. GoDaddy (*www.godaddy.com*) is an example of such a company (Figure 6-19).

GoDaddy, or a similar agency, will first determine if the desired name is unique worldwide. If so, then it will apply to register that name to the applicant. Once the registration is completed, the applicant can affiliate a public IP address with the domain name, much like your name is associated

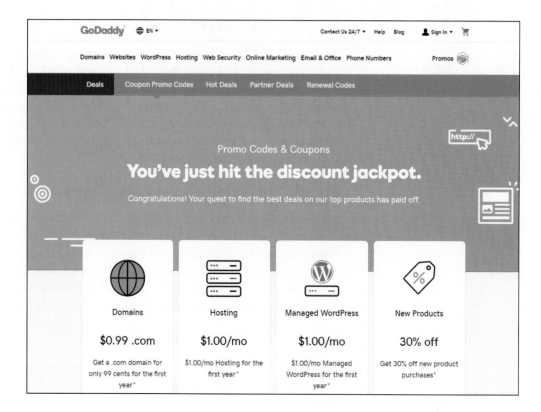

FIGURE 6-19
GoDaddy Screenshot
Source: © 2018 GoDaddy Operating
Company, LLC. All rights reserved.

with a single postal address. From that point onward, traffic for the new domain name will be routed to the affiliated IP address.

In 2016, the U.S. Department of Commerce gave up oversight of ICANN to a diverse group of governments and companies. Most tech companies applauded the handover. But critics worry that less-free countries may try to influence ICANN to disallow domain names for dissident groups, thereby kicking them off the Internet. At this point, ICANN is still located in the United States and must obey U.S. laws. Time will tell if the transition proves to be a good one.

Step 4: Put Address on Package (IP Address on Packet)

Every time you enter a domain name (e.g., *www.washington.edu*) into your Web browser, your computer sends a lookup (resolution) request to a DNS server asking it for the IP address that corresponds with that domain name. The DNS server responds with the IP address that your operating system then puts on packets to be sent to that site.

Note two important points: First, several (or many) domain names can point to the same IP address. This is the real-world equivalent of multiple people (i.e., a family) sharing the same postal mailing address. Second, the affiliation of domain names with IP addresses is dynamic. The owner of the domain name can change the affiliated IP addresses at its discretion, much like you can change your affiliation with a specific mailing address if you decide to move.

Before we leave addressing, you need to know one more term. A **URL (Uniform Resource Locator)** is an address on the Internet. Commonly, it consists of a protocol (such as *http://* or *ftp://*) followed by a domain name or public IP address. A URL is actually quite a bit more complicated than this description, but that detailed knowledge is beyond the scope of this text, so we'll hurry along. The preferred pronunciation of *URL* is to say the letters *U, R, L*.

Step 5: Put Registered Mail Sticker on Package (TCP)

After your package is addressed, you need to guarantee that it gets delivered using registered mail. Registered mail guarantees delivery by requiring the recipient to sign a receipt that is then sent back to the sender. The same is true of packets. The **Transmission Control Protocol (TCP)** is a core Internet protocol that guarantees the reliable delivery of packets. TCP is the equivalent of registered mail in the postal system. TCP information is added to packets just like registered mail stickers are added to postal packages. They guarantee delivery by requiring the receiver to send back an acknowledgement that the packet was received. If no acknowledgement is received, it will keep trying to sending the packet a certain number of times before it gives up.

Step 6: Ship Package (Packets Transported by Carriers)

Figure 6-20 illustrates a simplified path that your packet may take through the Internet. To begin, note that this example is an internet because it is a network of networks. It consists of two LANs (yours and the bank's) and four networks. (In truth, the real Internet consists of tens of thousands of networks, but to conserve paper, we don't show all of them.) A **hop** is the movement from one network to another. This term is frequently used by cloud vendors when they discuss provisioning servers to minimize the number of hops. As drawn, in Figure 6-20, the shortest path from you to the bank's LAN consists of four hops. Your box of cookies will take a similar number of hops between postal facilities as it moves across the country.

At this point, we should mention that most hosts connected to a LAN share a single public IP address, much like a family living in a house shares a single postal address. Each internal host receives a **private IP address** that identifies a particular device on a private network. Private IP addresses are used for traffic going to other devices on the LAN. But all traffic leaving the LAN uses the single shared public IP address to cross the Internet. All private IP addresses are managed by a LAN device like the one shown in Figure 6-16.

Carriers

In the U.S. postal system, your package weaves its way toward its destination through multiple airports. It does so aboard airplanes owned by airlines like Delta Air Lines, Southwest Airlines, and United Airlines. Similarly, as your packet moves across the Internet, it passes through **routers** (airports), which are devices that connect different networks together. Routers, and many of the networks they're connected to, are owned by large telecommunication providers (airlines) known as **carriers**. Some of these large carriers include Sprint, AT&T, Verizon Business, and XO Communications. These large carriers exchange Internet traffic freely at physical locations called **Internet exchange points (IXP)**. Large carriers exchange traffic without charging each other access fees via **peering** agreements. Carriers make revenue by collecting subscription fees from end users but not from peers.

The problem with peering is that some people use more bandwidth than others. Netflix, for example, accounts for more than 35 percent of all Internet traffic in North America between 9 PM and 12 AM.[10] Carriers argue that they should be able to charge varying rates based on content, application, or the user requesting the data.

FIGURE 6-20
Using the Internet to Request a Web Page

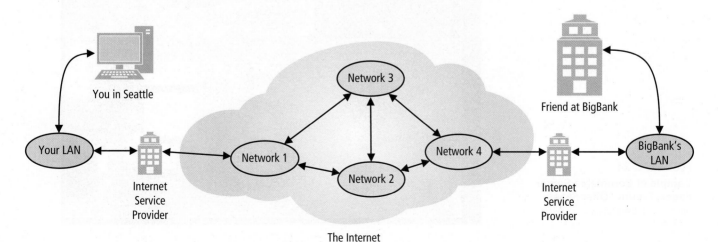

Net Neutrality

Netflix, eBay, Yahoo!, and Amazon say that allowing carriers to charge these varying rates could hurt consumers and innovation. They believe in the **net neutrality** principle, where all data is treated equally. They argue that carriers should not be allowed to decide which sites load quickly, which apps are allowed on a network, and which content is acceptable.

In 2015, the Federal Communications Commission (FCC) approved new net neutrality regulations that ensured ISPs could not discriminate between different types of Internet traffic. This meant all consumers would have access to content on an equal basis. This ruling in many ways rendered the Internet a *utility* like water or electricity that would be governed by comparable regulations.

However, in 2017 the FCC reversed the previous ruling and classified Internet services as an *information service*. This meant ISPs could manage the flow of network traffic over their networks. Several states have begun fighting these new regulations in court.

Q6-5 How Do Web Servers Support the Cloud?

At this point, you know basic networking terms and have a high-level view of how the Internet works. To understand the value of the cloud as well as how it works and how your organization can use it, you need to know a bit about the processing that occurs on a Web server. For this discussion, we will use the example of a Web storefront, which is a server on the Web from which you can buy products.

Suppose you want to buy an item from zulily, a private buyer's site that sells clothing. To do so, you go to *www.zulily.com* and navigate to the product(s) you want to buy (see Figure 6-21). When you find something you want, you add it to your shopping cart and keep shopping. At some point, you check out by supplying credit card data. But what happens when your order data arrives at the server?

FIGURE 6-21
Sample of Commerce Server Pages; Product Offer Pages
Source: Courtesy of Zulily Inc. Used by permission.

When you enter *www.zulily.com* in your browser, the browser sends a request that travels over the Internet to a computer in the server tier at the zulily site. In response to your request, a server-tier computer sends back a **Web page**, which is a document coded in, usually, html (and, as discussed in Chapter 4, probably includes CSS, JavaScript, and other data).

Three-Tier Architecture

Almost all Web applications use the **three-tier architecture**, which is a design of user computers and servers that consists of three categories, or tiers, as shown in Figure 6-22. The **user tier** consists of computers, phones, and other mobile devices that have browsers that request and process Web pages. The **server tier** consists of computers that run Web servers and process application programs. The **database tier** consists of computers that run a DBMS that processes requests to retrieve and store data. Figure 6-22 shows only one computer at the database tier. Some sites have multicomputer database tiers as well.

Web servers are programs that run on a server-tier computer and manage traffic by sending and receiving Web pages to and from clients. A **commerce server** is an application program that runs on a server-tier computer. Typical commerce server functions are to obtain product data from a database, manage the items in a shopping cart, and coordinate the checkout process. When a request comes to the server, the Web server examines it and sends it to the proper program for processing. Thus, the Web server passes e-commerce traffic to the commerce server. It passes requests for other applications to those applications. In Figure 6-22, the server-tier computers are running a Web server program, a commerce server application, and other applications having an unspecified purpose.

Watch the Three Tiers in Action!

Suppose the user of the Web page in Figure 6-21 clicks on shoes and then selects a particular shoe, say, the Darkish Gray Dorine Mary Jane shoe. When the user clicks on that shoe, the commerce server requests that shoe's data from the DBMS, which reads it from the database and then returns the data (including pictures) to the commerce server. That server then formats the Web page with the data and sends the html version of that page to the user's computer. The result is the page shown in Figure 6-23.

FIGURE 6-22
Three-Tier Architecture

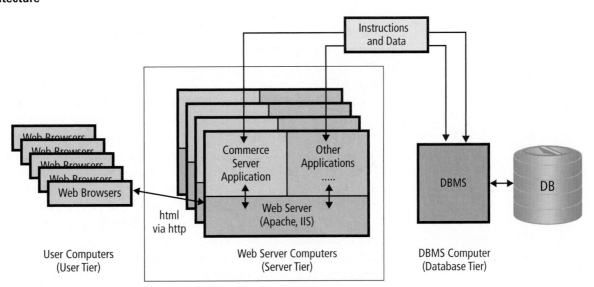

FIGURE 6-23
Product Page

Source: Courtesy of Zulily Inc. Used by permission.

Service-Oriented Architecture (SOA)

The cloud would be impossible without a design philosophy called the **service-oriented architecture (SOA)**. According to this philosophy, all interactions among computing devices are defined as services in a formal, standardized way. This philosophy enables all the pieces of the cloud to fit together, as you will see. However, understanding SOA (pronounced SO-ah) in depth requires you to learn more computer science than you need as a business professional. So, the best way for you to understand SOA is via a business analogy.

A SOA Analogy

Figure 6-24 shows an arrangement of departments at a hypothetical online bicycle part retailer named Best Bikes. The Sales Department receives order requests and follows a process to have them approved for shipping. On request, the Credit Department verifies customer credit as needed to approve orders, and the Inventory Department verifies the availability of the inventory needed to fulfill an order.

In an informal, non-SOA-type organization, one salesperson would contact someone he or she knows in Credit and ask something like "Can you approve an allocation of $10,000 of credit to the ABC Bicycle Company?" In response, the credit person might say, "Sure," and the salesperson might note the name of the person who approved the amount. Some days, he or she might remember to record the date; other days, not so. Another salesperson might do something else, say, contact a different person in Credit and ask something like, "I need $5,000 in credit for Order 12345," and that other person in Credit might say, "I don't know, send the order over, and if I can, I'll write 'Approved' on it." Other irregular, but similar, interactions could occur between the Sales and the Inventory departments.

Such operations are definitely *not* service-oriented. People are asking for credit verification in different ways and receiving responses in different ways. The process for approving an order

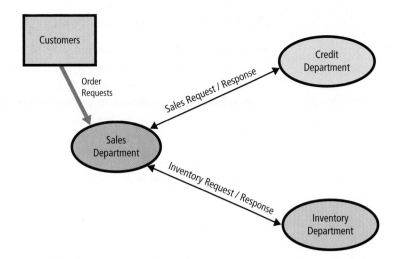

FIGURE 6-24
Approval Request Inter-actions Among Three Departments

varies from salesperson to salesperson, and possibly from day to day with the same salesperson. The records of approvals are inconsistent. Such an organization will have varying levels of process quality and inconsistent results, and should the company decide to open a facility in another city, these operations cannot be readily duplicated, nor should they be.

Using SOA principles, each department would formally define the services it provides. Examples are:

For the Credit Department:

- CheckCustomerCredit
- ApproveCustomerCredit

For the Inventory Department:

- VerifyInventoryAmount
- AllocateInventory
- ReleaseAllocatedInventory

Further, for each service, each department would formally state the data it expects to receive with the request and the data it promises to return in response. Every interaction is done exactly the same way. There is no personal contact between certain people in the departments; no salesperson need know who works in Credit or Inventory. Instead, requests are emailed to a generic email address in Credit or Inventory, and those departments decide who will process the request and how it will be processed. No department has or need have any knowledge of who works in another department nor how the department accomplishes its work. Each department is free to change personnel task assignments and to change the way it performs its services, and no other department needs to know that a change occurred. In SOA terms, we would say the work of the department is **encapsulated** in the department.

With this organization, if Best Bikes wants to add another Inventory Department in another city, it can do so and no salesperson need change the way he or she sets up, submits, or receives responses to requests. Sales continues to send a VerifyInventoryAmount service request, formatted in the standard way, to the same email address.

With multiple sites, the Inventory function would change the way it implements service requests to first identify which of the several Inventory Departments should process the request. Sales would not know, nor need to know, this happened. Best Bikes could dynamically create 1,000 Inventory Departments and the Sales Department need not change anything it does. Later, it could reduce those 1,000 Inventory Departments to three, and, again, sales need not make any change.

SOA for Three-Tier Architecture

From this discussion, you can see how SOA is used to enable cloud processing. The description and advantages and disadvantages of this analogy for SOA are the same for the cloud. Consider Figure 6-25, which shows the three-tier architecture with SOA drawn in. In this case, the commerce server application formally defines services that browsers can request, the data they must provide with the request, and the data that each will receive in response to the request. Sample services are:

- ObtainPartData
- ObtainPartImages
- ObtainPartQuantityOnHand
- OrderPart

And so forth. Again, each service also documents the data it expects and the data it will return.

Now, JavaScript (or another code language) is written to invoke these services correctly. That JavaScript is included as part of the Web pages the server sends to the browsers, and when users employ the browsers to purchase, the JavaScript behind the Web page invokes the services in the correct way.

The server tier can consist of three servers at 3 AM, 3,000 servers at 11 AM, 6,000 servers at 6 PM, and 100 servers at 10 PM. Furthermore, those servers can move around the world; at one time of day, they can be all located in the United States, and at another time of day, they can all be located in Europe, and so on. Nothing, absolutely nothing, in the browsers need change as these servers are adjusted.

To take advantage of the multiple Web servers, a load-balancing program receives requests and sends them to an available server. The load-balancing program keeps data about the speed and health of all its assigned Web servers and allocates work to maximize throughput.

In addition, on the back end, SOA services are defined between the Web server and the database server. Accordingly, the database server need do nothing as the number and location of Web servers is adjusted. And that's a two-way street. Nothing in the Web servers need be changed if the number and location of database servers is adjusted. However, load balancing for database servers is considerably more complicated.

Do not infer from this discussion that SOA services and the cloud are only used for three-tier processing. Such services and the cloud are used for multitudes of applications across the Internet. This three-tier application is just an example.

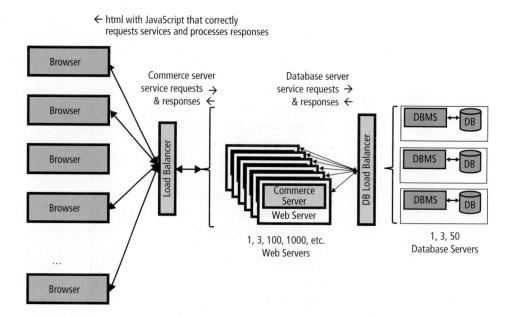

FIGURE 6-25

SOA Principles Applied to Three-Tier Architecture

From this discussion, you can understand how cloud elasticity is possible. However, for many organizations to use the cloud and to be able to mix and match Web services, they need to agree on standard ways of formatting and processing service requests and data. That leads us to cloud standards and protocols. Again, we discuss these at a very high level.

Internet Protocols

A protocol is a set of rules and data structures for organizing communication. Because the cloud's Web services use the Internet, the protocols that run the Internet also support cloud processing. We will start with them.

TCP/IP Protocol Architecture

The basic plumbing of the Internet is governed by protocols that are defined according to an arrangement called the **TCP/IP protocol architecture**. This architecture has five layers; one or more protocols are defined at each layer. Data communications and software vendors write computer programs that implement the rules of a particular protocol. (For protocols at the bottom layer, the physical layer, they build hardware devices that implement the protocol.)

Internet Protocols: http, https, smtp, and ftp

The only Internet protocols that you as a business professional are likely to encounter are those at the top, or the application layer of the TCP/IP architecture, shown in Figure 6-26. **Hypertext Transfer Protocol (http)** is the protocol used between browsers and Web servers. When you use a browser such as Chrome, Safari, or Firefox, you are using a program that implements the http protocol. At the other end there is a server that also processes http. Even though your browser and the server have never "met" before, they can communicate with one another because they both follow the rules of http. Similarly, in Figure 6-25, the browsers send and receive service requests to and from the commerce server using http.

As you will learn in Chapter 10, there is a secure version of http called **https**. Whenever you see *https* in your browser's address bar, you have a secure transmission and you can safely send sensitive data like credit card numbers. When you are on the Internet, if you do not see *https*, then you should assume that all of your communication is open and could be published on the front page of your campus newspaper tomorrow morning. Hence, when you are using http, email, text messaging, chat, videoconferencing, or anything other than https, know that whatever you are typing or saying could be known by anyone else.

Two additional TCP/IP application-layer protocols are common. **smtp**, or **Simple Mail Transfer Protocol**, is used for email transmissions (along with other protocols). **ftp**, or **File Transfer Protocol**, is used to move files over the Internet. Google Drive and Microsoft OneDrive use ftp behind the scenes to transmit files to and from their cloud servers to your computer.

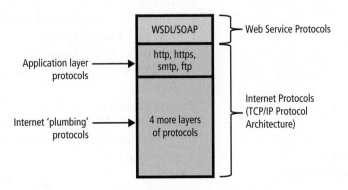

FIGURE 6-26
Protocols That Support Web Services

WSDL, SOAP, XML, and JSON

To wrap up the discussion, we will briefly consider four standards used extensively for Web services and the cloud. Those standards and their purpose are as follows:

WSDL (Web Services Description Language)	A standard for describing the services, inputs and outputs, and other data supported by a Web service. Documents coded according to this standard are machine readable and can be used by developer tools for creating programs to access the service.
SOAP (no longer an acronym)	A protocol for requesting Web services and for sending responses to Web service requests.
XML (eXtensible Markup Language)	A markup language used for transmitting documents. Contains much metadata that can be used to validate the format and completeness of the document, but includes considerable overhead (see Figure 6-27a).
JSON (JavaScript Object Notation)	A markup language used for transmitting documents. Contains little metadata and is preferred for transmitting volumes of data between servers and browsers. While the notation is the format of JavaScript objects, JSON documents can be processed by any language (see Figure 6-27b).

Service authors (computer programmers) create WSDL documents to describe the services they provide and the inputs and outputs required. These WSDL documents are seldom read by humans. Instead, developer tools like Microsoft Visual Studio read the WSDL to configure the programming environment for programmers who write code to access that service.

As shown in Figure 6-26, SOAP, which is not an acronym though it looks like one, is a protocol that sits on top of http and the lower-level Internet protocols. *Sits on top of* means that it uses http to send and receive SOAP messages. (SOAP can also use smtp.) Programs that use Web services issue SOAP messages to request services; the Web service uses SOAP messages to return responses to service requests.

Finally, XML and JSON are ways of marking up documents so that both the service requestor and the service provider know what data they're processing. Figure 6-27 shows a simple example of both. As you can see, XML documents contain as much metadata as they do application data. These metadata are used to ensure that the document is complete and properly formatted. XML is

```
<person>
    <firstName>Kelly</firstName>
    <lastName>Summers</lastName>
    <dob>12/28/1985</dob>
    <address>
        <streetAddress>309 Elm Avenue</streetAddress>
        <city>San Diego</city>
        <state>CA</state>
        <postalCode>98225</postalCode>
    </address>
    <phoneNumbers>
        <phoneNumber type="home">685 555-1234</phoneNumber>
        <phoneNumber type="cell">685 555-5678</phoneNumber>
    </phoneNumbers>
</person>
```

FIGURE 6-27A
Example XML Document

```
{
  "firstName": "Kelly",
  "lastName": "Summers",
  "dob": "12/28/1985",
  "address": {
    "streetAddress": "309 Elm Avenue",
    "city": "San Diego",
    "state": "CA",
    "postalCode": "98225"
  },
  "phoneNumber": [
    {
      "type": "home",
      "number": "685 555-1234"
    },
    {
      "type": "cell",
      "number": "685 555-5678"
    }
  ]
}
```

FIGURE 6-27B
Example JSON Document

used when relatively few messages are being transmitted and when ensuring a complete and correct document is crucial. Both WSDLs and SOAP messages are coded in XML.

As its name indicates, JSON uses the notation for JavaScript objects to format data. It has much less metadata and is preferred for the transmission of voluminous application data. Web servers use JSON as their primary way of sending application data to browsers.

With this technical background, you should no longer be skeptical that the benefits of the cloud are real. They are. However, this fact does not mean that every organization uses the cloud well. In the remainder of this chapter, we will describe generic ways that organizations can use the cloud, discuss how eHermes in particular can use the cloud, and, finally, discuss an exceedingly important topic: cloud security.

Q6-6   How Can eHermes Use the Cloud?

eHermes is an innovative startup company with a relatively small IT department. As such, it is unlikely to have the resources necessary to develop a large server infrastructure. Instead, it is far more likely to take advantage of cloud services provided by cloud vendors.

SaaS Services at eHermes

Software as a service requires little investment in the hardware and software system components. The SaaS vendor administers and manages the cloud servers and makes the software available, usually as a thin client. eHermes will, however, need to transfer existing data, create new data, develop procedures, and train users.

Some of the SaaS products that eHermes could use are:

- Google Mail
- Google Drive
- Office 365
- Salesforce.com
- Microsoft CRM OnLine
- And many others

You already know what the first three SaaS offerings are. Salesforce.com and Microsoft's CRM OnLine are customer relationship management systems, which you will learn about in Chapter 8.

PaaS Services at eHermes Security

With PaaS, eHermes leases hardware and operating systems in the cloud from the cloud vendor. For example, it can lease EC2 (Elastic Cloud 2, a PaaS product offered by Amazon), and Amazon will preinstall either Linux or Windows Server on the cloud hardware. Given that basic capability, eHermes would then install its own software. For example, it could install its own, in-house developed applications, or it could install other applications licensed from a software vendor. It could also license a DBMS, say, SQL Server from Microsoft, and place it on an EC2 Windows Server instance. In the case of software licensed from others, eHermes must purchase licenses that permit replication because Amazon will replicate it when it increases servers.

Some cloud vendors include DBMS products in their PaaS services. Thus, eHermes could obtain Windows Servers with SQL Server already installed from the Microsoft Azure cloud offerings. That option is likely what Seth was considering when he mentioned the $10 per TB per month.

DBMS are also included in other vendors' cloud offerings. As of May 2018, Amazon offers the following DBMS products with EC2:

Amazon Relational Database Service (RDS)	A relational database service supporting MySQL, Oracle, SQL Server, or PostgreSQL
Amazon DynamoDB	A fast and scalable NoSQL database service
Amazon ElastiCache	A very fast in-memory cache database service
Amazon Redshift	A petabyte-scale data warehouse
Amazon Neptune	A fast, fully managed graph database for complex hierarchical structures

Finally, eHermes might use a CDN to distribute its content worldwide as it grows and expands into new markets.

IaaS Services at eHermes

As stated, IaaS provides basic hardware in the cloud. Some companies acquire servers this way and then load operating systems onto them. Doing so requires a considerable technical expertise and management. A company like eHermes is more likely to spend its valuable resources on developing its own mobile storefronts and internal systems rather than spending time configuring servers.

eHermes might, however, obtain data storage services in the cloud. Amazon, for example, offers data storage with its S3 product. Using it, organizations can place data in the cloud and even have that data be made elastically available. Again, however, an organization like eHermes would more likely use SaaS and PaaS because of the added value they provide.

Q6-7 How Can Organizations Use Cloud Services Securely?

The Internet and cloud services based on Internet infrastructure provide powerful processing and storage services at a fraction of the cost of private data centers. However, the Internet is a jungle of threats to data and computing infrastructure, as discussed in Chapter 10. Some of the biggest threats to cloud services include insecure interfaces, data loss, and data leakage. How can organizations realize the benefits of cloud technology without succumbing to those threats?

The answer involves a combination of technologies that we will address, at a very high level, in this question. As you read, realize that no security story is ever over; attackers constantly strive to find ways around security safeguards, and occasionally they succeed. Thus, you can expect that cloud security will evolve beyond that described here throughout your career. We begin with a discussion of VPNs, a technology used to provide secure communication over the Internet.

Virtual Private Networks (VPNs)

A **virtual private network (VPN)** uses the Internet to create the appearance of private, secure connections. In the IT world, the term *virtual* means something that appears to exist but in fact does not. Here, a VPN uses the public Internet to create the appearance of a private connection on a secure network.

A Typical VPN

Figure 6-28 shows one way to create a VPN to connect a remote computer, perhaps used by an employee working at a hotel in Miami, to a LAN at a Chicago site. The remote user is the VPN client. That client first establishes a public connection to the Internet. The connection can be obtained by accessing a local ISP, as shown in Figure 6-28, or, in some cases, the hotel itself provides a direct Internet connection.

In either case, once the Internet connection is made, VPN software on the remote user's computer establishes a connection with the VPN server in Chicago. The VPN client and VPN server then have a secure connection. That connection, called a **tunnel**, is a virtual, private pathway over a public or shared network from the VPN client to the VPN server. Figure 6-29 illustrates the connection as it appears to the remote user.

To secure VPN communications over the public Internet, the VPN client software *encrypts*, or codes (see Chapter 10, page 395), messages so their contents are protected from snooping. Then the VPN client appends the Internet address of the VPN server to the message and sends that packet over the Internet to the VPN server. When the VPN server receives the message, it strips its address off the front of the message, *decrypts* the coded message, and sends the plain text message to the original address inside the LAN. In this way, secure private messages are delivered over the public Internet.

Using a Private Cloud

A **private cloud** is a cloud owned and operated by an organization for its own benefit. To create a *private* cloud, the organization creates a private internet and designs applications using Web services standards as shown in Figure 6-14 (page 214). The organization then creates a farm of

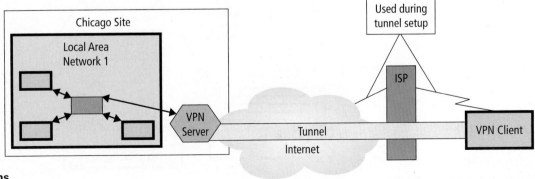

FIGURE 6-28
Remote Access Using VPN; Actual Connections

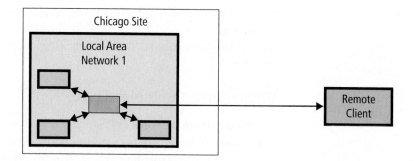

FIGURE 6-29
Remote Access Using VPN;
Apparent Connection

servers and manages those servers with elastic load balancing just as the cloud service vendors do. Because of the complexity of managing multiple database servers, most organizations choose not to replicate database servers. Figure 6-30 illustrates this possibility.

Private clouds provide security *within* the organizational infrastructure but do not provide secure access from outside that infrastructure. To provide such access, organizations set up a VPN and users employ it to securely access the private cloud as shown in Figure 6-31.

Private clouds provide the advantages of elasticity, but to questionable benefit. What can organizations do with their idle servers? They could realize some cost savings by shutting down the idle servers. But unlike the cloud vendors, they cannot repurpose them for use by other companies. Possibly a large conglomerate or major international company could balance processing loads across subsidiary business units and across different geographical regions. 3M, for example, might balance processing for its different product groups and on different continents, but it is difficult to imagine that, in doing so, it would save money or time. A company like eHermes is very unlikely to develop a private cloud.

Amazon, Microsoft, IBM, Google, and other major cloud service vendors employ thousands of highly trained, very highly skilled personnel to create, manage, administer, and improve their cloud services. It is unimaginable that any non-cloud company, even large ones like 3M, could build and operate a cloud service facility that competes. The only situation in which this might make sense is if the organization is required by law or business custom to maintain physical control over its stored data. Even in that case, however, the organization is unlikely to be required to maintain physical control over all data, so it might keep critically sensitive data on-premises and place the rest of the

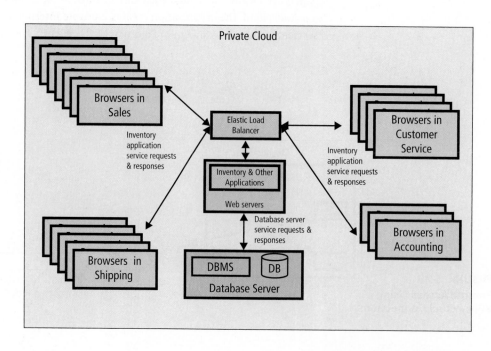

FIGURE 6-30
Private Cloud for Inventory
and Other Applications

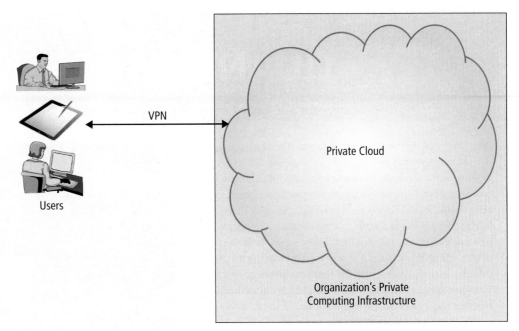

FIGURE 6-31
Accessing Private Cloud over a Virtual Private Network

data and related applications into the facilities of a public cloud vendor. It might also use a virtual private cloud, which we consider next.

Using a Virtual Private Cloud

A **virtual private cloud (VPC)** is a subset of a public cloud that has highly restricted, secure access. An organization can build its own VPC on top of public cloud infrastructure like AWS or that provided by other cloud vendors. The means by which this is done are beyond the scope of this text, but think of it as VPN tunneling on steroids.

Using a VPC, an organization can store its most sensitive data on its own infrastructure and store the less sensitive data on the VPC. In this way, organizations that are required to have physical control over some of their data can place that data on their own servers and locate the rest of their data on the VPC as shown in Figure 6-32. By doing so, the organization gains the advantages of cloud storage and possibly cloud processing for that portion of its data that it need not physically control.

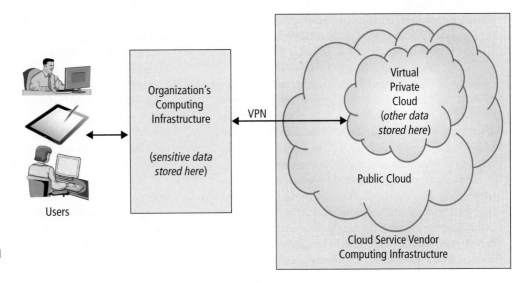

FIGURE 6-32
Using a Virtual Private Cloud (VPC)

SO WHAT? QUANTUM LEARNING

If you are reading this textbook as part of a college course, then you probably already recognize the value of learning. Learning has been a fundamental part of your life for as long as you can remember. Some of the knowledge you have acquired has been "book" knowledge learned in school, while some has been "street smarts" learned while interacting with new people in new places. For example, the first time someone broke a promise to you, it probably affected the way you perceive the trustworthiness of others. As a result, the next time someone promised you something, a small part of you might have questioned whether that person would actually keep his word.

This ability of humans to interpret complex situations and social interactions, and remember and learn from past experiences, enables us to survive and thrive in dynamic and rapidly changing environments. What you may not realize is that computers are becoming better at learning in this dynamic way, too.

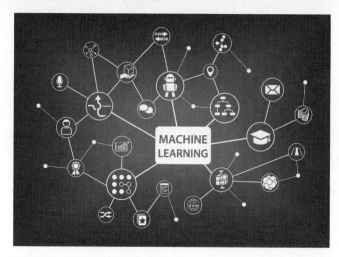

Source: Iconimage/Fotolia

Learning to Learn

Many people perceive computers to be systems with very rigid operations; they can only carry out finite sets of tasks based on seemingly endless lines of computer code that tell them what to do. However, the walls of rigid computer code are breaking down as machine learning becomes more widely used in a number of industries. *Machine learning*, in a basic sense, is the ability of computers to learn dynamically rather than being explicitly told what to do via restrictive sets of coded instructions. Machine learning is based on the iterative generation of models; the computer has the ability to adapt to these models and interpret them differently over time. This capability is important because it allows the computer to identify patterns and other insights without being directed to the features it should analyze or being told where to find those features in large sets of data.[11]

The ability of computers to learn iteratively and dynamically has important implications for many real-world applications. Machine learning techniques have been used for fraud detection, credit score analysis, network intrusion detection, and image recognition.[12] Future applications of machine learning will likely include the development of artificial intelligence personal assistants and autonomous cars.[13]

As a more specific example, think about the ways in which companies are turning to social media for insight about how their products and services are perceived by customers. Companies use machine learning tools to analyze customer tweets. Then they identify trends in how customers feel about different advertising campaigns. Based on the results,

companies can curtail campaigns that are not having the desired effect and roll out more effective campaigns on a larger scale.[14]

Computer scientists and executives are looking to the future of machine learning to see how advancements may change their industries. Many have an eye on the world of quantum computing as the next big advancement for machine learning due to its ability to increase the speed at which computers can process data.

One Quantum Step for Computers, One Giant Step for Learning

Quantum computing has been a topic of interest for scientists and innovators for many years. The fundamental difference between a quantum computer and a regular computer is the way in which computers manage information—bits. A standard computer uses 1s and 0s as the basis for all of its operations. For example, when you enter an *A* on the keyboard, the computer interprets this as "01000001." In contrast, a quantum computer can encode information in what are called *qubits*, which can be represented as a 1, a 0, or *both at the same time*. The capacity for this third state allows tasks to be carried out much more quickly and has the potential to yield exponential growth in the processing capability of computers.

Quantum computing also enhances computers' ability to learn. Right now there is still a huge gap between how computers adapt through machine learning and how humans learn. Quantum computing has the potential to narrow this gap as computers become increasingly able to learn how to interpret and adapt more complex datasets with little to no direction.[15]

The implications of quantum computing for machine learning and the creation of a more powerful artificial intelligence are profound. However, even if quantum computers have the capacity to process mammoth data sets, standardization of schemas and metadata will still be needed to ensure that the correct types of data are being considered for analysis.[16] Once infrastructure and data management hurdles are overcome, quantum computing stands to revolutionize almost everything that we do with 1s, 0s, or both!

Questions

1. Think about the last time you learned how to do something new. How long did it take for you to master it? What types of learning mechanisms did you use, and how varied were your approaches to learning? Think about the inherent limitations of computers in learning new operations. What would a computer have to do to master this same skill?

2. The feature provides the example of a company using social media analysis to evaluate customer sentiment and customize advertising based on consumers' tweets. Why would this type of analysis require a machine learning approach?

3. Conduct an Internet search to find the binary codes for ASCII keyboard characters. A common first task that programmers use to test their code is to have the system print "Hello World" on the screen. Use the binary codes for these characters to write "Hello World" as a computer would see it.

4. The article mentions that quantum computers will have tremendous processing power and revolutionize a number of computer applications. Conduct an Internet search to identify specific examples of how quantum computers may be used in the future.

Q6-8 2029?

So where does the cloud go in the next 10 years? Absent some unknown factor such as a federal tax on Internet traffic, cloud services will become faster, more secure, easier to use, and cheaper. Fewer and fewer organizations will set up their own computing infrastructure; instead, they will benefit from the pooling of servers across organizations and from the economies of scale produced by cloud vendors.

But, looking a bit deeper, the cloud brings both good and bad news. The good news is that organizations can readily obtain elastic resources at very low cost. This trend will benefit everyone from individuals on the iCloud or Google Drive, to small groups using Office 365, to companies like eHermes using PaaS, to huge organizations using IaaS.

The overall size of the cloud is getting bigger too. For example, Google's Project Loon looks to seed the atmosphere with high-altitude balloons capable of providing Internet access to previously unreachable parts of the planet. And Google isn't stopping there. It's also making the cloud faster. Google Fiber aims to offer users 1 Gbps connections to the Internet. That's 100 times faster than the average broadband connection. Comcast responded to Google's plans by announcing its own gigabit-per-second service.

So what's the bad news? Remember that 500,000-square-foot Apple Web farm in Figure 6-7? Note the size of the parking lot. That tiny lot accommodates the entire operations staff. According to *Computerworld*, that building employs an operations staff of 50 people, which, spread over three shifts, 24/7, means that not many more than eight people will be running that center at any one time. Seems impossible, but is it? Again, look at the size of the parking lot.

And it's not just large companies like Apple. In 2018, every city of almost any size still supports small companies that install and maintain in-house email Exchange and other servers. If SaaS products like Google Drive or Office 365 replace those servers, what happens to those local jobs? They're gone! See Collaboration Exercise 6, page 244, for more on this topic.

But, with computing infrastructure so much cheaper, there have to be new jobs somewhere. By 2029, where will they be? For one, there will be more startups. Cheap and elastic cloud services enable small startups like the football player evaluation company Hudl (*www.hudl.com*) to access

SECURITY GUIDE

IRS SYSTEMS OVERTAXED

The most common signs people look for when deciding to replace a computer or phone are rapidly depleted batteries, sluggish processing times, system crashes, and excessive physical abuse to the case or screen. If you have a device that is suffering from some (or all) of these symptoms, why haven't you replaced it? In many cases, people choose to delay replacing a device either because they do not have the resources to do so or they do not have the time. They simply wait until an absolute system failure, when they have no choice but to proceed with the upgrade.

Not surprisingly, companies often follow a similar strategy for managing their IT infrastructures. Outdated enterprise systems, also called legacy systems, can also show signs of duress over time. But as long as they don't severely disrupt business operations, they continue to be used. This is because executives and strategists within the organization often prefer to allocate resources to parts of the business with more glaring needs. In other words, if the system is not completely broken, why should we pay to fix it? Unfortunately, it is common for legacy systems to fail at the worst possible moment, like the middle of the holiday shopping season or, in the case of the IRS, April 17, 2018—Tax Day.

Be Right Back, in 7,981 Years!

The IRS experienced a critical system failure on the deadline for Americans to file their taxes. The system was inaccessible for direct bank account payments and e-filing services from the early morning hours on Tuesday until about 5 PM.[17] In spite of the poor timing of this failure, a number of high-ranking officials in the IRS expressed some degree of astonishment that this type of IT infrastructure breakdown had not already occurred. When describing the systems (some circa 1960s) used by the IRS for processing tax payments, the IRS Deputy Commissioner for operations support commented that about 64 percent of IRS systems are considered aged and 32 percent of software is multiple releases behind industry standards.[18]

Comically, visitors to the IRS site attempting to file were greeted with a message indicating that systems were down due to planned maintenance but that they would return on December 31, 9999. While some found this message humorous, the diminishing resources of the IRS over the past several years can be labeled anything but funny to those trying to manage the operations of this massive government agency. The IRS budget sank 80 percent from where it was in 2010.[19] Further exacerbating the problem is the constant barrage of daily cyberattacks against the IRS, which the organization must mitigate.[20]

Does the IRS Have Its Head in the Clouds? Should It?

Many organizations that maintain their own IT infrastructure are transitioning to cloud-based operations. This strategy allows highly specialized experts (benefiting from the economies of scale derived from managing numerous organizations' infrastructures) to manage your systems and data so that your organization can focus on its own expertise. In the case of the IRS, a cloud-based model seems especially appropriate due to the ability of cloud operations to more easily scale up during times of high demand and then ramp back down during times of little activity. (This clearly lines up with the frenzied activity of the tax season versus the rest of the year, as roughly 15 percent of Americans waited until the last possible week to file taxes in 2016.)[21] As a comparable example, consider

Source: Markus Mainka/Alamy Stock Photo

Amazon, which handles a constant stream of orders throughout the year but handles exceptional increases in traffic volume around the holiday season. Specifically, in 2017 Amazon handled just under 13 million orders over the 2 days spanning Thanksgiving Day and Black Friday.[22] Perhaps the IRS will follow the mass exodus of companies heading to the cloud so that we can all wait until the last minute to file our taxes without crashing their systems!

DISCUSSION QUESTIONS

1. Is it time for you to upgrade either your phone or your laptop? If so, what are the indicators that you look for to determine whether your device is beginning to become unstable or fail? What other types of legacy systems have you encountered?
2. The IRS system crash of 2018 is the most recent example of a high-profile IT-infrastructure debacle with the U.S. government. Can you think of any other recent examples of government-related IT problems?

3. From a security perspective, what are the pros and cons of the government using such outdated IT systems for handling tax filings?
4. What types of interactions do you have with the cloud? Do you back up personal documents, like photos and music, on the cloud? Do you use it strictly for productivity-related files and collaboration? What are the benefits and drawbacks of the cloud for you relative to storing files locally on your devices?

CDN and other cloud services for next to nothing, a capability that would have taken years and thousands of dollars in the past. Go to its site to check its response time; it's fast!

There may be additional new cloud services beyond IaaS, PaaS, and SaaS. Cloud service providers may provide Analytics as a Service (AaaS) to help companies analyze the mountains of big data they're collecting. They may go even further and provide Business Process as a Service (BPaaS). Companies could then outsource common business processes like shipping and procurement. In fact, the cloud may evolve into Everything as a Service (EaaS) where all aspects of your business can be outsourced to a service provider—except the one aspect where you add value.

But what else? The cloud will foster new categories of work. By 2029, everything will be connected to everything else. Consider **remote action systems**, IS that provide computer-based activity or action at a distance. By enabling action at a distance, remote action systems save time and travel expense and make the skills and abilities of an expert available in places where he or she is not physically located. They also enable experts to scale their expertise. Let's look at a few examples.

Telemedicine is a remote action system that healthcare professionals use to diagnose and treat patients in rural or remote areas. Doctors videoconference with patients at local drugstores, where they can transmit diagnostic readings like blood pressure and temperature. The telemedicine market is expected to exceed $49 billion by 2023.[23] In Canada, Dr. Mehran Anvari regularly performs **telesurgery**, in which telecommunications link the surgeon to robotic equipment at distant locations, on patients more than 400 kilometers away.[24] Such examples, which are still somewhat rare, have problems that must be overcome, but they will become more common by 2029. In fact, the largest healthcare provider in the United States, UnitedHealthcare, recently announced that all video-based doctor visits will be covered just like regular doctor visits.[25]

Other uses for remote systems include **telelaw enforcement**, such as the RedFlex system that uses cameras and motion-sensing equipment to issue tickets for red-light and speeding violations. The RedFlex Group, headquartered in South Melbourne, Victoria, Australia, earns 87 percent of its revenue from traffic violations in the United States. It offers a turnkey traffic citation information system that includes all five components.

Many remote systems are designed to provide services in dangerous locations, such as robots that clean nuclear reactors or biologically contaminated sites. Drones and other unoccupied military equipment are examples of remote systems used in war zones. Private security and law enforcement will increasingly take advantage of remotely controlled flying drones and robots. You may see an upgraded form of Knightscope's wheeled robot, named K7, patrolling your neighborhood in 2029.

But, even with these new opportunities, the news isn't all good. New York's Metropolitan Opera is arguably the finest opera company in the world. To see a live performance, you can drive to Manhattan, park your car, taxi to Lincoln Center, and pay $300 per seat. Or you can watch the same opera, remotely broadcast via Met Live, at a local movie theater, park your car for free, pay $12, and take a seat in the fourth row, where via the magic of digital broadcasting you can see details like the stitching on the singers' costumes. Details you just can't see from the $300 seats at the Met. And the sound quality is better. Wonderful, but now, who will go to a local opera performance?

Access to remote action systems reduces the value of local mediocrity. The claim "Well, I'm not the best, but at least I'm here" loses value in an interconnected world. In 1990, when former Secretary of Labor Robert Reich wrote *The Work of Nations*,[26] he could sensibly claim that those who provide routine face-to-face services are exempt from the dangers of offshoring. That claim loses validity in an interconnected world.

By 2029, the value of the top-notch performers increases, possibly exponentially. Four million people watch the average Met Live broadcast; agents for the artists who perform at that venue will negotiate a sizable part of that $120 million gate. A famous surgeon or skating coach can reach a bigger market, faster and better, and be much better paid. So, if you can be the world's best at something, do it!

But what about the rest of us? If you're not the world's expert at something, then find a way to be indispensable to someone who is. Own the theaters that broadcast Met Live. Own the skating rink for the remote figure skating coach. Be the vendor of the food at some teleaction event.

Or become essential to the development, use, and management of information systems that support these new opportunities. A business background with IS expertise will serve you very well between now and 2029. The next six chapters discuss many existing and new IS applications. Keep reading!

CAREER GUIDE

Source: Rebecca Cengiz Robbs, Carbonite, Senior Network Manager

Name: Rebecca Cengiz-Robbs
Company: Carbonite
Job Title: Senior Network Manager
Education: University of Utah

1 How did you get this type of job?

I think it's a combination of skill, attitude, and networking. I was working as a network engineer when I was promoted to manager. I had been an engineer for four and a half years and hoped to stay in a technical position for a few more years. However, with my strong organizational skills and my willingness to volunteer for projects, it evolved into a management position. I also have a manager who is motivated to help his employees improve and advance.

2 What attracted you to this field?

I worked in the tourism industry before making a career change. I was attracted to IT by the wide variety of disciplines and the abundant opportunities, especially for women. After working as a network administrator and being able to get exposure to storage, backups, computing, security, and networking, I realized I liked networking the best.

3 What does a typical workday look like for you (duties, decisions, problems)?

I have remote engineers, so I host a daily team call so we all stay connected and aware of short- and long-term projects. I am responsible for negotiating and maintaining support contracts for network equipment; purchasing equipment for new projects and upgrades; coordinating with other teams on projects that impact infrastructure; monitoring and managing bandwidth capacity, network assets, and inventory; and managing the work and advancement of network engineers.

4 What do you like most about your job?

I like how there is always something to learn from day-to-day tasks, new projects, and my colleagues. At first I was intimidated by how much I didn't know. Now I'm glad I don't know everything and that I am surrounded by smart engineers who are willing to learn, teach, and help each other.

5 What skills would someone need to do well at your job?

When I am interviewing potential candidates I look for someone who is smart and happy. I've hired less experienced people because they were educated, intelligent, and organized and had a good attitude. Technical skills are easy to teach; attitude and intelligence are not.

6 Are education or certifications important in your field? Why?

This question is frequently debated by my colleagues. Most of the engineers at my company do not have a college degree. Some have certifications. I often hear that the only thing that matters is what you can do on the job, not a piece of paper. I believe education and certifications are both important in addition to technical skills. My degree gave me an advantage when I was looking for my first job. I had very little experience, but my manager was impressed with my academic accomplishments and took a chance on me. Based on my experience as a manager, I see that engineers with education have more motivation, focus, and ability to juggle multiple projects. They often communicate (verbally and in writing) better than engineers without degrees.

7 What advice would you give to someone who is considering working in your field?

In addition to technical skills and a good work ethic, I'd develop emotional intelligence and build a personal network. Often in IT, it's who you know and how you get along with people that will help you stand out and advance.

8 What do you think will be hot tech jobs in 10 years?

Anything to do with cloud computing: software engineering, network infrastructure and engineering, storage, computing, and automation.

ACTIVE REVIEW

Use this Active Review to verify that you understand the ideas and concepts that answer the chapter's study questions.

Q6-1   Why are organizations moving to the cloud?

Define *cloud* and explain the three key terms in your definition. Describe the differences between mainframe, client-server, and cloud architectures. Explain the difference between scalability and elasticity. Using Figure 6-5 as a guide, compare and contrast cloud-based and in-house hosting. What factors encourage organizations to move to the cloud? When does it not make sense to use a cloud-based infrastructure?

Q6-2   How do organizations use the cloud?

Describe how an organization can benefit from the cloud's resource elasticity, pooling, and unique Internet connectivity. Define *SaaS*, *PaaS*, and *IaaS*. Provide an example of each. For each, describe the business situation in which it would be the most appropriate option. Define *CDN* and explain the purpose and advantages of a CDN. Explain how Web services can be used internally.

Q6-3   What network technology supports the cloud?

Define *computer network*. Explain the differences among PANs, LANs, WANs, intranets, internets, and the Internet. Describe protocol and explain the purpose of protocols. Explain the key distinction of a LAN. Describe the purpose of each component in Figure 6-16. Define *IEEE 802.3* and *802.11* and explain how they differ. List three ways of connecting a LAN or computer to the Internet. Explain the nature of each.

Q6-4   How does the Internet work?

Describe how the Internet and the U.S. postal system are similar. Define *IP address* and explain why public IP addresses are necessary to deliver packets. Describe the purpose of a domain name and explain how such names are associated with public IP addresses. Explain the purpose of TCP. Explain the role for agencies like GoDaddy. Define *URL*. Define peering agreements and explain why carriers make them. Would a company like Netflix be for or against net neutrality? Explain why.

Q6-5   How do Web servers support the cloud?

Define *three-tier architecture* and name and describe the role of each tier. Explain the role of each tier in Figure 6-22 as

well as how the pages in Figures 6-21 and 6-23 are processed. Using the department analogy, define *SOA* and explain why departments are encapsulated. Summarize the advantages of using SOA in the three-tier architecture. Define *TCP/IP protocol architecture* and explain, in general terms, the purpose of http, https, smtp, and ftp. Define the purpose and role of WSDL, SOAP, XML, and JSON. State a key difference between XML and JSON.

Q6-6   How can eHermes use the cloud?

First, state why eHermes is likely to use the cloud. Name and describe SaaS products that eHermes could use. Explain several ways that eHermes could use PaaS offerings. Summarize why it is unlikely that eHermes would use IaaS.

Q6-7   How can organizations use cloud services securely?

Explain the purpose of a VPN and describe, in broad terms, how a VPN works. Define the term *virtual* and explain how it relates to VPN. Define *private cloud*. Summarize why the benefits of a private cloud are questionable. What kind of organization might benefit from such a cloud? Explain why it is unlikely that even very large organizations can create private clouds that compete with public cloud utilities. Under what circumstance might a private cloud make sense for an organization? Define *VPC* and explain how and why an organization might use one.

Q6-8   2029?

What is the likely future for the cloud? Summarize the good and bad news the cloud brings. Explain why the photo in Figure 6-7 is disturbing. Describe three categories of remote action systems. Explain how remote systems will increase the value of super-experts but diminish local mediocrity. What can other-than-super-experts do? Summarize how this 2029 discussion pertains to your career hopes.

Using Your Knowledge with eHermes

Name the principal advantage of the cloud to eHermes. For hosting its data, which cloud offering—SaaS, PaaS, or IaaS—makes the most sense, given the size and nature of eHermes' business? Explain how eHermes could use that offering. If eHermes were larger and employed a more sophisticated IT staff, name another alternative that would make sense. Explain why.

KEY TERMS AND CONCEPTS

10/100/1000 Ethernet   215
Bluetooth   218
Cable line   219
Carrier   223
Client-server architecture   203
Cloud   203
Cloud computing architecture   204
Commerce server   225
Computer terminal   203
Content delivery network (CDN)   212
Database tier   225
Digital subscriber line (DSL)   219
Domain name   221
Domain Name System (DNS)   221
Elastic   205
Encapsulated   227
Ethernet   215
File Transfer Protocol (ftp)   229
Hop   223
https   229
Hypertext Transfer Protocol (http)   229
ICANN (Internet Corpora-
    tion for Assigned Names and
    Numbers)   221
IEEE 802.3 protocol   215

IEEE 802.11 protocol   218
Infrastructure as a service (IaaS)   210
Internet   215
Internet exchange points (IXP)   223
Internet service provider (ISP)   218
Intranet   215
IP address   221
IPv4   221
IPv6   221
Local area network (LAN)   214
Mainframe architecture   203
Mainframes   203
Net neutrality   224
Network   214
Over the Internet   205
Packet   221
Peering   223
Personal area network (PAN)   214
Platform as a service (PaaS)   211
Pooled   205
Private cloud   233
Private IP address   223
Protocol   215
Public IP address   221
Remote action system   239

Routers   223
Scalable   204
Server tier   225
Service-oriented architecture (SOA)   226
Simple Mail Transfer Protocol (smtp)   229
Small office/home office (SOHO)   215
Software as a service (SaaS)   211
TCP/IP protocol architecture   229
Telelaw enforcement   239
Telemedicine   239
Telesurgery   239
The Internet   215
Thin client   203
Three-tier architecture   225
Transmission Control Protocol
    (TCP)   222
Tunnel   233
URL (Uniform Resource Locator)   222
User tier   225
Virtual private cloud (VPC)   235
Virtual private network (VPN)   233
WAN wireless   220
Web page   225
Web servers   225
Wide area network (WAN)   214

MyLab MIS

To complete the problems with MyLab MIS, go to EOC Discussion Questions in the MyLab.

USING YOUR KNOWLEDGE

6-1. Define *cloud*, and explain the three key terms in your defi-
MyLab MIS nition. Compare and contrast cloud-based and in-house
hosting using the comparison presented in Q6-1 as a
guide. In your opinion, explain the three most important
factors that make cloud-based hosting preferable to in-
house hosting.

6-2. Apple invested more than $3B in the North Carolina data
MyLab MIS center mentioned in Q6-2. For Apple to spend such a sum,
it must perceive the iCloud as being a key component of
its future. Using the principles discussed in Q2-7 of Chapter 2, explain all the ways you believe the iCloud will give
Apple a competitive advantage over other mobile device
vendors.

6-3. Suppose you manage a group of seven employees in a small
MyLab MIS business. Each of your employees wants to be connected to
the Internet. Consider two alternatives:

Alternative A: Each employee has his or her own device
and connects individually to the Internet.

Alternative B: The employees' computers are connected
using a LAN, and the network uses a single device to connect to the Internet.

a. Sketch the equipment and lines required for each
alternative.

b. Explain the actions you need to take to create each
alternative.

c. Which of these two alternatives would you recommend?

6-4. Go to *http://aws.amazon.com*. and search for AWS database offerings. Explain the differences among Amazon's RDS, DynamoDB, ElastiCache, Redshift services, and Neptune. Which of these would you recommend for storing eHermes' data? (By the way, whenever you query the Internet for any AWS product, be sure to include the keyword *AWS* in your search. Otherwise, your search will result in Amazon's lists of books about the item you're searching for.)

6-5. Suppose Seth wants eHermes to set up a private internet, and he justifies this request on the basis of better security. Explain why that is not a good decision and rebut his claim about security by suggesting that eHermes use a VPC. Justify your suggestion.

6-6. In five sentences or fewer, explain how the cloud will affect job prospects for you between now and 2029.

COLLABORATION EXERCISE 6

Using the collaboration IS you built in Chapter 1 (page 32), collaborate with a group of students to answer the following questions.

The cloud is causing monumental changes in the information systems services industry. In every city, you will still see the trucks of local independent software vendors (ISVs) driving to their clients to set up and maintain local area networks, servers, and software. You'll know the trucks by the Microsoft, Oracle, and Cisco logos on their sides. For years, those small, local companies have survived, some very profitably, on their ability to set up and maintain LANs, connect user computers to the Internet, set up servers, sell Microsoft Exchange licenses, and install other software on both servers and user computers.

Once everything is installed, these companies continued to earn revenue by providing maintenance for problems that inevitably developed and support for new versions of software, connecting new user computers, and so forth. Their customers vary, but generally are smaller companies of, say, 3 to 50 employees—companies that are large enough to need email, Internet connections, and possibly some entry-level software applications such as QuickBooks.

6-7. Using the knowledge of this chapter and the intuition of the members of your team, summarize threats that cloud services present to such ISVs.

6-8. Suppose your team owns and manages one of these ISVs. You learn that more and more of your clients are choosing SaaS cloud services like Google for email, rather than setting up local email servers.
   a. What, if anything, can you do to prevent the encroachment of SaaS on your business?
   b. Given your answer to question 6-8a, identify three alternative ways you can respond.
   c. Which of the three responses identified in your answer to question 6-8b would you choose? Justify your choice.

6-9. Even if SaaS eliminates the need for email and other local servers, there will still remain viable services that you can provide. Name and describe those services.

6-10. Suppose instead of attempting to adapt an existing ISV to the threat of cloud services, you and your teammates decide to set up an entirely new business, one that will succeed in the presence of SaaS and other cloud services. Looking at businesses in and around your campus, identify and describe the IS needs those businesses will have in the cloud services world.

6-11. Describe the IS services that your new business could provide for the business needs you identified in your answer to question 6-10.

6-12. Given your answers to questions 6-7 through 6-11, would you rather be an existing ISV attempting to adapt to this new world or an entirely new company? Compare and contrast the advantages and disadvantages of each alternative.

6-13. Changing technology has, for centuries, eliminated the need for certain products and services and created the need for new products and services. What is new, today, however, is the rapid pace at which new technology is created and adapted. Using cloud services as an example, create a statement of the posture that business professionals should take with regard to technology in order to thrive in this fast-changing environment. Notice the verb in this assignment is *thrive* and not just *survive*.

Salesforce.com

In 1999, Marc Benioff was writing software in a small San Francisco apartment with two other cofounders of his new company. Together they created a cloud enterprise software used by millions of people today. Prior to starting the new company, Benioff was a successful executive at Oracle. But he was tired of the big company culture. He wanted to leave Oracle, but leaving such a successful job was a very hard decision. After some deep reflection and a bit of soul searching, Benioff decided to trust himself and start a new company called Salesforce.com.

Growing Salesforce.com

Benioff knew he wouldn't be able to go it alone. He didn't have the experience or the skills he needed to create what he envisioned. Finding the right people was a challenge. Even after he found the right people, he had to convince them that his vision of a people-focused software company would actually work. That was hard, too. Finally, once his team was in place, he faced a third challenge—he needed to raise a lot of money to develop the large systems the company needed.

Investors and venture capitalists weren't really interested in his idea, so Benioff turned to friends. Luckily, he had some successful friends, including founders and investors at companies like Oracle, Dropbox, and CNET. With money in hand, Benioff and his cofounders were able to launch one of the very earliest enterprise software as a service (SaaS) companies in the world.

A Force to Be Reckoned With

Today, Salesforce.com dominates the market for customer relationship management (CRM) software. It consistently outsells giants like SAP, Oracle, Microsoft, and IBM. About one-third of Salesforce.com customers are small businesses; the rest are larger

Source: Richard Levine/Alamy Stock Photo

organizations. It's estimated that Salesforce.com has a 20 percent share of the $40 billion CRM software market.[27]

As of 2018, Salesforce.com's market capitalization was more than $98 billion, and it is one of the most valued cloud computing companies in the United States. Even more amazing is how quickly Salesforce.com has grown. Since its initial public offering (IPO) in 2004, Salesforce.com's stock price has grown from $4 per share (adjusting for a stock split) to more than $130 per share (a P/E ratio of 147).[28] That's a 3,150 percent increase in stock price in 14 years, or 262 percent annual growth every year since its IPO. That is a tremendous amount of growth for any company. And Salesforce.com has gone worldwide, too. It has been translated into more than 15 different languages.

Salesforce.com has been more than just a financial success. It has been given numerous awards, including "100 Best Companies to Work For," "World's Most Admired Companies," and "Most Innovative Companies in the World."[29]

As an organization, Salesforce.com focuses on four pillars of success: trust, growth, innovation, and equality. To build trust, Salesforce.com communicates openly with its customers. It promises to do what it takes to keep customer data secure. To promote growth, Salesforce.com focuses on the success of its customers. By maintaining positive relationships with existing customers, the company continues to grow. Salesforce.com works to innovate in what it does with the hope that its ideas drive positive change in the company, the industry, and even the world. Finally, Salesforce.com pursues equality and is committed to hiring employees from every background. This focus helps it thrive.

QUESTIONS

6-14. Go to *www.salesforce.com*, and click on the "Try for Free" button. Fill in the required fields and start your free trial. This will take you to a test site full of data for a company named Acme. Click on the "Take a Tour of Salesforce.com" link on the upper left-hand side of the screen. Walk through the automated tour labeled "Manage Your Pipeline (13 steps)."

    a. Why would these dashboards be useful to a marketing or sales manager?

    b. How could Salesforce.com help a sales manager increase sales?

    c. How long do you think it would take you to learn the basics of Salesforce.com?

6-15. Explain why a company like Salesforce.com requires so much money to become successful. Once the software is built, what are the incremental costs of adding additional customers? How does this affect profitability?

6-16. Why was it critical to choose the right team of people to get Salesforce.com off the ground? What types of skills would be necessary to create a CRM like Salesforce.com?

6-17. Why did tech giants like SAP, Oracle, Microsoft, and IBM miss the opportunity to produce a SaaS CRM like Salesforce.com? What might keep large tech companies from identifying potential opportunities like Salesforce.com?

6-18. What could be driving the tremendous growth in Salesforce.com's stock price and revenue? Why do you think investors put such a high premium on Salesforce.com's stock?

6-19. Why do you think Salesforce.com chose trust, growth, innovation, and equality as its four pillars of success? Why are these important for a company that provides CRM software?

6-20. CRM software is just one type of software service. Companies might be open to trying additional types of SaaS after having a great experience with Salesforce.com. What other types of software might be good candidates for future expansion for Salesforce.com? Why?

MyMIS Lab

Go to the Assignments section of your MyLab to complete these writing exercises.

6-21. Suppose that you work at eHermes and Victor tells you that he doesn't believe that cheap, elastic provisioning of data storage is possible. "There has to be a catch somewhere," he says. Write a one-page memo to him explaining how the cloud works. In your memo, include the role of standards for cloud processing.

6-22. Suppose you manage a sales department that uses the SaaS product Salesforce.com. One of your key salespeople refuses to put his data into that system. "I just don't believe that the competition can't steal my data, and I'm not taking that risk." How do you respond to him?

ENDNOTES

1. Eric Jhonsa, "Amazon's New Cloud Deal with Verizon Signals a Bigger Trend," *The Street*, May 15, 2018, accessed June 5, 2018, *http://realmoney.thestreet.com/articles/05/15/2018/amazons-new-cloud-deal-verizon-signals-bigger-trend*.
2. Yahoo! Finance, *SEC Filings*, accessed June 5, 2018, *http://finance.yahoo.com/q/sec?s=AMZN+SEC+Filings*.
3. Bob Evans, "Top Cloud Vendors Will Crush $100 Billion in 2018 Revenue; Microsoft, Amazon, IBM Hit $75 Billion?," *Forbes*, May 21, 2018, accessed June 5, 2018, *www.forbes.com/sites/bobevans1/2018/05/21/top-cloud-vendors-will-crush-100-billion-in-2018-revenue-microsoft-amazon-ibm-hit-75-billion/*.
4. Jordan Novet, "Microsoft Narrows Amazon's Lead in Cloud, but the Gap Remains Large," *CNBC*, April 27, 2018, accessed June 5, 2018, *www.cnbc.com/2018/04/27/microsoft-gains-cloud-market-share-in-q1-but-aws-still-dominates.html*.
5. Patrick Thibodeau, "Apple, Google, Facebook Turn N.C. into Data Center Hub," *Computerworld*, June 3, 2011, accessed June 5, 2018, *www.computerworld.com/article/2508851/data-center/apple-googlefacebook-turn-n-c-into-data-center-hub.html*.
6. Signiant, "The Need for Speed Series Part 1: In a Changing Media Landscape," *Studiodaily*, March 20, 2018, accessed June 5, 2018, *http://partners.studiodaily.com/signiant/content/the-need-for-speed-series-part-1-in-a-changing-media-landscape*.
7. Hiawatha Bray, "When the Billboard Has a Brain," *The Boston Globe*, April 6, 2018, *www.bostonglobe.com/business/2016/05/18/when-billboard-has-brain/TjUFP907SOnUKmqsLihsaN/story.html*.
8. Christopher Mims, "Your Location Data Is Being Sold—Often Without Your Knowledge," *The Wall Street Journal*, April 6, 2018, *www.wsj.com/articles/your-location-data-is-being-soldoften-without-your-knowledge-1520168400*.
9. Swati Khandelwal, "Google Collects Android Location Data Even When Location Service Is Disabled," *The Hacker News*, April 6, 2018, *http://thehackernews.com/2017/11/android-location-tracking.html*.
10. Signiant, "The Need for Speed Series Part 1: In a Changing Media Landscape," *Studiodaily*, March 20, 2018, accessed June 5, 2018, *http://partners.studiodaily.com/signiant/content/the-need-for-speed-series-part-1-in-a-changing-media-landscape*.
11. SAS, "Machine Learning: What It Is & Why It Matters," SAS.com, accessed June 5, 2018, *www.sas.com/it_it/insights/analytics/machine-learning.html*.
12. Ibid.
13. Lukas Biewald, "How Real Businesses Are Using Machine Learning," TechCrunch.com, March 19, 2016, accessed June 5, 2018, *http://techcrunch.com/2016/03/19/how-real-businesses-are-usingmachine-learning*.
14. Ibid.
15. Tom Simonite, "Google's Quantum Dream Machine," *TechnologyReview.com*, December 18, 2015, accessed June 5, 2018, *www.technologyreview.com/s/544421/googles-quantum-dream-machine*.
16. Jennifer Ouellette, "How Quantum Computers and Machine Learning Will Revolutionize Big Data," *Wired*, October 14, 2013, accessed June 5, 2018, *www.wired.com/2013/10/computers-big-data*.

17. Elizabeth Weise, "IRS Site Back Up and Running—Drawing on Computer Codes That Date Back to the 1960s," *USA Today*, April 18, 2018, *www.usatoday.com/story/tech/news/2018/04/18/ irs-site-back-up-and-running-drawing-computer-codes-date-back- 1960-s/528468002/*.

18. Ibid.

19. Thomas Claburn, "It's US Tax Day, so of Course the IRS's Servers Have Taken a Swan Dive," *The Register*, April 17, 2018, *www.theregister .co.uk/2018/04/17/irs_systems_stumble/*.

20. Ibid.

21. Ben Casselman, "Everyone Files Their Taxes at the Last Minute," *FiveThirtyEight*, April 15, 2016, *http://fivethirtyeight.com/features/ everyone-files-their-taxes-at-the-last-minute/*.

22. Rob Stott, "Amazon's Share of Black Friday Transactions Will Shock You," *DealerScope*, November 27, 2017, *www.dealerscope.com/article/ hitwise-amazons-share-black-friday-transactions-will-shock*.

23. P&S Market Research, "Telemedicine Market to Cross $48.8 Billion by 2023: P&S Market Research," *Globenewswire.com*, May 30, 2018, accessed June 5, 2018, *http://globenewswire.com/news- release/2018/05/30/1513647/0/en/Telemedicine-Market-to-Cross-48- 8-Billion-by-2023-P-S-Market-Research.html*.

24. Rose Eveleth, "The Surgeon Who Operates from 400km Away," *BBC.com*, May 16, 2014, accessed June 5, 2018, *www.bbc.com/future/ story/20140516-i-operate-on-people-400km-away*.

25. Issie Lapowsky, "Video Is About to Become the Way We All Visit the Doctor," *Wired*, April 30, 2015, accessed June 5, 2018, *www.wired .com/2015/04/united-healthcare-telemedicine*.

26. Robert Reich, *Work of Nations: Preparing Ourselves for Twenty-First Century Capitalism* (New York: Vintage Books, 1992), p. 176.

27. PYMNTS, "Salesforce's Revenues Grow to $3B," June 4, 2018, accessed June 7, 2018, *www.pymnts.com/news/b2b-payments/2018/ salesforce-revenue-growth*.

28. Yahoo! Finance, "Salesforce.com, Inc. (CRM)," accessed June 7, 2018, *http://finance.yahoo.com/quote/CRM/http://finance.yahoo.com/quote/ CRM/*.

29. Salesforce.com, "Recognition," accessed June 7, 2018, *www.salesforce .com/company/recognition/*.

PART 3

Using IS for Competitive Advantage

In the previous six chapters, you gained a foundation of IS fundamentals. In Chapters 7–12, you will apply those fundamentals to learn how organizations use information systems to achieve their strategies. Part 3, Chapters 7–9, focuses on application of IS; Part 4, Chapters 10–12, focuses on management of IS.

Each of the remaining chapters is introduced using a cloud-based mobile application that integrates augmented reality (AR) headsets with stationary biking equipment. ARES (Augmented Reality Exercise System) allows users to bike holographic routes with friends in a virtual environment.

As far as we are aware, an application like ARES does not currently exist. However, AR application development is proceeding at a rapid rate by companies like Microsoft (HoloLens), Magic Leap, and Meta. Applications in education, entertainment, industrial design, collaboration, and medicine all show great potential.

The figure on the next page shows how different stakeholders interact with ARES. ARES collects and integrates user data from AR headsets, stationary exercise bikes,

and fitness bands. Cloud-based services are used to host and process all user data. Even the ARES application itself is hosted in the cloud.

ARES then allows users to share their data with friends, trainers, and employers. Expert trainers can lead custom spinning classes through famous bike routes, like stages of the Tour de France. Employers can give employees financial incentives for staying fit. ARES also has the capability

Source: Dragonstock/Fotolia

249

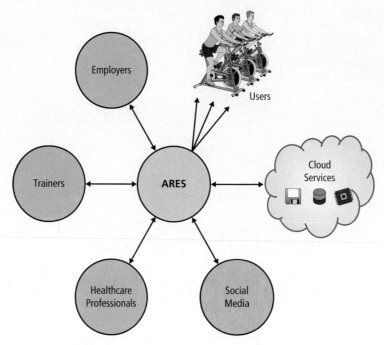

ARES: Augmented Reality Exercise System

to allow users to virtually bike with friends, famous cyclists, or even "pacers" that mimic their previous performance. Performance statistics can be shared using social media.

Zev Friedman, the owner of ARES, purchased an early prototype of the system from his cardiologist, Dr. Romero Flores. As a patient, Zev liked his experience with the system in spite of its rudimentary Web-based interface. It collected and analyzed workout data from exercise equipment and fitness bands, which helped Flores treat his patients. Unfortunately, the system wasn't being adopted outside of Flores's own medical practice.

Zev, a successful entrepreneur, saw the potential for the system to be used beyond medical applications. He'd also been watching the emergence of augmented reality and thinking about potential applications. This was perfect. He bought the company for a small amount of cash and a royalty agreement with Flores.

Source: Alexey Boldin/Shutterstock

Using his business contacts, he then found and hired a new general manager, Ashley Turnwood, a marketing professional, Cassie Castellon, and a customer server manager, Felix Ramos. He also brought Henri Kivi over as the technology manager from one of his other businesses and hired AR guru Raj Agarwal out of Stanford University.

CHAPTER 7

Collaboration Information Systems

Zev Friedman, the owner of ARES; Ashley Turnwood, general manager; Cassie Castellon, marketing professional; Henri Kivi, IS professional; and Raj Agarwal, augmented reality guru, are having an introductory meeting at Friedman's luxurious house on a Saturday morning. After polite conversation, Zev gets down to business.

"So . . . where did Flores go wrong?" Zev asks. His eyes quickly move around the group looking for a response. Zev rarely asks questions to which he already knows the answer, but he asked this question for a reason. He needs to know if he's found a dedicated team with a strong leader.

Cassie unabashedly jumps in. "I think Flores is a good doctor who sincerely cares about helping people. But, quite frankly, he doesn't know how to run a business. He didn't have any sales beyond his own practice, but he kept paying developers for more and more features."

MyLab MIS

Using Your Knowledge
Questions 7-1, 7-2, 7-3

Essay Questions 7-16, 7-17

Ashley can tell that Zev is looking for something more substantial. Zev glances over at his newly hired general manager for a response. "That's true, but Flores probably wasn't going to sell the system to many doctors anyway. Doctors make money from expensive tests and procedures—not hardware, software, and advertising. The data from Flores' system may be interesting to healthcare professionals, but it won't pay their mortgages. He needed to market to people who would actually buy it. Medicine cures physical problems, but sales cure business problems."

"OK, so to whom are we going to sell this?" Zev asks.

"Well, right now, probably no one," Ashley replies dryly. "Flores was able to collect and integrate data from exercise equipment, mobile devices, and fitness trackers using a cloud-based system. He even made some good-looking reporting tools that can share data with other systems. That's nice, but now upgraded fitness trackers and smartwatches can collect and report exercise data, too."

Cassie looks nervously at Ashley, and Zev leans back with a slight smile on his face.

"We could also sell virtual spinning classes . . . "

Source: Haiyin Wang/Alamy Stock Photo

Ashley continues, "But considering the people you've hired, that's not what you're going for anyway."

"What do you mean?" Zev replies.

"Well . . . Raj is an expert in augmented reality from Stanford, and the rest of us love cycling. OK, well, maybe that's overstating it a bit. Henri and I *love* cycling; everyone else enjoys cycling. If you add Flores' software to the mix, you've got a hybrid entertainment-fitness company."

Zev nods slightly and says, "Good, so how are we going to make money?"

Henri chimes in, "We'll definitely make money selling the app for the AR headsets. An augmented reality app for stationary bikes would be cool. Both the headset and bike manufacturers would love this app because it will help them sell more units. The integration with Flores' system is going to be tricky, though."

Raj sees his opening. "We could also sell virtual spinning classes led by expert instructors. Imagine a group of 20 riders biking through Arches National Park in the early morning. That would be really cool . . . " He pauses, clearly deep in thought, and then continues, "But I'm not sure if we have the bandwidth or back-end resources to handle that."

"Cassie, what do you think?" Zev asks.

"Well," Cassie says, "I think we should consider placing ads into the AR interface. Google, Facebook, and Twitter all make most of their money from ads. There's a real opportunity there. Certain companies would *love* to put ads in front of cyclists. We also might be able make money from celebrity rides, charity events, and promotional contests. I'm not sure how to make money using social media. Would users want to post their stats to Facebook? I'm not sure."

Ashley listens intently and then says, "You know, I think we could get referral fees from personal trainers if we could send them some of our users. They might even teach our virtual classes for free if they think it would attract clients. Large businesses might also be interested in using ARES for their wellness-at-work programs."

"Sounds good," Zev says approvingly. "Cassie, check into the ad revenue potential for ARES. Raj, see if it would be possible for our system to handle a virtual spinning class of 30 people. Henri, look at the costs of developing the apps and integrating the data on the back-end system. Ashley, you look into the trainers and employers. Any questions?"

Everyone looks around the table; no one says a word.

"OK, see you next week."

Study QUESTIONS

Q7-1   What are the two key characteristics of collaboration?

Q7-2   What are three criteria for successful collaboration?

Q7-3   What are the four primary purposes of collaboration?

Q7-4   What are the requirements for a collaboration information system?

Q7-5   How can you use collaboration tools to improve team communication?

Q7-6   How can you use collaboration tools to manage shared content?

Q7-7   How can you use collaboration tools to manage tasks?

Q7-8   Which collaboration IS is right for your team?

Q7-9   2029?

Chapter PREVIEW

Business is a social activity. While we often say that organizations accomplish their strategy, they don't. *People* in organizations accomplish strategy by working with other people, almost always working in groups. People do business with people.

Over the years, technology has increasingly supported group work. In your grandfather's day, communication was done using letter, phone, and office visits. Those technologies were augmented in the 1980s and 1990s with fax and email and more recently by texting, conference calls, and videoconferencing. Today, products such as Office 365 provide a wide array of tools to support collaborative work.

This chapter investigates ways that information systems can support collaboration. We begin by defining collaboration, discussing collaborative activities, and setting criteria for successful collaboration. Next, we'll address the kinds of work that collaborative teams do. Then we'll discuss requirements for collaborative information systems and illustrate important collaborative tools for improving communication and sharing content. After that, we'll bring this closer to your needs today and investigate the use of three different collaboration IS that can improve your student collaborations. Finally, we'll wrap up with a discussion of collaboration in 2029!

Q7-1 What Are the Two Key Characteristics of Collaboration?

To answer this question, we must first distinguish between the terms *cooperation* and *collaboration*. **Cooperation** is a group of people working together, all doing essentially the same type of work, to accomplish a job. A group of four painters, each painting a different wall in the same room, are working cooperatively. Similarly, a group of checkers at the grocery store or clerks at the post office are working cooperatively to serve customers. A cooperative group can accomplish a given task faster than an individual working alone, but the cooperative result is usually not better in quality than the result of someone working alone.

In this text, we define **collaboration** as a group of people working together to achieve a common goal *via a process of feedback and iteration.* Using feedback and iteration, one person will produce something, say, the draft of a document, and a second person will review that draft and provide critical feedback. Given the feedback, the original author or someone else will then revise the first draft to produce a second. The work proceeds in a series of stages, or *iterations,* in which something is produced, members criticize it, and then another version is produced. Using iteration and feedback, the group's result can be better than what any single individual can produce alone. This is possible because different group members provide different perspectives. "Oh, I never thought of it that way" is a typical signal of collaboration success.

Many, perhaps most, student groups incorrectly use cooperation rather than collaboration. Given an assignment, a group of five students will break it up into five pieces, work to accomplish their piece independently, and then merge their independent work for grading by the professor. Such a process will enable the project to be completed more quickly, with less work by any single individual, but it will not be better than the result obtained if the students were to work alone.

In contrast, when students work collaboratively, they set forth an initial idea or work product, provide feedback to one another on those ideas or products, and then revise in accordance with feedback. Such a process can produce a result far superior to that produced by any student working alone.

Importance of Constructive Criticism

Given this definition, for collaboration to be successful, members must provide and receive constructive criticism. **Constructive criticism** is both positive and negative advice given to improve an outcome. Most group members have no problem giving favorable feedback. It's easy and socially acceptable. It's *critical* feedback that is much more difficult for members to give—and receive. A group in which everyone is too polite to say anything critical cannot collaborate. In fact, groups that only provide positive feedback are susceptible to **groupthink**, a phenomenon where the desire for group cohesion leads to poor decision making.

On the other hand, a group that is so critical and negative that members come to distrust, even hate, one another cannot effectively collaborate either. Critical feedback needs to be presented in a friendly, well-reasoned manner. Learning how to effectively give critical feedback takes practice. For most groups, success is achieved when group members are able to give both favorable and critical feedback.

To underline this point, consider the research of Ditkoff, Allen, Moore, and Pollard. They surveyed 108 business professionals to determine the qualities, attitudes, and skills that make a good collaborator.[1] Figure 7-1 lists the most and least important characteristics reported in the survey. Most students are surprised to learn that 5 of the top 12 characteristics involve disagreement (highlighted in blue in Figure 7-1). Most students believe that "we should all get along" and more or less have the same idea and opinions about team matters. Although it is important for the team to be sociable enough to work together, this research indicates that it is also important for team members to have different ideas and opinions and to express them to each other.

When we think about collaboration as an iterative process in which team members give and receive feedback, these results are not surprising. During collaboration, team members learn from each other, and it will be difficult to learn if no one is willing to express different, or even unpopular, ideas. The respondents also seem to be saying, "You can be negative, as long as you care about what we're doing." These collaboration skills do not come naturally to people who have been taught to "play well with others," but that may be why they were so highly ranked in the survey.

The characteristics rated *not relevant* are also revealing. Experience as a collaborator or in business does not seem to matter. Being popular also is not important. A big surprise, however, is that being well organized was rated 31st out of 39 characteristics. Perhaps collaboration itself is not a very well-organized process.

> ### The Most Important Characteristics for an Effective Collaborator
>
> 1. Is enthusiastic about the subject of our collaboration.
>
> 2. Is open-minded and curious.
>
> 3. Speaks his or her mind even if it's an unpopular viewpoint.
>
> 4. Gets back to me and others in a timely way.
>
> 5. Is willing to enter into difficult conversations.
>
> 6. Is a perceptive listener.
>
> 7. Is skillful at giving/receiving negative feedback.
>
> 8. Is willing to put forward unpopular ideas.
>
> 9. Is self-managing and requires "low maintenance."
>
> 10. Is known for following through on commitments.
>
> 11. Is willing to dig into the topic with zeal.
>
> 12. Thinks differently than I do/brings different perspectives.
>
> …
>
> 31. Is well organized.
>
> 32. Is someone I immediately liked. The chemistry is good.
>
> 33. Has already earned my trust.
>
> 34. Has experience as a collaborator.
>
> 35. Is a skilled and persuasive presenter.
>
> 36. Is gregarious and dynamic.
>
> 37. Is someone I knew beforehand.
>
> 38. Has an established reputation in field of our collaboration.
>
> 39. Is an experienced businessperson.

FIGURE 7-1
**Important Characteristics
of a Collaborator**

Guidelines for Giving and Receiving Constructive Criticism

Giving and receiving constructive criticism is the single most important collaboration skill. You need to know how to give critical feedback in a positive way. So, before we discuss the role that information systems can play for improving collaboration, study the guidelines for giving and receiving critical feedback shown in Figure 7-2.

Many students have found that when they first form a collaborative group, it's useful to begin with a discussion of constructive criticism guidelines like those in Figure 7-2. Begin with this list, and then, using feedback and iteration, develop your own list. Of course, if a group member does not follow the agreed-upon guidelines, someone will have to provide constructive criticism to that effect as well.

Warning!

If you are like most undergraduate business students, especially freshmen or sophomores, your life experience is keeping you from understanding the need for collaboration. So far, almost everyone you know has the same experiences as you and, more or less, thinks like you. Your friends and associates have the same educational background, scored more or less the same on standardized tests,

Guideline	Example
Giving Constructive Criticism	
Be specific.	Unconstructive: "The whole thing is a disorganized mess." Constructive criticism: "I was confused until I got to Section 2."
Offer suggestions.	Unconstructive: "I don't know what to do with this." Constructive criticism: "Consider moving Section 2 to the beginning of the document."
Avoid personal comments.	Unconstructive: "Only an idiot would put the analysis section last." Constructive criticism: "The analysis section might need to be moved forward."
Set positive goals.	Unconstructive: "You have to stop missing deadlines." Constructive criticism: "In the future, try to budget your time so you can meet the deadline."
Accepting Constructive Criticism	
Question your emotions.	Unconstructive: "He's such a jerk. Why is he picking apart my work?" Constructive criticism: "Why do I feel so angry about the comment he just made?"
Do not dominate.	Unconstructive: You talk over others and use up half the time. Constructive criticism: If there are four group members, you get one fourth of the time.
Demonstrate a commitment to the group.	Unconstructive: "I've done my part. I'm not rewriting my work. It's good enough." Constructive criticism: "Ouch, I really didn't want to have to redo that section, but if you all think it's important, I'll do it."

FIGURE 7-2
Guidelines for Giving and Receiving Constructive Criticism

and have the same orientation toward success. So, why collaborate? Most of you think the same way, anyway: "What does the professor want, and what's the easiest, fastest way to get it to her?"

So, consider this thought experiment. Your company is planning to build a new facility that is critical for the success of a new product line and will create 300 new jobs. The county government won't issue a building permit because the site is prone to landslides. Your engineers believe your design overcomes that hazard, but your chief financial officer (CFO) is concerned about possible litigation in the event there is a problem. Your corporate counsel is investigating the best way to overcome the county's objections while limiting liability. Meanwhile, a local environmental group is protesting your site because it believes the site is too close to an eagle's nest. Your public relations director is meeting with these local groups every week.

Do you proceed with the project?

To decide, you create a working team of the chief engineer, the CFO, your legal counsel, and the PR director. Each of those people has different education and expertise, different life experience, and different values. In fact, the only thing they have in common is that they are paid by your company. That team will participate collaboratively in ways that are far different from your experience so far. Keep this example in mind as you read this chapter.

Bottom line: The two key characteristics of collaboration are iteration and feedback.

Q7-2 What Are Three Criteria for Successful Collaboration?

J. Richard Hackman studied teamwork for many years, and his book *Leading Teams* contains many useful concepts and tips for future managers.[2] According to Hackman, there are three primary criteria for judging team success:

- Successful outcome
- Growth in team capability
- Meaningful and satisfying experience

Successful Outcome

Most students are primarily concerned with the first criterion. They want to achieve a good outcome, measured by their grade, or they want to get the project done with an acceptable grade while minimizing the effort required. For business professionals, teams need to accomplish their goals: make a decision, solve a problem, or create a work product. Whatever the objective is, the first success criterion is "Did we do it?"

Although not as apparent in student teams, most business teams also need to ask, "Did we do it within the time and budget allowed?" Teams that produce a work product too late or far over budget are not successful, even if they did achieve their goal.

Growth in Team Capability

The other two criteria are surprising to most students, probably because most student teams are short-lived. But, in business, where teams often last months or years, it makes sense to ask, "Did the team get better?" If you're a football fan, you've undoubtedly heard your college's coach say, "We really improved as the season progressed." (Of course, for the team with 2 wins and 12 losses, you didn't hear that.) Football teams last only a season. If the team is permanent, say, a team of customer support personnel, the benefits of team growth are even greater. Over time, as the team gets better, it becomes more efficient; thus, over time the team provides more service for a given cost or the same service for less cost.

How does a team get better? For one, it develops better work processes. Activities are combined or eliminated. Linkages are established so that "the left hand knows what the right hand is doing" or needs or can provide. Teams also get better as individuals improve at their tasks. Part of that improvement is the learning curve; as someone does something over and over, he or she gets better at it. But team members also teach task skills and give knowledge to one another. Team members also provide perspectives that other team members need.

Meaningful and Satisfying Experience

The third element of Hackman's definition of team success is that team members have a meaningful and satisfying experience. Of course, the nature of team goals is a major factor in making work meaningful. But few of us have the opportunity to develop a life-saving cancer vaccine or engineer a new strain of wheat that could stop world hunger. For most of us, it's a matter of making the product, creating the shipment, accounting for the payment, or finding the prospects, and so on.

So, in the more mundane world of most business professionals, what makes work meaningful? Hackman cites numerous studies in his book, and one common thread is that the work is perceived as meaningful by the team. Keeping prices up to date in the product database may not be the most exciting work, but if that task is perceived by the team as important, it will become meaningful.

Furthermore, if an individual's work is not only perceived as important but the person doing that work is also given credit for it, then the experience will be perceived as meaningful. So, recognition for work well done is vitally important for a meaningful work experience.

Another aspect of team satisfaction is camaraderie. Business professionals, just like students, are energized when they have the feeling that they are part of a group, each person doing his or her own job and combining efforts to achieve something worthwhile that is better than any could have done alone.

Q7-3 What Are the Four Primary Purposes of Collaboration?

Collaborative teams accomplish four primary purposes:

- Become informed
- Make decisions
- Solve problems
- Manage projects

These four purposes build on each other. For example, making a decision requires that team members be informed. In turn, to solve a problem, the team must have the ability to make decisions (and become informed). Finally, to conduct a project, the team must be able to solve problems (and make decisions and become informed).

Before we continue, understand you can use the hierarchy of these four purposes to build your professional skills. You cannot make good decisions if you do not have the skills to inform yourself. You cannot solve problems if you are unable to make good decisions. And you cannot manage projects if you don't know how to solve problems!

In this question, we will consider the collaborative nature of these four purposes and describe requirements for information systems that support them, starting with the most basic: becoming informed.

Becoming Informed

Informing is the first and most fundamental collaboration purpose. Recall from Chapter 1 that two individuals can receive the same data but conceive different information. The goal of the informing is to ensure, as much as possible, that team members are conceiving information in the same way.

For example, as you read in the opening scenario, Zev has assigned the ARES team several tasks with the ultimate goal of increasing revenues. One of the team's first tasks is to ensure that everyone understands that goal and, further, understands the different ways they can achieve that goal.

Informing, and hence all of the purposes of collaboration, presents several requirements for collaborative information systems. As you would expect, team members need to be able to share data and to communicate with one another to share interpretations. Furthermore, because memories are faulty and team membership can change, it is also necessary to document the team's understanding of the information conceived. To avoid having to go "over and over and over" a topic, a repository of information, such as a wiki, is needed. We will say more about this in Q7-5.

Making Decisions

Collaboration is used for some types of decision making, but not all. Consequently, to understand the role of collaboration, we must begin with an analysis of decision making. Decisions are made at three levels: *operational, managerial,* and *strategic.*

Operational Decisions

Operational decisions are those that support operational, day-to-day activities. Typical operational decisions are: How many widgets should we order from vendor A? Should we extend credit to vendor B? Which invoices should we pay today?

Managerial Decisions

Managerial decisions are decisions about the allocation and utilization of resources. Typical decisions are: How much should we budget for computer hardware and programs for department A next year? How many engineers should we assign to project B? How many square feet of warehouse space do we need for the coming year?

In general, if a managerial decision requires consideration of different perspectives, then it will benefit from collaboration. For example, consider the decision of whether to increase employee pay in the coming year. No single individual has the answer. The decision depends on an analysis of inflation, industry trends, the organization's profitability, the influence of unions, and other factors. Senior managers, accountants, human resources personnel, labor relationships managers, and others will each bring a different perspective to the decision. They will produce a work product for the decision, evaluate that product, and make revisions in an iterative fashion—the essence of collaboration.

Strategic Decisions

Strategic decisions are those that support broad-scope, organizational issues. Typical decisions at the strategic level are: Should we start a new product line? Should we open a centralized warehouse in Tennessee? Should we acquire company A?

Strategic decisions are almost always collaborative. Consider a decision about whether to move manufacturing operations to China. This decision affects every employee in the organization, the organization's suppliers, its customers, and its shareholders. Many factors and many perspectives on each of those factors must be considered.

The Decision Process

Information systems can be classified based on whether their decision processes are *structured* or *unstructured*. These terms refer to the method or process by which the decision is to be made, not to the nature of the underlying problem. A **structured decision** process is one for which there is an understood and accepted method for making the decision. A formula for computing the reorder quantity of an item in inventory is an example of a structured decision process. A standard method for allocating furniture and equipment to employees is another structured decision process. Structured decisions seldom require collaboration.

An **unstructured decision** process is one for which there is no agreed-on decision-making method. Predicting the future direction of the economy or the stock market is a classic example. The prediction method varies from person to person; it is neither standardized nor broadly accepted. Another example of an unstructured decision process is assessing how well suited an employee is for performing a particular job. Managers vary in the manner in which they make such assessments. Unstructured decisions are often collaborative.

The Relationship Between Decision Type and Decision Process

The decision type and decision process are loosely related. Decisions at the operational level tend to be structured, and decisions at the strategic level tend to be unstructured. Managerial decisions tend to be both structured and unstructured.

We use the words *tend to be* because there are exceptions to the relationship. Some operational decisions are unstructured (e.g., "How many taxicab drivers do we need on the night before the homecoming game?"), and some strategic decisions can be structured (e.g., "How should we assign sales quotas for a new product?"). In general, however, the relationship holds.

Decision Making and Collaboration Systems

As stated, few structured decisions involve collaboration. Deciding, for example, how much of product A to order from vendor B does not require the feedback and iteration among members that typify collaboration. Although the process of generating the order might require the coordinated work of people in purchasing, accounting, and manufacturing, there is seldom a need for one person to comment on someone else's work. In fact, involving collaboration in routine, structured decisions is expensive, wasteful, and frustrating. "Do we have to have a meeting about everything?" is a common lament.

The situation is different for unstructured decisions because feedback and iteration are crucial. Members bring different ideas and perspectives about what is to be decided, how the decision will be reached, what criteria are important, and how decision alternatives score against those criteria. The group may make tentative conclusions and discuss potential outcomes of those conclusions, and members will often revise their positions. Figure 7-3 illustrates the change in the need for collaboration as decision processes become less structured.

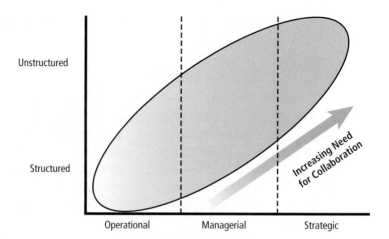

FIGURE 7-3
Collaboration Needs for Decision Making

Solving Problems

Solving problems is the third primary reason for collaborating. A **problem** is a perceived difference between what is and what ought to be. Because it is a perception, different people can have different problem definitions.

Therefore, the first and arguably the most important task for a problem-solving collaborative group is defining the problem. For example, the ARES team has been assigned the problem of finding ways to increase revenues. As stated as part of the informing purpose, the group needs first to ensure that the team members understand this goal and have a common understanding of the different ways they could increase revenues.

However, because a problem is a difference between what is and what ought to be, the statement "increase revenues" does not go far enough. Is generating $1 enough of an increase? Is generating $100,000 enough? Does it take $1,000,000 for the increase to be enough? A better problem definition would be to increase revenues by 10 percent or by $100,000 or some other more specific statement of what is desired.

Figure 7-4 lists the principal problem-solving tasks. Because this text is about information systems and not about problem solving per se, we will not delve into those tasks here. Just note the work that needs to be done, and consider the role of feedback and iteration for each of these tasks.

Managing Projects

Managing projects is a rich and complicated subject, with many theories and methods and techniques. Here we will just touch on the collaborative aspects of four primary project phases.

See the Career Guide on page 286 to learn more about the importance of real-world project management in MIS careers.

Projects are formed to create or produce something. The end goal might be a marketing plan, the design of a new factory, or a new product, or it could be performing the annual audit. Because projects vary so much in nature and size, we will summarize generic project phases here. Figure 7-5 shows project management with four phases, the major tasks of each, and the kinds of data that collaborative teams need to share.

- Define the problem.
- Identify alternative solutions.
- Specify evaluation criteria.
- Evaluate alternatives.
- Select an alternative.
- Implement solution.

FIGURE 7-4
Problem-Solving Tasks

Phase	Tasks	Shared Data
Starting	Set team authority. Set project scope and initial budget. Form team. Establish team roles, responsibilities, and authorities. Establish team rules.	Team member personal data Startup documents
Planning	Determine tasks and dependencies. Assign tasks. Determine schedule. Revise budget.	Project plan, budget, and other documents
Doing	Perform project tasks. Manage tasks and budget. Solve problems. Reschedule tasks as necessary. Document and report progress.	Work in process Updated tasks Updated project schedule Updated project budget Project status documents
Finalizing	Determine completion. Prepare archival documents. Disband team.	Archival documents

FIGURE 7-5
Project Management Tasks and Data

Starting Phase

The fundamental purpose of the starting phase is to set the ground rules for the project and the team. In industry, teams need to determine or understand what authority they have. Is the project given to the team? Or is part of the team's task to identify what the project is? Is the team free to determine team membership, or is membership given? Can the team devise its own methods for accomplishing the project, or is a particular method required? Student teams differ from those in industry because the team's authority and membership are set by the instructor. However, although student teams do not have the authority to define the project, they do have the authority to determine how that project will be accomplished.

Other tasks during the starting phase are to set the scope of the project and to establish an initial budget. Often this budget is preliminary and is revised after the project has been planned. An initial team is formed during this phase with the understanding that team membership may change as the project progresses. It is important to set team member expectations at the outset. What role will each team member play, and what responsibilities and authority will he or she have? Team rules are also established as discussed under decision making.

Planning Phase

The purpose of the planning phase is to determine "who will do what and by when." Work activities are defined, and resources such as personnel, budget, and equipment are assigned to them. As you'll learn when we discuss project management in Chapter 12, tasks can depend on one another. For example, you cannot evaluate alternatives until you have created a list of alternatives to evaluate. In this case, we say that there is a *task dependency* between the task *Evaluate alternatives* and the task *Create a list of alternatives*. The *Evaluate alternatives* task cannot begin until the completion of the *Create a list of alternatives* task.

Once tasks and resources have been assigned, it is possible to determine the project schedule. If the schedule is unacceptable, more resources can be added to the project or the project scope can be reduced. Risks and complications arise here, however, as will be discussed in Chapter 12. The project budget is usually revised at this point as well.

Doing Phase

Project tasks are accomplished during the doing phase. The key management challenge here is to ensure that tasks are accomplished on time and, if not, to identify schedule problems as early as possible. As work progresses, it is often necessary to add or delete tasks, change task assignments, add or remove task labor or other resources, and so forth. Another important task is to document and report project progress.

Finalizing Phase

Are we done? This question is an important and sometimes difficult one to answer. If work is not finished, the team needs to define more tasks and continue the doing phase. If the answer is yes, then the team needs to document its results, document information for future teams, close down the project, and disband the team.

Review the third column of Figure 7-5. All of this project data needs to be stored in a location accessible to the team. Furthermore, all of this data is subject to feedback and iteration. That means there will be hundreds, perhaps thousands, of versions of data items to be managed. We will consider ways that collaborative information systems can facilitate the management of such data in Q7-6.

What Are the Requirements for a Collaboration Information System?

As you would expect, a **collaboration information system**, or, more simply, a **collaboration system**, is an information system that supports collaboration. In this section, we'll discuss the components of such a system and use the discussions in Q7-1 and Q7-2 to summarize the requirements for a collaboration IS.

A collaboration information system is a practical example of IS, one that you and your teammates can, and should, build. Because you are new to thinking about IS, we begin first with a summary of the five components of such a system, and then we will survey the requirements that teams, including yours, should consider when constructing a collaboration IS.

The Five Components of an IS for Collaboration

As information systems, collaboration systems have the five components of every information system: hardware, software, data, procedures, and people. Concerning hardware, every team member needs a device for participating in the group's work, either a personal computer or a mobile device like an iPad. In addition, because teams need to share data, most collaboration systems store documents and other files on a server like Google Drive or Microsoft OneDrive.

Collaboration programs are applications like email or text messaging, Google Docs, Microsoft Office Online, and other tools that support collaborative work. We will survey those tools in Q7-5 through Q7-7.

Regarding the data component, collaboration involves two types. **Project data** is data that is part of the collaboration's work product. For example, for a team designing a new product, design documents are examples of project data. A document that describes a recommended solution is project data for a problem-solving project. **Project metadata** is data used to manage the project. Schedules, tasks, budgets, and other managerial data are examples of project metadata. Both types of data, by the way, are subject to iteration and feedback.

Collaboration information systems procedures specify standards, policies, and techniques for conducting the team's work. An example is procedures for reviewing documents or other work products. To reduce confusion and increase control, the team might establish a procedure that specifies who will review documents and in what sequence. Rules about who can do what to which data are also codified in procedures. Procedures are usually designed by the team; sometimes they need to be adjusted because of limitations in the collaboration tools being used.

The final component of a collaboration system is, of course, people. We discussed the importance of the ability to give and receive critical feedback in Q7-1. In addition, team members know how and when to use collaboration applications.

Primary Functions: Communication and Content Sharing

Figure 7-6 shows requirements categorized according to Hackman's three criteria for team success (discussed in Q7-2). For doing the work on time and on budget, teams need support from their collaboration system to communicate, to manage many versions of content, and to manage tasks. We will discuss tools that support each of those requirements in Q7-5 through Q7-7. Notice that these requirements support iteration and feedback, as you would expect for an IS that supports collaboration. Figure 7-6 also shows requirements for growth in team capability and for creating a meaningful and satisfying experience.

As you will learn, there are numerous alternatives for constructing an IS to meet those requirements. We will investigate three in Q7-8. Then in Collaboration Exercise 7 on page 289 you will look at the effectiveness—or ineffectiveness—of the collaboration system you created in Collaboration Exercise 1. Doing so will be greatly beneficial because it will allow you to reflect on your collaborative experiences and apply the principles presented in this chapter. It will also give you insights that you can use with other teams, in other courses, and, of course, during your career.

Figure 7-7 lists the four purposes of collaboration activities discussed in Q7-3 and summarizes IS requirements for collaboration systems for each purpose. When you analyze your own collaboration IS, first determine the type of effort you are engaged in and then use Figure 7-7 to help you determine your requirements.

Q7-5 How Can You Use Collaboration Tools to Improve Team Communication?

Because of the need to provide feedback, team communication is essential to every collaborative project. In addition to feedback, however, communication is important to manage content, project tasks, and the other requirements shown in Figures 7-6 and 7-7. Developing an effective communication facility is the first thing your team should do, and it is arguably the most important feature of a collaboration IS.

Criterion for Team Success	Requirement
Complete the work, on time, on budget	Communicate (feedback) Manage many versions of content (iteration) Manage tasks (on time, on budget)
Growth in team capability	Record lessons learned Document definitions, concepts, and other knowledge Support intra-team training
Meaningful and satisfying experience	Build team esprit Reward accomplishment Create sense of importance

FIGURE 7-6
Requirements for a Collaboration IS

Team Purpose	Requirements
Become informed	Share data Support group communication Manage project tasks Store history
Make decisions	Share decision criteria, alternative descriptions, evaluation tools, evaluation results, and implementation plan Support group communication Manage project tasks Publish decision, as needed Store analysis and results
Solve problems	Share problem definitions, solution alternatives, costs and benefits, alternative evaluations, and solution implementation plan Support group communication Manage project tasks Publish problem and solution, as needed Store problem definition, alternatives, analysis, and plan
Manage projects	Support starting, planning, doing, and finalizing project phases (Figure 7–5) Support group communication Manage project tasks

FIGURE 7-7
Requirements for Different Collaboration Purposes

The particular tools used depend on the ways that the team communicates, as summarized in Figure 7-8. **Synchronous communication** occurs when all team members meet at the same time, such as with conference calls or face-to-face meetings. **Asynchronous communication** occurs when team members do not meet at the same time. Employees who work different shifts at the same location or team members who work in different time zones around the world must meet asynchronously.

Most student teams attempt to meet face-to-face, at least at first. Arranging such meetings is always difficult, however, because student schedules and responsibilities differ. If you are going to arrange such meetings, consider creating an online group calendar in which team members post their availability, week by week. Also, use the meeting facilities in Microsoft Outlook to issue invitations and gather RSVPs. If you don't have Outlook, use an Internet site such as Evite (*www.evite.com*) for this purpose.

For most face-to-face meetings, you need little; the standard Office applications or their freeware lookalikes, such as LibreOffice, will suffice. However, research indicates that face-to-face

Synchronous		Asynchronous
Shared calendars Invitation and attendance		
Single location	Multiple locations	Single or multiple locations
Office applications such as Word and PowerPoint Shared whiteboards	Conference calls Multiparty text chat Screen sharing Webinars Videoconferencing	Email Discussion forums Team surveys

Virtual meetings

FIGURE 7-8
Collaboration Tools for Communication

meetings can benefit from shared, online workspaces, such as that shown in Figure 7-9.[3] With such a whiteboard, team members can type, write, and draw simultaneously, which enables more ideas to be proposed in a given period of time than when team members must wait in sequence to express ideas verbally. If you have access to such a whiteboard, try it in your face-to-face meetings to see if it works for your team.

The Ethics Guide on pages 274–275 addresses some of the ethical issues surrounding the sharing of data using new types of technology.

However, *given today's communication technology, most students should forgo face-to-face meetings*. They are too difficult to arrange and seldom worth the trouble. Instead, learn to use **virtual meetings** in which participants do not meet in the same place and possibly not at the same time.

If your virtual meeting is synchronous (all meet at the same time), you can use conference calls, multiparty text chat, screen sharing, webinars, or videoconferencing. Some students find it weird to use text chat for school projects, but why not? You can attend meetings wherever you are, without using your voice. Google Hangouts support multiparty text chat, as does Skype for Business. Google or Bing "multiparty text chat" to find other, similar products.

Screen-sharing applications enable users to view the same whiteboard, application, or other display. Figure 7-9 shows an example whiteboard for an ARES meeting. This whiteboard allows multiple people to contribute simultaneously. It allows users to simultaneously post their own notes, draw shapes, and insert pictures. Some groups save their whiteboards as minutes of the meeting.

A **webinar** is a virtual meeting in which attendees view one of the attendees' computer screens for a more formal and organized presentation. WebEx (*www.webex.com*) is a popular commercial webinar application used in virtual sales presentations.

If everyone on your team has a camera on his or her computer, you can also do **videoconferencing**, like that shown in Figure 7-10. You can use Google Hangouts, WebEx, or Skype for Business, which we will discuss in Q7-8. Videoconferencing is more intrusive than text chat (you have to comb your hair), but it does have a more personal touch.

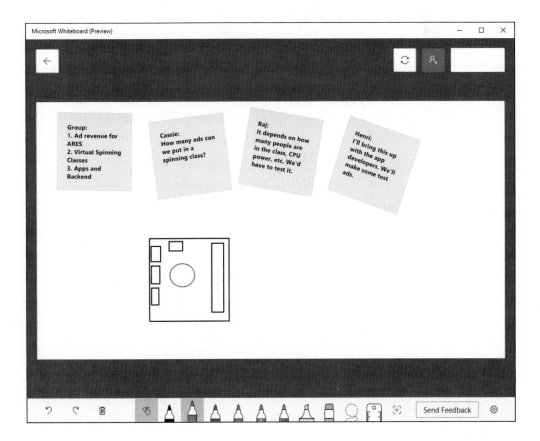

FIGURE 7-9
Microsoft Whiteboard Showing Simultaneous Contributions

Source: Windows 10, Microsoft Corporation.

FIGURE 7-10
Videoconferencing Example
Source: Tom Merton/OJO Images/
Getty Images

In some classes and situations, synchronous meetings, even virtual ones, are impossible to arrange. You just cannot get everyone together at the same time. In this circumstance, when the team must meet asynchronously, most students try to communicate via **email**. The problem with email is that there is too much freedom. Not everyone will participate because it is easy to hide from email. Email threads become disorganized and disconnected. After the fact, it is difficult to find particular emails, comments, or attachments.

Discussion forums are an alternative. Here, one group member posts an entry, perhaps an idea, a comment, or a question, and other group members respond. Figure 7-11 shows an example.

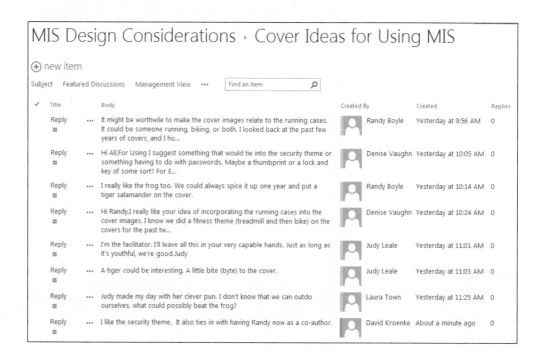

FIGURE 7-11
Example Discussion Forum
Source: Windows 10, Microsoft
Corporation.

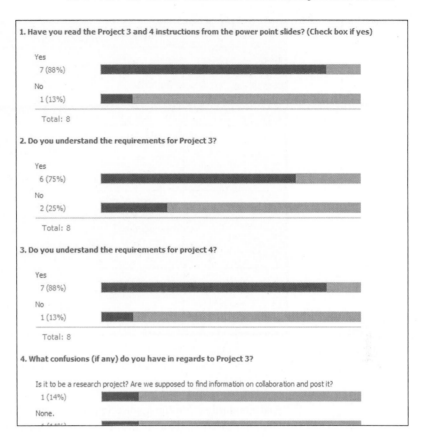

FIGURE 7-12
Example Survey Report

Such forums are better than email because it is harder for the discussion to get off track. Still, however, it remains easy for some team members not to participate.

Team surveys are another form of communication technology. With these, one team member creates a list of questions and other team members respond. Surveys are an effective way to obtain team opinions; they are generally easy to complete, so most team members will participate. Real-time surveying software like Socrative (*www.socrative.com*) or SurveyMonkey (*www.surveymonkey.com*) allows groups to generate ideas anonymously, provides instantaneous feedback, and generates detailed survey reports. Anonymous surveying can increase individual engagement and group buy-in because members are more willing to contribute ideas without worrying about being identified and criticized. Also, it is easy to determine who has not yet responded. Figure 7-12 shows the results of one team survey. Microsoft SharePoint has a built-in survey capability, as we discuss in Q7-8.

Video and audio recordings are also useful for asynchronous communication. Key presentations or discussions can be recorded and played back for team members at their convenience. Such recordings are also useful for training new employees.

Q7-6 How Can You Use Collaboration Tools to Manage Shared Content?

Content sharing is the second major function of collaboration systems. To enable iteration and feedback, team members need to share both project data (such as documents, spreadsheets, and presentations) and work-product data as well as project metadata (such as tasks, schedules, calendars, and budgets). The applications teams use and the means by which they share data depend on the type of content. Figure 7-13 provides an overview.[4]

Content Type	Desktop Application	Web Application	Cloud Drive
Office documents (Word, Excel, PowerPoint)	Microsoft Office LibreOffice OpenOffice	Google Docs (Import/Export non–Google Docs) Microsoft Office Online (Microsoft Office only)	Google Drive Microsoft OneDrive Microsoft SharePoint Dropbox
PDFs	Adobe Acrobat	Viewers in Google Drive, Microsoft OneDrive, and Microsoft SharePoint	Google Drive Microsoft OneDrive Microsoft SharePoint Dropbox
Photos, videos	Adobe Photoshop, Camtasia, and numerous others	Google Picasa	Google Drive Microsoft OneDrive Microsoft SharePoint Apple iCloud Dropbox
Other (engineering drawings)	Specific application (Google SketchUp)	Rare	Google Drive Microsoft OneDrive Microsoft SharePoint Dropbox

FIGURE 7-13
Content Applications and Storage Alternatives

For teams that are sharing Office documents such as Word, Excel, and PowerPoint, the gold standard of desktop applications is Microsoft Office. However, it is also the most expensive. To minimize costs, some teams use either LibreOffice (*www.libreoffice.org*) or Apache OpenOffice (*www.openoffice.org*). Both are license-free, open source products. These products have a small subset of the features and functions of Microsoft Office, but they are robust for what they do and are adequate for many businesses and students.

Teams that share documents of other types need to install applications for processing those particular types. For examples, Adobe Acrobat processes PDF files, Photoshop and Google Picasa process photos, and Camtasia produces computer screen videos that are useful for teaching team members how to use computer applications.

In addition to desktop applications, teams can also process some types of content using Web applications inside their browsers (Firefox, Chrome, and so on). Both Google Docs and Microsoft Office Online can process Word, Excel, and PowerPoint files. However, Google has its own versions of these files. Consequently, if the user uploads a Word document that was created using a desktop application and then wishes to edit that document, he or she must convert it into Google Docs format by opening it with Google Docs. After editing the document, if the user wants to place the document back into Word format, he or she will need to specifically save it in Word format. This is not difficult once the user is aware of the need to do so. Of course, if the team never uses a desktop application and instead uses Google Docs to create and process documents via the Web, then no conversion between the desktop and Google Docs formats is needed. Microsoft Office Online can be used in a similar way, but Office Online will edit only documents that were created using Microsoft Office file formats (e.g., .doc, .xls, etc.). Documents created using LibreOffice and OpenOffice's proprietary ODF format (e.g., .odt, .ods, etc.) cannot be edited using Microsoft Office Online. However, you can change the default settings in LibreOffice so documents are saved in Microsoft Office file formats.

Browser applications require that documents be stored on a cloud server. Google Docs documents must be stored on Google Drive; Microsoft Office Online must be stored on either Microsoft OneDrive or Microsoft SharePoint. We will illustrate the use of Google Docs and Google Drive when we discuss version management later in this chapter.

Documents other than Office documents can be stored (but not processed via the browser) on any cloud server. Team members store the documents on the server for other team members to access. Dropbox is one common alternative, but you can use Google Drive, Microsoft OneDrive, and SharePoint as well. You can also store photos and videos on Apple's iCloud.

Figure 7-14 lists collaboration tools for three categories of content: no control, version management, and version control.

Shared Content with No Control

The most primitive way to share content is via email attachments. However, email attachments have numerous problems. For one, there is always the danger that someone does not receive an email, does not notice it in his or her inbox, or does not bother to save the attachments. Then, too, if three users obtain the same document as an email attachment, each changes it, and each sends back the changed document via email, three different, incompatible versions of that document will be floating around. So, although email is simple, easy, and readily available, it will not suffice for collaborations in which there are many document versions or for which there is a desire for content control.

Another way to share content is to place it on a shared **file server**, which is simply a computer that stores files . . . just like the disk in your local computer. If your team has access to a file server at your university, you can put documents on the server and others can download them, make changes, and upload them back onto the server. You can also store files on the cloud servers listed in Figure 7-13.

Storing documents on servers is better than using email attachments because documents have a single storage location. They are not scattered in different team members' email boxes, and team members have a known location for finding documents.

However, without any additional control, it is possible for team members to interfere with one another's work. For example, suppose team members A and B download a document and edit it, but without knowing about the other's edits. Person A stores his version back on the server and then person B stores her version back on the server. In this scenario, person A's changes will be lost.

Furthermore, without any version management, it will be impossible to know who changed the document and when. Neither person A nor person B will know whose version of the document is on the server. To avoid such problems, some form of version management is recommended.

Shared Content with Version Management on Google Drive

Systems that provide **version management** track changes to documents and provide features and functions to accommodate concurrent work. For office documents, you can obtain version management services from Google Drive, Microsoft OneDrive, and Microsoft SharePoint. Here we will discuss the use of Google Drive.

Google Drive is a free service that provides a virtual drive in the cloud into which you can create folders and store files. You can upload files of any type, but only files that are processed by Google Docs receive version management. We'll restrict the rest of this discussion to files of those types.

To use Google Drive, you need a Google Account, which you obtain by creating a gmail address. (If you already have a gmail address, you already have a Google Account with the same name as your gmail address.) To create a Google account, go to *https://accounts.google.com* and fill out the form shown in Figure 7-15.

Alternatives for Sharing Content		
No Control	Version Management	Version Control
Email with attachments Shared files on a server	Google Docs Microsoft Office 365 Microsoft Office	Microsoft SharePoint

FIGURE 7-14
Collaboration Tools for
Sharing Content

Increasing degree of content control

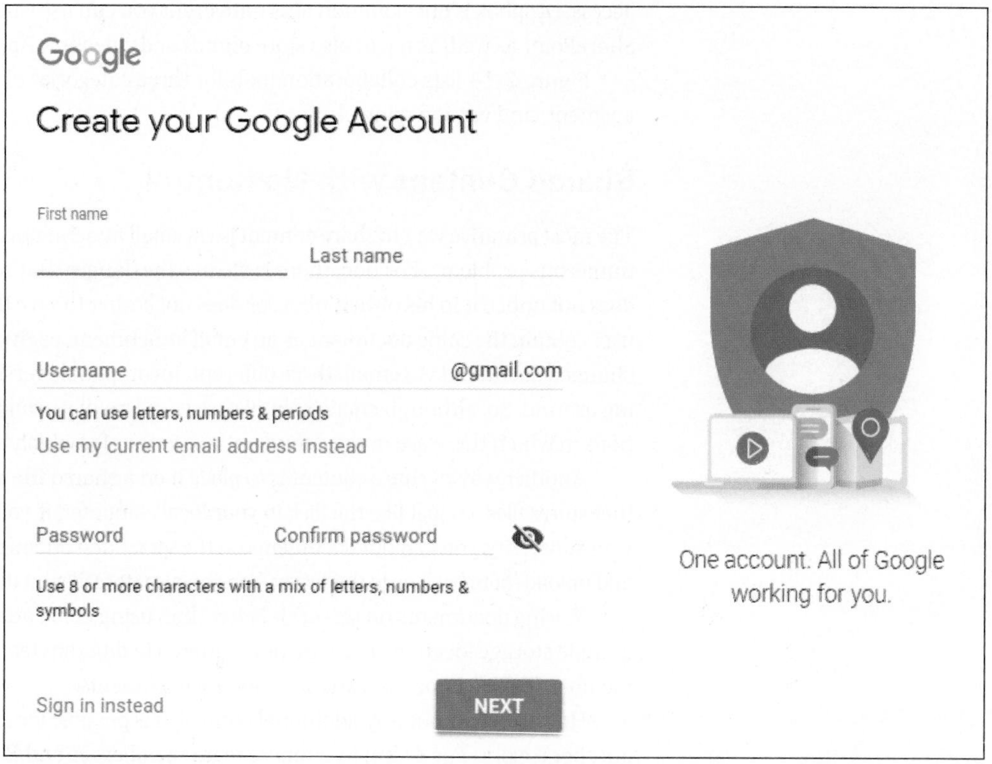

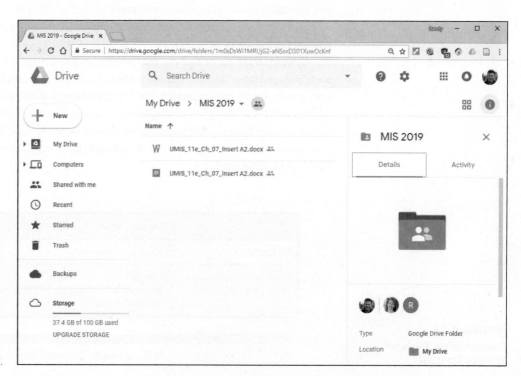

FIGURE 7-15
Form for Creating a Google Drive Account
Source: ©2018 Google LLC, used with permission. Google and the Google logo are registered trademarks of Google LLC.

In this form, you need not provide a value for your current email address, though it's a good idea to provide one if you can. That address is used by Google in the event you forget your password and for other security backup purposes.

To create a Google document, go to *https://drive.google.com.* (Note that there is no *www* in this address.) Sign in with your Google Account (your gmail address). From that point on, you can create, upload, process, save, and download documents. Figure 7-16 shows a folder named MIS 2019 with the same document in both Word and Google Docs format. After editing the user can save the

FIGURE 7-16
Available Types of Documents on Google Drive
Source: ©2018 Google LLC, used with permission. Google and the Google logo are registered trademarks of Google LLC.

Google Docs version back to Word if necessary. Types of documents that can be created on Google Drive are shown under the NEW button.

With Google Drive, you can make documents available to others by entering their email addresses or Google accounts. Those users are notified that the document exists and are given a link by which they can access it. If they have a Google account, they can edit the document; otherwise, they can just view the document. To see who can share one of the documents in Figure 7-16, right-click on any document on the screen, click Share, and click Advanced. A screen showing those who share the document will appear like that in Figure 7-17.

Because folders and documents are stored on Google Drive, server users can simultaneously see and edit documents. In the background, Google Docs merges the users' activities into a single document. You are notified that another user is editing a document at the same time as you are, and you can refresh the document to see his or her latest changes. Google tracks document revisions, with brief summaries of changes made. Figure 7-18 shows a sample revision document that has been edited by two users.

You can improve your collaboration activity even more by combining Google Drive with Google+.

Google Drive is free and very easy to use. Google Drive, Dropbox, and Microsoft OneDrive are all far superior to exchanging documents via email or via a file server. If you are not using one of these three products, you should. Go to *https://drive.google.com*, *www.dropbox.com*, or *www.onedrive.com* to check them out. You'll find easy-to-understand demos if you need additional instruction.

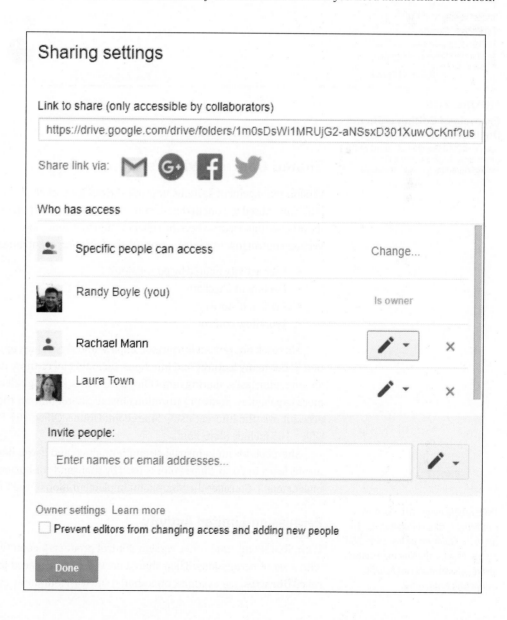

FIGURE 7-17
Document Sharing on Google Drive
Source: ©2018 Google LLC, used with permission. Google and the Google logo are registered trademarks of Google LLC.

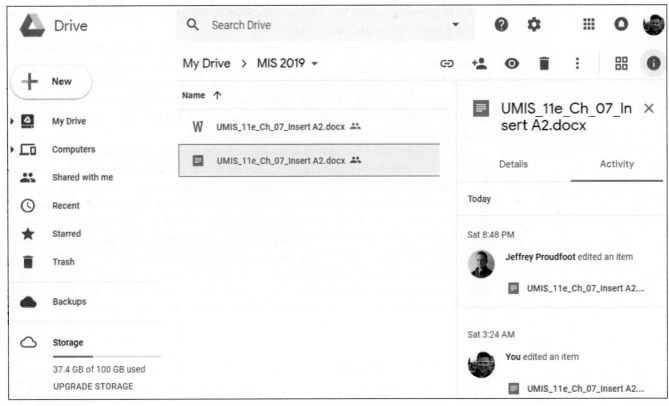

FIGURE 7-18
Example of Editing a Shared Document on Google Drive
Source: ©2018 Google LLC, used with permission. Google and the Google logo are registered trademarks of Google LLC.

Shared Content with Version Control

Version management systems improve the tracking of shared content and potentially eliminate problems caused by concurrent document access. They do not, however, provide **version control**, the process that occurs when the collaboration tool limits, and sometimes even directs, user activity. Version control involves one or more of the following capabilities:

- User activity limited by permissions
- Document checkout
- Version histories
- Workflow control

Microsoft SharePoint is a large, complex, and very robust application for all types of collaboration. It has many features and functions, including all of those just listed. It also contains features for managing tasks, sharing non-Office documents, keeping calendars, publishing blogs, and many more capabilities. Some organizations install SharePoint on their own Windows servers; others access it over the Internet using SharePoint Online. Office 365 Professional and other versions of Office 365 include SharePoint.

SharePoint is an industrial-strength product, and if you have an opportunity to use it, by all means learn to do so. SharePoint is used by thousands of businesses, and SharePoint skills are in high demand. Consider the SharePoint implementation of the four functions listed.

Permission-Limited Activity

Even highly competitive companies can benefit from collaborating. The Security Guide on pages 284–285 discusses why sharing information about cyberattacks can benefit competing companies.

With SharePoint (and other version control products), each team member is given an account with a set of permissions. Then shared documents are placed into shared directories, sometimes called **libraries**. For example, on a shared site with four libraries, a particular user might be given read-only permission for library 1; read and edit permission for library 2; read, edit, and delete permission for library 3; and no permission even to see library 4.

Document Checkout

With version control applications, document directories can be set up so that users are required to check out documents before they can modify them. When a document is checked out, no other user can obtain it for the purpose of editing it. Once the document has been checked in, other users can obtain it for editing.

Figure 7-19 shows a screen for a user of Microsoft SharePoint. The user is checking out the document UMIS 11e Chapter 7 Insert B. Once it has been checked out, the user can edit it and return it to this library. While it is checked out, no other user will be able to edit it, and the user's changes will not be visible to others.

With SharePoint, Microsoft manages concurrent updates on office documents (Word, Excel, etc.) and documents need not normally be checked out. In Figure 7-19, the user has checked out an Acrobat PDF (indicated by a green arrow next to the PDF icon), which is not an Office document.

Version History

Because collaboration involves feedback and iteration, it is inevitable that dozens, or even hundreds, of documents will be created. Imagine, for example, the number of versions of a design document for the Boeing 787. In some cases, collaboration team members attempt to keep track of versions by appending suffixes to file names. The result for a student project is a file name like *Project1_lt_kl_092911_most_recent_draft.docx* or something similar. Not only are such names ugly and awkward, no team member can tell whether this is the most current version.

Collaboration tools that provide version control have the data to readily provide histories on behalf of the users. When a document is changed (or checked in), the collaboration tool records the name of the author and the date and time the document is stored. Users also have the option of recording notes about their version.

Workflow Control

Collaboration tools that provide **workflow control** manage activities in a predefined process. If, for example, a group wants documents to be reviewed and approved by team members in a particular sequence, the group would define that workflow to the tool. Then the workflow is started, and the

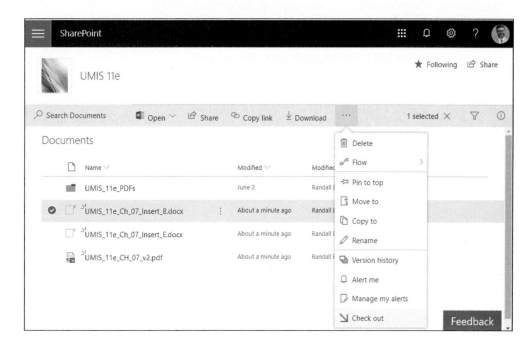

FIGURE 7-19
Checking Out a Document
Source: Windows 10, Microsoft Corporation.

BIG BROTHER WEARABLES

The sound of muffled keystrokes and distant phones ringing throughout the office lulled Richie Sagan into a daze. His new position at a top-tier investment bank was something he had aspired to for years, but the stress and pressure of performing at such a high level every day were beginning to take their toll.

His thoughts wandered off to last weekend's epic cycling adventure. He and some buddies had finished their first 100-mile ride. That was a serious accomplishment, especially for someone relatively new to the sport. Ironically, Richie had become interested in cycling *because* of work. His office recently launched a new program that gives employees monthly pay bonuses if they agree to wear a biological profiling/health tracking device. The company even gave him a really nice fitness tracker. The goal of the program is to reduce healthcare costs by making employees healthier. As long as Richie meets the company's "healthy" criteria and maintains a certain level of physical fitness, he will get a monthly bonus of $150. He will also get in shape.

When the HR department announced the new fitness program, it mentioned there would be *additional* reasons for having employees wear these devices. But all Richie cared about was earning some extra money to help pay the exorbitant rent for his new apartment in the city. He missed the majority of what was discussed during the information session about the fitness program. But he didn't really care. He had sat through so many orientation and HR meetings recently that they had all become a blur.

Richie's wandering attention was snapped back into focus by the arrival of an email. It was only Wednesday morning, and he still had several days of work ahead of him this week. He really wanted to get out on another serious ride this weekend. Right now, however, his inbox was growing by the minute. Richie hastily began responding to emails, quicker than usual, in order to get things under control.

Incoming

Several hours later, Richie saw his boss, Sal, heading in his direction with a stern look on his face. Much to Richie's

Source: rommma/Fotolia

chagrin, Sal came straight to his desk. "Come to my office, please," Sal said. Sal asked Richie to take a seat in one of the ritzy leather chairs in front of the desk. "We need to talk about your performance," Sal said.

"You have generally been one of our most consistent workers, but your performance this week has been unacceptable, to say the least. According to our new fitness monitoring initiative, you are underperforming." Richie was confused. Sal continued. "According to a report I received this morning, your biometric profile indicates you are showing physiological indicators we consider problematic. You are over-fatigued, and, as such, you are becoming a risk to the company. An analysis of your email habits also indicates that your emails are overly terse and not as thorough as usual; in other words, you have deviated from your usual baseline email activity. Your fatigue may prevent you from making sound decisions. In other words, in your current state, you are a liability to this firm."

Richie felt like he was sitting in the middle of some twisted science fiction movie. "Sir," Richie stammered, "I'm not sure what you are talking about." Sal pulled a document out of a file on his desk. He held it up and said, "This is the employee Security and Productivity Policy document that you signed when you joined the company. By signing it, you agreed to allow the company to monitor your biological profile and your computer activity. Didn't you read it before signing it?" Sal asked in an exasperated tone.

It was awkwardly silent for several seconds until Sal's office phone rang. Sal answered it, said a few words, and then told Richie he had to take the call. As Richie left, Sal interrupted his call and said, "Get yourself together, Richie—I want to see improvement by the end of the week, or we'll need to have a more serious talk about your performance."

DISCUSSION QUESTIONS

1. According to the definitions of the ethical principles defined in this book:
   a. Do you think that monitoring the physiology and computer behavior of employees is ethical according to the *categorical imperative* (page 23-24)?
   b. Do you think that monitoring the physiology and computer behavior of employees is ethical according to the *utilitarian* perspective (page 42-43)?
2. In the narrative presented, it's clear that Richie was fatigued from a weekend of physical exertion. His activity was probably having an effect on his work. How would you feel if your employer began monitoring your computer activity and physiological state? Would this type of monitoring change your behavior both inside and outside

of work? Would you consider this an invasion of your privacy?

3. It's clear that Richie didn't pay attention to the policies of his employer when he signed the employee fitness agreement. While this may seem hard to believe, you have likely agreed to specific terms of use policies when you started using your university's network. How familiar are you with those policies?
4. Patient data collected by healthcare providers is one of the most sensitive types of data. There are strict laws that govern how these data are captured, stored, and used. What are some of the risks and liabilities facing companies if they decide to use wearable technologies to monitor employees?

---

emails to manage the process are sent as defined. For example, Figure 7-20 shows a SharePoint workflow in which the group defined a document review process that involves a sequence of reviews by three people. Given this definition, when a document is submitted to a library, SharePoint assigns a task to the first person, Joseph Schumpeter, to approve the document and sends an email to him to that effect. Once he has completed his review (the green checkmark means that he has already done so), SharePoint assigns a task for and sends an email to Adam Smith to approve the document. When all three reviewers have completed their review, SharePoint marks the document as approved. If any of the reviewers disapprove, the document is marked accordingly and the workflow is terminated.

Numerous version control applications exist. For general business use, SharePoint is the most popular. Other document control systems include MasterControl (*www.mastercontrol.com*) and

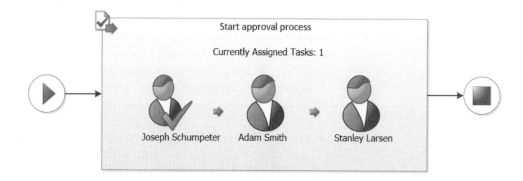

FIGURE 7-20
Example Workflow
Source: Windows 10, Microsoft Corporation.

Document Locator (*www.documentlocator.com*). Software development teams use applications such as CVS (*www.nongnu.org/cvs*) or Subversion (*http://subversion.apache.org*) to control versions of software code, test plans, and product documentation.

Q7-7   How Can You Use Collaboration Tools to Manage Tasks?

As you will learn in project management classes, one of the keys for making team progress is keeping a current task list. Good project managers make sure that every team meeting ends with an updated list of tasks, including who is responsible for getting each task done and the date by which he or she will get it done. We've all been to meetings in which many good ideas were discussed, even agreed upon, but nothing happened after the meeting. When teams create and manage task lists, the risks of such nonaction diminish. Managing with a task list is critical for making progress.

Task descriptions need to be specific and worded so it is possible to decide whether the task was accomplished. "Create a good requirements document" is not an effective, testable task description, unless all team members already know what is supposed to be in a good requirements document. A better task would be "Define the contents of the requirements document for the XYZ project."

In general, one person should be made responsible for accomplishing a task. That does not mean that the assigned person does the task; it means that he or she is responsible for ensuring that it gets done. Finally, no benefit will come from this list unless every task has a date by which it is to be completed. Further, team leaders need to follow up on tasks to ensure they are done by that date. Without accountability and follow-up, there is no task management.

As you'll learn in your project management classes, you can add other data to the task list. You might want to add critical resources that are required, and you might want to specify tasks that need to be finished before a given task can be started. We will discuss such task dependencies further in Chapter 12, when we discuss the management of systems development projects.

For team members to utilize the task list effectively, they need to share it. In this question, we will consider two options: sharing a task spreadsheet on Google Drive and using the task list feature in Microsoft SharePoint. Google gmail and Calendar also have a task list feature, but as of this writing, it is impossible to share it with others, so it is not useful for collaboration.

Sharing a Task List on Google Drive

Sharing a task list on Google Drive is simple. To do so, every team member needs to obtain a Google account. Then one team member can create a team folder and share it with the rest of the team, giving everyone edit permission on documents that it contains. One of the team members then creates a task spreadsheet on that folder.

Figure 7-21 shows a sample task list containing the name of each task, the name of the person to whom it is assigned, the date it is due, the task's status, and remarks. Because every member of the team has edit permission, everyone can contribute to this task list. Google Drive will allow simultaneous edits. Because Google Drive tracks version history, it will be possible, if necessary, to learn who made which changes to the task list.

Setting up such a list is easy, and having such a list greatly facilitates project management. The key for success is to keep it current and to use it to hold team members accountable.

Sharing a Task List Using Microsoft SharePoint

SharePoint includes a built-in content type for managing task lists that provides robust and powerful features. The standard task list can be readily modified to include user-customized columns, and many different views can be constructed to show the list in different ways for different users. Like the rest of SharePoint, its task lists are industrial-strength.

SO WHAT? FUTURE OF THE GIG ECONOMY

How did you spend your time last summer? Maybe you did some traveling or spent time at the beach. However, it is more likely that you spent at least some part of your summer working or completing an internship. Summer jobs and internships are a great way for college students to prepare for the workplace. These opportunities help you identify potential career paths or future employers that might interest you. They can also identify places or positions that would not be a good fit based on your aspirations and interests. But when it comes time to actually start full-time employment, many students struggle with the transition because of the rigidity of the schedule, the elevated expectations of employers, and being at the beginning of what seems like a long slog up the organizational ranks.

Some people in the workforce have decided to avoid the traditional employment model and pursue a more flexible and dynamic working arrangement. Instead of working for the same company until retirement (some of your grandparents did this for 30 years), they are embracing a new paradigm called the gig economy. The gig economy is where businesses hire many people as independent contractors for a short period of time. Many of these short-term employees can work remotely over high-speed Internet connections.

Businesses benefit because they don't have to pay for expensive office space, retirement, and benefits. Employees benefit because they can work as much or as little as they want and get paid well to do so. Younger employees are used to short-term services like Airbnb, Lyft, and Mechanical Turk, so the idea of working as a short-term contractor isn't that scary.[5] In fact, some projections estimate that the number of workers participating in the gig-economy model will surpass 40 percent of the workforce by 2020.[6]

The Stakes Are High

While increasing numbers of individuals are participating in the gig economy, it does not come without perils. Consistently finding new opportunities and contracts—and delivering on those agreements—can be more stressful than traditional work arrangements. This is especially true for gig workers who don't have the safety net of managers, colleagues, cultivated client leads, and other resources that are available to employees within a traditional organization. Furthermore, many gig workers operate remotely (primarily from home), which can present a host of challenges. A recent *Harvard Business Review* article discussed some of these perils and identified four factors that gig workers should consider to increase the likelihood of their success.[7]

Source: Keith Morris/Alamy Stock Photo

The first factor is *place*, meaning that gig workers should cultivate an environment at home in which they can avoid distractions and focus on their work. The second factor is *routines*, signifying that following a schedule consistently or sticking with certain traditions or rituals can help improve workflows and focus. The third factor is *purpose*, which is a unique aspect of the gig economy because employees can seek clients or contracts that adhere to their own beliefs, morals, and interests; this can provide incentives and motivation. (This is often not the case in the corporate world.) Finally, developing relationships with *people* who can provide support and encouragement can reduce the potential for the feelings of isolation and loneliness often associated with working remotely or alone.[8]

The Benefits Are Low

An additional challenge faced by workers in the gig economy is the lack of benefits they receive from clients. However, with the number of people working in this paradigm growing so rapidly, many believe that gig workers are entitled to better treatment. In fact, over the past several years, there have been lawsuits concerning the nature of gig workers and whether they should receive additional benefits from companies (like a standard employee).

For example, a delivery driver for Grubhub sued the company because he thought that he should be covered for more of his expenses. However, a federal district court judge ruled that the driver was correctly classified as an independent contractor.[9] Clearly, a legal precedent is being set that gig workers will not soon receive any benefits other than pay and that companies can continue abstaining from paying out payroll taxes and benefits.[10] Only time will tell if these legal implications will affect the growth of this employment model in years to come.

Questions

1. What are some of the downsides of being a worker in the gig economy? In spite of these downsides, it is likely that you will find yourself participating in the gig economy at some point in the future. Does this type of working arrangement interest you, and if so, what type of work would you do and for what type of organization?
2. Are there any technologies that may help gig workers feel more integrated with the clients for which they work?
3. The article references a *Harvard Business Review* piece that enumerates four factors to help gig workers be successful (namely, place, routines, purpose, and people). Can you think of any other elements that could help gig workers be more productive or satisfied?
4. A legal precedent is being set that continues to isolate gig workers from many of the benefits that traditional employees receive. Do you agree with this legal precedent? How has this precedent contributed to the growth of companies employing gig workers? How may it be harmful?

Figure 7-22 shows a task list that we used for the production of this text. The first three columns are built-in columns that SharePoint provides. The last column, named Book Title, is the book for which the task was assigned. For example, UMIS stands for the book titled *Using MIS.* When one of our team members opens this site, the view of the task list shown in Figure 7-23 is displayed. The tasks in this view are sorted by Due Date value and are filtered on the value of Task Status so any task that has been completed is not shown. Hence, this is a to-do list. Another view of this list, shown in Figure 7-24, includes only those tasks in which Status equals Completed. That view is a "what we've done so far" list.

Alerts are one of the most useful features in SharePoint task lists. Using alerts, team members can request SharePoint to send emails when certain events occur. Our team sets alerts so SharePoint sends a team member an email whenever a task is created that is assigned to him or her. We also have SharePoint send alerts to a task's creator whenever a task is modified.

SharePoint task lists provide features and functions that are far superior to the spreadsheet shown in Figure 7-21. Again, if you can obtain access to SharePoint, you should strongly consider using it, a possibility we address in the next question.

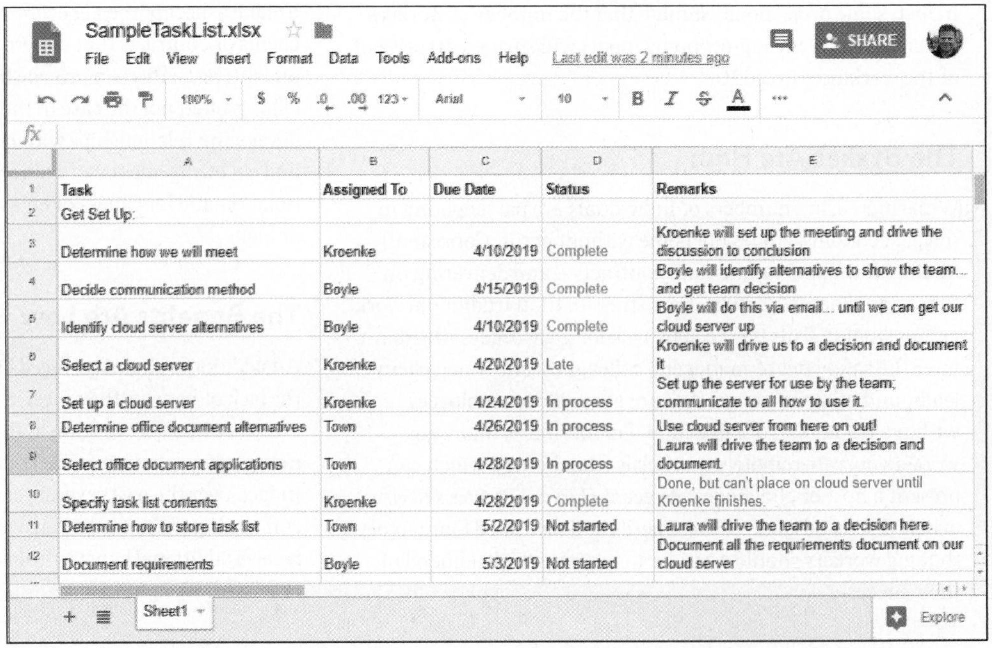

Task	Assigned To	Due Date	Status	Remarks
Get Set Up:				
Determine how we will meet	Kroenke	4/10/2019	Complete	Kroenke will set up the meeting and drive the discussion to conclusion
Decide communication method	Boyle	4/15/2019	Complete	Boyle will identify alternatives to show the team... and get team decision
Identify cloud server alternatives	Boyle	4/10/2019	Complete	Boyle will do this via email... until we can get our cloud server up
Select a cloud server	Kroenke	4/20/2019	Late	Kroenke will drive us to a decision and document it
Set up a cloud server	Kroenke	4/24/2019	In process	Set up the server for use by the team; communicate to all how to use it.
Determine office document alternatives	Town	4/26/2019	In process	Use cloud server from here on out!
Select office document applications	Town	4/28/2019	In process	Laura will drive the team to a decision and document.
Specify task list contents	Kroenke	4/28/2019	Complete	Done, but can't place on cloud server until Kroenke finishes.
Determine how to store task list	Town	5/2/2019	Not started	Laura will drive the team to a decision here.
Document requirements	Boyle	5/3/2019	Not started	Document all the requriements document on our cloud server

FIGURE 7-21
Sample Task List Using Google Drive
Source: ©2018 Google LLC, used with permission. Google and the Google logo are registered trademarks of Google LLC.

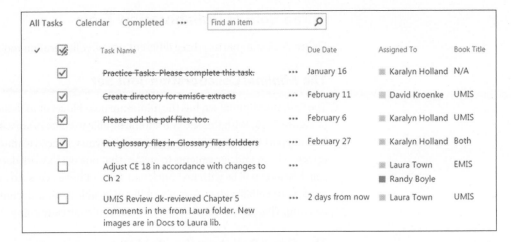

FIGURE 7-22
UMIS Production Task List in SharePoint

Source: Windows 10, Microsoft Corporation.

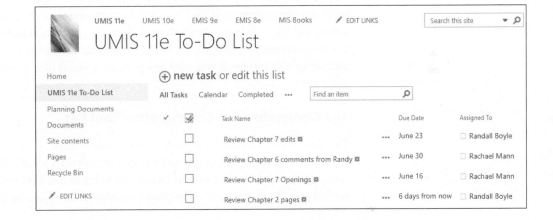

FIGURE 7-23
UMIS To-Do List in SharePoint

Source: Windows 10, Microsoft Corporation.

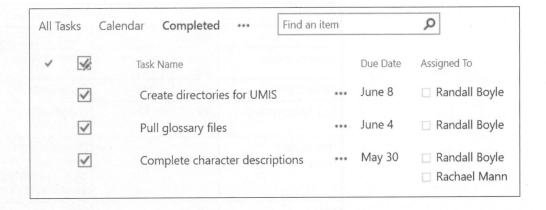

FIGURE 7-24
UMIS Completed Tasks in SharePoint

Source: Windows 10, Microsoft Corporation.

Q7-8 Which Collaboration IS Is Right for Your Team?

Your MIS class will help you gain knowledge and skills that you'll use throughout your business career. But why wait? You can benefit from this knowledge right now and put it to use tonight. Most business courses involve a team project; why not use what you've learned to construct a collaboration IS that will make teamwork easier and can help your team achieve a better product? In this question, we will define and set up your evaluation of three sets of collaboration tools.

Three Sets of Collaboration Tools

Figure 7-25 summarizes three different sets of collaboration tools that you might use.

The *Minimal* Collaboration Tool Set

The first, the Minimal set, has the minimum possible set of tools and is shown in the second column of Figure 7-25. With this set, you should be able to collaborate with your team, though you will get little support from the software. In particular, you will need to manage concurrent access by setting up procedures and agreements to ensure that one user's work doesn't conflict with another's. Your collaboration will be with text only; you will not have access to audio or video so you cannot hear or see your collaborators. You also will not be able to view documents or whiteboards during your meeting. This set is probably close to what you're already doing.

The *Good* Collaboration Tool Set

The second set, the Good set, shown in the third column of Figure 7-25, shows a more sophisticated set of collaboration tools. With it, you will have the ability to conduct multiparty audio and video virtual meetings, and you will also have support for concurrent access to document, spreadsheet, and presentation files. You will not be able to support surveys, wikis, and blogs and share pictures and videos with this set. If you want any of them, you will need to search the Internet to find suitable tools.

The *Comprehensive* Collaboration Tool Set

The third set of collaboration tools, the Comprehensive set, is shown in the last column of Figure 7-25. You can obtain this tool set with certain versions of Office 365. However, Microsoft continually revises the versions and what's included in them, so you'll need to investigate which version provides the features of the comprehensive tool set. Look for a version (perhaps a free trial)

	Three Collaboration Tool Sets		
	Minimal	Good	Comprehensive
Communication	Email; multiparty text chat	Google Hangouts	Microsoft Skype for Business
Content Sharing	Email or file server	Google Drive	SharePoint
Task Management	Word or Excel files	Google Calendar	SharePoint lists integrated with email
Nice-to-Have Features		Discussion boards, surveys, wikis, blogs, share pictures/videos from third-party tools	Built-in discussion boards, surveys, wikis, blogs, picture/video sharing
Cost	Free	Free	$10/month per user or Free
Ease of Use (time to learn)	None	1 hour	3 hours
Value to Future Business Professional	None	Limited	Great
Limitations	All text, no voice or video; no tool integration	Tools not integrated, must learn to use several products	Cost, learning curve required

FIGURE 7-25
Three Collaboration Tool Sets

Component	Features
Skype for Business	Multiparty text chat Audio- and videoconferencing Online content sharing Webinars with PowerPoint
SharePoint Online	Content management and control using libraries and lists Discussion forums Surveys Wikis Blogs
Exchange	Email integrated with Skype for Business and SharePoint Online
Office 2016	Concurrent editing for Word, Excel, PowerPoint, and OneNote
Hosted integration	Infrastructure built, managed, and operated by Microsoft

FIGURE 7-26

Office 365 Features You Need for the Comprehensive Tool Set

that includes all the products shown in Figure 7-26. If your school has adopted Office 365 for Education, then you should be able to obtain these features for free.

This set is the best of these three because it includes content management and control, workflow control, and online meetings with sharing as just described. Furthermore, this set is integrated; SharePoint alerts can send emails via the Microsoft email server Exchange when tasks or other lists and libraries change. You can click on users' names in emails or in SharePoint, and Office 365 will automatically start a Skype for Business text, audio, or video conversation with that user if he or she is currently available. All text messages you send via Skype for Business are automatically recorded and stored in your email folder.

Choosing the Set for Your Team

Which set should you choose for your team? Unless your university has already standardized on the Office 365 version you need, you will have to pay for it. You can obtain a 30-day free trial, and if your team can finish its work in that amount of time, you might choose to do so. Otherwise, your team will need to pay a minimum of $10 per month per user. So, if cost is the only factor, you can rule out the comprehensive tool set.

And even if you can afford the most comprehensive set, you may not want to use it. As noted in Figure 7-25, team members need to be willing to invest something on the order of 3 hours to begin to use the basic features. Less time, on the order of an hour, will be required to learn to use the Good tool set, and you most likely already know how to use the Minimal set.

When evaluating learning time, consider Figure 7-27. This diagram is a product **power curve**, which is a graph that shows the relationship of the power (the utility that one gains from a software product) as a function of the time using that product. A flat line means you are investing time without any increase in power. The ideal power curve starts at a positive value at time zero and has no flat spots.

The Minimal product set gives you some power at time zero because you already know how to use it. However, as you use it over time, your project will gain complexity and the problems of controlling concurrent access will actually cause power to decrease. The Good set has a short flat spot as you get to know it. However, your power then increases over time until you reach the most capability your team can do with it. The Comprehensive set has a longer flat spot in the beginning because it will take longer to learn. However, because it has such a rich collaboration feature set, you will be able to gain considerable collaborative power, much more so than the Good set, and the maximum capability is much greater than the Good set.

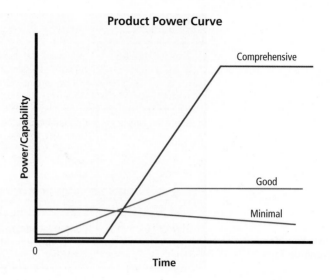

FIGURE 7-27
Product Power Curve

Finally, consider the next-to-last row in Figure 7-25. The Minimal set has no value to you as a future professional and contributes nothing to your professional competitive advantage. The Good set has some limited value; as you know, there are organizations that use Google Drive and Hangouts. The Comprehensive set has the potential to give you a considerable competitive advantage, particularly because SharePoint skills are highly valued in industry. You can use knowledge of it to demonstrate the currency of your knowledge in job interviews.

Don't Forget Procedures and People!

One last and very important point: Most of this chapter focuses on collaboration tools, the software component of an information system. Regarding the other four components, you need not worry about hardware, at least not for the Good or Comprehensive sets, because those tools are hosted on hardware in the cloud. The data component is up to you; it will be your content as well as your metadata for project management and for demonstrating that your team practiced iteration and feedback.

As you evaluate alternatives, however, you need to think seriously about the procedure and people components. How are team members going to use these tools? Your team needs to have agreement on tools usage, even if you do not formally document procedures. As noted, such procedures are especially necessary for controlling concurrent access in the minimal system. You need to have agreement not only on how to use these tools but also on what happens when teammates don't use these tools. What will you do, for example, if teammates persist in emailing documents instead of using Google Drive or SharePoint?

Additionally, how will your team train its members in the use of these tools? Will you divvy up responsibility for learning features and then teach the skills to one another? You will find a plethora of training materials on the Web.[11] But who will find them, learn them, and then teach the others?

Finally, does your team need to create any special jobs or roles? Do you want to identify, for example, someone to monitor your shared documents to ensure that deliverables are stored appropriately? Do you want someone identified to store minutes of meetings? Or to remove completed tasks from a task list? Or to keep the task list in agreement with current planning? Consider these and similar needs and, if needed, appoint such a person before problems develop.

Remember this example as a future business professional: In commerce, we are never selecting just software; to put that software to use as a system, we need to create all five of the IS components!

Q7-9 2029?

Collaboration in 2029 will look much different than it does today. *What* workers do, *how* they do it, and *why* they do it are changing rapidly. For example, consider a person who works as an Uber driver. That type of a job didn't exist 20 years ago. Yes, cab companies did exist, and they still do. But a non-employee driver giving customers rides during his or her free time didn't. There wasn't an app for that.

Workers in 2029 may be independent contractors or part of the **gig economy** where businesses hire many people as independent contractors for a short period of time. These short-term employees can work remotely over high-speed Internet connections. Collaboration among these types of employees will become even more important.

This same Uber driver is also part of the **sharing economy**, where consumers can temporarily share their assets or services with other consumers via renting or lending. This *collaborative consumption* allows the Uber driver to earn income from an otherwise idle unproductive asset. Enabling the collaboration between consumers has spawned companies like Uber, Airbnb, and DogVacay. By 2029, collaborative consumption will be even more important. Consider that Airbnb is the largest hotel chain in the world. And it doesn't own a single hotel property.

By 2029, the way people collaborate will be different. *Physical* face-to-face (F2F) meetings might be rare, and *holographic* face-to-face meetings could be commonplace. High-speed ubiquitous network connections will make collaboration systems cheaper, faster, and easier to use.

A surge in augmented reality (AR) glasses and 3D applications may make it possible for workers to holographically collaborate face-to-face from locations around the world. That might sound impossible at first. But consider how AR glasses are going to change the workplace. Holograms are cheap, take up little space, use little energy, and can be upgraded immediately. Employers may not buy physical monitors anymore. They may opt for a mixed-reality workspace where some objects are real and others are holograms in order to reduce costs. The same is true for all physical office objects—and employees.

Microsoft's demonstration of "holoportation" showed how people can interact with 3D holographic representations of other people. During the demonstration, detailed 3D holograms of remote users were created in a separate physical space using Hololens and several 3D cameras. Individuals in another room could see and hear everything the remote users did as if they were physically standing right in the same room. But the person holoporting to work may be physically located across town or even in another country. By 2029, you may be working with mixed-reality coworkers. Some may be real, and others may be holograms. Workers may come from different countries. Employers will get all the benefits of face-to-face interactions at a much lower cost. Remote holographic (virtual) collaboration may boost companies' bottom lines.

Think about all the costs that go away with virtual collaboration. No more expensive business air travel, waiting in TSA lines, checking into hotels, sitting in traffic, burning fuel, waiting in lobbies, or riding in elevators. By 2029, collaboration systems will greatly ease international business. If teams meet virtually most of the time and if it doesn't matter where team members are located, then projects can involve the best—or perhaps the most affordable—workers worldwide. From an employee's point of view, virtual work will be great. Getting a new job will be easy, but losing a job will be easy, too. The smartest, most talented knowledge workers will compete for jobs around the world.

Because of these trends, now is a great time for you to learn online, asynchronous collaboration skills. It's also a good time for you, as a future knowledge worker, to prepare yourself for global opportunities . . . and global competition. By 2029, you may be collaborating with people you've never met in person. And none of the people on your team may actually work for the company signing your paychecks! You'll be able to work anywhere in the world and do it all from your home office—wherever you want that to be.

SECURITY GUIDE

SECURITY IN THE SHARING ECONOMY

When was the last time you hailed a taxi? Maybe a better question is whether you have *ever* hailed a taxi. If not, then you have likely requested an Uber using your phone. If you have used a ride-sharing app or booked a vacation using Airbnb, then you have participated in the sharing economy, or a collaborative economy where goods and services are shared among participants in a peer-to-peer (P2P) network. While the concept of connecting peers who are interested in participating in transactions seems rudimentary, the companies cashing in on the sharing economy are no joke.

For example, Uber has disrupted countless taxi markets around the globe and the company is worth billions of dollars. Airbnb is worth billions of dollars, too. Clearly, the sharing economy is having an impact. It's becoming an increasingly important part of the overall economy, too. However, there is more to be gained from the sharing economy than just a convenient ride or a cheaper place to stay the night. In fact, many experts believe that adopting practices from the sharing economy could be beneficial in other areas, specifically information security.

Friend or Foe?

By their very nature, companies are competitive and secretive. They often invest heavily in producing a competitive advantage over rivals, which can take many forms—creation of disruptive new products, cultivation of a powerful brand, or development of an exceptional customer service reputation. None of these strategic plans requires sharing information or collaborating with competitors. However, all types of organizations are witnessing an increasing amount of cyber-security threats.

A survey of more than 50 U.S. organizations found that 100 percent reported cyberattacks in the form of viruses, worms, and Trojan horses; 97 percent reported malware; and just under 60 percent indicated they had experienced at least one phishing attack.[12] These incidents can result in millions of dollars in costs and can tarnish the brands of the affected organizations. Announcing that a company has been breached can also result in follow-up attacks as hackers

know that (1) the organization is vulnerable and (2) the organization is likely in a state of chaos as security practitioners try to determine the extent of the breach and recover from it. In light of these costs, many organizations choose to remain secretive about cyber-incidents. However, is it possible that organizations would be better off sharing information about breaches with others—even competitors—as quickly as possible?

Sharing Is Caring

Let's briefly compare cyberattacks to actual warfare. If one country attacks a number of other countries, are the targeted countries better off responding in isolation, or would they fare better by collaborating to defeat the enemy? Even if they do not join forces, the very act of sharing information about the enemy's weaponry, tactics, and capabilities would surely help. This concept holds true with cyberattacks. Proponents of this strategy believe that sharing information about attack methodologies, malware, and hacking groups helps companies improve their ability to defend against future attacks.

Companies like IBM are working to promote information sharing about cyberattacks and to promote government regulations that encourage sharing attack information.[13] For example, when a breach occurs in which personally identifiable information (PII) has been compromised, the targeted organization must publicly acknowledge the incident

Source: JIRAROJ PRADITCHAROENKUL/Alamy Stock Photo

per state and federal regulations.[14] The idea is that people should be aware that their data might have been leaked. Furthermore, the SEC requires that companies disclose information about material cyber-risks (to inform investors about the potential implications of a cyberattack against a company's stock value). However, what constitutes a material cyber-risk is not clearly defined. In short, while some regulations are in place, there are loopholes and wiggle room for organizations to not share—or share as little as possible—about the incident.

While there are clearly some benefits to increasing information sharing across organizations about cyberattacks,

some detractors think that doing so will be ineffective or that it is a bad idea. For example, some argue that not announcing a breach but collecting information about what hackers are doing can lead to better insights that can be used to stop future attacks. In fact, government agencies are still breached despite their own information sharing about attacks; this provides little evidence that sharing information across other types of organizations will actually make a difference. With threats and breaches on the rise, something needs to change, but it remains unclear how an environment of sharing could change the impact of and response to cyberattacks.

DISCUSSION QUESTIONS

1. Take a minute to consider this hypothetical scenario: You open up your laptop to find that your university email account and your social media accounts have been compromised. The attackers indicate that they are going to post your stolen data on the Web. After digging around, you are able to figure out some details about how they were able to access your system. The exploited vulnerability is one that most students at your school also have. Would you want to stand up at the beginning of each of your classes and share information about your breach to help other students avoid being compromised?

2. The article makes a comparison between cyberattacks and traditional warfare. Can you think of any ways in which cyberwar is actually different from traditional warfare?

3. Do you think that the SEC, state governments, and the federal government should articulate clearer regulations about disclosing cyberattack information? Why wouldn't the initial policies put in place be more clear or effective?

4. The article identifies some arguments against information sharing. Can you think of any other reasons why mandating cyberattack information sharing could be ineffective or harmful?

CAREER GUIDE

Name: Christi Wruck
Company: Instructure
Job Title: Software Product Manager
Education: University of Utah

Source: Christi Wruck, Instructure, Software Product Manager

1 How did you get this type of job?

I hired a friend who was working at Instructure Inc. at the time to come work for me. A few months later, that person decided to go back to Instructure. I asked them to take me with them . . . and they did.

2 What attracted you to this field?

I was working in a different field but was regularly considered the resident techie. I built Web sites and databases and set up networks and systems for the nonprofits that employed me. I was good at it, and I enjoyed it. So I decided to move into this field.

3 What does a typical workday look like for you (duties, decisions, problems)?

I spend a lot of time defining and documenting user problems. To do that, I talk to users on phone calls, I travel for site visits, and I engage in our user forums. I gather feedback from employees who frequently engage our clients. Once the problems are well documented, I work with a design team to try and solve the problems in innovative ways. Then we test with our users and iterate until we find the best solution. Once a solution is finalized, it's handed off to engineering to execute.

4 What do you like most about your job?

The best part of my job is doing site visits. Being able to see the pain points that users experience every day is incredibly valuable. There are some insights that can't be gained via email or forums or phone calls. Watching users has proven to be the most inspiring and motivating part of my job.

5 What skills would someone need to do well at your job?

Empathy, social skills, and curiosity. You have to be comfortable talking to strangers, and they need to trust you to solve their problems. If you are naturally curious and genuinely want to solve your users' problems, you will ask the right questions that help you gain the insights you need to solve their problems with innovative solutions.

6 Are education or certifications important in your field? Why?

Half of the product team I work with has a master's degree. And I've never met a product manager who doesn't have an undergraduate degree. So I guess the answer is yes. I think having a clear understanding of how business operates and how software engineering works is extremely important for a software product manager.

7 What advice would you give to someone who is considering working in your field?

Study Agile, UX/UI design, project management, and SCRUM, and learn how to write at least a little bit of code.

8 What do you think will be hot tech jobs in 10 years?

Software engineering. Especially in the United States. The rest of the world is already leaps and bounds ahead of us in this department. A lot of people understand a little bit about code, but we need a lot more people who are experts and pioneers in the field.

ACTIVE REVIEW

Use this Active Review to verify that you understand the ideas and concepts that answer the chapter's study questions.

Q7-1   What are the two key characteristics of collaboration?

In your own words, explain the difference between cooperation and collaboration. Name the two key characteristics of collaboration and explain how they improve group work. Describe how effectively giving and taking constructive criticism can help avoid groupthink. Summarize important skills for collaborators and list what you believe are the best ways to give and receive critical feedback.

Q7-2   What are three criteria for successful collaboration?

Name and describe three criteria for collaboration success. Summarize how these criteria differ between student and professional teams.

Q7-3   What are the four primary purposes of collaboration?

Name and describe four primary purposes of collaboration. Explain their relationship. Describe ways that collaboration systems can contribute to each purpose.

Q7-4   What are the requirements for a collaboration information system?

Name and describe the five components of a collaboration information system. Summarize the primary requirements for collaboration information systems and relate those requirements to the need for iteration and feedback as well as the three criteria for successful collaboration.

Q7-5   How can you use collaboration tools to improve team communication?

Explain why communication is important to collaboration. Define *synchronous* and *asynchronous communication* and explain when each is used. Name two collaboration tools that can be used to help set up synchronous meetings. Describe collaboration tools that can be used for face-to-face meetings. Describe tools that can be used for virtual, synchronous meetings. Describe tools that can be used for virtual, asynchronous meetings.

Q7-6   How can you use collaboration tools to manage shared content?

Summarize alternatives for processing Office documents on the desktop as well as over the Internet. Describe two ways that content is shared with no control and explain the problems that can occur. Explain the difference between version management and version control. Describe how user accounts, passwords, and libraries are used to control user activity. Explain how check-in/checkout works. Describe workflows and give an example.

Q7-7   How can you use collaboration tools to manage tasks?

Explain why managing tasks is important to team progress. Demonstrate how a task should be described. List the minimal content of a task list. Summarize the advantages and disadvantages of using a spreadsheet and Microsoft SharePoint for managing tasks.

Q7-8   Which collaboration IS is right for your team?

Describe the three collaboration tool sets described and indicate how each meets the minimum requirements for collaboration. Explain the differences among them. Summarize the criteria for choosing the right set for your team. Explain the meaning of the power curve and discuss the power curve for each of the three alternatives described.

Q7-9   2029?

Define *sharing economy* and *gig economy* and explain why they will make collaboration skills increasingly necessary. Explain why F2F meetings are expensive in both cost and time. Explain why mixed-reality workspaces might be desirable. Describe how holoportation may change collaboration. Summarize the ways collaboration systems reduce the costs and difficulties of international business. Explain how collaboration systems are changing the scope of workers with whom you will compete. If you disagree with any of the conclusions in this 2029, explain how and why.

Using Your Knowledge with ARES

Reread the ARES scenario at the start of this chapter. Using the knowledge you've gained from this chapter, explain how this team could use collaboration tools to complete the tasks assigned to them by Zev as well as result in better communication and higher-quality results for the team as a whole.

KEY TERMS AND CONCEPTS

Asynchronous communication   264
Collaboration   254
Collaboration information system   262
Collaboration system   262
Constructive criticism   254
Cooperation   253
Discussion forums   266
Email   266
File server   269
Gig economy   283
Google Drive   269

Groupthink   254
Libraries   272
Managerial decisions   258
Operational decisions   258
Power curve   281
Problem   260
Project data   262
Project metadata   262
Screen-sharing applications   265
Sharing economy   283
Strategic decisions   259

Structured decisions   259
Synchronous communication   264
Team surveys   267
Unstructured decisions   259
Version control   272
Version management   269
Videoconferencing   263
Virtual meetings   265
Webinar   265
Workflow control   273

MyLab MIS

To complete the problems with MyLab MIS, go to EOC Discussion Questions in the MyLab.

USING YOUR KNOWLEDGE

7-1. Reflect on your experience working on teams in previous classes as well as on collaborative teams in other settings, such as a campus committee. To what extent was your team collaborative? Did it involve feedback and iteration? If so, how? How did you use collaborative information systems, if at all? If you did not use collaborative information systems, describe how you think such systems might have improved your work methods and results. If you did use collaborative information systems, explain how you could improve on that use, given the knowledge you have gained from this chapter.

MyLab MIS

7-2. Using your experience working in past teams, give examples of unhelpful feedback according to the guidelines for providing critical feedback in Q7-1. Correct your examples to a more productive and helpful comment.

MyLab MIS

7-3. Using a past team project from your own experience, summarize how your team conducted the four phases (starting, planning, doing, and finalizing) in Q7-3. Evaluate how your team conducted problem-solving, decision-making, and informing activities. Rate your past team on Hackman's criteria as discussed in Q7-2.

MyLab MIS

7-4. This exercise requires you to experiment with Microsoft OneDrive. You will need two Office IDs to complete this exercise. The easiest way to do it is to work with a classmate. If that is not possible, set up two Office accounts using two different *Outlook.com* addresses.

   a. Go to *www.onedrive.com* and sign in with one of your accounts. Create a memo about collaboration tools

using the Word Online. Save your memo. Share your document with the email in your second Office account. Sign out of your first account.

      (If you have access to two computers situated close to each other, use both of them for this exercise. If you have two computers, do not sign out of your Office account. Perform step b and all actions for the second account on that second computer. If you are using two computers, ignore the instructions in the following steps to sign out of the Office accounts.)

   b. Open a new window in your browser. Access *www.onedrive.com* from that second window and sign in using your second Office account. Open the document you shared in step a.

   c. Change the memo by adding a brief description of content management. Do not save the document yet. If you are using just one computer, sign out from your second account.

   d. Sign in on your first account. Attempt to open the memo and note what occurs. Sign out of your first account and sign back in with your second account. Save the document. Now, sign out of your second account and sign back in with the first account. Now attempt to open the memo. (If you are using two computers, perform these same actions on the two different computers.)

   e. Sign in on your second account. Reopen the shared document. From the File menu, save the document as a Word document. Describe how OneDrive processed the changes to your document.

COLLABORATION EXERCISE 7

Using the collaboration IS you built in Chapter 1 (page 32), collaborate with a group of students to answer the following questions.

7-5. Collaboration:

   a. What is collaboration? Reread Q7-1 in this chapter, but do not confine yourselves to that discussion. Consider your own experience working in collaborative teams, and search the Web to identify other ideas about collaboration.

   b. What characteristics make for an effective team member? Review the survey of effective collaboration skills in Figure 7-1 and the guidelines for giving and receiving critical feedback, and discuss them as a group. Do you agree with them?

   c. What skills or feedback techniques would you add to this list? What conclusions can you, as a team, take from this survey? Would you change the rankings in Figure 7-1?

7-6. Ineffective collaboration:

   a. What would you do with an ineffective team member? First, define an ineffective team member. Specify five or so characteristics of an ineffective team member.

   b. If your group has such a member, what action do you, as a group, believe should be taken?

   c. In the business world, an ineffective team member can be fired. But in most academic environments, students can't fail other students for being an ineffective team member. Explain how differences or similarities in business and academic environments may affect how you deal with an ineffective team member.

7-7. Effective collaboration:

   a. How do you know *you* are collaborating well with your group?

   b. When working with a group, how do you know whether you are effectively giving or receiving constructive criticism?

   c. Specify five or so characteristics that indicate collaborative success. How can you measure those characteristics?

   d. Briefly describe what your team likes and doesn't like about using your collaboration system.

7-8. Types of communication:

   a. What *types* of communication (synchronous or asynchronous) does your team use most often?

   b. Why do you choose to use that type of communication?

   c. What factors influence your choice of collaboration tools?

   d. Which tools do you use most often?

   e. From your team experience, have virtual or face-to-face tools proved to be more effective? Give an example of when a face-to-face meeting was more effective. Give an example when a virtual meeting was more effective.

CASE STUDY 7

Airbnb

If someone gave you a penny every 2 seconds, how much money would you make in a year? Well, you would make $0.30 every minute. In an hour you would make $18. In a day you would make $432. In a month you would make $12,960. In a year you would make more than $155,000. All for earning just a penny every 2 seconds.

Every 2 seconds someone books an Airbnb room. (One Mississippi . . . two Mississippi . . .) There, someone just booked one again! It's not hard to see why Airbnb is a $25 billion company. In fact, Airbnb is the largest hotel chain in the world. It's even bigger than the next five largest hotel brands *combined.*[15] And it doesn't own a single hotel property.

From Airbeds to Billions

Creating this type of company and earning this amount of money were inconceivable when Airbnb got its start. In 2007,

two friends—Joe Gebbia and Brian Chesky—decided to rent out some spare air mattresses to make a little money to pay the rent for their San Francisco home. There was a popular conference coming to the city, and all the hotels were fully booked. The pair

Source: Smith Collection/Gado/Alamy Stock Photo

came up with the idea of hosting some guests by renting out three airbeds on their living room floor and cooking breakfast for the guests the next day. They created the Web site *www.airbed andbreakfast.com*, and within a few days they were hosting a man from India, a man from Utah, and a woman from Boston.

The experience proved that people were willing to rent rooms in a more sustainable and collaborative way. Airbnb began getting local people to list their rooms and travelers to book them. In 2008, Barack Obama was slated to speak at the Democratic National Convention in Denver. More than 75,000 people were expected to attend, and hotels were overbooked. A few weeks before the convention, Airbnb launched its new Web site. Within days the site had more than 800 listings for rooms to rent.

In 2009, Airbnb was able to raise more than $600,000 from venture capitalists. It worked out the details of how to make money on the site by charging 15 percent of the booking fee: The host pays 3 percent to Airbnb, and the guest pays 12 percent. The company's success led to another round of investing in 2010, when Airbnb raised more than $7 million. The following year it raised an incredible $112 million in venture funding.

Collaborative Consumption

Airbnb is a business based on sharing. This has been referred to as *collaborative consumption*. Consumers can temporarily share their assets with other consumers via renting or lending. Companies like Airbnb help consumers find each other, and they charge a fee for this service.

Airbnb founder Joe Gebbia said, "What we're doing with Airbnb feels like the nexus of everything that is right. We're helping people be more resourceful with the space they already have and we're connecting people around the world."[16] Effectively using idle resources is key to understanding the success behind Airbnb. In a recent TEDx Talk, urban planner Darren Cotton noted that the average power drill is used for only 12 to 13 minutes in its entire life. If true, why buy one? Why not rent or borrow one?

The same is true of underutilized space in people's homes. Airbnb logs more than 100 million stays per year in spaces that would have otherwise remained unused. Thanks to Airbnb, consumers are now able to generate income from their previously unused spaces by temporarily renting to other consumers. Imagine if this were also done with cars (Uber), pets (DogVacay), or loans (Lending Club). Collaborative consumption can be applied to many types of underutilized assets if done effectively.

A big part of collaborative consumption is feedback. Feedback in the accommodation industry, for example, gives consumers insight and understanding into the places they want to rent on Airbnb. After people book a room and stay there, they are encouraged to give feedback on their experience. If guests have a great experience, they may be inclined to give the host good reviews. Good reviews may encourage future guests to book

rooms. Likewise, if feedback is negative and the reviews are poor, future guests may not book rooms there in the future. Hosts use the feedback to improve the experience for future guests.

QUESTIONS

7-9. Airbnb launched its Web site and started renting rooms in 2008. But the Internet had been widely used starting in 1995. Why did it take 13 years for someone to start a company like Airbnb? Were there technological, social, or economic factors that kept this concept from becoming successful before 2008? Why didn't any of the existing large technology companies like Google, Apple, Microsoft, Amazon, or Facebook start a company like Airbnb?

7-10. Many successful companies are started to fulfill a need. What need did Airbnb fill? Why weren't hotels fulfilling this need? Are hotels and Airbnb fulfilling the same need, or are they offering different products for different needs? Would consumers use both traditional hotels and Airbnb for different purposes? Why?

7-11. Suppose you work for a large investing firm. Your boss asks you to determine the value of Airbnb as a company because he plans on buying stock in its upcoming initial public offering (IPO).
   a. How would you determine its value?
   b. Would you value Airbnb like a hotel chain, a tech startup, or another type of company?
   c. How would you determine Airbnb's future growth potential? Could it expand into other markets? Which ones?

7-12. Describe some of the economic impacts of collaborative consumption. Would companies like Airbnb and Uber help economies or hurt them? Why?

7-13. What are some other markets that could benefit from collaborative consumption? What might hinder these new markets from being profitable?

7-14. Why are customer reviews and ratings so important to hosts offering rooms on Airbnb? Why would reviews be more important to a smaller host compared to a large 200-room hotel? Would feedback be important to all collaborative consumption industries? Why?

7-15. Collaborative consumption utilizes idle resources. Could this same principle be applied to the human labor market? How? What impact might this have on the workforce? Airbnb doesn't own any hotels, yet it is the largest accommodation provider in the world. Could the largest organizations in the world have no employees? How?

MyLab MIS

Go to the Assignments section of your MyLab to complete these writing exercises.

7-16. Reread about 2029 in Q7-9. Do you agree with the conclusions? Why or why not? If F2F meetings become rare, what additional impacts do you see on the travel industry? In light of this change, describe travel industry investments that make sense and those that do not. What are promising investments in training? What are promising investments in other industries?

7-17. Consider how you might use information technology in group projects for your university classes. Using the discussion of IS requirements for collaboration presented in Q7-4, answer the following questions:

    a. Suppose that a group member wants to use nothing but face-to-face meetings, email, and texting for communication. What problems can you expect if you use only these methods? How might these methods affect group communication and content sharing?

    b. Assuming you are using only face-to-face meetings, email, texting, PowerPoint, and Excel, how will you share documents? What problems might you expect?

    c. Consider the four purposes of collaboration activities mentioned in Q7-3. For which purpose(s) might you use online data storage tools like Google Drive, Dropbox, and OneDrive?

    d. Describe what you think would be the single most important additional collaboration tool that you could add to your team.

ENDNOTES

1. Mitch Ditkoff, Tim Moore, Carolyn Allen, and Dave Pollard, "The Ideal Collaborative Team," *Idea Champions*, accessed June 8, 2018, *www.ideachampions.com/downloads/collaborationresults.pdf.*

2. J. Richard Hackman, *Leading Teams: Setting the Stage for Great Performances* (Boston: Harvard Business Press, 2002).

3. Wouter van Diggelen, *Changing Face-to-Face Communication: Collaborative Tools to Support Small-Group Discussions in the Classroom* (Groningen: University of Groningen, 2011).

4. Warning: The data in this figure is changing rapidly. The features and functions of both Web applications and cloud drives may have been extended from what is described here. Check the vendor's documentation for new capabilities.

5. Larry Alton, "Why the Gig Economy Is the Best and Worst Development for Workers Under 30," *Forbes*, January 24, 2018, *www.forbes.com/sites/larryalton/2018/01/24/why-the-gig-economy-is-the-best-and-worst-development-for-workers-under-30/#206321726d76.*

6. Ibid.

7. Gianpiero Petriglieri, Susan J. Ashford, and Amy Wrzesniewski, "Thriving in the Gig Economy," *Harvard Business Review*, March-April 2018 Issues, *https://hbr.org/2018/03/thriving-in-the-gig-economy.*

8. Ibid.

9. Megan Rose Dickey, "Judge Rules Grubhub Properly Classified Delivery Driver as Independent Contractor," *TechCrunch*, February 8, 2018, *https://techcrunch.com/2018/02/08/grubhub-v-lawson-ruling/.*

10. Ibid.

11. See also David Kroenke and Donald Nilson, *Office 365 in Business* (Indianapolis, IN: John Wiley & Sons, 2011).

12. Denise Zheng, "Should Companies Be Required to Share Information About Cyberattacks?," *The Wall Street Journal*, May 22, 2016, *www.wsj.com/articles/should-companies-be-required-to-share-information-about-cyberattacks-1463968801.*

13. Andrew Tannenbaum, "To Prevent Cyberattacks, Share the Threat Data," *The Wall Street Journal*, July 9, 2015, *www.wsj.com/articles/to-prevent-cyberattacks-share-the-threat-data-1436482349.*

14. Ibid.

15. Betty Wood, "Airbnb Is Now Bigger Than the World's Top Five Hotel Brands Put Together," *The Spaces*, August 15, 2017, accessed June 11, 2018, *https://thespaces.com/2017/08/15/airbnb-now-bigger-worlds-top-five-hotel-brands-put-together.*

16. Jessica Salter, "Airbnb: The Story Behind the $1.3bn Room-Letting Website," *The Telegraph*, September 7, 2012, accessed June 11, 2018, *www.telegraph.co.uk/technology/news/9525267/Airbnb-The-story-behind-the-1.3bn-room-letting-website.html.*

CHAPTER 8

Processes, Organizations, and Information Systems

"No, Felix! Not again! Over and over and over! We decide something one meeting and then go over it again the next meeting and again the next. What a waste!"

"What do you mean, Raj?" asks Felix, ARES' customer service manager. "I think it's important we get this right."

"Well, Felix, if that's the case, why don't you come to the meetings?"

"I just missed a couple."

"Right. Last week we met here for, oh, two, maybe three, hours, and we decided to meet with a spinning instructor Cassie knows. She teaches spinning classes at a local university and was open to the idea of leading the virtual classes."

MyLab MIS

Using Your Knowledge
Questions 8-1, 8-2, 8-3
Essay Questions 8-18, 8-19

"But, Raj, we don't even know if we'll have the bandwidth to handle the virtual classes or if anyone will actually sign up. What difference does it make if we offer spinning classes if no one signs up?"

"Felix! We discussed that last week. The university has an excellent high-speed Internet connection, and we share the same ISP. So, bandwidth won't be an issue at all. And users won't be a problem either. The spinning instructor has a class full of students who are more than willing to try the new virtual classes as long as we supply the headsets."

"Look, Raj, Henri just wants something reasonable to tell Ashley. If we tell him these new virtual spinning classes aren't going to fly, which they probably won't, Ashley will cancel this project and we can get back to work . . . focusing on home users and corporate clients!"

"Felix, you're driving me nuts. We discussed this *ad nauseam* last week. Let's make some progress. Cassie, what do you think?"

"Felix, Raj is right," Cassie chimes in. "We did have a long discussion on how to go about this—and we did agree to focus first on setting up this test class. This could be an important new revenue source. Yes, we'd have to change some of our internal processes, but it could be very profitable."

"Well, Cassie, I think it's a mistake. Why didn't anyone tell me? I put in a lot of time looking into selling ARES directly to corporate clients for their wellness programs."

"Did you read the email?" Cassie asks tentatively.

"What email?"

"The meeting summary email that I send out each week," Cassie says with a sigh.

"I got the email, but I couldn't download the attachment. Something weird about a virus checker couldn't access a gizmo or something like that . . ." Felix trails off.

"I got the email, but I couldn't download the attachment."

Source: Haiyin Wang/Alamy Stock Photo

Raj can't stand that excuse. "Here, Felix, take a look at mine. I'll underline the part where we concluded that we'd focus on testing the virtual spinning class."

"Raj, there's no reason to get snippy about this. I thought I had a good idea," Felix says, sounding hurt.

"OK, so we're agreed—*again this week*—that we're going to focus on testing the virtual spinning class at the university. Now, we've wasted enough time covering old ground. Let's get some new thinking on how we're going to do that."

Felix slumps back into his chair and looks down at his cell phone.

"Oh, no, I missed a call from Mapplethorpe. Ahhhh."

"Felix, what are you talking about?" Raj asks.

"Mapplethorpe, my human resource contact at GenTech. He wants to know what kind of data we can share with them for their wellness program. I'm sorry, but I've got to call him. I'll be back in a few minutes."

Felix leaves the room.

Raj looks at Cassie.

"Now what?" he asks. "If we go forward, we'll have to rediscuss everything when Felix comes back. Maybe we should just take a break?"

Cassie shakes her head. "Raj, let's not. It's tough for me to get to these meetings. I don't have to work until tonight, so I drove down here just for this. I've got to pick up Simone from day care. We haven't done anything yet. Let's just ignore Felix."

"OK, Cassie, but it isn't easy to ignore Felix. There's got to be a better way to get this done."

The door opens, and Henri walks in.

"Hi everyone! How's it going?" he asks brightly. "Is it OK if I sit in on your meeting?"

Study QUESTIONS

Q8-1   What are the basic types of processes?

Q8-2   How can information systems improve process quality?

Q8-3   How do information systems eliminate the problems of information silos?

Q8-4   How do CRM, ERP, and EAI support enterprise processes?

Q8-5   What are the elements of an ERP system?

Q8-6   What are the challenges of implementing and upgrading enterprise information systems?

Q8-7   How do inter-enterprise IS solve the problems of enterprise silos?

Q8-8   2029?

Chapter PREVIEW

This chapter explores processes and their supporting information systems within levels of an organization. We will extend the business process discussion from Chapter 2 to investigate three types of processes and the scope of information systems they use. We will also investigate the concept of process quality and explain how information systems can be used to increase it. Then we will discuss how the use of information systems at one level of organization leads to information silos, explain the problems of such silos, and then show how those problems can be solved by information systems at the next level of organization. In particular, we'll discuss how enterprise systems such as CRM, ERP, and EAI (you'll learn the meaning of those terms) solve problems caused by workgroup information silos. ERP systems play a particularly important role, and we'll discuss their purpose and components and the major ERP vendors. Then we'll survey the major challenges that occur when implementing enterprise systems. We'll wrap up the chapter by showing how inter-enterprise IS can solve the problems of enterprise-level silos and finally, in 2029, discuss the implications of mobility and the cloud on future enterprise and inter-enterprise IS.

Q8-1   What Are the Basic Types of Processes?

As you learned in Chapter 2, a business process is a network of activities that generate value by transforming inputs into outputs. Activities are subparts of processes that receive inputs and produce outputs. Activities can be performed by humans only, by humans augmented by computer systems, and by computer systems only.

Figure 8-1 shows a simplified view of a three-activity process for approving customer orders. Each of these activities is, itself, a subprocess of this overall process. You can see that each step—check inventory, check customer credit, and approve special terms—receives inputs and

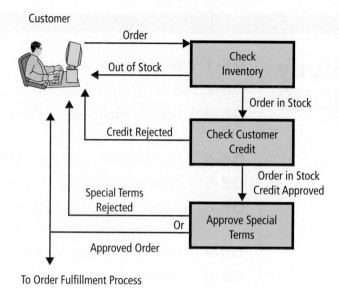

FIGURE 8-1
Business Process with Three Activities

transforms them into outputs. You will learn how to better diagram such processes in Chapter 12; for now, just view Figure 8-1 as showing the gist of a typical business process.

How Do Structured Processes Differ from Dynamic Processes?

Businesses have dozens, hundreds, even thousands of different processes. Some processes are stable, almost fixed sequences of activities and data flows. For example, the process of a salesclerk accepting a return at Nordstrom, or other quality retail stores, is fixed. If the customer has a receipt, take these steps . . . if the customer has no receipt, take these other steps. That process needs to be standardized so that customers are treated consistently and correctly, so that returned goods are accounted for appropriately, and so that sales commissions are reduced in a way that is fair to the sales staff.

Other processes are less structured, less rigid, and often creative. For example, how does Nordstrom's management decide what women's clothes to carry next spring? Managers can look at past sales, consider current economic conditions, and make assessments about women's acceptance of new styles at recent fashion shows, but the process for combining all those factors into orders of specific garments in specific quantities and colors is not nearly as structured as that for accepting returns.

In this text, we divide processes into two broad categories. **Structured processes** are formally defined, standardized processes that involve day-to-day operations: accepting a return, placing an order, purchasing raw materials, and so forth. They have the characteristics summarized in the left-hand column of Figure 8-2.

Dynamic processes are flexible, informal, and adaptive processes that normally involve strategic and less structured managerial decisions and activities. Deciding whether to open a new store location and how best to solve the problem of excessive product returns are examples, as is using Twitter to generate buzz about next season's product line. Dynamic processes usually require human judgment. The right-hand column of Figure 8-2 shows characteristics of dynamic processes.

We will discuss structured processes and information systems that support them in this chapter. We have already discussed one dynamic process, collaboration, in Chapter 7, and we will discuss another, social media, in Chapter 9.

For the balance of this chapter, we will use the term *process* to mean *structured process*.

Structured	Dynamic
Support operational and structured managerial decisions and activities	Support strategic and less structured managerial decision and activities
Standardized	Less specific, fluid
Usually formally defined and documented	Usually informal
Exceptions rare and not (well) tolerated	Exceptions frequent and expected
Process structure changes slowly and with organizational agony	Adaptive processes that change structure rapidly and readily
Example: Customer returns, order entry, purchasing, payroll, etc.	**Example:** Collaboration; social networking; ill-defined, ambiguous situations

FIGURE 8-2
Structured Versus Dynamic Processes

How Do Processes Vary by Organizational Scope?

Processes are used at three levels of organizational scope: workgroup, enterprise, and inter-enterprise. In general, the wider the scope of the process, the more challenging the process is to manage. For example, processes that support a single workgroup function, say, accounts payable, are simpler and easier to manage than those that support a network of independent organizations, such as a supply chain. Consider processes at each of these three organizational scopes.

Workgroup Processes

A **workgroup process** exists to enable workgroups to fulfill the charter, purpose, and goals of a particular group or department. A physicians' partnership is a workgroup that follows processes to manage patient records, issue and update prescriptions, provide standardized postsurgery care, and so forth.

Figure 8-3 lists common workgroup processes. Notice that each of these processes is largely contained within a given department. These processes may receive inputs from other departments, and they may produce outputs used by other departments, but all, or at least the bulk of, the processes' activities lay within a single department.

A **workgroup information system** exists to support one or more processes within the workgroup. For example, an Operations department could implement an IS to support all three of the operations processes shown in Figure 8-3. Or an Accounting department might implement two or three different IS to support the accounting processes shown. Sometimes, workgroup information systems are called **functional information systems**. Thus, an operations management system is a functional information system, as are a general ledger system and a cost accounting system. The program component of a functional information system is called a **functional application**.

General characteristics of workgroup information systems are summarized in the top row of Figure 8-4. Typical workgroup information systems support 10 to 100 users. Because the procedures for using them must be understood by all members of the group, those procedures are often formalized in documentation. Users generally receive formal training in the use of those procedures as well.

When problems occur, they almost always can be solved within the group. If accounts payable duplicates the record for a particular supplier, the accounts payable group can make the fix. If the Web storefront has the wrong number of items in the inventory database, that count can be fixed within the storefront group.

(Notice, by the way, that the consequences of a problem are not isolated to the group. Because the workgroup information system exists to provide a service to the rest of the organization, its

Workgroup	Workgroup Example Processes
Sales and marketing	• Lead generation • Lead tracking • Customer management • Sales forecasting • Product and brand management
Operations	• Order entry • Order management • Finished goods inventory management
Manufacturing	• Inventory (raw materials, goods-in-process) • Planning • Scheduling • Operations
Customer service	• Order tracking • Account tracking • Customer support
Human resources	• Recruiting • Compensation • Assessment • HR planning
Accounting	• General ledger • Financial reporting • Cost accounting • Accounts receivable • Accounts payable • Cash management • Budgeting • Treasury management

FIGURE 8-3
Common Workgroup Processes

problems have consequences throughout the organization. The fix to the problem can usually be obtained within the group, however.)

Two or more departments within an organization can duplicate data, and such duplication can be very problematic to the organization, as we discuss in Q8-3. Finally, because workgroup information systems involve multiple users, changing them can be problematic. But, again, when problems do occur, they can be resolved within the workgroup.

Scope	Example	Characteristics
Workgroup	Doctor's office/medical practice	Support one or more workgroup processes. 10–100 users; procedures often formalized; problem solutions within group; workgroups can duplicate data; somewhat difficult to change
Enterprise	Hospital	Support one or more enterprise processes. 100–1,000+ users; procedures formalized; problem solutions affect enterprise; eliminate workgroup data duplication; difficult to change
Inter-enterprise	Healthcare exchange	Support one or more inter-enterprise processes. 1,000+ users; systems procedures formalized; problem solutions affect multiple organizations; can resolve problems of duplicated enterprise data; very difficult to change

FIGURE 8-4
Characteristics of Information Systems

Enterprise Processes

The Ethics Guide on pages 310–311 demonstrates how one person's actions can affect an entire company

Enterprise processes span an organization and support activities in multiple departments. At a hospital, the process for discharging a patient supports activities in housekeeping, the pharmacy, the kitchen, nurses' stations, and other hospital departments.

Enterprise information systems support one or more enterprise processes. As shown in the second row of Figure 8-4, they typically have hundreds to thousands of users. Procedures are formalized and extensively documented; users always undergo formal procedure training. Sometimes enterprise systems include categories of procedures, and users are defined according to levels of expertise with the system as well as by level of authority.

The solutions to problems in an enterprise system involve more than one workgroup or department. As you will learn in this chapter, a major advantage of enterprise systems is that data duplication within the enterprise is either eliminated altogether or, if it is allowed to exist, changes to duplicated data are carefully managed to maintain consistency.

Because enterprise systems span many departments and involve potentially thousands of users, they are difficult to change. Changes must be carefully planned and cautiously implemented and users given considerable training. Sometimes users are given cash incentives and other inducements to motivate them to change.

CRM, ERP, and EAI are three enterprise information systems that we will define and discuss in Q8-4.

Inter-enterprise Processes

Inter-enterprise processes span two or more independent organizations. For example, the process of buying a healthcare insurance policy via a healthcare exchange (see Case Study 8, pages 330–332) involves many insurance companies and governmental agencies. Each of these organizations has activities to fulfill, all of which are affected by laws, governmental policy, and competitive concerns of the insurance companies.

Inter-enterprise information systems support one or more inter-enterprise processes. Such systems typically involve thousands of users, and solutions to problems require cooperation among different, usually independently owned, organizations. Problems are resolved by meeting, by contract, and sometimes by litigation.

Data are often duplicated among organizations; such duplication is either eliminated or carefully managed. Because of their wide span, complexity, and use by multiple companies, such systems can be exceedingly difficult to change. Supply chain management (discussed in the International Dimension, pages 494–514) is the classic example of an inter-enterprise information system. We will study inter-enterprise ARES examples throughout the remaining chapters of this text.

Q8-2 How Can Information Systems Improve Process Quality?

Processes are the fabric of organizations; they are the means by which people organize their activities to achieve the organization's goals. As such, process quality is an important, possibly the most important, determinant of organizational success.[1]

The two dimensions of process quality are efficiency and effectiveness. **Process efficiency** is a measure of the ratio of process outputs to inputs. If an alternative to the process in Figure 8-1 can produce the same order approvals/rejections (output) for less cost or produce more approvals/rejections for the same cost, it is more efficient.

Process effectiveness is a measure of how well a process achieves organizational strategy. If an organization differentiates itself on quality customer service and if the process in

Figure 8-1 requires 5 days to respond to an order request, then that process is ineffective. Companies that provide customized manufacturing might make their processes more effective by using 3D printing.

How Can Processes Be Improved?

Organizations can improve the quality (efficiency and/or effectiveness) of a process in one of three ways:

- Change the process structure.
- Change the process resources.
- Change both process structure and resources.

Change the Process Structure

In some cases, process quality can be changed just by reorganizing the process. The order approval process in Figure 8-1 might be made more efficient if customer credit was done first and inventory was checked second. This change might be more efficient because it would save the cost of checking inventory for customers whose credit will be denied. However, that change would also mean that the organization would pay for a credit check on customers for which it did not have appropriate inventory. We will investigate such changes further in Chapter 12. For now, just note that process structure has a strong bearing on process efficiency.

Changing process structure can also increase process effectiveness. If an organization chooses a cost-leader strategy, then that strategy might mean that no special terms should ever be approved. If the process in Figure 8-1 results in the authorization of orders with special terms, then eliminating the third activity will make it more effective (most likely it will save on operational costs as well).

Change Process Resources

Business process activities are accomplished by humans and information systems. One way to improve process quality is to change the allocation of those resources. For example, if the process in Figure 8-1 is not effective because it takes too long, one way to make it more effective is to identify the source of delays and then to add more resources. If delays are caused by the check customer credit activity, one way to increase process effectiveness is to add more people to that activity. Adding people should decrease delays, but it will also add cost, so the organization needs to find the appropriate balance between effectiveness and efficiency.

Another way to shorten the credit check process would be to use an information system to perform the customer credit checks. Depending on the development and operational costs of the new system, that change might also be less costly and therefore more efficient.

Change Both Process Structure and Process Resources

Of course, it is possible to improve process quality by changing both the process's structure and resources. In fact, unless a structure change is only a simple reordering of tasks, changing the structure of a process almost always involves a change in resources as well.

How Can Information Systems Improve Process Quality?

Information systems can be used to improve process quality by:

- Performing an activity.
- Augmenting a human who is performing an activity.
- Controlling data quality and process flow.

Performing an Activity

Information systems can perform the entirety of a process activity. In Figure 8-1, for example, the check credit activity could be entirely automated. When you purchase from Amazon or another major online retailer, information systems check your credit while your transaction is being processed. Reserving a seat on an airline is done automatically; all of the reservation activity is done by an information system. (Except, of course, the passenger's activities: When making a reservation, you must choose the seat from available locations, but your time is free to the airline.)

Augmenting a Human Performing an Activity

A second way that information systems can improve process quality is by augmenting the actions of a human who is performing that activity. Consider the process of managing patient appointments. To schedule an appointment, patients call the doctor's office and talk with a receptionist who uses an appointment information system. That information system augments the appointment creation activity.

Controlling Data Quality Process Flow

A third way that information systems can improve process quality is by controlling data quality and process flow.

One of the major benefits of information systems is to control data quality. The IS can not only ensure that correct data values are being input, it can also ensure that data are complete before continuing process activities. The cheapest way to correct for data errors is at the source, and it avoids the problems that develop when process activities are begun with incomplete data.

Information systems also have a role in controlling process flow. Consider the order approval process in Figure 8-1. If this process is controlled manually, then someone, say, a salesperson, will obtain the order data from the customer and take whatever actions are needed to push that order through the three steps in the order process. If the salesperson gets busy or is distracted or away from work for a few days, or if there are unexpected delays in one of the activities, it is possible for an order to be lost or the approval unnecessarily delayed.

If, however, an information system is controlling the order approval process, then it can ensure that steps are performed in accordance with an established schedule. The information system can also be relied upon to make correct process-routing decisions for processes that are more complicated than that in Figure 8-1. SharePoint workflows, discussed in the context of collaboration in Chapter 7, can be used to automate structured processes.

Q8-3 How Do Information Systems Eliminate the Problems of Information Silos?

An **information silo** is the condition that exists when data are isolated in separated information systems. For example, consider the six workgroups and their information systems in Figure 8-3. Reflect on these information systems for a moment, and you'll realize that each one processes customer, sales, product, and other data, but each uses that data for its own purposes and will likely store slightly different data. Sales, for example, will store contact data for customers' purchasing agents, while Accounting will store contact data for customers' accounts payable personnel.

It's completely natural for workgroups to develop information systems solely for their own needs, but, over time, the existence of these separate systems will result in information silos that cause numerous problems.

What Are the Problems of Information Silos?

Figure 8-5 lists the major problems caused by information silos at the workgroup level, in this case, between the Sales and Marketing department and the Accounting department. First, data are duplicated. Sales and Marketing and Accounting applications maintain separate databases that store some of the same customer data. As you know, data storage is cheap, so the problem with duplication is not wasted disk storage. Rather, the problem is data inconsistency. Changes to customer data made in the Sales and Marketing application may take days or weeks to be made to the Accounting application's database. During that period, shipments will reach the customer without delay, but invoices will be sent to the wrong address. When an organization has inconsistent duplicated data, it is said to have a **data integrity** problem.

Additionally, when applications are isolated, business processes are disjointed. Suppose a business has a rule that credit orders over $15,000 must be preapproved by the Accounts Receivable department. If the supporting applications are separated, it will be difficult for the two activities to reconcile their data, and the approval will be slow to grant and possibly erroneous.

In the second row of Figure 8-5, Sales and Marketing wants to approve a $20,000 order with Ajax. According to the Sales and Marketing database, Ajax has a current balance of $17,800, so Sales and Marketing requests a total credit amount of $37,800. The Accounting database, however, shows Ajax with a balance of only $12,300 because the accounts receivable application has credited Ajax for a return of $5,500. According to Accounting's records, a total credit authorization of only $32,300 is needed in order to approve the $20,000 order, so that is all the department grants.

FIGURE 8-5
Problems Created by Information Silos

Problem	Sales and Marketing	Accounting
Data duplication, data inconsistency	Ajax Construction Ship to: Reno, NV Bill to: Reno, NV	Ajax Construction Ship to: Reno, NV Bill to: Buffalo, NY
Disjointed processes	Get Credit Approval — Request $37,800 → Approve Customer Credit ← Approve $32,300	
Limited information and lack of integrated information	Order Data — ?? Is IndyMac a preferred customer?	Payment Data
Isolated decisions lead to organizational inefficiencies	Order Data Redouble sales efforts at IndyMac.	Payment Data OneWest has been slow to pay.
Increased expense	Sum of problems above.	

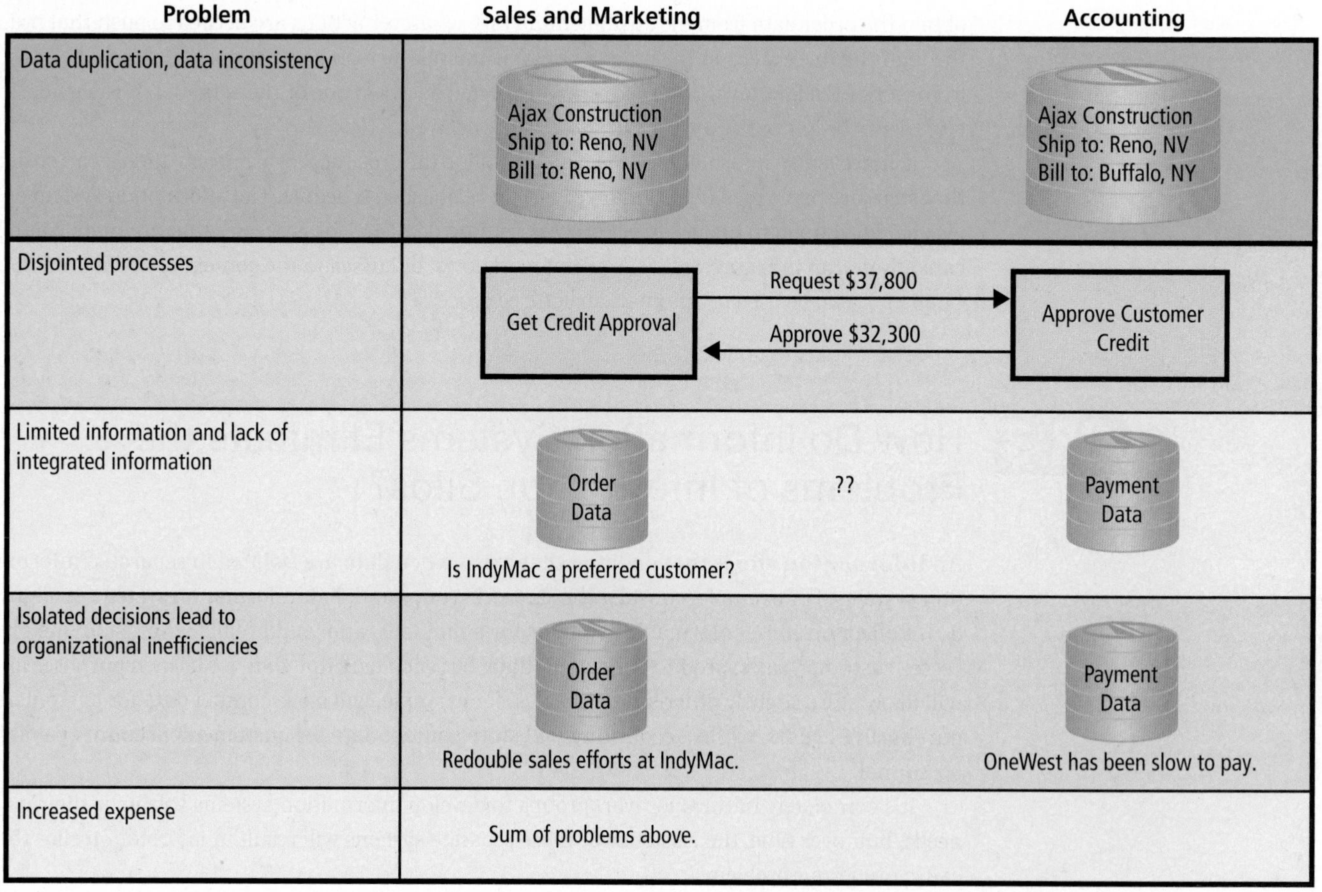

Sales and Marketing doesn't understand what to do with a credit approval of $32,300. According to its database, Ajax already owes $17,800, so if the total credit authorization is only $32,300, did Accounting approve only $14,500 of the new order? And why that amount? Both departments want to approve the order. It will take numerous emails and phone calls, however, to sort this out. These interacting business processes are disjointed.

A consequence of such disjointed activities is the lack of integrated enterprise information. For example, suppose Sales and Marketing wants to know if IndyMac is still a preferred customer. Assume that determining whether this is so requires a comparison of order history and payment history data. With information silos, that data will reside in two different databases and, in one of them, IndyMac is known by the name of the company that acquired it, OneWest Bank. Data integration will be difficult. Making the determination will require manual processes and days, when it should be readily answered in seconds.

This leads to the fourth consequence: inefficiency. When using isolated functional applications, decisions are made in isolation. As shown in the fourth row of Figure 8-5, Sales and Marketing decided to redouble its sales effort with IndyMac. However, Accounting knows that IndyMac was foreclosed by the FDIC and sold to OneWest and has been slow to pay. There are far better prospects for increased sales attention. Without integration, the left hand of the organization doesn't know what the right hand of the organization is doing.

Finally, information silos can result in increased cost for the organization. Duplicated data, disjointed systems, limited information, and inefficiencies all mean higher costs.

How Do Organizations Solve the Problems of Information Silos?

As defined, an information silo occurs when data is stored in isolated systems. The obvious way to fix such a silo is to integrate the data into a single database and revise applications (and business processes) to use that database. If that is not possible or practical, another remedy is to allow the isolation, but to manage it to avoid problems.

The arrows in Figure 8-6 show this resolution at two levels of organization. First, isolated data created by workgroup information systems are integrated using enterprise-wide applications.

Scope	Example	Example Information Silo	Enabling Technology
Workgroup	Doctor's office/ medical practice	Physicians and hospitals store separated data about patients. Unnecessarily duplicate tests and procedures.	Functional applications.
		⬇	Enterprise applications (CRM, ERP, EAI) on enterprise networks.
Enterprise	Hospital	Hospital and local drug store pharmacy have different prescription data for the same patient.	
		⬇	Distributed systems using Web service technologies in the cloud.
Inter-enterprise	Inter-agency prescription application	No silo: Doctors, hospitals, pharmacies share patients' prescription and other data.	

FIGURE 8-6
Information Silos as Drivers

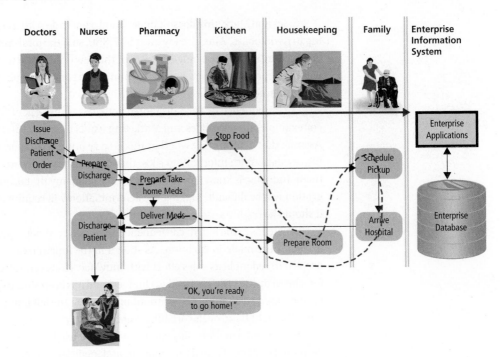

FIGURE 8-7
Example Enterprise Process and Information System

Second, today, isolated data created by information systems at the enterprise level are being integrated into inter-enterprise systems using distributed applications (such as ARES). These applications process data in a single cloud database or connect disparate, independent databases so that those databases appear to be one database. We will discuss inter-enterprise systems further in Q8-7.

For now, to better understand how isolated data problems can be resolved, consider an enterprise system at a hospital.

An Enterprise System for Patient Discharge

Figure 8-7 shows some of the hospital departments and a portion of the patient discharge process. A doctor initiates the process by issuing a discharge patient order. That order is delivered to the appropriate nursing staff, who initiates activities at the pharmacy, the patient's family, and the kitchen. Some of those activities initiate activities back at the nursing staff. In Figure 8-7, the enterprise process (supported by the IS) is represented by a dotted blue line.

Prior to the enterprise system, the hospital had developed procedures for using a paper-based system and informal messaging via the telephone. Each department kept its own records. When the new enterprise information system was implemented, not only was the data integrated into a database, but new computer-based forms and reports were created. The staff needed to transition from the paper-based system to the computer-based system. They also needed to stop making phone calls and let the new information system make notifications across departments. These measures involved substantial change, and most organizations experience considerable anguish when undergoing such transitions.

Q8-4 How Do CRM, ERP, and EAI Support Enterprise Processes?

Enterprise systems like the one in Figure 8-7 were not feasible until network, data communication, and database technologies reached a sufficient level of capability and maturity in the late 1980s and early 1990s. At that point, many organizations began to develop enterprise systems.

The Need for Business Process Engineering

As they did so, organizations realized that their existing business processes needed to change. In part, they needed to change to use the shared databases and to use new computer-based forms and reports. However, an even more important reason for changing business processes was that integrated data and enterprise systems offered the potential of substantial improvements in process quality. It became possible to do things that had been impossible before. Using Porter's language (Chapter 2, pages 44-46), enterprise systems enabled the creation of stronger, faster, more effective *linkages* among value chains.

For example, when the hospital used a paper-based system, the kitchen would prepare meals for everyone who was a patient at the hospital as of midnight the night before. It was not possible to obtain data about discharges until the next midnight. Consequently, considerable food was wasted at substantial cost.

With the enterprise system, the kitchen can be notified about patient discharges as they occur throughout the day, resulting in substantial reductions in wasted food. But when should the kitchen be notified? Immediately? And what if the discharge is cancelled before completion? Notify the kitchen of the cancelled discharge? Many possibilities and alternatives exist. So, to design its new enterprise system, the hospital needed to determine how best to change its processes to take advantage of the new capability. Such projects came to be known as **business process reengineering**, which is the activity of altering existing and designing new business processes to take advantage of new information systems.

Unfortunately, business process reengineering is difficult, slow, and exceedingly expensive. Business analysts need to interview key personnel throughout the organization to determine how best to use the new technology. Because of the complexity involved, such projects require high-level, expensive skills and considerable time. Many early projects stalled when the enormity of the project became apparent. This left some organizations with partially implemented systems, which had disastrous consequences. Personnel didn't know if they were using the new system, the old system, or some hacked-up version of both.

The stage was set for the emergence of enterprise application solutions, which we discuss next.

Emergence of Enterprise Application Solutions

When the process quality benefits of enterprise-wide systems became apparent, most organizations were still developing their applications in-house. At the time, organizations perceived their needs as being "too unique" to be satisfied by off-the-shelf or altered applications. However, as applications became more and more complex, in-house development costs became infeasible. As stated in Chapter 4, systems built in-house are expensive not only because of their high initial development costs, but also because of the continuing need to adapt those systems to changing requirements.

In the early 1990s, as the costs of business process reengineering were coupled to the costs of in-house development, organizations began to look more favorably on the idea of licensing preexisting applications. "Maybe we're not so unique, after all."

Some of the vendors who took advantage of this change in attitude were PeopleSoft, which licensed payroll and limited-capability human resources systems; Siebel, which licensed a sales lead tracking and management system; and SAP, which licensed something new, a system called *enterprise resource management*.

These three companies, and ultimately dozens of others like them, offered not just software and database designs. They also offered standardized business processes. These **inherent processes**, which are predesigned procedures for using the software products, saved organizations from the expense, delays, and risks of business process reengineering. Instead, organizations could license the software and obtain, as part of the deal, prebuilt processes that the vendors assured them were based on "industry best practices."

See the Career Guide on pages 324–325 to learn more about careers in managing the development of large-scale applications.

Some parts of that deal were too good to be true because, as you'll learn in Q8-5, inherent processes are almost never a perfect fit. But the offer was too much for many organizations to resist.

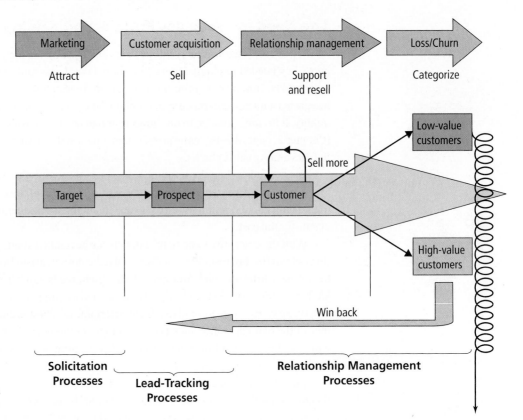

FIGURE 8-8

The Customer Life Cycle

Source: The Customer Life Cycle. Used with permission from Professor Douglas MacLachlan, Foster School of Business, University of Washington.

Over time, three categories of enterprise applications emerged: customer relationship management, enterprise resource planning, and enterprise application integration. Consider each.

Customer Relationship Management (CRM)

A **customer relationship management (CRM) system** is a suite of applications, a database, and a set of inherent processes for managing all the interactions with the customer, from lead generation to customer service. Every contact and transaction with the customer is recorded in the CRM database. Vendors of CRM systems claim that using their products makes the organization *customer-centric*. Though that term reeks of sales hyperbole, it does indicate the nature and intent of CRM packages.

Figure 8-8 shows four phases of the **customer life cycle**: marketing, customer acquisition, relationship management, and loss/churn. Marketing sends messages to the target market to attract customer prospects. When prospects order, they become customers who need to be supported. Additionally, relationship management processes increase the value of existing customers by selling them more product. Inevitably, over time the organization loses customers. When this occurs, win-back processes categorize customers according to value and attempt to win back high-value customers.

Figure 8-9 illustrates the major components of a CRM application. Notice that components exist for each stage of the customer life cycle. As shown, all applications process a common customer database. This design eliminates duplicated customer data and removes the possibility of inconsistent data. It also means that each department knows what has been happening with the customer at other departments. Customer support, for example, will know not to provide $1,000 worth of support labor to a customer that has generated $300 worth of business over time. However, it will know to bend over backward for customers that have generated hundreds of thousands of dollars of business. The result to the customers is that they feel like they are dealing with one entity, not many.

CRM systems vary in the degree of functionality they provide. One of the primary tasks when selecting a CRM package is to determine the features you need and to find a package that meets that set of needs. You might be involved in just such a project during your career.

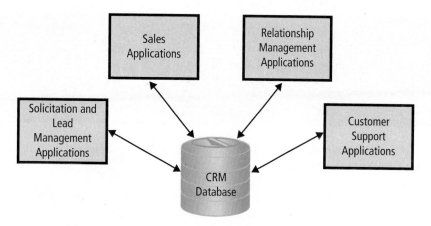

FIGURE 8-9
CRM Applications

Enterprise Resource Planning (ERP)

Large centralized databases can be attractive targets for disgruntled employees. For more information, see the Security Guide on pages 322–323.

Enterprise resource planning (ERP) is a suite of applications called **modules**, a database, and a set of inherent processes for consolidating business operations into a single, consistent, computing platform. An **ERP system** is an information system based on ERP technology. As shown in Figure 8-10, ERP systems include the functions of CRM systems but also incorporate accounting, manufacturing, inventory, and human resources applications.

The primary purpose of an ERP system is integration; an ERP system allows the left hand of the organization to know what the right hand is doing. This integration allows real-time updates globally, whenever and wherever a transaction takes place. Critical business decisions can then be made on a timely basis using the latest data.

To understand the utility of this integration, consider the pre-ERP systems shown in Figure 8-11. This diagram represents the processes used by a bicycle manufacturer. It includes five different databases, one each for vendors, raw materials, finished goods, manufacturing plan, and CRM. Consider the problems that appear with such separated data when the Sales department closes a large order, say, for 1,000 bicycles.

First, should the company take the order? Can it meet the schedule requirements for such a large order? Suppose one of the primary parts vendors recently lost capacity due to an earthquake,

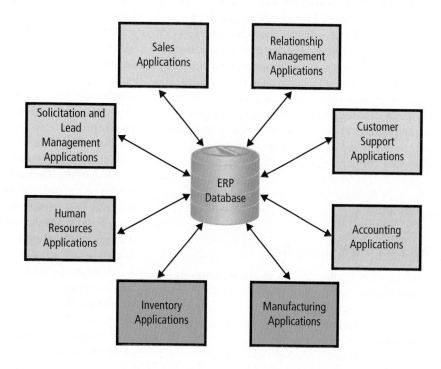

FIGURE 8-10
ERP Applications

DIGITAL DINING

Have you ever stopped to think about all of the complex processes that take place around you on a daily basis that you can't see? For example, ordering something online requires only a few keystrokes and mouse clicks. Before long, your order is delivered to your front door. However, this delivery is likely the result of countless business processes spanning multiple organizations—perhaps even in a global supply chain—and they *all* had to be conducted with precision for your package to arrive with the correct items, at the correct location, and at the indicated time.

We attribute the ease with which many processes seem to operate today to advancements in technology. For example, online retailers can track inventory levels and shipments in real time using RFID tags. Global supply chains leverage complex enterprise resource planning (ERP) systems to integrate operations and promote information sharing. And fulfillment centers now use robots to bring products to employees who pack shipments (instead of sending people to pick products from storage locations in massive warehouses). It feels as though most processes around us are being reevaluated and reengineered to promote efficiency and effectiveness, all using technology. No process is safe—not even at your local fast-food joint!

A Burger-Flipping Robot?

CaliBurger, a fast-food chain, recently started testing a burger-flipping robot named Flippy in its Pasadena restaurant. The robot is bolted to the floor in close proximity to the grill and can be fitted with a number of different tools that enable it to interact with the grill (e.g., a spatula and a scraper). The company that developed Flippy stated that the robot is a "cost-effective and highly efficient solution" that will not replace kitchen workers but augment them and allow them to focus on direct customer service (like asking customers about their food and experience at the restaurant).[2] Flippy uses a variety of sensors and cameras to monitor the environment and guide its movements around the grill. It can manage the cooking process for about 150 burgers per hour. CaliBurger plans to deploy Flippy robots in 50 of its locations in the near future. In light of the potential for competitors to invest in this technology, CaliBurger has exclusive rights to Flippy for the first 6months.[3]

Task Workers Are Flipping Out

While watching a robot make your next meal is an intriguing prospect, have you thought about what happens to the person who used to be paid to cook that burger? The reality of innovation and the transformation of processes mean that some people will inevitably lose their jobs to machines (even if companies state that machines will not replace human

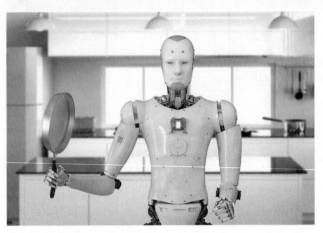

Source: Kittipong Jirasukhanont/Alamy Stock Photo

workers). The greatest risk of job loss is for workers who perform mundane and routine operations.

The real question becomes will these workers stay unemployed, or will they be able to retrain and transition into new jobs? Will younger workers choose to avoid jobs that can be easily automated? Consider that many of the best jobs available today didn't exist 50 years ago. In fact, current stock prices are reaching record highs, and unemployment rates are reaching near record lows in spite of the proliferation of automation and digitization in our lives. Nevertheless, some economists believe that this time it will be different and that the potential for mass unemployment is increasingly high.

Part of the driving force to automate many restaurant and hotel jobs is the plummeting cost of robots. One consulting company estimated that the cost of machines has dropped by about 40 percent since 2005.[4] Machines like Flippy are calculated to pay for themselves within a few years due in large part to the fact that they can run around the clock; do not take personal days or vacation time; and do not require extensive onboarding, training, or management. Consider the robotic barista from Café X. It costs $25,000, can make 150 cups of custom coffee per hour, and doesn't need to be tipped. The payback period is about 2 years, and then profits increase dramatically. How many baristas will need to be retrained after a major coffee shop chain sees the financial benefits of automation? Can they afford to stick with human labor if their competitors buy the Café X baristas?

Advocates for this type of automation also point out that the creation and use of machines add numerous jobs back into the economy. For example, the company developing these robots employs a lot of well-paid people. There are also people needed to sell, maintain, and replace these machines with newer models once they become antiquated. In fact, many argue that these new jobs provide better career opportunities than the jobs that are lost to automation. For you as a student, it has never been more important to choose the right college major—the first time around.

Questions

1. Take a few minutes to reflect on the nature of the work your friends do for a living. How many of those jobs could be outsourced to robots? What jobs wouldn't be outsourced?

2. When was the last time you interacted with a process that had been automated? What role did human workers previously fill? What roles are now carried out by machines? Is this automated process more efficient/effective now that it is automated? Are there ways in which humans were actually better at executing this process?

3. Flippy the burger-flipping robot has undergone rigorous testing before being deployed in restaurants. However, would you have any reservations about eating food prepared by a robot? Are there other applications of robots in which you would be uncomfortable with them replacing human workers?

4. The debate over promoting innovation/automation versus endangering jobs is a common theme in the news. Do you agree that workers and the overall economy will be able to adapt over time and replace as many jobs as are taken via automation?

and the manufacturer cannot obtain parts for the order in time. If so, the order schedule ought not to be approved. However, with such separated systems this situation is unknown.

Even if parts can be obtained, until the order is entered into the finished goods database, purchasing is unaware of the need to buy new parts. The same comment applies to manufacturing. Until the new order is entered into the manufacturing plan, the Production department doesn't know that it needs to increase manufacturing. And, as with parts, does the company have sufficient machine and floor capacity to fill the order on a timely basis? Does it have sufficient personnel with the correct skill sets? Should it be hiring? Can production meet the order schedule? No one knows before the order is approved.

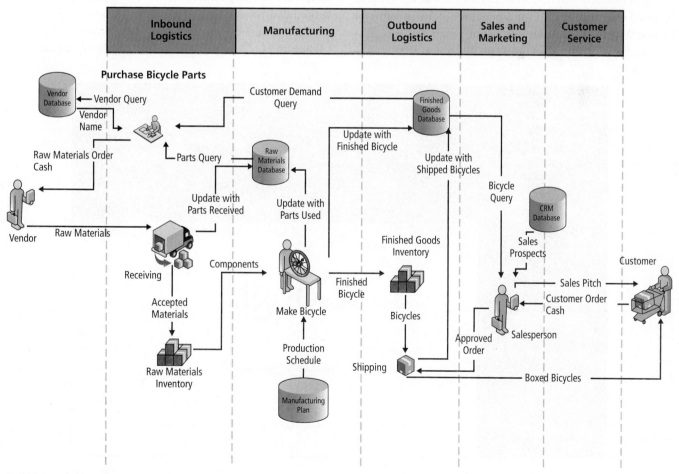

FIGURE 8-11
Pre-ERP Information Systems

ETHICS GUIDE

PAID DELETION

Robin wound her way up to the third floor of the parking garage. As she began backing up into her assigned spot, she noticed that the car she expected to see in her side mirror was not there. Rather, a shiny new luxury car was parked in that spot. The space occupied by the car belonged to Eric Pittman, a colleague on their employer's search engine optimization team. Robin and Eric had both worked for the company—a leading Web search provider—for about 5 years. Based on conversations they'd had while out for drinks after work, they had comparable salaries, too. Robin wondered how Eric could afford such a nice car considering they were both struggling to afford basic living expenses in such an expensive city.

Robin's thoughts turned to the meetings she had lined up all morning—she probably wouldn't be able to check her email until after lunch. With a grimace, she descended to the first floor in the elevator. She counted the number of days until the weekend and let out a groan.

Eraser for Hire

Eric and Robin burst out of the conference room as quickly as they could. It was almost 6 o'clock and they had just left their last meeting of the day. "Do you want to grab a bite to eat at that Greek place?" Eric asked. "Sure," Robin replied. "I am happy to go anywhere that's at least a mile from this office!" They jumped into their cars and met up at the restaurant. They gossiped about some of their colleagues and poked fun at their bosses while they waited for the food to arrive. Once it arrived and Eric picked up his gyro to take a bite, Robin noticed his brand-new luxury watch.

"Time out!" Robin exclaimed. "You need to tell me what is going on! I parked my car next to your brand-new set of wheels this morning. I didn't want to say anything, but I just noticed that you have a brand-new watch, too. Did you get some sort of bonus that I don't know about?" she asked, half-kidding and half-worried. She wondered why *she* wouldn't

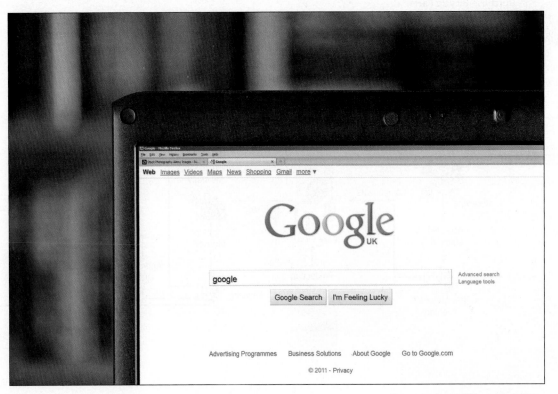

have received a bonus, too. Eric immediately had a concerned look on his face. "Can you keep a secret?" he asked.

Eric described an unraveling chain of events in which a number of companies operating in the area had approached him about the possibility of providing "reputation management" services. Each company had recently had some form of negative press, though each form was different. One large manufacturing company was dealing with environmental protection violations. A large retailer had to explain why it provided inadequate health benefits to its employees. A popular chain of restaurants had recently had a long list of health-code violations. The companies had come to Eric because his dad was a well-known consultant to many large companies in the area.

Each company had offered Eric a substantial financial incentive to tweak the results of Web searches using key terms relevant to these negative incidents. Eric had used his access to the search algorithms to make sure any negative press about these incidents showed up several pages deep in the search results, thus minimizing the likelihood that anyone would see them. In some cases, Eric even had the content completely removed from the search index.

Thanks to Eric, the negative stories had very little impact on the companies. His work limited the availability of information about these events via the search engine. "With what they paid me, I paid off my student loans, prepaid the lease on my apartment for a whole year, and still had some left over to treat myself a bit," he said with pride. "Are you interested in being a part of this?"

Robin was astounded. She couldn't imagine what would happen to Eric if someone found out what he had done. She also couldn't bring herself to think about what would happen to their employer if someone found out its search results had been manipulated. Not only could Eric be in trouble, but the company could be severely damaged. She could lose her job, too.

But now that she knew about Eric's actions, she worried that she might be considered an accessory to search engine manipulation if she didn't report his behavior. Robin took another bite of her gyro; it didn't taste nearly as good as it had about 20 minutes before.

DISCUSSION QUESTIONS

1. According to the definitions of the ethical principles previously defined in this book:
   a. Do you think that removing content on the Internet and manipulating search engine results for money is ethical according to the categorical imperative (page 23-24)?
   b. Do you think that removing content on the Internet and manipulating search engine results for money is ethical according to the utilitarian perspective (page 42-43)?

2. How might have Eric rationalized his fraudulent behavior?
3. How could an employer prevent this type of manipulation? What types of policies or procedures could be implemented to prevent this type of fraud?
4. Even if Eric were caught, would he be guilty of a crime? Which laws govern search engine management?
5. Would his employer be motivated to report this fraudulent behavior? Why or why not?

Figure 8-11 does not show accounting. We can assume, however, that the company has a separate accounting system that is similarly isolated. Eventually, records of business activity find their way to the Accounting department and will be posted into the general ledger. With such a pre-ERP system, financial statements are always outdated, available several weeks after the close of the quarter or other accounting period.

Contrast this situation with the ERP system in Figure 8-12. Here, all activity is processed by ERP application programs (called *modules*), and consolidated data are stored in a centralized ERP database. When Sales is confronted with the opportunity to sell 1,000 bicycles, the information it needs to confirm that the order, schedule, and terms are possible can be obtained from the ERP system immediately. Once the order is accepted, all departments, including purchasing, manufacturing, human resources, and accounting, are notified. Further, transactions are posted to the ERP database as they occur; the result is that financial statements are available quickly. In most cases, correct financial statements can be produced in real time. With such integration, ERP systems can display the current status of critical business factors to managers and executives, as shown in the sales dashboard in Figure 8-13.

Of course, the devil is in the details. It's one thing to draw a rectangle on a chart, label it "ERP Applications," and assume that data integration takes all the problems away. It is far more difficult

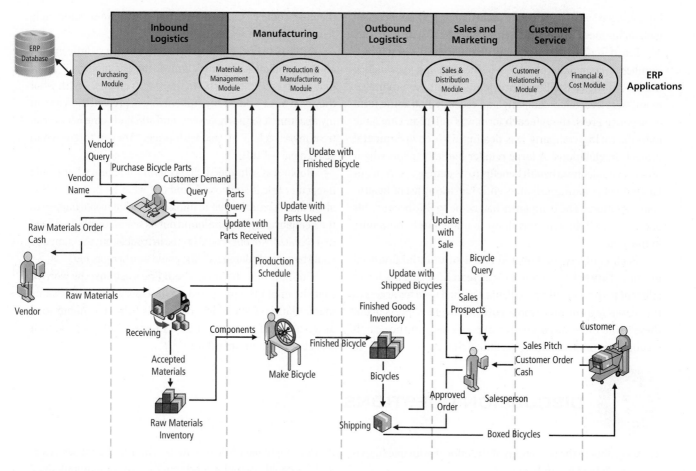

FIGURE 8-12
ERP Information Systems

to write those application programs and to design the database to store that integrated data. Even more problematic, what procedures should employees and others use to process those application programs? Specifically, for example, what actions should salespeople take before they approve a large order? Here are some of the questions that need to be answered or resolved:

- How does the Sales department determine that an order is considered large? By dollars? By volume?
- Who approves customer credit (and how)?
- Who approves production capacity (and how)?
- Who approves schedule and terms (and how)?
- What actions need to be taken if the customer modifies the order?
- How does management obtain oversight on sales activity?

As you can imagine, many other questions must be answered as well. Because of its importance to organizations today, we will discuss ERP in further detail in Q8-5. Before we do so, however, consider the third type of enterprise system: EAI.

Enterprise Application Integration (EAI)

ERP systems are not for every organization. For example, some nonmanufacturing companies find the manufacturing orientation of ERP inappropriate. Even for manufacturing companies, some find the process of converting from their current system to an ERP system too daunting. Others are quite satisfied with their manufacturing application systems and do not wish to change them.

Companies for which ERP is inappropriate still have the problems associated with information silos, however, and some choose to use **enterprise application integration (EAI)** to solve those

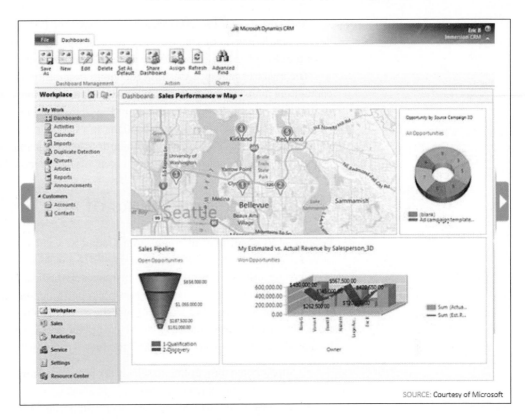

FIGURE 8-13

Sales Dashboard

Source: Windows 10, Microsoft Corporation.

problems. EAI is a suite of software applications that integrates existing systems by providing layers of software that connect applications together. EAI does the following:

- It connects system "islands" via a new layer of software/system.
- It enables existing applications to communicate and share data.
- It provides integrated information.
- It leverages existing systems—leaving functional applications as is but providing an integration layer over the top.
- It enables a gradual move to ERP.

The layers of EAI software shown in Figure 8-14 enable existing applications to communicate with each other and to share data. For example, EAI software can be configured to automatically carry out the data conversion required to make data compatible among different systems. When the CRM applications send data to the manufacturing application system, for example, the CRM system sends its data to an EAI software program. That EAI program makes the conversion and then sends the converted data to the ERP system. The reverse action is taken to send data back from the ERP to the CRM.

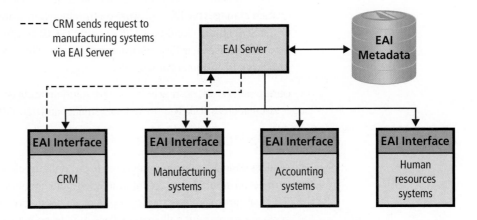

FIGURE 8-14

Design and Implementation for the Five Components

Although there is no centralized EAI database, the EAI software keeps files of metadata that describe data formats and locations. Users can access the EAI system to find the data they need. In some cases, the EAI system provides services that provide a "virtual integrated database" for the user to process.

The major benefit of EAI is that it enables organizations to use existing applications while eliminating many of the serious problems of isolated systems. Converting to an EAI system is not nearly as disruptive as converting to an ERP system, and it provides many of the benefits of ERP. Some organizations develop EAI applications as a stepping stone to complete ERP systems. Today, many EAI systems use Web services standards to define the interactions among EAI components. Some or all of the processing for those components can be moved to the cloud as well.

Q8-5 What Are the Elements of an ERP System?

Because of its importance to organizations today, we will consider ERP in more depth than CRM or EAI. To begin, the term *ERP* has been applied to a wide array of application solutions, in some cases erroneously. Some vendors attempted to catch the buzz for ERP by misapplying the term to applications that provided only one or two integrated functional applications.

The organization ERPsoftware360 publishes a wealth of information about ERP vendors, products, solutions, and applications. According to its Web site (*www.erpsoftware360.com/erp-101.htm*), for a product to be considered a true ERP product, it must include applications that integrate:

- Supply chain (procurement, sales order processing, inventory management, supplier management, and related activities)
- Manufacturing (scheduling, capacity planning, quality control, bill of materials, and related activities)
- CRM (sales prospecting, customer management, marketing, customer support, call center support)
- Human resources (payroll, time and attendance, HR management, commission calculations, benefits administration, and related activities)
- Accounting (general ledger, accounts receivable, accounts payable, cash management, fixed asset accounting)

An ERP solution is an information system and, as such, has all five components. We consider each in turn.

Hardware

Traditionally, organizations hosted ERP solutions on their own in-house, networked server computers. Such hosting is still the case for many large ERP applications, as well as for those ERP applications that were installed years ago and for which the hardware infrastructure is stable and well managed.

Increasingly, however, organizations are turning to cloud-based hosting in one of two modes:

- PaaS: Replace an organization's existing hardware infrastructure with hardware in the cloud. Install ERP software and databases on that cloud hardware. The using organization then manages the ERP software on the cloud hardware.
- SaaS: Acquire a cloud-based ERP solution. SAP, Oracle, Microsoft, and the other major ERP vendors offer their ERP software as a service. The vendor manages the ERP software and offers it to customers as a service.

During your career, existing in-house ERP solutions are likely to migrate to one of these two modes. Larger installations will likely move to PaaS; smaller and new ERP systems are likely to use SaaS.

ERP Application Programs

ERP vendors design application programs to be configurable so that development teams can alter them to meet an organization's requirements without changing program code. Accordingly, during the ERP development process, the development team sets configuration parameters that specify how ERP application programs will operate. For example, an hourly payroll application is configured to specify the number of hours in the standard workweek, hourly wages for different job categories, wage adjustments for overtime and holiday work, and so forth. Deciding on the initial configuration values and adapting them to new requirements is a challenging collaboration activity. It is also one that you might be involved in as a business professional.

Of course, there are limits to how much configuration can be done. If a new ERP customer has requirements that cannot be met via program configuration, then it needs to either adapt its business to what the software can do or write (or pay another vendor to write) application code to meet its requirements. As stated in Chapter 4, such custom programming is expensive, both initially and in long-term maintenance costs. Thus, choosing an ERP solution with applications that function close to the organization's requirements is critical to its successful implementation.

ERP Databases

An ERP solution includes a database design as well as initial configuration data. It does not, of course, contain the company's operational data. During development, the team must enter the initial values for that data as part of the development effort.

If your only experience with databases is creating a few tables in Microsoft Access, then you probably underestimate the value and importance of ERP database designs. SAP, the leading vendor of ERP solutions, provides ERP databases that contain more than 15,000 tables. The design includes the metadata for those tables, as well as their relationships to each other, and rules and constraints about how the data in some tables must relate to data in other tables. The ERP solution also contains tables filled with initial configuration data.

Reflect on the difficulty of creating and validating data models (as discussed in Chapter 5), and you will have some idea of the amount of intellectual capital invested in a database design of 15,000 tables. Also, consider the magnitude of the task of filling such a database with users' data!

Although we did not discuss this database feature in Chapter 5, large organizational databases contain two types of program code. The first, called a **trigger**, is a computer program stored within the database that runs to keep the database consistent when certain conditions arise. The second, called a **stored procedure**, is a computer program stored in the database that is used to enforce business rules. An example of such a rule would be never to sell certain items at a discount. Triggers and stored procedures are also part of the ERP solution. Developers and business users need to configure the operation of such code during the ERP implementation as well.

Business Process Procedures

Another component of an ERP solution is a set of inherent procedures that implement standard business processes. ERP vendors develop hundreds, or even thousands, of procedures that enable the ERP customer organization to accomplish its work using the applications provided by the vendor. Figure 8-15 shows a part of the SAP ordering business process; this process implements a portion of the inbound logistics activities. Some ERP vendors call the inherent processes that are defined in the ERP solution **process blueprints**.

Without delving into the details, you should be able to understand the flow of work outlined in this process. Every function (rounded rectangles in Figure 8-15) consists of a set of procedures for accomplishing that function. Typically, these procedures require an ERP user to use application menus, screens, and reports to accomplish the activity.

As with application programs, ERP users must either adapt to the predefined, inherent processes and procedures or design new ones. In the latter case, the design of new procedures may necessitate changes to application programs and to database structures as well. Perhaps you can begin to understand why organizations attempt to conform to vendor standards.

Training and Consulting

Because of the complexity and difficulty of implementing and using ERP solutions, ERP vendors have developed training curricula and numerous classes. SAP operates universities, in which customers and potential customers receive training both before and after the ERP implementation. In

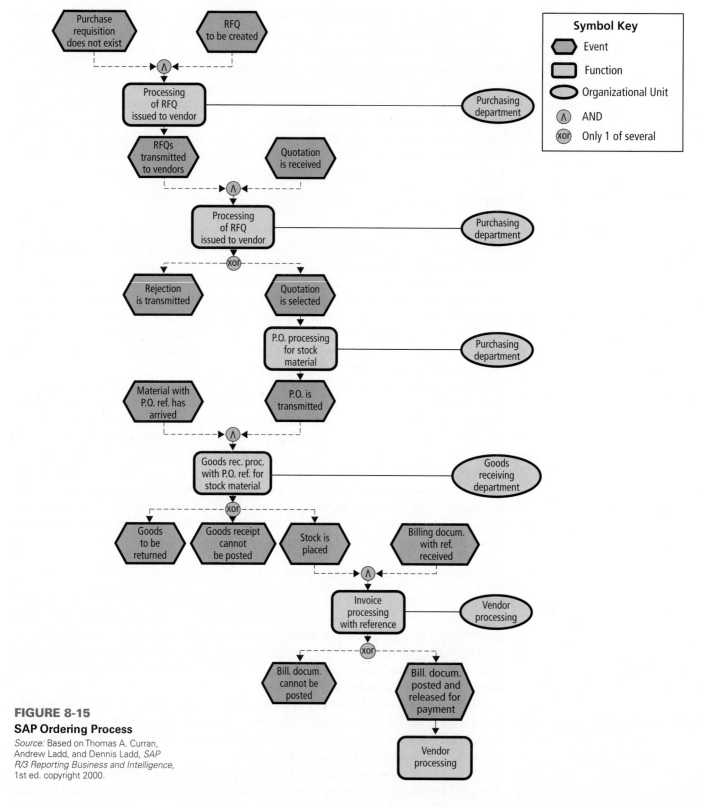

FIGURE 8-15
SAP Ordering Process

Source: Based on Thomas A. Curran,
Andrew Ladd, and Dennis Ladd, *SAP
R/3 Reporting Business and Intelligence,*
1st ed. copyright 2000.

addition, ERP vendors typically conduct classes on site. To reduce expenses, the vendors sometimes train the organization's employees, called Super Users, to become in-house trainers in training sessions called **train the trainer**.

ERP training falls into two broad categories. The first category is training about how to implement the ERP solution. This training includes topics such as obtaining top-level management support, preparing the organization for change, and dealing with the inevitable resistance that develops when people are asked to perform work in new ways. The second category is training on how to use the ERP application software; this training includes specific steps for using the ERP applications to accomplish the activities in processes such as those in Figure 8-15.

ERP vendors also provide on-site consulting for implementing and using the ERP system. Additionally, an industry of third-party ERP consultants has developed to support new ERP customers and implementations. These consultants provide knowledge gained through numerous ERP implementations. Such knowledge is valued because most organizations go through an ERP conversion only once. Ironically, having done so, they now know how to do it. Consequently, some employees, seasoned by an ERP conversion with their employer, leave that company to become ERP consultants.

Industry-Specific Solutions

As you can tell, considerable work needs to be done to customize an ERP application to a particular customer. To reduce that work, ERP vendors provide starter kits for specific industries called **industry-specific solutions**. These solutions contain program and database configuration files as well as process blueprints that apply to ERP implementations in specific industries. Over time, SAP, which first provided such solutions, and other ERP vendors created dozens of such starter kits for manufacturing, sales and distribution, healthcare, and other major industries.

Which Companies Are the Major ERP Vendors?

Although more than 100 different companies advertise ERP products, not all of those products meet the minimal ERP criteria. Of those that do, the bulk of the market is held by the five vendors shown in Figure 8-16.[5] SAP and Oracle serve the largest organizations. Microsoft, Infor ERP, and Epicor products primarily serve midsize to small companies.

The ERP market is mature and facing stiff competition from SaaS competitors. According to *Forbes*, four of 10 large organizations will have at least 60 percent of their ERP applications in the

FIGURE 8-16
Characteristics of Top ERP Vendors

Source: Based on Panorama Consulting Solutions, "Clash of the Titans 2017," Panorama-consulting.com, November 2015, *http://go.panorama-consulting.com/rs/603-UJX-107/images/Clash-of-the-Titans-2017.pdf.*

Company	Market Share	Remarks
SAP	21 percent	Market leader in client-server implementations. Expensive. Many consider it to be the gold standard of ERP.
Microsoft	16 percent	Microsoft AX, which is popular in Europe, is primarily used in manufacturing. Other products have smaller revenue. Dynamics CRM is offered as SaaS, but no full ERP solution is offered in the cloud.
Oracle	13 percent	Intensely competitive company with strong technology base. Large customer base. Flexible SOA architecture. Will leverage strong technology base into innovative and effective cloud-based solutions. Strong challenge to SAP market leadership.
Infor ERP	13 percent	Many solutions, not integrated, particularly specialized for manufacturing and supply chain management. Evolving with revolution in 3D printing practices.
Epicor	4 percent	Leading ERP provider for midsize companies. Many applications to provide clients with custom solutions.

cloud by 2020.[6] The $43 billion cloud ERP market will continue to mature, consolidation of vendors is likely, and smaller vendors will fall out entirely. In fact, the top 10 vendors own 64 percent of the market share, and the top five, listed in Figure 8-16, own 55 percent.[7]

The cloud is having a major impact on ERP vendors. Those with substantial resources (SAP) and deep technical talent (Oracle) are moving their product suites into some version of SaaS, PaaS, or IaaS. Others are unable to convert to the new technology and are gradually losing their customers to those who have converted or to new companies that have only ever offered cloud-based ERP solutions. Among organizations that use ERP, the movement from classical client/server ERP to the cloud will likely be a major business challenge during the early years of your career.

Q8-6 What Are the Challenges of Implementing and Upgrading Enterprise Information Systems?

Implementing new enterprise systems, whether CRM, ERP, or EAI, is challenging, difficult, expensive, and risky. It is not unusual for enterprise system projects to be well over budget and a year or more late. In addition to new ERP implementations, numerous organizations implemented ERP 15 or 20 years ago and now need to upgrade their ERP installation to meet new requirements. If you work in an organization that is already using enterprise systems, you may find yourself engaged in a significant upgrade effort. Whether from a new implementation or an upgrade, expense and risks arise from five primary factors (see Figure 8-17).

Collaborative Management

Unlike departmental systems in which a single department manager is in charge, enterprise systems have no clear boss. Examine the discharge process in Figure 8-7; there is no manager of discharge. The discharge process is a collaborative effort among many departments (and customers).

With no single manager, who resolves the disputes that inevitably arise? All of these departments ultimately report to the CEO, so there is a single boss over all of them, but employees can't go to the CEO with a problem about, say, coordinating discharge activities between nursing and housekeeping. The CEO would throw them out of his or her office. Instead, the organization needs to develop some sort of collaborative management for resolving process issues.

Usually this means that the enterprise develops committees and steering groups for providing enterprise process management. Although this can be an effective solution, and in fact may be the *only* solution, the work of such groups is both slow and expensive.

Requirements Gaps

As stated in Q8-4, few organizations today create their own enterprise systems from scratch. Instead, they license an enterprise product that provides specific functions and features and that includes inherent procedures. But such licensed products are never a perfect fit. Almost always there are gaps between the organization's requirements and the application's capabilities.

- Collaborative management
- Requirements gaps
- Transition problems
- Employee resistance
- New technology

FIGURE 8-17
Five Primary Factors

The first challenge is identifying the gaps. To specify a gap, an organization must know both what it needs and what the new product does. However, it can be very difficult for an organization to determine what it needs; that difficulty is one reason organizations choose to license rather than to build. Further, the features and functions of complex products like CRM or ERP are not easy to identify. Thus, gap identification is a major task when implementing enterprise systems.

The second challenge is deciding what to do with gaps, once they are identified. Either the organization needs to change the way it does things to adapt to the new application, or the application must be altered to match what the organization does. Either choice is problematic. Employees will resist change, but paying for alterations is expensive, and, as noted in Chapter 4, the organization is committing to maintaining those alterations as the application is changed over time. Here, organizations fill gaps by choosing their lesser regret.

Transition Problems

Transitioning to a new enterprise system is also difficult. The organization must somehow change from using isolated departmental systems to using the new enterprise system, while continuing to run the business. It's like having heart surgery while running a 100-yard dash.

Such transitions require careful planning and substantial training. Inevitably, problems will develop. Knowing this will occur, senior management needs to communicate the need for the change to the employees and then stand behind the new system as the kinks are worked out. It is an incredibly stressful time for all involved. We will discuss development techniques and implementation strategies further in Chapter 10.

Employee Resistance

People resist change. Change requires effort and engenders fear. Considerable research and literature exist about the reasons for change resistance and how organizations can deal with it. Here we will summarize the major principles.

First, senior-level management needs to communicate the need for the change to the organization and reiterate this, as necessary, throughout the transition process. Second, employees fear change because it threatens **self-efficacy**, which is a person's belief that he or she can be successful at his or her job. To enhance confidence, employees need to be trained and coached on the successful use of the new system. Word-of-mouth is a very powerful factor, and in some cases key users are trained ahead of time to create positive buzz about the new system. Video demonstrations of employees successfully using the new system are also effective.

Third, in many ways, the primary benefits of a new ERP system are felt by the accounting and finance departments and the senior management. Many of the employees who are asked to change their activities to implement ERP will not receive any direct benefit from it. Therefore, employees may need to be given extra inducement to change to the new system. As one experienced change consultant said, "Nothing succeeds like praise or cash, especially cash." Straight-out pay for change is bribery, but contests with cash prizes among employees or groups can be very effective at inducing change.

Implementing new enterprise systems can solve many problems and bring great efficiency and cost savings to an organization, but it is not for the faint of heart.

New Technology

Emerging, new technology affects all information systems, but it affects enterprise systems particularly because of their importance and their value. Consider, for example, the cloud. Because of the cost savings of cloud-based computing, organizations would like to move their enterprise systems to the cloud. But legal, risk, and business policy factors may make such a move infeasible. The organization may be required to keep physical control over its data. When moving it to the cloud, the cloud vendor controls the physical location of the data, and that location might not even be in the same country as the organization. So, some sort of hybrid model may need to be devised (see Q8-8).

Similar comments pertain to mobile technology. Employees want to use mobile devices to access and even modify enterprise system data. But mobile devices are just that—mobile. The enterprise system may be exposed to considerable risk while outside the control of the organization. And ERP data is a juicy target for crime. These factors don't mean organizations cannot use new technology with enterprise systems, but they do add challenges.

Q8-7 How Do Inter-Enterprise IS Solve the Problems of Enterprise Silos?

The discussion in Q8-4 illustrates the primary ways in which enterprise systems solve the problems of workgroup information silos. In this question, we will use the ARES example to show you how inter-enterprise systems can accomplish the same for enterprise silos. (The transition is shown by the lower arrow leading to the bottom row in Figure 8-6, page 303.)

Figure 8-18 shows the information silos that exist among employers, health clubs, and principal ARES home users. Employers may maintain records of exercise programs, diet, weight, lab test results (e.g., cholesterol, blood sugar, etc.), and biometric readings from wearables (e.g., steps taken, heart rate, sleep patterns, etc.). Health clubs store membership, class, personal trainer, and exercise performance data in a club database. Data is gathered automatically from virtual cycling classes or from on-premises exercise equipment and member heart monitors. At home, individuals generate exercise data on heart monitors and equipment; that data is recorded on mobile devices via wearable exercise devices.

The isolation of this exercise data causes problems. For example, employers would like to have reports on exercise data stored in user devices and in health clubs. Users would like to have data like lab test results from their employer, as well as exercise data from their time at health clubs. Health clubs would like to have lab results and home workout data to integrate with the data they have. All three entities would like to produce reports from the integrated data.

Figure 8-19 shows the structure of an inter-enterprise system that meets the goals of the three types of participants. In this figure, the labeled rectangles inside the cloud represent mobile applications that could be native, thin-client, or both. Some of the application processing might be done on cloud servers as well as on the mobile devices. Those design decisions are not shown. As illustrated, this system assumes that all users receive reports on mobile devices, but because of the large amount of keying involved, employers submit and manage lab results using a personal computer.

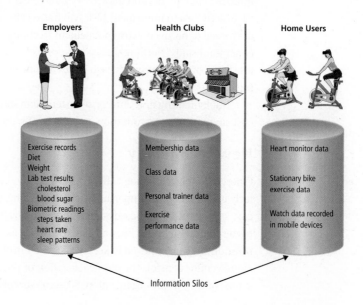

FIGURE 8-18
Information Silos Without ARES

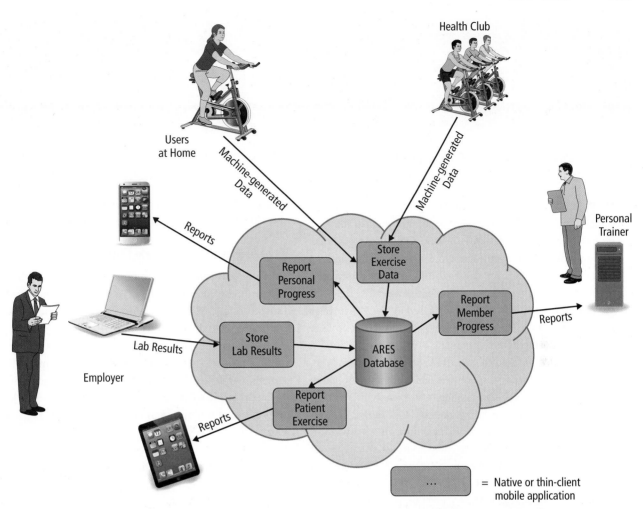

FIGURE 8-19
Inter-Enterprise ARES System

As you can see, lab results and exercise data are integrated in the ARES database; that integrated data is processed by a reporting application (Chapter 3) to create and distribute the reports as shown.

Systems like that shown in Figure 8-19 are referred to as **distributed systems** because applications processing is distributed across multiple computing devices. Standards such as http, https, html5, css3, JavaScript, and SOA using Web services enable programs to receive data from and display data to a variety of mobile and desktop devices.

ARES data is requested and delivered using JSON.

Q8-8 2029?

Within the next 10 years, ERP vendors and customers will have sorted out the problems of cloud-based ERP. In what is coming to be known as the **hybrid model**, ERP customers will store most of their data on cloud servers managed by cloud vendors and store sensitive data on servers that they manage themselves. Governmental agencies, financial analysts, and accountants will have defined standards against which organizations can be monitored for appropriate compliance. By the way, if you graduate as an accountant or financial analyst, this is interesting work in which you could be involved early in your career.

Mobility, however, will still present problems in 2029. Workers in the warehouse, loading dock, and shipping department will all carry mobile devices that enable them to process ERP and other

SECURITY GUIDE

IT'S NOT ME . . . IT'S YOU

If you have ever been asked to leave a job, then you understand how difficult it is. Learning that your services are no longer needed is stressful. Compounding the stresses are tense moments with managers and awkward interactions with coworkers. However, the realization that you now need to secure some other means of employment is often the most discouraging part. You may be surprised to learn that these factors commonly lead exiting employees to take advantage of their last moments with their employers.

A survey of 945 adults who had been laid off, been fired, or changed jobs in the past year revealed some startling statistics. Sixty percent reported stealing data from their employer before their employment ended. Seventy-nine percent admitted to knowing that taking company data with them was not permitted. They reported taking email lists, customers contact lists, employee records, and financial information.[8] It has been

estimated that the financial damages inflicted by these types of incidents range from $5,000 to $3 million per incident.[9]

White Collar . . . Dark Deeds

You may be wondering what factors contribute to the widespread theft of company data. To get "inside the minds" of data-stealing employees, we must look at the "fraud triangle." The fraud triangle contends that *pressure, opportunity,* and *rationalization* are the three key factors that govern an individual's propensity to commit white-collar crime.[10] In this context, employees in the process of leaving a company are pressured to find a job. They often think that they can increase the chances of finding a new position if they bring data assets with them. This is especially true if they are targeting a position at their employer's key competitor. What many employees fail to realize is that confidential customer lists and intellectual

property are considered proprietary and are often governed by nondisclosure agreements. Giving this information to a new employer will likely harm them, not help them.

Factor two—opportunity—has continually increased over the past decade as interactions among employees, systems, and data have drastically changed. The rise of *telecommuting*—employees working from home—and the ability of employees to access their employer's data in the cloud have opened up countless opportunities for theft of data and intellectual assets. Shockingly, the employee survey also revealed that almost a quarter of employees said they still had the ability to connect to their employer's network after their employment had ended.[11] That's an opportunity!

Finally, rationalization is an element of data theft because employees have often created the data that they are attempting to take with them. They feel a sense of justification for taking the data because they created it.

I'm Not Disgruntled . . . Are You?

In light of the ample opportunities for employees to take data from their companies and the feelings of pressure and rationalization for doing so, organizations are working to develop predictive tools that will help identify employees who may be preparing to steal data. A data loss prevention expert commented on the inadequacy of existing theft-prevention solutions by saying that most organizations fail to have the technological infrastructure in place to identify accidental employee dissemination of sensitive information. Identification of intentional, malicious incidents is even more difficult.[12]

The tools that are being developed to identify potential data theft search, monitor, analyze, and visualize the data originating from Web sites, applications, servers, networks, sensors, and mobile devices.[13] Encryption and continual monitoring of stored data are other tactics that can be used to thwart data theft. This includes encrypting and monitoring data stored within the organization and with third parties like the cloud vendors mentioned in Chapter 6.

Most importantly, companies need to ensure that HR departments and technology groups are collaborating in real time to ensure that employee access to internal systems is revoked when an employee's time with the company has come to an end.

DISCUSSION QUESTIONS

1. Have you ever witnessed someone stealing something at work? If so, it was probably apparent to both you and the perpetrator that he or she was doing something wrong. Why do you think employees are so willing to steal data but might be hesitant to steal tangible items like cash, laptops, or other expensive organizational assets?

2. Take a moment to search the Internet for cases of white-collar crime. Find a specific example and see if you can identify the three elements of the fraud triangle as being factors that contributed to that crime being committed.

3. How do you feel about the fact that many companies are investing in tools to monitor employee behavior? Would you want to work for a company that regularly audits your emails and analyzes your activity on the company's network?

4. The article mentions that encryption can be a tactic used to thwart employees from taking data with them. Explain how encryption can be used effectively in this context.

enterprise applications from wherever they happen to be. Managers, decision makers, and other knowledge workers will have similar applications on their own phones or other mobile devices, devices that they can access from work, other offices, the street, or home.

However—and it's an enormous however—mobile devices are subject to severe security threats. Putting data online does make it easier to access. That's true for the good guys, but it's also true for the bad guys. In 2015 Anthem Inc., the largest for-profit healthcare company in the United States, lost healthcare records for 80 million people. Consider the enormity of that single data breach. There are only 320 million people in the United States. That means a single company lost records for one out of every four people you know—including the author of your textbook! Even worse, in 2017 Yahoo! lost all of its 3 billion user accounts. That's nearly half the people on the planet.

Consider what would happen if some criminal, perhaps a malicious insider, were to infiltrate an ERP system. It would be possible to wreak havoc in, say, supply chain orders and inventories or in the operation of machinery on the factory floor. The hacked organization would have to shut down its ERP system, and thus its company, to sort out the mess. But allowing users mobile access to the ERP system will enable organizations to make significant improvements in process quality.

CAREER GUIDE

Source: Ben Peters, Anaconda, Inc, Software/Platform Engineer

Name: Ben Peters
Company: Anaconda, Inc.
Job Title: Software/Platform Engineer
Education: Carnegie Mellon University, Longwood University

1 How did you get this type of job?

I had been working in the industry for about 2 years after graduate school and was passively exploring new opportunities. An HR representative from Anaconda reached out to me about a job opening via LinkedIn, and it sounded exactly like what I was looking for. I spoke with the VP of engineering about the role and was given an interview assignment to complete over the weekend. I really wanted the job, so I spent a considerable amount of time working on the coding assignment. I went in for an onsite interview the following week where they asked me technical questions about data structures, cloud computing, and infrastructure tooling. We also went over the coding assignment. My hard work paid off, and I was given an offer later that week.

2 What attracted you to this field?

Big Data and machine learning are two of the hottest technology trends today, and Anaconda is an integral part of those communities. I love working to solve the challenges the industry faces and having the potential to change the world. When I was exploring majors in college, I looked at factors like job demand outlook and salary potential, too. I wanted to be a part of a growing industry with lots of potential.

3 What does a typical workday look like for you (duties, decisions, problems)?

We practice Agile software development at Anaconda, so each morning the team meets for a standup to discuss what each member is working on and whether there are any roadblocks. The rest of the day is spent coding and working through technical problems with other team members. As part of the Agile method, we commit to delivering new product features at the end of every 2-week period. This can be intense but is also enjoyable and rewarding.

4 What do you like most about your job?

Anaconda is a young and fairly small company, so I feel a great sense of ownership over the product. Before coming here, I was working for large Fortune 100 companies where I did not have that feeling. I get to work with and learn from some of the best talent in the field, and the company is highly respected among the open source and data science communities. It feels good to always get a positive reaction from other software engineers when I tell them where I work.

5 What skills would someone need to do well at your job?

Software engineers today need to be versatile. Technology is always changing, so you need to be willing to constantly learn and adapt. It's good to be fluent in multiple programming languages and frameworks and have a solid understanding of databases, Linux, and cloud computing. Modern software engineers should be knowledgable about DevOps and infrastructure automation tools as well.

6 Are education or certifications important in your field? Why?

Education and certifications are important because they give you a competitive advantage in the field. It's equivalent to having a trusted third party who can vouch for the skills you claim to have. Even though good software engineers are in high demand, the field is still very competitive for the positions that you likely want. There are many online courses and certifications you can pursue after graduating to help you stay on top and give you an edge.

7 **What advice would you give to someone who is considering working in your field?**

Practice, practice, and more practice! Try to get as much hands-on experience as you can while you are in school so you will stand out to future employers. Focus on grasping the fundamentals of software development, design, and architecture, and you will have a great career.

8 **What do you think will be hot tech jobs in 10 years?**

Internet of Things (IoT), virtual and augmented reality (VR/AR), machine learning and deep learning (ML/DL), artificial intelligence (AI), and quantum computing will all likely be hot engineering jobs in the near future. Some of these are already in high demand today, but I believe they will be a much bigger part of our daily life 10 years from now.

So, in the next 10 years, organizations must engage in a delicate balancing act between risk of loss and improvement to processes. We will discuss such trade-offs further in Chapter 10.

Consider also the effect of the Internet of Things. Future users of ERP systems will be not just people but also devices and machines. ERP vendors are adapting their software to the particular requirements of 3D printing. In the future, when a salesperson enters an order, he or she may be starting a machine to make that part on demand. In addition, factory automation will also add to process quality improvements. Inventory-picking robots are one example, but self-driving cars and trucks are likely to have an even larger effect. And within the next 10 years, machines will be able to employ the ERP system to schedule their own maintenance. For example, on the factory floor a milling machine will be able to order a replacement for a dull cutter, one possibly made by a 3D printer. Machines will schedule both routine and emergency maintenance for themselves, thus carrying factory automation to a new level.

As we have stated many times so far, the future belongs not to those who specialize in existing methods, technology, and processes but rather to those who can find and implement innovative applications of emerging trends. Technology's effect on enterprise systems will be widespread because enterprise systems are widespread. Many opportunities will occur in the early years of your career.

FIGURE 8-20
Designing a Future ERP System
Source: Tom Wang/Fotolia

ACTIVE REVIEW

Use this Active Review to verify that you understand the ideas and concepts that answer the chapter's study questions.

Q8-1   What are the basic types of processes?

Define *structured* and *dynamic processes* and compare and contrast them. Define *workgroup processes*, *enterprise processes*, and *inter-enterprise processes* and explain their differences and challenges. Define those same levels of information systems. Define *functional systems* and *functional applications*.

Q8-2   How can information systems improve process quality?

Name, define, and give an example of two dimensions of process quality. Name and describe three ways that organizations can improve process quality. Name and describe three ways that information systems can be used to improve process quality.

Q8-3   How do information systems eliminate the problems of information silos?

Define *information silo* and explain how such silos come into existence. When do such silos become a problem? Describe the two types of silos in Figure 8-6 and explain the meaning implied by the two arrows.

Q8-4   How do CRM, ERP, and EAI support enterprise processes?

Define *business process reengineering* and explain why it is difficult and expensive. Explain two major reasons why developing enterprise information systems in-house is expensive. Explain the advantages of inherent processes. Define and differentiate among *CRM*, *ERP*, and *EAI*. Explain how the nature of CRM and ERP is more similar to each other than that of EAI.

Q8-5   What are the elements of an ERP system?

Describe the minimum capability of a true ERP product. Explain the nature of each of the following ERP solution components: programs, data, procedures, and training and consulting. For each, summarize the work that customers must perform. List the top five ERP vendors in decreasing order of market share.

Q8-6   What are the challenges of implementing and upgrading enterprise information systems?

Name and describe five sources of challenges when implementing enterprise systems. Describe why enterprise systems management must be collaborative. Explain two major tasks required to identify requirements gaps. Summarize the challenges of transitioning to an enterprise system. Explain why employees resist change and describe three ways of responding to that resistance. Discuss the challenges that new technology poses for enterprise systems.

Q8-7   How do inter-enterprise IS solve the problems of enterprise silos?

Describe information silos that exist among employers health clubs, and individuals with regard to exercise data. Describe problems that those silos create. Explain how the system shown in Figure 8-19 will solve the problems caused by those silos. Define *distributed systems* and explain the benefits of SOA using Web services when implementing such systems.

Q8-8   2029?

Describe how the cloud, mobility, and the Internet of Things will affect enterprise systems in the next 10 years. Explain how these factors will create opportunities for business professionals. Explain how they will create opportunities for you!

Using Your Knowledge with ARES

Knowledge of this chapter will help you understand the fundamental value offered by solutions like ARES, namely the elimination of the problems of enterprise-level information silos. As you now know, silos caused by workgroup processes can be eliminated (or managed, in the case of EAI) with enterprise systems. Similarly, silos caused by enterprise processes can be eliminated with inter-enterprise systems like ARES Also, the knowledge of this chapter prepares you to understand the difficulty of adapting and of managing inter-enterprise systems. Finally, Figure 8-19 helps you understand how mobile devices and a cloud database can be used to implement an inter-enterprise system.

KEY TERMS AND CONCEPTS

Business process reengineering 305
Customer life cycle 305
Customer relationship management
    (CRM) system 306
Data integrity 302
Distributed systems 321
Dynamic processes 296
Enterprise application integration
    (EAI) 312
Enterprise information system 299
Enterprise processes 299

Enterprise resource planning (ERP) 307
ERP system 307
Functional application 297
Functional information systems 297
Hybrid model 321
Industry-specific solutions 317
Information silo 301
Inherent processes 305
Inter-enterprise information
    systems 299
Inter-enterprise processes 299

Modules 307
Process blueprints 315
Process effectiveness 299
Process efficiency 299
Self-efficacy 319
Stored procedure 319
Structured processes 296
Train the trainer 316
Trigger 315
Workgroup information system 297
Workgroup process 297

MyLab MIS

To complete the problems with MyLab MIS, go to EOC Discussion Questions in the MyLab.

USING YOUR KNOWLEDGE

8-1. *MyLab MIS* Using the example of your university, give examples of information systems for each of the three levels of scope (workgroup, enterprise, and inter-enterprise) discussed in Q8-1. Describe three departmental information systems likely to duplicate data. Explain how the characteristics of these systems relate to your examples.

8-2. *MyLab MIS* In your answer to question 8-1, explain how the three workgroup information systems create information silos. Describe the kinds of problems these silos are likely to cause. Refer to the discussion in Q8-3 as a guide.

8-3. *MyLab MIS* Using your answer to question 8-2, describe an enterprise information system that will eliminate the silos. Would the implementation of your system require business process reengineering? Explain why or why not.

8-4. Google or Bing each of the top five ERP vendors discussed in Q8-5. In what ways have their product offerings changed since this text was written? Do these vendors have new products? Have they made important acquisitions? Have they been acquired? Have any new companies made important inroads into their market share?

8-5. Using the knowledge you gained from Chapters 4 and 6, how do you think mobile systems and the cloud will affect ERP solutions? Explain how mobile ERP might benefit the types of personnel discussed in the bicycle manufacturing example from Q8-4.

COLLABORATION EXERCISE 8

Using the collaboration IS you built in Chapter 1 (page 32), collaborate with a group of students to answer the following questions.

The county planning office issues building permits, septic system permits, and county road access permits for all building projects in a county in an eastern state. The planning office issues permits to homeowners and builders for the construction of new homes and buildings and for any remodeling projects that involve

electrical, gas, plumbing, and other utilities, as well as the conversion of unoccupied spaces, such as garages, into living or working space. The office also issues permits for new or upgraded septic systems and permits to provide driveway entrances to county roads.

Figure 8-21 shows the permit process that the county used for many years. Contractors and homeowners found this process slow and very frustrating. For one, they did not like its sequential nature.

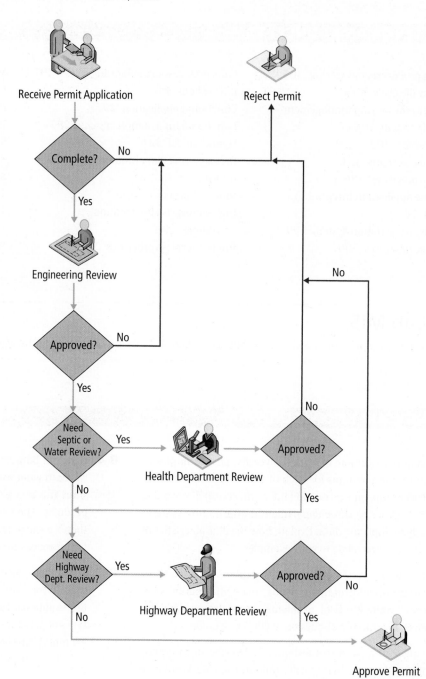

FIGURE 8-21
Building Permit Process, Old Version

Only after a permit had been approved or rejected by the engineering review process would they find out that a health or highway review was also needed. Because each of these reviews could take 3 or 4 weeks, applicants requesting permits wanted the review processes to be concurrent rather than serial. Also, both the permit applicants and county personnel were frustrated because they never knew where a particular application was in the permit process. A contractor would call to ask how much longer, and it might take an hour or longer just to find which desk the permits were on.

Accordingly, the county changed the permit process to that shown in Figure 8-22. In this second process, the permit office made three copies of the permit and distributed one to each department. The departments reviewed the permits in parallel; a clerk would analyze the results and, if there were no rejections, approve the permit.

Unfortunately, this process had a number of problems, too. For one, some of the permit applications were lengthy; some included as many as 40 to 50 pages of large architectural drawings. The labor and copy expense to the county was considerable.

Second, in some cases departments reviewed documents unnecessarily. If, for example, the highway department rejected an application, then neither the engineering nor health departments needed to continue their reviews. At first, the county

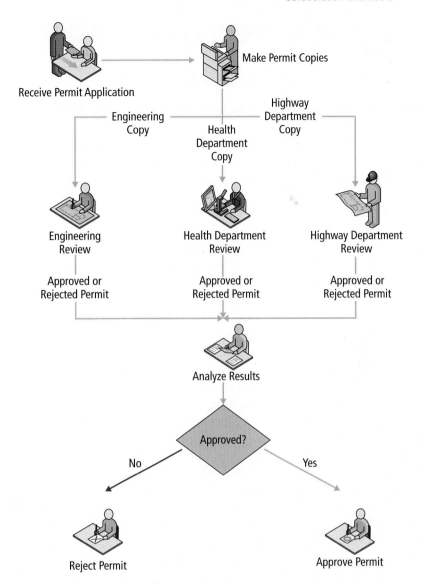

FIGURE 8-22
Building Permit Process,
Revised Version

Receive Permit Application

Make Permit Copies

Engineering Copy

Health Department Copy

Highway Department Copy

Engineering Review

Health Department Review

Highway Department Review

Approved or Rejected Permit

Approved or Rejected Permit

Approved or Rejected Permit

Analyze Results

Approved?

No

Yes

Reject Permit

Approve Permit

responded to this problem by having the clerk who analyzed results cancel the reviews of other departments when a rejection was received. However, that policy was exceedingly unpopular with the permit applicants, because once the problem in a rejected application was corrected, the permit had to go back through the other departments. The permit would go to the end of the line and work its way back into the departments from which it had been pulled. Sometimes this resulted in a delay of 5 or 6 weeks.

Cancelling reviews was unpopular with the departments as well, because permit-review work had to be repeated. An application might have been nearly completed when it was cancelled due to a rejection in another department. When the application came through again, the partial work results from the earlier review were lost.

8-6. Explain why the processes in Figures 8-21 and 8-22 are classified as enterprise processes rather than departmental processes. Why are these processes not interorganizational processes?

8-7. Using Figure 8-8 as an example, redraw Figure 8-21 using an enterprise information system that processes a shared database. Explain the advantages of this system over the paper-based system in Figure 8-21.

8-8. Using Figure 8-10 as an example, redraw Figure 8-22 using an enterprise information system that processes a shared database. Explain the advantages of this system over the paper-based system in Figure 8-22.

8-9. Assuming that the county has just changed from the system in Figure 8-21 to the one in Figure 8-22, which of your answers in questions 8-7 and 8-8 do you think is better? Justify your answer.

8-10. Assume your team is in charge of the implementation of the system you recommend in your answer to question 8-9. Describe how each of the five challenges discussed in Q8-6 pertain to this implementation. Explain how your team will deal with those challenges.

A Tale of Two Interorganizational IS

The Affordable Care Act (also known as Obamacare) requires the creation of healthcare exchanges that necessitate the development of interorganizational information systems. States were encouraged to set up exchanges for their own residents, but if they elected not to do so, the states' residents could use an exchange developed by the federal government. About half of the states decided to use the federal exchange. The remainder developed their own exchanges (and supporting information systems). These many parallel development projects give us a unique opportunity to learn from the experience of similar projects that had, in some cases, very different outcomes.

Consider, for example, Connecticut and Oregon. The state of Connecticut created an exchange named *Access CT*. It was delivered on time and on budget and has been such a success that the state of Maryland stopped developing its own system and licensed the Access CT solution instead.[14] Other states are considering licensing Access CT as well. On the other hand, the state of Oregon created an exchange named *Cover Oregon* that was a complete and utter failure. Cover Oregon was never operable despite costing more than $248 million in U.S. and Oregon tax dollars. In May 2014, the U.S. attorney's office in Portland opened a grand jury investigation into the project.[15]

Why were there such different outcomes? The two states started their projects about the same time, they had the same scope and goals, they began with about the same funding (Cover Oregon eventually spent nearly twice as much as Access CT), and they had the same required finish date. There is no substantial difference in the population of the two states; Connecticut has about 3.5 million people and Oregon about 3.9 million. What caused the different outcomes?

What Is a Healthcare Exchange?

To begin, a healthcare exchange is an online store that offers health insurance products to individuals and small businesses. Choosing medical insurance is a complex process with many different levels of coverage and costs, and selecting the right policy is difficult and confusing for most people. Exchanges are thus created not only to offer medical insurance policies, but also to simplify and partially automate the selection process. Exchanges also promote fair competition among health insurers.

Besides simplifying the selection of health insurance, another goal for exchanges is to help consumers navigate the complex array of governmental assistance options and possibilities. Depending on income, family size, and other circumstances, some consumers are entitled to Medicare and a variety of other governmental programs. Thus, when using an exchange, a consumer provides personal data about income and family situation, and the exchange uses automation to contact various governmental agencies to determine that consumer's eligibility. Given this determination, the exchange then offers insurance products appropriate to that particular consumer's situation. Exchanges are supposed to pay for themselves by charging a modest fee to insurers.

Figure 8-23 shows some of the organizations involved in a healthcare exchange. Clearly, an interorganizational information system is needed. As you know from this chapter, such projects are difficult to develop and manage, and it is not surprising that some states failed.

Access CT

Access CT is a quasi-public corporation. The chairman of the board is Connecticut's Lieutenant Governor, Nancy Wyman, who set out in the summer of 2012 to find an appropriate CEO. A nationwide search identified 74 candidates, and in July 2012, the Connecticut governor hired Kevin Counihan.

Counihan had more than 30 years of experience working in the insurance industry and had been a key player in the development of the Massachusetts healthcare system (widely regarded as the model for Obamacare). Most recently, he had been the president of a private health exchange in California.[16]

Counihan holds a master's degree in marketing, and it shows. As soon as he was hired, he began a series of press conferences to explain the nature and goals of the project to the public. Within a few months, Counihan hired senior staff with deep experience in insurance, including Jim Wadleigh, Chief Information Officer. Wadleigh had been director of application development for CIGNA, a health services organization.[17] Wadleigh's primary assignment was to hire and manage an outside contractor to develop the exchange Web site and supporting back-end code and to manage the implementation of the exchange information system.

By June 2012, Access CT had created a project plan and begun a search for the contractor to develop the site. By September 2012, it selected Deloitte Consulting LLP. At the time, Wadleigh stated, "With only 12 months until the Exchange goes live, we look forward to beginning our work with them immediately."[18]

That summer, in an interview on July 13, a local press reporter asked CEO Counihan, "Can you get it done on time?" His response: "This state's going to get it done in time."[19]

And it did. By the end of the federally mandated deadline, Access CT had enrolled 208,301 Connecticut residents,[20] and Connecticut had become a model for state-run exchanges.

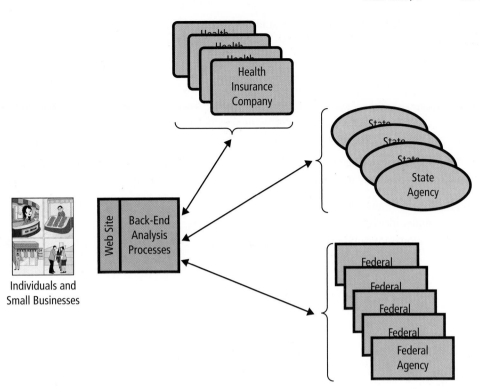

FIGURE 8-23
Healthcare Exchange
Interorganizational IS

Cover Oregon

The outcome was not so positive in Oregon. After spending nearly $250 million, the exchange was clearly inoperable, and the exchange's board of directors decided to stop development and utilize the federal exchange instead.[21] After this decision, the Oregon legislature hired an independent company, First Data Corporation, to investigate the causes of this debacle.[22]

Unlike in Connecticut, neither Oregon's governor nor any other elected official was directly involved in the project. In fact, in January 2014, the governor stated that he'd only become aware of the failure in "late October."[23] The site was to have gone operational on October 1, and it strains credulity to believe that it took 3 weeks for the news of the failure to reach him. In any case, it is safe to assume the governor was not a "hands-on manager" of the project, nor did he delegate any senior elected official to take that role.

According to First Data,[24] from the onset, the project suffered from divided direction. Cover Oregon is a quasi-independent corporation as is Access CT, but the exchange information system was to be developed by a different governmental agency, Oregon Health Authority (OHA). Personnel in the two agencies engaged in turf battles and held deep differences about project requirements. These differences resulted in always-changing, inconsistent direction to software developers.[25]

Further, unlike Access CT, OHA did not hire a supervising contractor for the project, but instead decided itself to take an active role in the software's development. Unfortunately, the agency suffered high employee turnover and had difficulty hiring and keeping qualified personnel. OHA did hire the services of a professional software development company to create major software components. However, of the three finalists for this work, two dropped out at the last minute, and the winner by default, Oracle Corporation, became in essence a sole source vendor. Consequently, Oracle was able to negotiate time and materials contracts rather than contracts for specific deliverables at specific prices. Later, when problems developed, Oracle was paid tens of millions of additional money for change orders on that same time and materials basis. OHA also attempted to do much of its own programming, but the team had no experience with Oracle and lacked both developers and managers.[26]

Ironically, because of prior problems with technology projects, the Oregon legislature required the state to hire a quality assurance contractor, Maximus Corporation, to oversee the project. From the project's start, Maximus reported significant problems involving divided control, lack of clear requirements, inappropriate contracting methodology, lack of project planning, and lack of progress. It is unclear to whom those reports were delivered or what was done with them. In January 2013, when the head of the OHA project received another negative report in a long string of such negative reports, she threatened to withhold Maximus' payment.[27]

Alas, when, in January 2013, *The Oregonian* asked Rocky King, the director of Cover Oregon, whether the system would work, he responded, "I haven't the foggiest idea."[28] Sadly, when the fog cleared, the exchange failed. In March 2015, Cover Oregon was shuttered.

QUESTIONS

8-11. Summarize the purpose and intended benefits of a healthcare exchange.

8-12. Explain why a healthcare exchange requires an interorganizational information system.

8-13. Using knowledge from this chapter, summarize the difficulties and challenges of developing interorganizational information systems.

8-14. Healthcare exchanges must utilize personal and confidential data about their users. Write a one-paragraph policy that stipulates responsible processing and storage of this data.

8-15. Explain what you believe are the reasons for the Access CT success.

8-16. Read the Executive Summary of the First Data report located at *https://digital.osl.state.or.us/islandora/object/ osl:16687*. Summarize the report's findings.

8-17. Using the facts described in this case and your answer to question 8-16, list five key learnings you can take from the Access CT and Cover Oregon projects.

MyLab MIS

Go to the Assignments section of your MyLab to complete these writing exercises.

8-18. Using the patient discharge process in Q8-3, explain how the hospital benefits from an ERP solution. Describe why integration of patient records has advantages over separated databases. Explain the value of an industry-specific ERP solution to the hospital.

8-19. Go to *www.microsoft.com* and search for *Microsoft Dynamics*. Ignore Dynamics CRM. Have any important changes occurred in Microsoft's ERP product offerings since this edition was written? Has Microsoft brought a cloud-based ERP solution to market? Have any of the four ERP systems described in the chapter been better integrated with Office or the Microsoft Developer's platform? Using your knowledge guided by experience, what do you think are Microsoft's intentions with regard to ERP?

ENDNOTES

1. The subject of this chapter is structured processes, and we will discuss process quality in terms of them. Note, however, that all of the concepts in this question pertain equally well to dynamic processes.
2. Scott Neuman, "'Flippy' the Fast Food Robot (Sort Of) Mans the Grill at Caliburger," *NPR*, March 29, 2018, *www .npr.org/sections/thetwo-way/2018/03/05/590884388/ flippy-the-fast-food-robot-sort-of-mans-the-grill-at-caliburger*.
3. Brian Heater, "Flippy, the Hamburger Cooking Robot, Gets Its First Restaurant Gig," *TechCrunch*, March 29, 2018, *https://techcrunch.com/2017/09/19/ flippy-the-hamburger-cooking-robot-gets-its-first-restaurant-gig/*.
4. Alana Semuels, "Robots Will Transform Fast Food," *The Atlantic*, March 29, 2018, *www.theatlantic.com/magazine/archive/2018/01/iron-chefs/546581/*.
5. Panorama Consulting Solutions, "Clash of the Titans 2017," *Panorama-consulting.com*, November 2015, *http://go.panorama-consulting.com/ rs/603-UJX-107/images/Clash-of-the-Titans-2017.pdf*.
6. Paul Taylor, "Tipping Point for Cloud-ERP and Big Companies," *Forbes*, February 6, 2017, accessed June 12, 2018, *www.forbes.com/sites/ sap/2017/02/06/tipping-point-for-cloud-erp-and-big-companies*.
7. Panorama Consulting Solutions, "Only the Best Will Rise to the Top," *Panorama-consulting.com*, February 2016, *http://go.panorama-consulting .com/rs/603-UJX-107/images/Top-10-ERP-Systems-Report.pdf*.

8. Brian Krebs, "Data Theft Common by Departing Employees," *The Washington Post*, March 7, 2016, *www .washingtonpost.com/wp-dyn/content/article/2009/02/26/ AR2009022601821.html*.
9. Devlin Barrett, "FBI Warns of Rise in Disgruntled Employees Stealing Data," *The Wall Street Journal*, March 7, 2016, *www.wsj.com/articles/ fbi-warns-of-rise-in-disgruntled-employees-stealing-data-1411516389*.
10. Bill Barrett, "Inside the Mind of the White-Collar Criminal," *Accounting Web*, March 7, 2016, *www.accountingweb.com/technology/ trends/inside-the-mind-of-the-white-collar-criminal*.
11. Krebs, "Data Theft Common by Departing Employees."
12. Ibid.
13. Stacy Collett, "5 Signs an Employee Plans to Leave with Your Company's Data," *CIO*, March 7, 2016, *www.cio.com/ article/2975774/data-protection/5-signs-an-employee-plans-to-leave-with-your-companysdata.html*.
14. Andrea Walker, Meredith Cohn, and Erin Cox, "Md. Votes to Adopt Health Exchange Software Used in Connecticut," *Baltimore Sun*, April 2, 2014, accessed June 11, 2018, *http://articles.baltimoresun .com/2014-04-02/health/bs-hs-exchange-board-vote-20140401_1_ isabel-fitzgerald-new-website-federal-exchange*.

15. Maeve Reston, "U.S. Prosecutors Investigate Oregon's Failed Health Insurance Exchange," *Los Angeles Times*, May 21, 2014, accessed June 11, 2018, *www.latimes.com/nation/nationnow/la-na-us-attorneys-officeprobes-oregons-health-insurance-exchange-20140521-story.html*.

16. Matthew Sturdevant, "CT Health Exchange Has a New Chief Executive," *Hartford Courant*, June 21, 2012, accessed June 11, 2018, *http://articles.courant.com/2012-06-21/health/hc-health-exchangeceo-20120621_1_health-insurance-exchange-health-care-victoria-veltri*

17. Healthcare IT Connect, "Jim Wadleigh," accessed June 11, 2018, *www.healthcareitconnect.com/jim-wadleigh/*.

18. Office of Lieutenant Governor Nancy Wyman, "Health Insurance Exchange Hires Key Technical Consultant," September 27, 2012, accessed June 11, 2018, *http://ct.gov/hix/lib/hix/HIX-DELOITTERELEASE.pdf*.

19. Matthew Sturdevant, "Health Exchange Chief Explains How It Will Work," *Hartford Courant*, July 13,2012, accessed June 11, 2018, *www.courant.com/health/connecticut/hc-healthexchange-20120712,0,4877364.story*.

20. Arielle Levin Becker, "Obamacare Exchange's Final Tally: 208,301 People Signed Up," *The CT Mirror*, April 17, 2014, accessed June 11, 2018, *http://ctmirror.org/2014/04/17/obamacare-exchanges-final-tally-208301-people-signed-up/*.

21. Jeff Manning, "Cover Oregon: State Moves to Federal Exchange, but Oracle Technology Lives On," *The Oregonian*, May 6, 2014, accessed June 11, 2018, *www.oregonlive.com/health/index.ssf/2014/05/cover_oregon_state_moves_to_fe.html*.

22. "Cover Oregon Website Implementation Assessment," April 23, 2014, accessed June 11, 2018, *http://portlandtribune.com/documents/artdocs/00003481205618.pdf*.

23. Dusty Lane, "'We Look Like Fools:' A History of Cover Oregon's Failure," *Katu.com*, January 10, 2014, accessed June 11, 2018, *www.althycommunitiesoregon.com/lanecounty/2014/01/we-look-like-fools-a-history-of-cover-oregons-failure/*.

24. "Cover Oregon Website Implementation Assessment."

25. Nick Budnick, "Cover Oregon: Health Exchange Failure Predicted, but Tech Watchdogs' Warnings Fell on Deaf Ears," *The Oregonian*, January18, 2014, accessed June 11, 2018, *www.oregonlive.com/health/index.ssf/2014/01/cover_oregon_health_exchange_f.html*.

26. Nick Budnick, "Oregon Health Exchange Technology Troubles Run Deep due to Mismanagement, Early Decisions," *The Oregonian*, December 14, 2013, accessed June 11, 2018, *www.oregonlive.com/health/index.ssf/2013/12/oregon_health_exchange_technol.html*.

27. Budnick, "Cover Oregon: Health Exchange Failure Predicted."

28. Ibid.

CHAPTER 9

Social Media Information Systems

"Henri, I'm trying to wrap my head around the types of ads we're going to sell," Cassie says hesitantly. Cassie is the new head of marketing at ARES. She was asked by Zev Friedman, the new owner, to look at ways of generating revenue from ads in a new augmented reality application. "Is it just banner ads, pop-ups, and short videos?"

Henri points at the screen Raj is working on. "Well, yes, of course we can put banner ads in the app. We could place them under the vital statistics panel. They'd get plenty of eyeball time for sure."

"Great, what about pop-up ads and short videos?"

"Umm . . . I'm not sure. Personally, pop-ups and videos would be really distracting to me if I were cycling . . ."

Raj interrupts, "You need to think bigger. You're not really seeing what we can do with AR."

"What do you mean?" Cassie asks.

"Things are shifting. It's similar to the shift that happened when static newspaper ads shifted into 30-second video commercials when television was invented."

MyLab MIS

Using Your Knowledge
Questions 9-1, 9-2, 9-3
Essay Questions 9-18, 9-19

"I don't follow."

Raj continues, "In a mixed-reality environment we can create anything, replace anything, and alter anything. Think about that for a minute. Imagine a user is cycling down Huntington Beach. We can replace the beach houses with a 40-foot power bar a company wants to sell."

"We can do that?"

"Sure, and a lot more than that. We can replace real ads on billboards—with our virtual ads. We can have virtual planes pull our banner ads. We can even have a 60-foot prehistoric megalodon shark swimming in the ocean to promote the next Hollywood blockbuster."

"You're kidding."

"In a mixed-reality environment we can create anything, replace anything, and alter anything."

Source: Haiyin Wang/Alamy Stock Photo

"Nope. And if users want to 'click' on the ad, they just reach out with a finger and tap on it. We can even tell which ads they look at using eye tracking."

"Wow, that's amazing."

"And it gets better. Users can cycle with their friends—virtually. If they look to the left, they see Jane. If they look to the right, they see John. They can bike anywhere, anytime, regardless of weather or location."

Henri interrupts, "Well, we're not quite there yet."

Cassie looks surprised. "What do you mean? This is great! Companies will eat this up. And there's a social angle too. When can we get that figured out?"

Henri shakes his head. "I don't know. We're not even sure how many people the system can support. It wasn't designed for an AR interface or people cycling together. It might be two people, and it might be 500. And the custom virtual ads . . . well, that would add even more development time."

Cassie looks frustrated. "So I'm back to selling banner ads."

"For now, yes. We're still trying to get the app and the existing back end working. Raj is checking into the load we can handle with multiple users."

Cassie thinks back to the advice her mentor gave her about working at a startup. She didn't think it was going to be *this* frustrating. She puts on a forced smile. "Couldn't we just hire someone to make these new ads? Can't we just figure it out?"

"Yes, we can," Henri responds calmly. "Everything Raj described is possible. But developing apps for virtual environments is different. It requires a big shift in the way we think about software development. We're moving from 2D windows to 3D holograms. Finding developers who can do this won't be easy or cheap. This is a big technological shift."

Raj looks up with a big smirk on his face. "Shift happens."

Study QUESTIONS

Q9-1 What is a social media information system (SMIS)?

Q9-2 How do SMIS advance organizational strategy?

Q9-3 How do SMIS increase social capital?

Q9-4 How do (some) companies earn revenue from social media?

Q9-5 How do organizations develop an effective SMIS?

Q9-6 What is an enterprise social network (ESN)?

Q9-7 How can organizations address SMIS security concerns?

Q9-8 2029?

Chapter PREVIEW

Changes to social media are happening so rapidly that we all struggle to keep up with the latest developments. We revise this textbook every year, and even still, writing in August, we know that by the time you read this in January or later, a good portion of it will be obsolete. Unfortunately, we don't know which parts they will be.

In our experience, the best response to rapid technological change is to learn and understand underlying principles. Rather than show you Facebook or Google+ features that we know will change before the ink on this page is dry, let's instead focus on principles, conceptual frameworks, and models that will be useful when you address the opportunities and risks of social media systems in the early years of your professional career.

This knowledge will also help you avoid mistakes. Every day, you hear business-people saying, "We're using Twitter" and "We've connected our Facebook page to our Web site." Or they mention that they are creating ads and news releases that say, "Follow us on Twitter." The important question is, for what purpose? To be modern? To be hip? And do they have a social media strategy? Will using social media affect their bottom line?

We'll begin in Q9-1 by defining and describing the components of a social media information system, which will help you understand the commitment that organizations make when they use social media. As you've learned, the purpose of information systems is to help organizations achieve their strategy, and, in Q9-2, we'll consider how social media information systems facilitate organizational strategies. Next, in Q9-3, we will address how social media information systems increase social capital. Q9-4 will address how some companies earn revenue from social media; Q9-5 will look at how you can develop an effective social media strategy; and Q9-6 will look at enterprise social networks. We will then describe in Q9-7 how organizations can address security concerns related to the use of social media. We'll wrap up in Q9-8 with an odd analogy about the change in the relationship between individuals and organizations heading into 2029.

Q9-1 What Is a Social Media Information System (SMIS)?

Social media (SM) is the use of information technology to support the sharing of content among networks of users. Social media enables people to form **communities of practice**, or simply **communities**, which are groups of people related by a common interest. A **social media information system (SMIS)** is an information system that supports the sharing of content among networks of users.

As illustrated in Figure 9-1, social media is a convergence of many disciplines. In this book, we will focus on the MIS portion of Figure 9-1 by discussing SMIS and how they contribute to organizational strategy. If you decide to work in the SM field as a professional, you will need some knowledge of all these disciplines, except possibly computer science.

Three SMIS Roles

Before discussing the components of an SMIS, we need to clarify the roles played by three organizational units:

- Social media providers
- Users
- Communities

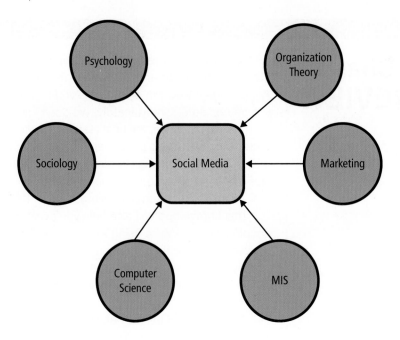

FIGURE 9-1

Social Media Is a Convergence of Disciplines

Social Media Providers

Social media providers such as Facebook, Google+, LinkedIn, Twitter, Instagram, and Pinterest provide platforms that enable the creation of **social networks**, or social relationships among people with common interests. The growth of SM over the past few years has been tremendous. Figure 9-2 shows the size of some well-known SM providers. In terms of the number of active users, several of these sites exceed the total population of the United States.[1] The growth of SM has generated extraordinary interest from businesses, advertisers, and investors. Social media providers compete with one another for the attention of users and for the associated advertising dollars.

FIGURE 9-2

Number of Social Media Active Users

Source: Based on 116 Amazing Social Media Statistics and Facts; https://www.brandwatch.com/blog/96-amazing-social-media-statistics-and-facts/

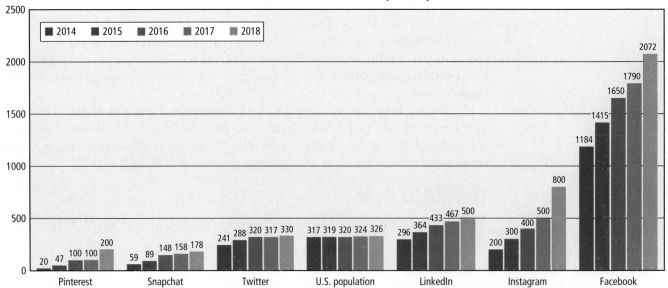

Users

Users include both individuals *and* organizations that use SM sites to build social relationships. More than 78 percent of people with Internet access use SM, and 80 percent of people access SM via their mobile phones.[2,3] Social media providers are attracting, and targeting, certain demographic groups. For example, about 81 percent of Pinterest users are female.[4] On LinkedIn, 61 percent of users are 30 or older.[5]

Organizations are SM users too. You may not think of an organization as a typical user, but in many ways it is. Organizations create and manage SM accounts just like you do. It's estimated that 88 percent of *Fortune* 500 companies maintain active Twitter accounts, 85 percent have Facebook pages, and 75 percent have YouTube accounts.[6] These companies hire staff to maintain their SM presence, promote their products, build relationships, and manage their image.

Depending on how organizations want to use SM, they can be users, providers, or both. For example, larger organizations are big enough to create and manage their own internal social media platforms such as wikis, blogs, and discussion boards. In this case, the organization would be a social media provider. We'll look at the ways social media can be used within organizations later in this chapter.

Communities

Forming communities is a natural human trait; anthropologists claim that the ability to form them is responsible for the progress of the human race. In the past, however, communities were based on family relationships or geographic location. Everyone in the village formed a community. The key difference of SM communities is that they are formed based on mutual interests and transcend familial, geographic, and organizational boundaries.

Because of this transcendence, most people belong to several, or even many, different user communities. Google+ recognized this fact when it created user circles that enable users to allocate their connections (*people*, using Google+ terminology) to one or more community groups. Facebook and other SM application providers are adapting in similar ways.

To better understand the concept of communities, take a look at Figure 9-3. This figure shows that, from the point of view of the SM site, Community A is a first-tier community. It consists of users who have a direct relationship to that site. User 1, in turn, belongs to three communities: A, B, and C (these could be, say, classmates, professional contacts, and friends). From the point of view of the SM site, Communities B–E are second-tier communities because the relationships in those communities are intermediated by first-tier users. The number of second- and third-tier community members grows exponentially. If each community had, for example, 100 members, then the SM site would have 100×100, or 10,000, second-tier members and $100 \times 100 \times 100$, or 1 million, third-tier members. However, that statement is not quite true because communities overlap; in Figure 9-3, for example, User 7 belongs to Communities C and E. Thus, these calculations reveal the maximum number of users, as opposed to the actual number.

How the SM site chooses to relate to these communities depends on its goals. If the SM site is interested in pure publicity, it will want to relate to as many tiers of communities as it can. If so, it will create a **viral hook**, which is some inducement, such as a prize or other reward, for passing communications along through the tiers. If, however, the purpose of the SM site is to solve an embarrassing problem, say, to fix a product defect, then it would endeavor to constrain, as much as it can, the communications to Community A.

The exponential nature of relationships via community tiers offers organizations both a blessing and a curse. An employee who is a member of Community A can share her sincere and legitimate pride in her organization's latest product or service with hundreds or thousands of people in her communities. However, she can also blast her disappointment at some recent development to that same audience or, worse, inadvertently share private and proprietary organizational data with someone in that audience who works for the competition.

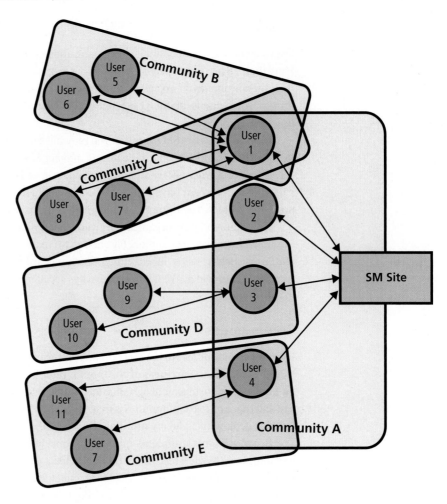

FIGURE 9-3
SM Communities

Social media is a powerful tool, and to use it well, organizations must know their goals and plan accordingly, as you'll learn.

SMIS Components

Because they are information systems, SMIS have the same five components as all IS: hardware, software, data, procedures, and people. Consider each component for the roles shown in Figure 9-4.

Hardware

Both users and organizations process SM sites using desktops, laptops, and mobile devices. In most cases, social media providers host the SM presence using elastic servers in the cloud.

Software

Users employ browsers and client applications to communicate with other users, send and receive content, and add and remove connections to communities and other users. These applications can be desktop or mobile applications for a variety of platforms, including iOS, Android, and Windows.

Social media providers develop and operate their own custom, proprietary, social networking application software. As you learned in Chapter 4, supporting custom software is expensive over the long term; SM application vendors must do so because the features and functions of their applications are fundamental to their competitive strategy. They can do so because they spread the development costs over the revenue generated by millions of users.

Component	Role	Description
Hardware	Social media providers	Elastic, cloud-based servers
	Users and communities	Any user computing device
Software	Social media providers	Application, NoSQL or other DBMS, Analytics
	Users and communities	Browser, IOS, Android, Windows 10, and other applications
Data	Social media providers	Content and connection data storage for rapid retrieval
	Users and communities	User-generated content, connection data
Procedures	Social media providers	Run and maintain application (beyond the scope of this text)
	Users and communities	Create and manage content, informal, copy each other
People	Social media providers	Staff to run and maintain application (beyond the scope of this text)
	Users and communities	Key users, adaptive, can be irrational

FIGURE 9-4
Five Components of SMIS

Many social networking vendors use a NoSQL database management system to process their data, though traditional relational DBMS products are used as well. Facebook began development of its own in-house DBMS (Cassandra) but later donated it to the open source community when it realized the expense and commitment of maintaining it. In addition to custom applications and databases, SM providers also invest in analytic software to understand how users interact with their site and application software.

Data

SM data falls into two categories: content and connections. **Content data** is data and responses to data that are contributed by users. You provide the source content data for your Facebook site, and your friends provide response content when they write on your wall, make comments, tag you, or otherwise publish on your site.

Connection data is data about relationships. On Facebook, for example, the relationships to your friends are connection data. The fact that you've liked particular organizations is also connection data. Connection data differentiates SMIS from Web site applications. Both Web sites and social networking sites present user and responder content, but only social networking applications store and process connection data.

SM providers store and retrieve SM data on behalf of users. They must do so in the presence of network and server failures, and they must do so rapidly. The problem is made somewhat easier, however, because SM content and connection data have a relatively simple structure.

Procedures

For social networking users, procedures are informal, evolving, and socially oriented. You do what your friends do. When the members of your community learn how to do something new and interesting, you copy them. SM software is designed to be easy to learn and use.

Such informality makes using SMIS easy, but it also means that unintended consequences are common. The most troubling examples concern user privacy. Many people have learned not to post pictures of themselves in front of their house numbers on the same publicly accessible site on which they're describing their new high-definition television. Many others, alas, have not.

For organizations, social networking procedures are more formalized and aligned with the organization's strategy. Organizations develop procedures for creating content, managing user responses, removing obsolete or objectionable content, and extracting value from content. For example, setting up an SMIS to gather data on product problems is a wasted expense unless procedures exist to extract knowledge from that social networking data. Organizations also need to develop procedures to manage SM risk, as described in Q9-7.

Procedures for operating and maintaining the SM application are beyond the scope of this text.

People

Users of social media do what they want to do depending on their goals and their personalities. They behave in certain ways and observe the consequences. They may or may not change their behavior. By the way, note that SM users aren't necessarily rational, at least not in purely monetary ways. See, for example, the study by Vernon Smith in which people walked away from free money because they thought someone else was getting more![7]

Organizations cannot be so casual. Anyone who uses his or her position in a company to speak for an organization needs to be trained on both SMIS user procedures and the organization's social networking policy. We will discuss such procedures and policies in Q9-7.

Social media is creating new job titles, new responsibilities, and the need for new types of training. For example, what makes a good tweeter? What makes an effective wall writer? What type of people should be hired for such jobs? What education should they have? How does one evaluate candidates for such positions? How do you find these types of people? All of these questions are being asked and answered today.

Q9-2   How Do SMIS Advance Organizational Strategy?

In Chapter 2, Figure 2-1 (page 40), you learned the relationship of information systems to organizational strategy. In brief, strategy determines value chains, which determine business processes, which determine information systems. Insofar as value chains determine *structured* business processes, such as those discussed in Chapter 8, this chain is straightforward. However, social media is by its very nature *dynamic*; its flow cannot be designed or diagrammed, and if it were, no sooner would the diagram be finished than the SM process would have changed.

Therefore, we need to back up a step and consider how value chains determine dynamic processes and thus set SMIS requirements. As you will see, social media fundamentally changes the balance of power among users, their communities, and organizations.

Figure 9-5 summarizes how social media contributes to the five primary value chain activities and to the human resources support activity. Consider each row of this table.

Social Media and the Sales and Marketing Activity

In the past, organizations controlled their relationships with customers using structured processes and related information systems. In fact, the primary purpose of traditional CRM was to manage customer touches. Traditional CRM ensured that the organization spoke to customers with one voice and that it controlled the messages, the offers, and even the support that customers received based on the value of a particular customer. In 1990, if you wanted to know something about an IBM product, you'd contact its local sales office; that office would classify you as a prospect and use that classification to control the literature, the documentation, and your access to IBM personnel.

Social CRM is a dynamic, SM-based CRM process. The relationships between organizations and customers emerge in a dynamic process as both parties create and process content. In addition to the traditional forms of promotion, employees in the organization create wikis, blogs, discussion lists, frequently asked questions, sites for user reviews and commentary, and other dynamic content. Customers search this content, contribute reviews and commentary, ask more questions, create user groups, and so forth. With social CRM, each customer crafts his or her own relationship with the company.

Activity	Focus	Dynamic process	Risks
Sales and marketing	Outward to prospects	Social CRM Peer-to-peer sales	Loss of credibility Bad PR
Customer service	Outward to customers	Peer-to-peer support	Loss of control
Inbound logistics	Upstream supply chain providers	Problem solving	Privacy
Outbound logistics	Downstream supply chain shippers	Problem solving	Privacy
Manufacturing and operations	Outward for user design; Inward to operations and manufacturing	User-guided design Industry relationships Operational efficiencies	Efficiency/effectiveness
Human resources	Employment candidates; Employee communications	Employee prospecting, recruiting, and evaluation SharePoint for employee-to-employee communication	Error Loss of credibility

FIGURE 9-5
SM in Value Chain Activities

Social CRM flies in the face of the structured and controlled processes of traditional CRM. Because relationships emerge from joint activity, customers have as much control as companies. This characteristic is anathema to traditional sales managers who want structured processes for controlling what the customer reads, sees, and hears about the company and its products.

Further, traditional CRM is centered on lifetime value; customers that are likely to generate the most business get the most attention and have the most effect on the organization. However, with social CRM, the customer who spends 10 cents but who is an effective reviewer, commentator, or blogger can have more influence than the quiet customer who purchases $10M a year. Such imbalance is incomprehensible to traditional sales managers.

However, traditional sales managers *are* happy to have loyal customers sell their products using peer-to-peer recommendations. A quick look at products and their reviews on Amazon will show how frequently customers are willing to write long, thoughtful reviews of products they like or do not like. Amazon and other online retailers also allow readers to rate the helpfulness of reviews. In that way, substandard reviews are revealed for the wary.

Today, many organizations are struggling to make the transition from controlled, structured, traditional CRM processes to wide-open, adaptive, dynamic social CRM processes; this struggle represents a significant job opportunity for those interested in IS, sales, and social media.

Social Media and Customer Service

Product users are amazingly willing to help each other solve problems. Even more, they will do so without pay; in fact, payment can warp and ruin the support experience as customers fight with one another. SAP, for example, learned that it was better to reward its SAP Developer Network with donations on their behalf to charitable organizations than to give them personal rewards.

Not surprisingly, organizations whose business strategy involves selling to or through developer networks have been the earliest and most successful at SM-based customer support. In addition to SAP, Microsoft has long sold through its network of partners. Its MVP (Most Valuable Professional) program is a classic example of giving praise and glory in exchange for customer-provided customer assistance (*http://mvp.support.microsoft.com*). Of course, the developers in these networks have a business incentive to participate because that activity helps them sell services to the communities in which they participate.

However, users with no financial incentive are also willing to help others. For instance, Amazon supports a program called Vine by which customers can be selected to give prerelease and new product reviews to the buyer community.[8] You'll need your psychology course to explain what drives people to strive for such recognition. MIS just provides the platform!

The primary risk of peer-to-peer support is loss of control. Businesses may not be able to control peer-to-peer content. Negative comments about cherished products and recommendations for competitor's products are a real possibility. We address these risks in Q9-7.

Social Media and Inbound and Outbound Logistics

Companies whose profitability depends on the efficiency of their supply chain have long used information systems to improve both the effectiveness and efficiency of structured supply chain processes. Because supply chains are tightly integrated into structured manufacturing processes, there is less tolerance for the unpredictability of dynamic, adaptive processes. Solving problems is an exception; social media can be used to provide numerous solution ideas and rapid evaluation of them. The Japanese earthquake in the spring of 2011 created havoc in the automotive supply chain when major Japanese manufacturers lacked power and, in some cases, facilities to operate. Social media was used to dispense news, allay fears of radioactive products, and address ever-changing needs and problems.

SM communities may provide better and faster problem solutions to complex supply chain problems. Social media is designed to foster content creation and feedback among networks of users, and that characteristic facilitates the iteration and feedback needed for problem solving, as described in Chapter 7.

Loss of privacy is, however, a significant risk. Problem solving requires the open discussion of problem definitions, causes, and solution constraints. Because suppliers and shippers work with many companies, supply chain problem solving via social media may be problem solving in front of your competitors.

Social Media and Manufacturing and Operations

Operations and manufacturing activities are dominated by structured processes. The flexibility and adaptive nature of social media would result in chaos if applied to the manufacturing line or to the warehouse. However, social media does play a role in designing products, developing supplier relationships, and improving operational efficiencies.

Crowdsourcing is the dynamic social media process of employing users to participate in product design or product redesign. eBay often solicits customers to provide feedback on their eBay experience. As its site says, "There's no better group of advisors than our customers." User-guided design has been used to create video games, shoes, and many other products.

Social media has been widely used in **businesses-to-consumer (B2C)** relationships to market products to end users. Now manufacturers are starting to use social media to become industry leaders, promote brand awareness, and generate new **business-to-business (B2B)** leads to retailers. Manufacturers can use social media by starting a blog that discusses the latest industry-related news, posts interviews with experts, and comments on new product innovations. They can also create a YouTube channel and post videos of product reviews and testing and factory walk-throughs. Facebook and Twitter accounts are useful to promote positive consumer stories, announce new products, and follow competitors. Retailers view manufacturers who engage in such SM efforts as industry leaders.

Operations can use social media to improve communication channels within the organization and externally with consumers. For example, an enterprise social networking service like Yammer can be used to provide managers with real-time feedback about how to resolve internal operational inefficiencies. Externally, a retailer could monitor its corporate Twitter account and respond to product shortages or spikes in demand for new products around holidays.

Social Media and Human Resources

The last row in Figure 9-5 concerns the use of social media in human resources. As previously mentioned, social media is used for finding employee prospects, for recruiting candidates, and—in some organizations—for candidate evaluation.

Organizations use social media sites like LinkedIn to hire the best people more quickly and at a lower cost. For about $900 a month, recruiters can search through 433 million LinkedIn members to find the perfect candidate.[9] That $900 a month may sound like a lot to you, but to corporate customers, it's peanuts. The cost of hiring just one new employee runs around $5,000.[10] If an independent recruiting company is involved, that cost can be as high as 10 percent of the new employee's salary. LinkedIn also gives employers access to *passive* candidates who might not be looking for a job but are a perfect fit for a particular position. Once the employee is hired, the employer can leverage that new employee's social network to hire more candidates just like him or her.

Jobvite, a social recruiting company, reports that 96 percent of recruiters it surveyed used social media in their recruiting process. Furthermore, 63 percent of recruiters reported that they view shared details about volunteer or social engagement work on social media sites positively. However, posts with spelling mistakes or poor grammar were viewed negatively by 48 percent of respondents. They also viewed posts about alcohol consumption (35 percent) and marijuana use (61 percent) negatively.[11]

Social media is also used for employee communications, using internal personnel sites such as MySite and MyProfile in SharePoint or other similar enterprise systems. SharePoint provides a place for employees to post their expertise in the form of "Ask me about" questions. When employees are looking for an internal expert, they can search SharePoint for people who have posted the desired expertise. SharePoint 2016 greatly extends support for social media beyond that in earlier SharePoint versions.

The risks of social media in human resources concern the possibility of error when using sites such as Facebook to form conclusions about employees. A second risk is that the SM site becomes too defensive or is obviously promulgating an unpopular management message.

Study Figure 9-5 to understand the general framework by which organizations can accomplish their strategy via a dynamic process supported by SMIS. We will now turn to an economic perspective on the value and use of SMIS.

Q9-3 How Do SMIS Increase Social Capital?

Business literature defines three types of capital. Karl Marx defined **capital** as the investment of resources for future profit. This traditional definition refers to investments into resources such as factories, machines, manufacturing equipment, and the like. **Human capital** is the investment in human knowledge and skills for future profit. By taking this class, you are investing in your own human capital. You are investing your money and time to obtain knowledge that you hope will differentiate you from other workers and ultimately give you a wage premium in the workforce.

According to Nan Lin, **social capital** is the investment in social relations with the expectation of returns in the marketplace.[12] You can see social capital at work in your personal life. You strengthen your social relationships when you help someone get a job, set a friend up on a date, or introduce a friend to someone famous. You weaken the strength of your social relationships by continually freeloading, declining requests for help, and failing to spend time with friends.

In your professional life, you are investing in your social capital when you attend a business function for the purpose of meeting people and reinforcing relationships. Similarly, you can use social media to increase your social capital by recommending or endorsing someone on LinkedIn, liking a picture on Facebook, retweeting a tweet, or commenting on an Instagram picture.

What Is the Value of Social Capital?

According to Lin, social capital adds value in four ways:

- Information
- Influence
- Social credentials
- Personal reinforcement

First, relationships in social networks can provide *information* about opportunities, alternatives, problems, and other factors important to business professionals. On a personal level, this could come in the form of a friend telling you about a new job posting or the best teacher to take for Business Law. As a business professional, this could be a friend introducing you to a potential new supplier or letting you know about the opening of a new sales territory.

Second, relationships provide an opportunity to *influence* decision makers at your employer or in other organizations who are critical to your success. For example, playing golf every Saturday with the CEO of the company you work for could increase your chances of being promoted. Such influence cuts across formal organizational structures, such as reporting relationships.

Third, being linked to a network of highly regarded contacts is a form of *social credential.* You can bask in the glory of those with whom you are related. Others will be more inclined to work with you if they believe critical personnel are standing with you and may provide resources to support you.

Finally, being linked into social networks *reinforces* a professional's identity, image, and position in an organization or industry. It reinforces the way you define yourself to the world (and to yourself). For example, being friends with bankers, financial planners, and investors may reinforce your identity as a financial professional.

As mentioned, a social network is a network of social relationships among individuals with a common interest. Each social network differs in value. The social network you maintain with your high school friends probably has less value than the network you have with your business associates, but not necessarily so. According to Henk Flap, the **value of social capital** is determined by the number of relationships in a social network, by the strength of those relationships, and by the resources controlled by those related.[13] If your high school friends happened to have been Mark Zuckerberg or Cameron and Tyler Winklevoss and if you maintain strong relations with them via your high school network, then the value of that social network far exceeds any you'll have at work. For most of us, however, the network of our current professional contacts provides the most social capital.

So, when you use social networking professionally, consider these three factors. You gain social capital by adding more friends and by strengthening the relationships you have with existing friends. Further, you gain more social capital by adding friends and strengthening relationships with people who control resources that are important to you. Such calculations may seem cold, impersonal, and possibly even phony. When applied to the recreational use of social networking, they may be. But when you use social networking for professional purposes, keep them in mind.

When it comes to social capital, one tool you might find particularly useful is *Klout.com.* This site searches social media activity on Facebook, Twitter, and other sites and creates what it calls a Klout score, which is a measure of an individual's social capital. Klout scores vary from 0 to 100; the more that others respond to your content, the higher your score. Also, responses from people who seldom respond are valued more than responses from those who respond frequently.[14]

How Do Social Networks Add Value to Businesses?

Organizations have social capital just as humans do. Historically, organizations created social capital via salespeople, customer support, and public relations. Endorsements by high-profile people are a traditional way of increasing social capital, but there are tigers in those woods.

Today, progressive organizations maintain a presence on Facebook, LinkedIn, Twitter, and possibly other sites. They include links to their social networking presence on their Web sites and make it easy for customers and interested parties to leave comments.

To understand how social networks add value to businesses, consider each of the elements of social capital: number of relationships, strength of relationships, and resources controlled by "friends."

Using Social Networking to Increase the Number of Relationships

In a traditional business relationship, a client (you) has some experience with a business, such as a restaurant or resort. Traditionally, you may express your opinions about that experience by word of mouth to your social network. If you are an **influencer** in your social network, your opinion may force a change in others' behavior and beliefs.

However, such communication is unreliable and brief: You are more likely to say something to your friends if the experience was particularly good or bad; but, even then, you are likely only to say something to those friends whom you encounter while the experience is still recent. And once you have said something, that's it; your words don't live on for days or weeks.

However, what if you could use SM to communicate your experience using text, pictures, and video instantly to everyone in your social network? For example, suppose a wedding photographer uses social media to promote her business by asking a recent client (user 1) to "like" her Facebook page and the wedding photos posted there (Figure 9-6). She also tags people in the client's pictures on Facebook. She may even ask the client to tweet about her experience.

All of the people in the client's social network (users 4–6) see the likes, tags, and tweets. If user 6 likes the pictures, they might be seen by users 10–12. It's possible that one of those users is looking for a wedding photographer. Using social media, the photographer has thus grown her social

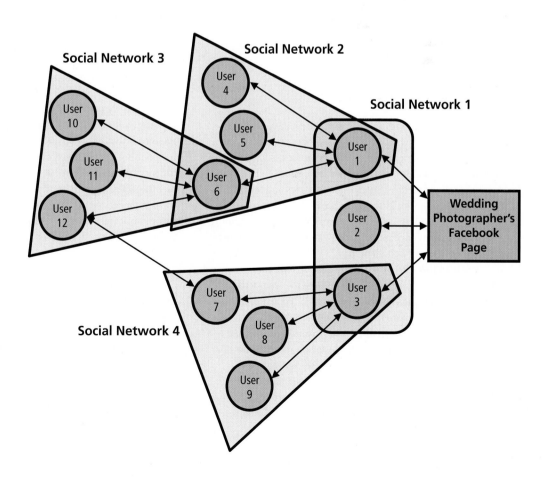

FIGURE 9-6
Growing Social Networks

ENHANCED GOLF FAN

If you have ever stopped by a yard sale on a Saturday afternoon, you know that it can be quite the experience. Treasure hunters stop by to see if they can find good deals on used items. Electronics are a common yard sale item because technology changes so quickly. Their value drops just as quickly.

It is worth thinking about how changes in technology have changed the way we *consume* entertainment. For example, advancements in television over several decades have been based on evolutions in the quality and functionality of the device. Not that long ago, your grandparents were manually tuning in to view a very limited set of black-and-white channels. In the 1960s, television broadcasts in color became the norm. That was followed decades later by the advent of digital television in the 1990s and then adoption of HDTV by the masses in the 2000s.

The clarity of the images we view today is much improved over the televisions of old. The content has improved as well. For example, the widespread adoption of HDTVs over the 2000s have changed how sports fans want to watch their favorite teams. A survey conducted in 1998 reported that 54 percent of respondents would rather attend a game than watch it at home; in 2011 that number had dropped to 29 percent.[15] New innovations in data analytics are going to change sports viewing even more.

Source: Anekoho/Fotolia

Now on the Tee, Big Data

For example, watching golf on TV has the potential to be revolutionized as new types of data analytics and social media capabilities are incorporated into broadcasts. Golf is an extremely difficult sport to broadcast because golfers play in small groups and are dispersed across acres and acres of the course. A majority of the shots are replays occurring minutes after the actual shot has occurred. Thus, maintaining a captivating viewing experience for a sport that is inherently disjointed can be very challenging.

The PGA has started providing data visualizations, advanced statistics, real-time updates, and live feeds to their events to improve the viewing experience.[16] For example, fans are now able to compare the putting and driving statistics of different players. They can also track players on the course in real time and view social media posts about the action happening with each group on the course. Specialized applications are also being developed that will allow fans to track the probabilities of each player getting certain outcomes (e.g., birdie, par, or bogey) on each hole.[17]

But these new applications all come at a cost. New infrastructure (Wi-Fi access points and tracking beacons) must be installed, software must be developed, and personnel must be paid to maintain the infrastructure and keep social media posts current. The upside is that the quality and interactivity of the viewing experience have improved.

Sports Analytics for the Win

Golf isn't the only sport adding sensors and real-time data analytics into the game. The National Football League (NFL) recently partnered with a company that specializes in using radio-frequency identification (RFID) tags to track the movement of objects. The company embeds RFID tags in the padding of NFL players and then uses them to measure the movement of players on the field with high levels of precision. The tags are outfitted with tiny antennae that transmit a beacon 12 times per second to receiver units located throughout the stadium.[18] The receiver units are able to determine where each player is located by triangulating this signal.

Metrics like speed, acceleration, and routes run by players can be digitized, stored, and used to enhance how fans view the game. Coaches can also use these data in the future to support decision making (e.g., identifying which players are fatigued by tracking downward trends in acceleration play after play or locating favorable speed mismatches on the field). As we witness continuous improvements to the experience of watching sports on television, we may soon eliminate the willingness of even the most stalwart fans to actually attend the big game.

Questions

1. Sports aren't the only type of television programming that has benefited from advances in technology. Think about how other types of programming have changed in light of new innovations in hardware, software, mobile devices, and Big Data.

2. Golf and football are two examples of sports that are working to incorporate data analytics into broadcasts. How could other sports use data analytics to enhance the viewing experience?

3. Analytics in sports can clearly enhance sports broadcasts and help coaches. How can access to this type of analysis help current or aspiring athletes?

4. What do you think the next great innovation will be in the paradigm of watching sports on television? Will it be based on advances in hardware, software, data, or some other factor?

network to reach potential clients who she wouldn't have otherwise had access to. She also used SM to grow the number of relationships she has with clients. Depending on the number, strength, and value of those relationships, her social capital within those networks could substantially increase.

Such relationship sales have been going on by word of mouth for centuries; the difference here is that SMIS allow such relationships to scale to levels not possible in the past. In fact, the photographer in our example might even consider *paying* the client for the opportunity to take the wedding pictures if the client were a famous celebrity with hundreds of thousands of followers. In this way, social media may allow users to convert social capital into financial capital. Some famous celebrities get paid more than $30,000 for a single 140-character tweet![19]

Using Social Networks to Increase the Strength of Relationships

To an organization, the **strength of a relationship** is the likelihood that the other entity (person or other organization) in the relationship will do something that benefits the organization. An organization may have a strong relationship with you if you write positive reviews about it, post pictures of you using the organization's products or services, tweet about upcoming product releases, and so on.

In the previous example, the photographer asked a client to like her Facebook page and wedding photos. To the photographer, the number of friends the client has in her social network is important, but equally important is the strength of the relationships. Will the client's friends like the photographer's page and photos? Will they retweet the client's success story? If none of the client's friends like the photographer's page and photos, then the strength of the relationships is weak. If all of the client's friends like the photographer's page and photos, then the strength of the relationships in the client's social network is strong.

In his autobiography, Benjamin Franklin provided a key insight. He said that if you want to strengthen your relationship with someone in power, ask him to do you a favor. Before Franklin invented the public library, he would ask powerful strangers to lend him their expensive books. In that same sense, organizations have learned that they can strengthen their relationships with you by asking you to do them a favor. When you provide that favor, it strengthens your relationship with the organization.

Traditional capital depreciates. Machines wear out, factories get old, technology and computers become obsolete, and so forth. Does social capital also depreciate? Do relationships wear out from use? So far, the answer seems to be both yes and no.

Clearly, there are only so many favors you can ask of someone in power. And there are only so many times a company can ask you to review a product, post pictures, or provide connections to your friends. At some point, the relationship deteriorates due to overuse. So, yes, social capital can be spent.

However, frequent interactions strengthen relationships and hence increase social capital. The more you interact with a company, the stronger your commitment and allegiance. But continued frequent interactions occur only when both parties see value in continuing the relationship. Thus, at some point, the organization must provide you an incentive to continue to do it a favor.

So, social capital can be spent, but it can also be earned by adding something of value to the interaction. If an organization can induce those in its relationships to provide more influence,

Highest-Paid YouTube Channels		
Rank	**Name**	**Annual Earnings (millions)**
1	Daniel Middleton (DanTDM)	$16.5
2	Evan Fong (VanossGaming)	$15.5
3	Dude Perfect	$14.0
4	Logan Paul	$12.5
5	Mark Fischbach (Markiplier)	$12.5

Most-Viewed YouTube Channels		
Rank	**Name**	**Annual Views (billions)**
1	T-Series	39.5
2	WWE	23.4
3	Ryan ToysReview	22.3
4	netd muzik	21.7
5	SET India	19.0

Most-Subscribed YouTube Channels		
Rank	**Name**	**Subscribers (millions)**
1	Felix Kjellberg (PewDiePie)	63.3
2	T-Series	48.6
3	Justin Bieber	39.4
4	Canal KondZilla	34.7
5	JustinBieberVEVO	34.5

FIGURE 9-7
Top YouTube Channels
Source: Data from Social Blade, "Top 50 Influential YouTube Channels," Socialblade.com, June 12, 2018, accessed June 12, 2018, *https://socialblade.com/youtube/top/50.*

information, social credentials, or personal reinforcement, it has strengthened those relationships. And, continuing a successful relationship over time substantially increases relationship strength.

Using Social Networks to Connect to Those with More Resources

Buying automated bot followers is a questionable practice. Read more about it in the Ethics Guide on pages 354–355.

The third measure of the value of social capital is the value of the resources controlled by those in the relationships. An organization's social capital is thus partly a function of the social capital of those to whom it relates. The most visible measure is the number of relationships. Someone with 1,000 loyal Twitter followers is usually more valuable than someone with 10. But the calculation is more subtle than that; for example, if those 1,000 followers are college students and if the organization's product is adult diapers, then the value of the relationship to the followers is low. A relationship with 10 Twitter followers who are in retirement homes would be more valuable.

To illustrate this point, Figure 9-7 shows rankings of YouTube channels by annual earnings, number of subscribers, and annual views.[20] Note that the channel with the highest annual earnings (DanTDM) does not have the most subscribers (PewDiePie) or the most annual views (T-Series). The resources (i.e., money) controlled by the viewers of the DanTDM channel are highly valued by paying advertisers even though DanTDM only ranks 24th in the number of annual views and 50th in number of subscribers.

There is no formula for computing social capital, but the three factors would seem to be more multiplicative than additive. Or, stated in other terms, the value of social capital is more in the form of

$$Social\ Capital = Number\ of\ Relationships \times Relationship\ Strength \times Entity\ Resources$$

than in the form of

$$Social\ Capital = Number\ of\ Relationships + Relationship\ Strength + Entity\ Resources$$

Again, do not take these equations literally; take them in the sense of the multiplicative interaction of the three factors.

This multiplicative nature of social capital means that a huge network of relationships with people who have few resources may be of less value than a smaller network of relationships with people who have substantial resources. Furthermore, those resources must be relevant to the organization. Students with pocket change are relevant to Pizza Hut; they are irrelevant to a BMW dealership.

This discussion brings us to the brink of social networking practice. Most organizations today ignore the value of entity assets and simply try to connect to more people with stronger relationships. This area is ripe for innovation. Data aggregators such as ChoicePoint and Acxiom maintain detailed data about people worldwide. It would seem that such data could be used by information systems to calculate the potential value of a relationship to a particular individual. This possibility would enable organizations to better understand the value of their social networks as well as guide their behavior with regard to particular individuals.

Stay tuned; many possibilities exist, and some ideas—maybe yours—will be very successful.

Q9-4 How Do (Some) Companies Earn Revenue from Social Media?

Having a large social network with strong relationships may not be enough. Facebook, for example, has more than 2.1 billion active users that have generated more than 1.13 trillion likes. YouTube has more than 1.6 billion active users that watch more than 5 billion videos each day.[21] Both companies have extremely large numbers of active users. The only problem is that they give it away for free. Billions of anything multiplied by zero is zero. Do all those users really matter if Facebook and YouTube can't make a single penny off of them?

As a business student, you know that nothing is free. Processing time, data communication, and data storage may be cheap, but they still cost something. Who pays for the hardware? Social media companies like Facebook, Twitter, and LinkedIn also need to pay people to develop, implement, and manage the SMIS. And where does Web content come from? *Fortune* pays authors for the content that it offers for free. Who is paying those authors? And from what revenue?

You Are the Product

Social media has evolved in such a way that users expect to use SM applications without paying for them. SM companies want to build up a large network of users quickly, but they have to offer a free product in order to attract users. The dilemma then becomes how do they **monetize**, or make money from, their application, service, or content.

The answer is by making *users* the product. That may sound strange at first. You don't want to think of yourself as a product. But try to look at it from the company's point of view. When a company runs an advertisement, it's essentially being paid to put the ad in front of its users. In a way, it's renting your eyeballs to an advertiser for a short period of time. Google is paid to target users with ads by using their search terms, sites they visit, and "scans" of their emails to place targeted ads in front of them. In essence, then, users are the product being sold to advertisers. As the old saying says, "If you're not paying, you're the product."

Revenue Models for Social Media

The two most common ways SM companies generate revenue are advertising and charging for premium services. On Facebook, for example, creating a company page is free, but Facebook charges a fee to advertise to communities that "like" that page.

Advertising

Most SM companies earn revenue through advertising. Facebook made 98 percent of its 2018 first quarter earnings ($11.80B) from advertising.[22] About 86 percent of Twitter's $665M first quarter earnings came from advertising as well.[23] Advertising on SM can come in the form of paid search, display or banner ads, mobile ads, classifieds, or digital video ads.

Google led the way in making digital advertising revenue with search, followed by Gmail and then YouTube. Today, it doesn't seem like any great insight to realize that if someone is searching for information about an Audi A5 Cabriolet, then that person may be interested in ads from local Audi dealers and BMW and Mercedes dealers as well. Or if someone is watching a soccer game on YouTube, maybe he or she likes soccer. While not mind-boggling to imagine, Google was the first to turn this notion into substantial revenue streams. Other tech companies followed.

Advertisers like digital ads because, unlike traditional media such as newspapers, users can respond directly to Web ads by clicking on them. Run an ad in the print version of *The Wall Street Journal*, and you have no idea of who responds to that ad and how strongly. But place an ad for that same product in the newspaper's online version, and you'll soon know the percentage of viewers who clicked that ad and what action they took next. This knowledge led to the **pay-per-click** revenue model, in which advertisers display ads to potential customers for free and pay only when the customer clicks.

Another way to grow ad revenue is to increase site value with user contributions. The term **use increases value** means the more people use a site, the more value it has, and the more people will visit. Furthermore, the more value a site has, the more existing users will return. This phenomenon led to user comments and reviews, blogging, and, within a few years, social media. If you can get people to connect their community of practice to a site, you will get more users, they will add more value, existing users will return more frequently, and, all things considered, the more ad clicks there will be.

Freemium

The **freemium** revenue model offers users a basic service for free and then charges a premium for upgrades or advanced features. LinkedIn earns part of its revenue by selling upgrades to its standard software as a service (SaaS) product. As of May 2018, regular users access LinkedIn for free; individual upgrades range from $29 to $99 a month and offer advanced search capabilities, greater visibility of user profiles, and more direct email messages to LinkedIn users outside one's network. Businesses that want to use LinkedIn for recruiting can purchase a Recruiter Corporate account for $120 to $1200 a month. LinkedIn's revenue consists of about 17 percent from premium subscriptions, 65 percent from online recruitment, and 18 percent from advertising.[24]

By diversifying its revenue streams, LinkedIn has reduced its dependence on fluctuating ad revenue and lessened the negative impact of ad-blocking software. A recent report by PageFair indicated that 11 percent of Web surfers use **ad-blocking software** to filter out advertising content and rarely, if ever, see Internet ads.[25] It also reported that the use of ad-blocking software grew by 30 percent over the past year. SM companies that rely solely on ad revenue may see their share prices plummet if the use of ad-blocking software becomes widespread.

Other ways of generating revenue on SM sites include the sale of apps and virtual goods, affiliate commissions, and donations. During the month of April 2018, the free-to-play game Fortnite generated $296 million dollars from the sale of virtual goods. Wikipedia took in about $87.5M in donations during 2017.[26] Interestingly, some SM companies, like Pinterest, don't generate any revenue at all. They just focus on building a large network of users now and figuring out how to make money later.

Social media is the ultimate expression of use increasing value. The more communities of practice there are, the more people, and the more incentive people will have to come back again and again. So, social media would seem to be the next great revenue generator, except, possibly, for the movement from PCs to mobile devices.

Does Mobility Reduce Online Ad Revenue?

The ad click revenue model successfully emerged on PC devices where there is plenty of space for lots of ads. However, as users move from PCs to mobile devices, particularly small-screen smartphones, there is much less ad space. Does this mean a reduction in ad revenue?

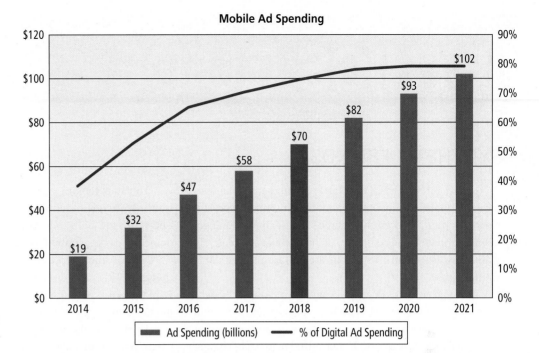

FIGURE 9-8
Mobile Ad Spending

Source: Based on data from "US Ad Spending The eMarketer Forecast for 2017", http://www.mobyaffiliates.com/blog/us-mobile-ad-spend-to-reach-52-8bn-by-2017/

On the surface, yes. According to eMarketer, mobile ad spending will increase more than 20 percent in 2018 to $70B accounting for 75 percent of total digital ad spending.[27] By 2021, as shown in Figure 9-8, mobile ad spending should reach $102B and account for 80 percent of total digital ad spending. However, growth in the number of mobile devices far exceeds PC growth. In 2016, global mobile data traffic increased by 63 percent, and the number of mobile devices worldwide exceeded 8 billion. By 2021, the number of mobile devices is expected to reach 12 billion, which will exceed the world's population.[28] Cisco predicts that by 2021, smartphones will account for 86 percent of total global mobile traffic.[29] So, even though the revenue per device may be lower for mobile devices than PCs, the sheer number of mobile devices may swamp the difference in revenue.

Furthermore, the number of devices is not the whole story. According to Marin Software, the average click-through rate of smartphones is 2.18 percent, while that same rate on PCs is 1.86 percent.[30] So, mobile users click ads more often and hence generate more revenue. This is especially true in Facebook's case. In the first quarter of 2018, 95 percent of Facebook users visited from a mobile device, and 91 percent of its total ad revenue came from mobile ads.[31]

However, clicks aren't the final story either. Because ads take up so much more space on mobile devices than they do on PCs, many of the mobile clicks could have been accidental. **Conversion rate** measures the frequency that someone who clicks on an ad makes a purchase, "likes" a site, or takes some other action desired by the advertiser. According to Monetate, conversion rates for PCs (3.77 percent) are higher than those for tablets (3.40 percent) or smartphones (1.53 percent). So, on average, PC ad clicks are more effective than mobile clicks.[32]

Clickstream data is easy to gather, and as we have seen, analyses of it are widespread. It's possible, for example, to measure click and conversion rates by type of mobile device. According to Moovweb, iOS users have higher conversion rates than Android users, 1.04 percent versus 0.79 percent.[33] But why? Is it the device? Is it the way the ads are integrated into the user experience? Is it the user? Are iOS users more curious than Android users? Or do they have more spendable income? We do not know for sure.

What we can conclude from this morass of confusing data, however, is that mobile devices are most unlikely to spell the death of the Web/social media revenue model. The users are there, the interest is there, and what remains is a design problem: how best to configure the mobile experience to obtain legitimate clicks and conversions. The computer industry is superb at solving design problems; given the current dynamic evolution of mobile interfaces and USX, active, interesting, and compelling ways of presenting ads in iOS/Android/Windows 10 environments are just around the corner.

ETHICS GUIDE

SYNTHETIC FRIENDS

You've just been hired as a marketing manager for a national clothing retailer. Your boss has made it crystal clear that your predecessor was fired because she couldn't get any traction with the company's social media campaign. He wants results—soon. This is your dream job, and you don't want to lose it.

You read an online news article about a person who bought an army of bots that would follow him on Instagram. This could immediately inflate your follower count and show your boss that you're making real progress. Of course, the bots wouldn't be real followers, but if your follower count goes up, it might be easier to attract real human followers. People like popular people.

You do some searching and find an online forum where users are bragging about how realistic their bots are. You even find Web sites (click farms) that advertise Facebook "likes" for sale. You decide to spend $100 and see what happens. You end up getting 15,000 followers that slowly trickle in over the next couple weeks. Not bad. Not bad at all. Real progress that you can show your boss. Well, maybe not "real" progress. But at least it's progress.

You start looking at the profiles of your newly minted synthetic friends and find that they're pretty easy to identify. They only put one word in their name field. But the photos, names, and other content look very believable. You also notice that you've started to attract annoying spammy accounts that leave URLs and discount codes in their comments. This is buggy, but it helps push up your follower count, and that might mean more real followers.

Then comes the purge. Only a few months into your campaign, Instagram starts deleting bots! You lose about 2,000 followers overnight. Ouch. But you still have loads of fictitious followers left. Justin Bieber had the worst hit—3.5 million followers deleted in one day.[34] Other celebrities lost millions of followers as well. You check the news, and it looks like nearly every company, actor, singer, politician, and popular user on Instagram lost followers. You immediately get a sinking feeling in the pit of your stomach. What if you're not the only one who bought followers?

Source: Gilbertc/Fotolia

DISCUSSION QUESTIONS

1. Consider your decision to use company funds to buy an army of bot followers.
   a. Is your action ethical according to the categorical imperative (page 23-24)?
   b. Is your action ethical according to the utilitarian perspective (page 42-43)?
   c. What would your boss say if he found out that all of the company's new corporate followers and Facebook likes are fake?
2. Consider Instagram's action to purge bot accounts.
   a. Is it ethical for Instagram to delete followers? Consider both the categorical imperative and utilitarian perspectives.
   b. Is it ethical for Instagram to allow any bots at all? Consider both the categorical imperative and utilitarian perspectives.
3. How hard should Instagram, or any other social media company, work to eliminate bots?
4. Suppose a social media startup decides to become a publicly traded company. It hasn't been profitable—yet. The number of average monthly users is one of the primary means of valuing the company.
   a. Does it have a *legal* obligation to find out how many of its users are bots?
   b. Does it have an *ethical* obligation to find out how many of its users are bots?
   c. Is there any way for investors to determine how many users are bots? How?
5. Consider the position of an advertising agency or social media company that sells your firm advertising.
   a. Suppose your company is charged based on the number of ads shown to users and the number of clicks on those ads. Does the advertising agency have an ethical obligation to find out how many of the ads it sells are seen by actual humans—not bots?
   b. The advertising agency offers to sell you "likes" for a new product line you're launching. It tells you that buying likes is just like hiring actors for a TV commercial. You're paying them to say they like your product. Is it ethical to buy or sell likes? Consider both the categorical imperative and utilitarian perspectives.

Geofencing

Mobility adds a different dimension in the ability to target customers with ads. Companies can use geofencing to target customers with ads when they are physically on company premises. **Geofencing** is a location service that allows applications to know when a user has crossed a virtual fence (specific location) and then triggers an automated action.

For example, suppose a user enters a coffee shop and her phone automatically connects to the free Wi-Fi. An app on her phone recognizes the coffee shop wireless network and pushes an in-store ad to her phone for a free donut. Her phone might also be able to use her cellular network to determine her location, and she could see that there's a sale on shoes at the outdoor mall down the street.

Geofencing has the potential to make a tremendous impact on a massive number of people because geofencing is technically supported by more than 90 percent of smartphones in the United States. Consumers may like it because they get the right coupon at the right time. Companies like it because it allows them to more accurately target potential customers.

Q9-5 How Do Organizations Develop an Effective SMIS?

The popularity of Bitcoin has attracted social engineers looking to cash in on user's inexperience. Read more about this in the Security Guide on pages 366–367.

At this point in your reading, you know what SMIS are, why they are important, and how they generate revenue. Now you need to know how to develop an effective SMIS that is strategically aligned with your organization's goals. In Q9-2, you saw that SM can be used to benefit an organization, but how do you get to that point? We're not talking about a recipe for turning your organization into the next Facebook. Rather, the steps shown in Figure 9-9 walk you through the process of developing a practical plan to effectively use existing social media platforms.

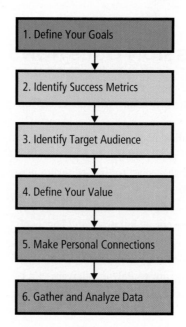

FIGURE 9-9
Social Media Plan Development

Many companies are still unsure how to use SM. They want to use it, but they're unsure how to facilitate their existing competitive strategy. Think back to Porter's model for competitive strategies from Chapter 2 (Figure 2-5). Organizations can focus their strategies on being the cost leader or on differentiating their products from the competition. Organizations can then employ the chosen strategy across an entire industry or focus on a particular segment within that industry. Depending on an organization's strategy, it will use different SM platforms in different ways. Again, the key is premeditated alignment of the SMIS with the organization's strategy.

Organizations know SM is popular and could be strategically beneficial. They hear about it constantly in the news. It's not entirely their fault if they want to jump on board. Social media is a relatively new development with a dizzying array of companies, platforms, and services. It's constantly changing, too.

It's important to understand the development process presented in Figure 9-9 because you may be the "social media expert" at your future job. You may be called in to help develop the organization's SMIS. In order to be successful, take a few minutes to consider the steps in the process.

Step 1: Define Your Goals

It may sound clichéd, but the first step in developing an SMIS is to clearly define what the organization wants to achieve with SM. As previously mentioned, your goals must be clear, deliberate, and aligned with the organization's competitive strategy. Without clearly defined goals, you won't know whether your SM effort was successful.

As you learned in Chapter 2, the goals for each organization are different. For organizations that choose a differentiation strategy, SM goals could include better employee recruiting, quicker product development, becoming an industry product leader, or increasing customer loyalty. In general, most organizations include increased brand awareness, conversion rates, Web site traffic, or user engagement as goals. Figure 9-10 gives you examples of how these might manifest themselves in social media.

Step 2: Identify Success Metrics

After you know what you want to accomplish using SM, you need to identify metrics that will indicate when you've achieved your goals. These are referred to as **success metrics** or **key performance indicators (KPI)**. **Metrics** are simply measurements used to track performance. Every organization has different metrics for success. For example, a law firm may measure billable hours, a hospital may measure patients seen or procedures performed, and a manufacturer may look at units produced or operational efficiency.

Goal	Description	Example
Brand awareness	Extent that users recognize a brand	Organization's brand mentioned in a tweet
Conversion rates	Measures the frequency that someone takes a desired action	Likes the organization's Facebook page
Web site traffic	Quantity, frequency, duration, and depth of visits to a Web site	Traffic from Google+ post mentioning the organization's site
User engagement	Extent to which users interact with a site, application, or other media	User regularly comments on organization's LinkedIn posts

FIGURE 9-10
Common SM Strategic Goals

The hard part in identifying success metrics is identifying the right ones. The right metrics help you make better decisions; the wrong metrics are meaningless and don't positively affect your decision making. For example, measuring the number of registered users on your site may be interesting but not really meaningful. What really matters is the number of *active* users on your site each month. Twitter, for example, had an estimated 700 million yearly active accounts but only 330 million monthly active users.[35] Metrics that don't improve your decision making are commonly referred to as **vanity metrics**.

Figure 9-11 shows examples of possible success metrics for the goals mentioned in Figure 9-10. Remember, in some circumstances you want to maximize the metric, while in others you want to minimize the metric. It's similar to sports in that respect: Sometimes you want a high score (basketball), and other times you want a low score (golf). It just depends on what you're measuring. Whereas you may want to maximize a metric like conversion rate,[36] or the percentage of people who achieve a certain result, you will probably want to minimize other metrics like **bounce rate**, or the percentage of people who visit your Web site and then immediately leave.

Step 3: Identify the Target Audience

The next step in creating an effective SMIS is to clearly identify your target audience. Chances are it's not going to be everyone. For example, if you're Caterpillar Inc. trying to use social media to sell more D11 dozers, your target audience probably won't include many teenagers. Organizations go to great lengths to identify their target audience because it helps them focus their marketing efforts.

Once you've identified your target audience, you need to find out which SM platforms they use. Certain social media platforms attract certain audiences. For example, more than 81 percent of Pinterest users are women,[37] 92 percent of Instagram users are under the age of 49,[38] and 61 percent of LinkedIn users are over 30.[39] Your target audience will influence which SM platforms you use.

Step 4: Define Your Value

After pinpointing your target audience, you'll need to define the value you'll provide your audience. Why should these users listen to you, go to your Web site, like your posts, or tweet about your products? Are you providing news, entertainment, education, employee recruiting, or information?

Goal	Metrics
Brand awareness	Total Twitter followers, audience growth rate, brand mentions in SM, Klout or Kred score
Conversion rates	Click rate on your SM content, assisted social conversions
Web site traffic	Visitor frequency rate, referral traffic from SM
User engagement	Number of SM interactions, reshares of SM content

FIGURE 9-11
Common SM Metrics

See what a typical workday would look like for someone who manages social media in the Career Guide on page 368.

In essence, you need to define what you are going to give your audience in exchange for making a connection with you.

Shopping is a good metaphor to explain how you can do this. When you go shopping, you see something of value and you exchange your *financial* capital (money) with the business for the item you value. The same is true of social media. Your audience members are constantly browsing for things of value, and they have *social* capital to spend. They may eventually spend financial capital at your Web site, but it's the social capital that is most important. You need to define what you're going to offer users in exchange for their social capital.

Take LinkedIn as an example. It helps users find jobs, build a professional network, join special interest groups, get introduced to prospective clients, and reconnect with past colleagues. From an organizational perspective, LinkedIn allows recruiters to quickly identify and contact potential hires from a large pool of candidates. This lowers hiring costs and improves the quality of new hires.

If you're unsure how your organization could add value, start by performing a **competitive analysis** to identify the strengths and weaknesses in your competitors' use of social media. Look at what they're doing right and what they're doing wrong.

Step 5: Make Personal Connections

The true value of social media can be achieved only when organizations use social media to interact with customers, employees, and partners in a more personal, humane, relationship-oriented way.

According to recent studies, younger users are more skeptical of organizational messages and may no longer listen to them. A CivicScience study found that 58 percent of younger consumers ages 18 through 29 were more influenced by social media chatter than either TV ads or Internet ads.[40] Interestingly, the study also found that only 29 percent of consumers over age 55 thought social media chatter was more influential than TV or Internet advertising. Such skepticism by younger consumers is understandable. They grew up with more sources of information and feel comfortable using social media. Skepticism of organizational messages gives a competitive advantage to organizations that can make personal connections with users via social media.

Today, people want informed, useful interactions that help them solve particular problems and satisfy unique needs. They increasingly ignore prepackaged organizational messages that tout product benefits. This requires you to engage audience members, ask them questions, and respond to their posts. It also means you must avoid hard-selling products, overwhelming audience members with content, and contacting them too often.

The sales force in Apple stores is an excellent example of how to make personal connections. Team members have been trained to act as customer problem-solving consultants and not as sellers of products. An organization's use of social media needs to mirror this behavior; otherwise, social media is nothing more than another channel for classic advertising.

Step 6: Gather and Analyze Data

Finally, when creating a social media strategy, you need to gather the right amount of data necessary to make the most informed decision you can. You can use online analytical tools like Google Analytics, Facebook Page Insights, Clicky, or KISSmetrics to measure the success metrics you defined earlier. These tools will show you statistical information such as which tweets get the most attention, which posts generate the most traffic, and which SM platform generates the most referrals.

Then you can refine your use of social media based on the performance of your success metrics. Be sure to rely on analysis of hard data, not anecdotes from friends. Also, remember that the SM landscape is changing rapidly, and today's winners could be tomorrow's losers. MySpace, for example, was the top SM site in late 2007 valued at $65B, but then succumbed to Facebook's success and was sold for $35M in 2011.[41] Users may shift away from current SM giants like Facebook toward a group of more customized applications like Instagram, Twitter, Snapchat, and WhatsApp.[42] Allow your use of social media to be flexible enough to change with the times.

Senior managers need to see regular progress reports about how SM is affecting the organization. They also need to be educated about changes in social media landscape. Watch for SM success stories and communicate them with upper management.

Q9-6 What Is an Enterprise Social Network (ESN)?

An **enterprise social network (ESN)** is a software platform that uses social media to facilitate cooperative work of people *within* an organization. Instead of using outward-facing SM platforms like Facebook and Twitter, it uses specialized enterprise social software designed to be used inside the organization. These applications may incorporate the same functionality used by traditional social media, including blogs, microblogs, status updates, image and video sharing, personal sites, and wikis. The primary goal of enterprise social networks is to improve communication, collaboration, knowledge sharing, problem solving, and decision making.

Enterprise 2.0

In 2006, Andrew McAfee wrote an article about how dynamic user-generated content systems, then termed **Web 2.0**, could be used in an enterprise setting. He described **Enterprise 2.0** as the use of emergent social software platforms within companies.[43] In other words, the term *Enterprise 2.0* refers to the *use* of enterprise social networks.

McAfee defined six characteristics that he refers to with the acronym **SLATES** (see Figure 9-12).[44] First, workers want to be able to *search* for content inside the organization just like they do on the Web. Most workers find that searching is more effective than navigating content structures such as lists and tables of content. Second, workers want to access organizational content via *links*, just as they do on the Web. They also want to *author* organizational content using blogs, wikis, discussion groups, published presentations, and so on.

According to McAfee, a fourth characteristic of ESNs is that their content is *tagged*, just like content on the Web, and these tags are organized into structures, as is done on the Web at sites like Delicious (*www.delicious.com*). These structures organize tags as a taxonomy does, but, unlike taxonomies, they are not preplanned; they emerge organically. In other words, ESNs employ a **folksonomy**, or a content structure that emerges from the processing of many user tags. Fifth, workers want applications that enable them to rate tagged content and to use the tags to predict content that will be of interest to them (as with Pandora), a process McAfee refers to as *extensions*. Finally, workers want relevant content pushed to them; or, in McAfee's terminology, they want to be *signaled* when something of interest to them happens in organizational content.

FIGURE 9-12
McAfee's SLATES Model
Source: Based on Andrew McAfee, "Enterprise 2.0: The Dawn of Emergent Collaboration," *MIT Sloan Management Review*, Spring 2006, *http://sloanreview. mit.edu/article/enterprise-the-dawn-of-emergent-collaboration*.

Enterprise 2.0 Component	Remarks
Search	People have more success searching than they do in finding from structured content.
Links	Links to enterprise resources (like on the Web).
Authoring	Create enterprise content via blogs, wikis, discussion groups, presentations, etc.
Tags	Flexible tagging (like Delicious) results in folksonomies of enterprise content.
Extensions	Using usage patterns to offer enterprise content via tag processing (like the style of Pandora).
Signals	Pushing enterprise content to users based on subscriptions and alerts.

The potential problem with ESNs is the quality of their dynamic process. Because the benefits of an ESN result from emergence, there is no way to control for either effectiveness or efficiency. It's a messy process about which little can be predicted.

Changing Communication

Prior to 1980, communication in the United States was restricted to a few **communication channels**, or means of delivering messages. There were three major national TV networks and no more than a half-dozen major national newspapers. Consumers got their news twice a day: from the morning paper and the evening news. A small number of people decided which stories were told. You got what you were given with few alternatives.

Communication within organizations was similarly restricted. Employees could communicate with their immediate supervisor and coworkers in their vicinity. It was difficult for employees of large corporations to get private meetings with the CEO or to communicate with their counterparts in other countries. If an employee had a good idea, it was passed up through his or her boss to senior management. As a result, it was common for bosses to claim subordinates' ideas as their own.

In recent decades, the Internet, Web sites, social networking, email, cable TV, and smartphones have radically altered existing communication channels. At the societal level, you can now get your news instantly from hundreds of different sources. Traditional news organizations have struggled to adapt to changes in traditional communication channels.

Communication channels within corporations have changed in equally dramatic ways. Using ESNs, employees can now bypass managers and post ideas directly for the CEO to read. They can also quickly identify internal subject matter experts to solve unforeseen problems. In addition, ESNs also enable collaboration with teams dispersed across the globe.

To better understand the potential impacts of ESNs, let's consider an example. In 2012, Yammer (a Microsoft subsidiary) conducted a case study analyzing how restaurant chain Red Robin used an ESN to transform its business.[45] The CIO of Red Robin Chris Laping rolled out Yammer to Red Robin's 26,000 employees across 450 restaurants in an effort to give line employees a voice. This effort yielded more than just stronger employee engagement.

When Red Robin rolled out its new Pig Out Style Double Tavern Burger, for instance, the customer response was disappointing. Employees used Yammer to give management immediate feedback about how the Pig Out recipe could be fixed. Within 4 months, the improved burger was ready to go. Here, using Yammer to improve internal communication resulted in an increase in organizational responsiveness. The result was a reduction in the amount of time needed to revamp the menu from 12 to 18 months to just 4 months.

In another example, Red Robin's CFO offered a $1,000 employee bonus for the best cost-saving idea. The winning idea was reusable kids' cups that saved hundreds of thousands of dollars. Laping attributes the cost savings to the ESN, stating, "I'm convinced that idea would never have surfaced if we didn't have a social network."[46]

Deploying Successful Enterprise Social Networks

The use of ESNs in organizations is new, and organizations are still learning how to use ESNs successfully (creating fascinating job opportunities for you, by the way.) Before deploying an ESN, organizations should develop a strategic plan for using SM *internally* via the same process they used for their *external* social media use. Once a strategic plan has been created, an ESN can then be implemented.

Deploying new systems—including ESNs—can be problematic, so the organization's strategic plan should be sure to address possible challenges, including the likelihood of employee resistance. Will employees adopt the new system? Not everyone uses every social media platform in their personal lives, so why should they use them at work?

In order to ensure a successful implementation of an ESN, organizations can also follow industry **best practices**, or methods that have been shown to produce successful results in prior implementations. You'll learn more about systems implementation in Chapter 12. When implementing an ESN, successful companies follow a process of four stages having the elements shown in Figure 9-13. Read

	ESN Deployment Best Practices
Strategy	1. Define how ESN supports the organization's existing goals and objectives. 2. Define success metrics. 3. Communicate the ESN strategy to all users. 4. Convey an expectation of organization-wide ESN adoption.
Sponsorship	5. Identify an executive sponsor to promote the ESN. 6. Identify ESN champions within each organizational unit. 7. Encourage champions to recruit users. 8. Identify groups that would benefit most from the ESN.
Support	9. Provide all users access to the ESN. 10. Mandate processes to be used within the ESN. 11. Provide incentives for ESN adoption and use. 12. Provide employee training and ESN demonstrations.
Success	13. Measure ESN effectiveness via success metrics. 14. Evaluate how ESN supports the organization's strategy. 15. Promote ESN success stories. 16. Continuously look for ways to use the ESN more effectively.

FIGURE 9-13
ESN Implementation Best Practices

through the items and reflect on what you went through when you first started using SM. Think about how important your friends were in your decision to start using SM. Having an internal champion or defender of your internal ESN is equally important.

Q9-7 How Can Organizations Address SMIS Security Concerns?

As you have seen, social media revolutionizes the ways that organizations communicate. Twenty years ago, most organizations managed all public and internal messaging with the highest degree of control. Every press conference, press release, public interview, presentation, and even academic paper needed to be preapproved by both the legal and marketing departments. Such approval could take weeks or months.

Today, progressive organizations have turned that model on its head. Employees are encouraged to engage with communities and, in most organizations, to identify themselves with their employer while doing so. All of this participation, all of this engagement, however, comes with risks. In this question, we will discuss the need for a social media policy, consider risks from nonemployee user-generated content, and look at risks from employee use of social media.

Managing the Risk of Employee Communication

The first step that any organization should take is to develop and publicize a **social media policy**, which is a statement that delineates employees' rights and responsibilities. You can find an index to 100 different policies at the Social Media Today Web site.[47] In general, the more technical the organization, the more open and lenient the social policies. The U.S. military has, perhaps surprisingly, endorsed social media with enthusiasm, tempered by the need to protect classified data.

Intel Corporation has pioneered open and employee-trusting SM policies, policies that continue to evolve as the company gains more experience with employee-written social media. The three key pillars of Intel's policy in 2018 are:

- Disclose
- Protect
- Use Common Sense[48]

3 Rules of Engagement

Disclose
Your presence in social media must be transparent.

Protect
Take extra care to protect both Intel and yourself.

Use Common Sense
Remember that professional, straightforward, and appropriate communication is best.

FIGURE 9-14
Intel's Rules of Social Media Engagement
Source: Based on Intel Corporation www.intel.com/content/ www/us/en/legal/intel-social-media-guidelines.html

Those policies are further developed as shown in Figure 9-14. Visit *www.intel.com/content/ www/us/en/legal/intel-social-media-guidelines.html* to read Intel's social media guidelines in full. Be sure to read carefully, as the guidelines contain great advice and considerable wisdom.

Two elements in this list are particularly noteworthy. The first is the call for transparency and truth. As an experienced and wise business professional once shared, "Nothing is more serviceable than the truth." Truth may not be convenient, but it is serviceable over the long term. Second, SM contributors and their employers should be open and candid. If you make a mistake, don't obfuscate; instead, correct it, apologize, and make amends. The SM world is too open, too broad, and too powerful to fool.

In 2015, BBC reporter Ahmen Khawaja sent out a tweet that "Queen Elizabeth has died." Fortunately for the Queen, she was still very much alive. Two hours later Khawaja tweeted that it was all a "silly prank," but the damage was done.

The best way to avoid these types of missteps is to include an SM awareness module in users' annual security training. Social media is still new to many users. Honestly, they may be unaware a policy even exists. When cell phones first became popular, they were constantly ringing in movie theaters. Over time, people learned to mute their phones before entering a crowded theater. It just takes time for society to catch up to technology. Training helps.

Managing the Risk of Inappropriate Content

As with any relationship, comments can be inappropriate or excessively negative in tone or be otherwise problematic. Organizations need to determine how they will deal with such content before engaging in social media. This is done by designating a single individual to be responsible for official organizational SM interactions and by creating a process to monitor and manage SM interactions. This allows the organization to have a clear, coordinated, and consistent message.

User-generated content (UGC), which simply means content on your SM site that is contributed by users, is the essence of SM relationships. Following are a few examples of inappropriate UGC that can negatively affect organizations.

Problems from External Sources

The major sources of UGC problems are:

- Junk and crackpot contributions
- Inappropriate content
- Unfavorable reviews
- Mutinous movements

When a business participates in a social network or opens its site to UGC, it opens itself to misguided people who post junk unrelated to the site's purpose. Crackpots may also use the network or UGC site as a way of expressing passionately held views about unrelated topics, such as UFOs, government cover-ups, fantastic conspiracy theories, and so forth. Because of the possibility of such content, organizations should regularly monitor the site and remove objectionable material immediately. Monitoring can be done by employees or by companies such as Bazaarvoice, which offer services not only to collect and manage ratings and reviews, but also to monitor sites for irrelevant content.

Unfavorable reviews are another risk. Research indicates that customers are sophisticated enough to know that few, if any, products are perfect. Most customers want to know the disadvantages of a product before purchasing it so they can determine whether those disadvantages are important for their application. However, if every review is bad, if the product is rated 1 star out of 5, then the company is using social media to publish its problems. In this case, some action must be taken.

Sometimes inappropriate social media content can come from unexpected places. In 2016 Microsoft released its artificial intelligence chatbot "Tay" on Twitter. Tay was supposed to increase user engagement by learning from them. Unfortunately it learned to be extremely racist and sexist from its interactions. Microsoft disabled Tay after a series of horribly offensive tweets.[49]

Responding to Social Networking Problems

Part of managing social networking risk is knowing the sources of potential problems and monitoring sites for problematic content. Once such content is found, however, organizations need to respond appropriately. Three possibilities in such situations are:

- Leave it
- Respond to it
- Delete it

If the problematic content represents reasonable criticism of the organization's products or services, the best response may be to leave it where it is. Such criticism indicates that the site is not just a shill for the organization but contains legitimate user content. Such criticism also serves as a free source of product reviews, which can be useful for product development. For the criticism to be useful, the development team needs to know about it, so, as stated, processes to ensure the criticism is found and communicated to the team are necessary.

A second alternative is to respond to the problematic content. However, this alternative is dangerous. If the response can be construed in any way as patronizing or insulting to the content contributor, it can enrage the community and generate a strong backlash. Also, if the response appears defensive, it can become a public relations negative.

In most cases, responses are best reserved for when the problematic content has caused the organization to do something positive as a result. For example, suppose a user publishes that he or she was required to hold for customer support for 45 minutes. If the organization has done something to reduce wait times, then an effective response to the criticism is to recognize it as valid and to state, nondefensively, what has been done to reduce wait times.

If a reasoned, nondefensive response generates continued and unreasonable UGC from that same source, it is best for the organization to do nothing. Never wrestle with a pig; you'll get dirty, and the pig will enjoy it. Instead, allow the community to constrain the user. It will.

Deleting content should be reserved for contributions that are inappropriate because they are contributed by crackpots, have nothing to do with the site, or contain obscene or otherwise inappropriate content. Deleting legitimate negative comments can result in a strong user backlash. In the early days of social media, Nestlé created a PR nightmare on its Facebook account with its response to criticism it received about its use of palm oil. Someone altered the Nestlé logo, and in response Nestlé decided to delete all Facebook contributions that used that altered logo and did so in an arrogant, heavy-handed way. The result was a negative firestorm on Twitter.[50]

A sound principle in business is to never ask a question to which you do not want the answer. We can extend that principle to social networking; never set up a site that will generate content for which you have no effective response!

Internal Risks from Social Media

The increased adoption of social media has created new risks within organizations as well. These risks include threats to information security, increased organizational liability, and decreased employee productivity.

First, the use of social media can directly affect the ability of an organization to secure its information resources. For example, suppose a senior-level employee tweets, "Married 20 years ago today in Dallas," or "Class of 1984 reunion at Central High School was awesome," or "Remembering my honeymoon to Hawaii." All of these tweets provide attackers with the answers to password reset questions. Once attackers reset the user's passwords, they could have full access to internal systems. Thus, seemingly innocuous comments can inadvertently leak information used to secure access to organizational resources. Unfortunately, it turns out that it's not a good idea to tell everyone it's your birthday because your date of birth (DOB) can be used to steal your identity.

Employees using social media also can unintentionally (or intentionally) leak information about intellectual property, new marketing campaigns, future products, potential layoffs, budget woes, product flaws, or upcoming mergers. It's not just information leakage, either. Employees may install unauthorized apps that deliver content using SM that bypasses existing security measures. Or worse, they may use their corporate password at less secure SM sites.

Second, employees may inadvertently increase corporate liability when they use social media. For example, suppose a coworker regularly looks at SM content with questionable sexual content on his or her own smartphone. The organization could be slapped with a sexual harassment lawsuit. Other organizations may face legal issues if employees leak information via social media. Schools, healthcare providers, and financial institutions must all follow specific guidelines to protect user data and avoid regulatory compliance violations. Thus, tweeting about students, patients, or customer accounts could have legal consequences.

Finally, increased use of social media can be a threat to employee productivity. Posts, tweets, pins, likes, comments, and endorsements all take time. This is time employers are paying for but not benefiting from. *Forbes* notes that 64 percent of employees visit non-work-related Web sites each day. Among the SM sites that are most detrimental to employee productivity are Tumblr (57 percent), Facebook (52 percent), Twitter (17 percent), Instagram (11 percent), and Snapchat (4 percent).[51]

From an employee's point of view, you might think a little lost productivity is OK. But imagine you're the employer or manager, which hopefully you'll be at some point. Would you mind if your employees spend their days using SM to look for another job, chat with friends, or look at vacation pictures when your paycheck is tied to their productivity? What if SM is being used for interoffice gossip that creates HR problems, morale issues, and possible lawsuits? Smart managers will understand that, like any technology, SM comes with both benefits and costs.

Q9-8   2029?

Social media has hit a rough patch lately. Facebook founder Mark Zuckerberg was recently asked to testify before the U.S. Congress about a large data breach affecting more than 80 million people. It turns out a researcher had siphoned off Facebook user data and then sold it to an analytics firm before Facebook enacted tighter data restrictions. This violation of user privacy resulted in a swarm of news articles critical of all social media.

Over the past decade, social media has been seen as something fun that could reach customers in new ways. And it was fun. It did reach customers in new ways that changed the marketing landscape. Social media companies received generous praise and huge market valuations. But there was always the question of how these companies were going to make money. Most of them relied on selling user data to increase ad revenue. The general belief was that users wouldn't mind the "small" loss of privacy if they got the service for free. But what if they did mind?

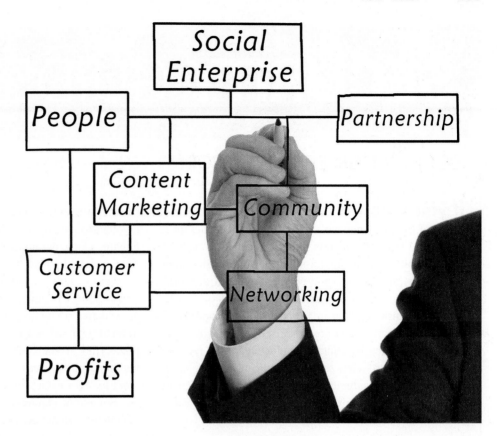

FIGURE 9-15
Redesigning Enterprises for Social Media
Source: Stephen VanHorn/Fotolia

By 2029, the social media landscape will look much different than it does now. The honeymoon phase of social media is over. Privacy is becoming important again, teens are leaving Facebook,[52] and quitting social media (or at least taking a break) is becoming a cool thing to do.[53]

In many ways, social media is like your driver's license. It made driving fun and exciting when you first got it. But over time, driving became more of a utility. It became something you had to do to get from point A to point B. What happens when social media becomes a utility? What happens to social media companies when their products (you) decide to leave? Whose information will they sell?

There are still tremendous opportunities for growth in the social media space. Enterprises are starting to use it internally (Enterprise 2.0). Is there an Enterprise 3.0 around the corner? New mobile devices with innovative mobile-device UX, coupled with dynamic and agile information systems based on cloud computing and dynamic virtualization, guarantee that monumental changes will continue to occur between now and 2029. (See Figure 9-15.)

The explosive growth of IoT devices has opened up entirely new markets for social media. For example, a network-enabled fitness tracker can now send workout data to the cloud where it can be used as part of a friendly competition with friends. Fitness trackers can now be part of a larger social interaction. Imagine the new types of social interactions that will come when mixed-reality devices become popular. You could sit in a virtual college class, play an online game with friends, and IM coworkers all while you're physically sitting at your desk at work.

Organizations like Harvard, Microsoft, and Starbucks are concerned enough with social media that they have hired chief digital officers (CDOs), a position responsible for developing and managing innovative social media programs.[54]

Think about your role as a manager in 2029. Say your team has 10 people, three of whom report to you; two report to other managers, and five work for different companies. Your company uses a variety of desktops, laptops, tablets, phones, and virtual devices. Some of these are issued by the company, but most are brought in by employees. All of these devices have features that enable employees and teams to instantly publish their ideas in blogs, wikis, videos, and whatever other means have become available.

SECURITY GUIDE

SOCIAL ENGINEERING BITCOIN

If you keep an eye on the nightly news, you are well aware of the frequency with which security breaches make headlines. Clearly, information security practitioners are fighting an uphill battle due to the volume of attacks that target companies, universities, and even government organizations. A common misconception is that the bulk of security threats organizations face are introduced by nefarious hackers or cybercriminals sponsored by foreign governments. However, a recent security analysis conducted by PwC reported that insiders, third-party suppliers, and contractors pose an increasingly serious threat.[55] In short, many of the security threats plaguing organizations today originate from within the company (or within its partner network).

The Weakest Link

This trend is due to the relative ease with which people can be manipulated and compromised. Hackers often resort to exploiting people's desire to be friendly and help others rather than exploiting vulnerabilities in hardware or software. This concept is often referred to as *social engineering*, or the process of manipulating individuals to access secure systems, gain confidential information, or violate the integrity of secure systems.

While social engineering presents a clear threat to organizational information security, it can also be highly effective in other contexts in which people feel pressured and make rash decisions. In fact, social engineering has introduced a number of new threats into the frenzied world of investing in cryptocurrencies.

Social Engineers Striking It Rich

The world of cryptocurrencies has evolved rapidly, and it recently reached the tipping point of becoming mainstream with the surge in value of Bitcoin. All types of people from finance gurus, tech investors, and savvy high school students have succumbed to their speculative side and tried to "get rich quick" from this trend. However, the world of cryptocurrency is complex. Due to its immaturity, there are virtually no controls or regulatory mechanisms in place to protect the people

participating in this market. In light of the frantic interest in cryptocurrency; the technical complexities associated with buying, selling, or mining it; and the lack of any sort of oversight, it is ripe for exploitation by social engineers.

For example, some scammers are targeting cryptocurrency mining equipment. *Cryptocurrency mining* is the process of validating recent cryptocurrency transactions and distributing the updated "ledger" to all of the devices associated with that cryptocurrency's network. In return for performing this function, miners can receive a payment in that cryptocurrency for a percentage of the transaction's value.

But mining requires an extremely powerful system or grid of systems, which may be infeasible for a single individual to purchase and manage. Social engineers have begun scamming people into investing in mining equipment that does not exist, convincing victims to contribute the idle computing power of their systems to mine cryptocurrencies but never paying them for their contribution, and soliciting would-be miners to buy fraudulent hardware (that is not as powerful as advertised) for use in mining.[56]

Another cryptocurrency scam currently involves selling people cryptocurrencies that do not actually exist. Bitcoin is certainly the most high-profile cryptocurrency market, but there has been a flurry of initial coin offerings (ICOs) in which new currencies are introduced. In fact, in the first quarter of

Source: Nils Ackermann/Alamy Stock Photo

2018, there were 101 ICOs.[57] Additionally, there have been more than 300 ICOs since the value of Bitcoin witnessed substantial gains in 2017.[58]

With all of this activity, it can be extremely difficult to keep track of and verify which currencies are legitimate and which have any sort of investment value. The market is so murky that even some financial institutions have been duped.[59] The best way to participate in the cryptocurrency gold rush is to use best practices that apply to general financial transactions. Always use common sense, verify the parties that are involved in the transaction, avoid investment opportunities that sound too good to be true, and, when in doubt, do not hesitate to do more research![60]

DISCUSSION QUESTIONS

1. Why might an insider pose a greater threat to an internal secure system than an outside attacker? How could an insider be a weak link?

2. What is social engineering? How could attackers use social engineering to compromise a secure internal system?

3. What is cryptocurrency mining? How does it generate money?

4. How would attackers use social engineering to scam users into mining?

Of course, your employees have their own accounts on Facebook, Twitter, LinkedIn, Foursquare, and whatever other social networking sites have become popular, and they regularly contribute to them. How do you manage this team? If "management" means to plan, organize, and control, how can you accomplish any of these functions in this emergent network of employees? If you and your organization follow the lead of tech-savvy companies such as Intel, you'll know you cannot close the door on your employees' SM lives, nor will you want to. Instead, you'll harness the power of the social behavior of your employees and partners to advance your strategy.

So what, then? Maybe we can take a lesson from biology. Crabs have an external exoskeleton. Deer, much later in the evolutionary chain, have an internal endoskeleton. When crabs grow, they must endure the laborious and biologically expensive process of shedding a small shell and growing a larger one. They are also vulnerable during the transition. When deer grow, the skeleton inside grows with the deer. No need for vulnerable molting. And, considering agility, would you take a crab over a deer? In the 1960s, organizations were the exoskeleton around employees. By 2029, organizations will be the endoskeleton, supporting the work of people on the exterior.

What all of this means for you is that social media + IoT + cloud will create fascinating opportunities for your nonroutine cognitive skills in the next 10 years!

CAREER GUIDE

Name: Adam Young
Company: RC Willey
Job Title: Social Media/Online Reputation Manager
Education: University of Utah

1 How did you get this type of job?

I started working at RC Willey in the marketing department while I was going to college at the University of Utah. I worked my way up and took on social media and other online marketing opportunites when RC Willey decided it needed to move in that direction. I worked hard, and I did what it took to make the people around me successful. Those people recognized my hard work and my dedication to making the company successful, and my dedication paid off.

2 What attracted you to this field?

As I was going through my degree and working to pay my way through school, some of the skills that came naturally to me were in marketing and technology. While looking for career opportunities, I saw that technology was always going to be important and was constantly evolving. I've always liked new challenges, and this looked like a good starting point.

3 What does a typical workday look like for you (duties, decisions, problems)?

Every day I go over the reports from the previous day. I also create new reports to help me understand the day-to-day trends. I use my marketing tools to respond to positive and negative feedback and reviews, and I work with management to address any concerns. I create content for the various social media platforms and schedule it to be posted. I also attend meetings with the marketing department.

4 What do you like most about your job?

One of the best things about my job is that I get to help people. Not everyone is happy with their current situation, and I get to reach out and do what I can to take care of those individuals and see what the company can do to address their concerns. One of the best things is when someone completely changes their mind-set about the company because I addressed their concerns when they thought nobody cared about or was willing to listen to them.

5 What skills would someone need to do well at your job?

Being able to manage your time is an essential part of being a social media manager. You also need to be a good communicator. Being able to analyze data and create the story that the marketing team wants to tell is key.

6 Are education or certifications important in your field? Why?

Most companies require an educational background in marketing and/or communications or something similar. Most are looking for experience as well. While other certifications in media buying, content creation, influencer marketing, etc., are beneficial, they are not always necessary.

7 What advice would you give to someone who is considering working in your field?

Do as much as you can to gain as much experience as you can before you graduate. A lot of companies are looking for experience. The more that you do now to develop those skill sets, the better you will stand out.

8 What do you think will be hot tech jobs in 10 years?

I think that most everything is going toward the tech industry right now. I think some of the hot tech jobs in industry will be programming engineers and digital marketing in different capacities.

ACTIVE REVIEW

Use this Active Review to verify that you understand the ideas and concepts that answer this chapter's study questions.

Q9-1 What is a social media information system (SMIS)?

Define *social media, communities of practice, social media information systems, social media provider,* and *social networks.* Name and describe three SMIS organizational roles. Explain the elements of Figure 9-3. In your own words, explain the nature of the five components of SMIS for each of the three SMIS organizational roles.

Q9-2 How do SMIS advance organizational strategy?

Summarize how social media contributes to sales and marketing, customer support, inbound logistics, outbound logistics, manufacturing and operations, and human resources. Name SM risks for each activity. Define *social CRM* and *crowdsourcing.*

Q9-3 How do SMIS increase social capital?

Define *capital, human capital,* and *social capital.* Explain four ways that social capital adds value. Name three factors that determine social capital and explain how "they are more multiplicative than additive." Define *influencer* and describe how you could use social media to increase the number and strength of your social relationships.

Q9-4 How do (some) companies earn revenue from social media?

Define *monetize* and describe why it's difficult for social media companies to generate revenue. Give examples of how social media companies generate revenue from advertising and charging for premium services. Define *pay-per-click, conversion rate,* and *freemium.* Define *ad blocking* and explain how it hurts online companies' ability to generate revenue. Summarize how growth in mobile devices affects revenue streams. Explain why concerns about mobile devices limiting ad revenue are overreactions.

Q9-5 How do organizations develop an effective SMIS?

Discuss why aligning the development of SMIS with the organization's strategy is important. Describe the process of developing an effective SMIS. List four common social media goals and describe why they are important. Define *metrics, success metrics,* and *vanity*

metrics and give examples of metrics that could be measured for the four goals mentioned previously. Describe the importance of making personal connections with users.

Q9-6 What is an enterprise social network (ESN)?

Define *enterprise social network (ESN)* and describe the primary goal of an ESN. Define *Web 2.0* and *Enterprise 2.0.* Explain each element of the model. Explain how changes in communication channels have changed the way organizations communicate with employees. Give an example of how an ESN could benefit an organization. Define *best practices* and explain how the ESN implementation best practices listed in Figure 9-13 could improve adoption of the ESN.

Q9-7 How can organizations address SMIS security concerns?

Name and describe two sources of SM risk. Describe the purpose of an SM policy and summarize Intel's guiding principles. Describe an SM mistake, other than one in this text, and explain the wise response to it. Name four sources of problems of UGC; name three possible responses and give the advantages and disadvantages of each. Explain how internal use of social media can create risks to information security, organizational liability, and employee productivity.

Q9-8 2029?

Describe ways in which the use of social media is changing today. Summarize possible management challenges when controlling employees in 2029. Describe the text's suggested response. Describe how a social media company might be able to benefit from an IoT device. Explain the relationship of the differences between crab and deer to this change.

Using Your Knowledge with ARES

This chapter has given you several important models for assessing the ARES system's social media program. You can apply the components of SMIS to understand the commitment that Zev Friedman and developers must make. You can use organizational strategy and social capital models to assess the desirability of social media to companies that participate in ARES. You can also consider whether ARES might want to generate revenue via a freemium model or by placing ads within the application. You can help craft an effective social media strategy for ARES and help Zev manage the risks of using social media.

KEY TERMS AND CONCEPTS

Ad-blocking software   352
Best practices   360
Bounce rate   357
Business-to-business
    (B2B)   344
Business-to-consumer
    (B2C)   344
Capital   345
Communication channels   360
Communities   337
Communities of practice   337
Competitive analysis   358
Connection data   341
Content data   341
Conversion rate   353

Crowdsourcing   344
Enterprise 2.0   359
Enterprise social network (ESN)   359
Folksonomy   359
Freemium   352
Geofencing   355
Human capital   345
Influencer   347
Key performance indicators (KPI)   356
Metrics   356
Monetize   351
Pay per click   352
SLATES   359
Social capital   345
Social CRM   342

Social media (SM)   337
Social media information system
    (SMIS)   337
Social media policy   361
Social media providers   338
Social networks   338
Strength of a relationship   349
Success metrics   356
Use increases value   352
User-generated content (UGC)   362
Users   339
Value of social capital   346
Vanity metrics   357
Viral hook   339
Web 2.0   359

MyLab MIS

To complete the problems with MyLab MIS, go to EOC Discussion Questions in the MyLab.

USING YOUR KNOWLEDGE

9-1. Using the Facebook page of a company that you have
MyLab MIS   "liked" (or would choose to), fill out the five components of an SMIS grid shown in Q9-1. Strive to replace the phrases in that grid with specific statements that pertain to Facebook, the company you like, and you and users whom you know. For example, if you and your friends access Facebook using an Android phone, enter that specific device.

9-2. Name a company for which you would like to work. Describe,
MyLab MIS   as specifically as you can, how that company could use social media in each of the areas from Q9-2 listed in parts a through f of this question. Include community type, specific focus, processes involved, risks, and any other observations.
   a. Sales and marketing
   b. Customer service
   c. Inbound logistics
   d. Outbound logistics
   e. Manufacturing and operations
   f. Human resources

9-3. Visit *www.lie-nielsen.com* or *www.sephora.com*. On the
MyLab MIS   site you chose, find links to social networking sites. In what ways are those sites sharing their social capital with you? In what ways are they attempting to cause you to share your social capital with them? Describe the business value of social networking to the business you chose.

9-4. Visit *www.intel.com/content/www/us/en/legal/intel-social-media-guidelines.html*. Explain why Intel's social media guidelines might accomplish one or more of the common social media strategic goals listed in Figure 9-10.

9-5. Visit *www.socialmediatoday.com/content/social-media-employee-policy-examples-over-100-organizations*. Find an organization with a very restrictive employee SM policy. Name the organization, and explain why you find that policy restrictive. Does that policy cause you to feel positive, negative, or neutral about that company? Explain.

COLLABORATION EXERCISE 9

Using the collaboration IS you built in Chapter 1 (page 32), collaborate with a group of students to answer the following questions.

Twitter's IPO on November 7, 2013, was one of the biggest tech IPOs in history. The social media giant's stock closed that day at $44.90 a share, making the company worth an estimated $25B.[61] Not bad for a company that had never made a profit. In fact, Twitter posted a $70M loss the quarter before listing! How could a company be worth $25B and never have made any money?

Analysts argue that tech companies, like those shown in Figure 9-16, should be valued based on growth potential, user base, consumer engagement, and market size. It turns out that Amazon, Instagram, and Pinterest weren't profitable when they went public, either.

Traditional IPO valuations focus on measures of profitability. This means investors look at revenues, profits, assets, liabilities, and new products. Figure 9-16 shows price-to-earnings ratios (P/E) for several well-known traditional and tech companies.

Using iteration and feedback, answer the following questions:

9-6. Compare the tech companies' P/E ratios to the traditional companies' P/E ratios. Note that some of the tech companies have *very* high P/E ratios. (A low P/E is good; a high P/E is bad.) Some don't even have a P/E ratio because they didn't turn a profit. As a group, list the reasons why the tech companies have such high P/E ratios. Are the prices of these companies' stocks justified given the earnings? Why?

9-7. Identify public tech stocks you believe are undervalued (not limited to this list). Design an investment portfolio consisting solely of tech stocks that you believe will be profitable. Justify your decision with regard to risk and return on those stocks.

9-8. Create a free online portfolio of these stocks (i.e., via Yahoo! Finance) and track its progress. Report on its performance.

9-9. Could overvalued tech stocks lead to a dot-com 2.0 crash like the original dot-com crash in 1999–2001? Discuss why this may or may not happen. Summarize your discussion in a couple of paragraphs.

Tech Companies	Market Cap (billions)	P/E
Apple	$940	18
Google	$788	30
Facebook	$554	28
Amazon	$819	266
Salesforce.com	$98	146
Netflix	$157	216
Twitter	$31	85

Traditional Companies	Market Cap (billions)	P/E
General Electric	$121	NA
Wal-Mart Stores	$249	28
Verizon Comm.	$203	14
Toyota	$202	9
General Motors	$63	11
Johnson & Johnson	$329	23
Ford	$47	6

FIGURE 9-16
Tech Company Valuations

LinkedIn

For a newly launched social networking company, having only 20 people sign up per day could indicate you are doomed to fail. This is especially true if the team of colleagues involved had worked for successful ventures like SocialNet and PayPal. However, in 2002, this was the case for LinkedIn, the business-oriented social networking site headquartered in Mountain View, California. Venture capitalist Reid Hoffman assembled the team of designers and engineers who created the social networking site.

Growing the Network

Growth for the company was very slow in the beginning. Some days, only 20 people per day would sign up to become members. Metcalfe's Law states that the value of a social network is proportional to the square of the number of connected users of the system. By this logic, if LinkedIn couldn't get users to sign up, the company wouldn't be worth anything.

However, the company finally became profitable in 2006 when it boasted more than 5 million members. In 2010, LinkedIn experienced hypergrowth and saw membership climb to 90 million, with more than 1,000 employees in 10 offices around the world.[62] The company was adding nearly two new members every second! One year later, in 2011, LinkedIn celebrated its eighth anniversary and enjoyed a membership of more than 115 million members.

That same year, LinkedIn became publicly traded on the New York Stock Exchange and was valued at more than $4.5 billion. At the time, LinkedIn was earning more than $150 million per year in advertising revenue, which was $15 million more than social networking giant Twitter was earning from advertising.

Professional Network

Unlike other popular social networks that focus on friendships and recreation, LinkedIn focuses on professional connections. People use the site to highlight career skills and promote professional résumés. LinkedIn allows people to be introduced via common connections and allows job seekers to become connected with people posting jobs.

Employers can target the exact type of person they are looking for and post jobs for those qualified individuals to see. Connecting colleagues, professionals, recruiters, job seekers, and employers is at the core of what LinkedIn is all about. LinkedIn is for all people interested in taking their professional life more seriously.

Leveraging Microsoft

In 2016, LinkedIn was acquired by Microsoft for $26 billion. At the time the company had more than 9,000 employees and claimed more than half a billion members in more than 200 countries worldwide. More than 20,000 companies buy LinkedIn Recruiter accounts to help find potential employees. Job seekers can comb through more than 11 million job openings posted by the largest companies in the world.

The acquisition of LinkedIn raised a lot of questions. Why did Microsoft's CEO Satya Nadella buy LinkedIn? Would the two companies be worth more together than apart? This was Microsoft's largest acquisition, and it was coming on the heels of a disastrous acquisition of mobile phone maker Nokia for $7 billion.

In separate blog posts, Satya Nadella and LinkedIn CEO Jeff Weiner outlined the ways the two companies plan to integrate products and leverage Microsoft's scale.[63] Some of the ways they're planning on achieving their shared vision include:

1. Incorporating LinkedIn's identity and network in Microsoft Outlook and the Office suite
2. Supporting LinkedIn notifications within the Windows action center
3. Enabling members drafting résumés in Word to update their profiles and to discover and apply to jobs on LinkedIn
4. Extending the reach of Sponsored Content across Microsoft properties

Source: Jejim120 / Alamy Stock Photo

5. Powering Enterprise LinkedIn Lookup by Active Directory and Office 365

6. Making LinkedIn Learning available across the Office 365 and Windows ecosystem

7. Developing a business news desk across the content ecosystem and MSN.com

8. Redefining social selling through the combination of Sales Navigator and Dynamics 365

Some of these ideas show real promise. They would allow the large core of Microsoft users much greater reach on LinkedIn. Nearly every corporation uses some form of Microsoft products. Its desktop operating system sits on more than 88 percent of all desktops. Within corporations, that percentage is even higher. If LinkedIn is successfully integrated across all Windows products, LinkedIn will have greater reach and more frequent contact with end users. Consequently, that could lead to rapid growth of its userbase and its profitability.

QUESTIONS

9-10. Why is growing the number of users such an important metric for social media companies? How does Metcalfe's Law relate to the profitability of social media companies?

9-11. Most social media companies rely on ad revenue as their main source of income. What are other ways that LinkedIn generates income? Why is it important for a company to have multiple ways of generating income?

9-12. Why do recruiters and job seekers like LinkedIn? Explain why an employer may dislike LinkedIn. Is there a strategic disadvantage to having your employees list detailed profiles on LinkedIn?

9-13. LinkedIn targets a specific demographic: working professionals. They tend to be older and better educated. Why might advertisers be more interested in this group over others?

9-14. Microsoft creates software focused on supporting businesses. LinkedIn focuses on creating a platform for business professionals. Does the acquisition of LinkedIn make sense? What type of synergies could come from integrating products from these two companies?

9-15. How would the integration of LinkedIn into the Microsoft Office Suite be beneficial?

9-16. How would enabling draft résumés in Microsoft Word to update connected LinkedIn profiles be beneficial?

9-17. Suppose you are advising Microsoft about future acquisitions. Which company would you recommend as a good acquisition? Why?

MyLab MIS

Go to the Assignments section of your MyLab to complete these writing exercises.

9-18. According to Paul Greenberg, Amazon is the master of the 2-minute relationship, and Boeing is the master of the 10-year relationship.[64] Visit *www.boeing.com* and *www.amazon.com*. From Greenberg's statement and from the appearance of these Web sites, it appears that Boeing is committed to traditional CRM and Amazon to social CRM. Give evidence from each site that this might be true. Explain why the products and business environment of both companies cause this difference. Is there any justification for traditional CRM at Amazon? Why or why not? Is there any justification for social CRM at Boeing? Why or why not? Based on these companies, is it possible that a company might endorse enterprise social networks but not endorse social CRM? Explain.

9-19. Suppose you are hired by a local farming cooperative to develop a SMIS. The cooperative wants to promote eating healthy foods, increase awareness about its weekly farmer's market, increase traffic to its Web site, and sell more of its products directly to consumers. Which success metrics would indicate that the cooperative has achieved its goals? Who would be the cooperative's target audience? What value would the cooperative's SMIS provide to its customers? How could the cooperative make personal connections with its customers? Which SM platform(s) would you recommend the cooperative use? Justify your recommendations.

ENDNOTES

1. Kit Smith, "116 Amazing Social Media Statistics and Facts," *Brandwatch.com*, April 2, 2018, accessed June 12, 2018, *www.brandwatch.com/blog/96-amazing-social-media-statistics-and-facts/*.

2. Greg Sterling, "Nearly 80 Percent of Social Media Time Now Spent on Mobile Devices," *Marketing Land*, April 4, 2016, accessed June 12, 2018, *http://marketingland.com/facebook-usage-accounts-1-5-minutes-spent-mobile-171561*.

3. Salman Aslam, "Pinterest by the Numbers: Stats, Demographics & Fun Facts," Omnicore, January 1, 2018, accessed June 12, 2018, *www.omnicoreagency.com/pinterest-statistics/*.

4. Statista, "Percentage of U.S. Internet Users Who Use LinkedIn as of January 2018, by Age Group," *Statista.com*, January 2018, accessed June 12, 2018, *www.statista.com/statistics/246172/share-of-us-internet-users-who-use-linkedin-by-age-group/*.

5. Dara Fontein, "Top LinkedIn Demographics That Matter to Social Media Marketers" *LinkedIn.com*, January 6, 2017 accessed June 12, 2018, *www.linkedin.com/pulse/top-linkedin-demographics-matter-social-media-dara-fontein*.

6. Ayaz Nanji, "Social Media and Blog Usage by Fortune 500 Companies in 2017," MarketingProfs, November 27, 2017, accessed June 12, 2018, *www.marketingprofs.com/charts/2017/33156/social-media-and-blog-usage-by-fortune-500-companies-in-2017*.

7. Vernon Smith, *Rationality in Economics: Constructivist and Ecological Forms* (Cambridge, UK: Cambridge University Press, 2007), pp. 247–250.

8. "About Customer Ratings," *Amazon.com*, accessed June 12, 2018, *www.amazon.com/gp/help/customer/display. html/ref=hp_200791020_vine?nodeId=200791020#vine*.

9. LinkedIn Talent Solutions, "Recruiter," accessed June 12, 2018, *https://business.linkedin.com/talent-solutions/recruiter*.

10. Recruiterbox, "The Cost of Hiring New Employees," *Recruiterbox.com*, accessed June 12, 2018, *https://recruiterbox.com/blog/the-cost-of-hiring-new-employees-infographic*.

11. Jobvite Inc., "2017 Jobvite Recruiter Nation Survey," *Jobvite.com*, September 22, 2017, accessed June 12, 2018, *http://web.jobvite.com/FY17_Website_2017RecruiterNation_LP.html*.

12. Nan Lin, *Social Capital: The Theory of Social Structure and Action* (Cambridge, UK: Cambridge University Press, 2002), Kindle location 310.

13. Henk D. Flap, "Social Capital in the Reproduction of Inequality," *Comparative Sociology of Family, Health, and Education*, Vol. 20 (1991), pp. 6179–6202. Cited in Nan Lin, *Social Capital: The Theory of Social Structure and Action* (Cambridge, UK: Cambridge University Press, 2002), Kindle location 345.

14. Accessed June 12, 2018, *http://klout.com/corp/how-it-works*.

15. Matthew Zajechowski, "How Big Data Is Changing the Sports Fan's Experience," *Smart Data Collective*, September 25, 2015, accessed June 12, 2018, *www.smartdatacollective.com/mattzajechowski/347799/how-big-data-changing-sports-fan-s-experience*.

16. Lauren Brousell, "How the PGA Uses Analytics, Beacons and Social to Enhance Fan Experience,"*CIO.com*, August 13, 2015, accessed June 12, 2018, *www.cio.com/article/2970499/consumer-technology/how-thepga-uses-analytics-beacons-and-social-to-enhance-fan-experience.html*.

17. John Armstrong, "U.S. Open Uses Technology to Reinvent Golf Fans' Experience," *Forbes*, June 9, 2014, accessed June 12, 2018, *www.forbes.com/sites/ibm/2014/06/09/u-s-open-uses-technology-to-reinventgolf-fans-experience*.

18. Nicola Twilley, "How Will Real-Time Tracking Change the N.F.L.?" *The New Yorker*, September 10, 2015, accessed June 12, 2018, *www.newyorker.com/news/sporting-scene/how-will-real-time-tracking-change-the-n-f-l*.

19. Stacy Jones, "A Comparison of the Paid Ad Tweet Vs the Celebrity Tweet," *Hollywood Branded*, May 7, 2018, accessed June 12, 2018, *https://blog.hollywoodbranded.com/a-comparison-of-the-paid-ad-tweet-vs-the-celebrity-tweet*.

20. Social Blade, "Top 50 Influential YouTube Channels," *Socialblade.com*, June 12, 2018, accessed June 12, 2018, *https://socialblade.com/youtube/top/50*.

21. Salman Aslam, "YouTube by the Numbers: Stats, Demographics & Fun Facts," Omnicore, February 5, 2018, accessed June 12, 2018, *www.omnicoreagency.com/youtube-statistics/*.

22. Facebook Inc., "Facebook Reports First Quarter 2018 Results," *Facebook.com*, April 25, 2018, accessed June 12, 2018, *https://investor.fb.com/investor-news/press-release-details/2018/Facebook-Reports-First-Quarter-2018-Results/default.aspx*.

23. Twitter Inc., "Q1 2018 Letter to Shareholders," *Twitterinc.com*, April 25, 2018, accessed June 12, 2018, *https://investor.twitterinc.com/releases.cfm*.

24. Aashish Pahwa, "How LinkedIn Makes Money? LinkedIn Business Model," *Feedough.com*, January 24, 2016, accessed June 12, 2018, *www.feedough.com/how-linkedin-makes-money/*.

25. PageFair, "2017 Ad Block Report," *PageFair.com*, February 1, 2017 accessed June 12, 2018, *https://pagefair.com/blog/2017/adblockreport/*.

26. Wikimedia Foundation, "2016–2017 Annual Report," *Wikimedia Foundation.org*, accessed June 12, 2018, *https://wikimediafoundation.org/wiki/Financial_reports#2016%E2%80%932017_fiscal_year*.

27. Corey McNair, "US Ad Spending The eMarketer Forecast for 2017," *eMarketer.com*, March 15, 2017, accessed June 12, 2018, *www.emarketer.com/content/global-ad-spending*.

28. Cisco, "Cisco Visual Networking Index: Global Mobile Data Traffic Forecast Update, 2016–2021," *Cisco.com*, June 6, 2017, accessed June 12, 2018, *www.cisco.com/c/en/us/solutions/service-provider/visual-networking-index-vni/index.html*.

29. Ibid.

30. Marin Software, "Mobile Search Advertising Around the Globe: 2016 Annual Report," *MarinSoftware.com*, April 2016, accessed June 12, 2018, *www.marinsoftware.com/resources/whitepapers*.

31. Facebook Inc., "Facebook Reports First Quarter 2018 Results," *Facebook.com*, April 25, 2018, accessed June 12, 2018, *https://investor.fb.com/investor-news/press-release-details/2018/Facebook-Reports-First-Quarter-2018-Results/default.aspx*.

32. Monetate, "EQ1 2018: First Impressions," *Monetate.com*, February 2018, accessed June 12, 2018, *https://info.monetate.com/ecommerce-quarterly-report-eq1-2018.html*.

33. Moovweb, "Are iOS Users Still More Valuable Than Android Users?" *Moovweb.com*, June11, 2015, accessed November 26, 2018, *http://moovweb.com/blog/are-ios-users-still-more-valuable-than-android-users*.

34. Rex Santus, "Justin Bieber Dethroned as King of Instagram in Massive Follower Purge," *Mashable*, December 19, 2013, accessed June 12, 2018, *http://mashable.com/2014/12/19/instagram-purge*.

35. Adam Levy, "Twitter Has 700 Million Yearly Active Users," *The Motley Fool*, November 6, 2016, accessed November 14, 2018, *https://www.fool.com/investing/2016/11/06/twitter-has-700-million-yearly-active-users.aspx*.

36. While a conversion is having someone take a desired action, an assisted social conversion is when social media helps the conversion take place.

37. Salman Aslam, "Pinterest by the Numbers: Stats, Demographics & Fun Facts," Omnicore, January 1, 2018, accessed June 12, 2018, *www.omnicoreagency.com/pinterest-statistics/*.

38. Salman Aslam, "Instagram by the Numbers: Stats, Demographics & Fun Facts," Omnicore, January 1, 2018, accessed June 12, 2018, *www.omnicoreagency.com/instagram-statistics/*.

39. Dara Fontein, "Top LinkedIn Demographics That Matter to Social Media Marketers," *LinkedIn.com*, January 6, 2017 accessed June 12, 2018, *www.linkedin.com/pulse/top-linkedin-demographics-matter-social-media-dara-fontein*.

40. CivicScience, "Social Media Now Equals TV Advertising in Influence Power on Consumption Decisions," *CivicScience.com*, September 2014, accessed June 12, 2018, *https://civicscience.com/library/insightreports/social-media-equals-tv-advertising-in-influence-power-onconsumptiondecisions*.

41. Nicholas Jackson, "As MySpace Sells for $35 Million, a History of the Network's Valuation," *The Atlantic*, June 29, 2011, accessed June 12, 2018, *www.theatlantic.com/technology/archive/2011/06/as-myspacesells-for-35-million-a-history-of-the-networksvaluation/241224/*.

42. Ryan Holmes, "As Facebook Shifts, Instagram Emerges as a New Home for Brands," *Forbes*, February 1, 2018, accessed June 12, 2018, *www.forbes.com/sites/ryanholmes/2018/02/01/as-facebook-shifts-instagram-emerges-as-a-new-home-for-brands/*.

43. Andrew McAfee, "Enterprise 2.0, Version 2.0," *AndrewMcAfee.org*, May 27, 2006, accessed June 12, 2018, *http://andrewmcafee.org/2006/05/enterprise_20_version_20/*.

44. Andrew McAfee, "Enterprise 2.0: The Dawn of Emergent Collaboration," *MIT Sloan Management Review*, Spring 2006, accessed June 12, 2018, *http://sloanreview.mit.edu/article/enterprise-the-dawn-of-emergent-collaboration*.

45. Yammer, "Empowering Employees for Improved Customer Service and a Better Bottom Line," *Yammer.com*, accessed June 12, 2018, *https://about.yammer.com/assets/Yammer-Case-Study-Red-Robin.pdf*.

46. Ibid.

47. Ralph Paglia, "Social Media Employee Policy Examples from Over 100 Organizations," July 3, 2010, *Social Media Today*, accessed June 12, 2018, *www.socialmediatoday.com/content/social-media-employee-policy-examples-over-100-organizations*.

48. "Intel Social Media Guidelines," *Intel*, accessed June 12, 2018, *www.intel.com/content/www/us/en/legal/intel-social-media-guidelines.html*.

49. Sarah Perez, "Microsoft Silences Its New A.I. Bot Tay, After Twitter Users Teach It Racism," *TechCrunch*, March 25, 2016, accessed June 12, 2018, *http://techcrunch.com/2016/03/24/microsoft-silences-its-new-a-i-bot-tay-after-twitter-users-teach-it-racism*.

50. Bernhard Warner, "Nestlé's 'No Logo' Policy Triggers Facebook Revolt," *Social Media Influence*, March 19,2010, *http://socialmediainfluence.com/2010/03/19/nestles-no-logo-policy-triggers-facebook-revolt/*.

51. Cheryl Conner, "Who Wastes the Most Time at Work," *Forbes*, September 7, 2014, accessed June 12, 2018, *www.forbes.com/sites/cherylsnappconner/2013/09/07/who-wastes-the-most-time-at-work/*.

52. Aatif Sulleyman, "Facebook Losing Its Grip on Young People, Who Are Quitting the Site in Their Millions," *The Independent*, February 12, 2018, accessed June 14, 2018, *www.independent.co.uk/life-style/gadgets-and-tech/news/facebook-quit-young-people-social-media-snapchat-instagram-emarketer-a8206486.html*.

53. Rieva Lesonsky, "Worried About the Gen Z Social Media Exodus? 3 Creative Ways Your Business Can Respond," *Small Business Trends*, June 4, 2018, accessed June 14, 2018, *https://smallbiztrends.com/2018/06/gen-z-social-media-exodus.html*.

54. Jennifer Wolfe, "How Marketers Can Shape the Chief Digital Officer Role," *CMO.com*, March 21, 2013, accessed June 12, 2018, *www.cmo.com/articles/2013/3/20/how_marketers_can_shape.html*.

55. PwC, *The Global State of Information Security® Survey 2018*, March 30, 2018, *www.pwc.com/us/en/cybersecurity/information-security-survey.html*.

56. Amanda, "Protect Yourself Against Social Engineering in the Age of Cryptocurrency," *Security Boulevard*, March 30, 2018, *https://securityboulevard.com/2017/12/protect-yourself-against-social-engineering-in-the-age-of-cryptocurrency/*.

57. Ryan Derousseau, "These Are the 5 Safest Cryptocurrencies to Invest In, According to a Prominent Rating Firm," *Money*, March 30, 2018, *http://time.com/money/5214911/these-are-the-5-safest-cryptocurrencies-to-invest-in-according-to-a-prominent-rating-firm/*.

58. Ibid.

59. Ibid.

60. Ibid.

61. Olivia Oran and Gerry Shih, "Twitter Shares Soar in Frenzied NYSE Debut," Reuters, November 7, 2013, accessed June 12, 2018, *www.reuters.com/article/2013/11/07/us-twitter-ipo-idUSBRE99N1AE20131107*.

62. LinkedIn, "A Brief History LinkedIn," *LinkedIn.com*, accessed June 14, 2018, *https://ourstory.linkedin.com*.

63. Satya Nadella, "Microsoft + LinkedIn: Beginning Our Journey Together," *LinkedIn.com*, December 8, 2016, accessed June 14, 2018, *www.linkedin.com/pulse/microsoft-linkedin-beginning-our-journey-together-satya-nadella*.

64. Paul Greenberg, *CRM at the Speed of Light*, 4th ed. (New York: McGraw-Hill, 2010), p. 105.

Information Systems Management

Part 4 addresses the management of information systems security, development, and resources. We begin with security because of its great importance today. With the Internet and the interconnectivity of systems and the rise of interorganizational IS, security problems in one organization become security problems in connected organizations as well. As you'll learn, the millions of dollars of damage that Target incurred was due to an interorganizational systems problem. You'll see how that affects ARES in the opening of Chapter 10.

While you can readily understand that IS security is important to you as a future manager, it may be more difficult for you to appreciate why you need to know about IS development. As a business professional, you will be the customer of development projects. You need basic knowledge of development processes to be able to assess the quality of the work being done on your behalf. As a manager, you may allocate budget and release funds for IS development. You need the knowledge that will allow you to be an active and effective participant is such projects.

Source: Julia Tim/Fotolia

Finally, you need to know how IS resources are managed so that you can better relate to your IS department. IS managers can sometimes seem rigid and overly protective of IS assets, but usually they have important reasons for their concerns. You need to understand the IS department's perspective and know both your rights and responsibilities as a user of IS resources at your organization. Having such knowledge is key to success for any business professional today.

CHAPTER 10

Information Systems Security

"Lindsey, thank you for talking with us today," Henri says with a broad smile as he gestures to Raj. Cassie set up a videoconference for Henri and Raj to talk with Lindsey Walsh. Lindsey is the CTO of the largest exercise equipment manufacturer in the United States—CanyonBack Fitness.

"No, thank you. I'm glad to finally meet you both. Cassie has told me a lot about the augmented reality project you are working on. It sounds really cool." Lindsey sounds upbeat and interested, not at all like Cassie described her.

Raj jumps in, "Yes, we're excited as well. It's going to create a completely new cycling experience for users. We're going to do things that no one has done before. Augmented reality is going to fundamentally change the way people exercise."

Henri watches Lindsey's eyes as she slowly nods in agreement and then looks down at her notes. She's obviously not convinced.

"Well, it certainly is a great opportunity for CanyonBack Fitness. Most of our upper management team is sold on the idea that integrating ARES with our stationary exercise bikes could really boost sales," Lindsey responds hesitantly.

MyLab MIS

Using Your Knowledge
Questions 10-1, 10-2, 10-3

Essay Questions 10-15, 10-16

"I think you'll see that we really do take security seriously."

Source: Haiyin Wang/Alamy Stock Photo

Henri can see that Lindsey is concerned. Cassie told Henri that Lindsey had security concerns about integrating ARES with CanyonBack exercise bikes. She really pushed back on the idea of allowing ARES to control the settings of the bikes. The CEO of CanyonBack Fitness trusts Lindsey's judgement when it comes to technical issues because she was in charge of the design and development of the software used on most of its exercise equipment. The CEO isn't going to sign off on anything until Lindsey is satisfied, and Lindsey doesn't want some untested app doing whatever it wants on her machines.

Henri responds calmly and patiently, "We hope so, but there are still a lot of details to work out. I've worked on a couple larger systems integration projects, but nothing like this before. No one has. AR is a whole new animal."

"I agree," Lindsey responds emphatically. "And quite frankly . . . I don't know much about AR at all. I'm just not sure how it will work with our equipment and systems."

"Yeah, Cassie mentioned that you had some security concerns. What type of questions did you have?"

"Well, I don't want to come across as negative on the idea of ARES. I really don't. I see the opportunity ARES represents. I'd like to see it work. But I'm concerned about allowing an outside system control over our exercise bikes. What if ARES gets hacked? Could some hacker halfway around the world mess with one of our bikes while a customer is using it? If the customer got hurt, would he sue us? Would he sue you?"

Henri just nods, listens intently, and makes notes as Lindsey talks.

Lindsey continues, "And what about protecting our customers' data? Is ARES being coded securely enough to protect against an SQL injection attack or a buffer overflow? Our bikes collect a lot of personal exercise data. We need to make sure it remains private. If we allow ARES access to this data stream, will it be secure on the back end? What type of data protections do you all have in place on the back end?"

Raj takes a sip of his coffee, looks down at his laptop, and tries to keep a neutral expression on his face. He can't believe Lindsey is worried about security. His new AR app is going to help them sell boatloads of new bikes, and she's worried about potential security issues.

Study QUESTIONS

Q10-1 What is the goal of information systems security?

Q10-2 How big is the computer security problem?

Q10-3 How should you respond to security threats?

Q10-4 How should organizations respond to security threats?

Q10-5 How can technical safeguards protect against security threats?

Q10-6 How can data safeguards protect against security threats?

Q10-7 How can human safeguards protect against security threats?

Q10-8 How should organizations respond to security incidents?

Q10-9 2029?

Henri keeps nodding and writing on his notepad. "You're completely right. Security is a big concern. We need to make sure we . . . "

Lindsey interrupts, "Oh, and if something does go wrong, guess who's going to get blamed *and* have to work day and night until it's fixed? Me. I mean, does this make sense to you? Can you see why I'm concerned? I need to make sure ARES doesn't create security problems for CanyonBack's equipment or our customers."

Henri gestures toward the video screen. "Yes, of course, I'd feel the same way. In fact, I saw an article a few months ago about how hackers broke into the operating system of a car and locked up the brakes. That's scary."

"Exactly, that's what I'm saying. You never know what's going to happen."

Henri points to his notes. "Lindsey, your concerns are legitimate. No doubt about it." He intentionally pauses, looks at his notes, and slowly looks down his list. He wants her to see that he is carefully thinking about what she said. Then he continues, "Well, how about we work through this list and see what we come up with. Raj is here to talk about the secure coding practices we are using, and I can talk about our secure data connections and back-end storage. I think you'll see that we really do take security seriously."

Henri motions to Raj. "Raj, do you want to talk about how we protect ourselves from SQL injection attacks?"

Raj, still irritated, forces a smile. "Yes, yes, I'd be happy to. We use parameterization to sanitize any data coming into our system, and we've eliminated the need for users to enter any data at all. Users interact with radio buttons, dropdown menus, and other interactive AR elements rather than typing in data. There's really no place for SQL injection to occur."

The videoconference continues for another 40 minutes, with Raj and Henri taking turns talking with Lindsey. Lindsey seems satisfied with the answers Raj and Henri provide. She even offers some suggestions about implementing ARES with other exercise equipment CanyonBack produces. They schedule a follow-up call in a week to talk about data integration. Lindsey wants one of her database administrators on the call to ask questions about ARES online storage and backup procedures. Henri and Lindsey end the call with some friendly discussion about biking routes they enjoy taking around California.

Chapter PREVIEW

This chapter provides an overview of the major components of information systems security. We begin in Q10-1 by defining the goals of IS security and then, in Q10-2, discuss the size of the computer security problem. Next, in Q10-3, we address how you, both as a student today and as a business professional in the future, should respond to security threats. Then, in Q10-4, we ask what organizations need to do to respond to security threats. After that, Q10-5 through Q10-7 address security safeguards. Q10-5 discusses technical safeguards that involve hardware and software components, Q10-6 addresses data safeguards, and Q10-7 discusses human safeguards that involve procedure and people components. Q10-8 then summarizes what organizations need to do when they incur a security incident, and we wrap up the chapter with a preview of IS security in 2029.

Unfortunately, threats to data and information systems are increasing and becoming more complex. In fact, the U.S. Bureau of Labor Statistics estimates that demand for security specialists will increase by more than 28 percent between 2016 and 2026 with a median salary of $92,600. This is strong growth considering computer occupations are projected to grow at 14 percent and all occupations at 7 percent.[1] If you find this topic attractive, majoring in information systems with a security specialty would open the door to many interesting jobs.

Later, Raj remarks to Henri as they're walking down the hall, "That wasn't too bad. I guess she had some legitimate concerns, but I'm not sure she really understands everything we're going to do with AR. This is going to be huge for them."

"Probably not, but I see it from her point of view. We're a small startup with a new technology that could cause a lot of problems for an already-successful business. We represent a risk with a potential reward. New technology is always risky."

"True, but sticking with old technology might be even more risky."

Q10-1   What Is the Goal of Information Systems Security?

Information systems security is really about trade-offs. In one sense, it's a trade-off between security and freedom. For example, organizations can increase the security of their information systems by taking away users' freedom to choose their own passwords and force them to choose stronger passwords that are difficult for hackers to crack.

Another way to look at information systems security, and the primary focus of this chapter, is that it's a trade-off between cost and risk. To understand the nature of this trade-off, we begin with a description of the security threat/loss scenario and then discuss the sources of security threats. Following that, we'll state the goal of information systems security.

The IS Security Threat/Loss Scenario

Figure 10-1 illustrates the major elements of the security problem that individuals and organizations confront today. A **threat** is a person or organization that seeks to obtain or alter data or other IS assets illegally, without the owner's permission and often without the owner's knowledge. A **vulnerability** is an opportunity for threats to gain access to individual or organizational assets. For example, when you buy something online, you provide your credit card data; when that data is transmitted over the Internet, it is vulnerable to threats. A **safeguard** is some measure that individuals or organizations take to block the threat from obtaining the asset. Notice in Figure 10-1 that safeguards are not always effective; some threats achieve their goal despite safeguards. Finally, the **target** is the asset that is desired by the threat.

Figure 10-2 shows examples of threats/targets, vulnerabilities, safeguards, and results. In the first two rows, a hacker (the threat) wants your bank login credentials (the target) to access your bank account. If you click on links in emails you can be directed to phishing sites that look identical to your bank's Web site. Phishing sites don't typically use https. If, as shown in the first row of Figure 10-2, you always access your bank's site using https rather than http (discussed in Q10-5), you will be using an effective safeguard, and you will successfully counter the threat.

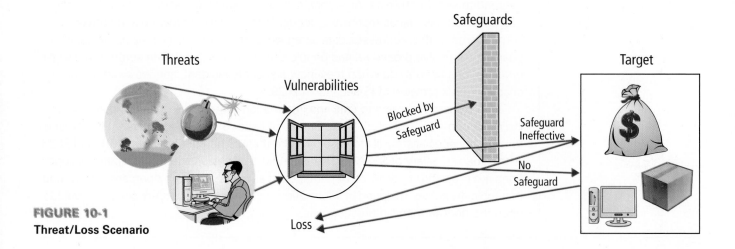

FIGURE 10-1
Threat/Loss Scenario

If, however, as described in the second row of Figure 10-2, you access what appears to be your bank's site without using https (i.e., an unsecured site), you have no safeguard at all. Your login credentials can be quickly recorded and resold to other criminals.

The bottom row of Figure 10-2 shows another situation. Here an employee at work obtains sensitive data and posts it on what he thinks is a work-only Google+ group. However, the employee errs and instead posts it to a public group. The target is the sensitive data, and the vulnerability is public access to the group. In this case, there are several safeguards that should have prevented this loss; the employee needed passwords to obtain the sensitive data and to join the private, work-only group. The employer has procedures that state employees are not to post confidential data to any public site, such as Google+, but these procedures were either unknown or ignored. A third safeguard is the training that all employees are given. Because the employee ignores the procedures, though, all of those safeguards are ineffective and the data is exposed to the public.

What Are the Sources of Threats?

Figure 10-3 summarizes the sources of security threats. The type of threat is shown in the columns, and the type of loss is shown in the rows.

Human Error

Human errors and mistakes include accidental problems caused by both employees and nonemployees. An example is an employee who misunderstands operating procedures and accidentally deletes customer records. Another example is an employee who, in the course of backing up a database, inadvertently installs an old database on top of the current one. This category also includes poorly written application programs and poorly designed procedures. Finally, human errors and mistakes include physical accidents, such as driving a forklift through the wall of a computer room.

Computer Crime

The second threat type is *computer crime*. This threat type includes employees and former employees who intentionally destroy data or other system components. It also includes hackers who break into a system and virus and worm writers who infect computer systems. Computer crime also includes terrorists and those who break into a system to steal for financial gain.

Natural Events and Disasters

Natural events and disasters are the third type of security threat. This category includes fires, floods, hurricanes, earthquakes, tsunamis, avalanches, and other acts of nature. Problems in this category include not only the initial loss of capability and service, but also losses stemming from actions to recover from the initial problem.

Threat/Target	Vulnerability	Safeguard	Result	Explanation
Hacker wants to steal your bank login credentials	Hacker creates a phishing site nearly identical to your online banking site	Only access sites using https	No loss	Effective safeguard
		None	Loss of login credentials	Ineffective safeguard
Employee posts sensitive data to public Google + group	Public access to not-secure group	Passwords Procedures Employee training	Loss of sensitive data	Ineffective safeguard

FIGURE 10-2
Examples of Threat/Loss

		Threat		
		Human Error	**Computer Crime**	**Natural Disasters**
Loss	**Unauthorized Data Disclosure**	Procedural mistakes	Pretexting Phishing Spoofing Sniffing Hacking	Disclosure during recovery
	Incorrect Data Modification	Procedural mistakes Incorrect procedures Ineffective accounting controls System errors	Hacking	Incorrect data recovery
	Faulty Service	Procedural mistakes Development and installation errors	Usurpation	Service improperly restored
	Denial of Service (DoS)	Accidents	DoS attacks	Service interruption
	Loss of Infrastructure	Accidents	Theft Terrorist activity	Property loss

FIGURE 10-3
Security Problems and Sources

What Types of Security Loss Exist?

Five types of security loss exist: unauthorized data disclosure, incorrect data modification, faulty service, denial of service, and loss of infrastructure. Consider each.

Unauthorized Data Disclosure

Unauthorized data disclosure occurs when a threat obtains data that is supposed to be protected. It can occur by human error when someone inadvertently releases data in violation of policy. An example at a university is a department administrator who posts student names, identification numbers, and grades in a public place, when the releasing of names and grades violates state and federal law. Another example is employees who unknowingly or carelessly release proprietary data to competitors or to the media. WikiLeaks is a famous example of unauthorized disclosure; the situation described in the third row of Figure 10-2 is another example.

The popularity and efficacy of search engines have created another source of inadvertent disclosure. Employees who place restricted data on Web sites that can be reached by search engines might mistakenly publish proprietary or restricted data over the Web.

Of course, proprietary and personal data can also be released and obtained maliciously. **Pretexting** occurs when someone deceives by pretending to be someone else. A common scam involves a telephone caller who pretends to be from a credit card company and claims to be checking the validity of credit card numbers: "I'm checking your Mastercard number; it begins with 5491. Can you verify the rest of the number?" Thousands of Mastercard numbers start with 5491; the caller is attempting to steal a valid number.

Phishing is a similar technique for obtaining unauthorized data that uses pretexting via email. The **phisher** pretends to be a legitimate company and sends an email requesting confidential data, such as account numbers, Social Security numbers, account passwords, and so forth.

Spoofing is another term for someone pretending to be someone else. If you pretend to be your professor, you are spoofing your professor. **IP spoofing** occurs when an intruder uses another site's IP address to masquerade as that other site. **Email spoofing** is a synonym for phishing.

Sniffing is a technique for intercepting computer communications. With wired networks, sniffing requires a physical connection to the network. With wireless networks, no such connection is required: **Wardrivers** simply take computers with wireless connections through an area and search for unprotected wireless networks. They use **packet sniffers**, which are programs that capture network traffic to monitor and intercept traffic on unsecured wireless (or wired) networks. Even protected wireless networks are vulnerable, as you will learn. Spyware and adware are two other sniffing techniques discussed later in this chapter.

Other forms of computer crime include **hacking**, which is breaking into computers, servers, or networks to steal data such as customer lists, product inventory data, employee data, and other proprietary and confidential data.

Finally, people might inadvertently disclose data during recovery from a natural disaster. During a recovery, everyone is so focused on restoring system capability that they might ignore normal security safeguards. A request such as "I need a copy of the customer database backup" will receive far less scrutiny during disaster recovery than at other times.

Incorrect Data Modification

The second type of security loss in Figure 10-3 is *incorrect data modification*. Examples include incorrectly increasing a customer's discount or incorrectly modifying an employee's salary, earned days of vacation, or annual bonus. Other examples include placing incorrect information, such as incorrect price changes, on a company's Web site or company portal.

Incorrect data modification can occur through human error when employees follow procedures incorrectly or when procedures have been designed incorrectly. For proper internal control on systems that process financial data or control inventories of assets, such as products and equipment, companies should ensure separation of duties and authorities and have multiple checks and balances in place.

A final type of incorrect data modification caused by human error includes *system errors*. An example is the lost-update problem discussed in Chapter 5 (pages 177–178).

Computer criminals can make unauthorized data modifications by hacking into a computer system. For example, hackers could hack into a system and transfer people's account balances or place orders to ship goods to unauthorized locations and customers.

Finally, faulty recovery actions after a disaster can result in incorrect data changes. The faulty actions can be unintentional or malicious.

Faulty Service

The third type of security loss, *faulty service*, includes problems that result because of incorrect system operation. Faulty service could include incorrect data modification, as just described. It also could include systems that work incorrectly by sending the wrong goods to a customer or the ordered goods to the wrong customer, inaccurately billing customers, or sending the wrong information to employees. Humans can inadvertently cause faulty service by making procedural mistakes. System developers can write programs incorrectly or make errors during the installation of hardware, software programs, and data.

Usurpation occurs when computer criminals invade a computer system and replace legitimate programs with their own, unauthorized ones that shut down legitimate applications and substitute their own processing to spy, steal and manipulate data, or achieve other purposes. Faulty service can also result when service is improperly restored during recovery from natural disasters.

Denial of Service

Human error in following procedures or a lack of procedures can result in **denial of service (DoS)**, the fourth type of loss. For example, humans can inadvertently shut down a Web server or corporate gateway router by starting a computationally intensive application. An OLAP application that uses the operational DBMS can consume so many DBMS resources that order-entry transactions cannot get through.

Computer criminals can launch an intentional denial-of-service attack in which a malicious hacker floods a Web server, for example, with millions of bogus service requests that so occupy the server that it cannot service legitimate requests. Also, computer worms can infiltrate a network with so much artificial traffic that legitimate traffic cannot get through. Finally, natural disasters may cause systems to fail, resulting in denial of service.

Loss of Infrastructure

Many times, human accidents cause loss of infrastructure, the last loss type. Examples are a bulldozer cutting a conduit of fiber-optic cables and a floor buffer crashing into a rack of Web servers.

Theft and terrorist events also cause loss of infrastructure. For instance, a disgruntled, terminated employee might walk off with corporate data servers, routers, or other crucial equipment. Terrorist events also can cause the loss of physical plants and equipment.

Natural disasters present the largest risk for infrastructure loss. A fire, flood, earthquake, or similar event can destroy data centers and all they contain.

You may be wondering why Figure 10-3 does not include terms such as viruses, worms, and Trojan horses. The answer is that viruses, worms, and Trojan horses are techniques for causing some of the problems in the figure. They can cause a denial-of-service attack, or they can be used to cause malicious, unauthorized data access or data loss.

Finally, a new threat term has come into recent use. An **Advanced Persistent Threat (APT)** is a sophisticated, possibly long-running computer hack that is perpetrated by large, well-funded organizations such as governments. APTs can be a means to engage in cyberwarfare and cyber-espionage. An example of an APT is a group called APT37 or Reaper, which is allegedly a state-sponsored hacking group based out of North Korea. In 2018, security researchers at FireEye released a detailed report describing APT37's tools, tactics, and procedures.[2] More specifically, it showed how APT37 used zero-day vulnerabilites to attack the South Korean military, government, and defense industries. APT37 then expanded operations to include strategic political targets in Japan, Vietnam, and the Middle East. If you work in the military or for intelligence agencies, you will certainly be concerned, if not involved, with APTs. We return to this topic in Q10-9.

Goal of Information Systems Security

As shown in Figure 10-1, threats can be stopped, or if not stopped, the costs of loss can be reduced by creating appropriate safeguards. Safeguards are, however, expensive to create and maintain. They also reduce work efficiency by making common tasks more difficult, adding additional labor expense. The goal of information security is to find an appropriate trade-off between the risk of loss and the cost of implementing safeguards.

Business professionals need to consider that trade-off carefully. In your personal life, you should certainly employ antivirus software. You should probably implement other safeguards that you'll learn about in Q10-3. Some safeguards, such as deleting browser cookies, will make using your computer more difficult. Are such safeguards worth it? You need to assess the risks and benefits for yourself.

Similar comments pertain to organizations, though they need to go about it more systematically. The bottom line is not to let the future unfold without careful analysis and action as indicated by that analysis. Get in front of the security problem by making the appropriate trade-off for your life and your business.

Q10-2 How Big Is the Computer Security Problem?

We do not know the full extent of the financial and data losses due to computer security threats. Certainly, the losses due to human error are enormous, but few organizations compute those losses, and even fewer publish them. However, a 2017 security report by Risk Based Security reported the loss of 7.89 billion personal records in a record 5,207 security incidents.[3] Some of the more notable data breaches include the loss of user accounts at DU Caller Group in China (2 billion); River City Media, LLC (1.3 billion); and FriendFinder Networks, Inc. (412 million).[4] And that's not even counting the loss of more than 145 million financial records from Equifax or the loss of 57 million Uber customer accounts. More than 82 percent of user records stolen were taken by external attackers via Web vulnerabilities (69 percent) or direct hacking (30 percent). Keep in mind that these are only the companies that made the news and voluntarily reported their losses.

Losses due to natural disasters are also enormous and nearly impossible to compute. The 2011 earthquake in Japan, for example, shut down Japanese manufacturing, and losses rippled through the supply chain from the Far East to Europe and the United States. One can only imagine the enormous expense for Japanese companies as they restored their information systems.

Furthermore, no one knows the cost of computer crime. For one, there are no standards for tallying crime costs. Does the cost of a denial-of-service attack include lost employee time, lost revenue, or long-term revenue losses due to lost customers? Or, if an employee loses a $2,000 laptop, does the cost include the value of the data that was on it? Does it include the cost of the time of replacing it and reinstalling software? Or, if someone steals next year's financial plan, how is the cost of the value that competitors glean determined?

Second, all the studies on the cost of computer crime are based on surveys. Different respondents interpret terms differently, some organizations don't report all their losses, and some won't report computer crime losses at all. Absent standard definitions and a more accurate way of gathering crime data, we cannot rely on the accuracy of any particular estimate. The most we can do is look for trends by comparing year-to-year data, assuming the same methodology is used by the various types of survey respondents.

Figure 10-4 shows the results of a survey done over 8 years.[5] It was commissioned by Hewlett-Packard and performed by the Ponemon Institute, a consulting group that specializes in computer crime. It shows the average cost and percent of total incidents of the seven most expensive types of attack. Without tests of significance, it's difficult to determine if the differences shown are random; they could be. But taking the data at face value, it appears the most common attack type was malicious code (23 percent). Fortunately, this seems to be decreasing. Over the past year, however, ransomware attacks and Web-based attacks have increased substantially. The cost of malicious code, ransomware, and phishing attacks also increased over the previous year (Figure 10-5). The average costs of the remaining categories are essentially flat or slightly decreasing.

FIGURE 10-4
Average Computer Crime Cost and Percent of Attacks by Type
Source: Data from Ponemon Institute. *2017 Cost of Cyber Crime Study: United States,* October 2017, p. 12.

	2010	2011	2012	2013	2014	2015	2016	2017
Denial of Service	NA	$187,506 (17%)	$172,238 (20%)	$243,913 (21%)	$166,545 (18%)	$255,470 (16%)	$133,453 (16%)	$129,450 (10%)
Malicious Insiders	$100,300 (11%)	$105,352 (9%)	$166,251 (8%)	$198,769 (8%)	$213,542 (8%)	$179,805 (10%)	$167,890 (11%)	$173,517 (9%)
Web-Based Attacks	$143,209 (15%)	$141,647 (12%)	$125,795 (13%)	$125,101 (12%)	$116,424 (14%)	$125,630 (12%)	$88,145 (12%)	$83,450 (20%)
Malicious Code	$124,083 (26%)	$126,787 (23%)	$109,533 (26%)	$102,216 (21%)	$91,500 (23%)	$164,500 (24%)	$92,336 (24%)	$112,419 (23%)
Phishing and Social Engineering	$35,514 (12%)	$30,397 (9%)	$18,040 (7%)	$21,094 (11%)	$45,959 (13%)	$23,470 (14%)	$95,821 (15%)	$105,900 (13%)
Stolen Devices	$25,663 (17%)	$24,968 (13%)	$23,541 (12%)	$20,070 (9%)	$43,565 (10%)	$16,588 (7%)	$31,870 (6%)	$29,883 (8%)
Ransomware							$78,993 (5%)	$88,496 (5%)

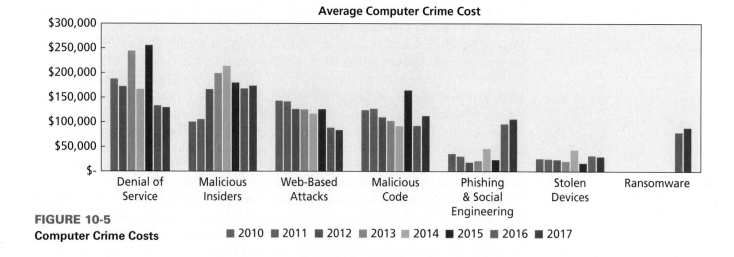

FIGURE 10-5
Computer Crime Costs

In addition to this data, Ponemon also surveyed losses by type of asset compromised. It found that information loss was the single most expensive consequence of computer crime, accounting for 43 percent of costs in 2017. Business disruption was the second highest cost, at 33 percent in 2017. Equipment losses and damages were only 3 percent of the lost value. Clearly, value lies in data and not in hardware!

Looking to the future, Ponemon reported that 76 percent of internal costs related to cybercrime come from detection (35 percent), containment (21 percent), and recovery (20 percent).[6] The next most costly activities were investigation (11 percent), incident management (8 percent), and after-the-fact response (5 percent).

The *2017 Cost of Computer Crime Study* includes an in-depth analysis of the effect of different security policies on the savings in computer crime. The bottom line is that organizations that spend more to create the safeguards discussed in Q10-4 through Q10-7 (later in this chapter) experience less computer crime and suffer smaller losses when they do. Security safeguards do work!

If you search for the phrase *computer crime statistics* on the Web, you will find numerous similar studies. Some are based on dubious sampling techniques and seem to be written to promote a particular safeguard product or point of view. Be aware of such bias as you read.

Using the Ponemon study, the bottom line, as of 2017, is:

- Ransomware and Web-based attacks are increasingly serious security threats.
- Data loss and business disruption are principal costs of computer crime.
- Detection and recovery account for more than half of the internal costs related to cyber intrusions.
- Security safeguards work.

Q10-3 How Should You Respond to Security Threats?

As stated at the end of Q10-1, your personal IS security goal should be to find an effective trade-off between the risk of loss and the cost of safeguards. However, few individuals take security as seriously as they should, and most fail to implement even low-cost safeguards.

Figure 10-6 lists recommended personal security safeguards. The first safeguard is to take security seriously. You cannot see the attempts that are being made, right now, to compromise your computer. However, they are there.

Unfortunately, the first sign you receive that your security has been compromised will be bogus charges on your credit card or messages from friends complaining about the disgusting email they just received from your email account. Computer security professionals run intrusion detection systems to detect attacks. An **intrusion detection system (IDS)** is a computer program that senses when another computer is attempting to scan or access a computer or network. IDS logs can record thousands of attempts each day. If these attempts come from outside the country, there is nothing you can do about them except use reasonable safeguards.

If you decide to take computer security seriously, the single most important safeguard you can implement is to create and use strong passwords. We discussed ways of doing this in Chapter 1 (pages 26–27). To summarize, do not use any word, in any language, as part of your password. Use passwords with a mixture of upper- and lowercase letters and numbers and special characters.

Such nonword passwords are still vulnerable to a **brute force attack** in which the password cracker tries every possible combination of characters. A brute force attack can crack a six-character password of either upper- or lowercase letters in a couple minutes. However, a brute force attack of a six-character password having a mixture of upper- and lowercase letters, numbers, and special characters can take hours. A 10-digit password of only upper- and lowercase letters can take years to crack, but one using a mix of letters, numbers, and special characters may require hundreds of years. A 12-digit, letter-only password may require thousands of years, and a 12-digit mixed password may take millions of years. All of these estimates assume, of course, that the password contains no word in any language. The bottom line is this: Use long passwords with no words, 12 or more characters, and a mix of letters, numbers, and special characters.

Data privacy has become an important issue as companies seek to extract value from user data, as discussed in the Ethics Guide on pages 394–395.

In addition to using long, complex passwords, you should also use different passwords for different sites. That way, if one of your passwords is compromised, you do not lose control of all of your accounts. Make sure you use very strong passwords for important sites (like your bank's site), and do not reuse those passwords on less important sites (like your social networking sites). Some sites are focused on innovating products and may not allocate the same amount of resources to protect your information. Guard your information with a password it deserves.

Never send passwords, credit card data, or any other valuable data in email or IM. As stated numerous times in this text, most email and IM is not protected by encryption (see Q10-5), and you should assume that anything you write in email or IM could find its way to the front page of *The New York Times* tomorrow.

Buy only from reputable online vendors using a secure https connection. If the vendor does not support https in its transactions (look for *https://* in the address line of your browser), do not buy from that vendor.

You can reduce your vulnerability to loss by removing high-value assets from your computers. Now, and especially later as a business professional, make it your practice not to travel out of your office with a laptop or other device that contains any data that you do not need. In general, store proprietary data on servers or removable devices that do not travel with you. (Office 365, by the

- Take security seriously
- Create strong passwords
- Use multiple passwords
- Send no valuable data via email or IM
- Use https at trusted, reputable vendors
- Remove high-value assets from computers
- Clear browsing history, temporary files, and cookies (CCleaner or equivalent)
- Regularly update antivirus software
- Demonstrate security concern to your fellow workers
- Follow organizational security directives and guidelines
- Consider security for all business initiatives

FIGURE 10-6
Personal Security Safeguards

way, uses https to transfer data to and from SharePoint. You can use it or a similar application for processing documents from public locations such as airports while you are traveling.)

Your browser automatically stores a history of your browsing activities and temporary files that contain sensitive data about where you've visited, what you've purchased, what your account names and passwords are, and so forth. It also stores **cookies**, which are small files that your browser receives when you visit Web sites. Cookies enable you to access Web sites without having to sign in every time, and they speed up processing of some sites. Unfortunately, some cookies also contain sensitive security data. The best safeguard is to remove your browsing history, temporary files, and cookies from your computer and to set your browser to disable history and cookies.

CCleaner is a free, open source product that will do a thorough job of securely removing all such data (*http://download.cnet.com/ccleaner/*). You should make a backup of your computer before using CCleaner, however.

Removing and disabling cookies presents an excellent example of the trade-off between improved security and cost. Your security will be substantially improved, but your computer will be more difficult to use. You decide, but make a conscious decision; do not let ignorance of the vulnerability of such data make the decision for you.

We will address the use of antivirus software in Q10-5. The last three items in Figure 10-6 apply once you become a business professional. With your coworkers, and especially with those whom you manage, you should demonstrate a concern and respect for security. You should also follow all organizational security directives and guidelines. Finally, consider security in all of your business initiatives.

Q10-4 How Should Organizations Respond to Security Threats?

Q10-3 discussed ways that you as an individual should respond to security threats. In the case of organizations, a broader and more systematic approach needs to be taken. To begin, senior management needs to address two critical security functions: security policy and risk management.

See what a typical workday would look like for someone who works as a security analyst in the Career Guide on pages 410–411.

Considering the first, senior management must establish company-wide security policies. Take, for example, a data security policy that states the organization's posture regarding data that it gathers about its customers, suppliers, partners, and employees. At a minimum, the policy should stipulate:

- What sensitive data the organization will store
- How it will process that data
- Whether data will be shared with other organizations
- How employees and others can obtain copies of data stored about them
- How employees and others can request changes to inaccurate data

The specifics of a policy depend on whether the organization is governmental or nongovernmental, on whether it is publically held or private, on the organization's industry, on the relationship of management to employees, and on other factors. As a new hire, seek out your employer's security policy if it is not discussed with you in new-employee training.

The second senior management security function is to manage risk. Risk cannot be eliminated, so *manage risk* means to proactively balance the trade-off between risk and cost. This trade-off varies from industry to industry and from organization to organization. Financial institutions are obvious targets for theft and must invest heavily in security safeguards. On the other hand, a bowling alley is unlikely to be much of a target, unless, of course, it stores credit card data on computers or mobile devices (a decision that would be part of its security policy and that would seem unwise, not only for a bowling alley but also for most small businesses).

NEW FROM BLACK
HAT 2017

Hackers, security professionals, and government agents flock to Las Vegas each year to attend an important security conference: Black Hat. Black Hat caters to hackers, security professionals, corporations, and government entities.

Each year speakers make briefings on how things can be hacked. Presenters show exactly how to exploit weaknesses in hardware, software, protocols, or systems. One session may show you how to hack your smartphone, while another may show you how to empty the cash out of an ATM.

Presentations encourage companies to fix product vulnerabilities and serve as an educational forum for hackers, developers, manufacturers, and government agencies. The following are highlights from the 2017 Black Hat conference:

- **Focusing on Defense:** The keynote presentation at Black Hat was given by Alex Stamos, Facebook's chief security officer (CSO).[7] Stamos made an empathetic and consolatory talk about trying to solve the real issues facing *users*. He asked attendees to focus more on stopping real threats that actually harm users, such as spam, DoS attacks, and malware. Too often, the security community focuses on presentations about obscure vulnerabilities that rarely happen but are dazzling to other security professionals.

  Stamos urged attendees to realize that organized groups are attacking things that matter to *everyone*, not just security professionals. This includes things like critical infrastructure, voting machines, and personal data (as evidenced by massive data breaches). Securing the systems that house this information helps everyone. Stamos pointed out that defending against these common types of attacks is far more important and beneficial than doing a demo of a rare attack to a small group of friends in a hotel.

- **Industroyer:** The most talked about presentation at Black Hat was a piece of malware designed to knock out entire power grids. It was used in December 2016 to knock out the power in the Ukraine for an hour. Robert Lipovsky (ESET) and Sergio Caltagirone (Dragos) led two different security research teams that outlined how Industroyer (also called CrashOverride by the Dragos researchers) was able to shut down power grids by taking advantage of the communication protocols used by the industrial control systems.[8] Attackers using the malware can force

Source: Ken Gillespie Photography/Alamy Stock Photo

power substations to isolate themselves by continually turning circuit breakers on and off until they automatically sever their connection with the rest of the power grid. This makes the malware effective against a wide variety of power grid systems produced by a variety of manufacturers.

This type of malware would likely be most valuable in a cyberwar. Knocking out power and communication systems is a top priority in a cyberwar. It effectively blinds the opposing country and makes counterattacks difficult. Industroyer could give organized nation-state actors the tools to launch an initial salvo in a cyberwar and knock out power for a couple of days. In developed countries like the United States, uninterrupted power is vital for daily operations at hospitals, online retailers, telecom providers, and many others. Prolonged power losses would be catastrophic.

- **Broadpwn:** Another widely discussed presentation by Nitay Artenstein showed how a WiFi worm could automatically spread from network to network and infect all WiFi devices with Broadcom wireless cards.[9] Artenstein identified a buffer overflow vulnerability that allowed him to remotely install malware that then spread to WiFi clients and access points. Any device with a Broadcom wireless card would be affected. This includes all Android and Apple devices. Fortunately, both Google and Apple released patches for the vulnerability just before Artenstein's presentation at Black Hat.

Questions

1. Why would Alex Stamos want security researchers to focus on fixing vulnerabilities rather than finding them?

2. Why would nation-states be interested in developing malware like Industroyer?

3. What type of consequences might follow if Industroyer was able to knock out power for more than a week?

4. Besides power grids, what other types of infrastructure might nation-states target in a cyberwar? Why would they target these types of infrastructure?

5. Suppose Broadpwn malware was released into the wild and was able to immediately propagate between all access points and wireless clients (i.e., smartphones, laptops, and tablets). How long do you think it would take for most systems to be infected? What might affect the rate of infections?

To make trade-off decisions, organizations need to create an inventory of the data and hardware they want to protect and then evaluate safeguards relative to the probability of each potential threat. Figure 10-3 is a good source for understanding categories and frequencies of threat. Given this set of inventory and threats, the organization needs to decide how much risk it wishes to take or, stated differently, which security safeguards it wishes to implement.

A good analogy of using safeguards to protect information assets is buying car insurance. Before buying car insurance you determine how much your car is worth, the likelihood of incurring damage to your car, and how much risk you are willing to accept. Then you transfer some of your risk to the insurer by buying a safeguard called an insurance policy. Instead of buying just one insurance policy, organizations implement a variety of safeguards to protect their data and hardware.

An easy way to remember information systems safeguards is to arrange them according to the five components of an information system, as shown in Figure 10-7. Some of the safeguards involve computer hardware and software. Some involve data; others involve procedures and people. We will consider technical, data, and human safeguards in the next three questions.

Q10-5 How Can Technical Safeguards Protect Against Security Threats?

Technical safeguards involve the hardware and software components of an information system. Figure 10-8 lists primary technical safeguards. Consider each.

Hardware	Software	Data	Procedures	People

Technical Safeguards	Data Safeguards	Human Safeguards
Identification and authorization	Data rights and responsibilities	Hiring
Encryption	Passwords	Training
Firewalls	Encryption	Education
Malware protection	Backup and recovery	Procedure design
Application design	Physical security	Administration
		Assessment
		Compliance
		Accountability

FIGURE 10-7

Security Safeguards as They Relate to the Five Components

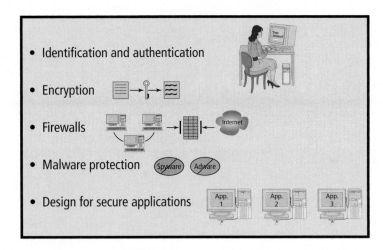

FIGURE 10-8
Technical Safeguards

Identification and Authentication

Every information system today should require users to sign on with a username and password. The username *identifies* the user (the process of **identification**), and the password *authenticates* that user (the process of **authentication**).

Passwords have important weaknesses. In spite of repeated warnings (don't let this happen to you!), users often share their passwords, and many people choose ineffective, simple passwords. In fact, a 2018 Verizon report noted that "63 percent of confirmed data breaches involved leveraging weak, default, or stolen passwords."[10] Because of these problems, some organizations choose to use smart cards and biometric authentication in addition to passwords.

Smart Cards

A **smart card** is a plastic card similar to an older credit card with a magnetic stripe but with an embedded microchip. The microchip, which holds far more data than a magnetic strip, is loaded with identifying data. Users of smart cards are required to enter a **personal identification number (PIN)** to be authenticated.

Biometric Authentication

Biometric authentication uses personal physical characteristics such as fingerprints, facial features, and retinal scans to authenticate users. Biometric authentication provides strong authentication, but the required equipment is expensive. Often, too, users resist biometric identification because they feel it is invasive.

Biometric authentication is in the early stages of adoption. Because of its strength, it likely will see increased usage in the future. It is also likely that legislators will pass laws governing the use, storage, and protection requirements for biometric data. For more on biometrics, search for *biometrics* at *http://searchsecurity.techtarget.com*.

Note that authentication methods fall into three categories: what you know (password or PIN), what you have (smart card), and what you are (biometric).

Single Sign-on for Multiple Systems

Information systems often require multiple sources of authentication. For example, when you sign on to your personal computer, you need to be authenticated. When you access the LAN in your department, you need to be authenticated again. When you traverse your organization's WAN, you will need to be authenticated to even more networks. Also, if your request requires database data, the DBMS server that manages that database will authenticate you yet again.

ETHICS GUIDE

WEB RECORDING EVERYTHING

The rhythm of the stop-and-go traffic on Robin's drive to the office was lulling her to sleep. She reached over to turn up the air conditioning and then increased the volume of the radio, too. In spite of the traffic—and her drowsiness—she enjoyed her commute into Cambridge. The road she took went past Walden Pond and towns like Lexington and Concord—some of the most meaningful landmarks in this part of the country. She loved visiting these historical sites on the weekends, but it felt like forever since she last had had the chance to do so. Her surge of enthusiasm waned, and she refocused on the road.

The past few months of work had been fraught with challenges. She had been working nights, weekends, and holidays to keep up. Her position of user experience manager on the company's e-commerce site was becoming more and more critical as major players like Amazon and other smaller (but growing) competitors continued to fight for market share. Retaining every potential sale was of the utmost importance. Her current charge from higher-level managers was to compile as much data about customer interactions as possible.

The idea was that if she could understand how and why users of the site made decisions to buy certain products or abandon items in a shopping cart, the site could be customized to increase purchases and diminish lost sales. The company could even customize the site for each specific visitor. Most e-commerce sites were doing this type of data collection, analysis, and customization. However, she was actually heading into the city today to meet with a data analytics expert to discuss new strategies for collecting and analyzing customer behavior. She was open to anything new that could help the company get even a shred of competitive advantage over its rivals!

The Devil Is in the Details

Robin parked in the underground garage, made her way up to street level, and began walking along the Charles River to the coffee shop where the meeting had been set. Upon arriving, she pulled open the door and immediately recognized Marianne from her LinkedIn profile. She was sitting in the corner making some final preparations for the meeting. After preliminary introductions and an overview of the company by Robin, Marianne began explaining some of the new types of data collection and analysis solutions that some of her most

recent clients had found useful. The first few approaches were things that Robin had already implemented at her company, but Robin perked up as soon Marianne began discussing the next approach.

Marianne explained, "One of the most exciting things about the Big Data movement is the ability not just to capture and store vast troves of data but to do so using new data input streams, things that people have never thought to explore or just didn't have the ability to explore. For example, many Web sites are now storing and analyzing *everything* that visitors do on the site—not just pages they visit or the products that they add to a shopping cart, but all of the mouse movements, keystrokes, and scrolling behavior, too.[11]

Marianne continued, "The level of detail that you can capture about site visitors will grow exponentially if you decide to incorporate this functionality into your site. Currently, you can see if someone adds or removes a product from the shopping cart. But the technology I am talking about will allow you to see if a visitor keeps moving their mouse toward specific products but never actually adds those products to the cart. Think about it this way—right now you are only able to read a written transcript of what your users are 'telling' you about their interaction on the site. With this new technology, you will be able to watch a video of their entire 'conversation.' You'll see what they do before and after they 'speak' and see *how* they are speaking. The best part is that there is very little you have to do to make this

happen. All of this data is piped to a third-party company that can do all of the analysis for you. You would just have to add the data collection piece to your site!"

Data Mine, Not Yours

While Marianne continued in this same vein, Robin couldn't help but let her mind wander to all of the possibilities and implications of this idea. This was not the first time she had heard about analyzing mouse movements to derive meaningful information. She had recently read an article in the *Wall Street Journal* about researchers who were analyzing mouse movements to uncover emotion.[12] But the more she thought about Marianne's pitch, the more she started to become concerned.

If the data collection tool captures everything users do during a Web session, some very sensitive data (like name, address, and credit card information) would be captured during the checkout process. If all of this data was sent to a third party, it could open up a potential vulnerability for customer data to be compromised. Tracking everything users did felt strange, too. It felt like some kind of breach of privacy, and if nothing else, it was kind of creepy. Finally, if customers caught wind that her company was doing this, it could cause a PR nightmare. Robin took a drink of her coffee and continued thinking about what to do. Maybe she wasn't quite as open to new ideas as she had thought.

DISCUSSION QUESTIONS

1. According to the definitions of the ethical principles defined previously in this book:
   a. Do you think covertly monitoring all user behavior on a Web site is ethical according to the categorical imperative (page 23-24)?
   b. Do you think covertly monitoring all user behavior on a Web site is ethical according to the utilitarian perspective (page 42-43)?
2. Were Robin's concerns about sharing customer data with a third-part company valid? What kind of problems might arise from sharing this type of data?

3. Should Robin's company change its site's terms and conditions policy if it implements the new technology? How might this protect the company and its customers?
4. Would this type of data collection be more problematic if it were enabled on a mobile application versus a Web site? What type of additional data could be collected from a mobile application versus a Web site?

It would be annoying to enter a name and password for every one of these resources. You might have to use and remember five or six different passwords just to access the data you need to perform your job. It would be equally undesirable to send your password across all of these networks. The further your password travels, the greater the risk it can be compromised.

Instead, today's operating systems have the capability to authenticate you to networks and other servers. You sign on to your local computer and provide authentication data; from that point on your operating system authenticates you to another network or server, which can authenticate you to yet another network and server, and so forth. Because this is so, your identity and passwords open many doors beyond those on your local computer; remember this when you choose your passwords!

Encryption

Encryption is the process of transforming clear text into coded, unintelligible text for secure storage or communication. Considerable research has gone into developing **encryption algorithms** (procedures for encrypting data) that are difficult to break. Commonly used methods are DES, 3DES, and AES; search the Web for these terms if you want to know more about them.

A **key** is a string of bits used to encrypt the data. It is called a *key* because it unlocks a message, but it is a string of bits, expressed as numbers or letters, used with an encryption algorithm. It's not a physical thing like the key to your apartment.

To encrypt a message, a computer program uses the encryption method (say, AES) combined with the key (say, the word "key") to convert a plaintext message (in this case, the word "secret") into an encrypted message. The resulting coded message ("U2FsdGVkX1+b637aTP80u+y2WYl UbqUz2XtYcw4E8m4=") looks like gibberish. Decoding (decrypting) a message is similar; a key is applied to the coded message to recover the original text. With **symmetric encryption**, the same key is used to encode and to decode. With **asymmetric encryption**, two keys are used; one key encodes the message, and the other key decodes the message. Symmetric encryption is simpler and much faster than asymmetric encryption.

A special version of asymmetric encryption, **public key encryption**, is used on the Internet. With this method, each site has a *public key* for encoding messages and a *private key* for decoding them. Before we explain how that works, consider the following analogy.

Suppose you send a friend an open combination lock (like you have on your gym locker). Suppose you are the only one who knows the combination to that lock. Now, suppose your friend puts something in a box and locks the lock. Now, neither your friend nor anyone else can open that box. That friend sends the locked box to you, and you apply the combination to open the box.

A *public key* is like the combination lock, and the *private key* is like the combination. Your friend uses the public key to code the message (lock the box), and you use the private key to decode the message (open the lock).

Now, suppose we have two generic computers, A and B. Suppose B wants to send an encrypted message to A. To do so, A sends B its public key (in our analogy, A sends B an open combination lock). Now B applies A's public key to the message and sends the resulting coded message back to A. At that point, neither B nor anyone other than A can decode that message. It is like the box with a locked combination lock. When A receives the coded message, A applies its private key (the combination in our analogy) to unlock or decrypt the message.

Again, public keys are like open combination locks. Computer A will send a lock to anyone who asks for one. But A never sends its private key (the combination) to anyone. Private keys stay private.

Most secure communication over the Internet uses a protocol called **https**. With https, data are encrypted using a protocol called the **Secure Sockets Layer (SSL)**, which is also known as **Transport Layer Security (TLS)**. SSL/TLS uses a combination of public key encryption and symmetric encryption.

The basic idea is this: Symmetric encryption is fast and is preferred. But the two parties (say, you and a Web site) don't share a symmetric key. So, the two of you use public key encryption to share the same symmetric key. Once you both have that key, you use symmetric encryption for the remainder of the communication.

Figure 10-9 summarizes how SSL/TLS works when you communicate securely with a Web site:

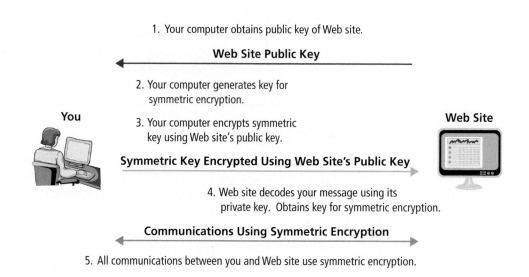

FIGURE 10-9
The Essence of https (SSL or TLS)

1. Your computer obtains the *public* key of the Web site to which it will connect.
2. Your computer generates a key for symmetric encryption.
3. Your computer encodes that key using the Web site's public key. It sends the encrypted symmetric key to the Web site.
4. The Web site then decodes the symmetric key using its *private* key.
5. From that point forward, your computer and the Web site communicate using symmetric encryption.

At the end of the session, your computer and the secure site discard the keys. Using this strategy, the bulk of the secure communication occurs using the faster symmetric encryption. Also, because keys are used for short intervals, there is less likelihood they can be discovered.

Use of SSL/TLS makes it safe to send sensitive data such as credit card numbers and bank balances. Just be certain that you see *https://* in your browser and not just *http://*. Most browsers have additional plug-ins or add-ons (like HTTPS Everywhere) that can force https connections when available.

Firewalls

A **firewall** is a computing device that prevents unauthorized network access. A firewall can be a special-purpose computer, or it can be a program on a general-purpose computer or on a router. In essence, a firewall is simply a filter. It can filter traffic in a variety of ways including where network traffic is coming from, what types of packets are being sent, the contents of the packets, and if the packets are part of an authorized connection.

Organizations normally use multiple firewalls. A **perimeter firewall** sits outside the organizational network; it is the first device that Internet traffic encounters. In addition to perimeter firewalls, some organizations employ **internal firewalls** inside the organizational network. Figure 10-10 shows the use of a perimeter firewall that protects all of an organization's computers and a second internal firewall that protects a LAN.

A **packet-filtering firewall** examines each part of a message and determines whether to let that part pass. To make this decision, it examines the source address, the destination address(es), and other data.

Packet-filtering firewalls can prohibit outsiders from starting a session with any user behind the firewall. They can also disallow traffic from particular sites, such as known hacker addresses. They can prohibit traffic from legitimate, but unwanted, addresses, such as competitors' computers, and filter outbound traffic as well. They can keep employees from accessing specific sites, such as competitors' sites, sites with pornographic material, or popular news sites. As a future manager, if you have particular sites with which you do not want your employees to communicate, you can ask your IS department to enforce that limit via the firewall.

Packet-filtering firewalls are the simplest type of firewall. Other firewalls filter on a more sophisticated basis. If you take a data communications class, you will learn about them. For

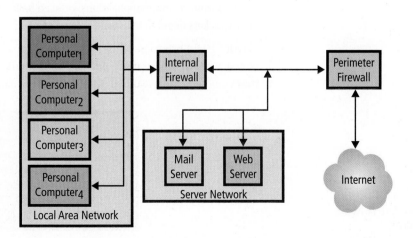

FIGURE 10-10
Use of Multiple Firewalls

now, just understand that firewalls help to protect organizational computers from unauthorized network access.

No computer should connect to the Internet without firewall protection. Many ISPs provide firewalls for their customers. By nature, these firewalls are generic. Large organizations supplement such generic firewalls with their own. Most home routers include firewalls, and Microsoft Windows has a built-in firewall as well. Third parties also license firewall products.

Malware Protection

The next technical safeguard in our list in Figure 10-8 concerns malware. **Malware** is a broad category of software that includes viruses, spyware, and adware.

- A **virus** is a computer program that replicates itself. Unchecked replication is like computer cancer; ultimately, the virus consumes the computer's resources. Furthermore, many viruses also take unwanted and harmful actions. The program code that causes the unwanted actions is called the payload. The **payload** can delete programs or data—or, even worse, modify data in undetected ways.
- **Trojan horses** are viruses that masquerade as useful programs or files. The name refers to the gigantic mock-up of a horse that was filled with soldiers and moved into Troy during the Trojan War. A typical Trojan horse appears to be a computer game, an MP3 music file, or some other useful, innocuous program.
- A **worm** is a virus that self-propagates using the Internet or other computer network. Worms spread faster than other virus types because they can replicate by themselves. Unlike nonworm viruses, which must wait for the user to share a file with a second computer, worms actively use the network to spread. Sometimes, worms can propagate so quickly that they overload and crash a network.
- **Spyware** programs are installed on the user's computer without the user's knowledge or permission. Spyware resides in the background and, unknown to the user, observes the user's actions and keystrokes, monitors computer activity, and reports the user's activities to sponsoring organizations. Some malicious spyware, called **key loggers**, captures keystrokes to obtain usernames, passwords, account numbers, and other sensitive information. Other spyware supports marketing analyses such as observing what users do, Web sites visited, products examined and purchased, and so forth.
- **Adware** is similar to spyware in that it is installed without the user's permission and resides in the background and observes user behavior. Most adware is benign in that it does not perform malicious acts or steal data. It does, however, watch user activity and produce pop-up ads. Adware can also change the user's default window or modify search results and switch the user's search engine.
- **Ransomware** is malicious software that blocks access to a system or data until money is paid to the attacker. Some forms of ransomware encrypt your data (CryptoLocker), prevent you from running applications, or even lock you out of your operating system (Reveton). Attackers demand to be paid before they will allow access to your data or system.

Figure 10-11 lists some of the symptoms of adware and spyware. Sometimes these symptoms develop slowly over time as more malware components are installed. Should these symptoms occur on your computer, remove the spyware or adware using antimalware programs.

- Slow system startup
- Sluggish system performance
- Many pop-up advertisements
- Suspicious browser homepage changes
- Suspicious changes to the taskbar and other system interfaces
- Unusual hard-disk activity

FIGURE 10-11
Spyware and Adware Symptoms

Malware Safeguards

Fortunately, it is possible to avoid most malware using the following malware safeguards:

1. *Install antivirus and antispyware programs on your computer.* Your IS department will have a list of recommended (perhaps required) programs for this purpose. If you choose a program for yourself, choose one from a reputable vendor. Check reviews of antimalware software on the Web before purchasing.

2. *Set up your antimalware programs to scan your computer frequently.* You should scan your computer at least once a week and possibly more often. When you detect malware code, use the antimalware software to remove it. If the code cannot be removed, contact your IS department or antimalware vendor.

3. *Update malware definitions.* **Malware definitions**—patterns that exist in malware code—should be downloaded frequently. Antimalware vendors update these definitions continuously, and you should install these updates as they become available.

4. *Open email attachments only from known sources.* Also, even when opening attachments from known sources, do so with great care. With a properly configured firewall, email is the only outside-initiated traffic that can reach user computers.

    Most antimalware programs check email attachments for malware code. However, all users should form the habit of *never* opening an email attachment from an unknown source. Also, if you receive an unexpected email from a known source or an email from a known source that has a suspicious subject, odd spelling, or poor grammar, do not open the attachment without first verifying with the known source that the attachment is legitimate.

5. *Promptly install software updates from legitimate sources.* Unfortunately, all programs are chock full of security holes; vendors are fixing them as rapidly as they are discovered, but the practice is inexact. Install patches to the operating system and application programs promptly.

6. *Browse only reputable Web sites.* It is possible for some malware to install itself when you do nothing more than open a Web page. Recently, malware writers have been paying for banner ads on legitimate sites that have malware embedded in the ad. One click and you're infected.

Design for Secure Applications

The final technical safeguard in Figure 10-8 concerns the design of applications. As you learned in the opening vignette, Henri and Raj are designing ARES with security in mind; ARES will store users' privacy settings in a database, and it will develop all applications to first read the privacy settings before revealing any data in exercise reports. Most likely, ARES will design its programs so that privacy data is processed by programs on servers; that design means that such data need be transmitted over the Internet only when it is created or modified.

By the way, a **SQL injection attack** occurs when users enter a SQL statement into a form in which they are supposed to enter a name or other data. If the program is improperly designed, it will accept this code and make it part of the database command that it issues. Improper data disclosure and data damage and loss are possible consequences. A well-designed application will make such injections ineffective.

As a future IS user, you will not design programs yourself. However, you should ensure that any information system developed for you and your department includes security as one of the application requirements.

Q10-6 How Can Data Safeguards Protect Against Security Threats?

Data safeguards protect databases and other organizational data. Two organizational units are responsible for data safeguards. **Data administration** refers to an organization-wide function that is in charge of developing data policies and enforcing data standards.

Database administration refers to a function that pertains to a particular database. ERP, CRM, and MRP databases each have a database administration function. Database administration develops procedures and practices to ensure efficient and orderly multiuser processing of the database, to control changes to the database structure, and to protect the database. Database administration was summarized in Chapter 5.

Both data and database administration are involved in establishing the data safeguards in Figure 10-12. First, data administration should define data policies such as "We will not share identifying customer data with any other organization" and the like. Then data administration and database administration(s) work together to specify user data rights and responsibilities. Third, those rights should be enforced by user accounts that are authenticated at least by passwords.

The organization should protect sensitive data by storing it in encrypted form. Such encryption uses one or more keys in ways similar to that described for data communication encryption. One potential problem with stored data, however, is that the key might be lost or that disgruntled or terminated employees might destroy it. Because of this possibility, when data are encrypted, a trusted party should have a copy of the encryption key. This safety procedure is sometimes called **key escrow**.

Another data safeguard is to periodically create backup copies of database contents. The organization should store at least some of these backups off premises, possibly in a remote location. Additionally, IT personnel should periodically practice recovery to ensure that the backups are valid and that effective recovery procedures exist. Do not assume that just because a backup is made that the database is protected.

Physical security is another data safeguard. The computers that run the DBMS and all devices that store database data should reside in locked, controlled-access facilities. If not, they are subject not only to theft, but also to damage. For better security, the organization should keep a log showing who entered the facility, when, and for what purpose.

When organizations store databases in the cloud, all of the safeguards in Figure 10-12 should be part of the cloud service contract.

Legal Safeguards for Data

Some organizations have legal requirements to safeguard the customer data they collect and store. Laws can dictate how long records must be kept, who companies can share the data with, and mandatory safe data storage requirements. Some data storage laws have direct implications for business.

For example, the **Payment Card Industry Data Security Standard (PCI DSS)** governs the secure storage and processing of credit card data. The **Gramm-Leach-Bliley (GLB) Act**, passed by Congress in 1999, protects consumer financial data stored by financial institutions, which are defined as banks; securities firms; insurance companies; and organizations that supply financial advice, prepare tax returns, and provide similar financial services.

For healthcare organizations, the privacy provisions of the **Health Insurance Portability and Accountability Act (HIPAA)** of 1996 give individuals the right to access health data created by doctors and other healthcare providers. HIPAA also sets rules and limits on who can read and receive your health information.

Data protection laws may be stronger in other countries than in the United States. In Australia, for example, the Privacy Principles of the Australian Privacy Act of 1988 govern not only government and healthcare data but also records maintained by businesses with revenues in excess of AU$3 million.

- Define data policies
- Data rights and responsibilities
- Rights enforced by user accounts authenticated by passwords
- Data encryption
- Backup and recovery procedures
- Physical security

FIGURE 10-12
Data Safeguards

Q10-7 ## How Can Human Safeguards Protect Against Security Threats?

Read about the largest data breach in the world in the Security Guide on pages 408–409.

Human safeguards involve the people and procedure components of information systems. In general, human safeguards result when authorized users follow appropriate procedures for system use and recovery. Restricting access to authorized users requires effective authentication methods and careful user account management. In addition, appropriate security procedures must be designed as part of every information system, and users should be trained on the importance and use of those procedures. In this section, we will consider the development of human safeguards for employees. According to the survey of computer crime discussed in Q10-2, crime from malicious insiders is a frequent and expensive problem. This fact makes safeguards even more important.

Human Safeguards for Employees

Figure 10-13 lists security considerations for employees. Consider each.

Position Definitions

Effective human safeguards begin with definitions of job tasks and responsibilities. In general, job descriptions should provide a separation of duties and authorities. For example, no single individual

- Position definition
  - Separate duties and authorities
  - Determine least privilege
  - Document position sensitivity

"OK to pay this."

- Hiring and screening

"Where did you last work?"

- Dissemination and enforcement
  - Responsibility
  - Accountability
  - Compliance

"Let's talk security..."

- Termination
  - Friendly

"Congratulations on your new job."

  - Unfriendly

"We've closed your accounts. Goodbye."

FIGURE 10-13
Security Policy for In-House Staff

should be allowed to both approve expenses and write checks. Instead, one person should approve expenses, another pay them, and a third should account for the payment. Similarly, in inventory, no single person should be allowed to authorize an inventory withdrawal and also to remove the items from inventory.

Given appropriate job descriptions, user accounts should be defined to give users the *least possible privilege* needed to perform their jobs. For example, users whose job description does not include modifying data should be given accounts with read-only privileges. Similarly, user accounts should prohibit users from accessing data their job description does not require.

Finally, the security sensitivity should be documented for each position. Some jobs involve highly sensitive data (e.g., employee compensation, salesperson quotas, and proprietary marketing or technical data). Other positions involve no sensitive data. Documenting *position sensitivity* enables security personnel to prioritize their activities in accordance with the possible risk and loss.

Hiring and Screening

Security considerations should be part of the hiring process. Of course, if the position involves no sensitive data and no access to information systems, then screening for information systems security purposes will be minimal. When hiring for high-sensitivity positions, however, extensive interviews, references, and background investigations are appropriate. Note, too, that security screening applies not only to new employees, but also to employees who are promoted into sensitive positions.

Dissemination and Enforcement

Employees cannot be expected to follow security policies and procedures that they do not know about. Therefore, employees need to be made aware of the security policies, procedures, and responsibilities they will have.

Employee security training begins during new-employee training, with the explanation of general security policies and procedures. That general training must be amplified in accordance with the position's sensitivity and responsibilities. Promoted employees should receive security training that is appropriate to their new positions. The company should not provide user accounts and passwords until employees have completed required security training.

Enforcement consists of three interdependent factors: responsibility, accountability, and compliance. First, the company should clearly define the security *responsibilities* of each position. The design of the security program should be such that employees can be held *accountable* for security violations. Procedures should exist so that when critical data are lost, it is possible to determine how the loss occurred and who is accountable. Finally, the security program should encourage security *compliance*. Employee activities should regularly be monitored for compliance, and management should specify the disciplinary action to be taken in light of noncompliance.

Management attitude is crucial: Employee compliance is greater when management demonstrates, both in word and deed, a serious concern for security. If managers write passwords on staff bulletin boards, shout passwords down hallways, or ignore physical security procedures, then employee security attitudes and employee security compliance will suffer. Note, too, that effective security is a continuing management responsibility. Regular reminders about security are essential.

Termination

Companies also must establish security policies and procedures for the termination of employees. Many employee terminations are friendly and occur as the result of promotion or retirement or when the employee resigns to take another position. Standard human resources policies should ensure that system administrators receive notification in advance of the employee's last day so that they can remove accounts and passwords. The need to recover keys for encrypted data and any other special security requirements should be part of the employee's out-processing.

Unfriendly termination is more difficult because employees may be tempted to take malicious or harmful actions. In such a case, system administrators may need to remove user accounts and passwords prior to notifying the employee of his or her termination. Other actions may be needed to protect the company's data assets. A terminated sales employee, for example, may attempt to take the company's confidential customer and sales-prospect data for future use at another company. The terminating employer should take steps to protect those data prior to the termination.

The human resources department should be aware of the importance of giving IS administrators early notification of employee termination. No blanket policy exists; the information systems department must assess each case on an individual basis.

Human Safeguards for Nonemployee Personnel

Business requirements may necessitate opening information systems to nonemployee personnel—temporary personnel, vendors, partner personnel (employees of business partners), and the public. Although temporary personnel can be screened, to reduce costs the screening will be abbreviated from that for employees. In most cases, companies cannot screen either vendor or partner personnel. Of course, public users cannot be screened at all. Similar limitations pertain to security training and compliance testing.

In the case of temporary, vendor, and partner personnel, the contracts that govern the activity should call for security measures appropriate to the sensitivity of the data and the IS resources involved. Companies should require vendors and partners to perform appropriate screening and security training. The contract also should mention specific security responsibilities that are particular to the work to be performed. Companies should provide accounts and passwords with the least privilege and remove those accounts as soon as possible.

The situation differs with public users of Web sites and other openly accessible information systems. It is exceedingly difficult and expensive to hold public users accountable for security violations. In general, the best safeguard from threats from public users is to *harden* the Web site or other facility against attack as much as possible. **Hardening** a site means to take extraordinary measures to reduce a system's vulnerability. Hardened sites use special versions of the operating system, and they lock down or eliminate operating systems features and functions that are not required by the application. Hardening is actually a technical safeguard, but we mention it here as the most important safeguard against public users.

Finally, note that the business relationship with the public, and with some partners, differs from that with temporary personnel and vendors. The public and some partners use the information system to receive a benefit. Consequently, safeguards need to protect such users from internal company security problems. A disgruntled employee who maliciously changes prices on a Web site potentially damages both public users and business partners. As one IT manager put it, "Rather than protecting ourselves from them, we need to protect them from us." This is an extension of the fifth safeguard in Figure 10-7.

Account Administration

The administration of user accounts, passwords, and help-desk policies and procedures is another important human safeguard.

Account Management

Account management concerns the creation of new user accounts, the modification of existing account permissions, and the removal of unneeded accounts. Information system administrators perform all of these tasks, but account users have the responsibility to notify the administrators of the need for these actions. The IS department should create standard procedures for this purpose. As a future user, you can improve your relationship with IS personnel by providing early and timely notification of the need for account changes.

The existence of accounts that are no longer necessary is a serious security threat. IS administrators cannot know when an account should be removed; it is up to users and managers to give such notification.

Password Management

Passwords are the primary means of authentication. They are important not just for access to the user's computer, but also for authentication to other networks and servers to which the user may have access. Because of the importance of passwords, the National Institute of Standards and Technology (NIST) recommends that employees be required to sign statements similar to those shown in Figure 10-14.

When an account is created, users should immediately change the password they are given to one of their own. In fact, well-constructed systems require the user to change the password on first use.

Additionally, users should change passwords frequently thereafter. Some systems will require a password change every 3 months or perhaps more frequently. Users grumble at the nuisance of making such changes, but frequent password changes reduce not only the risk of password loss, but also the extent of damage if an existing password is compromised.

Some users create two passwords and switch back and forth between those two. This strategy results in poor security, and some password systems do not allow the user to reuse recently used passwords. Again, users may view this policy as a nuisance, but it is important.

Help-Desk Policies

In the past, help desks have been a serious security risk. A user who had forgotten his password would call the help desk and plead for the help-desk representative to tell him his password or to reset the password to something else. "I can't get this report out without it!" was (and is) a common lament.

The problem for help-desk representatives is, of course, that they have no way of determining that they are talking with the true user and not someone spoofing a true user. But they are in a bind: If they do not help in some way, the help desk is perceived to be the "unhelpful desk."

To resolve such problems, many systems give the help-desk representative a means of authenticating the user. Typically, the help-desk information system has answers to questions that only the true user would know, such as the user's birthplace, mother's maiden name, or last four digits of an important account number. Usually, when a password is changed, notification of that change is sent to the user in an email. Email is sent as plaintext, however, so the new password itself ought not to be emailed. If you ever receive notification that your password was reset when you did not request such a reset, immediately contact IT security. Someone has compromised your account.

All such help-desk measures reduce the strength of the security system, and, if the employee's position is sufficiently sensitive, they may create too large a vulnerability. In such a case, the user may just be out of luck. The account will be deleted, and the user must repeat the account-application process.

FIGURE 10-14
Sample Account Acknowledgment Form

Source: National Institute of Standards and Technology, U.S. Department of Commerce. Introduction to Computer Security: The NIST Handbook, Publication 800–812.

> I hereby acknowledge personal receipt of the system password(s) associated with the user IDs listed below. I understand that I am responsible for protecting the password(s), will comply with all applicable system security standards, and will not divulge my password(s) to any person. I further understand that I must report to the Information Systems Security Officer any problem I encounter in the use of the password(s) or when I have reason to believe that the private nature of my password(s) has been compromised.

Systems Procedures

Figure 10-15 shows a grid of procedure types—normal operation, backup, and recovery. Procedures of each type should exist for each information system. For example, the order-entry system will have procedures of each of these types, as will the Web storefront, the inventory system, and so forth. The definition and use of standardized procedures reduces the likelihood of computer crime and other malicious activity by insiders. It also ensures that the system's security policy is enforced.

Procedures exist for both users and operations personnel. For each type of user, the company should develop procedures for normal, backup, and recovery operations. As a future user, you will be primarily concerned with user procedures. Normal-use procedures should provide safeguards appropriate to the sensitivity of the information system.

Backup procedures concern the creation of backup data to be used in the event of failure. Whereas operations personnel have the responsibility for backing up system databases and other systems data, departmental personnel have the need to back up data on their own computers. Good questions to ponder are, "What would happen if I lost my computer or mobile device tomorrow?" "What would happen if someone dropped my computer during an airport security inspection?" "What would happen if my computer was stolen?" Employees should ensure that they back up critical business data on their computers. The IS department may help in this effort by designing backup procedures and making backup facilities available.

Finally, systems analysts should develop procedures for system recovery. First, how will the department manage its affairs when a critical system is unavailable? Customers will want to order and manufacturing will want to remove items from inventory even though a critical information system is unavailable. How will the department respond? Once the system is returned to service, how will records of business activities during the outage be entered into the system? How will service be resumed? The system developers should ask and answer these questions and others like them and develop procedures accordingly.

Security Monitoring

Security monitoring is the last of the human safeguards we will consider. Important monitoring functions are activity log analyses, security testing, and investigating and learning from security incidents.

Many information system programs produce *activity logs*. Firewalls produce logs of their activities, including lists of all dropped packets, infiltration attempts, and unauthorized access attempts from within the firewall. DBMS products produce logs of successful and failed log-ins. Web servers produce voluminous logs of Web activities. The operating systems in personal computers can produce logs of log-ins and firewall activities.

None of these logs adds any value to an organization unless someone looks at them. Accordingly, an important security function is to analyze these logs for threat patterns, successful and unsuccessful attacks, and evidence of security vulnerabilities.

	System Users	Operations Personnel
Normal operation	Use the system to perform job tasks, with security appropriate to sensitivity.	Operate data center equipment, manage networks, run Web servers, and do related operational tasks.
Backup	Prepare for loss of system functionality.	Back up Web site resources, databases, administrative data, account and password data, and other data.
Recovery	Accomplish job tasks during failure. Know tasks to do during system recovery.	Recover systems from backed up data. Perform role of help desk during recovery.

FIGURE 10-15
Systems Procedures

Today, most large organizations actively investigate their security vulnerabilities. They may employ utilities such as Tenable's Nessus or IBM's Security AppScan to assess their vulnerabilities.

Many companies create **honeypots**, which are false targets for computer criminals to attack. To an intruder, a honeypot looks like a particularly valuable resource, such as an unprotected Web site, but in actuality the only site content is a program that determines the attacker's IP address. Organizations can then trace the IP address back using free online tools, like DNSstuff, to determine who has attacked them.[13] If you are technically minded, detail-oriented, and curious, a career as a security specialist in this field is almost as exciting as it appears on *CSI*. To learn more, check out DNSstuff, Nessus, or Security AppScan. See also *Applied Information Security*, 3rd ed.[14]

Another important monitoring function is to investigate security incidents. How did the problem occur? Have safeguards been created to prevent a recurrence of such problems? Does the incident indicate vulnerabilities in other portions of the security system? What else can be learned from the incident?

Security systems reside in a dynamic environment. Organization structures change. Companies are acquired or sold; mergers occur. New systems require new security measures. New technology changes the security landscape, and new threats arise. Security personnel must constantly monitor the situation and determine if the existing security policy and safeguards are adequate. If changes are needed, security personnel need to take appropriate action.

Security, like quality, is an ongoing process. There is no final state that represents a secure system or company. Instead, companies must monitor security on a continuing basis.

How Should Organizations Respond to Security Incidents?

The last component of a security plan that we will consider is incident response. Figure 10-16 lists the major factors. First, every organization should have an incident-response plan as part of the security program. No organization should wait until some asset has been lost or compromised before deciding what to do. The plan should include how employees are to respond to security problems, whom they should contact, the reports they should make, and steps they can take to reduce further loss.

Consider, for example, a virus. An incident-response plan will stipulate what an employee should do when he notices the virus. It should specify whom to contact and what to do. It may stipulate that the employee should turn off his computer and physically disconnect from the network. The plan should also indicate what users with wireless computers should do.

The plan should provide centralized reporting of all security incidents. Such reporting will enable an organization to determine if it is under systematic attack or whether an incident is isolated. Centralized reporting also allows the organization to learn about security threats, take consistent actions in response, and apply specialized expertise to all security problems.

When an incident does occur, speed is of the essence. The longer the incident goes on, the greater the cost. Viruses and worms can spread very quickly across an organization's networks, and a fast response will help to mitigate the consequences. Because of the need for speed,

- Have plan in place
- Centralized reporting
- Specific responses
  - Speed
  - Preparation pays
  - Don't make problem worse
- Practice

FIGURE 10-16
Factors in Incident Response

preparation pays. The incident-response plan should identify critical personnel and their off-hours contact information. These personnel should be trained on where to go and what to do when they get there. Without adequate preparation, there is substantial risk that the actions of well-meaning people will make the problem worse. Also, the rumor mill will be alive with all sorts of nutty ideas about what to do. A cadre of well-informed, trained personnel will serve to dampen such rumors.

Finally, organizations should periodically practice incident response. Without such practice, personnel will be poorly informed on the response plan, and the plan itself may have flaws that only become apparent during a drill.

Q10-9   2029?

What will be the status of information security by 2029? Will we have found a magic bullet to eliminate security problems? No. Human error is a constant; well-managed organizations will plan better for it and know how to respond better when it does occur, but as long as we have humans, we'll have error. Natural disasters are similar. The horrific events surrounding Hurricane Katrina in 2005 and the Japanese tsunami in 2011, as well as Hurricane Sandy in 2012, have alerted the world that we need to be better prepared, and more companies will set up hot or cold sites and put more data in well-prepared clouds. So, we'll be better prepared, but natural disasters are natural, after all.

Unfortunately, it is likely that sometime in the next 10 years some new, major incidents of cyberwarfare will have occurred. APTs will become more common, if indeed, they are not already common but we don't know it. Will some new nation or group enter the cyberwar picture? That also seems likely. Unless you're in the security and intelligence business, there isn't much you can do about it. But don't be surprised if some serious damage is inflicted somewhere in the world due to APTs.

In 2013, privacy advocates were outraged at the existence of **PRISM**, the intelligence program by which the National Security Agency (NSA) requested and received data about Internet activities from major Internet providers. They claimed their **privacy**, or freedom from being observed by other people, was being destroyed in the name of **security**, or the state of being free from danger. After the initial hullabaloo, it appears that Internet providers did not allow the government direct access to their servers but rather delivered only data about specific individuals, as legally requested according to security laws enacted after 9/11. If so, then PRISM represents a legal governmental request for data, different only in scale from a governmental request for banking data about an organized crime figure.

As of June 2018, Edward Snowden, the man who exposed the PRISM program, appears to be either an advocate for Internet freedom and privacy or a traitor who sold government secrets to China and Russia for private gain. Regardless of the reasons for the leak, the episode raises the question of what governmental intrusion should be allowed into private data. We can hope the revelation of the existence of PRISM will spark a public conversation on the balance of national security and data privacy. In 2018 the PRISM surveillance program was renewed by Congress and the President of the United States.

What about computer crime? It is a game of cat and mouse. Computer criminals find a vulnerability to exploit, and they exploit it. Computer security experts discover that vulnerability and create safeguards to thwart it. Computer criminals find a new vulnerability to exploit, computer security forces thwart it, and so it goes. The next major challenges will likely be those affecting mobile devices. But security on these devices will be improved as threats emerge that exploit their vulnerabilities. This cat-and-mouse game is likely to continue for at least the next 10 years. No super-safeguard will be devised to prevent computer crime, nor will any particular computer crime be impossible to thwart. However, the skill level of this cat-and-mouse activity is likely to increase,

SECURITY GUIDE

LARGEST! DATA! BREACH! EVER!

Source: dennizn/Alamy Stock Photo

If you think back to your earliest experiences with the World Wide Web, you may recall the atmosphere of a Web 1.0 world. Web 1.0 was an extremely stripped-down version of the Web that we know and love today. At the time, a majority of Web content was static text. Fancy animations, embedded videos, and rich graphics were not even possible due to a variety of constraints (e.g., limited bandwidth). Additionally, the vast majority of people accessing the Web at that time were content consumers, not content creators. The blogs, wikis, and social media platforms that are the juggernauts of the Internet today did not exist, and the search engines in use at that time were precursors to Google.

One of the core sites that attracted heavy usage at that time was Yahoo! Developed in 1994 by David Filo and Jerry Yang, Yahoo! was essentially a portal for accessing a variety of different types of content on the Web.[15] This included topics like arts, business, entertainment, news, recreation and sports, and science. Within 2 years, the company was worth more than $800 million, and at the peak of the dot-com bubble in 2000, Yahoo! was valued at more than $125 billion.[16] Over the next 15 years, the company attempted a number of acquisitions (including a failed acquisition attempt of Google in 2002).

In 2008, Microsoft tried to acquire Yahoo! but was denied. Yahoo! was finally purchased by Verizon in 2016 for more

than $4 billion.[17] Despite its permanent place as a pioneer on the early Web and its persisting prominence over the past 20 years, Yahoo!'s reputation has been permanently tainted by a recent breach in which more than 3 billion user accounts were compromised. That's nearly half the population of all people on the planet!

What Happened?

In December 2016, Yahoo! announced that a breach had occurred in August 2013 that resulted in roughly 1 billion user accounts being compromised. The company later announced in October 2017 that it believed 3 billion accounts had actually been compromised. In either case, Yahoo!'s breach is the largest of its kind in the history of the Internet. Even worse, it took over *3 years* for Yahoo! to disclose the data breach.[18] It was reported that the stolen account information included email addresses, names, phone numbers, hashed passwords, and, for some users, security questions and answers.[19]

Initial speculation about the breach concluded that the attack was likely attributable to state-sponsored actors, as very little account info from the breach was posted on the dark Web. This means the attackers were looking to compromise the accounts of specific individuals, likely associated with the government or military, and were not planning to just sell all of the stolen account data online.

These suspicions were later confirmed when a 22-year-old hacker was apprehended in Toronto and ultimately pleaded guilty in a San Francisco court to working with another hacker and aiding two Russian spies in stealing Yahoo!'s user account data. He was charged with hacking and aggravated identity theft.[20] The other three involved in the breach were located in Russia and were thus outside any legal ramifications from the U.S. court system.

Do You *Still* Yahoo!?

It can be very difficult for a company and its brand to recover from a security incident, especially one of this magnitude. An understandable outcome of any data breach is that consumers may choose to no longer engage with the compromised company. However, at the time that this breach was made public, Yahoo! was also in the process of being acquired by Verizon. The breach had an impact on the valuation of the company, which had initially been $4.85 billion, but the company was ultimately acquired for $4.5 billion (a loss of $350 million). While the acquisition may have brought closure to the Yahoo! breach, causing it to fade from our minds, it is only a matter of time before the next big cyber-incident reverberates through the tech world and we relive this process all over again.

DISCUSSION QUESTIONS

1. Most data breaches are found within a few days or weeks. Why did the Yahoo! data breach take so long to be discovered? Would the disclosure of the data breach have been harmful to Yahoo!'s efforts to sell their company?

2. Have you been a victim of one of the large security breaches over the past several years? If so, what was the impact of your data being compromised? Did you have to take any actions to try to secure your data or your identity? Have you continued being a customer (or using the site) of the company that was compromised? (If you have not been a victim, think about how you would likely respond in this situation.)

3. The article reports that several years transpired between the time when the breach occurred and the time when the breach was acknowledged and made public. Why is there so much latency between the incident and the response?

4. Compare this breach to the Equifax data breach that also happened recently. (If you are not familiar with the Equifax breach, take a few minutes to conduct an online search and read about it.) Was the Equifax breach or the Yahoo! breach worse? Be prepared to defend your opinion.

and substantially so. Because of increased security in operating systems and other software, and because of improved security procedures and employee training, it will become harder and harder for the lone hacker to find some vulnerability to exploit. Not impossible, but vastly more difficult.

So, what will happen? Cloud vendors and major organizations will continue to invest in safeguards; they'll hire more people (maybe you), train them well, and become ever more difficult to infiltrate. Although some criminals will continue to attack these fortresses, most will turn their attention to less protected, more vulnerable, midsized and smaller organizations and to individuals. You can steal $50M from one company or $50 from a million people with the same cash result. And, in the next 10 years, because of improved security at large organizations, the difficulty and cost of stealing that $50M will be much higher than stealing $50 a million times.

Part of the problem is porous national borders. People can freely enter the United States electronically without a passport. They can commit crimes with little fear of repercussions. There are no real electronic IDs. Cyber-gangs are well organized, financially motivated, and possibly state-sponsored. Electronic lawlessness is the order of the day. If someone in Romania steals from Google, Apple, Microsoft, or Boeing and then disappears into a cloud of networks in Uzbekistan, do those large organizations have the resources, expertise, and legal authority to pursue the attackers? What if that same criminal steals from you in Nashville? Can your local or state law enforcement authorities help? And, if your portion of the crime is for $50, how many calls to Uzbekistan do they want to make?

At the federal level, finances and politics take precedence over electronic security. The situation will likely be solved as it was in the past. Strong local "electronic" sheriffs will take control of their electronic borders and enforce existing laws. It will take at least a couple decades for this to happen. Technology is moving faster than either the public or elected officials can educate themselves.

Take another look at Figure 10-6. Send a copy to your loved ones.

CAREER GUIDE

Name: Marianne Olsen
Company: PwC
Job Title: Manager, Cybersecurity and Privacy
Education: Carnegie Mellon University

Source: Marianne Olsen, PwC, Manager, Cybersecurity and Privacy

1 How did you get this type of job?

While receiving my undergraduate degrees in information systems and accounting, I did a couple internships that really prepared me for my current job. At the first, I worked as a business analyst. This entailed gathering requirements from business stakeholders, planning the development of new features, and executing the design. It helped prepare me for my consulting interviews because understanding your client's needs is a major part of the work. I subsequently worked at a security operations center as an analyst. It was there I began delving deeper into information security and truly developed a passion for the field.

Honestly, I initially had misconceptions about being a consultant and did not plan on applying for any work in the field. I believed the "lifestyle of a consultant" wasn't for me. Fortunately, I had a classmate in grad school who pushed me to take the interview for a consulting internship because, at the very least, it would be good interview practice. Once I passed the first round, I was motivated to continue by the free trip. Finally, on the cab ride home, the cabbie asked me about my trip, and I told her I wasn't likely to take the job because the lifestyle wasn't conducive to some of my family goals. She wisely asked about my family, and at that time I wasn't even seriously dating anyone. She helped me see that I shouldn't limit myself for something that might be years down the road. I ended up taking the internship, and I am so grateful I did.

2 What attracted you to this field?

Information security as a whole is constantly growing to meet the ever-changing threat landscape, which is very exciting. Consulting gives you the freedom to work across many different organizations and see solutions in play. This makes it easier to see what is and isn't working and to understand the field and the technologies more deeply.

3 What does a typical workday look like for you (duties, decisions, problems)?

Regardless of the project, I am always working with a team of people to help deliver a solution. In my position, I focus on executing the project. This means working to ensure the associates have sufficient understanding of their tasks and are creating quality work, that any potential risks or issues are identified and communicated to leadership, and that the client is clear on the value we are delivering.

4 What do you like most about your job?

I love how different my days and weeks are and the many opportunities available both inside and outside the firm. Within the firm, there are opportunities for getting involved in different initiatives within your area of focus or across service offerings. So, even if you are on a client-facing project that is less than ideal, you can find fulfillment with internal involvement.

5 What skills would someone need to do well at your job?

Communication. Communication. Communication. In consulting, you are constantly working with people on your team and from the client to create meaningful solutions. You need to have clear communication within your team and to the client to ensure the needs of the project are satisfied.

6 **Are education or certifications important in your field? Why?**

At the very least a bachelor's degree is required. Beyond that, knowledge beyond the education/certifications is most important. However, taking those certifications helps to clearly demonstrate that you have the underlying skills.

7 **What advice would you give to someone who is considering working in your field?**

Begin to understand who you are and what you want your life to look like. In consulting, there are more opportunities than you have time for, so you need to understand where you want to go.

That being said, in the beginning of your career, you need to be flexible and understand that any opportunity you have can help you grow in a way that may be beneficial down the road.

8 **What do you think will be hot tech jobs in 10 years?**

While the tech industry is growing quickly in terms of innovation, maintenance of technology is suffering. Companies are struggling to fully realize the potential of the tools they already have. In addition, the world is starting to be aware of the importance of security to the business. Jobs that capture these elements will still be hot in 10 years.

ACTIVE REVIEW

Use this Active Review to verify that you understand the ideas and concepts that answer the chapter's study questions.

Q10-1 What is the goal of information systems security?

Define *threat, vulnerability, safeguard,* and *target.* Give an example of each. List three types of threats and five types of security losses. Give different examples for the three rows of Figure 10-2. Summarize each of the elements in the cells of Figure 10-3. Explain why it is difficult to know the true cost of computer crime. Explain the goal of IS security.

Q10-2 How big is the computer security problem?

Explain why it is difficult to know the true size of the computer security problem in general and of computer crime in particular. List the takeways in this question and explain the meaning of each.

Q10-3 How should you respond to security threats?

Explain each of the elements in Figure 10-6. Define *IDS,* and explain why the use of an IDS program is sobering, to say the least. Define *brute force attack.* Summarize the characteristics of a strong password. Explain how your identity and password do more than just open doors on your computer. Define *cookie* and explain why using a program like CCleaner is a good example of the computer security trade-off.

Q10-4 How should organizations respond to security threats?

Name and describe two security functions that senior management should address. Summarize the contents of a security policy. Explain what it means to manage risk. Summarize the steps that organizations should take when balancing risk and cost.

Q10-5 How can technical safeguards protect against security threats?

List five technical safeguards. Define *identification* and *authentication.* Describe three types of authentication. Explain how SSL/TLS works. Define *firewall,* and explain its purpose. Define *malware* and

name six types of malware. Describe six ways to protect against malware. Summarize why malware is a serious problem. Explain how ARES is designed for security.

Q10-6 How can data safeguards protect against security threats?

Define *data administration* and *database administration,* and explain the difference. List data safeguards. Explain how laws like GLBA, HIPAA, and PCI DSS protect consumer data.

Q10-7 How can human safeguards protect against security threats?

Summarize human safeguards for each activity in Figure 10-12. Summarize safeguards that pertain to nonemployee personnel. Describe three dimensions of safeguards for account administration. Explain how system procedures can serve as human safeguards. Describe security monitoring techniques.

Q10-8 How should organizations respond to security incidents?

Summarize the actions that an organization should take when dealing with a security incident.

Q10-9 2029?

What, in the opinion of the authors, is likely to happen regarding cyberwarfare in the next 10 years? Explain how the phrase *cat and mouse* pertains to the evolution of computer crime. Describe the types of security problems that are likely to occur in the next 10 years. Explain how the focus of computer criminals will likely change in the next 10 years. Explain how this is likely to impact smaller organizations, and you.

Using Your Knowledge with ARES

As an employee, investor, or advisor to ARES Systems, you can use the knowledge of this chapter to understand the security threats to which any business is subject. You know the need to trade off cost versus risk. You also know three categories of safeguards and the major types of safeguards for each. And you know what it means to design for security. You can also help ensure that ARES Systems employees and ARES users create and use strong passwords.

KEY TERMS AND CONCEPTS

Advanced Persistent Threat (APT)   386
Adware   398
Asymmetric encryption   396
Authentication   393
Biometric authentication   393
Brute force attack   389
Cookies   390
Data administration   399
Data safeguards   399
Database administration   400
Denial of service (DoS)   385
Email spoofing   384
Encryption   394
Encryption algorithms   394
Firewall   397
Gramm-Leach-Bliley Act (GLBA)   400
Hacking   385
Hardening   403
Health Insurance Portability and
    Accountability Act (HIPAA)   400
Honeypots   406
https   382

Human safeguards   392
Identification   393
Internal firewalls   397
Intrusion detection system (IDS)   389
IP spoofing   384
Key   394
Key escrow   400
Key loggers   398
Malware   398
Malware definitions   399
Packet-filtering firewall   397
Packet sniffers   385
Payload   398
Payment Card Industry Data Security
    Standard (PCI DSS)   400
Perimeter firewall   397
Personal identification number
    (PIN)   393
Phisher   384
Phishing   384
Pretexting   384
PRISM   407

Privacy   407
Public key encryption   396
Ransomware   398
Safeguard   382
Secure Sockets Layer (SSL)   396
Security   399
Smart cards   393
Sniffing   385
Spoofing   384
Spyware   385
SQL injection attack   399
Symmetric encryption   396
Target   382
Technical safeguards   392
Threat   382
Transport Layer Security (TLS)   396
Trojan horses   398
Usurpation   385
Virus   398
Vulnerability   382
Wardrivers   385
Worm   398

MyLab MIS

To complete the problems with MyLab MIS, go to EOC Discussion Questions in the MyLab.

USING YOUR KNOWLEDGE

10-1.
MyLab MIS
Credit reporting agencies are required to provide you with a free credit report each year. Most such reports do not include your credit score, but they do provide the details on which your credit score is based. Use one of the following companies to obtain your free report: *www.equifax.com*, *www.experion.com*, and *www.transunion.com*.

a. You should review your credit report for obvious errors. However, other checks are appropriate. Search the Web for guidance on how best to review your credit records. Summarize what you learn.

b. What actions can you take if you find errors in your credit report?

c. Define *identity theft*. Search the Web and determine the best course of action if someone thinks he or she has been the victim of identity theft.

10-2.
MyLab MIS
Suppose you lose your company laptop at an airport. What should you do? Does it matter what data are stored on your disk drive? If the computer contained sensitive or proprietary data, are you necessarily in trouble? Under what circumstances should you now focus on updating your résumé for your new employer?

10-3.
MyLab MIS
Suppose you alert your boss to the security threats discussed in Q10-1 and to the safeguards discussed in Q10-4. Suppose she says, "Very interesting. Tell me more." In preparing for the meeting, you decide to create a list of talking points.

a. Write a brief explanation of each threat discussed in Q10-1.

b. Explain how the five components relate to safeguards.

c. Describe two to three technical, two to three data, and two to three human safeguards.

d. Write a brief description about the safeguards discussed in Q10-4.

e. List security procedures that pertain to you, a temporary employee.

f. List procedures that your department should have with regard to disaster planning.

Using the collaboration IS you built in Chapter 1 (page 32), collaborate with a group of students to answer the following questions.

The purpose of this activity is to assess the current state of computer crime.

10-4. Search the Web for the term *computer crime* and any related terms. Identify what you and your teammates think are the five most serious recent examples. Consider no crime that occurred more than 6 months ago. For each crime, summarize the loss that occurred and the circumstances surrounding the loss, and identify safeguards that were not in place or were ineffective in preventing the crime.

10-5. Search the Web for the term *computer crime statistics* and find two sources other than the Ponemon surveys cited in Q10-2.

a. For each source, explain the methodology used and explain strengths and weaknesses of that methodology.

b. Compare the data in the two new sources to that in Q10-2 and describe differences.

c. Using your knowledge and intuition, describe why you think those differences occurred.

10-6. Go to *www.ponemon.org/library* and download the 2017 Cost of Cyber Crime Study (or a more recent report if one is available).

a. Summarize the survey with regard to safeguards and other measures that organizations use.

b. Summarize the study's conclusions with regard to the efficacy of organizational security measures.

c. Does your team agree with the conclusions in the study? Explain your answer.

10-7. Suppose that you are asked by your boss for a summary of what your organization should do with regard to computer security. Using the knowledge of this chapter and your answer to questions 10-4 through 10-6, create a PowerPoint presentation for your summary. Your presentation should include, but not be limited to:

a. Definition of key terms

b. Summary of threats

c. Summary of safeguards

d. Current trends in computer crime

e. What senior managers should do about computer security

f. What managers at all levels should do about computer security

Hitting the Target

On December 18, 2013, Target Corporation announced that it had lost 40 million credit and debit card numbers to attackers. Less than a month later Target announced an additional 70 million customer accounts were stolen that included names, emails, addresses, phone numbers, and so on.

After accounting for some overlap between the two data losses, it turns out that about 98 million customers were affected.[21] That's 31 percent of all 318 million people in the United States (including children and those without credit cards). This was one of the largest data breaches in U.S. history.

These records were stolen from point-of-sale (POS) systems at Target retail stores during the holiday shopping season (November 27 to December 15, 2013). If you were shopping at

a Target during this time, it's likely your data was lost. Following is a short summary of how attackers got away with that much data.

How Did They Do It?

The attackers first used spear-phishing to infect a Target third-party vendor named Fazio Mechanical Services (refrigeration and HVAC services).[22] Attackers placed a piece of malware called Citadel to gather keystrokes, login credentials, and screenshots from Fazio users.[23] The attackers then used the stolen login credentials from Fazio to access a vendor portal (server) on Target's network. The attackers escalated privileges on that server and gained access to Target's internal network.

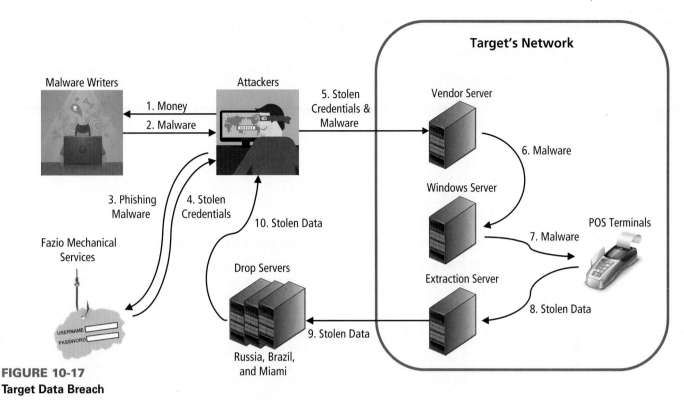

FIGURE 10-17
Target Data Breach

Once in, the attackers compromised an internal Windows file server. From this server the attackers used malware named Trojan.POSRAM (a variant of BlackPOS) to extract information from POS terminals. BlackPOS was developed by a 17-year-old from St. Petersburg, Russia, and can be purchased from underground sites for about $2,000.[24]

The customer data was continuously sent from the POS terminals to an extraction server within Target's network. It was then funneled out of Target's network to drop servers in Russia, Brazil, and Miami. From there the data was taken and sold on the black market. (See Figure 10-17.)

The Damage

For the attackers, the "damage" was great. It's estimated that the attackers sold about 2 million credit cards for about $26.85 each for a total profit of $53.7M.[25] Not bad for a few weeks of work. Incentives for this type of criminal activity are substantial. Payoffs like these encourage even more data breaches.

Target, on the other hand, incurred much greater losses than the hacker's gains. It was forced to upgrade its payment terminals to support chip-and-PIN enabled cards (to prevent cloning cards from stolen information), which cost more than $100M. In 2015, Target lost a legal battle with banks over reimbursement of costs associated with the data breach, which could exceed $160M. It also had to pay increased insurance premiums, pay legal fees, pay for consumer credit monitoring, and pay regulatory fines.

Target faced a loss of customer confidence and a drop in its revenues (a 46 percent loss for that quarter). Analysts put the direct loss to Target as high as $450M.[26] The company lost its CIO Beth Jacob and paid its CEO Gregg Steinhafel $16M to leave.[27] And in late 2015, Target paid banks $39 million for losses related to the data breach.[28]

The data breach affected more than just Target. The amount of media coverage related to the Target data breach likely accelerated the shift from magnetic swipe cards to EMV-compliant smart cards begun in 2015. This shift will force the eventual replacement of 800 million payment cards and 14 million POS terminals at a cost of $7B.[29]

The good news is that the adoption of EMV-compliant smart cards will greatly reduce the $10B in credit card fraud that occurs each year. It will also likely reduce the amount of credit card theft by hackers because stolen credit card numbers would be of little value without the physical card.

Just like car accidents, data breaches may not be viewed as important until *after* they occur. The data breach affected Target enough that it upgraded its infrastructure, changed internal systems, and hired a Chief Information Security Officer (CISO).[30]

Will there be a more severe data breach in the future? Probably. Are organizations ready for it? Based on past performance, we won't be ready for it until *after* it happens.

QUESTIONS

10-8. Why did the attackers spear-phish a contractor to Target?

10-9. Explain how a third-party contractor could weaken an organization's overall security.

10-10. Describe how data was stolen from Target.

10-11. How might a data loss at one organization affect other organizations?

10-12. Explain why large organizations are attractive targets for attackers.

10-13. Why might chip-and-pin cards reduce this type of theft?

10-14. Why didn't Target have a CISO before the data breach?

MyLab MIS

Go to the Assignments section of your MyLab to complete these writing exercises.

10-15. Suppose you need to terminate an employee who works in your department. Summarize security protections you must take. How would you behave differently if this termination were a friendly one?

10-16. Suppose you were just notified that your company has experienced a major data breach. You've lost customer records, including usernames, email addresses, passwords, addresses, and phone numbers for all 500,000 of your customers. Estimate the direct costs for notification, detection, escalation, remediation, and legal fees. Suppose the attackers contact you and offer to destroy all records, tell no one about the data breach, and show you how to patch the security hole. The only trick is they want to be hired as a "consultant" and have $600,000 deposited into their European bank account. Would you pay the "consulting" fee? Justify your decision.

ENDNOTES

1. Bureau of Labor Statistics, U.S. Department of Labor, *Occupational Outlook Handbook*, accessed June 16, 2018, *www.bls.gov/ooh/*. Information about information security analysts can be found in the Computer and Information Technology section.
2. FireEye, "APT37 (Reaper): The Overlooked North Korean Actor," *Fireeye.com*, February 2, 2018, accessed June 16, 2018, *www2.fireeye .com/rs/848-DID-242/images/rpt_APT37.pdf*.
3. Risk Based Security, "Data Breach QuickView Report Year End 2017," January 2017, *RiskedBasedSecurity.com*, accessed June 16, 2018, *www.rpsins.com/media/2884/mc_0000634a-yearendreport.pdf*.
4. Ponemon Institute, *2017 Cost of Cyber Crime Study* October 2017, accessed June 16, 2018, *www.ponemon.org/library*.
5. Ibid.
6. Ibid.
7. Jon Evans, "Facebook's CSO: The Security Industry Needs to Change," *TechCrunch*, July 26, 2017, accessed May 16, 2018, *https://techcrunch .com/2017/07/26/facebooks-cso-the-security-industry-needs-to-change/*.
8. Jai Vijayan, "First Malware Designed Solely for Electric Grids Caused 2016 Ukraine Outage," June 12, 2017, *DarkReading*, accessed May 16, 2018, *www.darkreading.com/threat-intelligence/first-malware-designed-specifically-to-attack-electric-grid-warn-dragos-eset-/d/d-id/1329114*.
9. Sean Michael Kerner, "Broadpwn Flaw Shown at Black Hat Could Have Enabled WiFi Worm Attack," July 27, 2017, *eWeek*, accessed May 16, 2018, *www.eweek.com/security/broadpwn-flaw-shown-at-black-hat-could-have-enabled-wifi-worm-attack*.
10. *Verizon 2018 Data Breach Investigations Report*, accessed June 2018, *www.verizonenterprise.com/verizon-insights-lab/dbir/2016/*.
11. Swati Khandelwal, "Over 400 Popular Sites Record Your Every Keystroke and Mouse Movement," *The Hacker News*, April 4, 2018, *https://thehackernews.com/2017/11/website-keylogging.html*.
12. Daniel Akst, "Your Moods Change the Way You Move Your Mouse," *The Wall Street Journal*, April 4, 2018, *www.wsj.com/articles/ your-moods-change-the-way-you-move-your-mouse-1452268410*.
13. For this reason, do *not* attempt to scan servers for fun. It won't take the organization very long to find you, and it will not be amused!
14. Randall Boyle and Jeffrey Proudfoot, *Applied Information Security*, 3rd ed. (2018).
15. Lauren Johnson, "Here's a Timeline of Yahoo's 22-Year History as a Digital Pioneer," *AdWeek*, July 25, 2016, *www.adweek.com/digital/ heres-timeline-yahoo-s-22-year-history-digital-pioneer-172663/*.
16. Ibid.
17. Ibid.
18. Lily Hay Newman, "Yahoo's 2013 Email Hack Actually Compromised Three Billion Accounts," *Wired*, October 3, 2017, *www.wired.com/ story/yahoo-breach-three-billion-accounts/*.
19. Mariella Moon, "US Judge Says Yahoo Data Breach Victims Have the Right to Sue," *Engadget*. September 1, 2017, *www.engadget .com/2017/09/01/judge-says-yahoo-data-breach-victims-can-sue/*.
20. Wang Wei, "22-Year-Old Hacker Pleads Guilty to 2014 Yahoo Hack, Admits Helping Russian Intelligence," *The Hacker News*, November 28, 2017, *https://thehackernews.com/2017/11/yahoo-email-hacker.html*.
21. Ben Elgin, "Three New Details from Target's Credit Card Breach," *Bloomberg Business*, March 26, 2014, accessed June 16, 2018, *www .bloomberg.com/bw/articles/2014-03-26/three-new-details-from-targets-credit-card-breach*.
22. Brian Krebs, "Target Hackers Broke in via HVAC Company," *KrebsonSecurity.com*, February 5, 2014, accessed June 16, 2018, *http://krebsonsecurity.com/2014/02/target-hackers-broke-in-via-hvac-company*.

23. Chris Poulin, "What Retailers Need to Learn from the Target Data Breach to Protect Against Similar Attacks," *Security Intelligence*, January 31, 2014, accessed June 16, 2018, *http://securityintelligence .com/target-breach-protect-against-similar-attacks-retailers/#.VYngl_lVikr*.

24. Swati Khandelwal, "BlackPOS Malware Used in Target Data Breach Developed by 17-Year-Old Russian Hacker," *The Hacker News*, January 17, 2014, accessed June 16, 2018, *http://thehackernews .com/2014/01/BlackPOS-Malware-russian-hacker-Target.html*.

25. Brian Krebs, "The Target Breach, by the Numbers," *KrebsonSecurity .com*, May 6, 2014, accessed June 16, 2018, *http://krebsonsecurity .com/2014/05/the-target-breach-by-the-numbers*.

26. Bruce Horovitz, "Data Breach Takes Toll on Target Profit," *USA Today*, February 26, 2014, accessed June 16, 2018, *www.usatoday.com/story/ money/business/2014/02/26/target-earnings/5829469*.

27. Fred Donovan, "Target Breach: A Timeline," *FierceITSecurity.com*, February 18, 2014, accessed June 16, 2018, *www.fierceitsecurity.com/ story/target-breach-timeline/2014-02-18*.

28. Ahiza Garcia, "Target Settles for $39 Million over Data Breach," *CNN Money*, December 2, 2015, accessed June 16, 2018, *http://money.cnn .com/2015/12/02/news/companies/target-data-breach-settlement*.

29. Dick Mitchell, "The EMV Migration Will Be a Rough, Risky Ride," *PaymentSource.com*, January 14, 2015, accessed June 16, 2018, *www.paymentssource.com/news/paythink/the-emv-migration-will-be- aroughrisky-ride-randstad-exec-3020311-1.html*.

30. Dune Lawrence, "Target Taps an Outsider to Revamp IT Security After Massive Hack," *BusinessWeek*, April 29, 2014, accessed June 16, 2018, *www.businessweek.com/articles/2014-04-29/target-turns-to- anoutsiderfor-cio-bob-derodes-to-revamp-it-security-after-massive-hack*.

CHAPTER 11

Information Systems Management

"Outsourcing the development of our apps might be the best option," Henri reluctantly says to Ashley. "We'll need apps for the exercise bikes and the AR headsets, and we're going to need developers for our back-end system."

"How many apps are we going to need for the bikes?" Ashley asks.

"Well, CanyonBack Fitness and three of the other top-10 exercise equipment manufacturers use embedded Linux for their operating systems. The rest of the manufacturers use either Windows Embedded or a real-time operating system. I think we should stick to embedded Linux and Windows Embedded."

"Why is that?"

"I think the Internet of Things push is going to force them to make all of their devices 'smarter.' That means they'll need a high-end operating system."

"What about apps for the AR headsets?" Ashley asks, looking at Raj.

"That's the fun part," Raj says, smiling hesitantly. "We might need a different app for each headset. Each AR headset manufacturer has its own software development kit and wants companies like us to develop for its platform."

Ashley shifts in her chair and leans forward. "Aren't we already developing our app for Microsoft HoloLens?"

MyLab MIS

Using Your Knowledge
Questions 11-1, 11-2, 11-3

Essay Questions 11-18, 11-19

"Yes," Raj explains, pointing to the AR headset on Ashley's desk, "but we don't want to limit ourselves to Microsoft HoloLens. What if Meta, Magic Leap, or another AR headset becomes the dominant technology? It's probably best to hedge our bets and make apps for the top two or three most popular headsets."

Henri motions to his smartphone. "It's like developing an app for a smartphone. You need an iOS app, an Android app, and maybe a Windows app."

"Wow, OK. How much is this going to cost?" Ashley asks surprised.

"Not as much as you might think," Raj responds. "I know a guy in India named Sandeep who could probably make them for us."

"Probably? What do you mean 'probably'?" Ashley knows Raj is smart and passionate about AR, but she's not going to start pouring money into a probable outcome.

"Outsourcing the development of a strategic application seems risky."

Source: Haiyin Wang/Alamy Stock Photo

"Well, I've worked with Sandeep before, and he did a great job developing a C# app I needed. I met him when I was an undergraduate student at Indian Institute of Science before I came to Stanford. But he's busier now, and his business has really grown. He's also in India."

"Raj, this makes me nervous. I don't know anything about doing business in India. What if the guy takes our money and runs? What do we do then?" Ashley asks emphatically.

"Well, we don't pay him until he delivers . . . or at least we don't pay him much. But I've had a positive experience with him, and his references are good on a recent app development project."

"India is a long way away. What if he gives our code to somebody else? Or our ideas? What if we find some horrible bug in his code, and we can't find him to fix it? What if he just disappears? What if he gets two-thirds done and then loses interest . . . or goes to work on someone else's project?" Ashley is on a roll.

"All are risks, I agree. But it will cost you four to six times as much to develop over here," Raj says as he shrugs his shoulders.

"Outsourcing the development of a strategic application seems risky," Ashley says, shaking her head.

"It is risky. Well, riskier than hiring local developers. But there's still risk involved with local developers. Do you want me to look into hiring local developers?"

"I'm not sure. Henri, what do you think? You've worked on larger systems development projects before."

Henri shakes his head slowly. "I'm not sure. Augmented reality application development is very new. Not a lot of people know how to create AR apps, and everyone is facing a steep learning curve. If Raj worked closely with Sandeep's team, we might be able to get this done for a fraction of the cost."

Raj nods in agreement. "Since this is probably his first AR app, he might even do it for a little less. He knows I've been working on AR for years, and I've told him this is

Study QUESTIONS

Q11-1 What are the functions and organization of the IS department?

Q11-2 How do organizations plan the use of IS?

Q11-3 What are the advantages and disadvantages of outsourcing?

Q11-4 What are your user rights and responsibilities?

Q11-5 2029?

the future of app development. He'll want the experience. We could buy him a couple HoloLens software development kits to sweeten the deal."

Henri sees the worry on Ashley's face. "We could structure the contract so we pay less up front and then more on the back end. That would reduce our risk somewhat."

"True, then we would only have to pay for it after we've seen that it works."

"We've also got a lot of other things on our plate," Henri says, counting on his fingers. "We've got to get imaging for the virtual bike rides, test the 3D webcam integration, and look into mapping executive bike tours in Europe."

"I'd also like to test a few HoloLens apps on a real bike," Raj says excitedly. "The ability to use ARES on stationary bikes *and* regular bikes would be amazing! We could include apps that give turn-by-turn directions, hands-free notifications, rear-view radar, and point-of-interest notifications. Cyclists would love it."

Ashley can feel the meeting slipping away. "OK, well, those are really great ideas. Definitely something we want to consider for the future. Let's put a pin in that for now. Raj, will you arrange a meeting with Sandeep? I'd like all three of us there to hear what he says."

"Sure, I'll call him later today. There's a 12-hour difference between California and India. It's 2:00 AM in India right now. I won't be able to get a bid from him because I haven't finished the requirements documents yet. I should have those in a few days," Raj says while making a note for himself on his phone.

"Good, and will you also get a bid from a local developer? I want to see what the difference is going to be if we decide to outsource this."

"Absolutely. There's just one problem . . . the local developer may outsource it anyway."

"You mean we might be paying Sandeep either way?"

Raj smiles. "Unfortunately . . . yes. Well . . . maybe not. Honestly, I'm not sure. We'll see."

Chapter PREVIEW

Information systems are critical to organizational success and, like all critical assets, need to be managed responsibly. In this chapter, we will survey the management of IS and IT resources. We begin by discussing the major functions and the organization of the IS department. Then we will consider planning the use of IT/IS. Outsourcing is the process of hiring outside vendors to provide business services and related products. For our purposes, outsourcing refers to hiring outside vendors to provide information systems, products, and applications. We will examine the pros and cons of outsourcing and describe some of its risks. Finally, we will conclude this chapter by discussing the relationship of users to the IS department. In this last section, you will learn both your own and the IS department's rights and responsibilities. We continue this discussion in 2029 with new challenges: the gig economy and automated labor.

Q11-1 What Are the Functions and Organization of the IS Department?

The major functions of the information systems department[1] are as follows:

- Plan the use of IS to accomplish organizational goals and strategy.
- Manage outsourcing relationships.
- Protect information assets.

- Develop, operate, and maintain the organization's computing infrastructure.
- Develop, operate, and maintain applications.

We will consider the first two functions in Q11-2 and Q11-3 of this chapter. The protection function was the topic of Chapter 10. The last two functions are important for IS majors but less so for other business professionals; therefore, we will not consider them in this text. To set the stage, consider the organization of the IS department.

How Is the IS Department Organized?

Figure 11-1 shows typical top-level reporting relationships. As you will learn in your management classes, organizational structure varies depending on the organization's size, culture, competitive environment, industry, and other factors. Larger organizations with independent divisions will have a group of senior executives such as those shown here for each division. Smaller companies may combine some of these departments. Consider the structure in Figure 11-1 as typical.

The title of the principal manager of the IS department varies from organization to organization. A common title is **chief information officer**, or **CIO**. Other common titles are *vice president of information services*, *director of information services*, and, less commonly, *director of computer services*.

In Figure 11-1, the CIO, like other senior executives, reports to the *chief executive officer* (CEO), though sometimes these executives report to the *chief operating officer* (COO), who, in turn, reports to the CEO. In some companies, the CIO reports to the *chief financial officer* (CFO). That reporting arrangement might make sense if the primary information systems support only accounting and finance activities. In organizations such as manufacturers that operate significant nonaccounting information systems, the arrangement shown in Figure 11-1 is more common and effective.

The structure of the IS department also varies among organizations. Figure 11-1 shows a typical IS department with four groups and a data administration staff function.

Most IS departments include a *Technology* office that investigates new information systems technologies and determines how the organization can benefit from them. For example, today many organizations are investigating social media and elastic cloud opportunities and planning how they can use those capabilities to better accomplish their goals and objectives. An individual called the **chief technology officer**, or **CTO**, often heads the technology group. The CTO evaluates

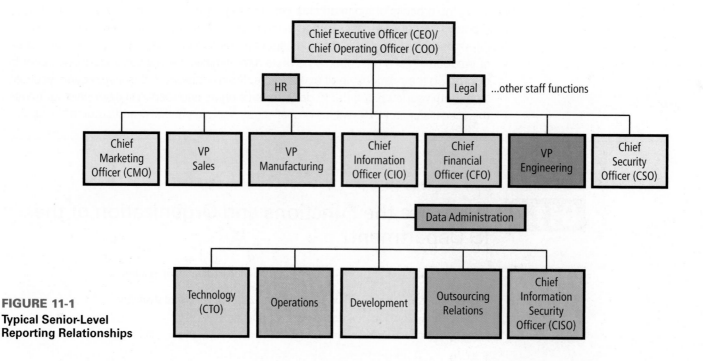

FIGURE 11-1
Typical Senior-Level Reporting Relationships

new technologies, new ideas, and new capabilities and identifies those that are most relevant to the organization. The CTO's job requires deep knowledge of information technology and the ability to envision and innovate applications for the organization.

The next group in Figure 11-1, *Operations*, manages the computing infrastructure, including individual computers, in-house server farms, networks, and communications media. This group includes system and network administrators. As you will learn, an important function for this group is to monitor the user experience and respond to user problems.

The third group in the IS department in Figure 11-1 is *Development*. This group manages the process of creating new information systems as well as maintaining existing ones.

The size and structure of the development group depend on whether programs are developed in-house. If not, this department will be staffed primarily by business and systems analysts who work with users, operations, and vendors to acquire and install licensed software and to set up the system components around that software. If the organization develops programs in-house, then this department will include programmers, test engineers, technical writers, and other development personnel.

The last IS department group in Figure 11-1 is *Outsourcing Relations*. This group exists in organizations that have negotiated outsourcing agreements with other companies to provide equipment, applications, or other services. You will learn more about outsourcing later in this chapter.

Figure 11-1 also includes a *Data Administration* staff function. The purpose of this group is to protect data and information assets by establishing data standards and data management practices and policies.

There are many variations on the structure of the IS department shown in Figure 11-1. In larger organizations, the operations group may itself consist of several different departments. Sometimes, there is a separate group for data warehousing and data marts.

As you examine Figure 11-1, keep the distinction between IS and IT in mind. *Information systems (IS)* exist to help the organization achieve its goals and objectives. Information systems have the five components we have discussed throughout this text. *Information technology (IT)* is simply technology. It concerns the products, techniques, procedures, and designs of computer-based technology. IT must be placed into the structure of an IS before an organization can use it.

Security Officers

After Target Corp. lost 98 million customer accounts, it created a new C-level security position to help prevent these type of losses.[2] Many organizations reeling from large-scale data breaches are creating similar executive security positions. A **chief security officer**, or **CSO**, manages security for all of the organization's assets: physical plant and equipment, employees, intellectual property, and digital. The CSO reports directly to the CEO. A **chief information security officer**, or **CISO**, manages security for the organization's information systems and information. The CISO reports to the CIO.

Both positions involve the management of staff, but they also call for strong diplomatic skills. Neither the CSO nor the CISO has line authority over the management of the activities he or she is to protect and cannot enforce compliance with the organization's security program by direct order. Instead, they need to educate, encourage, even cajole the organization's management into the need for compliance with the security program (discussed in Chapter 10, pages 406–407).

What IS-Related Job Positions Exist?

IS departments provide a wide range of interesting and well-paying jobs. Many students enter the MIS class thinking that the IS departments consist only of programmers and tech support engineers. If you reflect on the five components of an information system, you can understand why this cannot be true. The data, procedures, and people components of an information system require professionals with highly developed interpersonal communications skills.

Figure 11-2 summarizes the major job positions in the IS industry. With the exception of tech support engineers and possibly test QA engineers, all of these positions require a 4-year degree. Furthermore, with the exception of programmer and test QA engineer, they all require business knowledge. In most cases, successful professionals have a degree in business. Note, too, that most positions require good verbal and written communications skills. Business, including information systems, is a social activity.

Median salaries and approximate salary ranges for the positions discussed in Figure 11-2 are shown in Figure 11-3.[3] According to the U.S. Social Security Administration, the median salary in 2016 for the average U.S. worker was $30,533.[4] Salary ranges for CTO, CIO, and CISO are higher than the other positions because they require many more years of experience.

FIGURE 11-2
Job Positions in the Information Systems Industry

Title	Responsibilities	Knowledge, Skill, and Characteristics Requirements
Network administrator	Monitor, maintain, fix, and tune computer networks.	Diagnostic skills, in-depth knowledge of communications technologies and products.
Technical writer	Write program documentation, help-text, procedures, job descriptions, and training materials.	Quick learner, clear writing skills, high verbal communications skills.
Technical sales	Sell software, network, communications, and consulting services.	Quick learner, knowledge of product, superb professional sales skills.
Tech support engineer	Help users solve problems and provide training.	Communications and people skills. Product knowledge. Patience.
Systems analyst	Work with users to determine system requirements, design and develop job descriptions and procedures, and help determine system test plans.	Strong interpersonal and communications skills. Knowledge of both business and technology. Adaptable.
Programmer	Design and write computer programs.	Logical thinking and design skills, knowledge of one or more programming languages.
Business intelligence analyst	Collaborate with cross-functional teams on projects, and analyze organizational data.	Excellent analytical, presentation, collaboration, database, and decision making skills.
Business analyst, IT	Work with business leaders and planners to develop processes and systems that implement business strategy and goals.	Knowledge of business planning, strategy, process management, and technology. Can deal with complexity. Sees the big picture but works with the details. Strong interpersonal and communications skills needed.
Test QA engineer	Develop test plans, design and write automated test scripts, and perform testing.	Logical thinking, basic programming, superb organizational skills, eye for detail.
Database administrator	Manage and protect database.	Diplomatic skills, database technology knowledge.
Consultant, IT	Wide range of activities: programming, testing, database design, communications and networks, project management, security and risk management, social media, and strategic planning.	Quick learner, entrepreneurial attitude, communications and people skills. Responds well to pressure. Particular knowledge depends on work.
Manager, IT	Manage teams of technical workers and manage the implementation of new systems	Management and people skills, critical thinking, very strong technical skills.
Project manager, IT	Initiate, plan, manage, monitor, and close down projects.	Management and people skills, technology knowledge. Highly organized.
Chief technology officer (CTO)	Advise CIO, executive group, and project managers on emerging technologies.	Quick learner, good communications skills, business background, deep knowledge of IT.
Chief information officer (CIO)	Manage IT departments and communicate with executive staff on IT- and IS-related matters. Member of the executive group.	Superb management skills, deep knowledge of business and technology, and good business judgment. Good communicator. Balanced and unflappable.
Chief information security officer (CISO)	Manage IS security program, protect the organization's information systems and information, and manage IS security personnel.	Deep knowledge of security threats, protections, and emerging security threat trends. Excellent communication and diplomacy skills. Good manager.

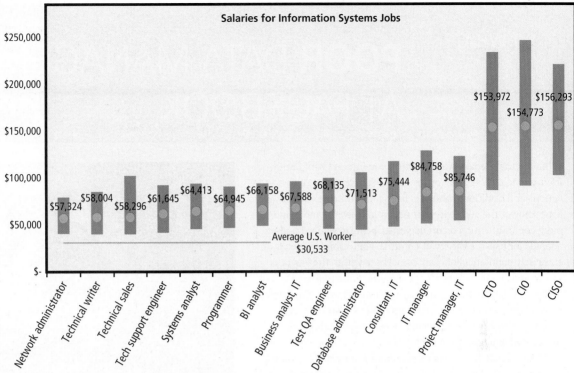

FIGURE 11-3
Salaries for Information Systems Jobs

Salaries for information systems jobs have a wide range. Higher salaries are for professionals with more experience, working for larger companies, and living in larger cities.[5] Do not expect to begin your career at the high end of these ranges. As noted, all salaries are for positions in the United States and are shown in U.S. dollars.

(By the way, for all but the most technical positions, knowledge of a business specialty can add to your marketability. If you have the time, a dual major can be an excellent choice. Popular and successful dual majors are accounting and information systems, marketing and information systems, and management and information systems.)

Q11-2 How Do Organizations Plan the Use of IS?

We begin our discussion of IS functions with planning. Figure 11-4 lists the major IS planning functions.

Align Information Systems with Organizational Strategy

The purpose of an information system is to help the organization accomplish its goals and objectives. In order to do so, all information systems must be aligned with the organization's competitive strategy.

Recall the four competitive strategies from Chapter 2. The first two strategies are that an organization can be a cost leader either across an industry or within an industry segment. Alternatively, for the second two strategies, an organization can differentiate its products or services either across

- Align information systems with organizational strategy; maintain alignment as organization changes.
- Communicate IS/IT issues to executive group.
- Develop/enforce IS priorities within the IS department.
- Sponsor steering committee.

FIGURE 11-4
Planning the Use of IS/IT

POOR DATA MANAGEMENT AT FACEBOOK

What are the primary ways in which you interact with family, friends, and colleagues? You probably use face-to-face inter- actions and traditional phone calls to communicate with at least some of the people in your network. However, more and more communication technologies are being developed and adopted for use in a variety of contexts. For example, Slack is an extremely popular collaboration tool used within the business world, and Discord is a popular communication tool used by millions of gamers to keep in touch and strategize during game play. It is likely that you engage with some of your contacts using Facebook, the social media juggernaut boasting more than 2 billion active users as of 2018.

One reason that Facebook continues to attract and retain so many users is Metcalfe's Law, which states that the value of a network is equal to the square of the number of users connected to it. In other words, the more users there are associated with a network, the more value is offered by that network. This incentivizes new users to join. When someone is considering joining their first social network, they are most likely to choose the platform that will already have the highest number of their friends, family members, and colleagues as users because their experience on that network will provide the greatest value relative to others. However, Metcalfe's Law doesn't just attract new users to a site. It also attracts app developers, researchers, and businesses seeking to glean insights—and make money—off the troves of data generated by users.

Click Here to Dislike

Due to Facebook's position as the most popular social media site in the world, countless third parties target the network for opportunities to collect data about users, their connections with others, and their interactions. Several years ago, Facebook had an extremely open model that allowed the integration of Facebook with a variety of other platforms and services (music- streaming sites, dating sites, and so forth). This integration allowed users to create accounts and log in to those sites using their Facebook accounts. Additionally, third parties developed apps for Facebook that could access the data of the people using those apps *as well as the data for all of their friends.*

Only recently did the company recognize the potential privacy risks of this model and finally restrict data access to only those users who had directly provided consent to third-party developers as of 2015. However, the damage had already been done: It recently came to light that a researcher had siphoned

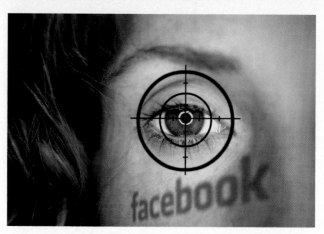

Source: Bildagentur-online/Ohde/Alamy Stock Photo

off data for more than 80 million Facebook users and then sold that data to an analytics firm prior to Facebook putting tighter data restrictions in place.[6] This violation of user privacy resulted in a firestorm about Facebook's poor data management practices and resulted in a statement that Facebook would conduct an investigation to evaluate the apps that had the ability to access user data during that time.

Pay for Play

In response to this incident, CEO and founder Mark Zuckerberg stated that Facebook had already taken steps to prevent future privacy missteps. He was later summoned to Washington, D.C., to testify before the Commerce and Judiciary Committees on Capitol Hill to explain how something like this could have happened and how something similar could be prevented in the future. However, Facebook's reputation was already tarnished by the incident. There was an active movement calling for people to delete their Facebook accounts. The scandal also had an impact on Wall Street. Major tech stocks (e.g., Facebook, Amazon, Apple, Netflix, and Alphabet) collectively lost $397 billion of market capitalization around this time as fears grew that other top tech companies likely had similar "skeletons in their closets."[7]

While Facebook's stock will likely recover, its data management practices, and possibly its business model, will change. Some experts have speculated that Facebook will begin offering the option for users to pay a monthly fee to access the network, which would protect their data from any sort of access by advertisers or other third parties.[8] It has been estimated that Facebook would need to charge roughly $7 per month from users in North America to compensate for the $82 per user that is collected in advertising revenues per user per year.[9] If nothing else, this situation has sent a shock wave through the tech world regarding privacy and the risks associated with careless management of user data—and the hard and soft costs that can occur as a result of such cavalier actions.

Questions

1. To what extent are social media platforms an important part of your daily interactions? Do you use a certain social media platform because your family or friends use it? Why do you think this is the case?

2. Are you one of the 87 million Facebook users who had their data shared with Cambridge Analytica? If so, did this situation bother you? Why or why not?

3. During Mark Zuckerberg's hearings on Capitol Hill, it became clear that many politicians have minimal knowledge about how Facebook operates as a business. How does this present challenges for the creation of regulations that may be put in place to ensure that Facebook and other tech companies properly manage user data?

4. Why would Facebook offer a pay option? Would it be worth it to you to pay a monthly fee to access Facebook and know that your personal data would be protected? Why or why not?

the industry or within a segment. Whatever the organizational strategy, the CIO and the IS department must constantly be vigilant to align IS with it.

Maintaining alignment between IS direction and organizational strategy is a continuing process. As strategies change, as the organization merges with other organizations, as divisions are sold, IS must evolve along with the organization. As you will learn in Chapter 12, maintaining that alignment is an important role for BPM and for COBIT, in particular.

Unfortunately, however, adapting IS to new versions of business processes is neither easy nor quick. For example, switching from in-house hosting to cloud hosting requires time and resources. Such a change must also be made without losing the organization's computing infrastructure. The difficulty of adapting IS is often not appreciated in the executive suite. Without a persuasive CIO, IS can be perceived as a drag on the organization's opportunities.

Communicate IS Issues to the Executive Group

This last observation leads to the second IS planning function in Figure 11-4. The CIO is the representative for IS and IT issues within the executive staff. The CIO provides the IS perspective during discussions of problem solutions, proposals, and new initiatives.

For example, when considering a merger, it is important that the company consider integration of information systems in the merged entities. This consideration needs to be addressed during the evaluation of the merger opportunity. Too often, such issues are not considered until after the deal has been signed. Such delayed consideration is a mistake; the costs of the integration need to be factored into the economics of the purchase. Involving the CIO in high-level discussions is the best way to avoid such problems.

Develop Priorities and Enforce Them Within the IS Department

The next IS planning function in Figure 11-4 concerns priorities. The CIO must ensure that priorities consistent with the overall organizational strategy are developed and then communicated to the IS department. At the same time, the CIO must also ensure that the department evaluates proposals and projects for using new technology in light of those communicated priorities.

Technology is seductive, particularly to IS professionals. The CTO may enthusiastically claim, "By moving all our reporting services to the cloud, we can do this and this and this . . . " Although true, the question that the CIO must continually ask is whether those new possibilities are consistent with the organization's strategy and direction.

Read more about the perspective of a senior data officer in the Career Guide on pages 440–441.

Thus, the CIO must not only establish and communicate such priorities, but enforce them as well. The department must evaluate every proposal, at the earliest stage possible, as to whether it is consistent with the organization's goals and aligned with its strategy.

Furthermore, no organization can afford to implement every good idea. Even projects that are aligned with the organization's strategy must be prioritized. The objective of everyone in the IS department must be to develop the most appropriate systems possible, given constraints on time and money. Well-thought-out and clearly communicated priorities are essential.

Sponsor the Steering Committee

The final planning function in Figure 11-4 is to sponsor the steering committee. A **steering committee** is a group of senior managers from the major business functions that works with the CIO to set the IS priorities and decide among major IS projects and alternatives.

The steering committee serves an important communication function between IS and the users. In the steering committee, information systems personnel can discuss potential IS initiatives and directions with the user community. At the same time, the steering committee provides a forum for users to express their needs, frustrations, and other issues they have with the IS department.

Typically, the IS department sets up the steering committee's schedule and agenda and conducts the meetings. The CEO and other members of the executive staff determine the membership of the steering committee.

Q11-3 What Are the Advantages and Disadvantages of Outsourcing?

Outsourcing is the process of hiring another organization to perform a service. Outsourcing is done to save costs, to gain expertise, and to free management time.

The father of modern management, Peter Drucker, is reputed to have said, "Your back room is someone else's front room." For instance, in most companies, running the cafeteria is not an essential function for business success; thus, the employee cafeteria is a "back room." Google wants to be the worldwide leader in search and mobile computing hardware and applications, all supported by ever-increasing ad revenue. It does not want to be known for how well it runs cafeterias. Using Drucker's sentiment, Google is better off hiring another company, one that specializes in food services, to run its cafeterias.

Because food service is some company's "front room," that company will be better able to provide a quality product at a fair price. Outsourcing to a food vendor will also free Google's management from attention on the cafeteria. Food quality, chef scheduling, plastic fork acquisition, waste disposal, and so on, will all be another company's concern. Google can focus on search, mobile computing, and advertising-revenue growth.

Outsourcing Information Systems

Many companies today have chosen to outsource portions of their information systems activities. Figure 11-5 lists popular reasons for doing so. Consider each major group of reasons.

Outsourcing information systems can reduce costs, but it can also create ethical dilemmas. For more on outsourcing issues, read the Ethics Guide on pages 429–430.

Management Advantages

First, outsourcing can be an easy way to gain expertise. As you'll learn in Chapter 12, ARES Systems wants to build 3D augmented reality apps, but no one on the staff knows the particulars of coding for Microsoft HoloLens. Outsourcing can be an easy and quick way to obtain that expertise.

For example, Figure 11-6 shows the top-10 highest-paid skills or experiences reported from Dice's annual Tech Salary Survey.[10] Note that only two of the top-10 skills in 2017 were ranked in the top 100 in 2012. Rapid changes in technology push rapid changes in demand for certain technical skills.

TRAINING YOUR REPLACEMENT

Scott Essex sat at his desk looking through the roster of employees he managed. As he flipped through the pages, he felt a sinking feeling in his stomach. Upper management had directed him to cut his team of software developers by nearly 75 percent. This directive came as a result of a recent initiative to reduce costs by outsourcing IT department projects. As he flipped back and forth between the pages, Scott didn't know how to identify which employees to retain and which employees to let go. All the employees brought value to the team—if they didn't, Scott wouldn't have hired them in the first place.

Scott flipped to the beginning of the roster and started putting stars next to the names of employees he would consider letting go. Some had worked for the company for many years. But, in spite of their time on the job, they honestly didn't add as much value as they should relative to their pay. Conversely, there were more recent hires who had tremendous potential and were low-cost relative to other employees. Scott paused and looked up from the roster—he wasn't sure how he was going to look these people in the eye when he told them the bad news. But he would have to do it. It was part of his job.

Then it got worse. Scott's boss sent him a portfolio of new development projects that had to be completed in the next 3 to 6 months. How could upper management expect the usual turnaround time for these projects when 75 percent of his staff was going to be replaced with new outsourced employees— working on the other side of the planet? These new employees would know nothing about the "vibe" of his team or the intangibles that made the team run smoothly. Letting employees go was one thing. But if he didn't get these projects completed on time, his own position could be in jeopardy.

To Train or Not to Train

The next morning, Scott walked into the office still feeling discouraged about losing so much of his team. But he felt confident in the selections he had made concerning the employees who would be staying. As long as the remaining team members could move past this process and get back to work, he figured they had a chance at sticking to the new project schedule. He walked down the hall to drop off his proposed personnel changes to his boss, Beth Birman. Beth asked him to close the door and take a seat.

Beth started the conversation. "Well, I bet you are wondering how you are going to make those new project deadlines with the employee changeover you will be managing." Scott tried to keep his true feelings from showing on his face. He replied optimistically, "Well, it is going to be a bit hectic, but I think we can manage!"

Beth smiled and retorted, "Well, you should know that I always try to take care of you. I wouldn't put you in such a bind without a little help." Scott wasn't sure what she was getting at. "I'm not exactly sure what you mean," he replied.

Source: HasanEROGLU/Fotolia

Beth continued, "We are going to have the employees who are being *released* from your team *train* the new outsourced employees. Training the replacements will be a condition of departing employees' severance package. If we do this, we ensure that the new employees do not spend a month or more getting up to speed and learning their responsibilities. Doing this will ensure that the outsourced hires are fully operational within a week or so. And you should be able to meet your project deadlines."

The rest of the meeting was a blur. Scott tried to come to terms with the fact that the employees he was about to fire would be forced to train their own replacements. If they didn't, they would forfeit most of their severance package. "Talk

about adding insult to injury," he muttered under his breath as he walked back to his desk.

He thought about it more and more as the day progressed, and he began to be deeply unsettled by what Beth was asking him to do. How is it fair to ask someone to train the person taking his or her job? This is going to be awkward, unpleasant, and insulting, Scott thought. If corporate felt good about this decision, what else would they be willing to make departing employees do as a condition of their termination? It seemed like a slippery slope. He wondered how long it would be before he was training his own replacement. He couldn't get his mother's famous saying out of his head, "If you lay down with the dogs, you wake up with fleas."

DISCUSSION QUESTIONS

1. According to the definitions of the ethical principles defined previously in this book:
   a. Do you think that forcing an employee to train his or her replacement is ethical according to the categorical imperative (page 23–24)?
   b. Do you think that forcing an employee to train his or her replacement is ethical according to the utilitarian perspective (page 42–43)?
2. How would you feel if you were asked to train your replacement after receiving notice that you were going

   to be terminated by your employer? Do you think that this sets a dangerous precedent for future termination conditions?
3. Aside from the tactic proposed by Beth in this scenario, what strategies could a company use to ensure that new replacement employees are better able to fulfill their responsibilities?
4. Building on question 3, how can technology be used to improve the change management process?

Organizations developing innovative products may not have the necessary in-house technical expertise to produce them. In fact, unless they're constantly training their current employees on the latest technology, they probably don't have the necessary expertise. Outsourcing and strategic partnerships enable organizations to make products they wouldn't have otherwise been able to make internally.

Another reason for outsourcing is to avoid management problems. At ARES Systems, building a large development and test team may be more than the company needs and require management

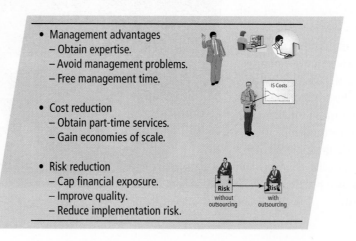

FIGURE 11-5
Popular Reasons for Outsourcing IS Services

FIGURE 11-6

Top-10 Tech Skills

Skill or Experience	Salary	Rank					
		2017	2016	2015	2014	2013	2012
PaaS (Platform as a Service)	$ 127,171	1	11	4	1	-	-
MapReduce	$ 125,378	2	2	9	3	3	-
Elasticsearch	$ 124,650	3	12	-	-	-	-
Amazon Redshift	$ 124,640	4	16	-	-	-	-
Cloudera	$ 124,221	5	19	3	4	19	-
Amazon DynamoDB	$ 124,054	6	26	-	-	-	-
CMMI (Capability Maturity Model Integration)	$ 123,970	7	15	27	21	16	11
webMethods	$ 123,578	8	50	25	50	-	-
ISO 27000	$ 123,575	9	44	26	-	-	-
SOA (Service Oriented Architecture)	$ 123,192	10	8	20	15	8	6

skills that neither Henri nor Raj has. Outsourcing the development function saves them from needing this expertise.

Similarly, some companies choose to outsource to save management time and attention. Henri at ARES has the skills to manage a new software development project, but he may choose not to invest the time.

Note, too, that it's not just Henri's time. It is also time from more senior managers who approve the purchase and hiring requisitions for that activity. And those senior managers, like Ashley, will need to devote the time necessary to learn enough about server infrastructure to approve or reject the requisitions. Outsourcing saves both direct and indirect management time.

Cost Reduction

Other common reasons for choosing to outsource concern cost reductions. With outsourcing, organizations can obtain part-time services. Another benefit of outsourcing is to gain economies of scale. If 25 organizations develop their own payroll applications in-house, then when the tax law changes 25 different groups will have to learn the new law, change their software to meet the law, test the changes, and write the documentation explaining the changes. However, if those same 25 organizations outsource to the same payroll vendor, then that vendor can make all of the adjustments once, and the cost of the change can be amortized over all of them (thus lowering the cost that the vendor must charge).

Risk Reduction

Another reason for outsourcing is to reduce risk. First, outsourcing can cap financial risk. In a typical outsourcing contract, the outsource vendor will agree to a fixed price contract for services. This occurs, for example, when companies outsource their hardware to cloud vendors. Another way to cap financial risk is as Henri recommends: delay paying the bulk of the fee until the work is completed and the software (or other component) is working. In the first case, it reduces risk by capping the total due; in the second, it ensures that little money need be spent until the job is done.

Second, outsourcing can reduce risk by ensuring a certain level of quality or avoiding the risk of having substandard quality. A company that specializes in food service knows what to do to provide a certain level of quality. It has the expertise to ensure, for example, that only healthy food is served. So, too, a company that specializes in, say, cloud-server hosting knows what to do to provide a certain level of reliability for a given workload.

Note that there is no guarantee that outsourcing will provide a certain level of quality or quality better than could be achieved in-house. If it doesn't outsource the cafeteria, Google might get lucky and hire only great chefs. Henri might get lucky and hire the world's best software developer. But, in general, a professional outsourcing firm knows how to avoid giving everyone food poisoning or how to develop new mobile applications. And, if that minimum level of quality is not provided, it is easier to hire another vendor than it is to fire and rehire internal staff.

Finally, organizations choose to outsource IS in order to reduce implementation risk. Hiring an outside cloud vendor reduces the risk of picking the wrong brand of hardware or the wrong virtualization software or implementing tax law changes incorrectly. Outsourcing gathers all of these risks into the risk of choosing the right vendor. Once the company has chosen the vendor, further risk management is up to that vendor.

International Outsourcing

Choosing to use an outsourcing developer in India is not unique to ARES. Many firms headquartered in the United States have chosen to outsource overseas. Microsoft and Dell, for example, have outsourced major portions of their customer support activities to companies outside the United States. India is a popular source because it has a large, well-educated, English-speaking population that will work for 20 to 30 percent of the labor cost in the United States. China and other countries are used as well. In fact, with modern telephone technology and Internet-enabled service databases, a single service call can be initiated in the United States, partially processed in India, then Singapore, and finalized by an employee in England. The customer knows only that he has been put on hold for brief periods of time.

International outsourcing is particularly advantageous for customer support and other functions that must be operational 24/7. Amazon for example, operates customer service centers in the United States, Costa Rica, Ireland, Scotland, Germany, Italy, Beijing, Japan, and India. During the evening hours in the United States, customer service reps in India, where it is daytime, can handle the calls. When night falls in India, customer service reps in Ireland or Scotland can handle the early morning calls from the east coast of the United States. In this way, companies can provide 24/7 service without requiring employees to work night shifts.

By the way, as you learned in Chapter 1, the key protection for your job is to become someone who excels at nonroutine symbolic analysis. Someone with the ability to find innovative applications of new technology is also unlikely to lose his or her job to overseas workers.

What Are the Outsourcing Alternatives?

Organizations have found hundreds of different ways to outsource information systems and portions of information systems. Figure 11-7 organizes the major categories of alternatives according to information systems components.

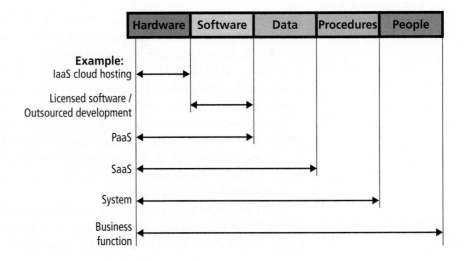

FIGURE 11-7
IS/IT Outsourcing Alternatives

Some organizations outsource the acquisition and operation of computer hardware. Electronic Data Systems (EDS) has been successful for more than 30 years as an outsource vendor of hardware infrastructure. Figure 11-7 shows another alternative: outsourcing the computers in the cloud via IaaS.

Acquiring licensed software, as discussed in Chapter 4 and Chapter 12, is a form of outsourcing. Rather than develop the software in-house, an organization licenses it from another vendor. Such licensing allows the software vendor to amortize the cost of software maintenance over all of the users, thus reducing that cost for all who use it. Another option is platform as a service (PaaS), which is the leasing of hardware with preinstalled operating systems as well as possibly DBMS systems. Microsoft's Azure is one such PaaS offering.

Some organizations choose to outsource the development of software. Such outsourcing might be for an entire application, as with ARES, or it could also be for making customizations to licensed software, as is frequently done with ERP implementations.

Yet another alternative is software as a service (SaaS), in which hardware and both operating system and application software are leased. Salesforce.com is a typical example of a company that offers SaaS.

It is also possible to outsource an entire system. PeopleSoft (now owned by Oracle) attained prominence by providing the entire payroll function as an outsourced service. In such a solution, as the arrow in Figure 11-7 implies, the vendor provides hardware, software, data, and some procedures. The company need provide only employee and work information; the payroll outsource vendor does the rest.

Finally, some organizations choose to outsource an entire business function. For years, many companies have outsourced to travel agencies the function of arranging for employee travel. Some of these outsource vendors even operate offices within the company facilities. Such agreements are much broader than outsourcing IS, but information systems are key components of the applications that are outsourced.

What Are the Risks of Outsourcing?

With so many advantages of outsourcing and so many different outsourcing alternatives, you might wonder why any company has in-house IS/IT functions. In fact, outsourcing presents significant risks, as listed in Figure 11-8.

Loss of Control

The first risk of outsourcing is a loss of control. For ARES, once Henri contracts with Sandeep, Sandeep is in control. At least for several weeks or months. If he makes ARES a priority project

- Loss of control
  - Vendor in driver's seat.
  - Technology direction.
  - Potential loss of intellectual capital.
  - Product fixes, enhancements in wrong priority.
  - Vendor management, direction, or identity changes.
  - CIO superfluous?

- Benefits outweighed by long-term costs
  - High unit cost, forever.
  - Paying for someone else's mismanagement.
  - In time, outsource vendor is de facto sole source.
  - May not get what you pay for but don't know it.

- No easy exit
  - Critical knowledge in minds of vendors, not employees.
  - Expensive and risky to change vendors.

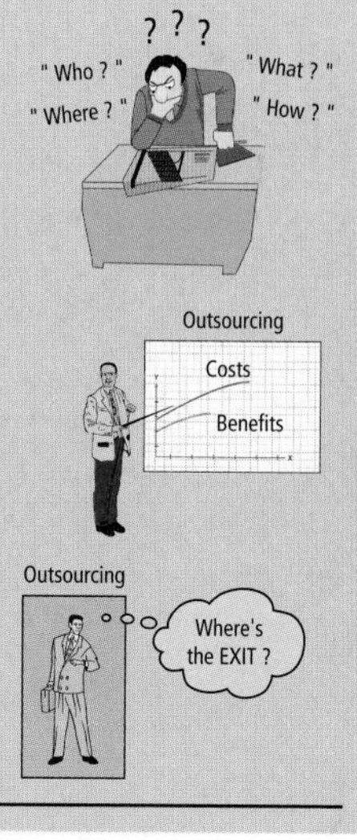

FIGURE 11-8
Outsourcing Risks

and devotes his attention and that of his employees as needed, all can work out well. On the other hand, if he obtains a larger, more lucrative contract soon after he starts ARES, schedule and quality problems can develop. Neither Henri nor Raj has any control over this eventuality. If they pay at the end, they may not lose money, but they can lose time.

For service-oriented outsourcing, say, the outsourcing of IT infrastructure, the vendor is in the driver's seat. Each outsource vendor has methods and procedures for its service. The organization and its employees will have to conform to those procedures. For example, a hardware infrastructure vendor will have standard forms and procedures for requesting a computer, for recording and processing a computer problem, or for providing routine maintenance on computers. Once the vendor is in charge, employees must conform.

When outsourcing the cafeteria, employees have only those food choices that the vendor provides. Similarly, when obtaining computer hardware and services, the employees will need to take what the vendor supports. Employees who want equipment that is not on the vendor's list will be out of luck.

Unless the contract requires otherwise, the outsource vendor can choose the technology that it wants to implement. If the vendor, for some reason, is slow to pick up on a significant new technology, then the hiring organization will be slow to attain benefits from that technology. An organization can find itself at a competitive disadvantage because it cannot offer the same IS services as its competitors.

Another concern is a potential loss of intellectual capital. The company may need to reveal proprietary trade secrets, methods, or procedures to the outsource vendor's employees. As part of its normal operations, that vendor may move employees to competing organizations, and the company may lose intellectual capital as that happens. The loss need not be intellectual theft; it could simply be that the vendor's employees learned to work in a new and better way at your company, and then they take that learning to your competitor.

Similarly, all software has failures and problems. Quality vendors track those failures and problems and fix them according to a set of priorities. When a company outsources a system, it no longer has control over prioritizing those fixes. Such control belongs to the vendor. A fix that might be critical to your organization might be of low priority to the outsource vendor.

Other problems are that the outsource vendor may change management, adopt a different strategic direction, or be acquired. When any of those changes occur, priorities may change, and an outsource vendor that was a good choice at one time might be a bad fit after it changes direction. It can be difficult and expensive to change an outsource vendor when this occurs.

The final loss-of-control risk is that the company's CIO can become superfluous. When users need a critical service that is outsourced, the CIO must turn to the vendor for a response. In time, users learn that it is quicker to deal directly with the outsource vendor, and soon the CIO is out of the communication loop. At that point, the vendor has essentially replaced the CIO, who has become a figurehead. However, employees of the outsource vendor work for a different company, with a bias toward their employer. Critical managers will thus not share the same goals and objectives as the rest of the management team. Biased, bad decisions can result.

Benefits Outweighed by Long-Term Costs

The initial benefits of outsourcing can appear huge. A cap on financial exposure, a reduction of management time and attention, and the release of many management and staffing problems are all possible. (Most likely, outsource vendors promise these very benefits.) Outsourcing can appear too good to be true.

In fact, it *can be* too good to be true. For one, although a fixed cost does indeed cap exposure, it also removes the benefits of economies of scale. If ARES demand takes off and it suddenly needs 200 servers instead of 20, the using organization will pay 200 times the fixed cost of supporting one server. It is possible, however, that because of economies of scale, the costs of supporting 200 servers are far less than 10 times the costs of supporting 20 servers. If they were hosting those servers in-house, they and not the vendor would be the beneficiary.

Also, the outsource vendor may change its pricing strategy over time. Initially, an organization obtains a competitive bid from several outsource vendors. However, as the winning vendor learns more about the business and as relationships develop between the organization's employees and those of the vendor, it becomes difficult for other firms to compete for subsequent contracts. The vendor becomes the de facto sole source and, with little competitive pressure, might increase its prices.

Another problem is that an organization can find itself paying for another organization's mismanagement, with little knowledge that that is the case. If ARES outsources its servers, it is difficult for it to know if the vendor is well managed. The ARES investors may be paying for poor management; even worse, ARES may suffer the consequences of poor management, such as lost data. It will be very difficult for ARES to learn about such mismanagement.

No Easy Exit

The final category of outsourcing risk concerns ending the agreement. There is no easy exit. For one, the outsource vendor's employees have gained significant knowledge of the company.

They know the server requirements in customer support, they know the patterns of usage, and they know the best procedures for downloading operational data into the data warehouse. Consequently, lack of knowledge will make it difficult to bring the outsourced service back in-house.

Also, because the vendor has become so tightly integrated into the business, parting company can be exceedingly risky. Closing down the employee cafeteria for a few weeks while finding another food vendor would be unpopular, but employees would survive. Shutting down the enterprise network for a few weeks would be impossible; the business would not survive. Because of such risk, the company must invest considerable work, duplication of effort, management time, and expense to change to another vendor. In truth, choosing an outsource vendor can be a one-way street.

At ARES, if, after the initial application development, the team decides to change development vendors, it may be very difficult to do. The new vendor will not know the application code as well as the current one who created it. It may become infeasible in terms of time and money to consider moving to another, better, lower-cost vendor.

Choosing to outsource is a difficult decision. In fact, the correct decision might not be clear, but time and events could force the company to decide.

Q11-4 What Are Your User Rights and Responsibilities?

As a future user of information systems, you have both rights and responsibilities in your relationship with the IS department. The items in Figure 11-9 list what you are entitled to receive and indicate what you are expected to contribute.

Your User Rights

You have a right to have the computing resources you need to perform your work as proficiently as you want. You have a right to the computer hardware and programs that you need. If you process huge files for data-mining applications, you have a right to the huge disks and the fast processor that you need. However, if you merely receive email and consult the corporate Web portal, then your right is for more modest requirements (leaving the more powerful resources for those in the organization who require them).

You have a right to reliable network and Internet services. *Reliable* means that you can process without problems almost all of the time. It means that you never go to work wondering, "Will the network be available today?" Network problems should be a rare occurrence.

You also have a right to a secure computing environment. The organization should protect your computer and its files, and you should not normally even need to think about security. From time to time, the organization might ask you to take particular actions to protect your computer and files,

You have a right to:
– Computer hardware and programs that allow you to perform your job proficiently
– Reliable network and Internet connections
– A secure computing environment
– Protection from viruses, worms, and other threats
– Contribute to requirements for new system features and functions
– Reliable systems development and maintenance
– Prompt attention to problems, concerns, and complaints
– Properly prioritized problem fixes and resolutions
– Effective training

You have a responsibility to:
– Learn basic computer skills
– Learn standard techniques and procedures for the applications you use
– Follow security and backup procedures
– Protect your password(s)
– Use computers and mobile devices according to your employer's computer-use policy
– Make no unauthorized hardware modifications
– Install only authorized programs
– Apply software patches and fixes when directed to do so
– When asked, devote the time required to respond carefully and completely to requests for requirements for new system features and functions
– Avoid reporting trivial problems

FIGURE 11-9
User Information Systems Rights and Responsibilities

and you should take those actions. But such requests should be rare and related to specific outside threats.

You have a right to participate in requirements meetings for new applications that you will use and for major changes to applications that you currently use. You may choose to delegate this right to others, or your department may delegate that right for you, but if so, you have a right to contribute your thoughts through that delegate.

You have a right to reliable systems development and maintenance. Although schedule slippages of a month or 2 are common in many development projects, you should not have to endure schedule slippages of 6 months or more. Such slippages are evidence of incompetent systems development.

Additionally, you have a right to receive prompt attention to your problems, concerns, and complaints about information services. You have a right to have a means to report problems and to know that your problem has been received and at least registered with the IS department. You have a right to have your problem resolved, consistent with established priorities. This means that an annoying problem that allows you to conduct your work will be prioritized below another's problem that interferes with his ability to do his job.

Finally, you have a right to effective training. It should be training that you can understand and that enables you to use systems to perform your particular job. The organization should provide training in a format and on a schedule that is convenient to you.

Your User Responsibilities

Users are given a responsibility to manage critical systems. They also have the opportunity to use this access to their own advantage. See the Security Guide on pages 438–439.

You also have responsibilities toward the IS department and your organization. Specifically, you have a responsibility to learn basic computer skills and to learn the techniques and procedures for the applications you use. You should not expect hand-holding for basic operations. Nor should you expect to receive repetitive training and support for the same issue.

You have a responsibility to follow security and backup procedures. This is especially important because actions that you fail to take might cause problems for your fellow employees and your organization as well as for you. In particular, you are responsible for protecting your password(s). This is important not only to protect your computer but, because of intersystem authentication, also to protect your organization's networks and databases.

You have a responsibility for using your computer resources in a manner that is consistent with your employer's policy. Many employers allow limited email for critical family matters while at work but discourage frequent and long casual email. You have a responsibility to know your employer's policy and to follow it. Further, if your employer has a policy concerning use of personal mobile devices at work, you are responsible for following it.

You also have a responsibility to make no unauthorized hardware modifications to your computer and to install only authorized programs. One reason for this policy is that your IS department constructs automated maintenance programs for upgrading your computer. Unauthorized hardware and programs might interfere with these programs. Additionally, the installation of unauthorized hardware or programs can cause you problems that the IS department will have to fix.

You have a responsibility to install computer updates and fixes when asked to do so. This is particularly important for patches that concern security and backup and recovery. When asked for input to requirements for new and adapted systems, you have a responsibility to take the time necessary to provide thoughtful, complete responses. If you do not have that time, you should delegate your input to someone else.

Finally, you have a responsibility to treat information systems professionals professionally. Everyone works for the same company, everyone wants to succeed, and professionalism and courtesy will go a long way on all sides. One form of professional behavior is to learn basic computer skills so that you avoid reporting trivial problems.

Q11-5 2029?

Over the next 10 years, changes in organizational management of IS and IT resources will be driven by the factors mentioned in Chapter 1, including exponential increases in processing power, storage, bandwidth, and connectivity. As a result, most organizations have already moved most of their internal hardware infrastructure to the cloud. This shift to the cloud will alter the way organizations function.

By 2029, conversion to the cloud will be complete. It may be difficult to find a single hard disk anywhere within the organization. The same might be true for applications and employees as more online applications are rented—not bought—and jobs are outsourced. What happens to an organization when *everything* is outside the organization? Organizational boundaries become fuzzy and potentially nonexistent. Security, privacy, and competitiveness will become even more important. Sharing and stealing confidential data will be much easier.

If workers shift from being traditional *employees* to being *consultants* in the gig economy, we could see companies becoming hypercompetitive for the best workers. Workers with the hottest skills and the best work experience could make five or 10 times as much as their contemporaries. Even now, companies that are perceived as cool places to work are attracting the most talented workers. This trend will likely accelerate by 2029.

Everyday work life will be different in 10 years, too. Consider that Amazon started using Kiva robots in 2014, and now those robots account for 17 percent of Amazon's workforce. More than 100,000 robots work alongside 566,000 employees. And it's not just physical labor, either. In 2017, former Citigroup CEO Vikram Pandit said advances in AI, robotics, and natural language processing could lead to a 30 percent reduction of all finance jobs by 2025.[11] JPMorgan CEO Jamie Dimon agreed, but said the loss of finance jobs would be somewhat offset by the hiring of more tech workers to manage these new systems. By 2029, it's likely you will be working alongside a synthetic coworker.

By 2029, creating and maintaining a distinct corporate culture may be increasingly difficult. Increased outsourcing and/or a large virtual workforce may make corporations much less cohesive. Employee loyalty may become a punchline at Christmas parties in 2029. In 10 years, mixed-reality devices will be commonplace. Workers will be able to virtually interact with coworkers around the world as if they were all meeting in the same room.

SECURITY GUIDE

WATCHING THE WATCHERS

What would you do with $14.3 million? It can be fun to sit and dream about the things you might buy or the luxuries you might enjoy with that kind of money. However, a much more important question is this: What would you be willing to do to get $14.3 million? Now *that* is a question you really need to stop and think about more earnestly. Would you be willing to violate your morals or break your code of ethics to get that kind of money? Would you be willing to break the law and face the potential penalties that accompany such behavior? An IT security manager in the state of Iowa likely pondered all of these questions not long ago. Unfortunately for him, his poor judgment led him to betray his employer.

This individual was the director of information security for the state lottery. In spite of his mandate to secure the Iowa state lottery's IT systems, he installed a rootkit on a computer used by the lottery system for the random number–generating software. Doing so allowed him to identify the numbers that would be drawn in the future so he could buy a winning ticket in advance.[12] To keep from getting caught, he wiped hard drives that may have provided further information about the crime. He also manipulated surveillance footage that had not been adequately managed. The penalty for committing this crime is up to 10 years in prison; that would give him plenty of time to dream about what he *could* have done with all of that money.

Person of Privilege

You may be wondering how a company or municipality can ensure that the director of its security operations is not abusing his or her power. Conducting audits and managing access are two common ways to ensure that IT security practitioners have not abused their roles. Audits are an effective way of assessing what has happened in the past. Unauthorized access to certain files or systems is recognized, and the perpetrating employee is identified. Audits should be conducted by organizational outsiders with no ties to the internal employees being evaluated.

However, IT security workers often manage and have access to log files. These log files can be used to identify potential misdeeds. IT security workers have the access, opportunity, and skill to potentially tamper with these log files.

A more preventative measure to securing systems is enforcing proper user access controls via superuser privilege management tools. These tools permit an administrator account to be created; other administrative privileges can then be created through this account. The benefit of this approach is that only one individual must be fully trusted, while other admins can be given only partial access.[13]

Other strategies to prevent abuses by security experts include (1) efforts to ensure that employees understand what

Source: Photographee.eu/Fotolia

438

behaviors are permitted within the organization, (2) separation of knowledge and duties, (3) and proper monitoring. Proper monitoring processes could include sending log files to external servers that are not accessible by internal employees.[14]

Watchers Are Everywhere

If you stop and think about it, you will soon realize that the "watchers" are not just IT security experts working for large companies. IT security practitioners do have a tremendous amount of power within the confines of their employer's networks and systems, but what about watchers outside of a business setting? What about watchers who have no limitations or constraints on the types of things that they can monitor? Can the maker of the flashlight app on your phone watch you?

You have likely heard of Edward Snowden and the revelations that he made about the U.S. government's pervasive surveillance and monitoring programs. The primary concern with these programs is that they pose a tremendous invasion of privacy. However, in many ways, everyday citizens are enabling the invasion of their own privacy. They buy and use devices that can be hacked or accessed remotely without their consent. Simple apps on your phone ask for a wide swath of permissions that may not even be necessary. Does your flashlight app need access to your contacts list?

These are examples of the inherent tensions between privacy and security. The use of new apps, IoT devices, and systems often introduces privacy risks and security vulnerabilities that are difficult to identify and mitigate. The biggest risk of all is that the designated watchers (i.e., IT security staff) often lack the proper oversight to ensure that they are not abusing their power. So the next time you think about buying a lottery ticket, keep your fingers crossed that the watchers are being watched!

DISCUSSION QUESTIONS

1. The article discusses the use of security audits to ensure that employees are not doing anything that they should not be doing on their employer's systems. In what other contexts are audits conducted?
2. Define what a rootkit is and conduct a search online for examples of how rootkits have been used.
3. One strategy for preventing IT employees from violating their extensive system access is "separation of duties." Can you think of any other examples of how a function or task is split into multiple pieces or assigned to multiple individuals to prevent abuse of that function?
4. Take a moment to think about all of the different types of devices that you use on a daily basis. How could these devices be compromised to invade your privacy? Is this risk of privacy invasion enough to make you stop using these devices?

Future workers may be more "connected" technologically but have fewer deep personal connections or shared experiences. You can already see this phenomenon with smartphones. How many times have you seen a group of people together physically, but most of them are silently staring down at their phones? Without a shared corporate culture or identity, it may be increasingly difficult for companies to hire, train, and keep the best employees.

By 2029, organizations will *need* to use social media inside the organization in true Enterprise 2.0 style. They will need to effectively engage their employees via internal social media. Similarly, employees will need to effectively engage customers in a world where social media interactions have a direct impact on the bottom line. IS will be seen no longer as a hindrance to organizational strategy and growth but as a key player for gaining competitive advantage. The ubiquity of social media and mobile devices will focus attention on the role that IS can play in achieving organizational goals.

CAREER GUIDE

Name: Susan M. Jones, DBA, CISA, OPST
Company: Utah State University
Job Title: Data Governance Officer
Education: Henley Business School, UK

Source: Susan M. Jones, DBA, CISA, OPST, Utah State University, Data Governance Officer

1 How did you get this type of job?

Early in my finance career, I watched technology advance and enhance business operations. I quickly realized that technology would provide a competitive advantage in the job market. Employers are always interested in individuals who have complementary technology skills. As the field evolved, threats to data became a focus, and I found myself addressing data security and data privacy issues. I studied "attackers" and how they were able to get into computer systems by exploiting technology and human psychology and trust. With this knowledge, my career advanced to my current position, where I help manage risk by setting clear ground rules for data access and handling.

2 What attracted you to this field?

Honestly, what *isn't* attractive about this field? The information technology (IT) field is exciting, innovative, and dynamic. IT connects every division in an organization. For example, IT connects marketing to manufacturing, reshaping not only the way we produce products but the way we market them. More than the excitement of technology, the field is attractive because of its service aspects.

3 What does a typical workday look like for you (duties, decisions, problems)?

Much of my work involves identifying data-related risks and recommending technical and administrative controls to mitigate them. My days are full of a wide range of interactions and activities, which ultimately become more management oriented than technology oriented. From the mapping of data flows to training employees about secure data collection, my daily interactions provide valuable insight into the organization and its use of data and technology.

4 What do you like most about your job?

Like others in the IT profession, I find myself learning many different business functions, legal requirements, and system controls. The more I learn, the more I can contribute to the organization. To truly accomplish our organizational mission, we need both people and technology. I enjoy that my work contributes both to the organization and to the employees.

5 What skills would someone need to do well at your job?

Project management, change management, problem solving, and communication skills are important for success in data governance. Data governance requires accountability; thus, if these skills are combined with a desire to learn and understand, a fulfilling career with strong relationships will follow. As a personal development goal, I consciously (and continually) work to hone these skills.

6 Are education or certifications important in your field? Why?

Yes, continual learning is valuable in any profession, but especially in technology. Technology is always progressing, so train, train, train! Education and certifications are very useful for professional development and career advancement, and they are listed as a base minimum in a majority of job descriptions in my field.

7 What advice would you give to someone who is considering working in your field?

Data governance requires the coordination of many roles and organizational areas. Therefore, my advice is to take time to analyze the big picture and make connections, whether working for yourself or for a large company. It is easy to learn about a single subject, but until you truly understand how one subject can enhance another, you will not recognize your full potential.

8 What do you think will be hot tech jobs in 10 years?

Tough question—tech forecasting can be a dangerous endeavor. In the next 10 years, I expect the hot tech jobs to involve more than just technology knowledge. In my dreams, all tech jobs will require a strong knowledge of data security and an understanding of privacy.

ACTIVE REVIEW

Use this Active Review to verify that you understand the ideas and concepts that answer the chapter's study questions.

Q11-1 What are the functions and organization of the IS department?

List the five primary functions of the IS department. Define *CIO* and explain the CIO's typical reporting relationships. Name the four groups found in a typical IS department and explain the major responsibilities of each. Define *CTO* and explain typical CTO responsibilities. Explain the purpose of the data administration function. Define *CSO* and *CISO* and explain the differences in their responsibilities.

Q11-2 How do organizations plan the use of IS?

Explain the importance of strategic alignment as it pertains to IS planning. Explain why maintaining alignment can be difficult. Describe the CIO's relationship to the rest of the executive staff. Describe the CIO's responsibilities with regard to priorities. Explain challenges to this task. Define *steering committee* and explain the CIO's role with regard to it.

Q11-3 What are the advantages and disadvantages of outsourcing?

Define *outsourcing*. Explain how Drucker's statement "Your back room is someone else's front room" pertains to outsourcing. Summarize the management advantages, cost advantages, and risks of outsourcing. Differentiate among IaaS, PaaS, and SaaS and give an example of each. Explain why international outsourcing can be particularly advantageous. Describe skills you can develop that will protect you from having your job outsourced.

Summarize the outsourcing risks concerning control, long-term costs, and exit strategy.

Q11-4 What are your user rights and responsibilities?

Explain in your own words the meaning of each of your user rights as listed in Figure 11-9. Explain in your own words the meaning of each of your user responsibilities in Figure 11-9 .

Q11-5 2029?

Explain how the adoption of the cloud may be a model for future outsourcing of applications and jobs. List some changes and developments that will have an effect on an organization's management of IS and IT. How might the gig economy affect organizational effectiveness? Explain how robotics and automation will affect the workplace. Describe how virtual workers and "connected" digital devices may actually make an organization less cohesive. Explain the organizational cultural change that will affect the IS department.

Using Your Knowledge with ARES

You now know the primary responsibilities of the IS department and can understand why it may implement the standards and policies that it does. You know the planning functions of IS and how they relate to the rest of your organization. You also know the reasons for outsourcing IS services, the most common and popular outsource alternatives, and the risks of outsourcing. Finally, you know your rights and responsibilities with regard to services provided by your IS department.

The knowledge of this chapter will help you understand what needs to be done, whether you work for ARES Systems, are a potential investor in ARES Systems, or are an advisor to a potential investor.

KEY TERMS AND CONCEPTS

Chief information officer (CIO) 422	Chief security officer (CSO) 423	Outsourcing 428
Chief information security officer (CISO) 423	Chief technology officer (CTO) 422	Steering committee 428
	Green computing 442	

MyLab MIS

To complete the problems with MyLab MIS, go to EOC Discussion Questions in the MyLab.

USING YOUR KNOWLEDGE

11-1.
MyLab MIS
According to this chapter, information systems, products, and technology are not malleable; they are difficult to change, alter, or bend. How do you think senior executives other than the CIO view this lack of malleability? For example, how do you think IS appears during a corporate merger?

11-2.
MyLab MIS
Suppose you represent an investor group that is acquiring hospitals across the nation and integrating them into a unified system. List five potential problems and risks concerning information systems. How do you think IS-related risks compare to other risks in such an acquisition program?

11-3.
MyLab MIS
What happens to IS when corporate direction changes rapidly? How will IS appear to other departments? What happens to IS when the corporate strategy changes frequently? Do you think such frequent changes are a greater problem to IS than to other business functions? Why or why not?

COLLABORATION EXERCISE 11

Using the collaboration IS you built in Chapter 1 (page 32), collaborate with a group of students to answer the following questions.

Green computing is environmentally conscious computing consisting of three major components: power management, virtualization, and e-waste management. In this exercise, we focus on power.

You know, of course, that computers (and related equipment, such as printers) consume electricity. That burden is light for any single computer or printer. But consider all the computers and printers in the United States that will be running tonight, with no one in the office. Proponents of green computing encourage companies and employees to reduce power and water consumption by turning off devices when not in use.

Is this issue important? Is it just a concession to environmentalists to make computing professionals appear virtuous? Form a team and develop your own, informed opinion by considering computer use at your campus.

11-4. Search the Internet to determine the power requirements for typical computing and office equipment. Consider laptop computers, desktop computers, CRT monitors, LCD monitors, and printers. For this exercise, ignore server computers. As you search, be aware that a *watt* is a measure of electrical power. It is *watts* that the green computing movement wants to reduce.

11-5. Estimate the number of each type of device in use on your campus. Use your university's Web site to determine the number of colleges, departments, faculty, staff, and students. Make assumptions about the number of computers, copiers, and other types of equipment used by each.

11-6. Using the data from items 11-4 and 11-5, estimate the total power used by computing and related devices on your campus.

11-7. A computer that is in screensaver mode uses the same amount of power as one in regular mode. Computers that are in sleep mode, however, use much less power, say, 6 watts per hour. Reflect on computer use on your campus and estimate the amount of time that computing devices are in sleep versus screensaver or use mode. Compute the savings in power that result from sleep mode.

11-8. Computers that are automatically updated by the IS department with software upgrades and patches cannot be allowed to go into sleep mode because if they are sleeping they will not be able to receive the upgrade. Hence, some universities prohibit sleep mode on university computers (sleep mode is never used on servers, by the way). Determine the cost, in watts, of such a policy.

11-9. Calculate the monthly cost, in watts, if:
  a. All user computers run full time night and day.
  b. All user computers run full time during work hours and in sleep mode during off-hours.
  c. All user computers are shut off during nonwork hours.

11-10. Given your answers to items 11-4 through 11-9, is computer power management during off-hours a significant concern? In comparison to the other costs of running a university, does this issue really matter? Discuss this question among your group and explain your answer.

Automating Labor

On May 24, 2016, former McDonald's CEO Ed Rensi was interviewed about recent protests for an increase in the minimum wage. Fast-food workers wanted a national minimum wage of $15 per hour. Rensi stated that a single $35,000 robotic worker would cost less and be more productive than a $15-an-hour human worker.[15] He also pointed out that pushing for higher wages will only accelerate the adoption of automated labor. He might be right.

A hamburger-making robot built by California-based Momentum Machines can make 400 burgers per hour, every hour, without a break. It can grind, grill, and assemble custom burgers more consistently, accurately, and cleanly than its human counterparts. It can completely replace three human fast-food workers.[16]

And it's not just fast-food companies that are jumping on the automation bandwagon. In 2018, Foxconn, a major supplier to Apple Inc. located in China, announced it was investing $4 billion after successfully replacing 60,000 factory workers with robots in 2016. The Foxconn implementation was so successful that nearly 600 other companies are looking at similar automation plans.[17] In Europe, airplane manufacturer Airbus announced a partnership with Japan's Joint Robotics Laboratory (JRL) to use its HRP-2 and HRP-4 humanoid robots to assemble its airplanes.[18] In the United States, Amazon is using 100,000 Kiva robots at 25 fulfillment centers to help process customer orders.[19]

A Brave New Automated World

No one fully understands the impact that robotic workers will have on organizations or society as a whole. Researchers estimate that by 2030, nearly 800 million workers will be taken out of the current worldwide labor force.[20] They will be replaced by robots with IQs higher than 90 percent of the U.S. population. Yes, some new jobs will be created to make, program, and manage the new robotic workforce.

What types of jobs will robots take? They will likely take jobs that involve routine physical and mental tasks. In the future you might interact with robots at kiosks, at grocery store checkout lines, at doctor's offices, in operating rooms, and on the road (e.g., self-driving cars).

Why these types of jobs? Consider some of the benefits of an automated labor force versus a human labor force, shown in Figure 11-10. Many of the traditional labor costs that come with a human workforce go away with an automated workforce. But there is still a need for human labor. Humans excel at higher-level, nonroutine cognitive tasks.

What If Labor Doesn't Matter?

In 2003, Nicholas Carr wrote a *Harvard Business Review* article titled "IT Doesn't Matter." He argued that information technology offered a few forward-looking companies a competitive advantage for a short period of time. Once information technology became widely used and commoditized, it was no longer a source of competitive advantage. Information technology was essential but wasn't strategically important anymore.

Carr's article was widely discussed and debated. He made a good argument. For example, suppose it's 1915 and you're in the shipping business. You're the first company to start using trucks to deliver goods. All of your competitors use trains or horse-drawn wagons. You've got a competitive advantage because you can deliver more quickly, cheaply, and consistently.

Benefits of Automated Labor	Benefits of Human Labor
1. No healthcare expenses.	1. Unique problem solving.
2. No time off, breaks, sick days, or vacations.	2. Create new products.
3. No accidents, injuries, workman's compensation claims.	3. Adaptable to rapidly changing environment.
4. No unions, arguments, complaints, bad attitudes, layoffs, severance packages.	4. Integrative systems thinking.
5. No smoke breaks, drinking on the job, sexual harassment, lawsuits.	5. Question poorly made decisions.
6. No minimum wage, raises, or paychecks.	6. Prior experience to predict future events.
7. Work 24 hours a day, 365 days a year.	7. Ethical decision making (hopefully).
8. Safer, more accurate, and more consistent work than humans.	8. Interact well with other humans (i.e., sales).

FIGURE 11-10
Automated Versus Human Labor

Once your competitors buy delivery trucks, you lose your competitive advantage. Now the competitive advantage comes from *how the trucks are used*, not the trucks themselves. The same is true of information technology. Once everyone can use cloud services, they cease to be a source of competitive advantage.

Will the same be true of an automated workforce once automated labor becomes widely used? Probably, but what should be more concerning about the widespread adoption of automated labor is this: You are labor. Your ability to earn income may be problematic if you are trying to compete against a horde of inexpensive automatons.

QUESTIONS

11-11. How might the automation of labor provide a competitive advantage for forward-looking companies? How would this new competitive advantage be affected if all competitors in an industry adopted automated workforces?

11-12. Automated workforces may replace certain types of jobs entirely. List three implications of an automated workforce for someone seeking a university education. Name three majors that might benefit from an automated workforce. Why might a university need to become nimbler in an era of automated labor?

11-13. List three new types of companies that might be created from an automated workforce. (e.g., Uber without drivers). Why might these new companies put existing companies out of business?

11-14. Government regulations like higher minimum wage rates, mandatory health insurance, and complex labor laws might make robots more attractive than human workers because they don't come with these additional costs. Describe how government regulations could be altered to support human workers.

11-15. Robots can be trained to do dangerous, stinky, and monotonous work that humans may not want to do. Name a job for which you think robots would be better suited than humans. Describe why you think humans would prefer to turn this job over to a robotic worker.

11-16. A personal robot could be purchased for your own use—to reduce your individual costs. It could do all your gardening, cooking, cleaning, home repairs, and so on. Explain why your personal income needs might change with an automated worker in your home. Can your personal robot meet all your needs?

11-17. Robots don't have the desire to stay alive, the desire to procreate, or the desire to improve their positions. How might the lack of these human characteristics prevent automatons from becoming our cybernetic overlords?

MyLab MIS

Go to the Assignments section of your MyLab to complete these writing exercises.

11-18. Consider the following statement: "In many ways, choosing an outsource vendor is a one-way street." Explain what this statement means. Do you agree with it? Why or why not? Does your answer change depending on what systems components are being outsourced? Why or why not?

11-19. A large multinational corporation experiences a severe data breach that results in the loss of customer data for nearly 250 million customers. The lost data included names, addresses, email addresses, passwords, credit card numbers, and dates of birth. During the first week, the entire company is in damage control mode. About 2 weeks after the data breach, the company's board of directors starts asking who was responsible. Heads are going to roll. They want to show their customers that they are taking steps so this won't happen again. Should they fire the CEO, CIO, CISO, CTO, database administrators, or line workers? Justify your choices.

ENDNOTES

1. Often, the department we are calling the *IS department* is known in organizations as the *IT department*. That name is a misnomer, however, because the IT department manages systems as well as technology. If you hear the term *IT department* in industry, don't assume that the scope of that department is limited to technology.

2. Nicole Norfleet, "Reporter Who Wrote About Target Breach Says Well-Trained Staff Is Best Defense Against Cyberattacks," *Star Tribune*, May 17, 2016, accessed June 18, 2018, *www.startribune.com/reporter-whowrote-about-target-breach-says-well-trained-staff-is-best-defense-againstcyberattacks/379831601.*

3. PayScale Inc., "Salary Data & Career Research Center (United States)," *PayScale.com*, accessed June 18, 2018, *www.payscale.com/research/US/Country=United_States/Salary*.

4. U.S. Social Security Administration, "Measures of Central Tendency for Wage Data," *SSA.gov*, accessed June 18, 2018, *www.ssa.gov/oact/cola/central.html*.

5. DHI Group Inc., "Dice Tech Salary Survey," *Dice.com*, February 21, 2018, accessed June 18, 2018, *https://marketing.dice.com/pdf/Dice_TechSalarySurvey_TechPro_2018.pdf*.

6. Deepa Seetharaman, "After Days of Silence, Facebook's Mark Zuckerberg Admits to 'Mistakes' with User Data," *Wall Street Journal*, March 21, 2018, *www.wsj.com/articles/after-days-of-silence-mark-zuckerberg-to-publicly-address-facebooks-user-data-uproar-1521659989*.

7. Akane Otani, Michael Wursthorn, and Ben Eisen, "Technology Shares Plunge Again amid Growing Backlash," *Wall Street Journal*, April 2, 2018, *www.wsj.com/articles/technology-shares-plunge-again-amid-growing-backlash-1522689491*.

8. Georgia Wells, "Facebook's Mark Zuckerberg Hints at Possibility of Paid Service," *Wall Street Journal*, April 10, 2018, *www.wsj.com/articles/facebooks-mark-zuckerberg-hints-at-possibility-of-paid-service-1523399467*.

9. Geoffrey A. Fowler, "What If We Paid for Facebook—Instead of Letting It Spy on Us for Free?" *Washington Post*, April 5, 2018, *www.washingtonpost.com/news/the-switch/wp/2018/04/05/what-if-we-paid-for-facebook-instead-of-letting-it-spy-on-us-for-free/?noredirect=on&utm_term=.4848b529a904*.

10. DHI Group Inc., "Dice Tech Salary Survey," *Dice.com*, February 21, 2018, accessed June 18, 2018, *https://marketing.dice.com/pdf/Dice_TechSalarySurvey_TechPro_2018.pdf*.

11. Chanyaporn Chanjaroen, "Technology Will Cut 30% of Banking Jobs Says Former Citigroup CEO Vikram Pandit," *The Independent*, September 13, 2017, accessed June 19, 2018, *www.independent.co.uk/news/business/news/fintech-technology-banking-jobs-30-per-cent-cut-replace-citigroup-ceo-vikram-pandit-a7944016.html*.

12. Iain Thomson, "Lottery IT Security Boss Guilty of Hacking Lotto Computer to Win $14.3M," *The Register*, March 13, 2016, *www.theregister.co.uk/2015/07/22/lotto_infosec_director_guilty*.

13. George V. Hulme, "Watching the Watchers," *CSO Online*, March 13, 2016, *www.csoonline.com/article/2130533/identity-management/watching-the-watchers.html*.

14. Ibid.

15. Julia Limitone, "Fmr. McDonald's USA CEO: $35K Robots Cheaper Than Hiring at $15 Per Hour," *FoxBusiness.com*, May 24, 2016, accessed June 18, 2018, *www.foxbusiness.com/features/2016/05/24/fmr-mcdonalds-usa-ceo-35k-robots-cheaper-than-hiring-at-15-per-hour.html*.

16. Dylan Love, "Here's the Burger-Flipping Robot That Could Put Fast-Food Workers Out of a Job," *Business Insider*, August 11, 2014, accessed June 18, 2018, *www.businessinsider.com/momentum-machines-burger-robot-2014-8*.

17. Sam Francis, "Foxconn to Invest $4 Billion in New Robotics and Automation Technology," *Robotics and Automation News*, February 24, 2018, accessed June 18, 2018, *https://roboticsandautomationnews.com/2018/02/24/foxconn-to-invest-4-billion-in-new-robotics-and-automation-technology/16182*.

18. Peggy Hollinger, "Airbus Plans to Develop Assembly Line Robots to Work with Humans," *The Financial Times*, May 4, 2016, accessed June 18, 2018, *https://next.ft.com/content/c2d9eea0-1072-11e6-91da-096d89bd2173*.

19. Alison DeNisco Rayome, "Amazon Doubles Down on Hybrid Human/Robot Workforce in Illinois Warehouse," *TechRepublic*, April 2, 2018, accessed June 18, 2018, *www.techrepublic.com/article/amazon-doubles-down-on-hybrid-humanrobot-workforce-in-illinois-warehouse/*.

20. Courtney Connley, "Robots May Replace 800 Million Workers by 2030. These Skills Will Keep You Employed," *CNBC*, November 30, 2017, accessed June 18, 2018, *www.cnbc.com/2017/11/30/robots-may-replace-up-to-800-million-workers-by-2030.html*.

Information Systems Development

"Hello, everyone, sorry I'm late," says Zev Friedman, ARES owner. "I was pushing as hard as I could to get a KOM for a segment between here and my house."

"Not a problem. You're the boss. We wouldn't have started without you," Ashley says, smiling. She can see Zev looking over everyone seated at the table. Even though he's old, he's clearly in good shape physically and mentally.

"Did you get it?" Henri asks.

"No, but it was close," Zev says. Zev looks around and sees Raj with a confused look on his face. "*KOM* stands for "King of the Mountain." You get a KOM if you bike a certain stretch of road the fastest."

"Ah, I see. I may need to get out of the office more often," Raj responds sheepishly.

"You should if you're working for a biking company," Zev says with a lighthearted smile and a laugh.

MyLab MIS

Using Your Knowledge
Questions 12-1, 12-2, 12-3

Essay Questions 12-15, 12-16

"Augmented reality is a dream come true."

Source: Haiyin Wang/Alamy Stock Photo

Zev sits down, looks directly at Ashley, and nods. "So you want to start spending some real money now, right?"

Ashley smiles nervously, reaches for a folder, and looks around the table. "Yes, well, actually it's *your* money we'd like to spend. So I thought I'd let you look at what we're considering."

Ashley hands Zev a folder with a few loose sheets of paper in it. "I'll let Henri and Raj tell you about the options we think would grow ARES the most quickly."

Henri leans forward and motions toward the first page. "The first page is an estimate for the development of the applications we'll need for the exercise equipment providers. Most of them use embedded Linux and Windows Embedded."

Zev looks carefully at the estimates. Henri knows Zev will find any error or faulty thinking. He continues, "It will be about $200,000 to $300,000 to make apps for the top 10 manufacturers. Then we'll need apps for the AR headsets. That will be somewhere between $100,000 and $250,000."

Zev looks up at Henri. "So it's somewhere between $300K and $550K? Why such a big range?"

"Well, we have to make apps for multiple equipment manufacturers and multiple AR headsets and integrate all of this into the existing back-end system we got from Dr. Flores. We're not certain how much we're going to have to spend to get that done. We also need to record the virtual bike routes in 3D and add information about local hotspots. And, quite frankly, estimating the costs for developing the augmented reality apps is nearly impossible."

Raj jumps in. "No one has experience developing AR apps. It's a huge opportunity, and the smart players know it. Everyone is scrambling to get something built, but no one has made holographic apps before. Estimating development costs is extremely difficult."

Henri can tell Zev wants more concrete answers. "We're looking at outsourcing development to Raj's friend Sandeep in India. It sounds like he's got a good team, and the estimates he sent us were much less than the ones from the local developers we talked with."

Zev puts the papers on the table and looks over to Cassie. "Cassie, can you sell this?"

Cassie smiles broadly. "Absolutely! The ad possibilities are *huge*. We could sell new kinds of ads that people have never seen before. Everyone I talked to wanted to be involved. The spinning classes, personal trainers, and employers also look like great revenue sources. Augmented reality is a dream come true."

Study QUESTIONS

Q12-1 How are business processes, IS, and applications developed?

Q12-2 How do organizations use business process management (BPM)?

Q12-3 How is business process modeling notation (BPMN) used to model processes?

Q12-4 What are the phases in the systems development life cycle (SDLC)?

Q12-5 What are the keys for successful SDLC projects?

Q12-6 How can scrum overcome the problems of the SDLC?

Q12-7 2029?

"That's good," Zev says smiling.

"Yes, but they want to see it work. They need to see the *wow* before we see the *money*."

Zev leans back and looks at the estimates again. No one is talking, and the pause in the conversation starts to become uncomfortable for the others, though it doesn't bother Zev.

Ashley slowly starts, "So . . . what do you think, Zev?"

Zev looks at Ashley. "I think we're getting ahead of ourselves. We're not ready for this yet."

"So what do you want to do?" Ashley asks hesitantly.

"We need to focus on getting a working prototype," Zev says flatly. "We'll develop one app for Microsoft HoloLens and ignore the other AR headsets for now. We'll develop one app to work with CanyonBack's exercise bikes because it's the industry leader, and we'll ignore the rest of the manufacturers."

Zev looks around the table and says in a clear voice, "Our focus now is the prototype. All of our efforts need to go into getting the prototype working. We need to get Cassie something to sell."

Zev pauses to make sure everyone understands. "Any questions?" Zev says with a smile. No one says a word. "Great, let's eat."

Chapter PREVIEW

As a future business professional, you will be involved in the development of new technology applications to your business. You may take the lead, as Henri has been doing in developing ARES, or you might be an office manager who implements procedures and trains people in the use of systems such as ARES. Or you might become a business analyst and work as a liaison between users and technical staff. If nothing else, you may be asked to provide requirements and to test the system to ensure those requirements have been met. Whatever your role, it is important that you understand how processes and systems are developed and managed.

We begin in Q12-1 by clarifying what we're developing and introducing three different development processes. Then, in the next series of questions, we'll go into more detail for each. In Q12-2, we'll discuss business process management, and in Q12-3 you'll learn how to interpret process diagrams that you may be called upon to evaluate during your career. Next, we'll discuss the stages of the systems development life cycle in Q12-4, and then in Q12-5 summarize the keys to successful SDLC project management. Q12-6 then presents a newer, possibly superior development process known as scrum, and we'll wrap up this chapter in Q12-7 with a discussion of how information systems careers are likely to change between now and 2029.

Q12-1   How Are Business Processes, IS, and Applications Developed?

Many business professionals become confused when discussing business processes, information systems, and applications. You can avoid this confusion by understanding that they are different, by knowing those differences, and by realizing how they relate to each other. That knowledge will make it easier for you to appreciate the ways that processes, systems, and applications are developed and, in turn, help you be more effective as a team member on development projects.

How Do Business Processes, Information Systems, and Applications Differ and Relate?

As you learned in Chapter 2, a business process consists of one or more activities. For example, Figure 12-1 shows activities in an ordering business process: A quotation is prepared and, assuming the customer accepts those terms, the order is processed. Inventory availability is verified, customer credit is checked, special terms, if any, are approved, and then the order is processed and shipped. Each of these activities includes many tasks, some of which involve processing exceptions (only part of the order is available, for example), but those exceptions are not shown.

The activities in a business process often involve information systems. In Figure 12-1, for example, all of the activities except Approve Special Terms use an information system. (For this example, we'll assume that special terms are rare and approved by having a salesperson walk down the hallway to the sales manager.) Each of these information systems has the five components that we've repeatedly discussed. The actors or participants in the business process are the users of the information systems. They employ IS procedures to use information systems to accomplish tasks in process activities.

Each of these information systems contains a software component. Developing software nearly always involves the data component, and it often involves the specification and characteristics of hardware (e.g., mobile devices). Consequently, we define the term **application** to mean a combination of hardware, software, and data components that accomplishes a set of requirements. In Figure 12-1, the Customer Credit IS contains an application that processes a customer database to approve or reject credit requests.

As you can see from the example in Figure 12-1, this one business process uses four different IS. In general, we can say that a single business process relates to one or more information systems. However, notice that not all process activities use an IS; some require just manual tasks. In Figure 12-1, the Approve Special Terms activity uses no IS. Instead, as stated, salespeople walk

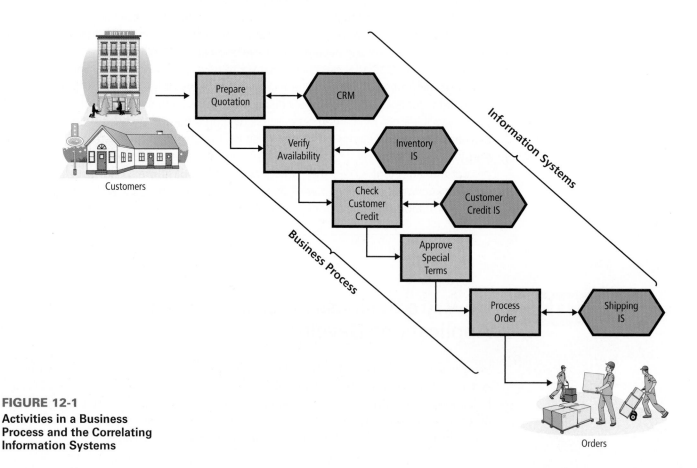

FIGURE 12-1

**Activities in a Business
Process and the Correlating
Information Systems**

FIGURE 12-2

Relationship of Business Processes and Information Systems

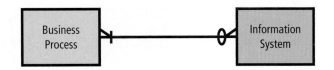

down the hallway to ask their manager if terms are acceptable. In some cases (not in this example, however), it is possible for none of the activities to use an IS, in which case the entire business process is manual.

Now, consider any of the information systems in Figure 12-1, say, the Inventory IS. In addition to providing features and functions to verify item availability, that IS has other features that support additional business processes. For example, the Inventory IS supports the item ordering process, the item stocking process, the item backorder process, and more. So, even though we cannot see it from Figure 12-1, we can correctly infer that IS supports many business processes. Further, every IS supports at least one business process; if it did not, it would have little utility to the organization that pays for it.

We can use the terminology of Chapter 5 to summarize these statements and state that the relationship of business processes and information systems is many-to-many. One business process can potentially use many IS, and a single IS can support potentially many business processes. Furthermore, a business process is not required to use an IS, but every IS supports at least one business process. Figure 12-2 shows the process/information system relationship using an entity-relationship diagram.

Every information system has at least one application because every IS includes a software component. We could further investigate the relationship between IS and applications, but that relationship is beyond the scope of this text.

So, to summarize:

1. Business processes, information systems, and applications have different characteristics and components.
2. The relationship of business processes to information systems is many-to-many, or N:M. A business process need not relate to any information system, but an information system relates to at least one business process.
3. Every IS has at least one application because every IS has a software component.

When you participate in development meetings, you'll sometimes hear people confuse these terms. They'll quickly switch back and forth among processes, systems, and applications without knowing that they've changed terms and contexts. With these understandings, you can add value to your team simply by clarifying these differences.

Which Development Processes Are Used for Which?

Developing secure applications for IoT devices is often an afterthought. Read the Security Guide on pages 484–485 to learn more.

Over the years, many different processes have been tried for the development of processes, IS, and applications. In this chapter, we'll investigate three: business process management (BPM), systems development life cycle (SDLC), and scrum.

Business process management is a technique used to create new business processes and to manage changes to existing processes. Except for startups, organizations already have processes, in one form or another, in varying levels of quality. If they did not, they wouldn't be able to operate. Therefore, BPM is, in most cases, used to manage the evolution of existing business processes from one version to an improved version. We'll discuss BPM in Q12-2 and Q12-3.

As shown in Figure 12-3, the systems development life cycle (SDLC) is a process that can be used to develop both information systems and applications. The SDLC achieved prominence in the 1980s when the U.S. Department of Defense required that it be used on all software and systems development projects. It is common, well-known, and often used but, as you'll learn, frequently problematic. You need to know what it is and when and when not to use it. We'll discuss the SDLC in Q12-4 and Q12-5.

		Development Processes		
		BPM	**SDLC**	**Scrum**
Scope	Business Processes	✓		✓
	Information Systems		✓	✓
	Applications		✓	✓

FIGURE 12-3
Scope of Development Processes

Scrum is a new development process that was created, in part, to overcome the problems that occur when using the SDLC. Scrum is generic enough that it can be used for the development (and adaptation) of business processes, information systems, and applications. We'll discuss scrum in Q12-6.

Personnel that take the most active and important role for each of these processes are shown in Figure 12-4. A **business analyst** is someone who is well versed in Porter's models (see Chapter 2) and in the organization's strategies and who focuses, primarily, on ensuring that business processes and information systems meet the organization's competitive strategies. As you would expect, the primary focus of a business analyst is business processes.

Systems analysts are IS professionals who understand both business and information technology. They focus primarily on IS development, but are involved with business analysts on the management of business processes as well. Systems analysts play a key role in moving development projects through the SDLC or scrum development process.

Applications are developed by technical personnel such as programmers, database designers, test personnel, hardware specialists, and other technical staff. Systems analysts play a key role in developing applications requirements and in facilitating the work of the programmers, testers, and users.

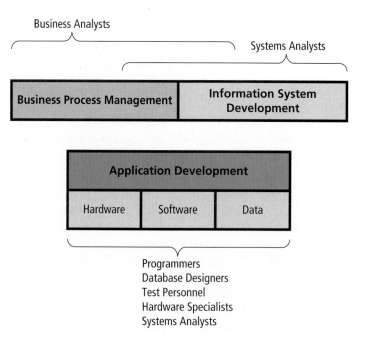

FIGURE 12-4
Role of Development Personnel

Because applications development involves technical details that are beyond the scope of this introductory class, we will only be peripherally concerned with applications development here. If you have a technical bent, however, you should consider these jobs because they are absolutely fascinating and are in extremely high demand.

Q12-2 How Do Organizations Use Business Process Management (BPM)?

For the purposes of this chapter, we will extend the definition of business processes that we used in Chapter 2. Here we will define a **business process** as a network of activities, repositories, roles, resources, and flows that interact to accomplish a business function. As stated in Chapter 2, *activities* are collections of related tasks that receive inputs and produce outputs. A *repository* is a collection of something; an inventory is a physical repository and a database is a data repository. The new terms in this definition are **roles**, which are collections of activities, and **resources**, which are people or computer applications that are assigned to roles. Finally, a flow is either a **control flow** that directs the order of activities or a **data flow** that shows the movement of data among activities and repositories.

To clarify these terms, think of roles as job titles. Example roles are *salesperson, credit manager, inventory supervisor*, and the like. Thus, an organization might assign three people (resources) to the salesperson role, or it might create an information system (resource) to perform the credit manager role.

Why Do Processes Need Management?

Business processes are not fixed in stone; they always evolve. To understand why, suppose you are a salesperson working at the company having the ordering process shown in Figure 12-1. When you joined the firm, they taught you to follow this process, and you've been using it for 2 years. It works fine as far as you know, so why does it need to be managed? Fundamentally, there are three reasons: to improve process quality, to adapt to changes in technology, and to adapt to changes in business fundamentals. Consider each.

Improve Process Quality

As you learned in Chapter 8, process quality has two dimensions: efficiency (use of resources) and effectiveness (accomplish strategy). The most obvious reason for changing a process is that it has efficiency or effectiveness problems. Consider a sales process. If the organization's goal is to provide high-quality service, then if the process takes too long or if it rejects credit inappropriately, it is ineffective and needs to be changed.

With regard to efficiency, the process may use its resources poorly. For example, according to Figure 12-1, salespeople verify product availability before checking customer credit. If checking availability means nothing more than querying an information system for inventory levels, that sequence makes sense. But suppose that checking availability means that someone in operations needs not only to verify inventory levels, but also to verify that the goods can be shipped to arrive on time. If the order delivery is complex, say, the order is for a large number of products that have to be shipped from three different warehouses, an hour or two of labor may be required to verify shipping schedules.

After verifying shipping, the next step is to verify credit. If it turns out the customer has insufficient credit and the order is refused, the shipping-verification labor will have been wasted. So, it might make sense to check credit before checking availability.

Similarly, if the customer's request for special terms is disapproved, the cost of checking availability and credit is wasted. If the customer has requested special terms that are not normally approved, it might make sense to obtain approval of special terms before checking availability or credit. However, your boss might not appreciate being asked to consider special terms for orders in which the items are not available or for customers with bad credit.

As you can see, it's not easy to determine what process structure is best. The need to monitor process quality and adjust process design, as appropriate, is one reason that processes need to be managed.

Change in Technology

Changing technology is a second reason for managing processes. For example, suppose the equipment supplier who uses the business process in Figure 12-1 invests in a new information system that enables it to track the location of trucks in real time. Suppose that with this capability the company can provide next-day availability of goods to customers. That capability will be of limited value, however, if the existing credit-checking process requires 2 days. "I can get the goods to you tomorrow, but I can't verify your credit until next Monday" will not be satisfying to either customers or salespeople.

Thus, when new technology changes any of a process's activities in a significant way, the entire process needs to be evaluated. That evaluation is another reason for managing processes.

Change in Business Fundamentals

A third reason for managing business processes is a change in business fundamentals. A substantial change in any of the following factors might result in the need to modify business processes:

- Market (e.g., new customer category, change in customer characteristics)
- Product lines
- Supply chain
- Company policy
- Company organization (e.g., merger, acquisition)
- Internationalization
- Business environment

To understand the implications of such changes, consider just the sequence of verifying availability and checking credit in Figure 12-1. A new category of customers could mean that the credit-check process needs to be modified; perhaps a certain category of customers is too risky to be extended credit. All sales to such customers must be cash. A change in product lines might require different ways of checking availability. A change in the supply chain might mean that the company no longer stocks some items in inventory but ships directly from the manufacturer instead.

Or the company might make broad changes to its credit policy. It might, for example, decide to accept more risk and sell to companies with lower credit scores. In this case, approval of special terms becomes more critical than checking credit, and the sequence of those two activities might need to be changed.

Of course, a merger or acquisition will mean substantial change in the organization and its products and markets, as does moving portions of the business offshore or engaging in international commerce. Finally, a substantial change in the business environment, say, the onset of a recession, might mean that credit checking becomes vitally important and needs to be moved to first in this process.

What Are BPM Activities?

The factors just discussed will necessitate changes in business processes, whether the organization recognizes that need or not. Organizations can either plan to develop and modify business processes, or they can wait and let the need for change just happen to them. In the latter case, the business will continually be in crisis, dealing with one process emergency after another.

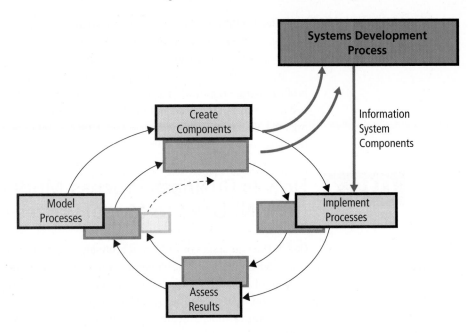

FIGURE 12-5
Four Stages of BPM

Figure 12-5 shows the basic activities in **business process management (BPM)**, a cyclical process for systematically creating, assessing, and altering business processes. This cycle begins by creating a model of the existing business process, called an **as-is model**. Then business users who are involved in the process (this could be you!) and business and systems analysts evaluate that model and make improvements. As you learned in Chapter 8, business processes can be improved by changing the structure of the process, by adding resources, or both. If the process structure is to be changed, a model of the changed process is constructed. Two common ways of adding resources to a process are to assign more people to process activities and to create or modify information systems.

The second activity in the BPM process is to create components. In this activity, the team designs changes to the business process at a depth sufficient for implementation. If the business process involves new information systems or changes to existing information systems then systems development projects are created and managed at this stage. Again, some activities involve IS, and some do not. For those that do, information systems procedures need to be created to enable users to accomplish their process tasks.

Implementing the new or changed process is the third activity in BPM. Here process actors are trained on the activities that they will perform and on the IS procedures that they will use. Converting from an existing process to a new or revised one usually meets with employee resistance, as you learned with regard to ERP implementations in Chapter 8. Thus, an important activity for you during implementation is softening that resistance. We will discuss four different conversion alternatives in Q12-4, when we discuss the SDLC. These four strategies pertain equally well to process implementation.

Once the process has been implemented, well-managed organizations don't stop there. Instead, they create policy, procedures, and committees to continually assess business process effectiveness. The Information Systems Audit and Control Association has created a set of standard practices called **COBIT (Control Objectives for Information and related Technology)** that are often used in the assessment stage of the BPM cycle. Explaining these standards is beyond the scope of this discussion, but you should know that they exist. See *www.isaca.org/cobit* for more information.

When the assessment process indicates that a significant need for change has arisen, the BPM cycle is repeated and adjusted. New process models are developed, and components are created, implemented, and assessed.

Effective BPM enables organizations to attain continuous process improvement. Like quality improvement, process improvement is never finished. Process effectiveness is constantly monitored, and processes are adjusted as and when required.

By the way, do not assume that business process management applies only to commercial, profit-making organizations. Nonprofit and government organizations have business processes just as commercial ones do, but most of these processes are service-oriented rather than revenue-oriented. Your state's Department of Labor, for example, has a need to manage its processes, as does the Girl Scouts of America. BPM applies to all types of organizations.

Q12-3 How Is Business Process Modeling Notation (BPMN) Used to Model Processes?

One of the four stages of BPM, and arguably the most important stage, is to model business processes. Such models are the blueprint for understanding the current process and for designing new versions of processes. They also set the stage for the requirements for any information systems and applications that need to be created or adapted. If models are incomplete and incorrect, follow-on components cannot be created correctly. In this question, you will learn standard notation for creating process documentation.

Learning this standard notation is important to you because, as a business professional, you may be involved in modeling projects. Unless you become a business or systems analyst, you are unlikely to lead such a project, but as a user, you may be asked to review and approve models and you may participate as a representative of your department or area of expertise in the creation of new models.

Need for Standard for Business Processing Notation

As stated, we define a *business process* as a network of activities, repositories, roles, resources, and flows that interact to accomplish a business function. This definition is commonly accepted, but unfortunately dozens of other definitions are used by other authors, industry analysts, and software products. For example, IBM, a key leader in business process management, has a product called WebSphere Business Modeler that uses a different set of terms. It has activities and resources, but it uses the term *repository* more broadly than we do, and it uses the term *business item* for *data flow*. Other business-modeling software products use still other definitions and terms. These differences and inconsistencies can be problematic, especially when two different organizations with two different sets of definitions must work together.

Accordingly, a software-industry standards organization called the **Object Management Group (OMG)** created a standard set of terms and graphical notations for documenting business processes. That standard, called **Business Process Modeling Notation (BPMN)**, is documented at *www.bpmn.org*. A complete description of BPMN is beyond the scope of this text. However, the basic symbols are easy to understand, and they work naturally with our definition of business process. Hence, we will use the BPMN symbols in the illustrations in the chapter. All of the diagrams in this chapter were drawn using Microsoft Visio, which includes several BPMN symbol templates. Figure 12-6 summarizes the basic BPMN symbols.

Documenting the As-Is Business Order Process

Figure 12-7 shows the as-is, or existing, order process introduced in Figure 12-1. First, note that this process is a model, an abstraction that shows the essential elements of the process but omits many details. If it were not an abstraction, the model would be as large as the business itself. This diagram is shown in **swim-lane layout**. In this format, each role in the business process is given its own swim lane. In Figure 12-7, there are five roles, hence five swim lanes. All activities for a given

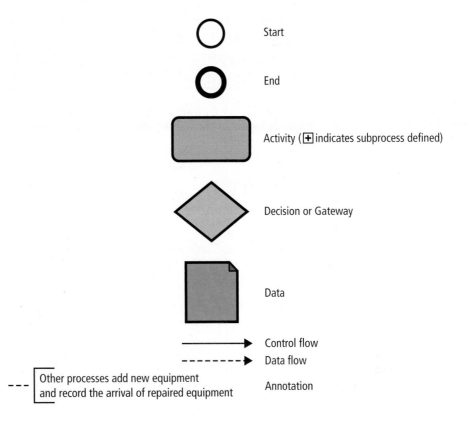

FIGURE 12-6

Business Process Management Notation (BPMN) Symbols

role are shown in that role's swim lane. Swim-lane layout simplifies the process diagram and draws attention to interactions among components of the diagram.

Two kinds of arrows are shown. Dotted arrows depict the flow of messages and data flows. Solid arrows depict the flow or sequence of the activities in the process. Some sequence flows have data associated with them as well. According to Figure 12-7, the customer sends an RFQ (request for quotation) to a salesperson (dotted arrow). That salesperson prepares a quotation in the first activity and then (solid arrow) submits the quotation back to the customer. You can follow the rest of the process in Figure 12-7. Allocate inventory means that if the items are available, they are allocated to the customer so that they will not be sold to someone else.

Diamonds represent decisions and usually contain a question that can be answered with yes or no. Process arrows labeled Yes and No exit two of the points of the diamond. Three of the activities in the as-is diagram contain a square with a plus (+) sign. This notation means that the activity is considered to be a subprocess of this process and that it is defined in greater detail in another diagram.

One of these three subprocesses, the Check Customer Credit subprocess, is shown in Figure 12-8. Note the role named *Customer Credit IS* in this subprocess. In fact, this role is performed entirely by an information system, although we cannot determine that fact from this diagram. Again, each role is fulfilled by some set of resources, either people or information systems or both.

Once the as-is model has been documented, that model can then be analyzed for problems or for improvement opportunities. For example, the process shown in Figure 12-7 has a serious problem. Before you continue, examine this figure and see if you can determine what the problem is.

The problem involves allocations. The Operations Manager role allocates inventory to the orders as they are processed, and the Credit Manager role allocates credit to the customer of orders in process. These allocations are correct as long as the order is accepted. However, if the order is rejected, these allocations are not freed. Thus, inventory is allocated that will not be ordered, and credit is extended for orders that will not be processed.

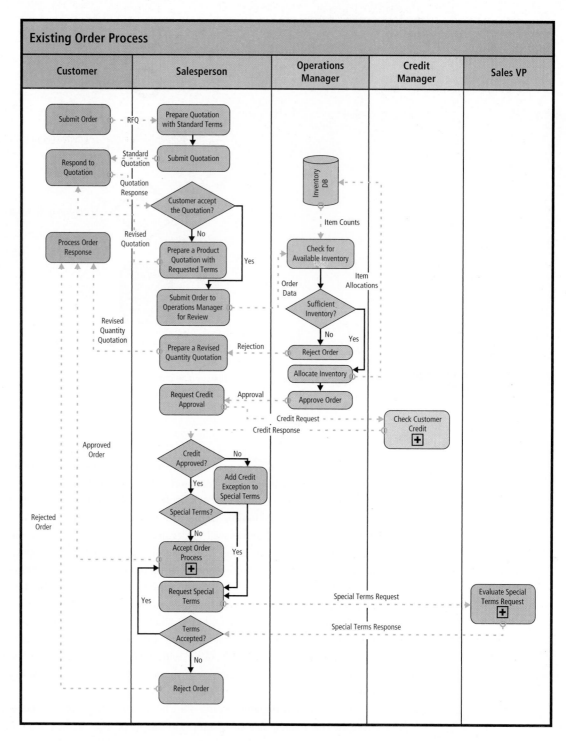

FIGURE 12-7
Existing Order Process

One fix (many are possible) is to define an independent process for Reject Order (in Figure 12-7 that would mean placing a box with a + in the Reject Order activity) and then designing the Reject Order subprocess to free allocations. Creating such a diagram is part of Exercise 12-3 in Using Your Knowledge (page 489).

Sometimes, BPMN diagrams are used to define process alternatives for discussion and evaluation. Another use is to document processes for employee training, and yet another use is to provide process requirements documentation for systems and application development. As a business professional, you may be asked to interpret and approve BPMN diagrams for any of these purposes.

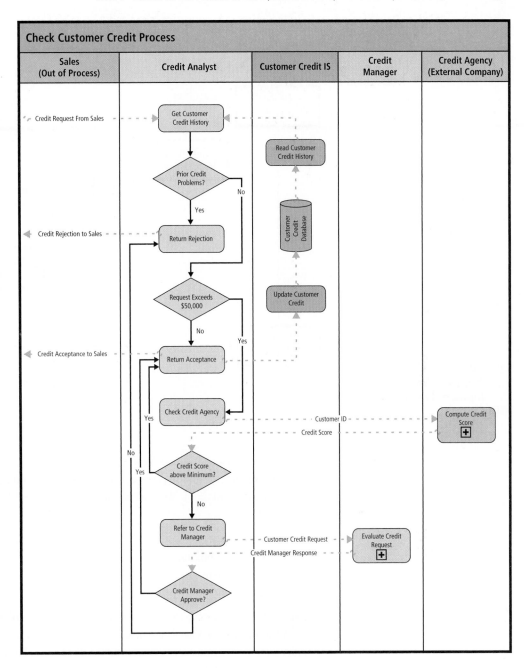

FIGURE 12-8
Check Customer Credit Process

Q12-4 What Are the Phases in the Systems Development Life Cycle (SDLC)?

The **systems development life cycle (SDLC)** is the traditional process used to develop information systems and applications. The IT industry developed the SDLC in the "school of hard knocks." Many early projects met with disaster, and companies and systems developers sifted through the ashes of those disasters to determine what went wrong. By the 1970s, most seasoned project managers agreed on the basic tasks that need to be performed to successfully build and maintain information systems. These basic tasks are combined into phases of systems development. As stated, SDLC rose to prominence when the U.S. Department of Defense required it on government contracts.

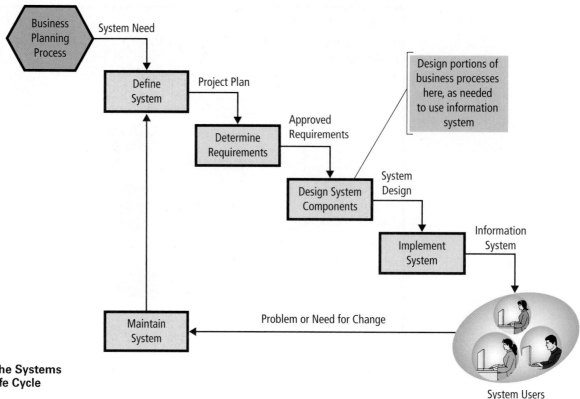

FIGURE 12-9
Five Phases of the Systems Development Life Cycle (SDLC)

Different authors and organizations package the tasks into different numbers of phases. Some organizations use an eight-phase process, others use a seven-phase process, and still others use a five-phase process. In this book, we will use the following five-phase process:

1. Define System
2. Determine Requirements
3. Design System Components
4. Implement System
5. Maintain System

Figure 12-9 shows how these phases are related. Development begins when a business-planning process identifies a need for a new system. This need may come from a BPM design activity, or it might come from some other business planning process. For now, suppose that management has determined, in some way, that the organization can best accomplish its goals and objectives by constructing a new information system.

For the potential ARES HoloLens application, Zev, the owner of the business, directs his team to create a prototype. That directive will start a systems development project.

Developers in the first SDLC phase—system definition—use management's statement of the system needs in order to begin to define the new system (for the HoloLens version of ARES, this statement is based on experience with the prototype). The resulting project plan is the input to the second phase—**requirements analysis**. Here, developers identify the particular features and functions of the new system. The output of that phase is a set of approved user requirements, which become the primary input used to design system components. In phase 4, developers implement, test, and install the new system.

Over time, users will find errors, mistakes, and problems. They will also develop new requirements. The description of fixes and new requirements is input into a system maintenance phase. The maintenance phase starts the process all over again, which is why the process is considered a cycle.

In the following sections, we will consider each phase of the SDLC in more detail.

Define the System

In response to the need for the new system, the organization will assign a few employees, possibly on a part-time basis, to define the new system, assess its feasibility, and plan the project. In a large organization, someone from the IS department leads the initial team, but the members of that initial team are both users and IS professionals. For small organizations, and for startups like ARES, the team will be led by IS-savvy managers like Henri.

Define System Goals and Scope

As Figure 12-10 shows, the first step is to define the goals and scope of the new information system. Information systems exist to facilitate an organization's competitive strategy by improving the quality of business processes. At this step, the development team defines the goal and purpose of the new system in terms of these reasons.

Consider ARES. The current system is built for a health professional, but the team wants a 3D augmented reality application for Microsoft HoloLens. What, exactly, does that mean? What kind of an application? How fancy of a user interface is needed? In broad strokes, what will the application do?

In other systems, the scope might be defined by specifying the users, or the business processes, or the organizations and healthcare providers that will be involved.

Assess Feasibility

Once we have defined the project's goals and scope, the next step is to assess feasibility. This step answers the question "Does this project make sense?" The aim here is to eliminate obviously non-sensible projects before forming a project development team and investing significant labor.

Feasibility has four dimensions: *cost, schedule, technical,* and *organizational.* Because IS development projects are difficult to budget and schedule, cost and schedule feasibility can be only an approximate, back-of-the-envelope analysis. The purpose is to eliminate any obviously infeasible ideas as soon as possible.

Cost feasibility is an assessment of whether the anticipated benefits of the system are likely to justify the estimated development and operational costs. In some cases, it also means whether the project can realistically be done within the budget provided. Clearly, costs depend on the scope of the project. Saying we're going to build a HoloLens augmented reality prototype with an interactive 3D interface doesn't provide much for the team to go on. So, at this point, all the team can do is to make rough estimates. Given those estimates, the team can then ask, "Does this project make sense? Will we obtain sufficient return to justify these estimated costs?" At ARES, Zev most likely asked for a prototype because he didn't like the $300K to $550K range for developing the full system.

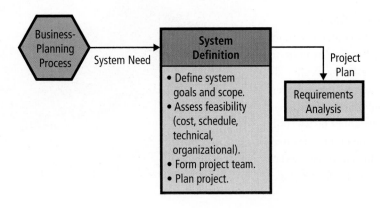

FIGURE 12-10
SDLC: System Definition Phase

ENGINEERED SLOWDOWN

Mike stared from his office into the conference room across the hallway. The glass panels partitioning off the conference room were frosted, so he couldn't determine exactly what was happening in the meeting. He could only gather that a pretty spirited discussion was taking place. Shadowy profiles of the meeting participants were standing and gesturing emphatically. The meeting had been going on for several hours, and it showed no signs of wrapping up. Mike looked at his watch and fought the urge to grimace—it was approaching 10 PM.

Mike had been working at the company—a tech startup developing tablet computers designed specifically for classroom use—for a few years. He was developing specialized software that made the graphical user interface customizable to the teaching preferences of each instructor. When he first took the job, he was extremely satisfied with the thought of innovating new tools to help teachers engage students and "cultivate the leaders of tomorrow."

However, project delays, increasing tension between the development teams, and recent growing concerns about the viability of their product among the core group of hardware engineers were creating an increasingly toxic workplace. All of these factors were beginning to make him think about seeking employment elsewhere. It had been a long week, and his eyelids began to droop. Then a sudden flurry of people coming out of the conference room brought him back into focus.

Assault and Battery

KJ exited the conference room last and headed straight to Mike's office. KJ wasn't officially the lead hardware engineer, but for all practical purposes, he was. No doubt he was brilliant, but sometimes his interactions with team members left something to be desired. Mike secretly tried to avoid KJ if at all possible. He just wasn't interested in being confronted by anyone in any situation, let alone at work; the current situation, however, was unavoidable. KJ abruptly entered the office, shut the door, and sat down.

"We need you to help us solve a problem," KJ stated slowly, while fixing Mike with an intense look. "If you can't fix this problem, the company's future is bleak, and we all may be out of a job."

KJ then explained the situation to Mike, and with each additional detail about what was going on, the company's prospects looked more and more grim. The problem was rooted in the lithium-ion batteries the company had ordered to power the first batch of tablets that were going out to 20 school districts. The testing team had noted a degradation in battery performance after a certain number of charges. The depleted battery integrity caused the tablets to shut off sporadically when resource-heavy applications were run.

The hardware team had tried a number of fixes, but none of them had prevented the device from shutting down when under stress. As KJ finished describing the problem—and all of the possible hardware solutions that had been tested and had failed—he finally told Mike what he wanted him to do.

"We need you to include some parameters in the software that slow the processing capacity of the tablet down as the battery ages. That will keep the tablets from becoming unstable and will extend the usable life of the tablets to the time frame we promised the school districts that have already signed contracts with us." He paused for a moment and then continued. "Just to be clear, if we don't resolve this somehow, our tablets will not function long enough to get us through the warranty. Further, we do not have the funds to replace all of these batteries once they start failing. We will develop a bad reputation for faulty products that we can't afford to fix, and we won't remain viable for long."

Apple Customers All Charged Up

KJ tried to assure Mike that no one would ever find out, but Mike still couldn't believe what he was hearing. He almost asked KJ why they couldn't just buy better batteries, but he knew that margins were already too thin. It really did sound like a software fix might be the only option. But it wasn't an option he wanted to think about.

Ironically, Apple was in the news for utilizing this exact same fix on its phones. When the lithium-ion batteries in iPhones started to degrade and cause problems, Apple resorted to a software fix that decreased the performance of the device. The result included apps that took longer to load and scrolling with a reduced frame rate. The changes kept the phones from becoming unstable,[1] but when Apple acknowledged the practice, there had been quite a customer backlash. Some customers even resorted to legal action against the company.[2] Critics claimed Apple was intentionally slowing down its devices so users would buy newer devices.

Mike wondered if the hardware team had come up with this idea on its own or if it was stealing a page out of Apple's playbook. Either way, Mike didn't know what to do. He wasn't happy at the company, but he certainly didn't want to lose his job right now. He didn't have anything to fall back on. He initially took this job because he liked the thought of being involved in education and developing innovative ways for kids to learn. He certainly didn't want to be complicit in duping school districts into buying a product that was intentionally flawed and would not last as long as advertised. Even worse, what if he made this fix and it subsequently came to light? Would there be a backlash similar to what Apple was going through? The thought of lawsuits being filed because of something he had done was difficult to imagine.

KJ could see the distress on his face. "Hey, look," he chimed in, "if Apple is doing this, all sorts of companies are doing things like it to eke out as much battery life in their devices as possible. I promise, if we can just get this first batch of tablets out to customers—and keep the customers happy long enough—they will never know the difference, and we will be sure to spend some of our profits investing in better batteries for the next version of the tablet!"

For a second, this sounded like a reasonable perspective, but Mike still didn't like what this meant for their customers. Mike slumped back in his chair, let out a sigh, and tried to decide what to say next.

DISCUSSION QUESTIONS

1. According to the definitions of the ethical principles previously defined in this book:
   a. Do you think intentionally slowing down a device without customers knowing is ethical according to the categorical imperative (page 23–24)?
   b. Do you think intentionally slowing down a device without customers knowing is ethical according to the utilitarian perspective (page 42–43)?
2. How would you feel if you were asked to write software that intentionally slowed down a product over time without customers knowing about it? Do you think other types of companies may be engaged in similar tactics? How would this benefit those companies?
3. Suppose the company producing the leading operating system slowly adds in more "features" that progressively increase processing power requirements (i.e., slow down the device). This would cause users to have to purchase a new device (laptop, desktop, tablet, or phone) every couple of years. How might hardware and software companies benefit from an increasingly inefficient operating system? Can you think of any other industry where something similar might be happening?
4. How could Mike justify introducing the intentional slowdown in processing power? Would you be OK calling this intentional slowdown a "feature" that increases battery life, knowing full well that it shortens the life of the device? Why?

Like cost feasibility, **schedule feasibility** is difficult to determine because it is hard to estimate the time it will take to build the system. However, if Raj and his team determine that it will take, say, no less than 6 months to develop the system and put it into operation, Henri and Zev can then decide if they can accept that minimum schedule. At this stage of the project, the organization should not rely on either cost or schedule estimates; the purpose of these estimates is simply to rule out any obviously unacceptable projects.

Technical feasibility refers to whether existing information technology is likely to be able to meet the needs of the new system. With regard to the Microsoft HoloLens prototype, the team would assess technical differences between the mobile devices it currently supports and the HoloLens. For example, can a HoloLens effectively connect to exercise equipment?

Finally, **organizational feasibility** concerns whether the new system fits within the organization's customs, culture, charter, or legal requirements. Dr. Flores, who developed the initial, medical application for ARES, did not sufficiently consider medical customs and culture. As a consequence, doctors avoided using it and he eventually had to sell the system to be used for a different purpose.

Form a Project Team

If the defined project is determined to be feasible, the next step is to form the project team. Normally the team consists of both IS professionals and user representatives. The project manager and IS professionals can be in-house personnel or outside contractors as described in Chapter 11.

Typical personnel on a development team are a manager (or managers for larger projects), business analysts, systems analysts, programmers, software testers, and users.

Systems analysts are closer to IT and are a bit more technical than business analysts, though, as stated, there is considerable overlap in their duties and responsibilities. Both are active throughout the systems development process and play a key role in moving the project through it. Business analysts work more with managers and executives; systems analysts integrate the work of the programmers, testers, and users. Depending on the nature of the project, the team may also include hardware and communications specialists, database designers and administrators, and other IT specialists.

The team composition changes over time. During requirements definition, the team will be heavy with business and systems analysts. During design and implementation, it will be heavy with programmers, testers, and database designers. During integrated testing and conversion, the team will be augmented with testers and business users.

User involvement is critical throughout the system development process. Depending on the size and nature of the project, users are assigned to the project either full or part time. Sometimes users are assigned to review and oversight committees that meet periodically, especially at the completion of project phases and other milestones. Users are involved in many different ways. *The important point is for users to have active involvement and to take ownership of the project throughout the entire development process.*

The first major task for the assembled team is to plan the project. Team members specify tasks to be accomplished, assign personnel, determine task dependencies, and set schedules.

Determine Requirements

Determining the system's requirements is the most important phase in the SDLC process. If the requirements are wrong, the system will be wrong. If the requirements are determined completely and correctly, then design and implementation will be easier and more likely to result in success.

Sources of Requirements

Examples of requirements are the contents and the format of Web pages and the functions of buttons on those pages, or the structure and content of a report, or the fields and menu choices

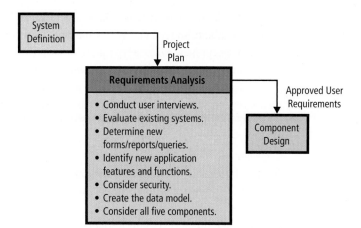

FIGURE 12-11
SDLC: Requirements Analysis Phase

in a data entry form. Requirements include not only what is to be produced, but also how frequently and how fast it is to be done. Some requirements specify the volume of data to be stored and processed.

If you take a course in systems analysis and design, you will spend weeks learning techniques for determining requirements. Here, we will just summarize that process. Typically, systems analysts interview users and record the results in some consistent manner. Good interviewing skills are crucial; users are notorious for being unable to describe what they want and need. Users also tend to focus on the tasks they are performing at the time of the interview. Tasks performed at the end of the quarter or end of the year are forgotten if the interview takes place mid-quarter. Seasoned and experienced systems analysts know how to conduct interviews to bring such requirements to light.

As listed in Figure 12-11, sources of requirements include existing systems as well as the Web pages, forms, reports, queries, and application features and functions desired in the new system. Security is another important category of requirements.

If the new system involves a new database or substantial changes to an existing database, then the development team will create a data model. As you learned in Chapter 5, that model must reflect the users' perspective on their business and business activities. Thus, the data model is constructed on the basis of user interviews and must be validated by those users.

Sometimes, the requirements determination is so focused on the software and data components that other components are forgotten. Experienced project managers ensure consideration of requirements for all five IS components, not just for software and data. Regarding hardware, the team might ask: Are there special needs or restrictions on hardware? Is there an organizational standard governing what kinds of hardware may or may not be used? Must the new system use existing hardware? What requirements are there for communications and network hardware?

Similarly, the team should consider requirements for procedures and personnel: Do accounting controls require procedures that separate duties and authorities? Are there restrictions that some actions can be taken only by certain departments or specific personnel? Are there policy requirements or union rules that restrict activities to certain categories of employees? Will the system need to interface with information systems from other companies and organizations? In short, requirements for all of the components of the new information system need to be considered.

These questions are examples of the kinds of questions that must be asked and answered during requirements analysis.

Role of a Prototype

Because requirements are difficult to specify, building a working prototype, as is being done for the ARES HoloLens application prototype, can be quite beneficial. Whereas future systems users often struggle to understand and relate to requirements expressed as word descriptions and sketches, working with a prototype provides direct experience. As they work with a prototype, users will assess usability and remember features and functions they have forgotten to mention. Additionally, prototypes provide evidence to assess the system's technical and organizational feasibility. Further, prototypes create data that can be used to estimate both development and operational costs.

To be useful, a prototype needs to work; mock-ups of forms and reports, while helpful, will not generate the benefits just described. The prototype needs to put the user into the experience of employing the system to do his or her tasks.

Prototypes can be expensive to create; however, this expense is often justified not only for the greater clarity and completeness of requirements, but also because parts of the prototype can often be reused in the operational system. Much of the code created for the HoloLens prototype at ARES can be reused for other augmented reality headset applications, if those applications are created.

Unfortunately, systems developers face a dilemma when funding prototypes; the cost of the prototype occurs early in the process, sometimes well before full project funding is available. A common complaint is "We need the prototype to get the funds, and we need the funds to get the prototype." Unfortunately, no uniform solution to this dilemma exists, except applying experience guided by intuition. Again we see the need for nonroutine problem-solving skills.

Approve Requirements

Once the requirements have been specified, the users must review and approve them before the project continues. The easiest and cheapest time to alter the information system is in the requirements phase. Changing a requirement at this stage is simply a matter of changing a description. Changing a requirement in the implementation phase may require weeks of reworking applications components and the database structure.

Design System Components

Each of the five components is designed in this stage. Typically, the team designs each component by developing alternatives, evaluating each of those alternatives against the requirements, and then selecting from among those alternatives. Accurate requirements are critical here; if they are incomplete or wrong, then they will be poor guides for evaluation.

Figure 12-12 shows that design tasks pertain to each of the five IS components. For hardware, the team determines specifications for what the system will need. (The team is not designing hardware in the sense of building a CPU or a disk drive.) Program design depends on the source of the programs. For off-the-shelf software, the team must determine candidate products and evaluate them against the requirements. For off-the-shelf with alteration programs, the team identifies products to be acquired off-the-shelf and then determines the alterations required. For custom-developed programs, the team produces design documentation for writing program code.

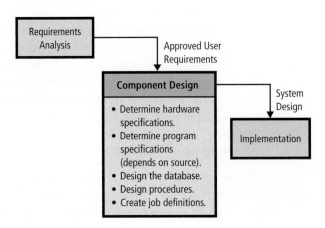

FIGURE 12-12
SDLC: Component Design Phase

If the project includes constructing a database, then during this phase database designers convert the data model to a database design using techniques such as those described in Chapter 5. If the project involves off-the-shelf programs, then little database design needs to be done; the programs will have been coded to work with a preexisting database design.

Procedure design differs, depending on whether the project is part of a BPM process or part of a systems development process. If the former, then business processes will already be designed, and all that is needed is to create procedures for using the application. If the latter, then procedures for using the system need to be developed, and it is possible that business processes that surround the system will be needed as well.

With regard to people, design involves developing job descriptions for the various roles. These descriptions will detail responsibilities, skills needed, training required, and so forth.

System Implementation

The term **implementation** has two meanings for us. It could mean to implement the information systems components only, or it could mean to implement the information system and the business processes that use the system. As you read the following task descriptions, keep in mind that the tasks can apply to both interpretations of implementation. Tasks in the implementation phase are to build and test system components and to convert users to the new system and possibly new business processes (see Figure 12-13).

Testing

Developers construct each of the components independently. They obtain, install, and test hardware. They license and install off-the-shelf programs; they write adaptations and custom programs as necessary. They construct a database and fill it with data. They document, review, and test procedures, and they create training programs. Finally, the organization hires and trains needed personnel. Once each component has been tested independently, the entire system is tested as an integrated whole.

Testing is important, time consuming, and expensive. A **test plan**, which is a formal description of the system's response to use and misuse scenarios, is written. Professional test engineers, called product quality assurance (PQA) test engineers, are hired for this task. Often, teams of these engineers are augmented by users as well.

System Conversion

Once the system has passed testing, the organization installs the new system. The term **system conversion** is often used for this activity because it implies the process of *converting* business activity from the old system to the new. Again, conversion can be to the new system only, or it can be to the new system, including new business processes.

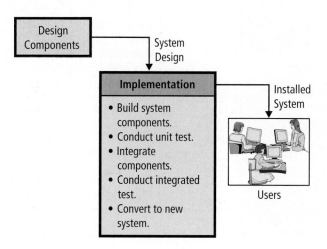

FIGURE 12-13
SDLC: Implementation Phase

Four types of conversion are possible: pilot, phased, parallel, and plunge. Any of the first three can be effective. In most cases, companies should avoid "taking the plunge"!

With **pilot installation**, the organization implements the entire system/business processes on a limited portion of the business, say, a single department. The advantage of pilot implementation is that if the system fails, the failure is contained within a limited boundary.

As the name implies, with **phased installation** the new system/business processes are installed in phases across the organization(s). Once a given piece works, then the organization installs and tests another piece of the system, until the entire system has been installed. Some systems are so tightly integrated that they cannot be installed in phased pieces. Such systems must be installed using one of the other techniques.

With **parallel installation**, the new system/business processes run parallel with the old one until the new system is tested and fully operational. Parallel installation is expensive because the organization incurs the costs of running both the existing and the new system/business processes. Users must work double-time, if you will, to run both systems. Then considerable work is needed to reconcile the results of the new with the old.

The final style of conversion is **plunge installation** (sometimes called *direct installation*). With it, the organization shuts off the old system/business processes and starts the new one. If the new system/business processes fail, the organization is in trouble: Nothing can be done until either the new system/business processes are fixed or the old ones are reinstalled. Because of the risk, organizations should avoid this conversion style if possible. The one exception is if the new system is providing a new capability that will not disrupt the operation of the organization if it fails.

Figure 12-14 summarizes the tasks for each of the five components during the design and implementation phases. Use this figure to test your knowledge of the tasks in each phase.

Maintain System

Sometimes maintenance updates can be harmful to consumers; see the Ethics Guide on pages 462–463.

With regard to information systems, **maintenance** is a misnomer; the work done during this phase is either to *fix* the system so that it works correctly or to *adapt* it to changes in requirements.

Figure 12-15 shows tasks during the maintenance phase. First, there needs to be a means for tracking both failures[3] and requests for enhancements to meet new requirements. For small systems, organizations can track failures and enhancements using word processing documents.

FIGURE 12-14
Design and Implementation for the Five Components

	Hardware	Software	Data	Procedures	People	
Design	Determine hardware specifications.	Select off-the-shelf programs. Design alterations and custom programs as necessary.	Design database and related structures.	Design user and operations procedures.	Develop user and operations job descriptions.	
Implementation	Obtain, install, and test hardware.	License and install off-the-shelf programs. Write alterations and custom programs. Test programs.	Create database. Fill with data. Test data.	Document procedures. Create training programs. Review and test procedures.	Hire and train personnel.	Unit test each component
Integrated Test and Conversion						

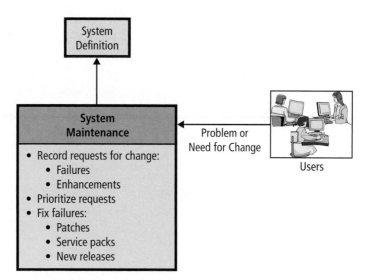

FIGURE 12-15
SDLC: System Maintenance Phase

As systems become larger, however, and as the number of failure and enhancement requests increases, many organizations find it necessary to develop a tracking database. Such a database contains a description of the failure or enhancement. It also records who reported the problem, who will make the fix or enhancement, what the status of that work is, and whether the fix or enhancement has been tested and verified by the originator.

Typically, IS personnel prioritize system problems according to their severity. They fix high-priority items as soon as possible, and they fix low-priority items as time and resources become available.

Because an enhancement is an adaptation to new requirements, developers usually prioritize enhancement requests separate from failures. The decision to make an enhancement includes a business decision that the enhancement will generate an acceptable rate of return.

Q12-5   What Are the Keys for Successful SDLC Projects?

SDLC projects are difficult to manage. In this question we will consider five keys to success:

- Create a work breakdown structure.
- Estimate time and costs.
- Create a project plan.
- Adjust the plan via trade-offs.
- Manage development challenges.

Create a Work Breakdown Structure

The key strategy for SDLC projects is to divide and conquer. Most such projects are too large, too complicated, and the duration too long to attempt to manage them as one piece. Instead, successful project managers break the project into smaller and smaller tasks until each task is small enough to estimate and to manage. Every task should culminate in one or more results called **deliverables**. Examples of deliverables are documents, designs, prototypes, data models, database designs, working data entry screens, and the like. Without a defined deliverable, it is impossible to know if the task was accomplished.

Tasks are interrelated, and to prevent them from becoming a confusing morass, project teams create a **work breakdown structure (WBS)**, which is a hierarchy of the tasks required to complete a project. The WBS for a large project is huge; it might entail hundreds or even thousands of tasks. Figure 12-16 shows the WBS for the system definition phase for a typical IS project.

```
System definition
1.1              Define goals and scope
                 1.1.1              Define goals
                 1.1.2              Define system boundaries
                 1.1.3              Review results
                 1.1.4              Document results
1.2              Assess feasibility
                 1.2.1              Cost
                 1.2.2              Schedule
                 1.2.3              Technical
                 1.2.4              Organizational
                 1.2.5              Document feasibility
                 1.2.6              Management review and go/no-go decision
1.3              Plan project
                 1.3.1              Establish milestones
                 1.3.2              Create WBS
                                    1.3.2.1              Levels 1 and 2
                                    1.3.2.2              Levels 3+
                 1.3.3              Document WBS
                                    1.3.3.1              Create WBS baseline
                                    1.3.3.2              Input to Project
                 1.3.4              Determine resource requirements
                                    1.3.4.1              Personnel
                                    1.3.4.2              Computing
                                    1.3.4.3              Office space
                                    1.3.4.4              Travel and Meeting Expense
                 1.3.5              Management review
                                    1.3.5.1              Prepare presentation
                                    1.3.5.2              Prepare background documents
                                    1.3.5.3              Give presentation
                                    1.3.5.4              Incorporate feedback into plan
                                    1.3.5.5              Approve project
1.4              Form project team
                 1.4.1              Meet with HR
                 1.4.2              Meet with IT Director
                 1.4.3              Develop job descriptions
                 1.4.4              Meet with available personnel
                 1.4.5              Hire personnel
```

FIGURE 12-16
Example Work Breakdown Structure (WBS)

In Figure 12-16, the overall task, *System definition*, is divided into *Define goals and scope*, *Assess feasibility*, *Plan project*, and *Form project team*. Each of those tasks is broken into smaller tasks until the work has been divided into small tasks that can be managed and estimated.

Estimate Time and Costs

As stated, it is exceedingly difficult to determine duration and labor requirements for many development tasks. Fred Brooks[4] defined software as "logical poetry." Like poetry, software is not made of wood or metal or plastic; it is pure thought-stuff. Some years ago, when a seasoned software developer was pressed for a schedule, he responded by asking, "What would Shakespeare have said if someone asked him how long it would take him to write *Hamlet?*" Another popular rejoinder is, "What would a fisherman say if you ask him how long it will take to catch three fish? He doesn't know, and neither do I."

Organizations take a variety of approaches to this challenge. One is to avoid scheduling problems altogether and never develop systems and software in-house. Instead, they license packages, such as ERP systems, that include both business processes and information systems components. As stated in Chapter 8, even if the vendor provides workable processes, those processes will need to be integrated into the business. However, the schedule risk of integration activities is far less than those for developing processes, programs, databases, and other components.

But what if no suitable package exists? In this case, companies can admit the impossibility of scheduling a date for the completion of the entire system and take the best result they can get.

Only the loosest commitments are made regarding the date of complete and final system functionality. Project sponsors dislike this approach because they feel like they are signing a blank check, and in fact, they are. But this approach doesn't treat fictional estimates and schedules as if they were real, which may be the only other alternative.

The third approach is to attempt to schedule the development project in spite of all the difficulties. Several different estimation techniques can be used. If the project is similar to a past project, the schedule data from that past project can be used for planning. When such similar past projects exist, this technique can produce quality schedule estimates. If there is no such past project, managers must make the best estimates they can. For computer coding, some managers estimate the number of lines of code that will need to be written and apply industry or company averages to estimate the time required. Other coding estimation techniques exist; visit *http://sunset.usc.edu/csse/research/ COCOMOII/cocomo_main.html*. Of course, lines of code and other advanced techniques estimate schedules only for software components. The schedules for processes, procedures, databases, and the other components must be estimated using different methods.

Create a Project Plan

A project plan is a list of WBS tasks, arranged to account for task dependencies, with durations and resources applied. Some tasks cannot be started or finished until other tasks are completed. You can't, for example, put electrical wires in a house until you've built the walls. You can define task dependencies in planning software such as Microsoft Project, and it will arrange the plan accordingly.

Given dependencies, estimates for task duration and resource requirements are then applied to the WBS to form a project plan. Figure 12-17 shows the WBS as input to Microsoft Project, with task dependencies and durations defined. The display, called a **Gantt chart**, shows tasks, dates, and dependencies.

The user has entered all of the tasks from the WBS and has assigned each task a duration. She has also specified task dependencies, although the means she used are beyond our discussion. The two red arrows emerging from task 4, *Define system boundaries*, indicate that neither the *Review results* task nor the *Assess feasibility* task can begin until *Define system boundaries* is completed. Other task dependencies are also shown; you can learn about them in a project management class.

The **critical path** is the sequence of activities that determine the earliest date by which the project can be completed. Reflect for a moment on that statement: The *earliest date* is the date determined by considering the *longest path* through the network of activities. Paying attention to task dependencies, the planner will compress the tasks as much as possible. Those tasks that cannot be

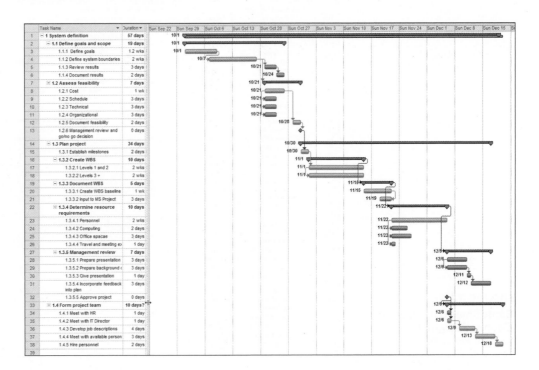

FIGURE 12-17

Gantt Chart of the WBS for the Definition Phase of a Project

Source: Windows 10, Microsoft Corporation.

further compressed lie on the critical path. Microsoft Project and other project-planning applications can readily identify critical path tasks.

Figure 12-17 shows the tasks on the critical path in red. Consider the first part of the WBS. The project planner specified that task 4 cannot begin until 2 days before task 3 ends. (That's the meaning of the red arrow emerging from task 3.) Neither task 5 nor task 8 can begin until task 4 is completed. Task 8 will take longer than tasks 5 and 6, and so task 8—not tasks 5 or 6—is on the critical path. Thus, the critical path to this point is tasks 3, 4, and 8. You can trace the critical path through the rest of the WBS by following the tasks shown in red, though the entire WBS and critical path are not shown.

Using Microsoft Project or a similar product, it is possible to assign personnel to tasks and to stipulate the percentage of time that each person devotes to a task. Figure 12-18 shows a Gantt chart for which this has been done. The notation means that Eleanore works only 25 percent of the time on task 3; Lynda and Richard work full time. Additionally, one can assign costs to personnel and compute a labor budget for each task and for the overall WBS. One can assign resources to tasks and use Microsoft Project to detect and prevent two tasks from using the same resources. Resource costs can be assigned and summed as well.

Managers can use the critical path to perform critical path analysis. First, note that if a task is on the critical path, and if that task runs late, the project will be late. Hence, tasks on the critical path cannot be allowed to run late if the project is to be delivered on time. Second, tasks not on the critical path can run late to the point at which they would become part of the critical path. Hence, up to a point, resources can be taken from noncritical path tasks to shorten tasks on the critical path. **Critical path analysis** is the process by which project managers compress the schedule by moving resources, typically people, from noncritical path tasks onto critical path tasks.

Adjust Plan via Trade-Offs

The project plan for the entire project results in a finish date and a total cost. In our experience in more than a dozen major development projects, the first response to a completed project plan is always "Good heavens! No way! We can't wait that long or pay that much!" And our experience is not unusual.

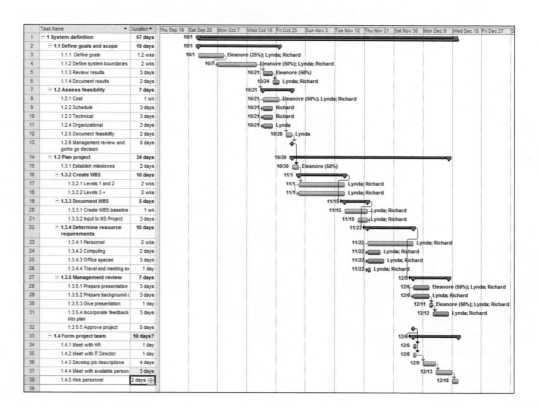

FIGURE 12-18
Gantt Chart with Resources (People) Assigned

Source: Windows 10, Microsoft Corporation.

Thus, the first response to a project plan is to attempt to reduce time and costs. Reductions can be made, but not out of thin air. An old adage in planning development projects is "Believe your first number." Believe what you have estimated before your desires and wishes cloud your judgment.

So, how can schedules and costs be responsibly reduced? By considering trade-offs. A **trade-off** is a balancing of three critical factors: requirements, cost, and time. To understand this balancing challenge, consider the construction of something relatively simple—say, a piece of jewelry, such as a necklace, or the deck on the side of a house. The more elaborate the necklace or the deck, the more time it will take. The less elaborate, the less time it will take. Further, if we embellish the necklace with diamonds and precious gems, it will cost more. Similarly, if we construct the deck from old crates, it will be cheaper than if we construct it of clear-grained, prime Port Orford cedar.

We can summarize this situation as shown in Figure 12-19. We can *trade off* requirements against time and against cost. If we make the necklace simpler, it will take less time. If we eliminate the diamonds and gems, it will be cheaper. The same trade-offs exist in the construction of anything: houses, buildings, ships, furniture, *and* information systems.

The relationship between time and cost is more complicated. Normally, we can reduce time by increasing cost *only to a point*. For example, we can reduce the time it takes to produce a deck by hiring more laborers. At some point, however, there will be so many laborers working on the deck that they will get in one another's way, and the time to finish the deck will actually increase. At some point, adding more people creates **diseconomies of scale**, the situation that occurs when adding more resources creates inefficiencies. A famous adage in the software industry is **Brooks' Law** (named for the Fred Brooks discussed earlier), which states that adding more people to a late project makes it later. This occurs, in part, because new team members need to be trained by existing team members, who must be taken off productive tasks.

In some projects, we can reduce costs by increasing time. If, for example, we are required to pay laborers time-and-a-half for overtime, we can reduce costs by eliminating overtime. If finishing the deck—by, say, Friday—requires overtime, then it may be cheaper to avoid overtime by completing the deck sometime next week. This trade-off is not always true, however. Extending the project interval means that we need to pay labor and overhead for a longer period; thus, adding more time can also increase costs.

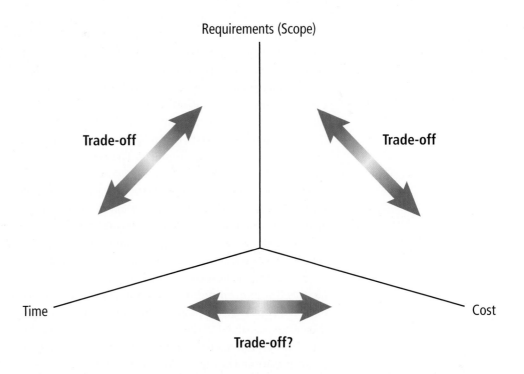

FIGURE 12-19
Primary Drivers of Systems Development

Consider how these trade-offs pertain to information systems. We specify a set of requirements for the new information system, and we schedule labor over a period of time. Suppose the initial schedule indicates the system will be finished in 3 years. If business requirements necessitate the project be finished in 2 years, we must shorten the schedule. We can proceed in two ways: reduce the requirements or add labor. For the former, we eliminate functions and features. For the latter, we hire more staff or contract with other vendors for development services. Deciding which course to take will be difficult and risky.

Using trade-offs, the WBS plan can be modified to shorten schedules or reduce costs. But they cannot be reduced by management fiat.

Manage Development Challenges

Given the project plan and management's endorsement and approval, the next stage is to do it. The final WBS plan is denoted as the **baseline WBS**. This baseline shows the planned tasks, dependencies, durations, and resource assignments. As the project proceeds, project managers can input actual dates, labor hours, and resource costs. At any point in time, planning applications can be used to determine whether the project is ahead of or behind schedule and how the actual project costs compare to baseline costs.

However, nothing ever goes according to plan, and the larger the project and the longer the development interval, the more things will violate the plan. Four critical factors need to be considered:

1. Coordination
2. Diseconomies of scale
3. Configuration control
4. Unexpected events

Development projects, especially large-scale projects, are usually organized into a variety of development groups that work independently. Coordinating the work of these independent groups can be difficult, particularly if the groups reside in different geographic locations or different countries. An accurate and complete WBS facilitates coordination, but no project ever proceeds exactly in accordance with the WBS. Delays occur, and unknown or unexpected dependencies develop among tasks.

The coordination problem is increased because software, as stated, is just thought-stuff. When constructing a new house, electricians install wiring in the walls as they exist; it is impossible to do otherwise. No electrician can install wiring in the wall as designed 6 months ago, before a change. In software, such physical constraints do not exist. It is entirely possible for a team to develop a set of application programs to process a database using an obsolete database design. When the database design was changed, all involved parties should have been notified, but this may not have occurred. Wasted hours, increased cost, and poor morale are the result.

Another problem is diseconomies of scale. The number of possible interactions among team members rises exponentially with the number of team members. Ultimately, no matter how well managed a project is, diseconomies of scale will set in.

As the project proceeds, controlling the configuration of the work product becomes difficult. Consider requirements, for example. The development team produces an initial statement of requirements. Meetings with users produce an adjusted set of requirements. Suppose an event then occurs that necessitates another version of requirements. After deliberation, assume the development team decides to ignore a large portion of the requirements changes resulting from the event. At this point, there are four different versions of the requirements. If the changes to requirements are not carefully managed, changes from the four versions will be mixed up, and confusion and disorder will result. No one will know which requirements are the correct, current ones.

Similar problems occur with designs, program code, database data, and other system components. The term **configuration control** refers to a set of management policies, practices, and tools that developers use to maintain control over the project's resources. Such resources include documents, schedules, designs, program code, test suites, and any other shared resource needed to complete the project. Configuration control is vital; a loss of control over a project's configuration is so expensive and disruptive that it can result in termination for senior project managers.

The last major challenge to large-scale project management is unexpected events. The larger and longer the project, the greater the chance of disruption due to an unanticipated event. Critical people can change companies; even whole teams have been known to pack up and join a competitor. A hurricane may destroy an office; the company may have a bad quarter and freeze hiring just as the project is staffing up; technology will change; competitors may do something that makes the project more (or less) important; or the company may be sold and new management may change requirements and priorities.

Because software is thought-stuff, team morale is crucial. Author David Kroenke once managed two strong-headed software developers who engaged in a heated argument over the design of a program feature. The argument ended when one threw a chair at the other. The rest of the team divided its loyalties between the two developers, and work came to a standstill as subgroups sneered and argued with one another when they met in hallways or at the coffee pot. How do you schedule that event into your WBS? As a project manager, you never know what strange event is heading your way. Such unanticipated events make project management challenging but also incredibly fascinating!

Q12-6 How Can Scrum Overcome the Problems of the SDLC?

The systems development life cycle (SDLC) process is falling out of favor in the systems development community, primarily for two reasons. First, the nature of the SDLC denies what every experienced developer knows to be true: systems requirements are fuzzy and always changing. They change because they need to be corrected, or more is known, or users change their minds about what they want after they use part of the system, or business needs change, or technology offers other possibilities.

According to the SDLC, however, progress goes in a linear sequence from requirements to design to implementation. Sometimes this is called the **waterfall method** because the assumption is that once you've finished a phase, you never go back; you go over the waterfall into the pool of the next stage. Requirements are done. Then you do design. Design is done; then you implement. However, experience has shown that it just doesn't work that way.

In the beginning, systems developers thought the SDLC might work for IS and applications because processes like the SDLC work for building physical things. If you're going to build a runway, for example, you specify how long it needs to be, how much airplane weight the surface must support, and so forth. Then you design it, and then you build it. Here waterfall processes work.

However, business processes, information systems, and applications are not physical; as stated, they're made of thought-stuff. They're also social; they exist for people to inform themselves and achieve their goals. But people and social systems are incredibly malleable; they adapt. That characteristic enables humans to do many amazing things, but it also means that requirements change and the waterfall development process cannot work.

The second reason that the SDLC is falling out of favor is that it is very risky. The people for whom the system is being constructed cannot see what they have until the very end. At that point, if something is wrong, all the money and time has already been spent. Furthermore, what if, as frequently happens, the project runs out of money or time before it is completed? The result is a form of management blackmail in which the developers say, "Well, it's not done yet, but give us another $100,000 and another 6 months, and *then* we'll have it done." If management declines, which it might because at that point, the time and money are sunk, it is left not only with the loss but also with the unmet need that caused it to start the SDLC in the first place.

In short, the SDLC assumes that requirements don't change, which everyone who has ever been within 10 feet of a development project knows is false, and it's very risky for the business that sponsors it.

If you are a sports fan, you know that nothing is more gratifying than watching your team come back from a deficit to win. In sports, it's not uncommon to see professional teams that are down 3–1 or 3–0 in a four-game series turn the tide and snatch victory from the jaws of defeat. But have you ever heard of a team on the verge of defeat winning eight consecutive matches for the overall series win? In what is considered by some to be the most prolific comeback in sports history, Oracle Team USA won eight consecutive days of sailing against the Royal New Zealand Yacht Squadron to win the 34th America's Cup in 2013 (the final series tally was 9–8). You may be wondering what contributed to Oracle Team USA turning the tide. Many people think that the key to its triumph was in the data.

Oracle Team USA leveraged an impressive network of sensors and data analytics tools to help it achieve victory. During each race, more than 300 sensors were used to collect roughly 3,000 variables about the performance of the boat.[5] Data for everything, from the strain on the mast to angle sensors on the wings, were captured, stored, and analyzed.[6] These data were transmitted to support teams nearby and to the sailors on the boat who could monitor key performance indicators in real time by looking at devices strapped to their wrists.

Immediate access to these analytics during the race allowed for better strategic decision making as well as opportunities for the support team servicing the boat to make modifications to the vessel between races. While the overall victory of Oracle Team USA was incredible, it is more profound to consider how sensor technologies and the ability to rapidly transmit, store, and analyze large data sets have redefined countless operations and industries. Welcome to the growing world of the Internet of Things (IoT)!

If You Can't Take the IoT, Get Out of the Kitchen

IoT is generally defined as the proliferation of Internet-connected devices. As more smart devices are connected to the Internet, increasing amounts of data are captured and transmitted by these devices. The potential impact of the IoT is tremendous. It's estimated that there will be roughly 25 billion Internet-connected devices by 2020.[7] As seen in the Oracle Team USA sailing example, having access to more data can result in more efficient processes and better decision making. But what does the IoT mean for business? Could IoT devices change the way businesses operate? Could they fundamentally change the way financial transactions are processed?

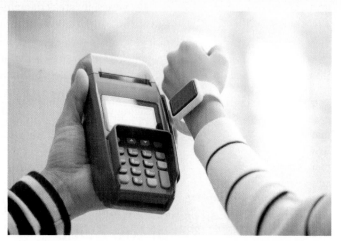

Source: Ryanking999/Fotolia

A hotbed of innovation for the IoT is the home kitchen. This is because kitchens are typically filled with a variety of appliances that are already plugged in and have embedded computers (of varying degrees of complexity). The cost of adding Wi-Fi connectivity to any of these devices is trivial, yet doing so can enhance functionality (e.g., you can start the coffee maker from bed by using an app on your phone).

Refrigerators are often considered prime targets for the IoT. Internet connectivity could allow remote viewing of fridge contents (in case you forget your shopping list at home when you go to the store) or tracking of items as they are consumed and need to be replenished. Could a smart refrigerator recognize that you are low on vegetables or fruit and automatically order replacement groceries? Could it complete the financial transaction for you—autonomously?

Banking institutions are starting to see the potential impact of IoT devices on their industry. They are interested in becoming the managers of these automated transactions that will be conducted by IoT devices, especially when you consider the potential for loyalty programs and rewards points to be paired with these transactions.[8] Imagine how the magnitude of financial transactions will change over the next decade if instead of making one or two payments at a grocery store each week your debit or credit card is being charged several times a day as various ingredients and foodstuffs run low and your appliances are reordering groceries for you. Now expand the scope to other appliances or even other parts of the home (e.g., 30 percent of the hangers on a rack in your closet are missing, so your IoT closet notifies a dry-cleaning service to come pick up your dirty shirts).

IoT = Winning

It is important to recognize that the IoT not only will revolutionize transactions for private consumers, but it will also change how businesses manage their transactions, loans, and other financial operations. For example, when a business takes out a loan, there is a declaration of some form of collateral. Or when a business is calculating balance sheets, inventories are assessed and reported. In manufacturing and agricultural industries, inventories of products or livestock could be tracked in real time, allowing financial statements to be current at all times,[9] not just when inventories are tallied and official statements are produced.

At an even higher level, as inventories of raw materials or trading goods are placed on ships and are transported around the world to various partners in a supply chain, these materials can be tracked in real time. So whether you are trying to win a race on a sailboat or win a race to get your products manufactured and delivered on time, in the high-tech business environment we are living in today, IoT can be invaluable to helping you win!

Questions

1. Sports are one area in which the collection and analysis of data have had a huge impact on how teams manage personnel and strategize during games. Take a minute to list or brainstorm all of the different types of data and analysis that could be useful in improving decisions for sports teams.

2. The article looked at the enhanced functionality that could come from a smart refrigerator with Internet connectivity. Can you identify any potential drawbacks or complications that may arise from this connectivity?

3. Take a minute to think about your home or apartment. What types of things would you like to see connect to the Internet? How would this connectivity make your life better or more efficient?

4. What are the potential pitfalls of drastically *increasing* the number of financial transactions you or a company is responsible for in a given period of time (e.g., buying groceries or raw materials in very small quantities)?

What Are the Principles of Agile Development Methodologies?

Over the past 40 years, numerous alternatives to the SDLC have been proposed, including *rapid application development*, the *unified process, extreme programming, scrum*, and others. All of these techniques addressed the problems of the SDLC, and by the turn of the last century, their philosophy had coalesced into what has come to be known as **agile development**, which means a development process that conforms to the principles in Figure 12-20.

Traditionally, agile development was thought to be done by small organizations, working on small projects. However, a 2018 study by VersionOne Inc. noted that this trend has reversed. For example, in 2006, nearly two-thirds of respondents worked for organizations with less than 100 people. By 2017, more than 65 percent of respondents worked for organizations with more than 1,000 people, and more than 28 percent worked for organizations with more than 20,000 people, as shown in Figure 12-21.[10]

Scrum is an agile methodology and conforms to the principles shown in Figure 12-20. While other agile methodologies are used, shown in Figure 12-22, more than 58 percent of agile projects use the scrum methodology.[11]

The first way in which scrum and the other agile techniques differ from the SDLC is that they expect and even welcome change. Given the nature of social systems, *expect* is not a surprise, but why *welcome*? Isn't welcoming requirements change a bit like welcoming a good case of the flu? No, because systems are created to help organizations and people achieve their strategies, and the

FIGURE 12-20
Principles of Agile (Scrum) Development

- Expect, even welcome, changes in requirements.
- Frequently deliver *working* version of the product.
- Work closely with customer for the duration.
- Design as you go.
- Test as you go.
- Team knows best how it's doing/how to change.
- Can be used for business processes, information systems, and applications development.

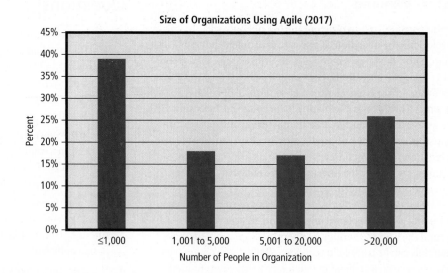

FIGURE 12-21
Size of Organizations Using Agile (2017)

more the requirements change, the closer they come to facilitating strategies. The result is better and more satisfying for both the users and the development team.

Second, scrum and other agile development processes are designed to frequently deliver a *working* version of some part of the product. Frequently means 1 to 8 weeks, not longer. This frequency means that management is at risk only for whatever costs and time have been consumed in that period. And, at the end of the period, they will have some usable product piece that has at least some value to the business.

Thus, unlike the SDLC, agile techniques deliver benefits early and often. The initial benefits might be small, but they are positive and increase throughout the process. With the SDLC, no value is generated until the very end. Considering the time value of money, this characteristic alone makes agile techniques more desirable.

The third principle in Figure 12-20 is that the development team will work closely with the customer until the project ends. Someone who knows the business requirements must be available to the development team and must be able and willing to clearly express, clarify, and elaborate on requirements. Also, customers need to be available to test the evolving work product and provide guidance on how well new features work.

The fourth principle is a tough one for many developers to accept. Rather than design the complete, overall system at the beginning, only those portions of the design that are needed to complete the current work are done. Sometimes this is called **just-in-time design**. Designing in

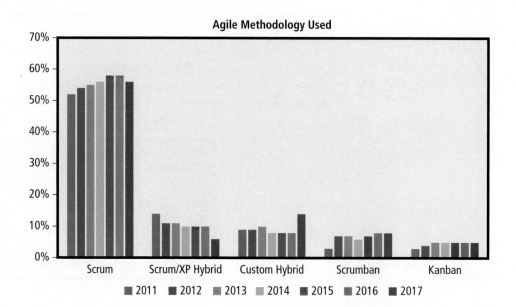

FIGURE 12-22
Agile Methodology Used

this way means that the design is constantly changing, and existing designs may need to be revised, along with substantial revision to the work product produced so far. On the surface, it is inefficient. However, experience has shown that far too many teams have constructed elaborate, fanciful, and complete designs that turned out to be glamorous fiction as the requirements changed.

Test as you go, the next principle, is obvious if the team is going to be delivering working versions. Testing is initially conducted among members of the team but involves the business customer as well.

Development teams know how well they're doing. You could go into any development environment today and ask the team how it's doing and, once team members understood you were not about to inflict a new management program on them, you would find they know their strengths, weaknesses, bottlenecks, and process problems quite well. That principle is part of agile development methodologies. At the end of every deliverable or some other (short) milestone, the team meets to assess how it's doing and how it can improve.

Finally, agile development methodologies are generic. They can be applied to the creation of business processes, information systems, and applications. They are applicable to other team projects as well, but that subject is beyond the scope of this text.

What Is the Scrum Process?

Scrum is an agile development methodology developed by Ken Schwaber and Jeff Sutherland[12] and extended by others over the past 15 years. *Scrum* is a rugby term and was first used for teamwork in a *Harvard Business Review* article written by Hirotaka Takeuchi and Ikujiro Nonaka.[13] In rugby, a *scrum* is a gathering of a team into a circle to restart play after a foul or other interruption. Think of it as a huddle in American football.

Scrum Essentials

As stated, scrum is one type of agile development process having the specific characteristics shown in Figure 12-23. First, the process is driven by a prioritized list of requirements that is created by the users and business sponsors of the new system. Scrum work periods can be as short as 1 week but, as with all agile processes, never longer than 8. Two to 4 weeks is recommended. Each work period, the team selects the top priority items that it will commit to delivering that period. Each workday begins with a **stand-up**, which is a 15-minute meeting in which each team member[14] states:

- What he or she has done in the past day
- What he or she will do in the coming day
- Any factors that are blocking his or her progress

- Requirements list drives process
- Each work period (1 to 4–8 weeks):
  - Select requirements to consider
  - Determine tasks to perform—select requirements to deliver
  - Team meets daily for 15 min (stand-up)
    - What I did yesterday
    - What I'm going to do today
    - What's blocking me
  - Test frequently
  - Paired work possible
  - Minimal documentation
  - Deliver (something) that works
  - Evaluate team's work process at end of period (and say thanks)
- Rinse and repeat until
  - Customer says we're done
  - Out of time
  - Out of money
- Three principal roles
  - Product owner (business professional who represents customer)
  - Scrum master
  - Team members (7±2 people)

FIGURE 12-23
Scrum Essentials

The purpose of the stand-up is to achieve accountability for team members' progress and to give a public forum for blocking factors. Oftentimes one team member will have the expertise to help a blocked team member resolve the blocking issue.

Testing is done frequently, possibly many times per day. Sometimes the business owner of the project is involved in daily testing as well. In some cases, team members work in pairs; in **paired programming**, for example, two team members share the same computer and write a computer program together. Sometimes, one programmer will provide a test, and the other will either demonstrate that the code passes that test or alter the code so that it will. Then the two members switch roles. Other types of paired work are possible as well.

Minimal documentation is prepared. The result of the team's work is not design or other documents but, rather, a working version of the requirements that were selected at the start of the scrum period.

At the end of the scrum period, the working version of the product is delivered to the customer, who can, if desired, put it to use at that time, even in its not-fully-finished state. After the product is delivered, the team meets to evaluate its own process and to make changes as needed. Team members are given an opportunity to express thanks and receive recognition for superior work at these meetings. (Review the criteria for team success in Chapter 7, and you will see how scrum adheres to the principles of a successful team.)

Figure 12-24 summarizes the scrum process.

When Are We Done?

Work continues in a repeating cycle of scrum periods until one of three conditions is met:

- The customer is satisfied with the product created and decides to accept the work product, even if some requirements are left unsatisfied.
- The project runs out of time.
- The project runs out of money.

Unlike the SDLC, if a scrum project terminates because of time or budget limitations, the customer will have some useful result for the time and money expended. It may not be the fully functioning version that was desired, but it is something that, assuming requirements are defined and prioritized correctly, can generate value for the project sponsors.

How Do Requirements Drive the Scrum Process?

Scrum is distinguished from other agile development methodologies, in part, by the way that it uses requirements to drive planning and scheduling. First, requirements are specified in a particular manner. One common format is to express requirements in terms of *who* does *what* and *why*.

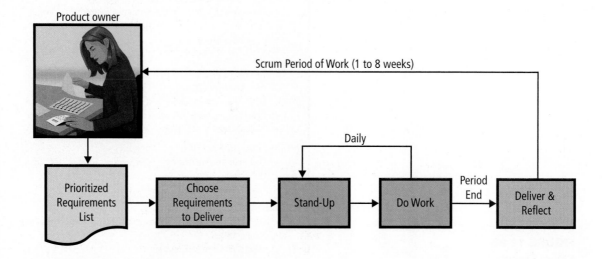

FIGURE 12-24
Scrum Process

For example, in the doctor's version of the ARES system, a requirement was expressed as:

"As a doctor, I want to view a patient's exercise records so I can make sure he is not doing too much."

Or,

"As a doctor, I want to view a patient's exercise records so I can make sure she is following her prescription."

Each of these requirements specifies who (the doctor) does what (view a patient's exercise data) and why (make sure she is following her prescription). It's not surprising that the requirement includes *who* and *what*, but the need for *why* may surprise you. The purpose of the why clause of the requirement is to set a context for the value that will be delivered by the requirement. Including it increases the likelihood that the product will deliver business value and not just blindly meet the requirement.

As stated, the product owner creates requirements and prioritizes them. For example, one of the two preceding requirements will be judged higher in importance than the other. All other things being equal, the team will satisfy the higher priority requirement first. This means, too, that if the project runs out of time or money, the highest priority requirements will have been completed first.

Creating Requirements Tasks

Given a requirement, the team meets to create tasks that must be accomplished to meet that requirement. In Figure 12-24, this work is done in the *Choose requirements to deliver* activity.

Figure 12-25 shows eight tasks that need to be done to accomplish an example requirement. In the *Choose requirements to deliver* activity, tasks for additional requirements that might also be implemented in this scrum period are created.

Tasks are created in a team meeting because the team as a whole can iterate and allow members to give feedback. One team member will think of a task that needs to be done, of which other members are not aware. Or the team member will realize that a particular task is incomplete, or is doable in some other way, or doesn't really need to be done.

Scheduling Tasks

As described so far, scrum is a good idea, one of many agile processes that might be used. What makes scrum particularly innovative, however, is the way that tasks are scheduled.

Scrum methodology recognizes that developers are terrible, even wretched, at determining how long a task will take. However, developers are quite good at determining how long something will take in comparison to something else. So, while a developer may be poor at estimating the time required to do, say, Task 2 in Figure 12-25, he or she will likely be accurate when saying that Task 2 will take twice as long as Task 1, or some other ratio.

So, according to the scrum process, once the tasks are known for a given set of requirements, the next step is to assign each task a difficulty score, called *points*. The easiest task has a point score of 1. A task that will take five times longer is given a point score of 5, etc. For reasons that are beyond

FIGURE 12-25

Example Requirement and Tasks

Requirement:
"As a doctor, I want to view the patient's exercise records so I can make sure she is following her prescription."

Tasks:
1. Authenticate the doctor.
2. Obtain patient identifying data from doctor.
3. Determine this doctor is authorized to view this patient's records.
4. Read the database to obtain exercise records.
5. Read the database to obtain most recent prescription record.
6. Format the data into a generic format.
7. Determine the type of mobile device the doctor is using.
8. Format the generic report into a report for that mobile device.

1. Team assigns 1 point to simplest task.
2. Times to deliver working tasks are compared to each other and assigned points (points are Fibonacci numbers). Use:
   a. Team estimation
   b. Planning poker
   c. Other
3. Using past experience, team computes its velocity … number of points it can accomplish per scrum period.
4. Working with product owner, team selects tasks for the upcoming scrum period, constrained by its velocity.

FIGURE 12-26
Summary of Scrum Estimation Techniques

the scope of this discussion, points are expressed in values from a sequence of integers known as the Fibonacci sequence: {1, 2, 3, 5, 8, 13, 21, 34, 55, 89, 144, and ?}. The question mark is used because any number larger than 144 is meaningless. Most likely 89 and 144 are meaningless as well. Tasks with such large point scores need to be subdivided into multiple requirements. When all tasks have received points, the points are summed to a total for the requirement.

Scrum includes several different techniques for assigning points. Team estimation and planning poker are two. You can learn more about them in *The Elements of Scrum*.[15] The gist of these techniques is to obtain team scores by applying the team's expertise in an iterative, feedback-generating process.

Committing to Finish Tasks

As teams work together, they will learn the total number of points of work they can accomplish each scrum period. That term is called the team's **velocity**. The team uses its velocity to determine how many requirements it can commit to accomplishing in the next scrum period. Of course, during the first period, the team will not know its velocity. In that case, senior members will need to make a guess. That guess may be far off, but it will get better as the team gains experience. Unlike the SDLC, there is at least well-founded hope that, over time, estimating will improve.

Suppose the five requirements on a team's prioritized requirements list total 125 points. If a team knows its velocity is 100 points per scrum period, it knows it cannot do all five. However, if the top four total, say, 80 points, it can commit to doing those four, plus something else. In this case, the team would go back to the product owner and ask if there is a requirement lower on the priority list that can be done for the available 20 points of capacity. This estimation technique is summarized in Figure 12-26.

Hocus-Pocus?

If you haven't participated in software or systems development, this process may sound like so much hocus-pocus. However, it has two very important characteristics that make it not so. First, scrum is a methodology that incorporates team iteration and feedback for scheduling and tasking, which, as you know by now, is a way for a team to create something together that exceeds what each member can do individually. Second, scrum provides a framework for process learning. As a team works more and more scrum periods together, it learns better and better how to assign points, and it learns more and more what its true velocity is.

But scrum isn't a magic bullet. It can't guarantee that the project will produce a high quality product, on time, and under budget. But, as an alternative to the traditional SDLC, it can limit potential financial losses and produce substantial results in just a few weeks.

Q12-7 2029?

By 2029, the way information systems are developed will have changed. In fact, it is already changing. Artificial intelligence (AI), machine learning, and deep neural networks are reshaping the way enterprise systems are developed. From a user's perspective, it will appear that information systems are being "trained" rather than "created." But why is this shift occurring?

Well, it's because machines are faster and more accurate than humans when it comes to certain tasks. Writing code for a calculator that does basic addition and subtraction is easy. The mathematical rules are straightforward. Write several lines of code and you're done. Developers who make this type of software *create* it line by line.

But what if the task is less clear—more abstract. For example, it is much more difficult to write software that can identify a specific face, translate content from one language to another, or determine which news stories are relevant to individual users. These types of applications are increasingly relevant and profitable. Developers are solving these types of problems via machine learning by *training* the system to make decisions that lead to the correct outcome. They don't *create* code for it.

Fetch!

Take Microsoft's new Fetch! application as an example (*www.what-dog.net*). The application takes any image and identifies the correct dog breed. That sounds simple enough. But how would you program that? Microsoft developers used machine learning to *train* Fetch! to identify the correct dog breed.

Developers kept giving Fetch! images of different dogs and told it when it correctly identified the correct dog breed. And Fetch! learned. It created the complex algorithms that it uses to analyze images. If the developers open up the application, they see an indecipherable set of mathematical equations that are constantly changing. They can't understand the code because it's not code in the traditional sense.

Identifying dog breeds is fun, but so what? Well, consider what will happen when AI and machine learning are applied to robotics, drones, self-driving cars, and 3D printing. Employees in accounting, manufacturing, finance, sales, and IS will all *train* a system to help them with their job—or do their job. Systems will, with help from their human partners, become their own developers.

Will all coding jobs go away? No, of course not. But software developers will become more like architects rather than builders.

User-Driven Systems

What does this mean for you as a business user? Well, you will be involved in a systems development project in the next 10 years. That's a near certainty. Software runs the world. Your current employer depends on software to keep making money. Your future employer will become even more dependent on these new types of applications. Even now, Facebook uses machine learning to determine stories in your News Feed, Google uses it to identify faces, and Microsoft Skype uses it to translate between languages.[16]

All management grads are going to play strong roles in developing new systems as well as managing the projects. You grew up using systems with great user experience (UX) designed into them. This experience will enable you to help create a closer alignment between processes and IS and business strategy, goals, and objectives. And later, you won't sit in your C-level job and complacently leave systems development to others.

Industry Will Push Change

That's it! You've reached the end of this text. Take a moment to consider how you can help your career by developing your personal brand, as described in the Career Guide on pages 486–487.

Finally, between now and 2029, the nature of the industry will change. First, as you learned in Chapter 5, the NoSQL DBMS products were not developed by existing DBMS vendors. They were developed by organizations that had unique needs and that developed software to meet those needs. The DBMS vendors caught on after the fact. In the next 10 years, we will see similar stories repeated again and again.

Software vendors will find ways to make their solutions more agile using SOA and Web services, and as a result, systems and processes will be more agile and better able to adapt to changing needs. New systems will come online fast, and the limiting factor will be humans' ability to cope. Business professionals have a key role in solving those coping problems.

In the end, user involvement will be the key to the success of systems development. Systems will depend on users to train them. Users will know how to create successful user interfaces. And users will be the ones to solve previously unknown problems. You as a business user will be the one to make a difference.

SECURITY GUIDE

IOT AND MIRAI

How many devices are connected to the Internet in your home or apartment? The answer may surprise you. It is hard to believe that most American households had just a single desktop computer with an Internet connection only 10 to 20 years ago (if they had computer or Internet access at all). Since then, the fulfillment of Moore's Law and Metcalfe's Law and increases in bandwidth have been catalysts for the proliferation of Internet-connected devices everywhere.

It is not uncommon today to walk into an average home to find dozens of devices connected to the Internet, including desktops, laptops, tablets, phones, game consoles, media-streaming devices, smart TVs, smart speakers, home safety devices (e.g., alarm systems, security cameras, smoke detectors, and video doorbells), baby monitors, AI assistants, appliances, and more. In addition to the core functionality of these devices, many are designed to interoperate with other Internet-connected devices to create systems and "systems of systems." This ecosystem of connected devices, which can communicate and interoperate without human intervention, is often referred to as the Internet of Things (IoT).

IoT, Not Securi-T

Companies developing IoT products have to create devices in such a way that they can communicate efficiently with other devices without requiring complex configuration. Early adopters aren't the only ones buying IoT devices; these products have become more mainstream, meaning that most IoT consumers lack the technical skills needed to troubleshoot problems. Subsequently, IoT devices are often designed with security as an afterthought rather than a priority. Each additional layer of security in an IoT device can slow its development and, eventually, its time to market.

As a result, IoT devices are another example of the trade-off between security and convenience (e.g., requiring a 50-character password for your online bank account is secure, but consumers won't tolerate the inconvenience of typing in 50 characters every time that they want to check their account balance). The only overt security feature of many IoT devices is the username and password needed to access/manage the settings for the device. However, users often neglect to create new credentials when setting up devices, which can create serious vulnerabilities.

In fact, because owners often neglect to create new passwords for their devices, hackers have identified IoT devices as prime targets for the purpose of creating massive botnets of zombies (a device with an Internet connection that has been compromised by a hacker). These botnets can then be used as part of a large coordinated denial-of-service (DoS) attack. Many DoS attacks are relatively minor in scale, and most larger organizations have the countermeasures in place to stave off these attacks. However, a group of three hackers recently took botnets and DoS attacks to an entirely new level.

Meet Mirai

A college student at Rutgers University, along with two other people, developed a piece of malware that specifically targeted IoT devices to create a botnet. The initial purpose of the botnet was to give the hackers an advantage when playing the popular game Minecraft. In essence, the botnet allowed the hackers to disrupt the connection of an opponent during a game and boot them offline, resulting in a victory over that opponent. However, the hackers were so savvy in the creation of the malware, named Mirai, that the size of the botnet grew to an unprecedented level. Mirai infected tens of thousands of devices in its first few hours and then doubled in size every hour until it reached about 600,000 infections.[17]

Source: JIRAROJ PRADITCHAROENKUL/Alamy Stock Photo

Upon recognizing the power of the digital monster they had created, the hackers worked to increase the sophistication of the botnet, and a number of attacks were launched at a variety of targets. When law enforcement agencies began ramping up their investigation, the hackers published their code online, a strategy often used to weaken claims about the identities of malware creators. However, posting the code online had much more of an impact than simply creating a smoke screen. Competing hacking groups started using the code to create their own botnets. Over the next 5 months, there were more than 15,000 Mirai-related DoS attacks.[18]

Even though the three original hackers were ultimately caught and pleaded guilty, the code lives on, and it's anyone's guess how long the code will be employed for nefarious purposes. The best bet for citizens is to change the passwords on IoT devices to ensure those devices are not a part of the next big botnet attack!

DISCUSSION QUESTIONS

1. Take a few minutes to think about your home network and your connected devices. How many IoT devices do you have? Have you created new credentials for each of them to ensure that they are not vulnerable? How might attackers gain access to these devices?

2. Think about your daily interactions with technology. Think of three other examples demonstrating the trade-off between security and convenience (besides the use of a long password as described in the article).

3. Why would IoT devices make good targets for attackers?

4. The hackers were able to avoid jail time for their actions. Do you think their direct disruption of numerous sites and companies' digital operations should have resulted in more serious penalties? How should the legal system apply penalties for the creation of malware that will continue to live on in spite of the hackers being caught and maybe even feeling sorry for their actions?

CAREER GUIDE

DEVELOPING YOUR PERSONAL BRAND

In the previous chapters, you read firsthand accounts from real people who have made successful careers in MIS. These unfiltered accounts explained how these people got their jobs, what attracted them to the field, what a typical workday looks like, and what they like most about their jobs. You also learned the kinds of skills and education necessary to do well in these types of jobs.

Now that you have completed this book, you also have a sense of what MIS is all about. You know the main content areas, understand the terminology, and have heard from real people who work in the field. Hopefully, this has given you a realistic view of MIS careers. If you are interested in such a career or even if you're going into another field, it's important to learn how to develop your personal brand.

Professionals use social media, such as LinkedIn, to build their personal brand. You may be too young, too inexperienced, and not yet unique enough to have a personal brand, but, then again, maybe not. And even if now isn't the right time to build a personal brand, you will need to have, build, and maintain your personal brand at some point in the future if you want to be a business leader.

So, what is "building a personal brand"? It's not embarrassing self-promotion. It's not self-advertising, and it's not a résumé of your recent experience. It is, instead, the means by which you conduct authentic relationships with the market for your talents and abilities. That market might be your professional colleagues, your employer, your fellow employees, your competition, or anyone who cares about what you care about.

As a business professional, how do you create authentic relationships that are less transactional and more personal? You start by realizing that the people who consume your services are not just bosses and colleagues, but rather full-fledged human beings with the rich stew of complexity that all humans have. With this idea in mind, can you use social media to transform your relationships from being transactional in nature to being more personal?

Such a transformation is possible but difficult. You don't want to share every detail of your personal life on LinkedIn or your professional blog. Few readers will care about your vacation in the Bahamas. However, they might want to know what you read while lying on the beach, why you read it, and what you learned from it—or perhaps how disappointed you were about what you didn't learn. But your report has to be authentic.

If you're reading Kierkegaard or Aristotle for the purpose of showing erudition on your personal blog, you missed the point. But if Kierkegaard has something interesting to say about the ethics of the latest business scandal that affects your professional interests, many readers who share those interests may want to know. And they will then have a way to approach you on a common interest. That common interest may lead to an exciting new job opportunity, or maybe it will lead to a fulfilling new relationship, or maybe it will go nowhere. You never know.

When engaging in personal branding efforts, always be guided by your personal strategy. Consider Figure 2-12 again in light of your personal competitive strategy. What is your personal competitive advantage? Why would someone choose you, your expertise, or your work products over others? Then, with answers to these questions in mind, start building your personal brand. Again, be sure your efforts focus on creating authentic relationships and not on shameless advertising.

Source: Anatolii Babii/Alamy Stock Photo

Realize, too, that a strong personal brand is essential to some careers. For example, if you want to be an independent consultant, say, an expert on privacy and control for cloud data storage, you'll need to invest considerable time developing and maintaining your professional brand. But whether or not it's essential, having a strong personal brand is an asset in any field, in any job. And you can be sure that if you don't have a good personal brand, one of your competitors will.

DISCUSSION QUESTIONS

1. Using your own words, define and describe a personal brand.
2. Describe how you could use social media (like LinkedIn) to make an existing professional contact more personal in nature while still maintaining your privacy.
3. Pick a contemporary topic of interest in your major field of study. For example, if you're an operations major, pick something like 3D printing. (Read question 4, however, before you pick.)
   a. Search the Web for opinions about the realities, contemporary uses, big issues and problems, or other interesting dimensions of your topic.
   b. Find two or three experts in that topic, and go to their professional brand sites. That brand might be a blog, a Web page, a collection of articles, an SM site on Facebook or LinkedIn, or some other public statement of their professionalism.
   c. Which of the sites is the best? Explain why you think so.

4. Suppose you become an expert in the topic you used in your answer to question 3. Think about your experiences in the past year that relate to that topic. It could be experiences in class, out of class with fellow students, or in conversations with roommates. It could be something that happened at your job at McDonald's. Whatever.
   a. Make a list of 10 such experiences.
   b. Describe how you could use social media, including blogs, to present five of the best of those 10 experiences in a way that helps build your professional brand.
5. Reflect on your answers to questions 1–4.
   a. Do you think having a personal brand is important for you? Explain why or why not. (The answer to this question may not be yes, and for good reasons.)
   b. What was the most difficult task for you when formulating your answers to question 4?
   c. Summarize what you have learned from this exercise about how you might get more value from your college experiences.

ACTIVE REVIEW

Use this Active Review to verify that you understand the ideas and concepts that answer the chapter's study questions.

Q12-1 How are business processes, IS, and applications developed?

Using your own words, explain the differences among business processes, information systems, and applications. State the components of each. Using the terminology from Chapter 5, describe the relationship of business processes and IS. Name three development processes and state which processes are used for the development of business processes, information systems, and applications. Explain the primary roles of business and systems analysts.

Q12-2 How do organizations use business process management (BPM)?

State the definition of business process used in this chapter and define *roles*, *resources*, and *data flows*. Explain three reasons why business processes need to be managed. Describe the need for BPM and explain why it is a cycle. Name the four stages of the BPM process and summarize the activities in each. Define *as-is model*. Explain the role of COBIT.

Q12-3 How is business process modeling notation (BPMN) used to model processes?

Explain the need for a process documentation standard. Describe swim-lane layout. Explain each of the symbols in Figures 12-7 and 12-8 and describe the relationship of these two diagrams. Describe the problems in the process in Figure 12-7 and suggest one solution. Name three uses for BPMN diagrams.

Q12-4 What are the phases in the systems development life cycle (SDLC)?

Describe the origins of the SDLC and how it came to prominence. Name five basic systems development activities. Describe tasks required for the definition, requirements, and design steps. Explain the tasks required to implement a system and describe four types of system conversion. State specific activities for each of the five components during the design and implementation stages. Explain why the term *maintenance* is a misnomer when applied to information systems; state tasks performed during systems maintenance.

Q12-5 What are the keys for successful SDLC projects?

Name five keys for successful development projects. Explain the purpose of a work breakdown structure. Summarize the difficulties of development estimation and describe three ways of addressing it. Explain the elements in the Gantt chart in Figure 12-17. Define *critical path* and explain critical path analysis. Summarize requirements, cost, and schedule trade-offs. List and explain four critical factors for development project management.

Q12-6 How can scrum overcome the problems of the SDLC?

Explain two reasons that the SDLC is falling out of favor. In your own words, explain the meaning and importance of each of the principles in Figure 12-20. Explain how each of the scrum essential items in Figure 12-23 is implemented in the scrum process shown in Figure 12-24. Name three elements in a scrum requirement. Describe what is unique about the way that scrum determines the time required to accomplish a task. Define *velocity* and explain how it is used in scheduling. Explain how scrum provides a framework for process learning.

Q12-7 2029?

Describe how machine learning will change systems development projects. Using Microsoft Fetch! as an example, explain why "training" will be an integral part of systems development. Explain why you will be involved in systems development projects during your professional career. How does the knowledge of your generation of businesspeople influence systems development? Explain why systems will be more easily adapted.

Using Your Knowledge with ARES

Henri, Ashley, and even Zev need to know the basics of development processes, which to use for what, and the advantages of using the SDLC and scrum. Before spending any money, they need to understand the difficulties and risks of developing processes, IS, and applications, particularly inter-enterprise systems, such as ARES.

At some point in your career, you will need this knowledge as well.

KEY TERMS AND CONCEPTS

Agile development   477
Application   450
As-is model   455
Baseline WBS   474
Brooks' Law   473
Business analyst   452
Business process   453
Business process management
   (BPM)   455
Business Process Modeling Notation
   (BPMN)   456
COBIT (Control Objectives for Informa-
   tion and related Technology)   455
Configuration control   474
Control flow   453
Cost feasibility   461

Critical path   471
Critical path analysis   472
Data flow   453
Deliverables   469
Diseconomies of scale   473
Gantt chart   471
Implementation   467
Just-in-time design   478
Maintenance   468
Object Management Group (OMG)   456
Organizational feasibility   464
Paired programming   480
Parallel installation   468
Phased installation   468
Pilot installation   468
Plunge installation   468

Requirements analysis   460
Resources   453
Roles   453
Schedule feasibility   464
Stand-up   479
Swim-lane layout   456
System conversion   467
Systems analyst   452
Systems development life cycle
   (SDLC)   459
Technical feasibility   464
Test plan   467
Trade-off   473
Velocity   482
Waterfall method   475
Work breakdown structure (WBS)   469

MyLab MIS

To complete the problems with MyLab MIS, go to EOC Discussion Questions in the MyLab.

USING YOUR KNOWLEDGE

12-1. *MyLab MIS* Search Google or Bing for the phrase *what is a business analyst*. Investigate several of the links that you find and answer the following questions:
  a. What are the primary job responsibilities of a business analyst?
  b. What knowledge do business analysts need?
  c. What skills/personal traits do business analysts need?

12-2. *MyLab MIS* Search Google or Bing for the phrase *what is a systems analyst*. Investigate several of the links that you find and answer the following questions:
  a. What are the primary job responsibilities of a systems analyst?
  b. What knowledge do systems analysts need?
  c. What skills/personal traits do systems analysts need?
  d. Would a career as a systems analyst be interesting to you? Explain why or why not.
  e. Using your answers to this question and to question 12-1, compare and contrast the jobs of business and systems analyst.

12-3. *MyLab MIS* Using your own experience and knowledge, create a process diagram for a Reject Order activity that would fix the allocation problem in the as-is order process in Q12-3. Use Visio 2016 and the standard BPMN shapes, if possible. Explain how your process fixes the allocation problem.

12-4. Choose an important project type in a business discipline of interest to you. In accounting it could be an audit; in marketing it could be a plan for using social media; in operations, it could be a project of opening a new warehouse. Choose a major activity that is important and that you find interesting. Compare and contrast the use of a process such as the SDLC to using a process such as scrum for your project. Which process would you recommend? Justify your recommendation.

12-5. Reread the opening vignette in Chapter 11. Explain how Henri and Raj could use a scrum process for managing Sandeep. Describe how doing so would reduce the risk of failure.

COLLABORATION EXERCISE 12

Using the collaboration IS you built in Chapter 1 (page 32), collaborate with a group of students to answer the following questions.

Wilma Baker, Jerry Barker, and Chris Bickel met in June 2018 at a convention of resort owners and tourism operators. They sat next to each other by chance while waiting for a presentation; after introducing themselves and laughing at the odd sound of their three names, they were surprised to learn that they managed similar businesses. Wilma Baker lives in Santa Fe, New Mexico, and specializes in renting homes and apartments to visitors to Santa Fe. Jerry Barker lives in Whistler Village, British Columbia, and specializes in renting condos to skiers and other visitors to the Whistler/Blackcomb Resort. Chris Bickel lives in Chatham, Massachusetts, and specializes in renting homes and condos to vacationers to Cape Cod.

The three agreed to have lunch after the presentation. During lunch, they shared frustrations about the difficulty of obtaining new customers, especially given the numerous travel opportunities available via the Internet today. Further, the rise in value of the dollar over the euro has created substantial competition for North American tourism.

As the conversation developed, they began to wonder if there was some way to combine forces (i.e., they were seeking a competitive advantage from an alliance). So, they decided to skip one of the next day's presentations and meet to discuss ways to form an alliance. Ideas they wanted to discuss further were sharing customer data, developing a joint reservation service, and exchanging property listings.

As they talked, it became clear they had no interest in merging their businesses; each wanted to stay independent. They also discovered that each was very concerned, even paranoid, about protecting their existing customer base from poaching. Still, the conflict was not as bad as it first seemed. Barker's business was primarily the ski trade, and winter was his busiest season; Bickel's business was mostly Cape Cod vacations, and she was busiest during the summer. Baker's high season was the summer and fall. So, it seemed there was enough difference in their high seasons that they would not necessarily cannibalize their businesses by selling the others' offerings to their own customers.

The question then became how to proceed. Given their desire to protect their own customers, they did not want to develop a common customer database. The best idea seemed to be to share data about properties. That way they could keep control of their customers but still have an opportunity to sell time at the others' properties.

They discussed several alternatives. Each could develop her or his own property database, and the three could then share those databases over the Internet. Or they could develop a centralized property database that they would all use. Or they could find some other way to share property listings.

Because we do not know Baker, Barker, and Bickel's detailed requirements, you cannot develop a plan for a specific system. In general, however, they first need to decide how elaborate an information system they want to construct. Consider the following two alternatives:

a. They could build a simple system centered on email. With it, each company sends property descriptions to the others via email. Each independent company then forwards these descriptions to its own customers, also using email. When a customer makes a reservation for a property, that request is then forwarded back to the property manager via email.

b. They could construct a more complex system using a Web-based, shared database that contains data on all their properties and reservations. Because reservations tracking is a common business task, it is likely that they can license an existing application with this capability.

In your answers to 12-6 and 12-7, use Microsoft Visio and BPMN templates to construct your diagram. If you don't have those templates, use the cross-functional and basic flowchart templates. If you do not have access to Visio, use PowerPoint instead.

12-6. Create a process diagram for alternative a, using Figure 12-8 as a guide. Each company will need to have a role for determining its available properties and sending emails to the other companies that describe them. They will also need to have a role for receiving emails and a role for renting properties to customers. Assume the companies have from three to five agents who can fulfill these roles. Create a role for the email system if you think it is appropriate. Specify roles, activities, repositories, and data flows.

12-7. Create a process diagram for alternative b, using Figure 12-8 as a guide. Each company will need to have a role for determining its available properties and adding them to the reservation database. They will also need a role for renting properties that accesses the shared database. Assume the companies have from three to five agents who can fulfill these roles. Create a role for the property database application. Specify roles, activities, repositories, and data flows.

12-8. Compare and contrast your answers in questions 12-6 and 12-7. Which is likely to be more effective in generating rental income? Which is likely to be more expensive to develop? Which is likely to be more expensive to operate?

12-9. If you were a consultant to Baker, Barker, and Bickel, which alternative would you recommend? Justify your recommendation.

When Will We Learn?

When David Kroenke, one of the authors of this text, was teaching at Colorado State in 1974, he participated in a study that investigated the primary causes of information systems development failures. The findings? The number one reason for failure was a lack of user involvement in creating and managing system requirements.

Technology has made enormous strides since that study. In 1974, computers consumed large rooms, and neither the minicomputer nor the personal computer had been invented. Alas, the development of information systems has not kept up; in fact, one can argue that nothing has changed.

Consider Case Study 8 (pages 330–332). The state of Oregon wasted more than $248M attempting to develop an information system to support its healthcare exchange. And very early in the project, Maximus Company, an independent consulting firm that had been hired to provide quality assurance, warned that requirements were vague, changing, and inconsistent. Those warnings made no difference. Why?

Why Are Requirements Not Managed?

In 1974, it might have been that managers were computer illiterate and thus couldn't know how to manage requirements. However, everyone involved in Cover Oregon has a cell phone and probably an iPad or Kindle, so they are hardly computer illiterate. So today, at least, computer literacy isn't the problem.

Does the problem of *managing requirements* lie with *management?* Or with *requirements?* In Case Study 8, you learned that Access CT, the Connecticut healthcare project, succeeded. Was it because the project was closely managed by the lieutenant governor? A woman with future political ambitions? Oregon has no lieutenant governor, but surely there was someone to manage the project. One indication of management problems in Oregon is that the information system was to be used by one healthcare agency (Cover Oregon) but developed by a different healthcare agency (Oregon Health Administration). The two agencies fought battles over requirements. Due to lack of senior-level management, not only were requirements unmanaged, they were fought over by two competing governmental agencies.

That might be the prime cause for Cover Oregon's failure. But is there something else? Even in well-managed organizations, is there something about requirements that makes them hard to manage? Fred Brooks provided one insight when he said that software is logical poetry. It's made of pure thought-stuff. If two governmental agencies were to construct a building and if they fought over, say, how many stories that building was to have, then their disagreement would be visible for all to see. People would notice one group of contractors adding a floor while another group is tearing it down.

So part of the problem is that the requirements are requirements for pure thought-stuff. But what else?

How do you know if the requirements are complete? If the blueprints for a building don't include any provisions for electrical systems, that omission is obvious. Less so with software and systems. For example, what if no one considers the need to do something when a client forgets his username or password and has no record of policy numbers? Software or procedures need to be developed for this situation, but if no one thinks to specify that requirement, then nothing will be done. The system will fail when such a client need appears.

And how do you know the quality of the requirements statements? A requirement like "Select a qualifying insurance policy for this client" is written at such a high level that it is useless. One of the reasons for building a prototype is to flush out missing and incomplete requirements.

Assess Feasibility and Make Trade-offs

But there's more we can learn from this example. All of the state and federal healthcare exchanges needed to be operating by October 1, 2013. So, the schedule was fixed with no chance for an adjustment. Considering cost, while funds were not fixed, they were not easily changed. The states initially provided some funding, as did the U.S. government. Once those financial allocations were made, it was difficult to obtain more money. Not impossible, but difficult.

Examine Figure 12-19 again. If schedule is fixed and if funding is nearly fixed, what is the one factor that can be traded off to reduce project difficulty and risk? The requirements. Reduce them to the bare minimum and get the system running. Then, after some success, add to the project. That seems to be the strategy that Access CT followed.

But this principle exposes another of the problems in Oregon. It wanted everything. It embarked on a policy called "No Wrong Door,"[19] a policy that would leave no person nor problem behind. Cover Oregon should provide a solution for all. Such statements make wonderful political messaging, but if the schedule is fixed and the funding is nearly so, how are those goals to be accomplished? Tell your roommate that you have 1 week between semesters and nearly no money and you plan to take a first-class, 2-month jungle excursion in Africa. Hello? Anyone home?

Software and systems are made of pure thought-stuff. Easy to imagine a glorious future of amazing capability. But they are constructed by costly human labor, and nine women can't make a baby in 1 month. Remember that sentence when you are asked to help determine requirements for your new information system.

Will this case still be relevant 40 years from now? It's up to you and your classmates.

QUESTIONS

12-10. Describe three reasons why cases like this will remain relevant 40 years from now. Describe three developments that could make these cases obsolete. Which will pertain? Will such cases be relevant 40 years from now? Justify your opinion.

12-11. Read the Executive Summary of the First Data report located at *http://portlandtribune.com/documents/artdocs/00003481205618.pdf*. Applying your knowledge about the SDLC, describe what you think are the three major reasons that Cover Oregon failed.

12-12. In Case Study 8 (pages 330–332), you learned that three vendors had been considered as outside contractors, but two of them bowed out of the competition. Describe three reasons that they may have done so.

12-13. The project was known to be in trouble, but it seemed to have a life of its own. Ying Kwong, a technology analyst at Oregon's Department of Administrative Services, said in May 2013 that the Cover Oregon project reminded him of the science fiction movie *The Blob*: "You simply don't know how to shoot this beast, because it does not have a known anatomy with the normal vital organs that make it tick."[20] Had you been a senior manager at Cover Oregon, what would you have done when the problems became apparent?

12-14. In a June 2014 survey, a majority of Oregonians held Governor Kitzhaber responsible.[21] But in 2015 Kitzhaber was reelected to a historic fourth term. Unfortunately, a month later he resigned amid an unrelated influence-peddling scandal.[22] Bruce Goldberg, former head of OHA and acting head of Cover Oregon, was fired on March 18, 2014, and continued to draw a full salary until July 18.[23] Given these results, does it seem likely that anyone will bear the consequences for these mistakes? Consider who that might be.

MyLab MIS

Go to the Assignments section of your MyLab to complete these writing exercises.

12-15. Assume that your company has just licensed a cloud-based SaaS CRM system. Your boss asks you what needs to be done to make it operational. Using the SDLC, summarize on one page the work to do to transform that SaaS into a working IS.

12-16. Suppose you work for a medium-sized oil and natural gas company as a systems developer. The CEO is interested in developing an application that will give him information about the amount of natural gas passing through pumping stations located around North America. He wants it to work on his desktop, iPad, and smartphone. The features he wants on the application seem to change every time you talk with him, and you're still in the planning phase. Now he's asked for a schedule. Why might it be difficult to develop a schedule for this project? How would you explain this to the CEO? Describe a metaphor you could use to explain how difficult it will be to accurately predict when the application will be completed.

ENDNOTES

1. Shara Tibken, "Apple's iPhone Slowdown: Your Questions Answered," *CNET*, April 2, 2018, *https://www.cnet.com/news/apple-is-slowing-down-older-iphones-batteries-faq/*.
2. Michelle Toh, "Global Backlash Spreads over Apple Slowing Down iPhones," *CNNTech*, April 2, 2018, *http://money.cnn.com/2018/01/12/technology/apple-iphone-slow-battery-lawsuit/index.html*.
3. A *failure* is a difference between what the system does and what it is supposed to do. Sometimes, you will hear the term *bug* used instead of failure. As a future user, call failures *failures* because that's what they are. Don't have a *bugs list*; have a *failures list*. Don't have an *unresolved bug*; have an *unresolved failure*. A few months of managing

an organization that is coping with a serious failure will show you the importance of this difference in terms.
4. Fred Brooks was a successful executive at IBM in the 1960s. After retiring from IBM, he authored a classic book on IT project management called *The Mythical Man-Month*. Published by Addison-Wesley in 1975, the book is still pertinent today and should be read by every IS manager. It's informative and quite enjoyable to read as well.
5. Asim Khan, "5 Ways Big Data Won the America's Cup for Ainslie and Oracle Team USA," *RealBusiness.co.uk*, September 27, 2013, accessed June 20, 2018, *http://realbusiness.co.uk/article/24276-5-ways-bigdata-won-the-americas-cup-for-ainslie-and-oracle-team-usa*.

6. Ibid.

7. Christoffer O. Hernaes, "Banks Should Prepare for the Internet of Things," *TechCrunch.com*, November 10, 2015, accessed June 20, 2018, *http://techcrunch.com/2015/11/10/banks-should-prepare-for-the-internet-of-things*.

8. Penny Crosman, "Why the Internet of Things Should Be a Bank Thing," *American Banker*, November 19, 2015, accessed June 20, 2018, *www.americanbanker.com/news/bank-technology/why-theinternet-of-things-should-be-a-bank-thing-1077911-1.html*.

9. Christoffer O.Hernaes, "Banks Should Prepare for the Internet of Things," *TechCrunch*, November 10, 2015, accessed June 20, 2018, *https://techcrunch.com/2015/11/10/banks-should-prepare-for-the-internet-of-things*.

10. VersionOne, "12th Annual State of Agile™ Report," *VersionOne.com*, April 9, 2018, accessed June 20, 2018, *http://stateofagile.versionone.com*.

11. Ibid.

12. Scrum Inc., the Creators of Scrum, Ken Schwaber and Jeff Sutherland, *Scrum.org*, November 7, 2017, accessed June 20, 2018, *www.scrum.org/resources/creators-scrum-ken-schwaber-and-jeff-sutherland-update-scrum-guide-0*.

13. Hirotaka Takeuchi and Ikujiro Nonaka, "New New Product Development Game," *Harvard Business Review*, January 1, 1986. Available for purchase at *http://hbr.org*.

14. Some scrum teams have the rule that only *pigs* can speak at stand-ups. The term comes from the joke about the difference between eggs and ham: The chicken was involved, but the pig was committed.

15. Sims and Johnson, *The Elements of Scrum*, pp. 125–133.

16. Jason Tanz, "The Rise of Artificial Intelligence and the End of Code," *Wired*, May 17, 2016, accessed June 20, 2018, *www.wired.com/2016/05/the-end-of-code*.

17. Garrett M. Graff, "How a Dorm Room Minecraft Scam Brought Down the Internet," *Wired*, December 13, 2017, *www.wired.com/story/mirai-botnet-minecraft-scam-brought-down-the-internet/*.

18. Ibid.

19. Maria L. La Ganga, "Oregon Dumps Its Broken Healthcare Exchange for Federal Website," *Los Angeles Times*, April 15, 2014, accessed June 20, 2018, *www.latimes.com/nation/politics/politicsnow/la-pn-oregondrops-broken-healthcare-exchange-20140425-story.html*.

20. Nick Budnick, "Cover Oregon: Health Exchange Failure Predicted, but Tech Watchdogs' Warnings Fell on Deaf Ears," *The Oregonian*, January 18, 2014, accessed June 20, 2018, *www.oregonlive.com/health/index.ssf/2014/01/cover_oregon_health_exchange_f.html*.

21. Hillary Lake, "Exclusive Poll: Majority Holds Kitzhaber Accountable for Cover Oregon Failure," *KATU News*, June 12, 2014, accessed June 20, 2018, *http://katu.com/news/local/exclusive-poll-majority-holds-kitzhaber-accountable-for-cover-oregon-failure*.

22. Rob Davis, "Oregon Governor John Kitzhaber Resigns amid Criminal Investigation, Growing Scandal," *OregonLive.com*, February 13, 2015, accessed June 20, 2018, *www.oregonlive.com/politics/index.ssf/2015/02/gov_john_kitzhaber_resigns_ami.html*.

23. Nick Budnick, "Long After Announced 'Resignation,' Ex-Cover Oregon Director Bruce Goldberg Draws $14,425 Monthly Salary," *The Oregonian*, May 21, 2014, accessed June 20, 2018, *www.oregonlive.com/politics/index.ssf/2014/05/long_after_publicized_resignat.html*.

THE INTERNATIONAL DIMENSION

International MIS

Study QUESTIONS

QID-1 How does the global economy affect organizations and processes?

QID-2 What are the characteristics of international IS components?

QID-3 How do inter-enterprise IS facilitate global supply chain management?

QID-4 What are the security challenges of international IS?

QID-5 What are the challenges of international IS management?

MyLab MIS

Using Your Knowledge
Questions ID-1, ID-2, ID-3
Essay Questions ID-5, ID-6

FIGURE ID-1
Growth in Internet Access
Source: Based on Klaus Schwab, "The Global Competitiveness Report 2017–2018," World Economic Forum, September 26, 2017, accessed June 16, 2018, *www3.weforum.org/docs/GCR2017-2018/05FullReport/TheGlobalCompetitivenessReport2017%E2%80%932018.pdf.*

QID-1 How Does the Global Economy Affect Organizations and Processes?

Today's businesses compete in a global market. International business has been sharply increasing since the middle of the 20th century. After World War II, the Japanese and other Asian economies exploded when those countries began to manufacture and sell goods to the West. The rise of the Japanese auto industry and the semiconductor industry in southeastern Asia greatly expanded international trade. At the same time, the economies of North America and Europe became more closely integrated.

Since then, a number of other factors have caused international business to mushroom. The fall of the Soviet Union opened the economies of Russia and Eastern Europe to the world market. Even more important, the telecommunications boom during the dot-com heyday caused the world to be encircled many times over by optical fiber that can be used for data and voice communications.

After the dot-com bust, optical fiber was largely underused and could be purchased for pennies on the dollar. Plentiful, cheap telecommunications enabled people worldwide to participate in the global economy. Before the advent of the Internet, if a young Indian professional wished to participate in the Western economy, he or she had to migrate to the West—a process that was politicized and limited. Today, that same young Indian professional can sell his or her goods or services over the Internet without leaving home. The Chinese economy has also benefitted from plentiful, cheap telecommunications and has become more open to the world.

Figure ID-1 shows the percent of individuals with Internet access in some of the largest countries in the world over the past few years.[1] Most developed countries have average Internet access rates around 80 to 90 percent and are relatively flat in terms of growth. But emerging countries are catching up very quickly.

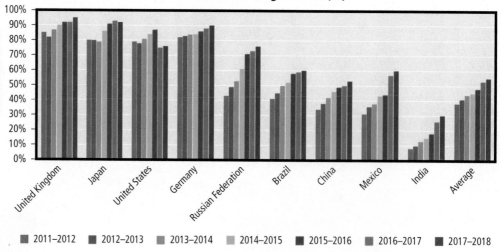

Individuals Using Internet (%)

■ 2011–2012   ■ 2012–2013   ■ 2013–2014   ■ 2014–2015   ■ 2015–2016   ■ 2016–2017   ■ 2017–2018

Developments such as these led columnist and author Thomas Friedman to claim, now famously, that "the world is flat," implying seamless integration among the world's economies. That claim and the popular book[2] of the same name fit with the business press's biases and preconceptions, and it seemed to make intuitive sense. A general sense that the world's economies were integrated came to pervade most business thinking.

However, Harvard professor Pankaj Ghemawat decided to look deeper, and the data he found prompted him to write a *Foreign Policy* article titled "Why the World Isn't Flat."[3] His article was published in 2007; the fact that it took such solid research and more than 8 years to gain widespread attention is a testament to the power of bias and preconception.

Some of Ghemawat's data is summarized in Figure ID-2. Notice that, even including cross-border telecommunications, Internet and voice averages less than 22 percent. Even international commerce, which most people think is a large factor in all economies, is less than 23 percent, when corrected for double-counting.[4]

Does this mean that international business is not important to you? No, it does not. What it does mean, as Ghemawat points out, is that most of the opportunity of international commerce is ahead of us. The world is not (yet) flat. While information systems have already played a key role in international commerce, their effect in the future is likely to be larger. As Web services become more widespread, it becomes easier to link information systems together. As mobile devices continue their exploding growth in developing countries, even more users will enter the world economy via the Internet.

Consider the difference between fixed and mobile Internet subscriptions shown in Figure ID-3. Mobile subscriptions far outweigh fixed subscriptions, especially in developing countries.[5] As more people gain access to the Internet through more types of devices, it becomes easier to provide Web-based services and products on the international stage. Opportunity abounds.

How Does the Global Economy Change the Competitive Environment?

To understand the effect of globalization, consider each of the elements in Figure ID-4.

The enlarging Internet-supported world economy has altered every one of the five competitive forces. Suppliers have to reach a wider range of customers, and customers have to consider a wider range of vendors. Suppliers and customers benefit not just from the greater size of the economy, but from the ease with which businesses can learn about each other using tools such as Google and Bing and, in China, Baibu.com.

FIGURE ID-2

Percent of Cross-Border Commerce

Source: Based on Pankaj Ghemawat and Steven Altman, "DHL Global Connectedness Index 2016," DHL International GmbH, October 2016, accessed June 21, 2018, *www.dhl.com/content/dam/downloads/g0/about_us/logistics_insights/gci_2016/DHL_GCI_2016_full_study.pdf.*

Commerce Type	Cross-Border Percent
Telecommunication	Voice: 5 percent Internet and voice: 22 percent
Immigration	3 percent immigrants
Investment	10 percent direct investment
Exports	23 percent commerce

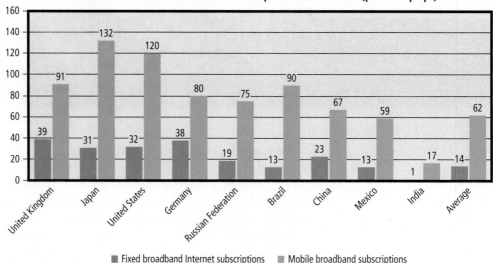

FIGURE ID-3
Fixed and Mobile Internet Subscriptions

Source: Based on Klaus Schwab, "The Global Competitiveness Report 2017–2018," World Economic Forum, September 26, 2018, accessed June 21, 2018, *www.weforum.org/reports/the-global-competitiveness-report-2017-2018.*

Because of the data available on the Internet, customers can also learn of substitutions more easily. The Internet has made it substantially easier for new market entrants, although not in all cases. Amazon, Apple, and Google, for example, have garnered such a large market share that it would be difficult for any new entrant to challenge them. Still, in other industries, the global economy facilitates new entrants. Finally, the global economy has intensified rivalry by increasing product and vendor choices and by accelerating the flow of information about price, product, availability, and service.

How Does the Emerging Global Economy Change Competitive Strategy?

The emerging global economy changes thinking about competitive strategies in two major ways: product localization and product differentiation. First, the sheer size and complexity of the global economy means that any organization that chooses a strategy allowing it to compete industry-wide is taking a very big bite! Competing in many different countries, with products localized to the language and culture of those countries, is an enormous and expensive task.

For example, to promote Windows worldwide, Microsoft must produce versions of Windows in dozens of different languages. Even in English, Microsoft produces a UK version, a U.S. version, an Australian version, and so forth. The problem for Microsoft is even greater because different countries use different character sets. In some languages, writing flows from left to right. In other languages, it flows from right to left. When Microsoft set out to sell Windows worldwide, it embarked on an enormous project.

FIGURE ID-4
Organizational Strategy Determines Information Systems

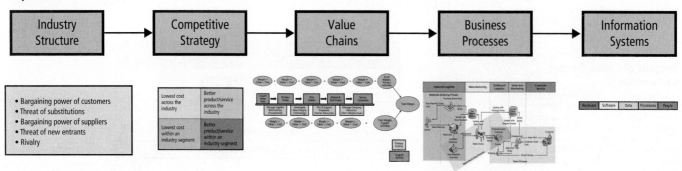

CAREER GUIDE

Name: Christin Dunlop
Company: Venafi
Job Title: Senior Learning and Development Specialist
Education: University of Utah

Source: Christin Dunlop, Venafi, Senior Learning and Development Specialist

1 How did you get this type of job?

I have worked my way up "the corporate ladder." I graduated with my MSIS degree and started as a consultant at EMC performing all sorts of technical projects for Fortune 100 companies. I was traveling almost every week, sitting in conference rooms and running calls with CTO/CIOs of some of the world's largest companies, banks, and government agencies. At the same time, I spent extra time working on internal tools, methodologies, and templates. I realized I really enjoyed internal development, so I made a career move to managing a team of consultants. I kept looking for additional responsibilities and experience and worked my way into global methodology and practice management, overseeing my local team and global teams in Egypt and India as well. Recently, I jumped from a large corporation to a small company and I started at Venafi, where I was able to define my own role thanks to my broad experience.

2 What attracted you to this field?

I wasn't one of those people who grew up building computers, always destined to be in the technical field. As I started taking computer courses in college, I quickly discovered that was how my brain worked. I would solve homework problems while trying to fall asleep at night. Learning how things worked and the "magic" behind the scenes really excites me. An unexpected perk is how much fun it is to be part of the IT community and one of the "geeks."

3 What does a typical workday look like for you (duties, decisions, problems)?

I start each day looking at the meetings I have for that day, reading email, and organizing my daily priorities. Each day is a little different after that; some days are heavily loaded with customer communication, while others are full of internal development tasks like spreadsheets, PowerPoints, internal meetings, and various developmental responsibilities. I actually really enjoy putting on my headphones and spending hours on spreadsheets and PowerPoint presentations.

4 What do you like most about your job?

The best thing about my job is the incredible opportunities I have before me. I am able to choose my own career path, work from home when I want, and travel when I choose, including attending conventions and conferences. It's incredible to be able to do what you truly enjoy doing.

5 What skills would someone need to do well at your job?

Self-motivation and people skills are absolutely critical in my position. You have to have drive and organization because you have responsibilities from many areas of the business. Building relationships with customers and coworkers is crucial. You enjoy your job more, and it gives you more brains to pick.

6 Are education or certifications important in your field? Why?

I'm a huge proponent of education, so I will always say education is important. Technology is always changing, and the only way to stay relevant is through continued learning. Certifications are a great way to learn and let others know you have an understanding of something, but they cannot replace actual experience. You really need a combination of formal education, certifications, and hands-on experience. Nothing is implemented or operates as cleanly as described in school.

7 What advice would you give to someone who is considering working in your field?

The biggest key to success within technology is a sense of adventure, confidence in yourself, and a willingness to try something new and step outside your comfort zone. My advice is be confident you can learn something and go for it! You'll fail sometimes, but you'll always learn, and it's amazing to see what you are capable of when you give yourself the chance.

8 What do you think will be hot tech jobs in 10 years?

As technology and automation advance, I foresee high demand placed on the ability to bridge the gap between technology and business. Nearly all industries rely on technology in some way and a good portion of employees don't have the slightest understanding of technology and often suffer from severe technophobia. "Translators" who are fluent in both the technical and business worlds will be the key to success across the board.

The second major way today's world economy changes competitive strategies is that its size, combined with the Internet, enables unprecedented product differentiation. If you choose to produce the world's highest quality and most exotic oatmeal—and if your production costs require you to sell that oatmeal for $350 a pound—your target market might contain only 200 people worldwide. The Internet allows you to find them—and them to find you. The decision involving a global competitive strategy requires the consideration of these two changing factors.

How Does the Global Economy Change Value Chains and Business Processes?

Because of information systems, any or all of the value chain activities in Figure ID-2 can be performed anywhere in the world. An international company can conduct sales and marketing efforts locally, for every market in which it sells. 3M divisions, for example, sell in the United States with a U.S. sales force, in France with a French sales force, and in Argentina with an Argentinean sales force. Depending on local laws and customs, those sales offices may be owned by 3M, or they may be locally owned entities with which 3M contracts for sales and marketing services. 3M can coordinate all of the sales efforts of these entities using the same CRM system. When 3M managers need to roll up sales totals for a sales projection, they can do so using an integrated, worldwide system.

Manufacturing of a final product is frequently distributed throughout the world. Components of the Boeing 787 are manufactured in Italy, China, England, and numerous other countries and delivered to Washington and South Carolina for final assembly. Each manufacturing facility has its own inbound logistics, manufacturing, and outbound logistics activity, but those activities are linked via information systems.

For example, Rolls-Royce manufactures an engine and delivers that engine to Boeing via its outbound logistics activity. Boeing receives the engine using its inbound logistics activity. All of this activity is coordinated via shared, inter-enterprise information systems. Rolls-Royce's CRM is connected with Boeing's supply processes, using techniques such as CRM and enterprise resource planning (ERP). We discuss global supply chains further in QID-3.

World time differences enable global virtual companies to operate 24/7. Boeing engineers in Los Angeles can develop a design for an engine support strut and send that design to Rolls-Royce in England at the end of their day. The design will be waiting for Rolls-Royce engineers at the start of their day. They review the design, make needed adjustments, and send it back to Boeing in Los Angeles, where the reviewed, adjusted design arrives at the start of the workday in Los Angeles. The ability to work around the clock by moving work into other time zones increases productivity.

Because of the abundance of low-cost, well-educated, English-speaking professionals in India, many organizations have chosen to outsource their service and support functions to India. Some accounting functions are outsourced to India as well.

QID-2 What Are the Characteristics of International IS Components?

To understand the effect of internationalization on information systems, consider the five components. Computer hardware is sold worldwide, and most vendors provide documentation in at least the major languages, so it has always been possible to obtain local hardware and set up local networks. Today, however, the emergence of the international cloud makes it even easier for any company, anywhere in the world, to obtain the latest in server technology. It does need to know how to do so, however, pointing to a possible future role for you as an international IS major.

Regarding software, consider the user interface for an international information system. Does it include a local-language version of Windows? What about the software application itself? Does an inventory system used worldwide by Boeing suppose that each user speaks English? If so, at what level of proficiency? If not, what languages must the user interface support?

Next, consider the data component. Suppose that the inventory database has a table for parts data, and that table contains a column named Remarks. Further suppose Boeing needs to integrate parts data from three different vendors: one in China, one in India, and one in England. What language is to be used for recording remarks? Does someone need to translate all of the remarks into one language? Into three languages?

The human components—procedures and people—are obviously affected by language and culture. As with business processes, information systems procedures need to reflect local cultural values and norms. For systems users, job descriptions and reporting relationships must be appropriate for the setting in which the system is used. We will say more about this in QID-5.

What's Required to Localize Software?

The process of making a computer program work in a second language is called **localizing** software. It turns out to be surprisingly hard to do. To localize a document or the content of a Web page, all you need to do is hire a translator to convert your document or page from one language to another. The situation is much more difficult for a computer program, however.

Consider a program you use frequently—say, Microsoft Word—and ask what would need to be done to translate it to a different language. The entire user interface needs to be translated. The menu bar and the commands on it will need to be translated. It is possible that some of the icons will need to be changed because some graphic symbols that are harmless in one culture are confusing or offensive in another.

What about an application program such as CRM that includes forms, reports, and queries? The labels on each of these will require translation. Of course, not all labels translate into words of the same length, and so the forms and reports may need to be redesigned. The questions and prompts for queries, such as "Enter part number for back order," must also be translated.

All of the documentation will need to be translated. That should be just a matter of hiring a translator, except that all of the illustrations in the documentation will need to be redrawn in the second language.

Think, too, about error messages. When someone attempts to order more items than there are in inventory, the application produces an error message. All of those messages will need to be translated. There are other issues as well. Sorting order is one. Spanish uses accents on certain letters, and it turns out that an accented ó will sort after z when you use the computer's default sort ordering. Figure ID-5 summarizes the factors to address when localizing software.

Programming techniques can be used to simplify and reduce the cost of localization. However, those techniques must be used in design, long before any code is written. For example, suppose that when a certain condition occurs, the program is to display the message "Insufficient quantity in stock." If the programmer codes all such messages into the computer program, then, to localize that program, a programmer will have to find every such message in the code and then ask a translator to change that code. A preferred technique is to give every error message a unique identifier and to create a separate

- Translate the user interface, including menu bars and commands.
- Translate, and possibly redesign, labels in forms, reports, and query prompts.
- Translate all documentation and help text.
- Redraw and translate diagrams and examples in help text.
- Translate all error messages.
- Translate text in all message boxes.
- Adjust sorting order for different character set.
- Fix special problems in Asian character sets and in languages that read and write from right to left.

FIGURE ID-5
Factors to Address When Localizing a Computer Program

error file that contains a list of identifiers and their associated text. Then, when an error occurs, program code uses the identifier to obtain the text of the message to be displayed from the error file. During localization, translators simply translate the file of error messages into the second language.

The bottom line for you, as a future manager, is to understand two points: (1) Localizing computer programs is much more difficult, expensive, and time consuming than translating documents. (2) If a computer program is likely to be localized, then plan for that localization from the beginning, during design. In addition, when considering the acquisition of a company in a foreign country, be sure to budget time and expense for the localization of information systems.

IBM's Watson Learns Korean

A good example of the inherent problems with localization can be seen in the recent partnership between IBM and the large Korean IT services provider SK Holdings C&C.[6] SK C&C wants to use IBM's Watson, an artificial intelligence platform able to answer questions using a person's natural language, to improve mobile concierge services and call center interactions. In order to do this, Watson has started learning Korean.

This is no easy task. The Korean language uses different characters (Hangul) and, relative to English, can be contextually difficult to decipher. Watson uses an iterative process to learn Korean. It processes some text in Korean, gets feedback from humans who speak Korean, and then processes more text. It continues this process until it learns how to speak Korean.

The localization of IBM's Watson won't be easy, but the potential benefits are tremendous. Watson doesn't forget, sleep, or take vacations. It's continually learning and processing more information. It could potentially provide customer service to billions of customers worldwide across many different industries at the same time. And it could do it in the customer's native language, not a secondary language (Figure ID-6). Korean is the eighth language Watson has learned; the others are English, Japanese, French, Brazilian Portuguese, Spanish, Italian, and Arabic.[7]

What Are the Problems and Issues of Global Databases?

When we discussed CRM and ERP in Chapter 8, you learned the advantage of having all data stored in a single database. In brief, a single database reduces data integrity problems and makes it possible to have an integrated view of the customer or the operations of the organization.

International companies that have a single database must, however, declare a single language for the company. Every Remark or Comment or other text field needs to be in a single language. If not, the advantages of a single database disappear. This is not a problem for companies that commit to a single company language.

A single database is not possible, however, for companies that use multiple languages. Such companies often decide to give up on the benefits of a single database to let divisions in different countries use different databases, with data in local languages. For example, an international manufacturer might allow a component manufacturing division in South Korea to have a database in Korean and a final assembly division in Brazil to have a different database in Portuguese. In this scenario, the company needs applications to export and import data among the separate databases.

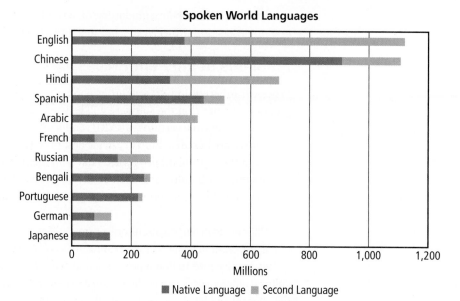

FIGURE ID-6
Spoken World Languages

Based on the source: Statista Inc.,
"The Most Spoken Languages Worldwide," *Statista.com*, February 21, 2017,
*www.statista.com/statistics/266808/
the-most-spoken-languages-worldwide.*

Besides language, performance is a second issue that confronts global databases. When using a single database, data transmission speeds are often too slow to process data from a single geographic location. If so, companies sometimes distribute their database to locations around the world.

Distributed database processing refers to the processing of a single database that resides in multiple locations. If the distributed database contains copies of the same data items, it is called a **replicated database**. If the distributed database does not contain copies of the same data, but rather divides the database into nonoverlapping segments, it is called a **partitioned database**. In most cases, querying either type of distributed database can improve performance without too much development work. However, updating a replicated database so that changes are correctly made to all copies of the data is full of challenges that require highly skilled personnel to solve. Still, companies like Amazon, which operates call centers in the United States, India, and Ireland, have invested in applications that are able to successfully update distributed databases worldwide. Given this infrastructure, Amazon then made this distributed database technology available via its Web services, as you learned in Chapters 5 and 6. The cloud has made the international distribution of data much easier.

Challenges of International Enterprise Applications?

As you learned in Chapter 8, workgroup business processes and functional applications support particular activities within a single department or business activity. Because the systems operate independently, the organization suffers from islands of automation. Sales and marketing data, for example, are not integrated with operations or manufacturing data.

You learned that many organizations eliminate the problems of information silos by creating enterprise systems. With international IS, however, such systems may not be worthwhile.

Advantages of Functional Systems

Lack of integration is disadvantageous in many situations, but it has *advantages* for international organizations and international systems. For example, if an order-processing functional system located in the United States is independent from the manufacturing systems located in Taiwan, it becomes unnecessary to accommodate language, business, and cultural differences within a single system. U.S. order-processing systems can operate in English and reflect the practices and culture of the United States. Taiwanese manufacturing information systems can operate in Chinese and reflect the business practices and culture of Taiwan. As long as there is an adequate data interface between the two systems, they can operate independently, sharing data when necessary.

Enterprise systems, such as ERP, solve the problems of data isolation by integrating data into a database that provides a comprehensive and organization-wide view. However, that advantage requires that the company standardize on a single language and, most likely, place that database in a single location. Otherwise, separated, functional databases are needed.

Problems of Inherent Processes

Processes inherent in ERP and other applications are even more problematic. Each software product assumes that the software will be used by people filling particular roles and performing their actions in a certain way. ERP vendors justify this standardization by saying that their procedures are based on industry-wide best practices and that the organization will benefit by following these standard processes. That statement may be true, but some inherent processes may conflict with cultural norms. If they do, it will be very difficult for management to convince the employees to follow those processes. Or at least it will be difficult in some cultures to do so.

Differences in language, culture, norms, and expectations compound the difficulties of international process management. Just creating an accurate as-is model is difficult and expensive; developing alternative international processes and evaluating them can be incredibly challenging. With cultural differences, it can be difficult just to determine what criteria should be used for evaluating the alternatives, let alone performing the evaluation.

Because of these challenges, in the future it is likely that international business processes will be developed more like inter-enterprise business processes. A high-level process will be defined to document the service responsibilities of each international unit. Then Web services will be used to connect those services into an integrated, enterprise, international system. Because of encapsulation, the only obligation of an international unit will be to deliver its defined service. One service can be delivered using procedures based on autocratic management policies, and another can be delivered using procedures based on collaborative management policies. The differences will not matter in a Web service-based enterprise system.

QID-3 How Do Inter-Enterprise IS Facilitate Global Supply Chain Management?

A **supply chain** is a network of organizations and facilities that transforms raw materials into products delivered to customers. Figure ID-7 shows a generic supply chain. Customers order from retailers, who in turn order from distributors, who order from manufacturers, who order from suppliers. In addition to the organizations shown here, the supply chain also includes transportation companies, warehouses, and inventories and some means for transmitting messages and information among the organizations involved.

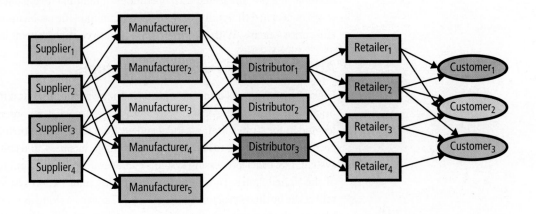

FIGURE ID-7
Supply Chain Relationships

Because of disintermediation, not every supply chain has all of these organizations. Some companies sell directly to the customer. Both the distributor and retailer organizations are omitted from their supply chains. In other supply chains, manufacturers sell directly to retailers and omit the distribution level.

The term *chain* is misleading. *Chain* implies that each organization is connected to just one company up the chain (toward the supplier) and down the chain (toward the customer). That is not the case. Instead, at each level an organization can work with many organizations both up and down the supply chain. Thus, a supply chain is a *network*.

To appreciate the international dimension of a supply chain, consider Figure ID-8. Suppose you decide to take up cross-country skiing. You go to REI (by visiting either one of its stores or its Web site) and purchase skis, bindings, boots, and poles. To fill your order, REI removes those items from its inventory of goods. Those goods have been purchased, in turn, from distributor/importers.

According to Figure ID-8, REI purchases the skis, bindings, and poles from one distributor/importer and the boots from a second. The distributor/importers, in turn, purchase the required items from the manufacturers, which, in turn, buy raw materials from their suppliers.

In Figure ID-8, notice the national flags on the suppliers and manufacturers. For example, the pole manufacturer is located in Brazil and imports plastic from China, aluminum from Canada, and fittings from Italy. The poles are then imported to REI in the United States by the Importer/Distributor.

The only source of revenue in a supply chain is the customer. In the REI example, you spend your money on the ski equipment. From that point all the way back up the supply chain to the raw materials suppliers, there is no further injection of cash into the system. The money you spend on the ski equipment is passed back up the supply chain as payments for goods or raw materials. Again, the customer is the only source of revenue.

The Importance of Information in the Supply Chain

In order to stay competitive, the focus of many businesses, worldwide, is to reduce costs. Supply chain costs are a primary target for such reductions, especially among companies that have a global supply chain. Figure ID-9 illustrates how Walmart overhauled its supply chain to eliminate distributors and other intermediaries, enabling it to buy directly from manufacturers. Walmart's goal is to increase sales and revenues from its private-label goods. At the same time, it also has consolidated

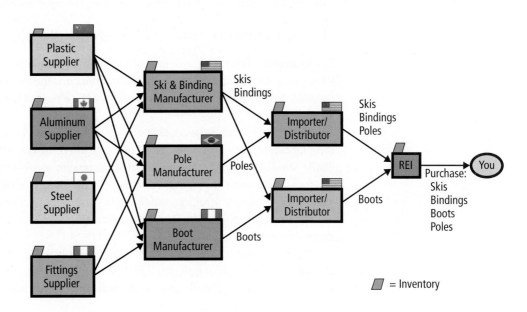

FIGURE ID-8
Supply Chain Example

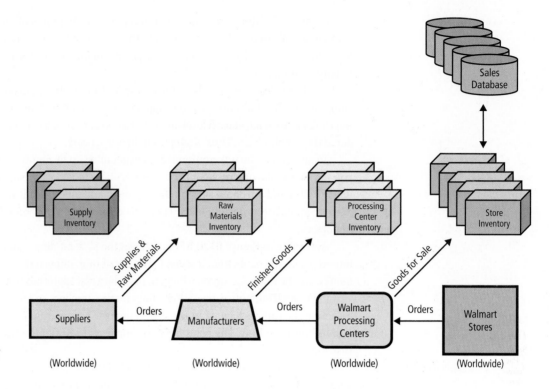

FIGURE ID-9
Example Walmart Supply Chain

purchasing and warehousing into four global merchandising centers, such as the one near Mexico City that processes goods for emerging markets.[8]

As you'll learn in your production and supply chain courses, many different factors determine the cost and performance of a supply chain. However, information is one of the most important. Consider, for example, inventory management at each of the companies in Figure ID-9. How do those companies decide when and how much to purchase? How does the new Walmart processing center in Mexico City determine how many pairs of jeans, ice chests, or bottles of vitamin C to order? How large should the orders be? How frequently should orders be placed? How are those orders tracked? What happens when a shipment disappears? Information is a major factor in making each of those decisions, along with dozens of others. To provide insight into the importance of information, consider just one example, the bullwhip effect.

How Can Information Relieve the Bullwhip Effect?

The **bullwhip effect** is a phenomenon in which the variability in the size and timing of orders increases at each stage up the supply chain, from customer to supplier. Figure ID-10 depicts the situation. In a famous study, the bullwhip effect was observed in Procter & Gamble's supply chain for diapers.[9]

Except for random variation, diaper demand is constant. Diaper use is not seasonal; the requirement for diapers does not change with fashion or anything else. The number of babies determines diaper demand, and that number is constant or possibly slowly changing.

Retailers do not order from the distributor with the sale of every diaper package. The retailer waits until the diaper inventory falls below a certain level, called the *reorder quantity*. Then the retailer orders a supply of diapers, perhaps ordering a few more than it expects to sell to ensure that it does not have an outage.

The distributor receives the retailer's order and follows the same process. It waits until its supply falls below the reorder quantity, and then it reorders from the manufacturer, with perhaps an increased amount to prevent outages. The manufacturer, in turn, uses a similar process with the raw-materials suppliers.

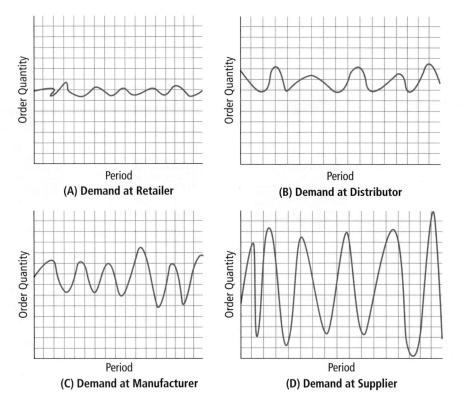

FIGURE ID-10
The Bullwhip Effect
Source: Based on Hau L. Lee, V. Padmanabhan, and S. Whang, "The Bullwhip Effect in Supply Chains," *Sloan Management Review*, Spring 1997, pp. 93–102.

Because of the nature of this process, small changes in demand at the retailer are amplified at each stage of the supply chain. As shown in Figure ID-10, those small changes become quite large variations on the supplier end.

The bullwhip effect is a natural dynamic that occurs because of the multistage nature of the supply chain. It is not related to erratic consumer demand, as the study of diapers indicated. You may have seen a similar effect while driving on the freeway. One car slows down, the car just behind it slows down a bit more abruptly, which causes the third car in line to slow down even more abruptly, and so forth, until the thirtieth car or so is slamming on its brakes.

The large fluctuations of the bullwhip effect force distributors, manufacturers, and suppliers to carry larger inventories than should be necessary to meet the real consumer demand. Thus, the bullwhip effect reduces the overall profitability of the supply chain. Eliminating or at least reducing the bullwhip effect is particularly important for international supply chains where logistics costs are high and shipping times are long.

One way to eliminate the bullwhip effect is to give all participants in the supply chain access to consumer-demand information from the retailer. Each organization can thus plan its inventory or manufacturing based on the true demand (the demand from the only party that introduces money into the system) and not on the observed demand from the next organization up the supply chain. Of course, an *inter-enterprise information system* is necessary to share such data.

Consider the Walmart example in Figure ID-11. Along the bottom, each entity orders from the entity up the supply chain (the entity to its left in Figure ID-11). Thus, for example, the Walmart processing centers order finished goods from manufacturers. Without knowledge of the true demand, this supply chain is vulnerable to bullwhip effects. However, if each entity can, via an information system, obtain data about the true demand—that is, the demand from the retail customers who are the source of funds for this chain—then each can anticipate orders. The data about true demand will enable each entity to meet order requirements, while maintaining a smaller inventory.

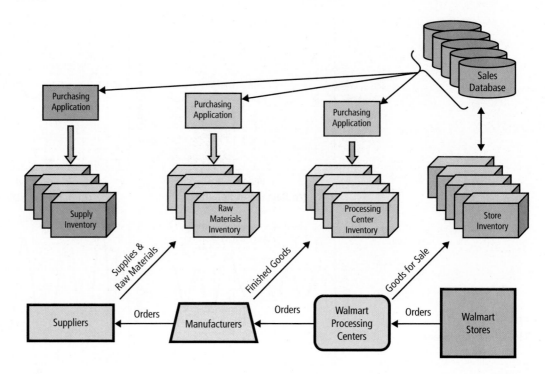

FIGURE ID-11
Eliminate Bullwhip Effect with True Demand Information

QID-4   What Are the Security Challenges of International IS?

Managing international systems creates unique security challenges that derive from differences in legal systems, physical environments, and cultural norms. These security challenges represent very real threats to an organization's ability to operate in another country.

Legal Environment

First, differences in legal environments between countries have a direct impact on the daily operation of information systems. The legal differences related to the use of encryption, distribution of content, and personal privacy protections can substantially affect international IS.

Encryption

Most people are unaware that encryption is *illegal* or highly restricted in many countries. Yes, you read that correctly, illegal. In Russia and China, a license is required to import or export encryption products.[10] The use of any encryption product requires a license. Other countries like England, India, and Australia have laws that can force decryption.

In fact, in 2015 British Prime Minister David Cameron suggested that back doors be placed in all software that would effectively circumvent all encryption. In 2016, the UK House of Commons passed the "Snooper's Charter" bill that requires companies to remove encryption when asked by law enforcement.

In the United States, Apple was sued by the FBI to unlock an encrypted cell phone used in a terror attack in San Bernardino. The FBI eventually dropped the lawsuit, claiming it had purchased limited software that could break Apple's encryption.[11]

Companies that use encryption need to be aware that encryption laws differ between countries and may affect their ability to operate effectively.

Distribution of Content

Laws regarding the legality of the nature of the content stored in an organization's systems are also different between countries. For example, in 2010 Google moved its search engine service from China to Hong Kong over censorship problems. The People's Republic of China (PRC) regularly forced Google to remove content that the PRC found unacceptable. Google subsequently saw its search market share drop from 30 percent to about 10 percent in 2016. In 2018, Google tried to restart operations in China by making Google Maps available within China. Unfortunately, in order to do so, Google must use a special map application that is different from its regular worldwide application and that runs through Alibaba.[12]

In fact, dozens of countries regularly block access to certain Internet companies. Brazil blocked Facebook's messaging app, WhatsApp, for 72 hours when it implemented end-to-end encryption.[13] Turkey's government blocked Twitter and YouTube once in 2014 to suppress an embarrassing video showing officials talking about starting a war and again in 2016 to block communications during an attempted military coup.[14]

Personal Privacy

Variations in privacy laws can also affect the operation of an organization's international systems. For example, in parts of Europe employers cannot read their workers' emails, personal data cannot be collected without an individual's permission, organizations must provide individuals with the ability to correct inaccuracies in the data they collect, and personal data cannot be shared by companies without express permission. None of these apply to organizations in the United States.

Differences in privacy laws may become even more pronounced. In 2018, the EU passed a comprehensive privacy law named the **General Data Protection Regulation (GDPR)** that lets people request their online data and limits how businesses can use customer data. As of 2018, Google had received more than 693,441 removal requests for more than 2,593,414 URLs. It has removed 44 percent of the requested URLs.[15]

The GDPR will likely be applied to other tech companies like Facebook, Bing, and Twitter as well. Unfortunately, none of these privacy protections applies to U.S. citizens. In fact, Google assembled its own panel of advisers, which recommended that the GDPR law not apply to any of Google's properties outside the European Union (EU). This means EU users can still see their removed URLs if they visit *www.google.com* rather than *www.google.co.uk*.

A few days after the passage of the GDPR, a high-profile privacy advocate filed a $4.3B lawsuit against Google. Facebook was also sued for $4.5B.[16]

Privacy laws have the potential to force international technology companies to change the way they operate and, more importantly, reshape international law.

Organizations need to be aware that laws related to encryption, content, and privacy will affect the way they collect, process, and store data. Consider how these laws might affect organizations that use cloud-based services to store data. Organizations could operate in a country with loose content laws and then store all of their data and applications in another country with stricter privacy laws in order to protect their users. In other words, the intersection of international law and technology is forcing organizations to carefully evaluate how they manage their information systems, in particular, the location of their data.

Physical Security

Second, operating information systems internationally can be problematic because of different physical environments. This includes threats to infrastructure in the form of natural disasters, geopolitical risks, civil unrest, and terrorist attacks.

Place your data center in Kansas, and it's subject to tornados. Place your data center internationally, and it's potentially subject to typhoons/hurricanes, earthquakes, floods, volcanic eruptions, or mudslides. For example, the data centers in Japan survived the terrible effects of the 2011 earthquake, tsunami, and nuclear reactor meltdowns. They survived the shaking, flooding, and widespread power outages because they were housed in special facilities with shock-absorbing structures and had backup power generators.

An organization's physical infrastructure is also vulnerable to outright seizure. In 2018, Peter Levashov, also known as the Russian spam king, was arrested in Barcelona, Spain, for allegedly operating one of the top-10 largest spam networks named Kelihos.[17] Federal agents seized two of Levashov's Luxembourg servers that were being used as a proxy to hide his alleged criminal activities.

Employees who run critical infrastructure can be targeted as well. In 2014, Russian president Vladimir Putin revoked visas for nearly 1,000 foreign workers when tensions flared between Russia and Western countries. Deloitte & Touche's local chief operating officer, Quentin O'Toole, was deported for his wife's speeding tickets.

Cultural Norms

Finally, cultural norms can affect the way organizations manage their international information systems. For example, bribery is generally considered unacceptable in the United States, but in other countries it is accepted as a normal way of doing business.

In 2018, the large French bank Societe Generale agreed to a $1.3 billion fine for bribing Libyan officials in order to secure government-sponsored investments ($585 million) and for manipulating LIBOR, a key global interest rate ($750 million).[18] It's important to note that this is just one company in one industry. Graft is a worldwide problem across many industries. This example points out how differences in cultural norms can affect an organization's daily operations.

Apply these cultural differences to the management of international information systems. Can an organization depend on the control of separation of duties and authorities in a culture for which graft is an accepted norm? Could an organization lose valuable intellectual property in such an environment? Or what is the utility of a personal reference in a culture in which it is considered exceedingly rude to talk about someone when he or she is not present?

Organizations need to carefully examine how the deployment of international information systems might be affected by cultural norms. Because of differences in cultural norms, safeguards need to be chosen and evaluated on a culture-by-culture basis. Additional safeguards may be needed, but the technical and data safeguards described in Chapter 10 still apply to international systems.

 ## What Are the Challenges of International IS Management?

In addition to security, size and complexity make international IS management challenging. The components of international information systems are larger and more complex. Projects to develop them are larger and more complicated to manage. International IS departments are bigger and composed of people from many cultures with many different native languages. International organizations have more IS and IT assets, and those assets are exposed to more risk and greater uncertainty. Because of the complexity of international law, security incidents are more complicated to investigate.

Why Is International IS Development More Challenging?

The factors that affect international information systems development are more challenging than those that affect international software development. If the *system* is truly international, if many people from many different countries will be using the system, then the development project is exceedingly complicated.

To see why, consider the five components. Running hardware in different countries is not a problem, especially using the cloud, and localizing software is manageable, assuming programs were designed to be localized. Databases pose more difficulties. First, is a single database to be used, and if so, is it to be distributed? If so, how will updates be processed? Also, what language, currency, and units of measure will be used to store data? If multiple databases are to be used, how are data going to be transported among them? Some of these problems are difficult, but they are solvable, and cloud-based databases make them more so.

The same cannot be said for the procedure and people components. An international system is used by people who live and work in cultures that are vastly different from one another. The way customers are treated in Japan differs substantially from the way customers are treated in Spain, which differs substantially from the way they are treated in the United States. Therefore, the procedures for using a CRM will be correspondingly different.

Consider the relationship of business processes and information systems as discussed in Chapter 12. Information systems are supposed to facilitate the organization's competitive strategy and support business processes. But what if the underlying business processes differ? Customer support in Japan and customer support in Spain may involve completely different processes and activities.

Even if the purpose and scope can be defined in some unified way, how are requirements to be determined? Again, if the underlying business processes differ, then the specific requirements for the information system will differ. Managing requirements for a system in one culture is difficult, but managing requirements for international systems can be many times more difficult.

There are two responses to such challenges: (1) either define a set of standard business processes or (2) develop alternative versions of the system that support different processes in different countries. Both responses are problematic. The first response requires conversion of the organization to different work processes, and, as you learned in Chapter 8, such conversion can be exceedingly difficult. People resist change, and they will do so with vehemence if the change violates cultural norms.

The second response is easier to implement, but it creates system design challenges. It also means that, in truth, there is not one system, but many.

In spite of the problems, both responses are used. For example, SAP, Oracle, and other ERP vendors define standard business processes via the inherent procedures in their software products. Many organizations attempt to enforce those standard procedures. When it becomes organizationally infeasible to do so, organizations develop exceptions to those inherent procedures and develop programs to handle the exceptions. This choice means high maintenance expense.

What Are the Challenges of International Project Management?

Managing a global IS development project is difficult because of project size and complexity. Requirements are complex, many resources are required, and numerous people are involved. Team members speak different languages, live in different cultures, work in different time zones, and seldom meet face to face.

One way to understand how these factors affect global project management is to consider each of the project management knowledge areas as set out by the International Project Management Institute's document, the *PMBOK® Guide* (*www.pmi.org/PMBOK-Guide-and-Standards.aspx*). Figure ID-12 summarizes challenges for each knowledge area. Project integration is more difficult because international development projects require the complex integration of results from distributed work groups. Also, task dependencies can span teams working in different countries, increasing the difficulty of task management.

The scope and requirements definition for international IS is more difficult, as just discussed. Time management is more difficult because teams in different cultures and countries work at different rates. Some cultures have a 35-hour workweek, and some have a 60-hour workweek. Some cultures expect 6-week vacations, and some expect 2 weeks. Some cultures thrive on efficiency of labor, and others thrive on considerate working relationships. There is no standard rate of development for an international project.

Knowledge Areas	Challenge
Project integration	Complex integration of results from distributed work groups. Management of dependencies of tasks from physically and culturally different work groups.
Requirements (scope)	Need to support multiple versions of underlying business processes. Possibly substantial differences in requirements and procedures.
Time	Development rates vary among cultures and countries.
Cost	Cost of development varies widely among countries. Two members performing the same work in different countries may be paid substantially different rates. Moving work among teams may dramatically change costs.
Quality	Quality standards vary among cultures. Different expectations of quality may result in an inconsistent system.
Human resources	Worker expectations differ. Compensation, rewards, work conditions vary widely.
Communications	Geographic, language, and cultural distance among team members impedes effective communication.
Risk	Development risk is higher. Easy to lose control.
Procurement	Complications of international trade.

FIGURE ID-12
Challenges for International IS Project Management

In terms of cost, different countries and cultures pay vastly different labor rates. Using critical path analysis, managers may choose to move a task from one team to another. Doing so, however, may substantially increase costs. Thus, management may choose to accept a delay rather than move work to an available (but more expensive) team. The complex trade-offs that exist between time and cost become even more complex for international projects.

Quality and human resources are also more complicated for international projects. Quality standards vary among countries. The IT industry in some nations, such as India, has invested heavily in development techniques that increase program quality. Other countries, such as the United States, have been less willing to invest in quality. In any case, the integration of programs of varying quality results in an inconsistent system.

Worker expectations vary among cultures and nations. Compensation, rewards, and worker conditions vary, and these differences can lead to misunderstandings, poor morale, and project delays.

Because of these factors, effective team communication is exceedingly important for international projects, but because of language and culture differences and geographic separation, such communication is difficult. Effective communication is also more expensive. Consider, for example, just the additional expense of maintaining a team portal in three or four languages.

If you consider all of the factors in Figure ID-12, it is easy to understand why project risk is high for international IS development projects. So many things can go wrong. Project integration is complex; requirements are difficult to determine; cost, time, and quality are difficult to manage; worker conditions vary widely; and communication is difficult. Finally, project procurement is complicated by the normal challenges of international commerce.

What Are the Challenges of International IS Management?

Chapter 11 defined the four primary responsibilities of the IS department: plan, operate, develop, and protect information systems and supporting infrastructure. Each of these responsibilities becomes more challenging for international IS organizations.

Regarding planning, the principal task is to align IT and IS resources with the organization's competitive strategy. The task does not change character for international companies; it just becomes more complex and difficult. Multinational organizations and operations are complicated; thus, the business processes that support their competitive strategies also tend to be complicated. Furthermore, changes in global economic factors can mean dramatic changes in processes and necessitate changes in IS and IT support. Technology adoption can also cause remarkable change. The increasing use of cell phones in developing countries, for example, changes the requirements for local information systems. The price of oil and energy can change international business processes. For these reasons, planning tasks for international IS are larger and more complex.

Three factors create challenges for international IS operations. First, conducting operations in different countries, cultures, and languages adds complexity. Go to the Web site of any multinational corporation, say, *www.3m.com* or *www.dell.com*, and you'll be asked to click on the country in which you reside. When you click, you are likely to be directed to a Web server running in some other country. Those Web servers need to be managed consistently, even though they are operated by people living in different cultures and speaking various languages.

The second operational challenge of international IS is the integration of similar, but different, systems. Consider inventory. A multinational corporation might have dozens of different inventory systems in use throughout the world. To enable the movement of goods, many of these systems need to be coordinated and integrated.

Or consider customer support that operates from three different support centers in three different countries. Each center may have its own information system, but the data among those systems will need to be exported or otherwise shared. If not, then a customer who contacts one center will be unknown to the others.

The third complication for operations is outsourcing. Many organizations have chosen to outsource customer support, training, logistics, and other backroom activities. International outsourcing is particularly advantageous for customer support and other functions that must be operational 24/7. Many companies outsource logistics to UPS because doing so offers comprehensive, worldwide shipping and logistical support. The organization's information systems usually need to be integrated with outsource vendors' information systems, and this may need to be done for different systems, all over the world.

The fourth IS department responsibility is protecting IS and IT infrastructure. We consider that function next.

Setting Up Information Systems in Foreign Offices

The fourth IS department responsibility is protecting IS and IT infrastructure. To illustrate the challenges of international IS management, suppose that eHermes decides to open an office in Europe. How might it go about developing information systems for that office?

Before answering that question, consider how the Mahr Group, a midsized, multinational firm headquartered in Germany manages its foreign offices. The Mahr Group purchases its hardware and Internet access from local vendors but has its corporate employees install and configure the same software worldwide. It also has corporate employees perform standardized IT audits worldwide at each foreign office.[19]

Because it is a manufacturer, Mahr operates an ERP system, for which it maintains a centralized database in Germany that is accessed via its own leased communication lines worldwide. It also requires that the same computer-assisted-design (CAD) software be used worldwide. Doing so allows Mahr employees to exchange designs with offices around the world without worrying about compatibility problems.

ACTIVE REVIEW

Use this Active Review to verify that you understand the ideas and concepts that answer the study questions.

QID-1   How does the global economy affect organizations and processes?

Describe how the global economy has changed since the mid-20th century. Explain how the dot-com bust influenced the global economy and changed the number of workers worldwide. Summarize why the idea that the world is flat gained momentum and why that notion is incorrect. State how the lack of a "flat" world presents business opportunities. Summarize the ways in which today's global economy influences the five competitive forces. Explain how the global economy changes the way organizations assess industry structure. How does the global economy change competitive strategy? How do global information systems benefit the value chain? Using Figure 2-6 (page 44) as a guide, explain how each primary value chain activity can be performed anywhere in the world.

QID-2   What are the characteristics of international IS components?

Explain how internationalization affects the five components of an IS. What does it mean to localize software? Summarize the work required to localize a computer program. In your own words, explain why it is better to design a program to be localized rather than attempt to adapt an existing single-language program to a second language. Explain the problems of having a single database for an international IS. Define *distributed database*, *replicated database*, and *partitioned database*. State a source of problems for processing replicated databases.

Summarize the advantages of functional systems for international companies. Summarize the issues of inherent processes for multinational ERP. Explain how SOA services could be used to address the problems of international enterprise applications.

QID-3   How do inter-enterprise IS facilitate global supply chain management?

Define *supply chain*, and explain why the term *chain* is misleading. Under what circumstances are not all of the organizations in Figure ID-8 part of the supply chain? Name the only source of revenue in a supply chain. Explain how Walmart is attempting to reduce supply costs. Describe the bullwhip effect and explain why it adds costs to a supply chain. Explain how the system shown in Figure ID-11 can eliminate the bullwhip effect.

QID-4   What are the security challenges of international IS?

Explain legal differences between countries with respect to the use of encryption, distribution of content, and personal privacy protections. Describe how natural disasters, geopolitical risks, civil unrest, and terrorist attacks could threaten the physical security of international IS. Give an example of how differences in cultural norms may affect international IS.

QID-5   What are the challenges of international IS management?

State the two characteristics that make international IS management challenging.

Explain the difference between international systems development and international software development. Using the five-component framework, explain why international systems development is more difficult. Give an example of one complication for each knowledge area in Figure ID-12. State the four responsibilities for IS departments. Explain how each of these responsibilities is more challenging for international IS organizations. Describe three factors that create challenges for international IS operations. Summarize the strategy that Mahr uses when creating IS infrastructure in foreign offices.

KEY TERMS AND CONCEPTS

Bullwhip effect   504
Distributed database processing   501
General Data Protection Regulation (GDPR)   507
Localizing   499
Partitioned database   501
Replicated database   501
Supply chain   502

MyLab MIS

To complete the problems with MyMISLab, go to EOC Discussion Questions in the MyLab.

USING YOUR KNOWLEDGE

ID-1.
MyLab MIS

Suppose you are about to have a job interview with a multinational company, such as 3M, Starbucks, or Coca-Cola. Further suppose you wish to demonstrate an awareness of the changes for international commerce that the Internet and modern information technology have made. Using the information in QID-1, create a list of three questions that you could ask the interviewer regarding the company's use of IT in its international business.

ID-2.
MyLab MIS

Suppose you work for a business that has $100M in annual sales that is contemplating acquiring a company in Mexico. Assume you are a junior member of a team that is analyzing the desirability of this acquisition. Your boss, who is not technically savvy, has asked you to prepare a summary of the issues that she should be aware of in the merging of information systems of the two companies. She wants your summary to include a list of questions that she should ask of both your IS department and the IS department personnel in the prospective acquisition. Prepare that summary.

ID-3.
MyLab MIS

Using the data in this module as well as in Chapter 8, summarize the strengths and weaknesses of functional systems, CRM, and ERP. How do the advantages and disadvantages of each change in an international setting? For your answer, create a table with strength and weakness columns and with one row for each of the four systems types.

ID-4. Suppose you are the CISO for a *Fortune* 500 company with offices in 15 different countries. Your company has substantial intellectual property to protect, and the CEO has suggested that the company move part of its R&D offshore to reduce costs. Using the information from QID-4, describe the potential threats that might arise from moving R&D to an offshore site.

MyLab MIS

Go to the Assignments section of your MyLab to complete these writing exercises.

ID-5. Suppose you are working for a well-known social media company based in the United States. You've been placed in charge of expanding the company internationally. The first day on the job the chief information security officer (CISO) informs you that there have been repeated intrusions into corporate servers located in Asia. The hackers targeted accounts of well-known political dissidents. And they continue to do so on a regular basis. They make little effort to cover their tracks. The problem is that they're based in the country in which you're focusing your expansion efforts. Explain how different legal and cultural norms may hamper your expansion plans. Why might foreign government officials be hesitant to help you catch the hackers? What types of concessions or changes might the foreign government ask you to make to your social media platform before you're given permission to operate in the country?

ID-6. Assume you are Seth Wilson (Director of IT services) at eHermes. Using your knowledge from QID-5, write a one-page memo to Victor Vazquez (COO) explaining what needs to be done to set up information systems in a new European office. State and justify any assumptions you make.

ENDNOTES

1. Klaus Schwab, "The Global Competitiveness Report 2017–2018," *World Economic Forum*, September 26, 2017, accessed June 21, 2018, *www.weforum.org/reports/the-global-competitiveness-report-2017-2018.*

2. Thomas L. Friedman, *The World Is Flat 3.0: A Brief History of the Twenty-First Century* (New York: Farrar, Strauss and Giroux, 2007).

3. Pankaj Ghemawat, "Why the World Isn't Flat," *Foreign Policy*, March 2007, *www.foreignpolicy.com/articles/2007/02/14/why_the_world_isnt_flat.*

4. Pankaj Ghemawat and Steven Altman, "DHL Global Connectedness Index 2016," DHL International GmbH, October 2016, accessed June 21, 2018, *www.dhl.com/content/dam/downloads/g0/about_us/logistics_insights/gci_2016/DHL_GCI_2016_full_study.pdf.*

5. Klaus Schwab, "The Global Competitiveness Report 2017–2018," *World Economic Forum*, September 26, 2018, accessed June 21, 2018, *www.weforum.org/reports/the-global-competitiveness-report-2017-2018.*

6. Fiona Doherty, "The Science of Tutoring Watson to Understand Korean," *IBM Research*, May 18, 2016, accessed June 21, 2018, *www.ibm.com/blogs/research/2016/05/science-tutoring-watsonunderstand-korean.*

7. Statista Inc., "The Most Spoken Languages Worldwide," *Statista.com*, February 21, 2017, *www.statista.com/statistics/266808/the-most-spoken-languages-worldwide.*

8. Wal-Mart Stores, Inc., "Walmart Leverages Global Scale to Lower Costs of Goods, Accelerate Speed to Market, Improve Quality of Products," Wal-Mart press release, last updated January 28, 2010, *http://corporate.walmart.com/_news_/news-archive/2010/01/28/walmartleverages-global-scale-to-lower-costs-of-goods-accelerate-speed-to-marketimprove-quality-of-products.*

9. Hau L. Lee, V. Padmanabhan, and S. Whang, "The Bullwhip Effect in Supply Chains," *Sloan Management Review*, Spring 1997, pp. 93–102.

10. Bert-Jaap Koops, "Crypto Law Survey," *Cryptolaw.org*, February 2013, *www.cryptolaw.org*, accessed June 21, 2018.

11. Caroline Craig, "Apple vs. FBI Is Over, but the Encryption Battle Rages On," March 25, 2016, accessed June 21, 2018, *www.infoworld.com/article/3048237/security/apple-vs-fbi-is-over-but-the-encryption-battlerages-on.html.*

12. Charlotte Gao, "Google Stumbles Back to China," *TheDiplomat.com*, January 16, 2018, accessed June 21, 2018, *https://thediplomat.com/2018/01/google-stumbles-back-to-china/.*

13. Kate Conger, "Brazil Orders Cell Phone Carriers to Block WhatsApp for 72 Hours," *TechCrunch*, May 2, 2016, accessed June 21, 2018, *https://techcrunch.com/2016/05/02/brazil-orders-cell-phone-carriers-to-block-whatsapp-for-72-hours.*

14. Jonathan Vanian, "Turkey Blocks Facebook, Twitter, and YouTube Amid Military Coup," *Fortune*, July 15, 2016, accessed June 21, 2018, *http://fortune.com/2016/07/15/turkey-facebook-twitter-youtube-military-coup/.*

15. Google Inc., "Search Removals Under European Privacy Law," *Google.com*, June 21, 2018, accessed June 21, 2018, *https://transparencyreport.google.com/eu-privacy/overview.*

16. Josiah Motley, "It's Only Day One of the GDPR and Google and Facebook Have Been Hit with $8.8 Billion in Lawsuits," *KnowTechie*, May 25, 2018, accessed November 13, 2018, *https://knowtechie.com/google-and-facebook-8-billion-dollar-lawsuit/.*

17. Russell Brandom, "Feds Tracked Down Russian Spam Kingpin with Help from His iCloud Account," *The Verge*, February 5, 2018, accessed June 21, 2018, *www.theverge.com/2018/2/5/16975896/icloud-warrant-kelihos-botnet-levashov-affidavit.*

18. CBS/AP, "France's Societe Generale Hit with $1.3B in U.S. Fines," *CBSNews.com*, June 4, 2018, accessed June 21, 2018, *www.cbsnews.com/news/frances-societe-generale-hit-with-1-3b-in-u-s-fines/.*

19. Private correspondence with the author, August 2011.

APPLICATION EXERCISES

All exercise files can be found on the following Web site: *www.pearsonhighered.com/kroenke.*

Chapter 1

AE1-1. The spreadsheet in Microsoft Excel file **Ch01Ex01_U11e.xlsx** contains records of employee activity on special projects. Open this workbook and examine the data that you find in the three spreadsheets it contains. Assess the accuracy, relevancy, and sufficiency of this data to the following people and problems.

    a. You manage the Denver plant, and you want to know how much time your employees are spending on special projects.

    b. You manage the Reno plant, and you want to know how much time your employees are spending on special projects.

    c. You manage the Quota Computation project in Chicago, and you want to know how much time your employees have spent on that project.

    d. You manage the Quota Computation project for all three plants, and you want to know the total time employees have spent on that project.

    e. You manage the Quota Computation project for all three plants, and you want to know the total labor cost for all employees on that project.

    f. You manage the Quota Computation project for all three plants, and you want to know how the labor-hour total for your project compares to the labor-hour totals for the other special projects.

    g. What conclusions can you make from this exercise?

AE1-2. The database in the Microsoft Access file **Ch01Ex02_U11e.accdb** contains the same records of employee activity on special projects as in AE1-1. Before proceeding, open that database and view the records in the Employee Hours table.

    a. Eight queries have been created that process this data in different ways. Using the criteria of accuracy, relevancy, and sufficiency, select the single query that is most appropriate for the information requirements in AE1-1, parts a–f. If no query meets the need, explain why.

    b. What conclusions can you make from this exercise?

    c. Comparing your experiences on these two projects, what are the advantages and disadvantages of spreadsheets and databases?

AE1-3. In this project, you will look at statistics related to information systems jobs. For several years, the demand for IT workers has been increasing. So have average annual wages for IT workers. Projections for future job demand and salary growth are also well above average.

    The sites in this exercise allow you to search by job code (e.g., 15-1071) or by job title. The data is aggregated by state, but you can look up statistics for your individual city through the Department of Labor's (DOL's) Web site (*www.dol.gov/dol/location.htm*). The DOL site links to your local state government's Web page.

This project gives you a realistic look at expected IT salaries. You can also use the sites from this project to look at wage data for other occupations (i.e., jobs in your major).

(1) Go to O*NET at *http://online.onetcenter.org/*.

(2) Type "network administrator" into the Occupation Quick Search in the top right of the screen.

(3) Press Enter.

(4) Click on the first link.

(5) Click on *Wages & Employment*.

(6) Take a screenshot. (You can take a screenshot by pressing Alt-PrintScreen.)

(7) Select your state from the State Wages dropdown box.

(8) Click *Go*.

(9) Click on the *Yearly Wage Chart*.

(10) Take a screenshot.

(11) Go to the U.S. Bureau of Labor Statistics at *www.bls.gov/OES/*.

(12) Click on *Subjects* and then *Pay & Benefits*.

(13) Click *Wages by Area and Occupation*.

(14) Click the link labeled *By State* under the Wage Data by State section.

(15) Click on a state. (Choose the state you want to work in after you graduate.)

(16) Click on the link labeled *15-0000 Computer and Mathematical Occupations*.

(17) Take a screenshot.

(18) Click on the link labeled *Network and Computer Systems Administrators*. (Note the mean annual wage.)

(19) Click on the link labeled *Geographic profile for this occupation*. (This will show you the states with the highest concentration of workers in this job category. It will also show you the states that have the highest annual salaries for this job category.)

(20) Take a screenshot.

a. Could you find statistics for employment by city within your state? *Hint*: Visit the U.S. Department of Labor at *www.dol.gov/dol/location.htm*.

b. Is the demand for IT jobs (network administrators) projected to increase more than the national average? Why or why not?

c. Is the average salary for IT workers (network administrators) projected to increase more than the national average? Why or why not?

d. Why do you think the projections for job demand and salary increase for IT workers are so high?

Chapter 2

AE2-1.   Figure AE-1 shows an Excel spreadsheet that the resort bicycle rental business uses to value and analyze its bicycle inventory. Examine this figure to understand the meaning of the data. Now use Excel to create a similar spreadsheet. Note the following:

- The top heading is in 20-point Calibri font. It is centered in the spreadsheet. Cells A1 through H1 have been merged.
- The second heading, Bicycle Inventory Valuation, is in 18-point Calibri, italics. It is centered in cells A2 through H2, which have been merged.
- The column headings are set in 11-point Calibri, bold. They are centered in their cells, and the text wraps in the cells.

a. Make the first two rows of your spreadsheet similar to that in Figure AE-1. Choose your own colors for background and type, however.

b. Place the current date so that it is centered in cells C3, D3, and E3, which must be merged.

	A	B	C	D	E	F	G	H
1				Resort Bicycle Rental				
2				Bicycle Inventory Valuation				
3				Saturday, May 27, 2018				
4	Make of Bike	Bike Cost	Number on Hand	Cost of Current Inventory	Number of Rentals	Total Rental Revenue	Revenue per Bike	Revenue as Percent of Cost of Inventory
5	Wonder Bike	$325	12	$3,900	85	$6,375	$531	163.5%
6	Wonder Bike II	$385	4	$1,540	34	$4,570	$1,143	296.8%
7	Wonder Bike Supreme	$475	8	$3,800	44	$5,200	$650	136.8%
8	LiteLift Pro	$655	8	$5,240	25	$2,480	$310	47.3%
9	LiteLift Ladies	$655	4	$2,620	40	$6,710	$1,678	256.1%
10	LiteLift Racer	$795	3	$2,385	37	$5,900	$1,967	247.4%

FIGURE AE-1
Excel Spreadsheet
Source: Microsoft Excel, Microsoft Corporation

c. Outline the cells as shown in Figure AE-1.

d. Figure AE-1 uses the following formulas:

Cost of Current Inventory = Bike Cost × Number on Hand

Revenue per Bike = Rental Revenue/Number on Hand

**Revenue as a Percent of Cost of Inventory = Total Rental Revenue/
Cost of Current Inventory**

Use these formulas in your spreadsheet, as shown in Figure AE-1.

e. Format the cells in the columns as shown.

f. Give three examples of decisions that management of the bike rental agency might make from this data.

g. What other calculation could you make from this data that would be useful to the bike rental management? Create a second version of this spreadsheet in your worksheet document that has this calculation.

AE2-2.   In this exercise, you will learn how to create a query based on data that a user enters and how to use that query to create a data entry form.

a. Download the Microsoft Access file **Ch02Ex02_U11e.accdb**. Open the file and familiarize yourself with the data in the Customer table.

b. Click *Create* in the Access ribbon. Click the icon labeled *Query Design*. Select the Customer table as the basis for the query by double-clicking on *Customer*. Close the Show Table dialog. Drag CustomerName, CustomerEmail, DateOfLastRental, BikeLastRented, TotalNumberOfRentals, and TotalRentalRevenue into the columns of the query results pane (the table at the bottom of the query design window).

c. In the CustomerName column, in the row labeled Criteria, place the following text:

[Enter Name of Customer:]

Type this exactly as shown, including the square brackets. This notation tells Access to ask you for a customer name to query.

d. In the ribbon, click the red exclamation mark labeled *Run*. Access will display a dialog box with the text *Enter Name of Customer:* (the text you entered in the query Criteria row). Enter the value *Maple, Rex* and click *OK*.

e. Save your query with the name *Parameter Query*.

f. Click the Home tab on the ribbon and click the Design View (upper left-hand button on the Home ribbon). Replace the text in the Criteria column of the CustomerName column with the following text. Type it exactly as shown:

Like "*"& [Enter part of Customer Name to search by:]&"*"

g. Run the query by clicking *Run* on the ribbon. Enter *Maple* when prompted *Enter part of Customer Name to search by*. Notice that the two customers who have the name Maple are displayed. If you have any problems, ensure that you have typed the preceding phrase *exactly* as shown into the Criteria row of the CustomerName column of your query.

h. Save your query again under the name *Parameter Query*. Close the query window.

i. Click *Create* on the Access ribbon. Under the Forms group, choose *Form Wizard*. In the dialog that opens, in the Tables/Queries box, click the down arrow. Select *Query: Parameter Query*. Click the double chevron << symbol and all of the columns in the query will move to the Selected Fields area.

j. Click *Next* two times. In the box under *What title do you want for your form?* enter *Customer Query Form* and click *Finish*.

k. Enter *Maple* in the dialog box that appears. Access will open a form with the values for Maple, Rex. At the bottom of the form, click the right-facing arrow, and the data for the second customer named Maple will appear. *What is that customer's first name?* will appear.

l. Close the form. Select *Object Type* and *Forms* in the Access Navigation Pane. Double-click the Customer Query Form and enter the value *Amanda*. Access will display data for all three customers having the value Amanda in their name.

Chapter 3

AE3-1. OLAP cubes are very similar to Microsoft Excel pivot tables. For this exercise, assume that your organization's purchasing agents rate vendors on a scale from 1 to 5, with 5 being the best.

a. Open the Excel file **Ch03Ex01_U11e.xlsx**. The spreadsheet has the following column names: *VendorName, EmployeeName, Date, Year*, and *Rating*.

b. Under the *INSERT* ribbon in Excel, click *Pivot Table*.

c. When asked to provide a data range, drag your mouse over the column names and data values so as to select all of the data. Excel will fill in the range values in the open dialog box. Place your pivot table in a new worksheet. Click *OK*.

d. Excel will create a field list on the right-hand side of your spreadsheet. Underneath it, a grid labeled *Drag fields between areas below*: should appear. Drag and drop the field named *VendorName* into the area named ROWS. Observe what happens in the pivot table to the left (in column A). Now drag and drop *EmployeeName* on to COLUMNS and *Rating* on to VALUES. Again, observe the effect of these actions in the pivot table to the left. Voilà! You have a pivot table.

e. To see how the pivot table works, drag and drop more fields onto the grid in the bottom right-hand side of your screen. For example, drop *Year* just underneath *EmployeeName*. Then move *Year* above *Employee*. Now move *Year* below *Vendor*. All of this action is just like an OLAP cube, and, in fact, OLAP cubes are readily displayed in Excel pivot tables. The major difference is that OLAP cubes are usually based on thousands or more rows of data.

AE3-2. Suppose you work for the bicycle parts distributor mentioned in Q3-2 of Chapter 3. The team was investigating the possibility of selling 3D printable plans for bike parts rather than the parts themselves. The team needed to identify qualifying parts and compute how much revenue potential those parts represent. Download the Access file **Ch03Ex02_U11e.accdb**, which contains the data extract the team used.

a. Suppose Desert Gear Supply decides not to release its 3D design files at any price. Remove parts provided by it from consideration and repeat the data analysis in Chapter 3.

b. The team decides, in light of the absence of Desert Gear Supply's part designs, to repeat its analysis with different criteria as follows:

- Large customers are those who have ordered more than 900 parts.
- Frequent purchases occur at least 25 times per year.

- Small quantities have an average order size of 3 or less.
- Inexpensive parts cost less than $75.
- Shipping weight is less than 4 pounds.

Repeat the data analysis in Chapter 3.

c. How does the second set of criteria change the results?

d. What recommendations would you make in light of your analysis?

AE3-3. Microsoft Fetch! is an AI application that is designed to automatically identify dog breeds. Identifying dog breeds is difficult because there are many dog breeds with similar traits. Fetch! analyzes numerous facial traits to try to identify the correct dog breed. It turns out to be amazingly accurate. The fun part is when you upload a picture of yourself and see which dog breed you most closely match. Another AI-driven Microsoft application (*www.how-old.net*) guesses how old you look based on your picture. We will consider both of these applications in this exercise.

a. Go to *www.what-dog.net*. (Microsoft Fetch! runs the application on this site.)

b. Click *Use your own photo*.

c. Select a picture of yourself from your computer.

d. Take a screenshot of the results. (One of the authors, Boyle, was identified as an Irish Setter. The other author, Kroenke, was identified as a Boerboel.)

e. Go to *www.how-old.net*.

f. Click *Use your own photo*.

g. Select a picture of yourself from your computer.

h. Take a screenshot of the results.

i. Explain how AI applications like these could be useful beyond identifying dog breeds and ages.

j. How could this type of AI-driven vision system be commercialized (i.e., be used to make money)?

Chapter 4

AE4-1. Sometimes you will have data in one Office application and want to move it to another Office application without rekeying it. Often this occurs when data was created for one purpose but then is used for a second purpose. For example, Figure AE-2 presents a portion of an Excel spreadsheet that shows the assignment of computers to employees.

	A	B	C	D	E	F	G	H
1	EmpLastName	EmpFirstName	Plant	Computer Brand	CPU (GHz)	Memory (GB)	Disk (TB)	OS
2	Ashley	Linda	Denver	Dell	3	32	4	Windows 10
3	Davidson	Victor	Denver	Dell	3	24	4	Windows 10
4	Ching	Diem Thi	Denver	HP	3	16	6	Windows 8
5	Collins	James	Denver	Dell	2.5	12	3	Windows 7
6	Corning	Haley	Denver	HP	3	16	4	Windows 8
7	Scott	Richard	Denver	HP	2.5	16	6	Windows 8
8	Corovic	Anna	Denver	Dell	4	24	8	Windows 10
9	Lane	Kathy	Denver	Lenovo	2.5	12	2	Windows 7
10	Wei	James	Denver	IBM	3	32	4	Windows 10
11	Dixon	Mary	Denver	IBM	2	12	2	Windows 7
12	Lee	Matthew	Denver	Dell	2.5	12	2	Windows 7
13	Duong	Steven	Denver	Dell	2	4	2	Vista
14	Bosa	William	Denver	HP	3	16	6	Windows 8
15	Drew	Tony	Denver	HP	3	16	4	Windows 8
16	Adams	Mark	Denver	HP	2.5	8	2	Windows 7
17	Lunden	Nicole	Denver	Lenovo	4	24	8	Windows 10
18	Utran	Bryan	Denver	Dell	3	16	4	Windows 8
19								
20		Primary Contact:	Kaye Davidson					
21								

FIGURE AE-2
Sample Excel Data for Import
Source: Microsoft Excel, Microsoft Corporation

Suppose you want to use this data to help you assess how to upgrade computers. Let's say, for example, that you want to upgrade all of the computers' operating systems to Windows 10. Furthermore, you want to first upgrade the computers that most need upgrading, but suppose you have a limited budget. To address this situation, you would like to query the data in Figure AE-2, find all computers that do not have Windows 10, and then select those with slower CPUs or smaller memory as candidates for upgrading. To do this, you need to move the data from Excel into Access.

Once you have analyzed the data and determined the computers to upgrade, you want to produce a report. In that case, you may want to move the data from Access back to Excel or perhaps into Word. In this exercise, you will learn how to perform these tasks.

a. To begin, download the Excel file **Ch04Ex01_U11e.xlsx** into one of your directories. We will import the data in this file into Access, but before we do so, familiarize yourself with the data by opening it in Excel. Notice that there are three worksheets in this workbook. Close the Excel file.

b. Create a blank Access database. Name the database Ch04Ex01_Answer. Place it in some directory; it may be the same directory into which you have placed the Excel file, but it need not be. Close the default table that Access creates and delete it.

c. Now, we will import the data from the three worksheets in the Excel file **Ch04Ex01_U11e.xlsx** into a single table in your Access database. On the ribbon, select *External Data* and in the Import & Link section, click *Excel*. Start the import. For the first worksheet (Denver), you should select *Import the source data into a new table in the current database*. Ignore the warning about the first row by clicking *OK*. Be sure to click *First Row Contains Column Headings* when Access presents your data. You can use the default Field types and let Access add the primary key. Name your table *Employees* and click *Finish*. There is no need to save your import script.

For the Miami and Boston worksheets, again click *External Data, Import Excel*, but this time select *Append a copy of the records to the table Employees*. Select the Miami worksheet, and click *Finish*. Repeat to import the Boston office employees.

d. Open the *Employee* table, and examine the data. Notice that Access has erroneously imported a blank line and the *Primary Contact* data into rows at the end of each data set. This data is not part of the employee records, and you should delete it (in three places—once for each worksheet). The *Employee* table should have a total of 40 records.

e. Create a parameterized query on this data. Place all of the columns except *ID* into the query. In the *OS* column, set the criteria to select rows for which the value is not *Windows 10*. In the *CPU* (GHz) column, enter the criterion: $<=[Enter\ cutoff\ value\ for\ CPU]$ and in the *Memory* (GB) column, enter the criterion: $<=[Enter\ cutoff\ value\ for\ Memory]$. Test your query. For example, run your query and enter a value of 4 for CPU and 16 for memory. Verify that the correct rows are produced.

f. Use your query to find values of CPU and memory that give you as close to a maximum of 10 computers to upgrade as possible.

g. When you have found values of CPU and memory that give you 10, or nearly 10, computers to upgrade, leave your query open. Now, click *External data, Word*, and create a Word document that contains the results of your query. Adjust the column widths of the created table so that it fits on the page. Write a memo around this table explaining that these are the computers that you believe should be upgraded.

AE4-2. Assume you have been asked to create a spreadsheet to help make a buy-versus-lease decision about the servers for your organization. Assume that you are considering the servers for a 5-year period, but you do not know exactly how many servers you will need. Initially, you know you will need five servers, but you might need as many as 50, depending on the success of your organization's e-commerce activity. (By the way, many organizations are still making these calculations. However, those that have moved to the cloud no longer need to do so!)

a. For the buy-alternative calculations, set up your spreadsheet so that you can enter the base price of the server hardware, the price of all software, and a maintenance expense that is some percentage of the hardware price. Assume that the percent you enter covers both hardware and software maintenance. Also assume that each server has a 3-year life, after which it has no value. Assume straight-line depreciation for computers used less than 3 years, and that at the end of the 5 years you can sell the computers you have used for less than 3 years for their depreciated value. Also assume that your organization pays 2 percent interest on capital expenses. Assume the servers cost $2,500 each, and the needed software costs $1,250. Assume that the maintenance expense varies from 2 to 7 percent.

b. For the lease-alternative calculations, assume that the leasing vendor will lease the same computer hardware you can purchase. The lease includes all the software you need as well as all maintenance. Set up your spreadsheet so that you can enter various lease costs, which vary according to the number of years of the lease (1, 2, or 3). Assume the cost of a 3-year lease is $285 per machine per month, a 2-year lease is $335 per machine per month, and a 1-year lease is $415 per machine per month. Also, the lessor offers a 5 percent discount if you lease from 20 to 30 computers and a 10 percent discount if you lease from 31 to 50 computers.

c. Using your spreadsheet, compare the costs of buy versus lease under the following situations. (Assume you either buy or lease. You cannot lease some and buy some.) Make assumptions as necessary and state those assumptions.

   (1) Your organization requires 20 servers for 5 years.
   (2) Your organization requires 20 servers for the first 2 years and 40 servers for the next 3 years.
   (3) Your organization requires 20 servers for the first 2 years, 40 servers for the next 2 years, and 50 servers for the last year.
   (4) Your organization requires 10 servers the first year, 20 servers the second year, 30 servers the third year, 40 servers the fourth year, and 50 servers the last year.
   (5) For the previous case, does the cheaper alternative change if the cost of the servers is $4,000? If it is $8,000?

AE4-3. As you read in Chapter 4, open source software is popular because it's stable, customizable, and free. But you may not have used open source software before. In this project, you will download an alternate to the Microsoft Office suite called LibreOffice. It has applications for making documents (Writer), spreadsheets (Calc), presentations (Impress), databases (Base), and graphics (Draw) similar to those in Microsoft Office.

If you're used to Microsoft Office, it will take some time to become familiar with the LibreOffice interface. LibreOffice can do just about everything Microsoft Office can do, but it does it in a slightly different way. The main benefit of using LibreOffice is that it's totally free. You can install it as many times as you'd like on as many computers as you'd like.

a. Browse to *www.libreoffice.org*.
b. Click on the Download menu and select LibreOffice Fresh.
c. Download and install the latest version of LibreOffice. (There are LibreOffice versions for Windows, macOS, and Linux.)
d. Open LibreOffice Calc. (There will be a shortcut on your desktop.)

e. Enter your name, date, and time into the new spreadsheet in cells A1, A2, and A3, respectively.

f. Click *Tools and Options*.

g. Expand the Load/Save menu and click on General.

h. Change the "Always save as" dropdown from *ODF Spreadsheet* to *Microsoft Excel 2007-2013 XML* and click *OK*. (You can do the same thing for documents and presentations.)

i. Click *File*, *Save*, and *Save*.

j. Take a screenshot with your name showing and paste it into your document. (You can take a screenshot by pressing *Alt + Print Screen*.)

k. Explain why more people don't use LibreOffice if it's free.

l. Explain why a systems administrator, who manages hundreds of servers (with Linux and Windows operating systems), might like using LibreOffice.

m. Explain why LibreOffice might be an important application for users or organizations in developing countries.

Chapter 5

AE5-1.   In some cases, users want to use Access and Excel together. They process relational data with Access, import some of the data into Excel, and use Excel's tools for creating professional-looking charts and graphs. You will do exactly that in this exercise.

Download the Access file **Ch05Ex01_U11e.accdb**. Open the database, and select *DATABASE TOOLS/Relationships*. As you can see, there are three tables: *Product*, *Vendor-ProductInventory*, and *Vendor*. Open each table individually to familiarize yourself with the data.

For this problem, we will define *InventoryCost* as the product of *Industry-Standard-Cost* and *QuantityOnHand*. The query *InventoryCost* computes these values for every item in inventory for every vendor. Open that query, and view the data to be certain you understand this computation. Open the other queries as well so that you understand the data they produce.

a. Sum this data by vendor and display it in a pie chart like that shown in Figure AE-3 (your totals will be different from those shown). Proceed as follows:

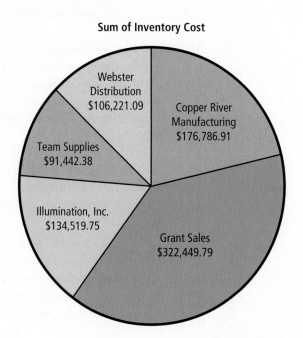

Sum of Inventory Cost

Webster Distribution $106,221.09

Copper River Manufacturing $176,786.91

Team Supplies $91,442.38

Illumination, Inc. $134,519.75

Grant Sales $322,449.79

FIGURE AE-3
Data Displayed in Pie-Chart Format
Source: Microsoft Corporation

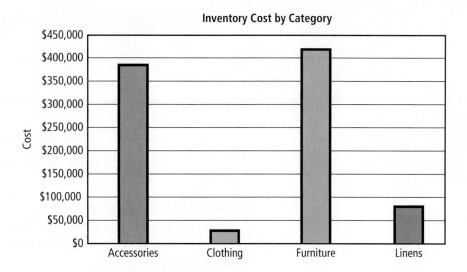

FIGURE AE-4
Data Displayed in Bar-Chart Format
Source: Microsoft Corporation

(1) Open Excel and create a new spreadsheet.

(2) Click *DATA* on the ribbon and select *From Access* in the *Get External Data* ribbon category.

(3) Navigate to the location in which you have stored the Access file **Ch05Ex01_U11e.accdb**.

(4) Select the query that contains the data you need for this pie chart.

(5) Import the data into a worksheet.

(6) Format the appropriate data as currency.

(7) Select the range that contains the data, press the Function key, and proceed from there to create the pie chart. Name the data and pie chart worksheets appropriately.

b. Follow a similar procedure to create the bar chart shown in Figure AE-4. Again, your data will be different. Place the data and the chart in separate worksheets and name them appropriately.

AE5-2. Read Case Study 5 on pages 195–199. A copy of Dean's database is stored in the Access file **Ch05Ex02_U11e.accdb**. Download a copy of this file and create queries to provide the following data:

a. Sort the pianos from high quality to low.

b. Sort the pianos from high quality to low, and within each quality, sort by Building and then by Location within that building.

c. List the pianos in the shed, and sort the results by manufacturer.

d. List all of the pianos with a Type of *Spinet*.

e. Count the pianos for each value of quality (ranging from 1 to 5).

f. Write a query to produce the report in Figure 5-35 on page 199.

AE5-3. In this exercise, you will create a two-table database, define relationships, create a form and a report, and use them to enter data and view results.

a. Download the Excel file **Ch05Ex03_U11e.xlsx**. Open the spreadsheet, and review the data in the *Employee* and *Computer* worksheets.

b. Create a new Access database with the name *Ch05Ex03_Solution*. Close the table that Access automatically creates, and delete it.

c. Import the data from the Excel spreadsheet into your database. Import the *Employee* worksheet into a table named *Employee*. Be sure to check *First Row Contains Column Headings*. Select *Choose my own primary key* and use the ID field as that key.

d. Import the *Computer* worksheet into a table named *Computer*. Check *First Row Contains Column Headings*, but let Access create the primary key.

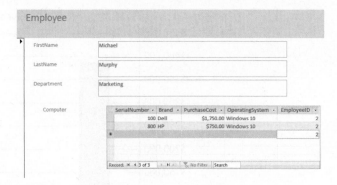

FIGURE AE-5
Employee Computer Assignment Form
Source: Windows 10, Microsoft Corporation

e. Open the relationships window, and add both *Employee* and *Computer* to the design space. Drag ID from *Employee* and drop it on *EmployeeID* in *Computer*. Check *Enforce Referential Integrity* and the two checkmarks below. Ensure you know what these actions mean.

f. Open the Form Wizard dialog box (under *Create, More Forms*), and add all of the columns for each of your tables to your form. Select *View your data by Employee*. Title your form *Employee* and your subform *Computer*.

g. Open the *Computer* subform, and delete *EmployeeID* and *ComputerID*. These values are maintained by Access, and it is just a distraction to keep them. Your form should appear like the one shown in Figure AE-5. (Your data will be different.)

h. Use your form to add two new computers to *Michael Murphy*. Both computers are Dells, both use Windows 10, one costs $750, and the other costs $1,400.

i. Delete the Lenovo computer for Stan Larsen.

j. Use the Report Wizard (under *Create*) to create a report having all data from both the *Employee* and *Computer* tables. Adjust the report design until you find a design you like. Correct the label alignment if you need to.

Chapter 6

AE6-1. Numerous Web sites are available that will test your Internet data communications speed. You can find one good example at *www.measurementlab.net/tests/ndt/*. (If that site is no longer active, Google "What is my Internet speed?" to find another speed-testing site. Use it.)

a. While connected to your university's network, go to *www.measurementlab.net/tests/ndt/* and click *Start Test*. Record your average upload speed, download speed, network latency, and jitter.

b. Go home or to a public wireless site, and run the *www.measurementlab.net/tests/ndt/* test again. Compute your average upload and download speeds. If you are performing this test at home, are you getting the performance you are paying for?

c. Contact a friend or relative in another state. Ask him or her to run the *www.measurementlab.net/tests/ndt/* test. Report the upload and download speeds.

d. Compare the results in parts a–c. What conclusion, if any, can you draw from these tests?

AE6-2. Assume you have been asked to create an Office application to estimate cloud computing costs. You decide to create a spreadsheet into which your customers can provide their cloud computing needs and which you can then import into an Access database and use queries to compute cloud computing costs.

Figure AE-6 shows the structure of the spreadsheet into which your customers will input their requirements. You can download this spreadsheet in the Excel file **Ch06Ex02_U11e.xlsx**. Figure AE-7 shows an Access table that has costs corresponding to the requirements in Figure AE-6. You can download this database in the Access file **Ch06Ex02_U11e.accdb**.

FIGURE AE-6
Worksheet for Inputting Cloud Computing Requirements
Source: Microsoft Excel, Microsoft Corporation

	A	B	C	D	E	F	G
1		Jan-20	Feb-20	Mar-20	Apr-20	May-20	Jun-20
2	Compute requirements (hours):						
3							
4	Extra Small Instance	1200	1200	1200	1200	1200	1200
5	Small Instance	2000	2000	2400	2400	0	3000
6	Medium Instance	900	1800	2700	3600	3600	3600
7	Large Instance	0	500	1000	1500	2000	2000
8	Extra Large Instance	0	0	0	1000	1500	2000
9							
10	Storage requirements:						
11	Storage Required (GB)	30	35	40	45	50	55
12	Storage Transactions (1000s)	30	30	35	35	40	50
13							
14	Database requirements (number of instances)						
15	10GB Database	2	2	2	2	1	1
16	20GB Database	0	3	3	3	3	3
17	30GB Database		4	5	6	6	7
18	40GB Database	0	0	0	3	3	4
19	50GB Database	0	0	2	2	3	0
20							

FIGURE AE-7
Cloud Computing Costs
Source: Microsoft Access, Microsoft Corporation

CloudCosts

ID	Resource Name	Units	Cost
1	Extra Small Instance	Hours	$0.03
2	Small Instance	Hours	$0.09
3	Medium Instance	Hours	$0.12
4	Large Instance	Hours	$0.37
5	Extra Large Instance	Hours	$0.55
6	StorageRequired	GB / month	$0.15
7	StorageTransactions	10,000	$0.01
8	10GB Database	Each	$9.99
9	20GB Database	Each	$149.98
10	30GB Database	Each	$199.97
11	40GB Database	Each	$299.96
12	50GB Database	Each	$399.95

a. Import the spreadsheet data into the Access database.

b. Write queries to compute the cost of each resource.

c. Create a report that shows the cost for each type of resource for each month. Show the total costs for the 6-month period for each resource as well. Include a grand total of all the costs.

d. Create a pie chart that breaks out the total costs by resource. *Hint:* You can import the query data back into Excel.

e. Create a pie chart that breaks out the total costs by month. *Hint:* You can import the query data back into Excel.

f. Assume that processing costs increase by 10 percent across the board. Repeat parts c, d, and e for the changed costs.

AE6-3. There are a few problems with cloud-based storage. First, it seems like there's never enough of it. This is especially true if it's free. Second, you always wonder if it's really secure. Yes, your storage provider says your data is secure. But is it really? Is there some way to be sure?

In this project, you will learn how to use 7-Zip to solve both of these problems. You'll learn how to compress and encrypt important files and directories. If you are storing confidential data in the cloud, it's important to make sure it's encrypted—by you. Using a third-party encryption tool like 7-Zip means only *you* can access your data. Trusting your cloud providers isn't necessary. 7-Zip is also a very efficient file archiver that will save you a lot of space.

a. Browse to *www.7-zip.org*.

b. Click on *Download* and install the latest version of 7-Zip for your operating system. (There are 7-Zip versions for Windows, macOS, Linux, BSD, and UNIX.)

c. Go to your Downloads folder. (You can go to any folder that contains large files.)

d. Right-click on a large file.

e. Click *7-Zip* and *Add to archive*.

f. Rename the file *YourName.7z*. (Replace "YourName" with your first and last names. If your name was John Doe, the file would be named JohnDoe.7z.)

g. In the Encryption section, enter a password—twice. (Choose a simple password you can remember.)

h. Take a screenshot, and paste it into your document. (You can take a screenshot by pressing *Alt + Print Screen*.)

i. Click *OK*. (Notice that your original file remains unchanged.)

j. After your new YourName.7z file is compressed, right-click it and select *7-Zip* and *Extract to "YourName\"*.

k. Enter the password you set, and click *OK*. (Your file should start extracting.)

l. Explain why third-party encryption is important for highly confidential files.

m. Explain why compressing large files is important when using cloud-based storage.

AE6-4. In this exercise, you will learn to use two of the most commonly used networking commands—*ping* and *ipconfig*. Both of these commands are commonly used to troubleshoot network problems.

Ping is a command that will tell you if a computer (host) is reachable and alive. It works just like pings in submarines (think back to the movie *The Hunt for Red October*). It sends out a packet that asks the target computer to send it back a message saying it's actually there. It also tells you how long it took the message to get back from the target computer and if any of the packets were lost. This is very useful when you need to see if a server/computer is running. You can also use it to diagnose latency and/or packet loss issues.

This example pings *www.weber.edu*. Feel free to ping your own university or Web site of your choice. Instead of using *www.weber.edu*, please use *www.[YourUniversity].edu*. Time stamps will also be included at the end of each example.

Ipconfig will give you a listing of the basic network information for the computer you are using. You will get your Internet Protocol (IP) address and default gateway (the computer that connects you to the Internet). Network administrators use ipconfig to diagnose a variety of issues like network outages, faulty hardware, and misconfigured computers.

a. Click *Start*.

b. In the search box, type *cmd*

c. Press *Enter*.

d. Type *ping www.weber.edu*

e. Press *Enter*. (This will ping *www.weber.edu* with four packets.)

f. Type *time*

g. Press *Enter* twice.

h. Take a screenshot.

i. Type *ipconfig*

j. Press *Enter*. (This will display basic network configuration information for adapters on your computer.)

k. Type *ipconfig /all*

l. Press *Enter*. (This will display extended network configuration information for all adapters on your computer.)

m. Take a screenshot.

n. What is the Default Gateway?

o. What do DNS servers do?

p. Why would you experience packet loss?

Chapter 7

AE7-1.   Suppose that you have been asked to assist in the managerial decision about how much to increase pay in the next year. Assume you are given a list of the departments in your company, along with the average salary for employees in each department for major companies in your industry. Additionally, you are given the names and salaries of 10 people in each of three departments in your company.

Assume you have been asked to create a spreadsheet that shows the names of the 10 employees in each department, their current salary, the difference between their current salary and the industry average salary for their department, and the percent their salary would need to be increased to meet the industry average. Your spreadsheet should also compute the average increase needed to meet the industry average for each department and the average increase, company-wide, to meet industry averages.

a. Use the data in the file **Ch07Ex01_U11e.docx** and create the spreadsheet.

b. How can you use this analysis to contribute to the employee salary decision? Based on this data, what conclusions can you make?

c. Suppose other team members want to use your spreadsheet. Name three ways you can share it with them and describe the advantages and disadvantages of each.

AE7-2.   Suppose that you have been asked to assist in the managerial decision about how much to increase pay in the next year. Specifically, you are tasked to determine if there are significant salary differences among departments in your company.

You are given an Access database with a table of employee data with the following structure:

EMPLOYEE (Name, Department, Specialty, Salary)

where *Name* is the name of an employee who works in a department, *Department* is the department name, *Specialty* is the name of the employee's primary skill, and *Salary* is the employee's current salary. Assume that no two employees have the same name. You have been asked to answer the following queries:

(1) List the names, department, and salary of all employees earning more than $100,000.

(2) List the names and specialties of all employees in the Marketing department.

(3) Compute the average, maximum, and minimum salary of employees in your company.

(4) Compute the average, minimum, and maximum salary of employees in the Marketing department.

(5) Compute the average, minimum, and maximum salary of employees in the Information Systems department.

(6) *Extra credit*: Compute the average salary for employees in every department. Use *Group By*.

a. Design and run Access queries to obtain the answers to these questions, using the data in the file **Ch07Ex02_U11e.accdb**.

b. Explain how the data in your answer contributes to the salary increase decision.

c. Suppose other team members want to use your Access application. Name three ways you can share it with them and describe the advantages and disadvantages of each.

Chapter 8

AE8-1. Suppose your manager asks you to create a spreadsheet to compute a production schedule. Your schedule should stipulate a production quantity for seven products that is based on sales projections made by three regional managers at your company's three sales regions.

a. Create a separate worksheet for each sales region. Use the data in the Word file **Ch08Ex01_U11e.docx**. This file contains each manager's monthly sales projections for the past year, actual sales results for those same months, and projections for sales for each month in the coming quarter.

b. Create a separate worksheet for each manager's data. Import the data from Word into Excel.

c. On each of the worksheets, use the data from the prior four quarters to compute the discrepancy between the actual sales and the sale projections. This discrepancy can be computed in several ways: You could calculate an overall average, or you could calculate an average per quarter or per month. You could also weight recent discrepancies more heavily than earlier ones. Choose a method that you think is most appropriate. Explain why you chose the method you did.

d. Modify your worksheets to use the discrepancy factors to compute an adjusted forecast for the coming quarter. Thus, each of your spreadsheets will show the raw forecast and the adjusted forecast for each month in the coming quarter.

e. Create a fourth worksheet that totals sales projections for all of the regions. Show both the unadjusted forecast and the adjusted forecast for each region and for the company overall. Show month and quarter totals.

f. Create a bar graph showing total monthly production. Display the unadjusted and adjusted forecasts using different colored bars.

AE8-2. Figure AE-8 is a sample bill of materials (BOM), a form that shows the components and parts used to construct a product. In this example, the product is a child's wagon. Such bills of materials are an essential part of manufacturing functional applications as well as ERP applications.

This particular example is a form produced using Microsoft Access. Creating such a form is a bit tricky, so this exercise will guide you through the steps required. You can then apply what you learn to produce a similar report. You can also use Access to experiment on extensions of this form.

a. Create a table named *PART* with columns *PartNumber, Level, Description, QuantityRequired*, and *PartOf*. *Description* and *Level* should be text, *PartNumber* should be AutoNumber, and *QuantityRequired* and *PartOf* should be numeric, long integer. Add the *PART* data shown in Figure AE-8 to your table.

b. Create a query that has all columns of *PART*. Restrict the view to rows having a value of 1 for *Level*. Name your query *Level1*.

c. Create two more queries that are restricted to rows having values of 2 or 3 for *Level*. Name your queries *Level2* and *Level3*, respectively.

d. Create a form that contains *PartNumber, Level*, and *Description* from *Level1*. You can use a wizard for this if you want. Name the form *Bill of Materials*.

e. Select the Subform/Subreport tool in the Controls section of the DESIGN ribbon and create a subform in your form in part d. Set the data on this form to be all of the columns of *Level2*. After you have created the subform, ensure that the Link Child Fields property is set to *PartOf* and that the Link Master Fields property is set to *PartNumber*. Close the *Bill of Materials* form.

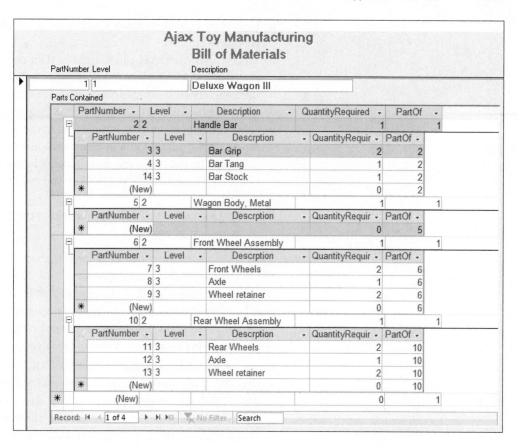

Ajax Toy Manufacturing
Bill of Materials

PartNumber Level   Description

| | | 1 | 1 | | Deluxe Wagon III | | | | |

Parts Contained

PartNumber	Level	Description	QuantityRequired	PartOf
2 2		Handle Bar	1	1

	PartNumber	Level	Descrption	QuantityRequir	PartOf
	3 3		Bar Grip	2	2
	4 3		Bar Tang	1	2
	14 3		Bar Stock	1	2
*	(New)			0	2

PartNumber	Level	Description	QuantityRequired	PartOf
5 2		Wagon Body, Metal	1	1

	PartNumber	Level	Descrption	QuantityRequir	PartOf
*	(New)			0	5

PartNumber	Level	Description	QuantityRequired	PartOf
6 2		Front Wheel Assembly	1	1

	PartNumber	Level	Descrption	QuantityRequir	PartOf
	7 3		Front Wheels	2	6
	8 3		Axle	1	6
	9 3		Wheel retainer	2	6
*	(New)			0	6

PartNumber	Level	Description	QuantityRequired	PartOf
10 2		Rear Wheel Assembly	1	1

	PartNumber	Level	Descrption	QuantityRequir	PartOf
	11 3		Rear Wheels	2	10
	12 3		Axle	1	10
	13 3		Wheel retainer	2	10
*	(New)			0	10

*	(New)			0	1

Record: I◄ ◄ 1 of 4 ► ►I ►⧉ ⟋ No Filter   Search

FIGURE AE-8
Bill of Materials Example
Source: Microsoft Excel, Microsoft Corporation

f. Open the subform created in part e, and create a subform on it using the Subform/Subreport control. Set the data on this subform to be all of the columns of *Level3*. After you have created the subform, ensure that the Link Child Fields property is set to *PartOf* and that the Link Master Fields property is set to *PartNumber*. Close the *Bill of Materials* form.

g. Open the *Bill of Materials* form. It should appear as in Figure AE-8. Open and close the form and add new data. Using this form, add sample BOM data for a product of your own choosing.

h. Following the process similar to that just described, create a *Bill of Materials Report* that lists the data for all of your products.

i. *Optional, challenging extension*: Each part in the BOM in Figure AE-8 can be used in at most one assembly (there is space to show just one *PartOf* value). You can change your design to allow a part to be used in more than one assembly as follows: First, remove *PartOf* from PART. Next, create a second table that has two columns: *AssemblyPartNumber* and *ComponentPartNumber*. The first contains a part number of an assembly, and the second contains a part number of a component. Every component of a part will have a row in this table. Extend the views described previously to use this second table and to produce a display similar to Figure AE-8.

Chapter 9

AE9-1. Suppose you are the manager of social media policy for an organization having 1,000 employees with seven different offices throughout North America. Further suppose that the CEO has requested a report showing a list of all of the employees' blogs, the employees' job titles and departments, and the purpose and URL of each blog. She doesn't want to control employees; she just wants to know where they are.

a. Explain the conditions under which using a spreadsheet to track this data would be appropriate.

b. Suppose that employees can have more than one blog, but that a blog is only supported by a single employee. Further suppose that you decide that you need to track the dates on which a blog was first created and the date of the last posting, if the blog is no longer active. Design a database for these requirements.

c. Fill your database with the sample data in the Word document **Ch09Ex01_U11e .docx**. EmployeeID is a unique identifier; a null value for EndDate means the blog is still active. Do not retype this data; import it instead. You can either import it several times, each time to a different table, or you can import it once and use queries to fill the tables.

d. Create a report that you believe is suitable for the CEO's needs. Justify the content and structure of your report.

AE9-2. Assume that you have been given the task of compiling evaluations that your company's purchasing agents make of their vendors. Each month, every purchasing agent evaluates all of the vendors that he or she has ordered from in the past month on three factors: price, quality, and responsiveness. Assume the ratings are from 1 to 5, with 5 being the best. Because your company has hundreds of vendors and dozens of purchasing agents, you decide to use Access to compile the results.

a. Create a database with three tables: VENDOR (*VendorNumber, Name, Contact*), PURCHASER (*EmpNumber, Name, Email*), and RATING (*EmpNumber, VendorNumber, Month, Year, Price Rating, QualityRating, ResponsivenessRating*). Assume that *VendorNumber* and *EmpNumber* are the keys of VENDOR and PURCHASER, respectively. Decide what you think is the appropriate key for RATING.

b. Create appropriate relationships.

c. Import the data in the Excel file **Ch09Ex02_U11e.xlsx**. Note that data for Vendor, Purchaser, and Rating are stored in three separate worksheets.

d. Create a query that shows the names of all vendors and their average scores.

e. Create a query that shows the names of all employees and their average scores.
Hint: In this and in part f, you will need to use the *Group By* function in your query.

f. Create a parameterized query that you can use to obtain the minimum, maximum, and average ratings on each criterion for a particular vendor. Assume you will enter *VendorName* as the parameter.

g. Using the data created by your queries, what conclusions can you make about vendors or purchasers?

Chapter 10

AE10-1. Adblock Plus® is a Web browser add-on that can block advertisements. It can also block trackers and domains that are known sources of malware. In addition, it allows you to create custom filters that can block specific Web content. Adblock Plus can make Web surfing safer and more enjoyable by eliminating annoying ads.

In this project, you will compare the same Web site in two browsers. You will install Adblock Plus in Firefox. You'll then compare the filtered Web site to an unfiltered version in Google Chrome.

(1) Open Google Chrome and browse to *www.amazon.com*.

(2) Fill the right-hand side of your screen with your Google Chrome browser by pressing the Window key and right arrow (⊞ + →).

(3) Open Firefox and browse to *www.amazon.com*.

(4) Fill the left-hand side of your screen with your Firefox browser by pressing the

Window key and left arrow (▦ + ←). You should now have two browsers displaying side by side.

(5) In your Firefox browser, type your name into the Amazon search box, but don't press *Enter*.

(6) Take a screenshot. (You can take a screenshot of your entire desktop by pressing *Ctrl + PrintScreen*.)

(7) Click the Firefox menu, then click *Add-ons*.

(8) Click *Get Add-ons*.

(9) In the search box, enter *Adblock Plus*.

(10) Press *Enter*.

(11) Click *Install* for the latest version of Adblock Plus.

(12) Click *Restart now*.

(13) Refresh the Amazon Web page in your Firefox browser. (You can press F5 or the Refresh button.)

(14) Enter your name in the Amazon search bar in your Firefox browser, but don't press *Enter*. (Note the reduced number of trackers and ads along the right-hand side when compared to the exact same page in your Google Chrome browser.)

(15) Take a screenshot of your entire desktop.

(16) Select another Web site that you know has advertising, and visit it in both browsers. (Major news Web sites typically have lots of ads and trackers.)

(17) Take another screenshot of your entire desktop, showing the difference in browsers.

a. Would online retailers dislike Adblock Plus? Why?

b. Some Web sites pay for their operations through ad revenue. Could Adblock Plus put them out of business?

c. Can you make exceptions (i.e., not block content) for specific Web sites?

AE10-2. Most users want an easy way to identify which Web sites are trustworthy and which Web sites they should avoid. Web of Trust® (WOT) provides a "scorecard" for each Web site you visit. This scorecard gives you a summary of four ratings: trustworthiness, vendor reliability, privacy, and child safety. The values shown on the scorecard are based on ratings from members of the WOT community who have contributed their evaluations of that Web site.

After installing WOT, you will notice a slight addition to the search results from major search engines (e.g., Google, Bing, and Yahoo!). You will see a WOT evaluation at the end of each search result. This evaluation provides a scorecard for each Web site displayed in the search results. The WOT evaluation can serve as a quick visual indicator of Web sites to avoid.

a. Open Firefox, click the Firefox menu, and click *Add-ons*.

b. Search for *WOT*.

c. Click *Install (WOT)* and *Restart now*. (You should see a small flag in the navigation bar.)

d. Browse to *www.google.com*, and search for your full name.

e. Take a screenshot of the results, and paste it into your document. (You can take a screenshot by pressing *Alt + Print Screen*. Notice the WOT icons next to each of the search results.)

f. Click on the WOT icon for one of the search results. (This will show you the WOT scorecard for that specific Web site.)

g. Using *Google.com*, search for *warez keygen*. (You should get a few Web sites with red circles, meaning they have a poor reputation.)

h. Click on the WOT icon for one of the Web site's WOT scorecard.

i. Take a screenshot, and paste it into your document.

j. Describe how WOT gets the values for its Web site scorecards.

k. Describe how you can evaluate Web sites using WOT.

l. Explain how WOT can protect users when surfing the Internet.

m. Uninstall WOT from your Web browser.

AE10-3. Recuva® is a program by Piriform® that recovers previously deleted files. Recuva scans the entire empty memory space for possible files to recover. Most users erroneously believe that data is gone forever when they empty it from the Recycle Bin. This is incorrect. It merely marks the space as available to be written over if another file needs to be stored. Your operating system writes over these available spaces and subsequently "damages" the previously deleted file. Recovery software can easily recover the undamaged part of the file if it knows how the file is structured.

In this project you will recover a file you delete from your USB drive. You can also run Recuva on your main hard drive if you accidently lose an important file.

a. Download and install Recuva from *www.recuva.com/download*.

b. If the program doesn't automatically open, you can click on the newly created desktop icon or click Start and search for Recuva.

c. Insert a USB drive into your computer.

d. Select your USB drive as the drive from which you want to recover files. (You can always scan your C: drive. Your USB will finish much quicker than your C: drive.)

e. Click *Scan*.

f. After the scan completes, click on any of the recovered files listed with a graphic extension (e.g., .jpg or .bmp) until you see a picture on the right-hand side of the screen. (If you don't see an image file, you can put a file on your USB, delete it, and then run the scan again. Remember the name of the file you delete so you can easily find it after you recover it.)

g. Click on the Info tab to see the details for the file and take a screenshot.

h. Check one of the recoverable graphic files. (Even some of the "unrecoverable" files are actually recoverable.)

i. Click *Recover* and save it to your desktop.

j. Open the picture you recovered, and take a screenshot.

k. Would Recuva work on your cell phone if it were connected to your computer?

l. What effect does the condition of the file have on its ability to be recovered?

Chapter 11

AE11-1. Suppose you have just been appointed manager of a help desk with an IS department. You have been there for just a week, and you are amazed to find only limited data to help you manage your employees. In fact, the only data kept concerns the processing of particular issues, called *Tickets*. The following data are kept: *Ticket#, Date_Submitted, Date_Opened, Date_Closed, Type (new or repeat), Reporting_ Employee_Name, Reporting_Employee_Division, Technician_Name_Problem_System,* and *Problem_Description.* You can find sample Ticket data in the Excel file **Ch11Ex01_U11e.xlsx**.

As a manager, you need information that will help you manage. Specifically, you need information that will help you learn who are your best- and worst-performing technicians, how different systems compare in terms of number of problems reported and the time required to fix those problems, how different divisions compare in terms of problems reported and the time required to fix them, which technicians are the best and worst at solving problems with particular systems, and which technicians are best and worst at solving problems from particular divisions.

a. Use Access, Excel, or a combination of the two to produce the information you need using the data in the Excel file **Ch11Ex01_U11e.xlsx**. In your answer, you may use queries, formulas, reports, forms, graphs, pivot tables, pivot charts, or any other type of Access or Excel display. Choose the best display for the type of information you are producing.

b. Explain how you would use these different types of information to manage your department.

c. Specify any additional information that you would like to have produced from this data to help you manage your department.

d. Use Access, Excel, or a combination to produce the information in part c.

Chapter 12

AE12-1. In this exercise, you will use Visio to create process diagrams in BPMN notation.

a. Download the Visio file **Ch12Ex01_U11e.vsd** from this text's support site. Open the file, and familiarize yourself with this diagram, which is a copy of Figure 12-7.

b. Notice that Visio includes the BPMN shapes. Go to the Shape organizer to see other types of flowchart shapes that Visio supports.

c. Create a new Visio diagram. Add BPMN shapes that you may want to use.

d. Model the customer process Respond to Quotation. Make sure your process accepts the inputs shown in **Ch12Ex01_U11e.vsd** and produces the outputs shown in that figure. Create your process so that your company checks prices and delivery dates, and requests changes if appropriate. Include other logic if necessary.

e. Show your work by saving your document as a PDF file.

AE12-2. Suppose you are given the task of comparing labor costs of meetings for systems development projects to budgets. Download the Word file **Ch12Ex02_U11e.docx** and the Excel file with the same name. The Word file has records of meeting dates, times, and attendees. The document was created from informal notes taken at the meetings. The Excel file has the project budgets as well as labor costs for different categories of employees.

Assume your company uses the traditional systems-first process illustrated in Figure 12-12. Further assume that each SDLC step requires two types of meetings: *Working meetings* involve users, business analysts, systems analysts, programmers, and PQA test engineers. *Review meetings* involve all of those people plus level-1 and level-2 managers of both user departments and the IS department.

a. Using either Access or Excel, whichever you think is better suited to the task, import the Word data to a work file and compute the total labor for each type of employee for each meeting.

b. Using the file you created in part a, compute the total labor for each type of employee for each phase of the project.

c. Combine your answer in part b with the data in the Excel file **Ch12Ex02_U11e.xlsx** to compute the total cost of meetings of each phase of the project.

d. Use a graphic chart of the type you think best to show the differences between meeting cost and budget.

e. Comment on your choice of Excel or Access for your work file. If you were to do this exercise over, would you use that same tool again? Why or why not?

GLOSSARY

10/100/1000 Ethernet A type of Ethernet that conforms to the IEEE 802.3 protocol and allows for transmission at a rate of 10, 100, or 1,000 Mbps (megabits per second). 215

Abstract reasoning The ability to make and manipulate models. One of four key skills for nonroutine cognitive thinking. 10

Access A popular personal and small workgroup DBMS product licensed by Microsoft. Included with some versions of Microsoft Office. 170

ACID An acronym standing for atomic, consistent, isolated, and durable. Used to describe the processing of transactions such that all of the transaction is processed or none of it is (atomic), transactions are processed in the same manner (consistent) whether processed alone or in the presence of millions of other transactions (isolated), and that once a transaction is stored it never goes away—even in the presence of failure (durable). 189

Activity A business function that receives inputs and produces outputs. An activity can be performed by a human, by a computer system, or by both. 46

Ad-blocking software Software that filters out advertising content. 352

Advanced Persistent Threat (APT) A sophisticated, possibly long-running, computer hack that is perpetrated by large, well-funded organizations like governments. APTs are a means to engage in cyberwarfare. 386

Adware Programs installed on the user's computer without the user's knowledge or permission that reside in the background and, unknown to the user, observe the user's actions and keystrokes, modify computer activity, and report the user's activities to sponsoring organizations. Most adware is benign in that it does not perform malicious acts or steal data. It does, however, watch user activity and produce pop-up ads. 398

Agile development An adaptive project management process based on the principles listed in Figure 12-20. Can be used for the management of many types of projects, including processes, information systems, and applications. 477

Algorithm A set of procedures used to solve a mathematical problem. 98

Android A mobile operating system that is a version of Linux. Android runs on the Google Nexus 7 and the Amazon Kindle Fire as well as many other mobile devices. 131

Application (1) Synonym for application software. (2) A combination of hardware, software, and data that is to be developed for an information system. 450

Application software Programs that perform a business function. Some application programs are general purpose, such as Excel or Word. Other application programs are specific to a business function, such as accounts payable. 133

Artificial intelligence (AI) The ability of a machine to simulate human abilities such as vision communication, recognition, learning, and decision making in order to achieve a goal. 89

As-is model A model that represents the current situation and processes. 455

Asymmetric encryption An encryption method whereby different keys are used to encode and to decode the message; one key encodes the message, and the other key decodes the message. Asymmetric encryption is slower and more complicated than symmetric encryption. 396

Asynchronous communication Information exchange that occurs when all members of a work team do not meet at the same time, such as those who work different shifts. 264

Attributes Characteristics of an entity. Example attributes of Order are *OrderNumber*, *OrderDate*, *SubTotal*, *Tax*, *Total*, and so forth. Example attributes of Salesperson are *Salesperson-Name*, *Email*, *Phone*, and so forth. 179

Augmented reality (AR) The altering of reality by overlaying digital information on real world objects. 123

Authentication The process whereby an information system verifies (validates) a user. 393

Automation The process of making systems operate without human intervention. 89

Baseline WBS The initial work breakdown structure that shows the planned tasks, dependencies, durations, and resource assignments. 474

Bell's Law A new computer class forms roughly each decade, establishing a new industry. 6

Best practices Methods that have been shown to produce successful results in prior implementations. 360

BI analysis The process of creating business intelligence. The four fundamental categories of BI analysis are reporting, data mining, Big Data, and knowledge management. 70

BI application The software component of a BI system. 68

Big Data A term used to describe data collections that are characterized by huge volume, rapid velocity, and great variety. 83

Binary digits See *bits*. 119

Biometric authentication The use of personal physical characteristics, such as fingerprints, facial features, and retinal scans, to authenticate users. 393

BI server A Web server application that is purpose-built for the publishing of business intelligence. 87

Bitcoin Currently the most well-known cryptocurrency. 127

Bits The means by which computers represent data; also called binary digits. A bit is either a zero or a one. 119

BlackBerry OS One of the most successful early mobile operating systems; was primarily used by business users on Black-Berry devices. 131

Blockchain The decentralized public ledgering system used to record cryptocurrency transactions. 128

Bluetooth A common wireless protocol designed for transmitting data over short distances, replacing cables. 218

Bounce rate Percent of people who visit a Web site and then immediately leave. 357

Bring your own device (BYOD) policy An official organizational policy that states employees' permissions and responsibilities when using personal mobile devices for organizational business. 147

Brooks' Law The adage that states: Adding more people to a late project makes the project later. Brooks' Law is true not only because a larger staff requires increased coordination, but also because new people need to be trained. The only people who can train the new employees are the existing team members, who are thus taken off productive tasks. The costs of training new people can overwhelm the benefit of their contributions. Named for Fred Brooks, author of *The Mythical Man-Month*. 473

Brute force attack A password-cracking program that tries every possible combination of characters. 389

Bullwhip effect A phenomenon in which the variability in the size and timing of orders increases at each stage up the supply chain, from customer to supplier. 504

Business analyst (1) A person who understands business strategies, goals, and objectives and who helps businesses develop and manage business processes and information systems. (2) Someone who is well versed in Porter's models, organizational strategy, and systems alignment theory, like COBIT, and who also understands technology sufficiently well to communicate with systems analysts and developers. Compare with systems analyst. 452

Business intelligence (BI) The processing of operational data, social data, purchased data, and employee knowledge to expose solutions, patterns, relationships, and trends of importance to the organization. 68

Business intelligence (BI) systems Information systems that produce business intelligence. 68

Business process (1) A network of activities that generate value by transforming inputs into outputs. (2) A network of activities, repositories, roles, resources, and flows that interact to achieve some business function; sometimes called a business system. 46, 453

Business process management (BPM) A cyclical process for systematically creating, assessing, and altering business processes. 47, 455

Business Process Modeling Notation (BPMN) Standard set of terms and graphical notations for documenting business processes. 456

Business process reengineering The activity of altering existing and designing new business processes to take advantage of the capabilities of new information systems technology. 305

Business-to-business (B2B) Relationships through which businesses generate new retail leads. 344

Business-to-consumer (B2C) Relationships through which businesses market their products to end users. 344

Bytes (1) 8-bit chunks of data. (2) Characters of data. 119

Cable line Cable television lines that provide high-speed data transmission. 219

Capital Resources that are invested with the expectation of future gain. 345

Carrier A telecommunications company that provides voice and data transportation services. 223

Central processing unit (CPU) The portion of a computer that selects instructions, processes them, performs arithmetic and logical comparisons, and stores results of operations in memory. 118

Chief information officer (CIO) The title of the principal manager of the IS department. Other common titles are vice president of information services, director of information services, and, less commonly, director of computer services. 422

Chief information security officer (CISO) The title of the person who manages security for the organization's information systems and information. 423

Chief security officer (CSO) The title of the person who manages security for all of the organization's assets: physical plant and equipment, employees, intellectual property, and digital. 423

Chief technology officer (CTO) The title of the head of the technology group. The CTO filters new ideas and products to identify those that are most relevant to the organization. The CTO's job requires deep knowledge of information technology and the ability to envision how new IT could affect an organization over time. 422

Client PCs, tablets, and smartphones that access servers via the cloud. 119

Client-server architecture Computing architecture that allows clients (users) to send requests across the Internet to servers, which respond and send data back. 203

Closed source Source code that is highly protected and only available to trusted employees and carefully vetted contractors. 137

Cloud A term that refers to elastic leasing of pooled computer resources over the Internet. 203

Cloud computing architecture Computing architecture that allows employees and customers to access organizational data and applications located in the cloud. 204

Cluster analysis Unsupervised data mining using statistical techniques to identify groups of entities that have similar characteristics. A common use for cluster analysis is to find groups of similar customers in data about customer orders and customer demographics. 82

COBIT (Control Objectives for Information and related Technology) A set of standard practices, created by the Information Systems Audit and Control Association, that are used in the assessment stage of the BPM cycle to determine how well an information system complies with an organization's strategy. 455

Collaboration The activity of two or more people working together to achieve a common goal via a process of feedback and iteration. One of four key skills for nonroutine cognitive thinking. 254

Collaboration information system An information system that supports collaboration. See also *collaboration system*. 262

Collaboration system See *collaboration information system*. 262

Columns Also called fields, or groups of bytes. A database table has multiple columns that are used to represent the attributes of an entity. Examples are PartNumber, EmployeeName, and SalesDate. 165

Commerce server An application program that runs on a server tier computer. A typical commerce server obtains product data from a database, manages items in users' shopping carts, and coordinates the checkout process. 225

Communication channels Means of delivering messages. 360

Communities See *communities of practice*. 337

Communities of practice Also called communities; groups of people related by a common interest. 337

Competitive analysis Process of identifying the strength and weaknesses in competitors' use of social media. 358

Competitive strategy The strategy an organization chooses as the way it will succeed in its industry. According to Porter, there are four fundamental competitive strategies: cost leadership across an industry or within a particular industry segment and product or service differentiation across an industry or within a particular industry segment. 41

Computer-based information system An information system that includes a computer. 15

Computer hardware Electronic components and related gadgetry that input, process, output, store, and communicate data according to the instructions encoded in computer programs or software. One of the five fundamental components of an information system. 14, 118

Computer terminal A computing device consisting of a screen, keyboard, and network connection. Also called a *thin client*. 203

Configuration control A set of management policies, practices, and tools that systems developers use to maintain control over a project's resources. 474

Connection data In social media systems, data about relationships. 341

Constructive criticism Both positive and negative advice given to improve an outcome. 254

Content data In social media systems, data and responses to data that are contributed by users and SM sponsors. 341

Content delivery network (CDN) An information system that serves content to Web pages over the Internet. To reduce wait time, data is typically stored and served from many geographic locations. 212

Content management systems (CMS) Information systems that support the management and delivery of documentation including reports, Web pages, and other expressions of employee knowledge. 89

Control flow A BPMN symbol that documents the flow of activity in a business process. 453

Conversion rate Measures the frequency with which someone who clicks on an ad makes a purchase, "likes" a site, or takes some other action desired by the advertiser. 353

Cookie A small file that is stored on the user's computer by a browser. Cookies can be used for authentication, for storing shopping cart contents and user preferences, and for other legitimate purposes. Cookies can also be used to implement spyware. 108

Cooperation The process by which a group of people having the same skills work in parallel to shorten the time required to accomplish a job (e.g., four painters each painting one wall of a room). 253

Corpus of knowledge A large set of related data and texts. 100

Cost The cost of a business process is equal to the cost of the inputs plus the cost of activities. 46

Cost feasibility An assessment of the cost of an information system development project that compares estimated costs to the available budget. Can also refer to a comparison of development plus operational costs versus value delivered. 461

Critical path The sequence of activities that determine the earliest date by which the project can be completed. 471

Critical path analysis The process by which project managers compress a schedule by moving resources, typically people, from noncritical path tasks to critical path tasks. 472

Crowdsourcing The dynamic social media process of employing users to participate in product design or redesign. 344

Crow's feet Lines on an entity-relationship diagram that indicate a 1:N relationship between two entities. 181

Crow's-foot diagram A type of entity-relationship diagram that uses a crow's foot symbol to designate a 1:N relationship. 181

Cryptocurrencies Digital-only currencies that use cryptographic protections to manage and record secure transactions. 127

Custom-developed software Software tailor-made for a particular organization's requirements. 134

Customer life cycle Taken as a whole, the processes of marketing, customer acquisition, relationship management, and loss/churn that must be managed by CRM systems. 305

Customer relationship management (CRM) system A suite of applications, a database, and a set of inherent processes for managing all the interactions with the customer, from lead generation to customer service. 306

Data Recorded facts or figures. One of the five fundamental components of an information system. 14

Data acquisition In business intelligence systems, the process of obtaining, cleaning, organizing, relating, and cataloging source data. 69

Data administration An organization-wide function that develops and enforces data policies and standards. 399

Data flow A BPMN symbol that documents the movement of data among activities and repositories in a business process. 453

Data integrity In a database or a collection of databases, the condition that exists when data values are consistent and in agreement with one another. 302

Data integrity problem In a database, the situation that exists when data item values disagree with one another. An example is two different names for the same customer. 183

Data mart A data collection, smaller than a data warehouse, that addresses the needs of a particular department or functional area of a business. 75

Data mining The application of statistical techniques to find patterns and relationships among data for classification and prediction. 80

Data model A logical representation of the data in a database that describes the data and relationships that will be stored in the database. Akin to a blueprint. 178

Data safeguards Measures used to protect databases and other data assets from threats. Includes data rights and responsibilities, encryptions, backup and recovery, and physical security. 399

Data warehouse A facility for managing an organization's BI data. 73

Database A self-describing collection of integrated records. 165

Database administration A person or department that develops procedures and practices to ensure efficient and orderly multiuser processing of the database, to control changes to database structure, and to protect the database. 171, 400

Database application A collection of forms, reports, queries, and application programs that facilitates users' processing of a database. A database can be processed by many different database applications. 174

Database management system (DBMS) A program for creating, processing, and administering a database. A DBMS is a large and complex program that is licensed like an operating system. Microsoft Access and Oracle Database are example DBMS products. 170

Database tier In the three-tier architecture, the tier that runs the DBMS and receives and processes requests to retrieve and store data. 225

DB2 A popular, enterprise-class DBMS product licensed by IBM. 170

Decision support systems Some authors define business intelligence (BI) systems as supporting decision making only, in which case they use this older term as a synonym for decision-making BI systems. 69

Deep learning A method for stimulating multiple layers of neural networks rather than just a single layer. 91

Deliverables Work products that are the result of the completion of tasks in a development project. 469

Denial of service (DoS) Security problem in which users are not able to access an information system; can be caused by human errors, natural disaster, or malicious activity. 385

Desktop virtualization Also called client virtualization and PC virtualization. The process of storing a user's desktop on a remote server. It enables users to run their desktop from many different client computers. 133

Digital Revolution The conversion from mechanical and analog devices to digital devices. 5

Digital subscriber line (DSL)   A communications line that operates on the same lines as voice telephones but does so in such a manner that its signals to not interfere with voice telephone service. 219

Dimension   A characteristic of an OLAP measure. Purchase date, customer type, customer location, and sales region are examples of dimensions. 79

Discussion forums   Forms of asynchronous communication in which one group member posts an entry and other group members respond. A better form of group communication than email because it is more difficult for one person to monopolize the discussion or for the discussion to go off track. 266

Diseconomies of scale   A principle that states as development teams become larger, the average contribution per worker decreases. 473

Distributed database processing   The processing of a single database that resides in multiple locations. 501

Distributed systems   Systems in which application processing is distributed across multiple computing devices. 321

Domain name   A worldwide unique name registered in the domain name system (DNS) and affiliated with a public IP address. 221

Domain Name System (DNS)   A directory naming system that assigns domain names to IP addresses. 221

Drill down   With an OLAP report, to further divide the data into more detail. 80

Dual processor   A computer with two CPUs. 118

Dynamic processes   Flexible, informal, and adaptive processes that normally involve strategic and less specific managerial decisions and activities. 296

Dynamic reports   Business intelligence documents that are updated at the time they are requested. 86

Elastic   In cloud computing, the situation that exists when the amount of resource leased can be dynamically increased or decreased, programmatically, in a short span of time, and organizations pay for just the resources that they use. This term was first used in this way by Amazon. 205

Email   A form of asynchronous communication in which participants send comments and attachments electronically. As a form of group communication, it can be disorganized, disconnected, and easy to hide from. 266

Email spoofing   A synonym for phishing. A technique for obtaining unauthorized data that uses pretexting via email. The phisher pretends to be a legitimate company and sends email requests for confidential data, such as account numbers, Social Security numbers, account passwords, and so

forth. Phishers direct traffic to their sites under the guise of a legitimate business. 384

Encapsulated   A characteristic of systems design in which the details of a process are hidden from users of that process. A formal interface is defined for the process that specifies how the process is to be accessed, what data it requires, and the data that it will produce. The means by which that process creates those results are never exposed, nor do they need to be. 227

Encryption   The process of transforming clear text into coded, unintelligible text for secure storage or communication. 394

Encryption algorithms   Algorithms used to transform clear text into coded, unintelligible text for secure storage or communication. 394

Enterprise 2.0   The use of emergent social software platforms within companies or between companies and their partners or customers. 359

Enterprise application integration (EAI)   A suite of software applications that integrates existing systems by providing layers of software that connect applications together. 312

Enterprise information system   Information systems that support cross-functional processes and activities in multiple departments. 299

Enterprise processes   Processes that span an organization and support activities in multiple departments. 299

Enterprise resource planning (ERP)   A suite of applications called modules, a database, and a set of inherent processes for consolidating business operations into a single, consistent, computing platform. 307

Enterprise social network (ESN)   A software platform that uses social media to facilitate cooperative work of people within an organization. 359

Entity   In the E-R data model, a representation of some thing that users want to track. Some entities represent a physical object; others represent a logical construct or transaction. 179

Entity-relationship (E-R) data model   A tool for constructing data models that defines the entities stored in a database and the relationships among those entities. 179

Entity-relationship (E-R) diagrams   A type of diagram used by database designers to document entities and their relationships to each other. 181

ERP system   An information system based upon ERP technology. 307

Ethernet   Another name for the IEEE 802.3 protocol, Ethernet is a communications standard that specifies how messages are to be packaged, processed, and transmitted for wired transmission over a LAN. 215

Exabyte (EB)   1,024 PB. 120

Exception reports   Reports produced when something out of predefined bounds occurs. 79

Experimentation   A careful and reasoned analysis of an opportunity, envisioning potential products or solutions or applications of technology and then developing those ideas that seem to have the most promise, consistent with the resources you have. One of four key skills for nonroutine cognitive thinking. 11

Fiat currencies   Government-approved legal tender. 128

Fields   Also called columns; groups of bytes in a database table. A database table has multiple columns that represent the attributes of an entity. Examples are PartNumber, EmployeeName, and SaleDate. 165

File   A group of similar rows or records. In a database, sometimes called a table. 165

File server   A networked computer that stores files. 269

File Transfer Protocol (ftp)   An applications-layer protocol used to transfer files over the Internet. 229

Firewall   Computing devices located between public and private networks that prevent unauthorized access to or from the internal network. A firewall can be a special-purpose computer, or it can be a program on a general-purpose computer or on a router. 397

Firmware   Computer software installed into devices such as printers, print servers, and various types of communication devices. The software is coded just like other software, but it is installed into special, programmable memory of the printer or other device. 134

First mover advantage   The benefit of gaining market share by being the first to develop a new technology in a market segment. 52

Five-component framework   The five fundamental components of an information system—computer hardware, software, data, procedures, and people—present in every information system, from the simplest to the most complex. 14

Five forces model   Model, proposed by Michael Porter, that assesses industry characteristics and profitability by means of five competitive forces—bargaining power of suppliers, threat of substitution, bargaining power of customers, rivalry among firms, and threat of new entrants. 40

Folksonomy   A structure of content that emerges from the activity and processing of many users. 359

Foreign keys   A column or group of columns used to represent relationships. Values of the foreign key match values of the primary key in a different (foreign) table. 167

Freemium   A revenue model offering a basic service for free and charging a premium for upgrades or advanced features. 352

Functional application   Software that provides features and functions necessary to support a particular business activity or department (function). 297

Functional information systems   Workgroup information systems that support a particular business function. 297

Gantt chart   A timeline graphical chart that shows tasks, dates, dependencies, and possibly resources. 471

General Data Protection Regulation (GDPR)   A comprehensive privacy law in the European Union that lets people request their online data and limits how businesses can use customer data. 507

Geofencing   A location service that allows applications to know when a user has crossed a virtual fence (specific location) and then trigger an automated action. 84, 355

Gigabyte (GB)   1,024 MB. 120

Gig economy   Economic system in which businesses hire many people as independent contractors for a short period of time. 283

GNU   A set of tools for creating and managing open source software. Originally created to develop an open source Unix-like operating system. 135

GNU general public license (GPL) agreement   One of the standard license agreements for open source software. 135

Google Drive   Cloud-based hardware used for sharing documents, spreadsheets, presentations, drawings, and other types of data. Includes version tracking. Used in conjunction with Google Docs. 269

Gramm-Leach-Bliley (GLB) Act   Passed by Congress in 1999, this act protects consumer financial data stored by financial institutions, which are defined as banks, securities firms, insurance companies, and organizations that provide financial advice, prepare tax returns, and provide similar financial services. 400

Granularity   The level of detail in data. Customer name and account balance is large granularity data. Customer name, balance, and details of all contacts with that customer, orders, and payments is smaller granularity. 75

Graphical queries   Queries in which criteria are created when the user clicks on a graphic. 176

Green computing   Environmentally conscious computing consisting of three major components: power management, virtualization, and e-waste management. 442

Groupthink   A phenomenon where the desire for group cohesion leads to poor decision making. 254

Hacking   A form of computer crime in which a person gains unauthorized access to a computer system. Although some people hack for the sheer joy of doing it, other hackers invade systems for the malicious purpose of stealing or modifying data. 385

Hadoop   An open source program supported by the Apache Foundation that manages thousands of computers and that implements MapReduce. 85

Hardening   A term used to describe server operating systems that have been modified to make it especially difficult for them to be infiltrated by malware. 403

Health Insurance Portability and Accountability Act (HIPAA)   The privacy provisions of this 1996 act give individuals the right to access health data created by doctors and other healthcare providers. HIPAA also sets rules and limits on who can read and receive a person's health information. 400

HoloLens   Microsoft's head-mounted mixed-reality computing device capable of producing holographic objects that appear in the real world. 155

Honeypots   False targets for computer criminals to attack. To an intruder, a honeypot looks like a particularly valuable resource, such as an unprotected Web site, but in actuality the only site content is a program that determines the attacker's IP address. 406

Hop   In an internet, the movement from one network to another. 223

Horizontal-market application   Software that provides capabilities common across all organizations and industries; examples include word processors, graphics programs, spreadsheets, and presentation programs. 134

Host operating system   In virtualization, the operating system that hosts the virtual operating systems. 131

https   An indication that a Web browser is using the SSL/TLS protocol to provide secure communication. 229, 382

Human capital   The investment in human knowledge and skills with the expectation of future gain. 345

Human safeguards   Steps taken to protect against security threats by establishing appropriate procedures for users to follow during system use. 392

Hybrid model   An enterprise system in which some of the data is stored in the cloud and managed by cloud vendors and other data is stored in the premises of the using organization and managed by it. 321

Hypertext Transfer Protocol (http)   An application-layer protocol used between browsers and Web servers. 229

ICANN (Internet Corporation for Assigned Names and Numbers)   The organization responsible for managing the assignment of public IP addresses and domain names for use on the Internet. Each public IP address is unique across all computers on the Internet. 221

Identification   The process whereby an information system identifies a user by requiring the user to sign on with a username and password. 393

Identifier   An attribute (or group of attributes) whose value is associated with one and only one entity instance. 179

IEEE 802.3 protocol   A standard for packaging and managing traffic on wired local area networks. 215

IEEE 802.11 protocol   A standard for packaging and managing traffic on wireless local area networks. 218

Implementation   In the context of the systems development life cycle, the phase following the design phase consisting of tasks to build, test, and convert users to the new system. 467

Industry-specific solutions   An ERP template designed to serve the needs of companies or organizations in specific industries. Such solutions save time and lower risk. The development of industry-specific solutions spurred ERP growth. 317

Influencer   An individual in a social network whose opinion can force a change in others' behavior and beliefs. 347

Information   (1) Knowledge derived from data, where *data* is defined as recorded facts or figures; (2) data presented in a meaningful context; (3) data processed by summing, ordering, averaging, grouping, comparing, or other similar operations; (4) a difference that makes a difference. Information exists only in the minds of humans. 19

Information Age   A period in history where the production, distribution, and control of information is the primary driver of the economy. 5

Information silo   A condition that exists when data are isolated in separated information systems. 301

Information system (IS)   A group of hardware, software, data, procedure, and people components that interacts to produce information. 14

Information technology (IT)   The products, methods, inventions, and standards used for the purpose of producing information. 14

Infrastructure as a service (IaaS)   Hosting of a bare server computer, data storage, network, and virtualization by a vendor. 210

Inherent processes   The procedures that must be followed to effectively use licensed software. For example, the processes inherent in ERP systems assume that certain users will take specified actions in a particular order. In most cases, the organization must conform to the processes inherent in the software. 305

In-memory DBMS   DBMS products that process databases stored in (very large) memories. Usually such DBMS utilize or extend the relational model. ACID support is common. 189

Inter-enterprise information systems   Information systems that support one or more inter-enterprise processes. 299

Inter-enterprise processes   Processes that support activities in multiple, independent companies or other organizations. 299

Internal firewalls   Firewalls that sit inside the organizational network. 397

Internet   When spelled with a small i, as in *internet*, a private network of networks. When spelled with a capital I, as in *Internet*, the public internet known as the Internet. 215

Internet exchange points (IXP)   Physical locations where large carriers exchange traffic. 223

Internet of Things (IoT)   The idea that objects are becoming connected to the Internet so they can interact with other devices, applications, or services. 121

Internet service provider (ISP)   An ISP provides users with Internet access. An ISP provides a user with a legitimate Internet address; it serves as the user's gateway to the Internet; and it passes communications back and forth between the user and the Internet. ISPs also pay for the Internet. They collect money from their customers and pay access fees and other charges on the users' behalf. 218

Intranet   A private internet (note small i) used within a corporation or other organization. 215

Intrusion detection system (IDS)   A computer program that senses when another computer is attempting to scan the disk or otherwise access a computer. 389

iOS   The operating system used on the iPhone, iPod Touch, and iPad. 131

IP address   A series of dotted decimals in a format like 192.168.2.28 that identifies a unique device on a network or internet. 221

IP spoofing   A type of spoofing whereby an intruder uses another site's IP address as if it were that other site. 384

IPv4   The most commonly used Internet layer protocol; has a four-decimal dotted notation, such as 165.193.123.253. 221

IPv6   An Internet layer protocol that uses 128-bit addresses and is gradually replacing IPv4. 221

Just-in-time data   Data delivered to the user at the time it is needed. 145

Just-in-time design   Rather than design the complete, overall system at the beginning, only those portions of the design needed to complete the current work are done. Common for agile development techniques such as scrum. 478

Key   (1) A column or group of columns that identifies a unique row in a table. Also referred to as a primary key. (2) A string of bits used to encrypt data. The encryption algorithm applies the key to the original message to produce the coded message. Decoding (decrypting) a message is similar; a key is applied to the coded message to recover the original text. 167, 394

Key escrow   A control procedure whereby a trusted party is given a copy of a key used to encrypt database data. 400

Key logger   Malicious spyware that captures keystrokes without the user's knowledge. Used to steal usernames, passwords, account numbers, and other sensitive data. 398

Key performance indicators (KPI)   See *success metrics*. 356

Kilobyte (KB)   1,024 bytes. 120

Knowledge management (KM)   The process of creating value from intellectual capital and sharing that knowledge with employees, managers, suppliers, customers, and others who need it. 88

Kryder's Law   The storage density on magnetic disks is increasing at an exponential rate. 8

Libraries   In SharePoint and other version-control collaboration systems, shared directories that allow access to various documents by means of permissions. 272

License   A contract that stipulates how a program can be used. Most specify the number of computers on which the program can be installed; some specify the number of users who can connect to and use the program remotely. Such agreements also stipulate limitations on the liability of the software vendor for the consequences of errors in the software. 133

Linkages   In Porter's model of business activities, interactions across value chain activities. 45

Linux   A version of Unix developed by the open source community. The open source community owns Linux, and there is no fee to use it. Linux is a popular operating system for Web servers. 130

Local area network (LAN)   A network that connects computers that reside in a single geographic location on the premises of the company that operates the LAN. The number of connected computers can range from two to several hundred. 214

Localizing   The process of making a computer program work in a second language. 499

Lost-update problem   A problem that exists in database applications in which two users update the same data item, but only one of those changes is recorded in the data. Can be resolved using locking. 178

Machine code   Code compiled from source code and ready to be processed by a computer. Cannot be understood by humans. 137

Machine learning   The extraction of knowledge from data based on algorithms created from training data. 98

macOS   An operating system developed by Apple Computer, Inc., for the Macintosh. The current version is macOS High Sierra. Initially, Macintosh computers were used primarily by graphic artists and workers in the arts community, but today Macs are used more widely. 130

Main memory   Memory that works in conjunction with the CPU. Stores data and instructions read by the CPU and stores the results of the CPU's computations. 118

Mainframe architecture   Computing architecture that supports connections between a central mainframe and numerous thin clients. 203

Mainframes   Large-scale high-speed centralized computers used for internal data processing needs. 203

Maintenance   In the context of information systems, (1) to fix the system to do what it was supposed to do in the first place or (2) to adapt the system to a change in requirements. 468

Malware   Viruses, worms, Trojan horses, spyware, and adware. 398

Malware definitions   Patterns that exist in malware code. Antimalware vendors update these definitions continuously and incorporate them into their products in order to better fight against malware. 399

Management information systems (MIS)   The management and use of information systems that help organizations achieve their strategies. 14

Managerial decisions   Decisions that concern the allocation and use of resources. 258

Many-to-many (N:M) relationships   Relationships involving two entity types in which an instance of one type can relate to many instances of the second type, and an instance of the second type can relate to many instances of the first. For example, the relationship between Student and Class is N:M. One student may enroll in many classes, and one class may have many students. Contrast with one-to-many relationships. 181

MapReduce   A two-phase technique for harnessing the power of thousands of computers working in parallel. During the first phase, the Map phase, computers work on a task in parallel; during the second phase, the Reduce phase, the work of separate computers is combined, eventually obtaining a single result. 83

Margin   The difference between the value that an activity generates and the cost of the activity. 44

Maximum cardinality   The maximum number of entities that can be involved in a relationship. Common examples of maximum cardinality are 1:N, N:M, and 1:1. 182

M-commerce   E-commerce transacted using mobile devices. 140

Measure   The data item of interest on an OLAP report. It is the item that is to be summed, averaged, or otherwise processed in the OLAP cube. Total sales, average sales, and average cost are examples of measures. 79

Megabyte (MB)   1,024 KB. 120

Metadata   Data that describes data. 167

Metcalfe's Law   The value of a network is equal to the square of the number of users connected to it. 7

Metrics   Measurements used to track performance. 356

Microsoft Windows   The most popular nonmobile client operating system. Also refers to Windows Server, a popular server operating system that competes with Linux. 130

Minimum cardinality   The minimum number of entities that must be involved on one side of a relationship, typically zero or one. 182

Mixed reality (MR)   The combination of the real physical world with interactive virtual images or objects. 123

Mobile device   A small, lightweight, power-conserving, computing device that is capable of wireless access. 140

Mobile device management (MDM) software   Products that install and update mobile device software, back up and restore mobile devices, and wipe software and data from devices in the event the device is lost or the employee leaves the company. Such products also report usage and provide other mobile device management data. 148

Mobile systems   Information systems that support users in motion. 140

Modern-style applications   Windows applications that are touch-screen oriented and provide context-sensitive, popup menus. 130

Modules   A suite of applications in an ERP system. 307

Monetize   A social media company's ability to make money from its application, service, or content. 351

MongoDB   An open source, document-oriented, nonrelational DBMS. 188

Moore's Law   A law, created by Gordon Moore, stating that the number of transistors per square inch on an integrated chip doubles every 18 months. Moore's prediction has proved generally accurate in the 40 years since it was made. Sometimes this law is stated that the performance of a computer doubles every 48 months. Although not strictly true, this version gives the gist of the idea. 6

Multi-user processing   The situation in which multiple users process the database at the same time. 177

MySQL   A popular open source DBMS product that is license-free for most applications. 170

Naïve Bayes Classifier   An algorithm that predicts the probability of a certain outcome based on prior occurrences of related events. 98

Native application   A thick-client application designed to work with a particular operating system and sometimes further limited to work only with a particular mobile device that runs that operating system. 129

Natural language processing (NLP) The ability of a computer system to understand spoken human language. 100

Net neutrality The idea that all data should be treated equally as it passes between networks regardless of its type, source, or quantity. 224

Network A collection of computers that communicate with one another over transmission lines. 214

Neural network A computing system modeled after the human brain that is used to predict values and make classifications. 91

NewSQL DBMS Relational DBMS with ACID support that provide processing speeds equivalent to those of NoSQL DBMS products. 189

Nielsen's Law Network connection speeds for high-end users will increase by 50 percent per year. 8

Nonvolatile Memory that preserves data contents even when not powered (e.g., magnetic and optical disks). With such devices, you can turn the computer off and back on, and the contents will be unchanged. 121

Normal forms Definitions of table characteristics that identify various problems to which a table is subject. 184

Normalization The process of converting poorly structured tables into two or more better-structured tables. 182

NoSQL DBMS Nonrelational DBMS that support very high transaction rates processing relatively simple data structures, replicated on many servers in the cloud. No ACID support. 189

Object Management Group (OMG) A software industry standards organization that created a standard set of terms and graphical notations for documenting business processes. 456

Object-oriented When referring to languages, ones that can be used to create difficult, complex applications and, if used properly, will result in high-performance code that is easy to alter when requirements change. 138

Off-the-shelf software Software used without making any changes. 134

Off-the-shelf with alterations software Software bought off the shelf but altered to fit an organization's specific needs. 134

OLAP cube A presentation of an OLAP measure with associated dimensions. The reason for this term is that some products show these displays using three axes, like a cube in geometry. Same as OLAP report. 80

One-of-a-kind application Software developed for a specific, unique need, usually for a single company's requirements. 134

One-to-many (1:N) relationships Relationships involving two entity types in which an instance of one type can relate to many instances of the second type, but an instance of the second type can relate to at most one instance of the first. For example, in most businesses, the relationship between Department and Employee is 1:N. A department may relate to many employees, but an employee relates to at most one department. 181

Online analytical processing (OLAP) A dynamic type of reporting system that provides the ability to sum, count, average, and perform other simple arithmetic operations on groups of data. Such reports are dynamic because users can change the format of the reports while viewing them. 79

Open source (1) Source code available for a community to access. (2) A collaborative effort by which software developers create a product such as Linux; the developers often volunteer their time. In most cases, the jointly developed product can be used without paying a license fee. 137

Operating system (OS) A computer program that controls the computer's resources: It manages the contents of main memory, processes keystrokes and mouse movements, sends signals to the display monitor, reads and writes disk files, and controls the processing of other programs. 128

Operational decisions Decisions that concern the day-to-day activities of an organization. 258

Oracle Database A popular, enterprise-class DBMS product from Oracle Corporation. 170

Organizational feasibility Whether an information system fits within an organization's customer, culture, and legal requirements. 464

Outsourcing The process of hiring another organization to perform a service. Outsourcing is done to save costs, to gain expertise, and to free up management time. 428

Over the Internet When applied to cloud computing, the provisioning of worldwide servers over the Internet. 205

Packet A formatted message that passes through networks. 221

Packet-filtering firewall A firewall that examines each packet and determines whether to let the packet pass. To make this decision, it examines the source address, the destination addresses, and other data. 397

Packet sniffers A program that captures network traffic. 385

Paired programming The situation in which two computer programmers share the same computer and develop a computer program together. 480

Parallel installation A type of system conversion in which the new system runs in parallel with the old one and the results of the two are reconciled for consistency. Parallel installation is expensive because the organization incurs the costs of running both systems, but it is the safest form of installation. 468

Partitioned database Distributed database that does not contain copies of the same data, but rather divides the database into nonoverlapping segments. 501

Payment Card Industry Data Security Standard (PCI DSS) Standard that governs the secure storage and processing of credit card data. 400

Pay per click Revenue model in which advertisers display ads to potential customers for free and pay only when the customer clicks. 352

Payload The program codes of a virus that causes unwanted or hurtful actions, such as deleting programs or data, or even worse, modifying data in ways that are undetected by the user. 398

PC virtualization Synonym for desktop virtualization. 132

Peering Exchanging information between telecommunication providers without charging an access fee. 223

People As part of the five-component framework, one of the five fundamental components of an information system; includes those who operate and service the computers, those who maintain the data, those who support the networks, and those who use the system. Information exists only in the minds of people. 14

Perimeter firewall A firewall that sits outside the organizational network; it is the first device that Internet traffic encounters. 397

Personal area network (PAN) A network connecting devices located around a single person. 214

Personal computers Classic computing devices used by individuals. Examples of PCs include laptop or desktop computers. 118

Personal identification number (PIN) A form of authentication whereby the user supplies a number that only he or she knows. 393

Petabyte (PB) 1,024 TB. 120

Phablet A mobile device that combines the functionality of a smartphone with the larger screen of a tablet. 118

Phased installation A type of system conversion in which the new system is installed in pieces across the organization(s). Once a given piece works, then the organization installs and tests another piece of the system, until the entire system has been installed. 468

Phisher An individual or organization that spoofs legitimate companies in an attempt to illegally capture personal data, such as credit card numbers, email accounts, and driver's license numbers. 384

Phishing A technique for obtaining unauthorized data that uses pretexting via email. The phisher pretends to be a legitimate company and sends an email requesting confidential data, such as account numbers, Social Security numbers, account passwords, and so forth. 384

Pig Query language used with Hadoop. 85

Pilot installation A type of system conversion in which the organization implements the entire system on a limited portion of the business. The advantage of pilot implementation is that if the system fails, the failure is contained within a limited boundary. This reduces exposure of the business and also protects the new system from developing a negative reputation throughout the organizations. 468

Platform as a service (PaaS) Hosting of an operating system, runtime environment, and middleware by a vendor. 211

Plunge installation A type of system conversion in which the organization shuts off the old system and starts the new system. If the new system fails, the organization is in trouble: Nothing can be done until either the new system is fixed or the old system is reinstalled. Because of the risk, organizations should avoid this conversion style if possible. Sometimes called direct installation. 468

Pooled The situation in which many different organizations use the same physical hardware. 205

Power curve A graph that shows the relationship of the power (the utility that one gains from a software product) as a function of the time using that product. 281

Pretexting Deceiving someone over the Internet by pretending to be another person or organization. 384

Primary activities Activities that contribute directly to the production, sale, or service of a product. In Porter's model they are inbound logistics, operations and manufacturing, outbound logistics, sales and marketing, and customer service. 44

Primary key One or more columns in a relation whose values identify a unique row of that relation. Also known as a key. 167

PRISM Code name for a secret global surveillance program by which the National Security Agency (NSA) requested and received data about Internet activities from major Internet providers. 407

Privacy The freedom from being observed by other people. 407

Private cloud In-house hosting, delivered via Web service standards, which can be dynamically configured. 233

Private IP address A type of IP address used within private networks and internets. Private IP addresses are assigned and managed by the company that operates the private network or internet. 223

Problem A *perceived* difference between what is and what ought to be. 260

Procedures Instructions for humans. One of the five fundamental components of an information system. 14

Process blueprints In an ERP application, comprehensive sets of inherent processes for all organizational activities, each of which is documented with diagrams that use a set of standardized symbols. 315

Process effectiveness A measure of how well a process achieves organizational strategy. 299

Process efficiency A measure of the ratio of process outputs to inputs. 299

Project data Data that is part of a collaboration's work product. 262

Project metadata Data that is used to manage a project. Schedules, tasks, budgets, and other managerial data are examples. 262

Protocol A set of rules and data structures for organizing communication. 215

Public IP address An IP address used to identify a particular device on the Internet. Such IP addresses are assigned to major institutions in blocks by the Internet Corporation for Assigned Names and Numbers (ICANN). Each IP address is unique across all computers on the Internet. 221

Public key encryption A special version of asymmetric encryption that is popular on the Internet. With this method, each site has a public key for encoding messages and a private key for decoding them. 396

Publish results The process of delivering business intelligence to the knowledge workers who need it. 70

Pull publishing In business intelligence (BI) systems, the mode whereby users must request BI results. 70

Push publishing In business intelligence (BI) systems, the mode whereby the BI system delivers business intelligence to users without any request from the users, according to a schedule, or as a result of an event or particular data condition. 70

Quad processor A computer with four CPUs. 118

RAM Random access memory. Another name for a computer's main memory. 118

Ransomware Malicious software that blocks access to a system or data until money is paid to the attacker. 398

Reality The state of things as they actually exist. 123

Records Also called rows, groups of columns in a database table. 165

Regression analysis A type of supervised data mining that estimates the values of parameters in a linear equation. Used to determine the relative influence of variables on an outcome and also to predict future values of that outcome. 82

Relation A formal name for a database table. 167

Relational databases Databases that store data in the form of relations (tables with certain restrictions) and that represents record relationships using foreign keys. 167

Relationships Associations among entities or entity instances in an E-R model or an association among rows of a table in a relational database. 180

Remote action system An information system that provides action at a distance, such as telesurgery or telelaw enforcement. 239

Replicated database A distributed database that contains copies of the same data items. 501

Reporting analysis The process of sorting, grouping, summing, filtering, and formatting structured data. 78

Reporting application A business intelligence application that inputs data from one or more sources and applies reporting operations to that data to produce business intelligence. 78

Repository In a business process model, a collection of something; for example, a database is a repository of data. 46

Requirements analysis The second phase in the SDLC, in which developers conduct user interviews; evaluate existing systems; determine new forms/reports/queries; identify new features and functions, including security; and create the data model. 460

Resources People or information system applications that are assigned to roles in business processes. 453

RFM analysis A technique readily implemented with basic reporting operations to analyze and rank customers according to their purchasing patterns. 79

Roles In a business process, collections of activities. 453

Routers Devices that connect different networks together. 223

Rows Also called records, groups of columns in a database table. 165

Safeguard Any action, device, procedure, technique, or other measure that reduces a system's vulnerability to a threat. 382

Satoshi 1/100,000,000 of one bitcoin. 128

Scalable Easily able to respond to incremental growth in demand. 204

Schedule feasibility Whether an information system can be developed within the time available. 464

Screen-sharing applications Applications that offer users the ability to view the same whiteboard, application, or other display over a network. 265

Second mover advantage The benefit of gaining market share by following a pioneering company into a market segment and imitating their product or service, thereby reducing costly research and development expenditures. 52

Secure Sockets Layer (SSL) A protocol that uses both asymmetric and symmetric encryption. When SSL is in use, the browser address will begin with https://. The most recent version of SSL is called TLS. 396

Security The state of being free from danger. 399

Self-driving car A driverless car that uses a variety of sensors to navigate like a traditional car but without human intervention. 125

Self-efficacy A person's belief that he or she can successfully perform the tasks required in his or her job. 319

Sense of presence The illusion that a virtual experience is real. 124

Server A computer that provides some type of service, such as hosting a database, running a blog, publishing a Web site, or selling goods. Server computers are faster, larger, and more powerful than client computers. 131

Server farm A large collection of server computers organized to share work and compensate for one another's failures. 119

Server tier In the three-tier architecture, the tier that consists of computers that run Web servers for generating Web pages and responding to requests from browsers. Web servers also process application programs. 225

Server virtualization The process of running two or more operating system instances on the same server. The host operating system runs virtual operating system instances as applications. 132

Service-oriented architecture (SOA) A design philosophy that dictates that all interactions among computing devices are defined as services in a formal, standardized way. SOA makes the cloud possible. 226

Sharing economy Economic system in which consumers temporarily share their assets or services with other consumers via renting or lending. 283

Simple Mail Transfer Protocol (smtp) The protocol used for email transmission. 229

Site license A license purchased by an organization to equip all the computers on a site with certain software. 133

SLATES Acronym developed by Andrew McAfee that summarizes key characteristics of Enterprise 2.0: search, links, author, tagged, extensions, signaled. 359

Small office/home office (SOHO) A business office with usually fewer than 10 employees often located in the business professional's home. 215

Smart cards Plastic cards similar to credit cards that have microchips. The microchip, which holds much more data than a magnetic strip, is loaded with identifying data. Normally requires a PIN. 393

Smart device A device that has processing power, memory, network connectivity, and the ability to interconnect with other devices and applications. 121

Smartphone A cell phone with processing capability. 118

Sniffing A technique for intercepting computer communications. With wired networks, sniffing requires a physical connection to the network. With wireless networks, no such connection is required. 385

Social capital The investment in social relations with expectation of future returns in the marketplace. 345

Social CRM CRM that includes social networking elements and gives the customer much more power and control in the customer/vendor relationship. 342

Social media (SM) The use of information technology to support the sharing of content among networks of users. 337

Social media information system (SMIS) An information system that supports the sharing of content among networks of users. 337

Social media policy A statement that delineates employees' rights and responsibilities when generating social media content. 361

Social media providers Companies that provide platforms that enable the creation of social networks. Facebook, Twitter, LinkedIn, and Google are all social media providers. 338

Social networks The social relationships among people with common interests. 338

Software Instructions for computers. One of the five fundamental components of an information system. 14

Software as a service (SaaS) Hosting of hardware infrastructure and operating system as well as application programs and databases by a vendor. 211

Solid-state storage (SSD) Stores information using nonvolatile electronic circuits. 118

Source code Computer code written by humans and understandable by humans. Source code must be translated into machine code before it can be processed. 137

Spoofing When someone pretends to be someone else with the intent of obtaining unauthorized data. If you pretend to be your professor, you are spoofing your professor. 384

Spyware Programs installed on the user's computer without the user's knowledge or permission that reside in the background and, unknown to the user, observe the user's actions and keystrokes, modify computer activity, and report the user's activities to sponsoring organizations. Malicious spyware captures keystrokes to obtain usernames, passwords, account numbers, and other sensitive information. Other spyware is used for marketing analyses, observing what users do, Web sites visited, products examined and purchased, and so forth. 385

SQL injection attack The situation that occurs when a user obtains unauthorized access to data by entering a SQL statement into a form in which one is supposed to enter a name or other data. If the program is improperly designed, it will accept this statement and make it part of the SQL command that it issues to the DBMS. 399

SQL Server A popular enterprise-class DBMS product licensed by Microsoft. 170

Stand-up In scrum, a 15-minute meeting in which each team member states what he or she has done in the past day, what he or she will do in the coming day, and any factors that are blocking his or her progress. 479

Static reports Business intelligence documents that are fixed at the time of creation and do not change. 86

Steering committee A group of senior managers from a company's major business functions that works with the CIO to set the IS priorities and decide among major IS projects and alternatives. 428

Storage hardware Hardware that saves data and programs. Magnetic disks are by far the most common storage device, although optical disks, such as CDs and DVDs, also are popular. 118

Stored procedure A computer program stored in the database that is used to enforce business rules. 319

Strategic decisions Decisions that concern broad-scope, organizational issues. 259

Strength of a relationship In social media, the likelihood that a person or other organization in a relationship will do something that will benefit the organization. 349

Strong AI Artificial general intelligence that can complete all of the same tasks a human can. 95

Strong password A password with the following characteristics: at least 12 characters; does not contain the user's username, real name, or company name; does not contain a complete dictionary word in any language; is different from the user's previous passwords; and contains both upper- and lowercase letters, numbers, and special characters. 26

Structured data Data in the form of rows and columns. 78

Structured decisions A type of decision for which there is a formalized and accepted method for making the decision. 259

Structured processes Formally defined, standardized processes that involve day-to-day operations; accepting a return, placing an order, and purchasing raw materials are common examples. 296

Structured Query Language (SQL) An international standard language for processing database data. Can also be used to create and modify database structure. 171

Subscriptions User requests for particular business intelligence results on a stated schedule or in response to particular events. 86

Success metrics Also called key performance indicators (KPI); measures that indicate when you've achieved your goals. 356

Superintelligence An AI system capable of intelligence more advanced than human intelligence. 95

Supervised data mining A form of data mining in which data miners develop a model prior to the analysis and apply statistical techniques to determine the validity of that model and to estimate values of the parameters of the model. 82

Supply chain A network of organizations and facilities that transforms raw materials into products delivered to customers. 502

Support activities In Porter's value chain model, the activities that contribute indirectly to value creation: procurement, technology, human resources, and the firm's infrastructure. 44

Swift Apple's programming language for OS X and iOS applications. 138

Swim-lane layout A process diagram layout similar to swim lanes in a swimming pool; each role in the process is shown in its own horizontal rectangle, or lane. 456

Switching costs Business strategy of locking in customers by making it difficult or expensive to change to another product or supplier. 52

Symbian A mobile client operating system popular on phones in Europe and the Far East but less so in North America. 131

Symmetric encryption An encryption method whereby the same key is used to encode and to decode the message. 396

Synchronous communication Information exchange that occurs when all members of a work team meet at the same time, such as face-to-face meeting or conference calls. 264

System A group of components that interacts to achieve some purpose. 14

System conversion The process of converting business activity from the old system to the new. 467

Systems analyst IS professionals who understand both business and technology. They are active throughout the systems development process and play a key role in moving the project from conception to conversion and, ultimately, maintenance. Systems analysts integrate the work of the programmers, testers, and users. Compare with business analyst. 452

Systems development life cycle (SDLC) The classical process used to develop information systems. The basic tasks of systems development are combined into the following phases: system definition, requirements analysis, component design, implementation, and system maintenance (fix or enhance). 459

Systems thinking   The mental activity of making one or more models of the components of a system and connecting the inputs and outputs among those components into a sensible whole, one that explains the phenomenon observed. One of four key skills for nonroutine cognitive thinking.   11

Table   Also called files, groups of similar rows or records in a database.   165

Tablets   Computing devices that allow interaction through a flat touch screen.   118

Target   The asset that is desired by a security threat.   382

TCP/IP protocol architecture   A protocol architecture having five layers and one or more protocols defined at each layer. Programs are written to implement the rules of a particular protocol.   229

Team surveys   Forms of asynchronous communication in which one team member creates a list of questions and other team members respond. Microsoft SharePoint has built-in survey capability.   267

Technical feasibility   Whether existing information technology will be able to meet the requirements of a new information system.   464

Technical safeguards   Procedures designed to protect the hardware and software components of an information system. Examples include identification and authorization, encryption, firewalls, malware protection, and application design.   392

Technology skills gap   The mismatch between the high level of tech skills demanded by employers and the low level of tech skills held by employees.   12

Telelaw enforcement   A remote access system that provides law enforcement capability.   239

Telemedicine   A remote action system that healthcare professionals use to diagnose and treat patients in rural or remote areas.   239

Telesurgery   A remote access system that links surgeons to robotic equipment and patients at a distance.   239

Terabyte (TB)   1,024 GB.   120

Test plan   Groups of action and usage sequences for validating the capability of new software.   467

The Internet   The public collection of networks used for transmitting data, worldwide.   215

The Singularity   According to Ray Kurzweil, the point at which computer systems become sophisticated enough that they can create and adapt their own software and hence adapt their behavior without human assistance.   101

Thick-client application   A software application that requires programs other than just the browser on a user's computer; that is, requires code on both client and server computers. See also *native application*.   129

Thin client   A computing device that consists of a screen, keyboard, and network connection. Also called a computer terminal.   203

Thin-client application   A software application that requires nothing more than a browser. Also called a Web application.   129

Third-party cookie   A cookie created by a site other than the one visited.   108

Threat   A person or organization that seeks to obtain or alter data or other IS assets illegally, without the owner's permission and often without the owner's knowledge.   382

Three-tier architecture   Architecture used by most e-commerce server applications. The tiers refer to three different classes of computers. The user tier consists of users' computers that have browsers that request and process Web pages. The server tier consists of computers that run Web servers and in the process generate Web pages and other data in response to requests from browsers. Web servers also process application programs. The third tier is the database tier, which runs the DBMS that processes the database.   225

Trade-off   In project management, a balancing of three critical factors: requirements, cost, and time.   473

Train the trainer   Training sessions in which vendors train the organization's employees, called Super Users, to become in-house trainers in order to improve training quality and reduce training expenses.   316

Transmission Control Protocol (TCP)   A core Internet protocol that guarantees the reliable delivery of packets.   222

Transport Layer Security (TLS)   The new name for a later version of Secure Sockets Layer (SSL).   396

Trigger   A computer program stored within the database that runs to keep the database consistent when certain conditions arise.   315

Trojan horses   Viruses that masquerade as useful programs or files. A typical Trojan horse appears to be a computer game, an MP3 music file, or some other useful, innocuous program.   398

Tunnel   A virtual, private pathway over a public or shared network from the VPN client to the VPN server.   233

Turing test   Idea proposed by Alan Turing that a machine can be considered intelligent if a human can have a conversation with it and not be able to tell if it is a machine or a human.   96

Unified Modeling Language (UML)   A series of diagramming techniques that facilitates OOP development. UML has dozens of different diagrams for all phases of system development. UML does not require or promote any particular development process. Generally less popular that the E-R model.   179

Unix An operating system developed at Bell Labs in the 1970s. It has been the workhorse of the scientific and engineering communities since then. 130

Unstructured decisions A type of decision for which there is no agreed-on decision-making method. 259

Unsupervised data mining A form of data mining whereby the analysts do not create a model or hypothesis before running the analysis. Instead, they apply the data mining technique to the data and observe the results. With this method, analysts create hypotheses after the analysis to explain the patterns found. 82

URL (Uniform Resource Locator) An address on the Internet. Consists of a protocol followed by a domain name or public IP address. 222

Use increases value The concept that the more people use a site, the more value it has, and the more people will visit. Furthermore, the more value a site has, the more existing users will return. 352

User-generated content (UGC) Content on an organization's social media presence contributed by nonemployee users. 362

User tier In the three-tier architecture, the tier that consists of computers, phones, and other mobile devices that have browsers and request or process Web pages and other services. 225

Users Individuals and organizations that use social media sites to build social relationships. 339

Usurpation Occurs when unauthorized programs invade a computer system and replace legitimate programs. Such unauthorized programs typically shut down the legitimate system and substitute their own processing to spy, steal and manipulate data, or achieve other purposes. 385

Value As defined by Porter, the amount of money that a customer is willing to pay for a resource, product, or service. 44

Value chain A network of value-creating activities. 44

Value of social capital Value determined by the number of relationships in a social network, by the strength of those relationships, and by the resources controlled by those related. 346

Vanity metrics Measures that don't improve decision making. 357

Velocity In scrum, the total number of points of work that a team can accomplish in each scrum period. 482

Version control The process that occurs when the collaboration tool limits and sometimes even directs user activity. 272

Version management Tracking of changes to documents by means of features and functions that accommodate concurrent work. 269

Vertical-market application Software that serves the needs of a specific industry. Examples of such programs are those used by dental offices to schedule appointments and bill patients, those used by auto mechanics to keep track of customer data and customers' automobile repairs, and those used by parts warehouses to track inventory, purchases, and sales. 134

Videoconferencing Communication technology that enables online conferencing using video. 263

Viral hook An inducement that causes someone to share an ad, link, file, picture, movie, or other resource with friends and associates over the Internet. 339

Virtualization The process whereby multiple operating systems run as clients on a single host operating system. Gives the appearance of many computers running on a single computer. 131

Virtual A computer-generated world with interactive digital objects. 123

Virtual machines (vm) Computer programs that present the appearance of an independent operating system within a second host operating system. The host can support multiple virtual machines, possibly running different operating system programs (Windows, Linux), each of which is assigned assets such as disk space, devices, and network connections over which it has control. 131

Virtual meetings Meetings in which participants do not meet in the same place and possibly not at the same time. 265

Virtual private cloud (VPC) A subset of a public cloud that has highly restricted, secure access. 235

Virtual private network (VPN) A WAN connection alternative that uses the Internet or a private internet to create the appearance of private point-to-point connections. In the IT world, the term virtual means something that appears to exist that does not exist in fact. Here a VPN uses the public Internet to create the appearance of a private connection. 233

Virtual reality (VR) A completely computer-generated virtual world with interactive digital objects. 124

Virus A computer program that replicates itself. 398

Volatile Data that will be lost when the computer or device is not powered. 121

Vulnerability An opportunity for threats to gain access to individual or organizational assets. Some vulnerabilities exist because there are no safeguards or because the existing safeguards are ineffective. 382

WAN wireless A communications system that provides wireless connectivity to a wide area network. 220

Wardriver People who use computers with wireless connections to search for unprotected wireless networks. 385

Waterfall method The assumption that one phase of the SDLC can be completed in its entirety and the project can progress, without any backtracking, to the next phase of the

SDLC. Projects seldom are that simple; backtracking is normally required. 475

Weak AI   Artificial intelligence that is focused on completing a single specific task. 95

Web 2.0   A dynamic system that uses user-generated content. 359

Web application   A software application that requires nothing more than a browser. Also called a thin-client application. 129

Webinar   A virtual meeting in which attendees can view a common presentation on the computer screen of one of the attendees for formal and organized presentations. 265

Web page   Document encoded in html that is created, transmitted, and consumed using the World Wide Web. 225

Web servers   Programs that run on a server-tier computer and that manage http traffic by sending and receiving Web pages to and from clients and by processing client requests. 225

Wide area network (WAN)   A network that connects computers at different geographic locations. 214

Windows 10 (mobile)   A Windows operating system designed for mobile devices. 131

Windows Server   A version of Windows specifically designed and configured for server use. It has much more stringent and restrictive security procedures than other versions of Windows and is popular on servers in organizations that have made a strong commitment to Microsoft. 131

Work breakdown structure (WBS)   A hierarchy of the tasks required to complete a project; for a large project, it might involve hundreds or thousands of tasks. 469

Workflow control   Collaboration tool feature in which software manages the flow of documents approvals, rejections, and other characteristics among a collaborating team. 273

Workgroup information system   An information system that supports a particular department or workgroup. 297

Workgroup process   A process that exists to enable workgroups to fulfill the charter, purpose, and goals of a particular group or department. 297

Worm   A virus that propagates itself using the Internet or some other computer network. Worm code is written specifically to infect another computer as quickly as possible. 398

Zettabyte (ZB)   1,024 EB. 120

INDEX

Numbers

3D Printing, 6, 13, 62, 70, 127, 127f
3M, 89
10/10/1000 Ethernet, 215
2017 Cost of Cyber Crime Study, 387f, 388, 397

A

abstract reasoning, 10
access, 170
Access CT, 330–331, 491
account administration, 388–390, 389f,
    391–392, 403–404
account management, 403–404, 404f
Acemoglu, Daron, 12
ACID, 189
activities, 46. *See also* primary activities; support
    activities
    of business intelligence (BI), 69–70, 69f
    of business process, 296f
    of business process management (BPM),
        454–456
    outsourcing of, 428
    swim-lane layout depiction of, 456
    in the value chain, 44–45
Acxiom Corporation, 351
ad-blocking software, 352
Advanced Persistent Threat (APT), 386
advertising, 351–352
adware, 398, 398f
Affordable Care Act, 330
agile
    methodology, 478f
    size of organizations using in
        2917, 478f
agile development, 477, 477f
AI. *See* artificial intelligence
Airbnb, 289, 290
algorithms, 98, 394
Alibaba Holdings Group, 5
Alphabet Inc., 18–19
Altavista, 52
Amazon, 2, 56, 343
    3D printing from, 62
    business categories of, 61
    innovation, 61f
    stock history, 20, 20f, 61–62
    Whole Foods acquisition by, 50–52
Amazon Dash, 62
Amazon Echo, 62
Amazon Go, 62
Amazon Go model, 50
Amazon Marketplace Web Service (MWS), 62
Amazon Web Services (AWS), 61, 205–206,
    206f
American Express, 104
America's Cup, 476
Android, 18
    loyal following of, 131
    mobile operating system of, 129f
antimalware programs, 398

Apache Foundation, 85
Apache OpenOffice, 268
Apache Struts, 102
Apple App Store, 150, 157
Apple data centers, 209f
Apple Genius Bar, 157
Apple II PC, 157
Apple Inc., 5, 8, 89, 156–157, 483
    encryption and, 506
    Steve Jobs and, 158
    stock history, 156, 156f
applications, 129f, 450
    design for secure, 398
    development of, 449–453
    malware and, 150
    permissions and, 143
    privacy and, 143
    software for, 133
    types of, 133–134
approval request interactions, 227f
APT37, 386
ARES, 379–380, 432
Artenstein, Nitay, 391
artificial intelligence (AI), 89. *See also* Watson
    advances, 90
    applications, 90, 91f
    effects of, 91–95, 94
    employment and, 94–95
    as enabler of other technology, 97
    evolution of abilities, 95f
    forces driving innovation in, 90f
    future of, 483
    goal of, 95–97
    how it works, 97–101
    importance of, 89–91
    machine learning and, 98–100
    major research area, 96f
    organizations and, 91–95
    saying no to, 97
as-is model, 455, 456–457
Ask.com, 52
Association of Certified Fraud Examiners
    (ACFE), 93
asymmetric encryption, 396
asynchronous communication, 264
AT&T, 68
attributes, 179
augmented reality (AR), 56, 123
authentication, 393. *See also* biometric
    authentication
automated labor, 447
    benefits of, 92–94, 93f
    employee costs per hour (US), 92f
    employment and, 94–95
    productivity gains from, 93f
    retraining and retooling, 94–95
automation, 89, 91–95
    effects on organizations of, 91–95
    restaurants and, 308–309
Autor, David, 12

B

Baibu.com, 495
Bank of America, 89
banking institutions, 89, 476
baseline WBS, 474
Bateson, Gregory, 20
battery life, 463
Bell, Gordon, 6
Bell's Law, 6
Benioff, Marc, 245
best practices, 360
Bezos, Jeff, 62
BI analysis, 70
BI application, 68
BI data
    Big Data, 83–86
    data mining analysis, 80–84
    online analytical processing (OLAP), 81f
    processing techniques, 78–84
    reporting analysis, 78–79
    RFM analysis, 79
BI server, 87–88
BI systems, 87f
Bieber, Justin, 354
Big Data, 68, 83–86, 109
    Hadoop, 85–86
    losses and, 190–191
    MapReduce, 83
    security and, 190–191
binary digits, 119
Bing, 495, 507
biometric authentication, 393
bitcoin, 168–169, 366–367
bits, 119, 120f
Black Hat, 391–392
BlackBerry OS, 129f, 131
BlackPOS, 415
Blockbuster LLC, 9
blockchain, 128
Bluetooth, 218
Boeing 787, 498
botnet, 484
bots, 42–43, 354–355
bounce rate, 357
BPMN. *See* Business Process Management
    Notation (BPMN)
brand awareness, 357f
Brazil, 507
bribery, 508
Brin, Sergey, 18
bring your own device (BYOD) policy, 147–148
    advantages of, 148f
    common practices of, 147f
Brooks, Fred, 491
Brooks' Law, 473
Brown, Keith, 33
browser based applications
    account creation form for, 177f
    database applications
browser report, 177f

551

brute force attack, 389
bullwhip effect, 504–506, 505f, 506f
Bureau of Labor Statistics, U.S., 12–13, 13f
business analyst, 452
business intelligence (BI), 68, 70
   alternative publishing for, 86–89, 86f
   BI analysis, 69
   data acquisition, 69
   primary activities of, 69–70, 69f
   publishing results, 70
   searching with, 70–73
   users, 74
business intelligence (BI) systems, 65, 68–73
   data processing techniques, 85–86
   future of, 101
   types of, 69f
business model, 61
business process, 46, 453
   activities, 296f
   competitive advantages impacted by, 53
   development of, 450–451
   engineering, 305
   examples of, 46, 46f
   for high-service business, 49f
   IS for, 49
   value and, 46–47
business process engineering, 305
business process management (BPM), 46–47,
   451–454, 455
   activities, 454–456
   business fundamentals in, 454
   improved process quality and, 453–454
   need for, 453–454
   stages of, 455f
   technology change in, 454
   uses of, 453–456, 461
Business Process Management Notation
   (BPMN), 456
   the As-Is Business Order Process, 456–457
   modeling processes, 456–459
   standard of, 456
   symbols of, 457f
business process reengineering, 305
business-to-business (B2B), 344
business-to-consumer (B2C), 344
bytes, 119, 165

C

cable line, 219, 219–220
CaliBurger, 308
Caltagirone, Sergio, 391
Cameron, David, 506
capital, 345
careers, 104
   components of, 28–29
   in data and analytics, 104–105
   data governance officer, 440–441
   director of data engineering, 192
   manager, data and analytics, 104–105
   network manager, 241
   senior learning and development specialist,
     497–498
   senior software engineer, 152–153
   in social media, 368
   software engineer, 152–153
   software product manager, 286–287
   software/platform engineer, 324–325

Carr, Nicholas, 443
carriers, 223, 223–224
cars, hacking of, 55
Case Western Reserve University, 124
CCleaner, 390
CDN. *See* content delivery network (CDN)
central processing unit (CPU), 118
CES. *See* Consumer Electronics Show (CES) 2018
Challenges for International Project
   Management, 510f
Check Customer Credit Process, 459f
Chesky, Brian, 289
chief information officer (CIO), 422
chief information security officer (CISO),
   415, 423
chief security officer (CSO), 415, 423
chief technology officer (CTO), 422
China. *See* People's Republic of China (PRC)
Chino, Gabe, 57
ChoicePoint, 351
Chrome, 18
Citadel, 414
Clicky, 358
client, 119
client-server architecture, 203, 204f
closed source, 137
cloud, 203
   future of, 239–240
   IaaS Services, 232
   network technology and, 203–207,
     214–215, 218–220
   operation of the Internet and, 220–224
   organizations and, 203–214, 213–214
   PaaS Services, 232
   resources and, 207–209, 208f
   SaaS Services, 231
   security and, 232–235
   uses of, 207–214, 231–232
   web servers and, 224–231
cloud analytics, 172
cloud computing, 85, 89, 141
   architecture of, 204–205
   network technology and, 218–220
   storage hardware, 172
cloud services, 61, 207f
   future of, 237
   offerings of, 211f
   pros and cons of, 207
   security of, 221–222, 232–235
   types of, 210f
   virtual private networks (VPNs), 233
cloud vendors, 209–212
cluster analysis, 82
CNBC, 157
CNET, 245
COBIT (Control Objectives for Information and
   Related Technology), 455
CogniToys Dino, 91
collaboration, 10–11, 254, 255f, 259
   characteristics of, 253–256
   vs cooperation, 253
   criteria for success, 256–257
   decision-making and, 258–260
   feedback and, 255–256, 290
   future of, 283
   information and, 258
   iteration, 255–256

problem solving with, 260
project management and, 257–262
purposes of, 257–262
role in decision-making, 258–260, 260f
sharing content for, 258–260, 275–276
successful, 256–257
collaboration information systems (IS),
   251–291, 262
   choosing, 279–283
   managing shared content with, 267–273
   managing tasks with, 276, 277–279
   requirements for, 262–263, 263f, 264f
   team communication with, 263–267
collaboration system, 262
   communication and, 263
   components of, 262–263
   content sharing and, 263
   requirements for, 262–263
collaboration tools
   for communication, 264f
   comprehensive set of, 280–281
   good set of, 281–282, 282
   minimal set of, 281–282
   task management with, 276–279
   team communication and, 263–267
   three sets of, 280–281, 280f
collaborative consumption, 290
columns, 165
commerce server, 224f, 225
communication channels, 360
communities, 337
communities of practice, 337
competitive advantages
   business processes role in, 52
   IS provision of, 52–53, 53
   principles of, 49, 49f
   products and, 51–52
competitive analysis, 358
competitive strategy, 41. *See also* Porter's Four
   Competitive Strategies
   business process and, 48–49
   future of, 53, 56–57
   value chain structure and, 44–46, 53, 55
component design, 466–467, 466f, 468f
computer crime, 383, 387f
   cost of, 388f
   studies on, 387
computer data, 119–121
computer hardware, 14, 117–121, 118
   computer data sizes and, 120–121
   mobile systems and, 115–159
computer terminal, 203
computer vision systems, 97
computer-based information systems, 15
computing power, 89
configuration control, 474
connection data, 341
constructive criticism, 254–255, 256f
consumer data purchasing, 74f
Consumer Electronics Show (CES) 2018, 136
content, distribution of, 507
content data, 341
content delivery network (CDN). *See* One-to-many,
   212–213, 213f
content management systems (CMS), 89
content sharing, 269–272
   applications for, 268f

collaborative tools for, 269f
levels of control in, 267–273, 275–276
with no control, 269
storage alternatives and, 268f
with version control, 272–274, 275–276
control flow, 453
conversion rate, 353, 357f
Cook, Tim, 89, 158
cookies, 89, 108, 390
cooperation, 253
coordination, 474
corpus of knowledge, 100
cost, of computer crime, 46, 387f, 388f
cost feasibility, 461
cost leader, 44
Cotton, Darren, 290
Counihan, Kevin, 330, 331
Cover Oregon, 330–331, 491
CrashOverride, 391
critical path, 471
critical path analysis, 472
CRM. *See* customer relationship
management (CRM)
cross-border commerce, 495f
crowdsourcing, 344
crow's feet, 181
crow's-foot diagram, 181
cryptocurrencies, 127–128, 366
benefits of, 127–128
future of, 128
mining of, 168–169
risks of, 128
at work, 168–169
custom-developed software, 134
customer life cycle, 305, 306f
customer relationship management (CRM)
system, 245, 305–307, 307f, 311–314
customer service, 508
customer summary, 72f
cyber attacks, 55
cyber security, 102

D

Daqri Smart Helmet, 123
data, 14. *See also* project data;
project metadata
accuracy of, 21
availability of, 74f
characteristics of, 21–22, 21f
from cookies, 108
data sizes, 119–120
information and, 20
legal safeguards for, 400
metadata on, 74
possible problems with, 74f
relevance of, 22
sufficiency of, 22
timeliness of, 21–22
unauthorized disclosure of, 384–385
value of, 22
data acquisition, 69, 70–71
data administration, 400, 422f
data analysis, 71–72
data breaches, 408–409
Equifax, 102–103
Target Corporation, 414–415, 415f
Yahoo! 408–409

data elements, 165f
data flow, 453
data marts, 75
data acquisition and, 77–78
data warehouse difference from, 75–78
examples of, 78f
data mining, 80, 81f
data mining analysis, 80
changes in purchasing patterns, 82–83
supervised data mining, 82
unsupervised data mining, 82
data model, 178
database design converted with, 170,
182–187
database development and, 178–182
transformed into database design, 184f
data quality, 301
data safeguards, 399–400, 400f
data warehouse, 73–75, 78
components of, 73f
data acquisition and, 77–78
data marts difference from, 75–78
metadata from, 74, 78f
database administration (DBA), 171, 173f, 400
database applications, 174–178
browser based applications, 176–177
components of, 174f
traditional, 174–178
database design
data model and, 184f
data model converted with, 178–187
normalization stage of, 182–184
database development, 179f
data models and, 178–182
entity-relationship (E-R) data model and,
179–182
database management system (DBMS),
170–171
database processing, 161–200, 189, 191
database security, 190–191
database system, 187–188
database tier, 225
databases, 165–167
in browser based application, 177–178
components of, 166f
database processing and, 165–167
for ERP, 315
examples of, 195–196
integrity and, 183–184, 302
metadata and, 167
purpose of, 163–165
traditional applications, 174–175
user role in, 187
DB2, 170
DBMS. *See* database management system
(DBMS)
Deano the Clown, 195, 196f
decision process, 259
decision support systems, 69
decision type, 259
deep learning, 91
deliverables, 469
Deloitte & Touche, 508
Deloitte Consulting LLP, 331
denial of service (DoS), 385–386
desktop virtualization, 132–133
development personnel, 452f

development processes, 452f
devices, intentional slow down of, 463
Dice's Annual Tech Salary Survey, 170,
428, 431f
differentiation strategy, 44
digital change, 8
digital reality
applications, 124f
impact of, 124–125
levels of, 123f
services, 123–125
digital revolution, 5–6, 14
digital subscriber line (DSL), 219
digital technology, 6
dimension, 79
dimensionality, 75
discussion forums, 266, 266f
diseconomies of scale, 473, 474
distributed CDN servers, 213f
distributed database processing, 501
distributed systems, 321
DNS. *See* Domain Name System (DNS)
document checkout, 273
DogVacay, 290
domain name, 221
Domain Name System (DNS), 221,
221–222
DoS. *See* denial of service (DoS)
DoubleClick, 108
Dragos, 391
drill down, 80
drone delivery, 62
Dropbox, 172, 245
DU Caller Group, 387
dual processor, 118
dynamic processes, 296–297, 297f
dynamic reports, 86

E

EAI. *See* enterprise application integration
eBay, 1, 40
e-commerce, 394
elastic, 205
Elastic Cloud 2 (EC2), 61, 232
Electronic Data Systems (EDS), 433
Ellison, Larry, 143
email, 266
email spoofing, 384
eMarketer, 363
employee resistance, 319
employees
enforcement of security policies and, 402
required to train replacements, 429–430
security safeguards and, 401–403
security training for, 402
termination, 322, 402–403
theft by disgruntled, 322–323
encapsulated, 227
encryption, 394–397, 506–507
Enterprise 2.0, 359–360
enterprise application integration (EAI),
305–306, 311–314, 312
enterprise information systems
collaborative management in, 318
enterprise processes supported by, 304–307
implementing and upgrading, 301–304,
318–320, 318f

enterprise processes, 299
  CRM and, 304–307
  enterprise information systems support for, 304–307
  and information system, 304f
  organizational scope and, 299
enterprise resource planning (ERP), 305–307, 309, 311–314
  applications, 307f, 314–315
  business process procedures, 315
  databases for, 315
  elements of, 314–318
  hardware, 314
  information system (IS), 312f
  major vendors of, 317–318, 317f
  system, 308, 325f
  training for, 315–317
enterprise social network (ESN), 359–361
  best practices for implementation, 361f
  communication and, 360
  successful, 360–361
enterprise system for patient discharge, 304
enterprise systems, neural networks changing of, 482
entities, 179
  entity-relationship (E-R) data model and, 179–181
  examples of, 180f
  relationships among, 180–182
entity-relationship (E-R) data model, 179–182, 188f
entity-relationship (E-R) diagrams, 181
Epson's Moverio Smart Glasses, 123
Equifax, 102–103
E-R. See entity-relationship
ERP. See enterprise resource planning
ESET, 391
estimation techniques, 482, 482f
Ethernet, 7, 215
ethics
  bots, 354–355
  brokering data and, 143
  engineered slowdown, 462–463
  manipulation of information, 76–77
  mining cryptocurrencies on work computer, 168–169
  monitoring with wearables, 274–275
  in online matchmaking, 42–43
  paid deletion of data, 310–311
  professional responsibility and, 23–24
  requiring fired employees to train replacements, 429–430
  reverse engineering privacy, 216–217
  trading free apps for personal data, 143–145, 143f
  web recording, 394–395
European Union (EU), 507
exabyte (EB), 120
exception reports, 79
Experian, 102
experimentation, 10, 11, 14
eXtensible Markup Language (XML), 220, 230, 230f
extracted data, 71f

F

Facebook, 363–365
  advertising on, 351
  in Brazil, 507
  chief security officer (CSO), 391
  data management on, 120, 426–427
  Fortune 500 companies with, 339
  future of, 439
  Oculus Rift from, 124
  Page Insights, 358
  presence on, 14
  privacy issues and, 426–427
  selling likes on, 354
  stock price, 426
  user-driven systems and, 483
  What's App and, 507
facial identity, 483
faulty service, 385
Fazio Mechanical Services, 414
Federal Bureau of Investigation, 506
feedback, 290
Fetch! 483
fiat currencies, 128
fields, 165
file, 165
file server, 269
File Transfer Protocol (ftp), 228, 229
Filo, David, 408
Firefox Lightbeam, 108
firewalls, 397–398, 397f
firmware, 134–135
First Data Corporation, 331
first mover advantage, 52
five forces model, 40, 41f.
       See also Porter's Five Forces Model of Industry Structure
five-component framework, 14, 14f, 16–19
  characteristics of, 16f
  components of, 17, 19
  computer hardware, 14
  data, 14
  design and implementation of, 313f
  high-tech versus low-tech information systems, 17
  of IS, 14, 16f
  using, 16–17, 19
Flap, Henk, 346
Flash, 157
folksonomy, 359
foreign keys, 167
Foreign Policy, 495
Foxconn, 443
freemium, 352
FriendFinder Networks, Inc., 387
ftp. See File Transfer Protocol (ftp)
Fulfillment by Amazon (FBA), 62
functional application, 297
functional information systems, 297

G

Gantt chart, 471
  creating a project plan, 471f
  with resources (people) assigned, 472f
Gebbia, Joe, 289, 290
General Data Protection Regulation (GDPR), 507
General Electric (GE), 122
geofencing, 85, 355
  business and, 84–85
  growth in, 84–85
location services and, 84
privacy and, 84–85
Ghemawat, Pankaj, 495
gig economy, 277–278, 283
gigabyte (GB), 120
global databases, 500–501
global economy, 496–497
  competitive environment and, 498
  organizations and processes, 494–496
  value chains and business processes, 498
global supply chain management, 503–504
GNU, 135
GNU general public license (GPL) agreement, 135
GoDaddy, 222f
Google, 8, 143, 483, 495
  advertising on, 351
  AI projects, 91
  data and, 68
  Google Maps, 18, 507
  Hong Kong, 507
  People's Republic of China (PRC) and, 507
  Project Loon, 7
  second mover advantage and, 52
Google (Alphabet), 52
Google+, 383
Google Analytics, 358
Google Docs, 262
Google Drive, 172
  available types of documents on, 270f
  document sharing on, 271f
  editing a shared document on, 272f
  form for creating an account, 279f
  shared content with version management, 269–272
  sharing task list on, 276, 278f
Google Glass, 123
Google Hangouts, 265
Google Maps, 18, 507
Google Search, 143
Google Trends, 86
GPS, 97, 143
graft, 508
Gramm-Leach-Bliley (GLB) Act, 400
granularity, 75
graphical queries, 176
green computing, 442
groupthink, 254

H

hacking, 385
Hackman, Richard J., 256
Hadoop, 85, 85f, 106
hamburger-making robot, 308–309, 443
hardening, 403
hardware, 117–121
  advances in, 121–128, 136
  competitive strategies and, 121–128
  components of, 118
  for ERP, 314
  of SMIS, 340
  types of, 118–119, 118f
Harvard Business Review, 443, 479
Health Insurance Portability and Accountability Act (HIPAA), 413
healthcare exchange, 330, 331f
help-desk policies, 404

Hewlett-Packard, 141, 387
high definition TV (HDTV), 348–349
hiring process, 402
Hoffman, Reid, 372
HoloLens, 155
home automation, 54
honeypots, 406
hop, 223
horizontal-market application, 134
host operating system, 131
http. *See* Hypertext Transfer Protocol (http)
https, 228–229, 382, 396f
human capital, 345
human error
    DoS caused by, 383
    security issue of, 383
human safeguards, 392, 401–406
    for employees, 401–403
    for nonemployee personnel,
        395, 403–404
hybrid model, 321
Hypertext Transfer Protocol (http), 228, 229

I

IBM, 56, 245
    Watson from, 56, 100–101, 500
iBookstore, 157
ICANN (Internet Corporation for Assigned
    Names and Numbers), 221
identification, 393
identifier, 179
identity theft, 102, 364
IEEE 802.11 protocol, 218
IEEE 802.3 protocol, 215
incorrect data modification, 385
India, outsourcing and, 432, 498
industry structure
    competitive advantages and, 41–42
    Five Forces Model, 40–41
industry-specific solutions, 317
influencer, 347
information, 19–20
    definitions of, 19–20
    derivation from data of, 20–21
    manipulation of, 76
Information Age, 5
information silos, 301, 303f, 320–321
    problems of, 302–303, 302f
    without ARES, 320f
information systems development, 449–453
    future of, 482–484
    scrum and, 477–482
information systems (IS), 14, 467. *See also*
    Collaboration Information Systems
    business processes and, 52, 293–333, 450f,
        451f
    careers in, 28–29
    characteristics of, 298f
    competitive advantages, 49–53
    competitive strategy, 49–53
    components of, 14–15
    development of, 450–451
    executives and, 427
    five-component framework, 14, 19
    future of, 321, 323, 325
    high-tech vs. low-tech, 17
    humans role in, 301

information silos and, 301–304, 309
    jobs in, 9–13
    management of, 15, 425
    organizational strategy and, 39–40, 427, 496f
    outsourcing of, 430–435, 430f
    planning for, 425–428, 425f
    priorities and, 427–428
    process quality improvement in, 299–301
    roles regarding products for, 51f
    security of, 382–386, 382f
    strategy and, 48–53
    user rights and responsibilities of, 435–437,
        436f
information systems (IS) department
    chief information officer (CIO) in, 422
    functions of, 421–425
    jobs in, 423–425, 424f
    organization of, 422–423
    salaries for, 425f
    security officers, 423
information systems (IS) management, future
    of, 437, 439
information technology (IT), 14
    architecture of, 57–58
    oversight of security staff, 438–439
Infrastructure as a service (IaaS). *See*
        Infrastructure as a service (IaaS), 210, 210f
inherent processes, 305
in-memory DBMS, 189
innovations, technological, 56f
Instagram, 354, 358, 364
Intel Corporation, 6
    social media guidelines, 362
Inter-Enterprise ARES System, 321f
inter-enterprise information systems, 299,
    320–321, 503–505
inter-enterprise processes, 299
interface, example of modern style, 130f
internal firewalls, 397
Internal Revenue Service (IRS)
    cloud computing and, 238
    system failure and, 238
international enterprise applications, challenges
    of, 501
international information systems
    challenges of, 508–511
    components of, 499–502
    cultural norms and, 508
    development projects and, 510
    functional systems and, 501–502
    inherent processes and, 502
    legal environment, 506–507
    physical security and, 507–508
    security and, 506–507, 506–509
    security challenges and, 494–514
    setting up in foreign offices, 511
international IS management
    challenges of, 510–511
    development of, 508–509
    security of, 407
International MIS, 498
    challenges of, 508–511
    global economy and, 494–496
    global supply chain management and,
        502–506
    international IS components, 499–502
    security challenges and, 506–509

international outsourcing, 432
    India and, 432
    People's Republic of China (PRC) and, 432
international project management, 509–510
International Project Management Institute, 509
Internet, 7, 18, 215, 220–224
    fixed and mobile connections to, 496f
    growth in users of, 494f
    postal service comparison to, 220f, 221–223
Internet exchange points (IXP), 223
Internet of Things (IoT), 54–55, 121–123,
        476–477, 484, 484–485
    banking industry and, 476
    impact of, 122
Internet service provider (ISP), 218
Intranet, 215
intrusion detection system (IDS), 389
iOS, 129f, 131, 150
iOS application, 157
IP addresses, 221, 222
IP spoofing, 384
iPad, 157
iPhone, 141, 157
iPod, 157
IPv4, 221
IPv6, 221
IT. *See* information technology (IT)
"IT Doesn't Matter" (Carr), 443
iTunes, 157

J

Japan earthquake, 387, 508
JavaScript, 140
JavaScript Object Notation (JSON), 220, 230,
    231f
jobs, 11, 28
    growth of, 12f
    in information systems, 9–10
    tradable type of, 9–10
Jobs, Steve, 156, 157, 158
    death of, 157
    return to Apple of, 157
Joint Robotics Laboratory (JRL), 443
JRL. *See* Joint Robotics Laboratory (JRL)
JSON. *See* JavaScript Object Notation (JSON)
just-in-time data, 145
just-in-time design, 478

K

Kant, Immanuel, 23–24
KB. *See* kilobyte (KB)
key, 167, 394
key escrow, 400
key loggers, 398
key performance indicators (KPI), 356
Khawaja, Ahmen, 362
kilobyte (KB), 120
Kindle, 62, 141
King, Rocky, 331
KISSmetrics, 358
Klout.com, 346
KM. *See* knowledge management
knowledge management (KM), 88
knowledge sharing, resistance to, 88–89
knowledge workers, 74
Korean language, 500
Kroenke, David, 491

Kryder, Mark, 8
Kryder's Law, 8, 8f, 9
Kurzweil, Ray, 101

L

LAN. *See* local area network (LAN)
languages, 501f
Laping, Chris, 360
Laredo Petroleum, 172
Leading Teams (Hackman), 256
legal safeguards, 400
Lending Club, 290
Levashov, Peter, 508
libraries, 272
LibreOffice, 268
license, 133
Lightbeam, 108
Lin, Nan, 345
linkages, 45
LinkedIn, 352, 372, 486
Linux, 129f, 130
Linux Mint Virtual Machine, 132f
Lipovsky, Robert, 391
local area network (LAN), 214, 218–220
localizing software, 499–500, 500f
location services, 84
lost-update problem, 178
Lycos, 52

M

macOS, 129f, 130
machine code, 137
machine learning, 98–100, 99f, 483
Macintosh, 157
main memory, 118, 120
mainframes, 203
    architecture of, 203
    era of, 203f
maintenance, 468
malware, 391, 398, 414
    cyberwar and, 391
    definitions of, 399
    safeguards against, 398–399
management information systems (MIS), 1–4,
        13–16
    careers and, 28, 29f
    future of, 22, 25
    importance of, 5–13
managerial decisions, 258–259
many-to-many (N:M) relationship, 181, 186f
MapReduce, 83, 83f
margin, 44
material ordering process, 47, 47f
maximum cardinality, 182, 182f
Maximus Corporation, 331, 491
Mayer, Marissa, 25
McAfee, Andrew, 358
McAfee's SLATES Model, 359f
m-commerce, 141
measure, 79
megabyte (MB), 120
Merrill Lynch, 89
metadata, 74, 87, 167
    on data, 74
    from data warehouses, 78f
    databases and, 167
    project, 262

sample of, 170f
Metcalfe, Robert, 7
Metcalfe's Law, 8f, 9, 372, 426, 484
metrics, 356
Microsoft, 122, 143, 245, 343, 372, 408, 432
    Azure, 433
    HoloLens, 6, 25
    password guidelines from, 26
    "Tay" chatbox from, 363
    versions of Windows in different countries, 496
Microsoft Access database, 196, 197f, 198f
Microsoft Office, 143
Microsoft Office 2019, 89
Microsoft Office Online, 262
Microsoft OneDrive, 262
Microsoft Project, 472
Microsoft SharePoint, 267, 345
    completed tasks in, 279f
    to-do list, 279f
    production task list in, 279f
    sharing task list on, 276–278
Microsoft Skype, 483
Microsoft SQL Server Report manager, 87
Microsoft SQL Server Reporting Services, 87
Microsoft Whiteboard Showing, 265f
Microsoft Windows, 130, 132f
Microsoft Word, 7–8, 14
minimal collaboration tools, 281–282
minimum cardinality, 182, 182f
Mirai, 484–485
MIS. *See* management information systems
mixed reality (MR), 123
mobile change and opportunity, 142f
mobile client operating systems, 131
mobile device management (MDM) software,
        148
mobile devices, 140
    ad spending on, 352–353, 355, 355f
    future of, 151
    security threats to, 150–151
    at work, 147–148, 147f, 148f
mobile information system, 141f
mobile systems, 140
    data and, 142–143
    employees use of, 146–147, 147f
    future of, 149, 151
    hardware and, 141–142
    importance of, 140–142, 144–146
    people and, 146
    procedures and, 145
    software and, 142
mobile workers, 146
modern-style application, 130
modules, 307
Momentum Machines, 447
monetize, 351
MongoDB, 188
monthly active users (MAU), 7
Moore, Gordon, 6
Moore's Law, 6–7, 8f, 9, 484
multi-user processing, 177–178
Murphy USA, 157
MySQL, 170

N

Nadella, Satya, 372
Naïve Bayes Classifier, 98

National Security Agency (NSA), 120
native applications, 129, 138–140
    characteristics of, 139f
    costs of, 139
    development of, 138–139
natural disasters, 383
natural language processing (NLP), 100
Nestlé, 363
net neutrality, 224
Netscape Navigator, 18
networks, 7, 8f, 214
neural network, 91, 482
NewSQL DBMS, 189
NeXT, 157
Nielson, Jacob, 8
Nielson's Law, 8, 8f
Nike, 127
Nonaka, Ikujiro, 479
nonmobile client operating systems, 130–131
nonroutine cognitive skills, 10–13, 10f
nonvolatile, 121
normal forms, 184
normalization, 182–184, 184f
    goals of, 183–184
    stage in database design process of, 182–184
    of tables, 184f
NoSQL DBMS, 189
NSA. *See* National Security Agency (NSA)
NSA data centers, 120

O

Object Management Group (OMG), 456
object-oriented, 138
Oculus Rift, 124
Office 365, 281f
off-the-shelf software, 134
off-the-shelf with alterations software, 134
OLAP. *See* online analytical processing (OLAP)
OneDrive, 172
one-of-a-kind application, 134
one-to-many (1:N) relationships, 172–174,
        181, 185f
Onion, Fritz, 33
online advertising, 355
online analytical processing (OLAP), 79–80
    cube, 80
    dimension, 79
    example reports of, 80f, 81f
    measure, 79
online banking, 92
online dating and matchmaking, 42–43
open source, 137
    collaboration and, 137–138
    community of, 135
    skill and, 137
    viability of, 135, 137–138
operating systems (OS), 128
    categories of, 129–131, 129f
    of servers, 131
operational data, 74–75
operational decisions, 258
Oracle, 56, 143, 245, 331, 433
Oracle Database, 170
Oracle Team USA, 476
order process, 458f
Oregon Health Authority (OHA), 331, 491
organizational feasibility, 464

organizational strategy, information system (IS)
    structure and, 39–40, 40f
outsourcing, 428
    advantages of, 428–431
    alternatives to, 432–433, 432f
    benefits of, 434–435
    cost reduction from, 431
    disadvantages of, 428–431
    gaining expertise and, 428
    information system (IS), 430f
    of IS activities, 428
    loss of control from, 433–434
    relations and, 423
    risk reduction, 431–432
    risks of, 433–435, 433f, 435
over the Internet, 205

P

PaaS. *See* platform as a service (PaaS)
PaaS Services, 232
packet, 221–224
packet sniffers, 385
packet-filtering firewall, 397
Page, Larry, 18, 143
paired programming, 480
Pandit, Vikram, 437
parallel installation, 468
partitioned database, 501
password etiquette, 26–27
password management, 389, 404
pay per click, 352
payload, 398
Payment Card Industry Data Security Standard
    (PCI DSS), 400
PayPal, 372
PC. *See* personal computer (PC)
PC virtualization, 132
peering, 223
Peleton Tread, 136
people, 14
People's Republic of China (PRC), 506–507
PeopleSoft, 305, 433
permission-limited activity, 272–273
personal area network (PAN), 214
personal computer (PC), 6, 7f, 118
personal identification number (PIN), 393
personally identifiable information (PII), 102
petabyte (PB), 120
Petrich, Dean, 195
phased installation, 468
phisher, 384
phishing, 384
Pig, 85
pilot installation, 468
Pinterest, 352
platform as a service (PaaS), 210f, 211
PlayStation VR, 124
plunge installation, 468
Pluralsight, 33
PMBOK" Guide (www.pmi.org/PMBOK-Guide-
    and-Standards.aspx), 509
point-of-sale (POS) systems, 414
Ponemon Institute, 387–388
pooled, 205
Porter, Michael, 39–41, 40
Porter's Five Forces Model of Industry Structure,
    40–41, 41f

Porter's Four Competitive Strategies, 43f
POSRAM, 415
postal system, Internet compared to, 221–224
power grids, malware and, 391
Pre-ERP Information Systems, 309f
pretexting, 384
PricewaterhouseCoopers, 67
primary activities, 44
    task descriptions of, 45f
    in the value chain, 44–45
primary key, 167
PRISM, 407
privacy, 394, 407
    GPS and, 143
    laws on, 507
    SM concerns of, 426–427
privacy protections, 507
private cloud, 233–235, 234f
private IP address, 223
problems, 260
problem-solving, 260, 260f
procedures, 14
process, improving, 300
process activity, 301
process blueprints, 315
process effectiveness, 299
process efficiency, 299
process resources, 300
process structure, 300
processes
    organizational scope and, 297–299
    types of, 297–299
product offer pages (example), 224f
product page, 226f
Product Power Curve, 282f
programming languages, 138
project data, 262
project management, 260–262. *See also*
    International Project Management
    Institute
    phases of, 260–262
    tasks and data, 261f
project metadata, 262
protocols, 215
    for internet, 228–229
    Web services supported by, 229f
public IP address, 221
public key encryption, 396
publish results, 70
pull publishing, 70
purchasing patterns, 82–83
push publishing, 70

Q

quad processor, 118
quantum computing, 236–237
QUANTUM learning, 225–226
qubits, 236
query operation, 72f, 175f, 197f, 198f

R

Rackspace, Inc., 129f, 206, 210, 498
RAM, 118
RAND Corporation, 9–10
ransomware, 398
RFID tags, 348
reality, 123

Reaper, 386
records, 165
Red Robin, 360
refrigerators, smart, 476
regression analysis, 82
Reich, Robert, 10, 240
relation, 167
relational databases, 167
relationships, 180, 181f
    among rows, 166–167, 166f
    of data administrative reporting, 422f
    examples of, 180f, 182f
    representation of, 184–187
    of senior level reporting, 422f
remote access
    actual connections, 233f
    apparent connections, 234f
remote action system, 239
Rensi, Ed, 443
reorder quantity, 504
replicated database, 501
reporting analysis, 78, 78–80
reporting application, 78
reporting relationships, 422f
repository, 46
requirement gaps, 318–319
requirements analysis, 460, 466
resources, 453
revenue models, social media (SM) and, 338f
RFM analysis, 79
RFM Scores, 79f
Risk Based Security, 386
River City Media, 387
robotics, 56, 308–309
roles, 453
Rolls-Royce, 498
rootkit, 438
routers, 223
rows, 165, 166f
Russia, encryption and, 506
Rutgers University, 484

S

SaaS. *See* software as a service (SaaS)
safeguard, 382
sales dashboard, 313f
sales history, 72f
Salesforce.com, 211, 245, 245–246, 384
SAP, 245
SAP Developer Network, 343
SAP ordering process, 316f
Satoshi, 128
scalable, 204
schedule feasibility, 464
Schwaber, Ken, 479
screen-sharing applications, 265
scrum, 451–453, 479
    completion and, 480, 482
    effectiveness of, 482
    essentials of, 479–480, 479f
    estimation techniques, 482–483, 482f
    principles of, 477f
    process of, 479–480, 480f
    requirements of, 480–482, 481f
    systems development life cycle (SDLC), 475
    tasks, 481, 481f
Sculley, John, 157

Seagate Corp., 8
search engines, 507
Sears, Roebuck and Company, 50
second mover advantage, 52
Secure Sockets Layer (SSL), 396, 396f
security, 15, 45f, 366–367, 399
    data breaches, 102–103
    human error in, 383
    of international IS, 506–509
    Internet of Things (IoT) and, 484–485
    of IS, 382–383, 382–386, 382f
    loss of Infrastructure, 386
    losses to, 383–386
    magnitude of problem, 386–388
    natural disasters threat to, 383
    passwords, 26–27
    privacy and, 438–439
    safeguards for, 392f
    sharing economy and, 284–285
    sources of problems, 384f
    system failure and, 238–239
    threats to, 383–384
security incidents
    response to, 406f
    of Target Corporation, 414–415
security monitoring, 405–406
security policy, 401f
security threats
    applications and, 150
    organizations response to, 406–407
    responding to, 388–394
self-driving cars, 97, 124–128
    cost of, 126
    as disrupters, 126–127
    ease of, 125–126
    future of, 125f
    safety of, 126
self-efficacy, 319
senior level reporting, relationships of, 422f
sense of presence, 124
server, 131
server content distribution, 212f
server farm, 119, 119f
server tier, 225
server virtualization, 132
servers, 235
    cloud and, 224–231
    operating systems (OS) of, 131
    SQL, 170
service-oriented architecture (SOA), 226–227,
        228–229, 228f, 230
sharing economy, 283
Simple Mail Transfer Protocol (smtp),
        228–229
single sign-on for multiple systems, 393, 395
The Singularity, 101
site license, 133
Skonnard, Aaron, 33
Skype for Business, 265
SLATES, 358, 359
small office/home office (SOHO), 215, 218f
    Internet and, 55
smart cards, 393
smart device, 54, 121
smart things, hacking of, 54–55
smartphone, 118, 122f
SMIS. See social media information system (SMIS)

Smith, Vernon, 342
smtp. See Simple Mail Transfer Protocol (smtp)
Snapchat, 358, 364
sniffing, 385
"Snooper's Charter," 506
Snowden, Edward, 407, 439
SOA. see service-oriented architecture (SOA)
social capital, 345–346, 346
social CRM, 342
social engineering, 366
social media information system (SMIS),
        335–375, 337–342
    components of, 340–342, 341f
    connections, 358
    data on, 358–359
    database processing, 341
    description of, 337–342
    developing, 355–359
    future of, 364–365, 367
    goals for, 356
    hardware, 340
    metrics for, 356–357
    organizational strategy and, 342–345
    people, 342
    procedures, 341–342
    roles of, 337–340
    security concerns, 361–364
    social capital and, 345–351
    social media providers, 338
    software for, 340–341
    target audience, 357
    users, 338–339
    values, 357–358
social media policy, 361
social media providers, 338
social media (SM), 337, 343–344
    advertising on, 351–352
    communities on, 339–340, 340f
    customer service and, 343–344
    employees on, 361–362
    external risks, 362–363
    freemium, 352
    human resources and, 345
    inappropriate content and, 362–364
    internal risks, 364, 367
    metrics, 357f
    monetizing, 342–343
    plan development, 356f
    redesigning enterprises, 365f
    responses to problems on, 363
    revenue and, 351–354, 355
    revenue models for, 337–340, 338f
    strategic goals, 357f
    user as product, 351
    in value chain, 343f
social networks, 7, 338, 347f
    added value to business, 346–347
    connections with more resources and,
        350–351
    relationships and, 347, 349
SocialNet, 372
Société Générale, 508
Socrative, 267
software, 14, 128–135
    application software, 133
    categories of, 128f
    for localizing, 499–500, 500f

mobile systems and, 115–159
    own versus license, 133
    of SMIS, 340–341
    sources and types of, 134f
software as a service (SaaS), 210f, 211
SOHO. See small office/home office (SOHO)
solid-state storage (SSD), 118
Sony, 124
Sony Aibo, 136
source code, 137, 137f
spear-phishing, 414
spoofing, 384
sports, 348–349
    analytics, 348–349, 476
    Big Data, 348
    HDTV and, 348–349
    user of, 338f
spreadsheets, student grades on, 175f
spyware, 385, 398f
SQL. See Structured Query Language (SQL)
SQL server, 170
SSL. See Secure Sockets Layer (SSL)
Stamos, Alex, 391
stand-up, 479
static reports, 86
steering committee, 428–429
Steinhafel, Gregg, 415
storage capacity
    custom-developed, 134
    price per GB, 9f
    terminology, 120f
storage hardware, 118
stored procedure, 319
strategic decisions, 259
strategies, 16
strategy, information system (IS) and, 49–53
strength of a relationship, 349
strong AI, 95
strong password, 26
structured data, 78
structured decisions, 259
structured processes, 296–297, 297f
Structured Query Language (SQL), 171
student table, 165f
subscriptions, 86
success metrics, 356
superintelligence, 95
supervised data mining, 81–82
supply chain, 502, 503f
    information in, 503–504
    international dimensions of, 502–506
    relationships, 502
    of Walmart, 503–504, 504f
support activities, 44–45
Survey Monkey, 267
survey report example, 267f
Sutherland, Jeff, 479
Swift, 138
swim-lane layout, 456
switching costs, 52
Symbian, 129f
symbian, 131
symmetric encryption, 396
synchronous communication, 264
system, 14, 461
system conversion, 467
system maintenance, 469f

systems analyst, 452
systems development life cycle (SDLC), 459
   agile techniques and, 477–479
   component design phase of, 466–467, 466f
   definition phase of, 461, 461f, 464
   estimating time and costs, 470–471
   implementation phase, 467–468, 467f
   keys for success of, 456–459, 469–475
   managing development challenges, 474–475
   phases of, 459–462, 460f, 486–487
   primary drivers of, 473f
   project plan and, 471–472
   prototyping in, 465–466
   requirements analysis phase of, 464–466, 465f
   scrum and, 475
   system maintenance phase of, 468–469, 469f
   team formation in, 464
systems procedures
   reasons for, 405
   types of, 405f
systems thinking, 10–11

T

Tableau Software, 189
tables, 165
   normalization of, 184f
   poor design of, 183f
tablet, 118
Takeuchi, Hirotaka, 479
Target Corporation, 382, 385, 423
   security breach of, 414–415, 415f
TCP, 222–223
TCP/IP protocol architecture, 214–215, 228–230
team surveys, 267
tech skills, 431f
technical feasibility, 464
technical safeguards, 392–393, 393f
technology
   advances in, 319–320
   forces creating change in, 8f
   skills gap, 11–12
   sports viewing and, 348–349
technology companies, innovations, 55
TEDx, 290
telelaw enforcement, 239
telemedicine, 239
telesurgery, 239
terabyte (TB), 120
Tesla, 125
test plan, 467
thick-client application, 129
thin client, 203
third-party apps, 426
third-party cookie, 108, 109f
threat / loss, 118, 383f
   example of, 383f
   scenario of, 382–383, 382f
three-tier architecture, 225, 225f, 228–229, 228f
Tiffany & Co., 157
TLS. *See* Transport Layer Security (TLS)
Toyota e-Palette, 136
trade-offs, planning and, 472–474
training, 94–95, 315–317, 402

transition problems, 319
translation, 483
Transmission Control Protocol (TCP), 222, 228
Transport Layer Security (TLS), 396, 396f
transportation services, 210, 210f
Transunion, 102
trigger, 315
Trojan, 415
trojan horses, 398
true demand information, 506f
Tumblr, 364
tunnel, 233
Turing Test, 96, 96f, 129
Turkey, 507
Twitter, 358, 360, 363–364, 507
   Fortune 500 companies with, 339
   "Tay" chatbox on, 363

U

Uber, 125, 290
UGC. *See* user-generated content (UGC)
UMI. *See* Unified Modeling Language
unauthorized data disclosure, 384–385
unexpected events, 474
Unified Modeling Language, 179
Unix, 129f, 130
unstructured decisions, 259
unsupervised data mining, 81, 82
URL (Uniform Resource Locator), 222
U.S. Department of Defense, 451, 459
use increases value, 352
user engagement, 357f
user rights and responsibilities, 435–436
user tier, 225
user-driven systems, 483
user-generated content (UGC), 362
users, 339
usurpation, 385
utilitarianism, 43

V

value, 44
value chain, 44, 48f
   of drone manufacturer, 44f
   linkages in, 45–46
   primary activities of, 44–45
   support activities in, 45
value chain structure
   competitive strategy and, 44–46
   future of, 56–57
value of social capital, 346
vanity metrics, 357
velocity, 482
Verizon, 407–408
version control, 272
version history, 273
version management, 269
vertical-market application, 134
videoconferencing, 263, 266f
Vine, 344
viral hook, 339
virtual, 123
virtual machine (vm), 131, 132f
virtual meetings, 265
virtual private cloud (VPC), 235
virtual private network (VPNs), 233, 233f,

234f, 235f
virtual reality (VR), 56, 124
virtualization, 131, 131–133, 132
virus, 398
volatile, 121
VPC. *See* virtual private cloud (VPC)
VPN. *See* virtual private network (VPN)
vulnerability, 382

W

Wadleigh, Jim, 150, 330, 331
The Wall Street Journal, 395
Walmart, 2, 50, 505
   data processing of, 120
   supply chain of, 503–504, 504f
WAN Wireless, 220
wardrivers, 385
waterfall method, 475
Watson (artificial intelligence), 56, 100–101
   future for, 101
   how it works, 100
   IBM's Question-and-Answer Process, 100f
   learns Korean, 500
Waymo (Google), 125
WBS. *See* work breakdown structure (WBS)
weak AI, 95
wearables, monitoring and, 274–275
Web 2.0, 85f, 359
web applications, 129, 138–140
   characteristics of, 139f
   costs of, 139
   development of, 139–140
Web page, 223f, 225
Web server computer, application programs and, 176f
Web services
   inventory applications and, 214f
   using internally, 213–214
Web Services Description Language (WSDL), 230
Web site traffic, 357f
WebCrawler, 52
WebEx, 265
webinar, 265
Weiner, Jeff, 372
WhatsApp, 358, 507
Whole Foods, 50–51, 62
"Why the World Isn't Flat" (Ghemawat), 495
wide area network (WAN), 214
Wi-Fi, 476
Wikipedia, 352
Williams, Bill, 33
Windows, 415
Windows server, 131, 132f
WordPerfect, 14
work breakdown structure (WBS), 469–470, 470f
The Work of Nations (Reich), 240
workflow, 414–415
workflow control, 273–274, 275f, 281
workgroup information system, 297
workgroup process, 297–298, 298f
world time differences, 498
worm, 398
WSDL. *See* Web Services Description Language (WSDL)
Wyman, Nancy, 330

X

XcodeGhost, 150
XML. *See* eXtensible Markup Language (XML)
XML (eXtensible Markup Language),
    220, 230

Y

Yahoo! 25, 408–409
Yammer, 344
Yang, Jerry, 408
YouTube, 8, 18, 339, 350f, 351, 507

Z

zettabyte (ZB), 120
Zuckerberg, Mark, 141, 143, 426
Zulily, 129f, 131, 224–225,
    224f, 226f

OTHER MIS TITLES OF INTEREST

Introductory MIS

Experiencing MIS, 7/e
Kroenke & Boyle ©2017

Using MIS, 10/e
Kroenke & Boyle ©2018

Management Information Systems, 15/e
Laudon & Laudon ©2018

Essentials of MIS, 12/e
Laudon & Laudon ©2017

IT Strategy, 3/e
McKeen & Smith ©2015

Processes, Systems, and Information: An Introduction to MIS, 2/e
McKinney & Kroenke ©2015

Information Systems Today, 8/e
Valacich & Schneider ©2018

Introduction to Information Systems, 3/e
Wallace ©2018

Database

Hands-on Database, 2/e
Conger ©2014

Modern Database Management, 12/e
Hoffer, Ramesh & Topi ©2016

Database Concepts, 8/e
Kroenke, Auer, Vandenburg, Yoder ©2018

Database Processing, 14/e
Kroenke & Auer ©2016

Systems Analysis and Design

Modern Systems Analysis and Design, 8/e
Hoffer, George & Valacich ©2017

Systems Analysis and Design, 9/e
Kendall & Kendall ©2014

Essentials of Systems Analysis and Design, 6/e
Valacich, George & Hoffer ©2015

Decision Support Systems

Business Intelligence, Analytics, and Data Science, 4/e
Sharda, Delen & Turban ©2018

Business Intelligence and Analytics: Systems for Decision Support, 10/e
Sharda, Delen & Turban ©2014

Data Communications & Networking

Applied Networking Labs, 2/e
Boyle ©2014

Digital Business Networks
Dooley ©2014

Business Data Networks and Security, 10/e
Panko & Panko ©2015

Electronic Commerce

E-Commerce: Business, Technology, Society, 13/e
Laudon & Traver ©2018

Enterprise Resource Planning

Enterprise Systems for Management, 2/e
Motiwalla & Thompson ©2012

Project Management

Project Management: Process, Technology and Practice
Vaidyanathan ©2013